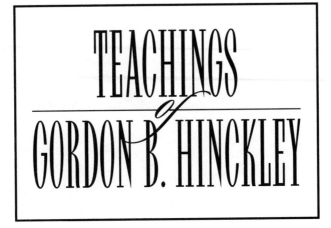

TEACHINGS of GORDON B. HINCKLEY

DESERET BOOK COMPANY
SALT LAKE CITY, UTAH

Library of Congress Cataloging-in-Publication Data

Hinckley, Gordon Bitner, 1910-
    Teachings of Gordon B. Hinckley.
        p.   cm.
    Includes index.
    ISBN 1-57345-262-9
    1. Church of Jesus Christ of Latter-day Saints—Doctrines.
2. Mormon Church—Doctrines.   I. Title.
BX8635.2.H55   1997
230'.9332—dc21   97-36519
                                                               CIP

Printed in the United States of America

10   9   8   7   6   5   4   3   2   72082

Contents

Preface

Gordon Bitner Hinckley, fifteenth President of The Church of Jesus Christ of Latter-day Saints, became a General Authority in April 1958, when he was called as an Assistant to the Twelve. Today, nearly forty years later, his words have been heard and treasured by Saints around the globe.

The quotations in this volume reflect, as much as possible, the broad scope of President Hinckley's teachings over the past four decades. In the course of his ministry, he has seen the Church's membership grow from less than 2 million to five times that number. His timely emphasis on missionary work, temple building, and maintaining standards in an era of declining morality and "shifting values," as he describes it, has blessed countless lives. He has counseled us to strengthen our families, build tolerance in our communities, reach out to the less fortunate, and increase our faith. He has borne strong and certain testimony of the Savior Jesus Christ, the Prophet Joseph Smith, and the going forth of the kingdom of God. Now, in this volume, many of President Hinckley's words of encouragement, inspiration, exhortation, and guidance have been gathered and arranged topically.

The entries in the book were collected from a variety of sources, including conference speeches, other published addresses, and writings. In addition, because President Hinckley has traveled so extensively since becoming prophet, transcripts of talks he has given throughout the world have provided rich source materials, as have various media interviews in which he has participated. With his permission and approval, many previously unpublished excerpts appear in this volume.

These materials have been arranged alphabetically according to topic for ease of reference. Within categories, the entries appear in chronological order from earliest to most recent. Complete references help the reader place the excerpts in their appropriate context.

It is our belief that these words of counsel from a latter-day prophet of the Lord will enlighten the understanding and enrich the spirit of every honest reader.

AARONIC PRIESTHOOD

See Priesthood: Aaronic Priesthood

ABORTION

Abortion is not the answer. This only compounds the problem. It is an evil and repulsive escape that will someday bring regret and remorse. ("Save the Children," *Ensign*, November 1994, p. 53.)

ABUSE

Spouse Abuse

I feel likewise that it ill becomes any man who holds the priesthood of God to abuse his wife in any way, to demean or injure or take undue advantage of the woman who is the mother of his children, the companion of his life, and his companion for eternity if he has received that greater blessing. Let us deal in kindness and with appreciation with those for whom the Lord will hold us accountable. ("Reach Out in Love and Kindness," *Ensign*, November 1982, p. 77.)

My heart reaches out to . . . [those] who by the circumstances in which they find themselves feel oppressed and smothered—all but destroyed. I regret that there are some men who are egotistical and evil, who are insensitive and even brutal. They are to be both condemned and pitied. I believe that any man who offends a daughter of God will someday be held accountable, and the time will come when he will stand before the bar of judgment with sorrow and remorse. ("Rise to the Stature of the Divine within You," *Ensign*, November 1989, p. 95.)

[I] call attention to the statement in the scriptures that Adam should rule over Eve. (See Gen. 3:16.) . . . I regrettably recognize that some men have used this through centuries of time as justification for abusing and demeaning women. But I am confident also that in so doing they have demeaned themselves and offended the Father of us all, who, I am confident, loves His daughters just as He loves His sons.

I sat with President David O. McKay on one occasion when he talked about that statement in Genesis. His eyes flashed with anger as he spoke of despotic husbands and stated that they would have to make an accounting of their evil actions when they stand to be judged by the Lord. He indicated that the very essence of the spirit of the gospel demands that any governance in the home must be done only in righteousness.

My own interpretation of that sentence is that the husband shall have a governing responsibility to provide for, to protect, to strengthen and shield the wife. Any man who belittles or abuses or terrorizes, or who rules in unrighteousness, will deserve and, I believe, receive the reprimand of a just God who is the Eternal Father of both His sons and daughters. ("Daughters of God," *Ensign,* November 1991, p. 99.)

Unfortunately a few of you may be married to men who are abusive. Some of them put on a fine face before the world during the day and come home in the evening, set aside their self-discipline, and on the slightest provocation fly into outbursts of anger.

No man who engages in such evil and unbecoming behavior is worthy of the priesthood of God. No man who so conducts himself is worthy of the privileges of the house of the Lord. I regret that there are some men undeserving of the love of their wives and children. There are children who fear their fathers, and wives who fear their husbands. If there be any such men within the hearing of my voice, as a servant of the Lord I rebuke you and call you to repentance. Discipline yourselves. Master your temper. Most of the things that make you angry are of very small consequence. And what a terrible price you are paying for your anger. Ask the Lord to forgive you. Ask your wife to forgive you. Apologize to your children. ("Women of the Church," *Ensign,* November 1996, p. 68.)

Child Abuse

There appears to be a plague of child abuse spreading across the world. Perhaps it has always been with us but has not received the attention it presently receives. I am glad there is a hue and cry going up against this terrible evil, too much of which is found among our own. Fathers, you cannot abuse your little ones without offending God. Any man involved in an incestuous relationship is unworthy to hold the priesthood. He is unworthy to hold membership in the Church and should be dealt with accordingly. Any man who beats or in other ways abuses his children will be held accountable before the great judge of us all. If there be any within the sound of my voice who are guilty of such practices, let them repent forthwith, make amends where possible, develop within themselves that discipline which can curb such evil practices, plead with the Lord for forgiveness, and resolve within their hearts henceforth to walk with clean hands. ("To Please Our Heavenly Father," *Ensign*, May 1985, p. 50.)

We deplore [child abuse,] which seems to be growing in the world. Of course, it is not new. It has gone on for generations. It is serious, and we so regard it. Sexual abuse of children on the part of fathers, or anyone else, has long been a cause for excommunication from the Church. No man who has been ordained to the priesthood of God can with impunity indulge in either spouse or child abuse. Such activity becomes an immediate repudiation of his right to hold and exercise the priesthood and to retain membership in the Church.

. . . The exploitation of children, or the abuse of one's spouse, for the satisfaction of sadistic desires is sin of the darkest hue. ("Questions and Answers," *Ensign*, November 1985, p. 51.)

Then there is the terrible, inexcusable, and evil phenomenon of physical and sexual abuse.

It is unnecessary. It is unjustified. It is indefensible.

In terms of physical abuse, I have never accepted the principle of "spare the rod and spoil the child." I will be forever grateful for a father who never laid a hand in anger upon his children. Somehow he had the wonderful talent to let them know what was expected of them and to give them encouragement in achieving it.

I am persuaded that violent fathers produce violent sons. I am satisfied that such punishment in most instances does more damage than good. Children don't need beating. They need love and encouragement. They need fathers to whom they can look with respect rather than fear. Above all, they need example.

I recently read a biography of George H. Brimhall, who at one time served as president of Brigham Young University. Concerning him, someone said that he reared "his boys with a rod, but it [was] a fishing rod" (Raymond Brimhall Holbrook and Esther Hamilton Holbrook, *The Tall Pine Tree: The Life and Work of George H. Brimhall*, n.p., 1988, p. 62). That says it all. ("Save the Children," *Ensign*, November 1994, pp. 53–54.)

And then there is the terrible, vicious practice of sexual abuse. It is beyond understanding. It is an affront to the decency that ought to exist in every man and woman. It is a violation of that which is sacred and divine. It is destructive in the lives of children. It is reprehensible and worthy of the most severe condemnation.

Shame on any man or woman who would sexually abuse a child. In doing so, the abuser not only does the most serious kind of injury. He or she also stands condemned before the Lord.

It was the Master himself who said, "But whoso shall offend one of these little ones which believe in me, it were better for him that a millstone were hanged about his neck, and that he were drowned in the depth of the sea" (Matt. 18:6). How could he have spoken in stronger terms?

If there be any within the sound of my voice who may be guilty of such practice, I urge you with all of the capacity of which I am capable to stop it, to run from it, to get help, to plead with the Lord for forgiveness and make amends to those whom you have offended. God will not be mocked concerning the abuse of his little ones. ("Save the Children," *Ensign*, November 1994, p. 54.)

ACCOUNTABILITY

See Choice and Accountability

ADDICTION

See Drugs; Gambling; Pornography

ADULTERY

The Church lays great stress on the sanctity of the home and teaches that children are a blessing from the Lord. There is no principle on which the Latter-day Saints lay greater emphasis than the sacredness of the marriage covenant. In Mormon theology adultery is next to murder in gravity. Strict morality is taught, and the Church has used its means and facilities liberally to teach its youth the necessity for moral cleanliness and the blessings of happy marriage. (*What of the Mormons?* pamphlet, 1982, p. 11.)

Was there ever adultery without dishonesty? In the vernacular, the evil is described as "cheating." And cheating it is, for it robs virtue, it robs loyalty, it robs sacred promises, it robs self-respect, it robs truth. It involves deception. It is personal dishonesty of the worst kind, for it becomes a betrayal of the most sacred of human relationships and a denial of covenants and promises entered into before God and man. It is the sordid violation of a trust. It is a selfish casting aside of the law of God, and like other forms of dishonesty its fruits are sorrow, bitterness, heartbroken companions, and betrayed children. ("An Honest Man—God's Noblest Work," *Ensign*, May 1976, p. 61.)

The temple recommend which you carry, if honestly obtained, is certification of your moral worthiness. It is inconceivable to think that a man who is a philanderer and unfaithful to his wife would consider himself eligible for the temple. ("Keeping the Temple Holy," *Ensign*, May 1990, p. 52.)

ADVERSITY

I know something of the frustrations of life in general. I have had my head bumped and my shins barked. On some of these occasions when I have needed a laugh I have turned to a letter which . . . was first published in the Manchester, England, *Guardian* and later reprinted in the *Deseret News*.

A hurricane had hit the West Indies, and a bricklayer was sent to repair the damage. He wrote to the home office as follows, and I hope you can get this delightful picture:

"Respected Sirs:

"When I got to the building I found that the hurricane had knocked some bricks off the top. So I rigged up a beam with a pulley at the top of the building and hoisted up a couple of barrels full of bricks. When I had fixed the building, there was a lot of bricks left over. I hoisted the barrel back up again and secured the line at the bottom, and then went up and filled the barrel with the extra bricks. Then I went to the bottom and cast off the line. Unfortunately the barrel of bricks was heavier than I was, and before I knew what was happening the barrel started down, jerking me off the ground. I decided to hang on, and halfway up I met the barrel coming down and received a severe blow on the shoulder. I then continued to the top, banging my head against the beam and getting my finger jammed in the pulley. When the barrel hit the ground it bursted its bottom, allowing all the bricks to spill out. I was now heavier than the barrel and so started down again at high speed. Halfway down, I met the barrel coming up and received severe injuries to my shins. When I hit the ground I landed on the bricks, getting several painful cuts from the sharp edges. At this point I must have lost my presence of mind because I let go of the line. The barrel then came down, giving me another heavy blow on the head and putting me in hospital. I respectfully request sick leave."

Life is like that—ups and downs, a bump on the head, and a crack on the shins. It was ever thus. Hamlet went about crying, "To be or not to be," but that didn't solve any of his problems. There is something of a tendency among us to think that everything must be lovely and rosy and beautiful without realizing that even adversity has some sweet uses. ("God Shall Give unto

You Knowledge by His Holy Spirit," *BYU Speeches of the Year,* September 25, 1973, pp. 105–6.)

If as a people we will build and sustain one another, the Lord will bless us with the strength to weather every storm and continue to move forward through every adversity. ("Five Million Members—A Milestone and Not a Summit," *Ensign,* May 1982, p. 46.)

We may know much of loneliness. We may know discouragement and frustration. We may know adversity and trouble and pain. I would hope not. But you know, and I know, that suffering comes to many. Sometimes it is mental. Sometimes it is physical. Sometimes it may even be spiritual.

Ours is the duty to walk by faith. Ours is the duty to walk in faith, rising above the evils of the world. We are sons and daughters of God. Ours is a divine birthright. Ours is a divine destiny. We must not, we cannot sink to the evils of the world—to selfishness and sin, to hate and envy and backbiting, to the "mean and beggarly" elements of life.

You and I must walk on a higher plane. It may not be easy, but we can do it. Our great example is the Son of God whom we wish to follow. (Ellen Pucell Unthank Monument Dedication, Cedar City, Utah, August 3, 1991.)

AGENCY

See Choice and Accountability

AGING

Sister Hinckley and I are learning that the so-called golden years are laced with lead. But I think I can honestly say that I do not feel old. I cannot repudiate my birth certificate, but I can still experience a great, almost youthful exuberance in my enthusiasm for this precious work of the Almighty. ("This Is the Work of the Master," *Ensign,* May 1995, p. 70.)

We have reached that age where you shrink instead of growing tall. You can't do a thing about it. You can't take any pills that will help you. You just accept it. (Oahu Hawaii Regional Conference, February 18, 1996.)

Age is more a matter of how you feel, how you think, and what's going on in your head than what's going on in your feet—although I wouldn't want to be challenged to a foot race this morning. (Colorado Springs Young Adult Meeting, April 14, 1996.)

AIDS/SEXUALLY TRANSMITTED DISEASE

There is a plague of fearsome dimensions moving across the world. Public health officials are greatly concerned, and everyone else should be. . . .

AIDS is a commonly fatal malady caused primarily from sexually transmitted disease and secondarily from drug abuse. Unfortunately, as in any epidemic, innocent people also become victims.

We, with others, hope that discoveries will make possible both prevention and healing from this dread affliction. But regardless of such discoveries, the observance of one clearly understandable and divinely given rule would do more than all else to check this epidemic. That is chastity before marriage and total fidelity after marriage.

Prophets of God have repeatedly taught through the ages that practices of homosexual relations, fornication, and adultery are grievous sins. Sexual relations outside the bonds of marriage are forbidden by the Lord. We reaffirm those teachings. . . .

The Lord has proclaimed that marriage between a man and a woman is ordained of God and is intended to be an eternal relationship bonded by trust and fidelity. Latter-day Saints, of all people, should marry with this sacred objective in mind. Marriage should not be viewed as a therapeutic step to solve problems such as homosexual inclinations or practices, which first should clearly be overcome with a firm and fixed determination never to slip to such practices again.

Having said this, I desire now to say with emphasis that our concern for the bitter fruit of sin is coupled with Christlike sympathy for its victims, innocent or culpable. We advocate the example of the Lord, who condemned the sin, yet loved the sinner. We should reach out with kindness and comfort to the afflicted, ministering to their needs and assisting them with their problems. We repeat, however, that the way of safety and the road to happiness lie in abstinence before marriage and fidelity following marriage. ("Reverence and Morality," *Ensign,* May 1987, pp. 46–47.)

ALCOHOL

See Word of Wisdom

AMERICA (THE UNITED STATES)

It has been my privilege to travel widely over this earth. I have encircled the globe again and again. I have known the beauties of New Zealand and the broad breadth of Australia. I have admired the industry of Japan and the fortitude of Korea. I have crisscrossed South America and been in every nation of that great continent. I have marveled at the architecture of the great cities of Europe, the magnificence of the Alps, the loveliness of the English countryside. I have been in Singapore, in India, in Tehran, and Turkey, and Lebanon, and Israel. I have come to know and admire and respect great people everywhere, but I always return to my homeland with gratitude and appreciation and thanksgiving to the Almighty.

Notwithstanding the trouble, notwithstanding the argument, notwithstanding the increasingly heavy hand of government, notwithstanding the spirit of arrogance we so often display, notwithstanding the growing tide of pornography and permissiveness, notwithstanding occasional corruption in public office and betrayal of sacred trust—I marvel at the miracle of America, the land which the God of Heaven long ago declared to be a land choice above all other lands and concerning which He has made a promise and given a warning in these remarkable words: "Behold, this is a choice land, and whatsoever nation shall possess it shall be free from bondage, and from captivity, and from all other nations under heaven, if they will but serve the God of the land, who is Jesus Christ" (Ether 2:12).

God bless America, for she is His creation. (National Advisory Council of BYU College of Business, November 2, 1973.)

I should like to say a few words about America. . . . No land is without its beauty, no people without their virtues, and I hope that you who come from elsewhere will pardon my saying a few words concerning my own native land, America. I know that she has problems. We have heard so much of them for so long. But surely this is a good land, a choice land, a chosen land. To me it is a miracle, a creation of the Almighty. . . .

There is too much fruitless, carping criticism of America. Perhaps the times are dark. There have been dark days in every nation. I should like to repeat the words of Winston Churchill spoken exactly thirty-three years ago today. Bombs were then dropping on London. The German juggernaut had overrun Austria, Czechoslovakia, France, Belgium, Holland, Norway, Russia. All of Europe was in the dread grasp of tyranny, and England was to be next. In that dangerous time, when the hearts of many were failing, this great Englishman said:

"Do not let us speak of darker days; let us speak rather of sterner days. These are not dark days; these are great days—the greatest days our country has ever lived; and we must all thank God that we have been allowed, each of us according to our stations, to play a part in making these days memorable in the history of our race." (Address at Harrow School, 29 October 1941.)

Earlier he had said to his people and to the whole world, following the catastrophe at Dunkirk when the prophets of doom foretold the end of Britain:

"We shall not flag or fail. . . . We shall fight in France, we shall fight on the seas and oceans, we shall fight with growing confidence and growing strength in the air, we shall defend our island, whatever the cost may be, we shall fight on the beaches, we shall fight on the landing grounds, we shall fight in the fields and in the streets, we shall fight in the hills; we shall never surrender." (Speech on Dunkirk, House of Commons, 4 June 1940.)

It was such talk as this, and not the critical faultfinding of glib cynics, that preserved the great people of Britain through those dark and deadly days when all the world thought their little island would go under.

It shall be so with America if we will do less speaking of her weaknesses and more of her goodness and strength and capacity. I was stirred in my heart by the words of our late, great President Harold B. Lee, who, speaking to a group such as this, said:

"This nation, founded on principles laid down by men whom God raised up, will never fail. . . . I have faith in America. You and I must have faith in America if we understand the teachings of the gospel of Jesus Christ." (*Deseret News*, 27 October 1973.)

I doubt not that we shall have days of trial. . . . But I am certain that if we will emphasize the greater good and turn our time and talents from vituperative criticism, from constantly looking for evil, and lift our sights to what may be done to build strength and goodness in our nation, America will continue to go forward with the blessing of the Almighty and stand as an ensign of strength and peace and generosity to all the world. ("Let Not Your Heart Be Troubled," *BYU Speeches of the Year,* October 29, 1974, pp. 267–68.)

I love America for her great and brawny strength, the products of her vital factories, and the science of her laboratories. I love her for the great intellectual capacity of her people. I love her for their generous hearts. I love her for her tremendous spiritual strengths. She is unique among the nations of the earth—in her discovery, in her birth as a nation, in the amalgamation of the races that have come to her shores, in the consistency and strength of her government, in the goodness of her people.

We first visited Jerusalem long ago, before the 1967 war. It was then a divided city. We retained the services of a guide who was an Arab. We stood on an elevation where we could see the other side of Jerusalem. With tears in his eyes he pointed to the home of which he had been dispossessed. And then he said with deep emotion: "You belong to the greatest nation on the face of the earth. Yours is the only nation which has been victorious in war and never claimed any territory as a prize of conquest.

"Your people have given millions, yes billions, to the poor of the earth and never asked for anything in return."

That I learned from a man in Jerusalem. I had never thought of it before. It is tremendously significant. I have stood in the American military cemetery in Suresnes, France, where are buried some who died in the First World War. It is a quiet and hallowed place, a remembrance of great sacrifice "to make the world safe for democracy." No additional territory was claimed by America as recompense for the sacrifices of those buried there.

I have stood in reverent awe and wonder in the beautiful American military cemetery on the outskirts of Manila in the Philippines. Here, standing row on row in perfect symmetry, are marble crosses and the Star of David marking the burial places of some 17,000 Americans who lost their lives in the Second World War. Surrounding that sacred ground are stone colon-nades on which are incised the names of another 35,000 who were lost in the battles of the Pacific during that terrible conflict. There was victory, but not a claim for territory.

I have been up and down South Korea from the 38th parallel on the north to Pusan on the south and seen the ridges and the valleys where Americans fought and died, not to save their own land, but to preserve freedom for people who were strangers to them but whom they acknowledged to be brothers under the Fatherhood of God. Not an inch of territory was sought nor added to the area of the United States during that conflict.

I have been up and down South Vietnam in the days of war, during those years when 55,000 Americans died in the sultry heat of that strange and foreign place fighting in the cause of human liberty without ambition for territory.

In no instance—in the First World War, in the Second World War, in the Korean War, in the Vietnam struggle—did this nation seize and hold territory for itself as a prize of conquest.

I love America for the tremendous genius of its scientists, its researchers, its laboratories, its universities, and the tens of thou-sands of facilities devoted to the increase of human health and comfort, to the sustenance of life, to improved communication and transportation. Its great, throbbing industries have blessed the entire world. The standard of living of its people has been the envy of the entire earth. Its farmlands have yielded an abundance undreamed of in many other places. The entrepreneurial environment in which has grown its industry has been the envy of all nations.

I love America for its great spiritual strength. It is a land of churches and synagogues, of temples and tabernacles, of pulpits and altars. (Freedom Festival Address, Provo, Utah, June 26, 1988.)

I believe in America. I am grateful for the Constitution under which this nation lives and moves and has its being. I am profoundly grateful that somehow for more than two centuries of time we have existed as a nation and grown to become the strongest and most free in the entire world. I am grateful for those men whom the God in Heaven raised up and inspired and who pledged their lives, their fortunes, and their sacred honor to establish this nation and its government.

I believe in America—one nation under God, indivisible, with liberty and justice for all. We are, of course, not without fault. We have more than our share of crime and of every other evil to be found on the earth. I fear that we have become an arrogant people, but when all is said and done, there is no other nation quite like this nation. ("Articles of Belief," Bonneville International Corporation Management Seminar, February 10, 1991.)

American Bill of Rights

The first ten amendments to the Constitution, which became our Bill of Rights, were ratified and came into effect on December 15, 1791. On December 15, 1941, President Franklin D. Roosevelt signed a resolution naming December 15th of each year as "Bill of Rights Day."

We pay relatively little attention to it. It is not a national holiday. It scarcely receives notice. And yet it marks one of the most significant accomplishments in the history of the United States, if not in the history of all mankind. It represents the codification of the basic, inclusive, and fundamental law of the liberties of the people which our forefathers regarded as gifts from God and not as gifts of government. These amendments prohibit the encroachment of government on these rights. We must never take them for granted. They are of the very essence of that freedom which we describe as American. I regard it as a miracle that we have them. (Sons of American Revolution Dinner, May 4, 1990.)

When you speak to the average citizen concerning the provisions of the Constitution he is likely to think of it in terms of the Bill of Rights rather than the Constitution itself. The Constitution sets up the machinery of government. The Bill of Rights denies to government those basic and fundamental elements of freedom which belong to the people as their divine inheritance and which they refuse to surrender to the whims of politicians. (Sons of American Revolution Dinner, May 4, 1990.)

I was in Seoul, Korea, in May of 1961 when a coup occurred. The president of the nation fled for his life as the military took over the affairs of the country. I was awakened in my hotel room at 4:30 in the morning by the sound of cannon fire in the street below. From my window I watched shells hit the wall and break the windows of the government building which stood next to the hotel. I turned on the radio. I discovered it had become the first target of those taking over the government. The newspapers followed. Freedom of the press was abridged. Freedom of speech was muzzled. Freedom of assembly was denied. These were primary targets in taking control of the nation and its people.

. . . [Such events] stand as evidence to each of us of the inspired vision of our forebears two centuries ago in demanding a written Constitutional prohibition against the enactment of any law concerning an establishment of religion, the free exercise thereof, freedom of speech, or of the press, or of the right of the people peaceably to assemble and to petition the government for a redress of grievances. ("The Bill of Rights," Bonneville International Corporation "Gathering of Eagles," June 20, 1991.)

American Constitution

There were men whom the God of Heaven had raised up who saw with a greater vision and dreamed a better and more inspired dream. On May 14, 1787, fifty-five of them met in Philadelphia. The heat of that summer was oppressive, the worst in the memory of man. There were differences of opinion, sharp and deep and bitter. But somehow, under the inspiration of the Almighty, there was forged the Constitution of the United States. On September 17, 1787, thirty-nine of the fifty-five signed the document. It began with these remarkable words:

"We, the people of the United States, in order to form a more perfect union, establish justice, insure domestic tranquillity, provide for the common defense, promote the general welfare, and secure the blessings of liberty to ourselves and our posterity, do ordain and establish this Constitution of the United States of America."

Of it, the great Gladstone said: "As the British Constitution is the most subtle organism which has proceeded from progressive history, so the American Constitution is the most wonderful work ever struck off at a given time by the brain and purpose of man."

It is the keystone of our nation.

It is my faith and my conviction that it came not alone of the brain and purpose of man, but of the inspiration of God, for He Himself has declared, "I established the Constitution of this land, by the hands of wise men whom I raised up unto this very purpose, . . . for the rights and protection of all flesh, according to just and holy principles; that every man may act in doctrine and principle . . . according to the moral agency which I have given unto him, that every man may be accountable for his own sins in the day of judgment." [D&C 101:80, 77–78.]

America was born of that miracle. (National Advisory Council of BYU College of Business, November 2, 1973.)

In a few months we shall celebrate the two hundredth anniversary of the founding of the nation. Is it not a miracle that through these two centuries of time our system of government has remained intact, our Constitution has held while storms have beaten about us from within and without? ("Let Not Your Heart Be Troubled," *BYU Speeches of the Year,* October 29, 1974, p. 267.)

Challenges to America

More than a century ago Alexis de Tocqueville, a French philosopher, visited America and out of the impressions of that tour wrote these interesting words:

"I sought for the greatness and genius of America in her commodious harbors and her ample rivers, and it was not there; in her fertile fields and boundless prairies, and it was not there; in her rich mines and her vast world commerce, and it was not there. Not until I went to the churches of America and heard her pulpits aflame with righteousness did I understand the secret of her genius and power. America is great because she is good, and if America ever ceases to be good, America will cease to be great."

Where has gone the goodness of America? What happened to her pulpits aflame with righteousness? . . .

I am not one who believes that all is wrong with this land. There is so much that is right and so much that is good.

But neither do I believe that all is well. Our problems are legion, but we are not alone in these. Other lands, most lands, are similarly afflicted.

But this need not be a terminal illness. The course can be changed. . . .

The place to begin to reform the world is not Washington or Paris or Tokyo or London. The place to begin is with oneself. A wise man once declared: "Make of yourself an honest man and there will be one fewer rascal in the world." ("'Rise, and Stand upon Thy Feet,'" *Improvement Era,* December 1968, pp. 68–69.)

Jim Bishop, prominent columnist, recently wrote as follows: "This is the twentieth year of America's Rotten Revolution. Two decades ago, this nation began its slide down the drain. It moved faster, more destructively, than the fall of the Roman Empire." He quoted from a book by Marvin Harris . . . [entitled] *Why America Changed.* He spoke of the moral decline, the decline of ethics and principle. And then he concluded: "It was, no matter how you gauge it, a Rotten Revolution. America has paid dearly for greed on all levels. We cannot wish our way back to strength. The only way is to restore the morals we had in our innocence."

I am, by nature, an optimist. But no one, it seems to me, can be blind to the tremendous forces that are slapping our society. I received my baccalaureate degree . . . in the depression-ridden year of 1932. . . . To be thrown onto the employment market in those times was like being cast into the sea to swim through heavy waves. Unemployment exceeded 30 percent. People committed suicide in despair. If a man had a job earning a hundred dollars a month, he was considered fortunate. Men who had been profitably employed found themselves standing in soup lines and living in shantytowns.

But with all of this, it seems to me, as I reflect on those days, there was something of tremendous good in the people. There was a spirit of mutual helpfulness, a spirit of respect one for another and, generally speaking, a high moral tone. Of course there was crime, even gang crime. There were the rumrunners and the moonshiners. There were even those who wished for arrest and conviction so that they could trade the cold of the outside for the warmth of jail. But, at least in the society of which I was a part as a young man, there was a great—and what I regard as wonderful—respect for women. Homosexuality was almost unheard of. The use of hard drugs was practically unknown.

We have traveled far since then, and the results are told in our statistics, of crime, divorce, and a long and sickening train of various immoralities.

. . . [We encourage you to] make the very most of the great and challenging opportunities you have before you—on the one hand, to equip yourselves for the changing and competitive world in which you will earn your livelihood, and, on the other hand, to cultivate a compelling loyalty to the unchanging and ever-constant principles of morality, integrity, and eternal truth which must undergird the character of every good man and woman, and every progressive society. ("Dedication of the John Taylor Building," *BYU 1982–83 Fireside and Devotional Speeches,* September 14, 1982, pp. 16–17.)

Today we face challenges we have scarcely known in the past. We have come through wars, both civil and international, with victory and have found peace. Now we are a people of contention with strident and accusatory voices heard in argument across the nation. We rose from scratch to become the greatest industrial power in the history of the earth. Now we have lost much of our competitive edge, and seen other nations move ahead of us in various fields in both research and production. We spend millions upon millions of our resources in litigation one against another. Our spiritual power is sapped by a flood tide of pornography, by a debilitating epidemic of the use of narcotics and drugs that destroy both body and mind.

We are forgetting God, whose commandments we have forgotten and obey not. In all too many ways we have substituted human sophistry for the wisdom of the Almighty. (Freedom Festival Address, Provo, Utah, June 26, 1988.)

We who believe in the Book of Mormon accept these great words: "Behold, this is a choice land, and whatsoever nation shall possess it shall be free from bondage, and from captivity, and from all other nations under heaven, if they will but serve the God of the land, who is Jesus Christ." (Ether 2:12.)

Declared the Psalmist: "Blessed is the nation whose God is the Lord." (Psalm 33:12.)

An acknowledgment of the Almighty and a return to the teachings of God will do more than all else to keep our ship of state on a steady course as she sails into the third century of nationhood. Here is the answer to the conflicts that best us. Here is the answer to the evils of pornography, abortion, drugs, and the squandering of our resources on evil pursuits. Here is the answer to the great epidemic of litigation which consumes time, saps our financial strength, and shackles our entrepreneurial spirit. Here is the answer to tawdry politics which place selfish interest above the common good. (Freedom Festival Address, Provo, Utah, June 26, 1988.)

Trust is what makes a government work, and maybe a lack of trust is one reason for the serious problems we are experiencing. ("Trust and Accountability," *BYU 1992–93 Devotional and Fireside Speeches*, October 13, 1992, p. 26.)

This is a wonderful season in the history of the world, the best ever, I truly believe. I have a profound feeling of gratitude for life in this remarkable age. I never get over the wonder of it. . . .

What tremendous technical progress you and I have witnessed during our lifetimes. I stand in respect, almost reverence, before the men and women of science who have made life better for each of us. When I was born, the life expectancy in the United States was 50 years. Today, it is 75 years. Is it not a thing of wonder that 25 years have been added to the average life span of an American? The same is happening in other areas of the world. . . .

We have achieved technical miracles, but, tragically, we are experiencing a moral and ethical disaster. I take you back to the homes of your childhood and mine. I think that in almost every case, there was prayer in those homes. Families knelt together in the morning and invoked the watch care of the Lord. At night they joined again in prayer. Something wonderful came of this. It is difficult to describe. It did something for children. The very act of expressing gratitude to God our Eternal Father brought with it a feeling of respect and reverence and appreciation. The sick were remembered in those prayers, as were the poor and the needy. The President of the United States, the Congress, and others of the government were remembered in those prayers. This cultivated a spirit of respect for those in public office. Where is the respect today, I ask? ("Saving the Nation by Changing Our Homes," BYU Management Society, Washington, D.C., March 5, 1994, pp. 1–2.)

I was intrigued with a statement by Ted Koppel at commencement exercises at Duke University four or five years ago. Speaking of the entertainment industry of which he has been a prominent part, he said:

"We require nothing of you; only that you watch. . . . And gradually, it must be said, we are beginning to make our mark on the American psyche. We have actually convinced ourselves that slogans will save us. 'Shoot up if you must; but use a clean needle.' 'Enjoy sex whenever and with whomever you wish; but wear a condom.'

"No! The answer is 'no!' Not 'no' because it isn't cool . . . or smart . . . or because you might end up in jail or dying in an AIDS ward—but 'no' . . . because it's wrong. Because we have spent 5,000 years as a race of rational human beings trying to drag ourselves out of the primeval slime by searching for truth . . . and moral absolutes. . . .

"Our society finds truth too strong a medicine to digest undiluted. In its purest form, truth is not a polite tap on the shoulder; it is a howling reproach.

"What Moses brought down from Mt. Sinai were not the 'Ten Suggestions' . . . they are commandments." (Duke University Archives, Commencement Speech, May 10, 1987.)

Now, I know that we have always had crime, and that we will always have crime. We have had and will have pornography, immorality, and other problems. But we cannot continue the trend that we are presently experiencing without catastrophe overtaking us. . . .

If we continue on a diet of pornography and filth and profanity, the mores that govern civility and respect and reverence will crumble around us.

I am more concerned about the moral deficit than I am about the budget deficit. ("Saving the Nation by Changing Our Homes," BYU Management Society, Washington, D.C., March 5, 1994, pp. 5–6.)

I have faith in the future of my beloved America. . . . And yet, I am deeply concerned. . . . There has been going on in this nation for a good while a process which I call "secularizing America." . . .

A few months ago Lady Margaret Thatcher, former Prime Minister of Great Britain . . . [visited] Utah. She spoke of the goodness and strength of America, which was settled by people from the British Isles who, as she said, came with the English Bible and the English common law. Those early settlers from the British Isles were Christian people who came with the Judeo-Christian concepts of right and wrong, of truth and error, which they derived from reading that Bible. They were people who looked to God for strength and inspiration and expressed their gratitude to Him for every blessing.

Lady Thatcher said, "You use the name of Deity in the Declaration of Independence and in the Constitution of the United States, and yet you cannot use it in the schoolroom." . . . I heard her make the statement more than once, and I have not forgotten it. This is symptomatic of what I refer to as the secularizing of America. Reverence for the Almighty, gratitude for His beneficent blessings, pleadings for His guidance, are increasingly being dropped from our public discourse. I take you back to George Washington's first inaugural address, spoken April 30, 1789, in Federal Hall in New York. Said he on that occasion:

" . . . It would be peculiarly improper to omit, in this first official act, my fervent supplications to that Almighty Being, who rules over the universe, who presides in the councils of nations, and whose providential aids can supply every human defect, that His benediction may consecrate to the liberties and happiness of the people of the United States a government instituted by themselves for these essential purposes. . . . In tendering this homage to the great Author of every public and private good, I assure myself that it expresses your sentiments not less than my own; nor those of my fellow citizens at large. . . . No people can be bound to acknowledge and adore the invisible hand, which conducts the affairs of men, more than the people of the United States. Every step, by which they have advanced to the character of an independent nation, seems to have been distinguished by some token of providential agency" (*Harvard Classics*, vol. 43, p. 242).

Wonderfully significant words are these spoken more than 200 years ago by him whom we idolize as the Father of our country. (Provo City Community Centennial Service, August 4, 1996.)

It is acknowledgment of the Almighty that gives civility and refinement to our actions. It is accountability to Him that brings discipline into our lives. It is gratitude for His gracious favors that takes from us the arrogance to which we are so prone.

I believe that one of the root causes of the terrible social illnesses that are running rampant among us is the almost total secularizing of our public attitudes. People who carry in their hearts a strong conviction concerning the living reality of the Almighty, and of accountability to Him for what we do with our lives and our society, are far less likely to become enmeshed in those problems which inevitably weaken our society. . . . We are shutting the doors of our homes against the God of the universe. Divine law has become a meaningless phrase. What was once so commonly spoken of as sin is now referred to only as poor judgment. Transgression has been replaced by misbehavior.

Family prayer was once the norm in the homes of the people across the nation. It has largely been forgotten. Marriage was once regarded as the most sacred of institutions, to be upheld through sunshine and storm. Now, the epidemic of divorce rages on, and while parents quarrel children suffer. The very foundation of their lives—a secure and happy home—is pulled from under them.

An editorial in the *Wall Street Journal* speaks of a report issued by the Council on Families in America after two years of intense study. The conclusion of that report is this: "American society would be better off if more people got married and stayed married." What a remarkable conclusion that is. Any of us in this hall could have said that without a long and costly study. . . .

The editorial in the *Journal* concludes: "Marriage may be an imperfect institution, but so far in human history no one has come up with a better way to nurture children in a stable society" (*Wall Street Journal,* April 25, 1995). (Provo City Community Centennial Service, August 4, 1996.)

Can we doubt that there is a sickness in our society? We cannot build prisons, even here, fast enough to accommodate the need. We have in this nation more than a million people in prison. The number is constantly increasing. Why is this happening? I believe that a substantial factor in all of this is that we as a nation are forsaking the Almighty, and He is forsaking us. . . . A recent poll indicated that a majority of Americans believe that the private lives of public officials need not be considered as a factor in their eligibility for public office. How far we have come from the time of George Washington, who stated in that first inaugural address the mandate "that the foundations of our national policy will be laid in the pure and immutable principles of private morality." (Provo City Community Centennial Service, August 4, 1996.)

Before disembarking from the *Mayflower*, our pilgrim fathers drafted and signed a compact which was to become the instrument of their governance, the first such document drafted on this continent. It began with these words: "In the name of God, amen." It went on to say that the signers "by these presents solemnly and mutually in the presence of God, and one another, covenant and combine ourselves together into a civil body politic . . ." (*Harvard Classics*, vol. 43, p. 62). . . . Once the people of our nation gathered their families together in daily prayer. They remembered before Deity this nation and its leaders. . . . That salutary practice of family prayer is largely disappearing from our society. Are we forgetting the Almighty, who in times of last resort is our greatest strength? ("Preserving Our Trust in God," American Legion Patriotic Religious Service, September 1, 1996.)

The Psalmist wrote, "The counsel of the Lord standeth forever, . . . Blessed is the nation whose God is the Lord" (Psalm 33:11–12). It was said of old by Paul the Apostle: "Where the spirit of the Lord is, there is liberty" (2 Corinthians 3:17).

One of the stirring pictures of our national heritage is that of General Washington kneeling in prayer at Valley Forge, pleading with the Almighty in behalf of his hungry, freezing, dying men of the Continental Army. . . .

We sing, "God Bless America." I pray that America will always be worthy of His blessing. ("Preserving Our Trust in God," American Legion Patriotic Religious Service, September 1, 1996.)

We have on our currency and our coinage a national motto: "In God We Trust." I know of no other nation that has such a motto. Others use the phrase, "By the Grace of God." But none other categorically states, "In God We Trust."

When that statement was adopted, it was believed in. It came of our great Judeo-Christian inheritance. I think we were then a humbler people than perhaps we are today. The recognition of

God, seeking His help in prayer, and giving honor and glory to Him, have been characteristic of our nation's history. . . .

We repeat the Pledge of Allegiance to the flag of the United States and "to the republic for which it stands." We say, "One nation under God, indivisible, with liberty and justice for all." I pray that we will never forget that we are in very deed a nation under God and that with the strength which comes from Him, we will remain "indivisible, with liberty and justice for all." . . .

In recent years the Boy Scouts of America have been challenged in the courts on the language of the Scout Oath: "On my honor, I will do my best, to do my duty to God, and my country."

Oaths of office and oaths in other legal procedures have concluded with the phrase, "So help me God."

Now, according to the *Wall Street Journal,* the state of New Jersey has passed a law banishing the mention of God from state courtroom oaths. Following this action by the legislature, a county judge decided to ban the use of Bibles for such oaths "because you-know-who is mentioned inside" the Bible. (*Wall Street Journal,* July 31, 1996.) (National Prayer Breakfast Ceremony, Salt Lake City, Utah, February 25, 1997.)

ANGER

[May we resolve] in our hearts to live the gospel, to be faithful and true, to have the strength to look above small things that could lead to argument and trouble, to be forgiving one to another, to "look to God and live." (Alma 37:47.)

It is so easy to stumble. It is sometimes so hard to keep our voices low when small things provoke us. ("Small Acts Lead to Great Consequences," *Ensign,* May 1984, p. 83.)

Love is the very essence of family life. Why is it that the children we love become so frequently the targets of our harsh words? Why is it that these children who love their fathers and mothers sometimes speak as if with daggers that cut to the quick? "There is beauty all around," *only* "when there's love at home." (*Hymns,* 1985, no. 294.) ("Let Love Be the Lodestar of Your Life," *Ensign,* May 1989, p. 67.)

A violent temper is such a terrible, corrosive thing. And the tragedy is that it accomplishes no good; it only feeds evil with resentment and rebellion and pain. To any man or boy within the sound of my voice who has trouble controlling his tongue, may I suggest that you plead with the Lord for the strength to over-come your weakness, that you apologize to those you have offended, and that you marshal within yourselves the power to discipline your tongue.

To the boys who are here, may I suggest that you watch your temper, now, in these formative years of your life. . . . This is the season to develop the power and capacity to discipline yourselves. You may think it is the macho thing to flare up in anger and swear and profane the name of the Lord. It is not the macho thing. It is an indication of weakness. Anger is not an expression of strength. It is an indication of one's inability to control his thoughts, words, his emotions. Of course it is easy to get angry. When the weakness of anger takes over, the strength of reason leaves. Cultivate within yourselves the mighty power of self-discipline. ("Our Solemn Responsibilities," *Ensign*, November 1991, p. 51.)

There is too much trouble in our homes. There is too much anger, that corrosive, terrible thing called anger. I make a plea with you, you men of the priesthood: Control your tongues. Walk out the door instead of shouting. Get control of yourselves. Love your children. Respect them. No good will come of beating them. It will only make them resentful. Treat them with love, kindness, and respect, and I do not hesitate to promise you that the day will come that you will get on your knees and thank the Lord for his blessings upon you and your family. (Anchorage Alaska Regional Conference, June 18, 1995.)

I appreciated the music of this wonderful men's chorus singing that song of Charles W. Penrose:

> *School thy feelings, O my brother;*
> *Train thy warm, impulsive soul.*
> *Do not its emotions smother,*
> *But let wisdom's voice control.*

> (HYMNS, NO. 336)

Do you know how that came to be written? He had been pre-siding in England. He was there for eleven years. He had never been to America, had never really known it—the organization of the Church. He thought they had forgotten him. He was presid-ing in Liverpool, and finally when he got his release, he was get-ting ready to move. During those eleven years he had accumulated a few sticks of furniture, besides that which the Church furnished. He had called the shipping agent and was bringing things out of the house and putting them in the wagon, and some of the Saints came along and said, "Look. President Penrose is stealing the Church's furniture."

He was a fiery Englishman. He had a great temper and he just flared up when he heard that kind of remark and then pulled himself down and went up into his room and wrote those words and put them to a popular tune. "School thy feelings, O my brother; Train thy warm, impulsive soul. . . ." That's the story of the song they sang. It's a great hymn, and there is a message for each of us in that, each of us. So many people get so mad over such little things. We lose our tempers. We don't know how to control our emotions. You come home tired at night, riding that commuter train, getting home about seven o'clock, and you take it out on your wives and your children. "School thy feelings, O my brother." Please, watch your temper. Whatever you do, watch your temper. (Potomac Virginia Regional Conference, priesthood leadership session, April 26, 1997.)

APPRECIATION

See Gratitude

ATONEMENT OF JESUS CHRIST

See also Jesus Christ

No member of this Church must ever forget the terrible price paid by our Redeemer who gave his life that all men might live—the agony of Gethsemane, the bitter mockery of his trial, the vicious crown of thorns tearing at his flesh, the blood cry of the mob before Pilate, the lonely burden of his heavy walk along the way to Calvary, the terrifying pain as great nails pierced his hands and feet, the fevered torture of his body as he hung that tragic day, the Son of God crying out, "Father, forgive them; for they know not what they do." (Luke 23:34.)

This was the cross, the instrument of his torture, the terrible device designed to destroy the Man of Peace, the evil recompense for his miraculous work of healing the sick, of causing the blind to see, of raising the dead. This was the cross on which he hung and died on Golgotha's lonely summit.

We cannot forget that. We must never forget it, for here our Savior, our Redeemer, the Son of God, gave himself a vicarious sacrifice for each of us. ("The Symbol of Christ," *Ensign*, May 1975, p. 93.)

I wish to remind everyone within my hearing that the comforts we have, the peace we have, and, most important, the faith and knowledge of the things of God that we have, were bought with a terrible price by those who have gone before us. Sacrifice has always been a part of the gospel of Jesus Christ. The crowning element of our faith is our conviction of our living God, the Father of us all, and of His Beloved Son, the Redeemer of the world. It is because of our Redeemer's life and sacrifice that we are here. It is because of His sacrificial atonement that we and all of the sons and daughters of God will partake of the salvation of the Lord. "For as in Adam all die, even so in Christ shall all be made alive." (1 Cor. 15:22.) It is because of the sacrificial redemption wrought by the Savior of the world that the great plan of the eternal gospel is made available to us under which those who die in the Lord shall not taste of death but shall have the opportunity of going on to a celestial and eternal glory.

In our own helplessness, He becomes our rescuer, saving us from damnation and bringing us to eternal life. ("Our Mission of Saving," *Ensign*, November 1991, p. 54.)

I cannot be grateful enough for the Atonement wrought by my Savior and my Redeemer. Through His sacrifice at the culmination of a life of perfection—that sacrifice offered in pain unspeakable—the bonds of death were broken, and the resurrection of all became assured. Beyond this, the doors of celestial glory have been opened to all who will accept divine truth and obey its precepts. ("My Testimony," *Ensign,* November 1993, p. 52.)

I sense in a measure the meaning of His atonement. I cannot comprehend it all. It is so vast in its reach and yet so intimate in its effect that it defies comprehension. When all is said and done, when all of history is examined, when the deepest depths of the human mind have been explored, there is nothing so wonderful, so majestic, so tremendous as this act of grace when the Son of the Almighty, the prince of His Father's royal household, . . . gave His life in ignominy and pain so that all of the sons and daughters of God, of all generations of time, every one of whom must die, might walk again and live eternally. ("Jesus Christ," First Presidency Christmas Devotional, Salt Lake Tabernacle, December 4, 1994.)

For all of Christendom, for all of mankind, [Easter] is observed as the anniversary of the greatest miracle in human history. It is the miracle that encompasses all who have lived upon the earth, all who now live upon the earth, and all who will yet live upon the earth. Nothing done before or since has so affected mankind as the atonement wrought by Jesus of Nazareth, who died on Calvary's cross and rose from the grave the third day as the living Son of the living God, the Savior and Redeemer of all mankind. . . . The Holy Spirit testifies of the truth, the validity, of what really occurred. His was the ultimate sacrifice; His the sublime victory. (St. Louis Missouri Regional Conference, April 16, 1995.)

The greatest salient truth of life is that the Son of God came into the world and atoned for the sins of mankind and opened the gate by which we may go on to eternal life. (Charlotte North Carolina Regional Conference, priesthood leadership session, February 24, 1996.)

When all else fails, our Lord is there to help us. He has said, "Come unto me, all ye that labour and are heavy laden, and I will give you rest" (Matt. 11:28). Each of you has burdens. Let the

Lord help you in carrying those burdens. Again He has said, "Take my yoke upon you, . . . for my yoke is easy, and my burden is light" (Matt. 11:29–30). He stands ready to help—to help each of us—with every burden. He loves us so much that He shed drops of blood in Gethsemane, then permitted evil and wicked men to take Him, to compel Him to carry the cross to Golgotha, to suffer beyond any power of description terrible pain when He was nailed to the cross, to be lifted up on the cross, and to die for each of us.

He was the one perfect man, without blemish, to walk the earth. He was the Savior and Redeemer of mankind. Because of His sacrifice, because of His Atonement, all of us will at some time arise in the Resurrection, and beyond that there will be marvelous opportunities to go forward on the road of immortality and eternal life. ("Stand True and Faithful," *Ensign,* May 1996, p. 94.)

I was in Jerusalem yesterday, and while we were there we went out to Shepherd's Field. A slit of a moon was in the sky, a band of sheep nearby, and Bethlehem over on the hill on the other side. There, in the shadows of the evening, we read together the story of the birth of the Son of God and sang a Christmas carol or two and had prayer together. It was not December; it was not April. It was June. But it was a wonderful thing, a thing of great inspiration. I wish everyone in the Church could have an experience of that kind. I've had it before. I am glad to have had it again.

To sense that, and to go again to the Garden of Gethsemane and there to sit in the shadow of an old olive tree and read of that terrible wrestling of the Son of God as He faced the certain future, sweating drops of blood and praying to His Father to let the cup pass if it might—but saying, Nevertheless, Thy will be done, not mine. As we sat there, I had an overwhelming feeling that He wasn't making His plea, He wasn't facing that ordeal in terms of the physical pain He was about to face, the terrible, brutal crucifixion on the cross. That was part of it, I am sure. But in larger measure it was, I think, a sense on His part of His role in the eternal welfare of all of the sons and daughters of God, of all generations of time.

Everything depended on Him—His atoning sacrifice. That was the key. That was the keystone in the arch of the great plan which the Father had brought forth for the eternal life of His sons and daughters. Terrible as it was to face it, and burdensome as it was to realize it, He faced it, He accomplished it, and it was a marvelous and wonderful thing. It is beyond our comprehension, I believe. Nevertheless, we glimpse it in small part and must learn to appreciate it more and more and more. (Mission Presidents Seminar, June 23, 1996.)

ATTITUDE

See also Optimism

For some eleven years I had responsibility for the work of the Church in Asia. I have been in that part of the world scores of times. I have seen firsthand the economic miracle of Japan. . . . I have seen that nation rise from the ashes of war to its present economic summit. Its secret has not been in its natural resources. It must import every quart of oil, every pound of iron ore. Its secret lies in the attitude of its people. At one time, within my memory, the label "Made in Japan" usually stood for a shoddy copy. Today, it stands for the highest quality. The difference does not lie in its minerals, in its scenery, in fertile fields or abundant rain or whatever of nature. I repeat, the difference lies in the attitude of its people. It must be so with us if we are to shape the future. . . .

I finished [at the university] in the Class of '32. I spoke at our class reunion in 1982 after 50 years had passed. People came to that reunion from across the nation. They were my friends of school days. They have filled positions of leadership in many parts of the land. There never was a darker time in this state to have been graduated from the university. . . . Those were the darkest days of the dark depression. We worried. Of course we worried. We were poor, and we knew it, but we were not bitter. We were young and we went to work at whatever we could find. Somehow we made it. The journey has been like a ride on an old steam train. There have been bumps and jolts and cinders in the eye. But there has also been a magnificent and exciting vista along the way. In my imagination, I can hear the old steam whistle blow, singing out as we move along the rails to our present station. Now there is a stronger engine and a better roadbed, and as we go forward, I hope we can sing together: "We're moving. We're on the right track. Here we come. The future never looked so bright." (Governor's Conference on Utah's Future, University of Utah, September 7, 1988.)

We see some around us who are indifferent concerning the future of this work, who are apathetic, who speak of limitations, who express fears, who spend their time digging out and writing about what they regard to be weaknesses which really are of no consequence. With doubt concerning its past, they have no vision concerning its future.

Well was it said of old, "Where there is no vision, the people perish" (Prov. 29:18). There is no place in this work for those who believe only in the gospel of doom and gloom. The gospel is good news. It is a message of triumph. It is a cause to be embraced with enthusiasm.

The Lord never said that there would not be troubles. Our people have known afflictions of every sort as those who have opposed this work have come upon them. But faith has shone through all their sorrows. ("Stay the Course—Keep the Faith," *Ensign*, November 1995, p. 71.)

BALANCE

See also Priorities

Grow with balance. An old cliche states that modern education leads a man to know more and more about less and less. I want to plead with you to keep balance in your lives. Do not become obsessed with what may be called "a gospel hobby." A good meal always includes more than one course. You ought to have great strength in your chosen and assigned field of expertise. But I warn you against making that your only interest. I glory in the breadth of this commandment to the people of the Church:

"And I give unto you a commandment that you shall teach one another the doctrine of the kingdom.

"Teach ye diligently and my grace shall attend you, that you may be instructed more perfectly in theory, in principle, in doctrine, in the law of the gospel, in all things that pertain unto the kingdom of God, that are expedient for you to understand;

"Of things both in heaven and in the earth, and under the earth; things which have been, things which are, things which must shortly come to pass; things which are at home, things which are abroad; the wars and the perplexities of the nations and the judgments which are on the land; and a knowledge also of countries and of kingdoms—

"That ye may be prepared in all things. . . ." (D&C 88:77–80.)

In my life I have had opportunity to serve in many different capacities in the Church. Every time I was released in connection with a new calling, I felt reluctant to leave the old. But every call brought with it an opportunity to learn of another segment of the great program of the Church. I carry in my heart something of pity for those who permit themselves to get locked into one situation and never have an opportunity to experience any other. Missionaries not infrequently plead with their presidents that they be permitted to extend their missions. This is commendable and is usually indicative of the fact that they have been effective in their work. But a missionary's release usually is as providential as his call, as thereby there are opened to him other opportunities. And out of it all will come a balance in his life. ("Four Imperatives for Religious Educators," Church Educational System Address, September 15, 1978, p. 2.)

Now and then as I have watched a man become obsessed with a narrow segment of knowledge, I have worried about him. I have seen a few such. They have pursued relentlessly only a sliver of knowledge until they have lost a sense of balance. At the moment I think of two who went so far and became so misguided in their narrow pursuits, that they who once had been effective teachers of youth have been found to be in apostasy and have been excommunicated from the Church. Keep balance in your lives. Beware of obsession. Beware of narrowness. Let your interests range over many good fields while working with growing strength in the field of your own profession. ("Four Imperatives for Religious Educators," Church Educational System Address, September 15, 1978, p. 3.)

I think every officer in the Church, all of us in this Church, serve in a part-time capacity and have a fourfold responsibility. One, they have a responsibility to their families, to see that their families have a measure of their time. What should it profit a man if he gain the whole world and lose his own, paraphrasing the Savior's words. Every man has a responsibility toward his family. None of us can evade that. . . . We must have time to be with family. That is basic and it is fundamental.

If we are employed, we have a responsibility to our employer. We are not at liberty to short-change him, as it were, in order to take care of the business of the elders quorum. We have a responsibility as men of integrity and honesty to deal right with our employer.

We have a responsibility to the Lord, of course, to do that which is expected of us as a servant in His house.

And I may add, we have a responsibility to ourselves to take some time to do a little meditating, to do a little exercise, whatever.

Now, that is a fourfold responsibility. How do you balance them? I don't think that is difficult. I served in many capacities in this Church. I am the father of five children, who were young and growing up when I was serving in those various capacities. I think we had a good time and we took vacations together. We enjoyed life. We had family home evenings. We just did what the Church expected us to do. There is safety in that program; it's inspired.

As a stake president I think I can say I did not neglect my family. I think my children would so testify if they were here. I think I will never get over feeling grateful that they have grown up to be faithful Latter-day Saints, who carry responsibilities of their own in an excellent way. I give the credit to their wonderful mother. She did the job while I was away. . . .

You have to sit down now and look at your resources. The major resource in this matter is time. I think you can do it. You balance it. You organize yourselves, as the Lord said, so that you can make that balance. (Heber City/Springville Utah Regional Conference, priesthood leadership session, May 13, 1995.)

BAPTISM

If a man or woman has truly repented of his or her sins, then he or she may be eligible to be baptized by immersion with the understanding that those sins will be forgiven and that life can begin anew.

It is no small or unimportant thing to baptize an individual. You as a young priest, acting in the name of the Lord and under divine authority, wipe out, as it were, by the marvelous process of baptism, the sins of the past and bring about a birth into a new and better life. What a tremendous responsibility you have to live worthy of the exercise of this sacred power! ("The Priesthood of Aaron," *Ensign*, November 1982, p. 46.)

I assume there is no Christian who does not acknowledge the necessity for and the importance of baptism "of water and of the Spirit." None could legitimately deny this necessity in view of the statement given by the Master to Nicodemus: "Except a man be born of water and of the Spirit, he cannot enter into the kingdom of God." (John 3:5.) ("Rejoice in This Great Era of Temple Building," *Ensign*, November 1985, p. 59.)

This Aaronic Priesthood, bestowed by John the Baptist, also includes the keys of baptism by immersion for the remission of sins. It is one thing to repent. It is another to have our sins remitted or forgiven. The power to bring this about is found in the Aaronic Priesthood.

Baptism is the primary ordinance of the gospel. It is the gate through which all come into the Church. It is so important that it is performed not only for the living but also for the dead. ("The Aaronic Priesthood—a Gift from God," *Ensign*, May 1988, p. 46.)

Baptism into this Church is a serious thing. It represents a covenant made with our Eternal Father. It is much more than a rite of passage. It is the gateway to a new manner of living, and a new road on which to walk that leads to immortality and eternal life. It was never intended as a dead end. It was intended to open a glorious and wonderful new way of life to all who would walk in obedience to the commandments of God. (General Authority Training Meeting, October 2, 1990.)

Baptism is only the gate through which a man or woman enters. Our real objective is to make of that stranger, who is rapidly taught in a few lessons, a strong and faithful member of The Church of Jesus Christ of Latter-day Saints, one who loves the Lord, who understands the gospel, who fellowships with the Saints, who partakes of the beauties and wonders of this great and marvelous thing which we call the gospel of Jesus Christ. (General Authority Training Meeting, April 2, 1991.)

Some people wonder why we don't accept the baptisms of other churches. We don't for two reasons: It isn't done in the proper way and it isn't done by the proper authority. And so, when a convert comes into this Church he must be baptized in the name of Jesus Christ, by immersion, by one holding the proper priesthood. . . . What a wonderful thing that is, to know that in similitude of the death and burial and resurrection of the Son of God we have gone down into the water and been immersed in the water and brought forth out of the water. Baptism is a great and sacred and marvelous ordinance that brings with it the remission of sins, but in a larger measure, it is symbolic of the death, burial, and resurrection of our Divine Redeemer. (Copenhagen Denmark Fireside, June 14, 1996.)

BIRTH CONTROL

Much has been said . . . about birth control. I like to think of the positive side of the equation, of the meaning and sanctity of life, of the purpose of this estate in our eternal journey, of the need for the experiences of mortal life under the great plan of God our Father, of the joy that is to be found only where there are children in the home, of the blessings that come of good posterity. When I think of these values and see them taught and observed, then I am willing to leave the question of numbers to the man and the woman and the Lord. ("If I Were You, What

Would I Do?" *BYU 1983–84 Fireside and Devotional Speeches,* September 20, 1983, p. 11.)

BOOK OF MORMON

[Parley P. Pratt] was traveling from Ohio to eastern New York. At Newark, along the Erie Canal, he left the boat and walked ten miles into the country where he met a Baptist deacon by the name of Hamlin, who told him "of a *book*, a STRANGE BOOK, a VERY STRANGE BOOK! . . . This book, he said, purported to have been originally written on plates either of gold or brass, by a branch of the tribes of Israel; and to have been discovered and translated by a young man near Palmyra, in the State of New York, by the aid of visions, or the ministry of angels. I inquired of him how or where the book was to be obtained. He promised me the perusal of it, at his house the next day. . . . Next morning I called at his house, where, for the first time, my eyes beheld the 'BOOK OF MORMON'—that book of books . . . which was the principal means, in the hands of God, of directing the entire course of my future life.

"I opened it with eagerness, and read its title page. I then read the testimony of several witnesses in relation to the manner of its being found and translated. After this I commenced its contents by course. I read all day; eating was a burden, I had no desire for food; sleep was a burden when the night came, for I preferred reading to sleep.

"As I read, the spirit of the Lord was upon me, and I knew and comprehended that the book was true, as plainly and manifestly as a man comprehends and knows that he exists" (*Autobiography of Parley P. Pratt,* 3d ed., Salt Lake City: Deseret Book Co., 1938, pp. 36–37).

Parley Pratt was then twenty-three years of age. The reading of the Book of Mormon affected him so profoundly that he was soon baptized into the Church and became one of its most effective and powerful advocates. . . .

Parley Pratt's experience with the Book of Mormon was not unique. As the volumes of the first edition were circulated and read, strong men and women by the hundreds were so deeply touched that they gave up everything they owned, and in the years that followed not a few even gave their lives for the witness they carried in their hearts of the truth of this remarkable volume. ("'An Angel from on High, the Long, Long Silence Broke,'" *Ensign*, November 1979, p. 7.)

I know of no other writing [than the Book of Mormon] which sets forth with such clarity the tragic consequences to societies that follow courses contrary to the commandments of God. Its pages trace the stories of two distinct civilizations that flourished on this Western Hemisphere. Each began as a small nation, its people walking in the fear of the Lord. But with prosperity came growing evils. The people succumbed to the wiles of ambitious and scheming leaders who oppressed them with burdensome taxes, who lulled them with hollow promises, who countenanced and even encouraged loose and lascivious living, who led them into terrible wars that resulted in the death of millions and the final and total extinction of two great civilizations in two different eras.

No other written testament so clearly illustrates the fact that when men and nations walk in the fear of God and in obedience to his commandments, they prosper and grow, but when they disregard him and his word, there comes a decay that, unless arrested by righteousness, leads to impotence and death. The Book of Mormon is an affirmation of the Old Testament proverb, "Righteousness exalteth a nation: but sin is a reproach to any people" (Prov. 14:34). ("'An Angel from on High, the Long, Long Silence Broke,'" *Ensign*, November 1979, p. 8.)

The great and stirring burden of [the message of the Book of Mormon] is a testimony, vibrant and true, that Jesus is the Christ, the promised Messiah, he who walked the dusty roads of Palestine healing the sick and teaching the doctrines of salvation; who died upon the cross of Calvary; who on the third day came forth from the tomb, appearing to many; and who, prior to his final ascension, visited the people of this Western Hemisphere, concerning whom he earlier had said: "And other sheep I have, which are not of this fold: them also I must bring, and they shall hear my voice; and there shall be one fold, and one shepherd" (John 10:16).

For centuries the Bible stood alone as a written testimony of the divinity of Jesus of Nazareth. Now, at its side, stands a second and powerful witness which has come forth "to the convincing of the Jew and Gentile that Jesus is the Christ, the Redeemer of the world" (Book of Mormon, title page). ("'An Angel from on High, the Long, Long Silence Broke,'" *Ensign*, November 1979, pp. 8–9.)

Today, a century and a half after its first publication, [the Book of Mormon] is more widely read than at any time in its history. . . .

Its appeal is as timeless as truth, as universal as mankind. It is the only book that contains within its covers a promise that by divine power the reader may know with certainty of its truth.

Its origin is miraculous; when the story of that origin is first told to one unfamiliar with it, it is almost unbelievable. But the book is here to be felt and handled and read. No one can dispute its presence. All efforts to account for its origin, other than the account given by Joseph Smith, have been shown to lack substance. It is a record of ancient America. It is a scripture of the New World, as certainly as the Bible is the scripture of the Old. Each speaks of the other. Each carries with it the spirit of inspiration, the power to convince and to convert. Together they become two witnesses, hand in hand, that Jesus is the Christ, the resurrected and living Son of the living God. ("'An Angel from on High, the Long, Long Silence Broke,'" *Ensign*, November 1979, pp. 7–8.)

As has been demonstrated for a hundred and fifty years, the truth of the book will not be determined by literary analysis or by scientific research, although these are reassuring and most welcome. The truth will be determined today and tomorrow, as it has been throughout the yesterdays, by the reading of it in a spirit of reverence and respect and prayer. . . .

. . . To think that anyone less than one inspired could bring forth a book which should have so profound an effect for good upon others is to imagine that which simply cannot be. The evidence for the truth of the Book of Mormon is found in the lives of the millions, living and gone, who have read it, prayed about it, and received a witness of its truth. ("'Praise to the Man,'" *BYU Devotional Speeches of the Year*, November 4, 1979, p. 205.)

Unbelievers may doubt the First Vision and say there were not witnesses to prove it. Critics may scorn every divine manifestation incident to the coming forth of this work as being of such an intangible nature as to be unprovable to the pragmatic mind, as if the things of God could be understood other than by the Spirit of God. They may discount our theology. But they cannot in honesty dismiss the Book of Mormon. It is here. They can feel it. They can read it. They can weigh its substance and its content. They can witness its influence. . . .

. . . The Book of Mormon has gone forth to change for good the lives of men and women in many nations. What a concourse of the people of the earth we would have if all of those who have read this book and been influenced by its message were gathered together in one place. (*Be Thou an Example* [Salt Lake City: Deseret Book, 1981], p. 103–4.)

Each time we encourage a man to read the Book of Mormon we do him a favor. If he reads it prayerfully and with a sincere desire to know the truth, he will know by the power of the Holy Ghost that the book is true. And from that knowledge there will flow a conviction of the truth of many other things.

For if the Book of Mormon is true, then God lives. Testimony upon testimony runs through its pages of the solemn fact that our Father is real, that he is personal, that he loves his children and seeks their happiness.

If the Book of Mormon is true, then Jesus is the Son of God, the Only Begotten of the Father in the flesh, born of Mary, "a virgin most beautiful above all other virgins," for the book so testifies in a description unexcelled in all literature.

If the Book of Mormon is true, then Jesus is verily our Redeemer, the Savior of the world.

If the Book of Mormon is true, then this land is choice above all other lands; but if it is to remain such, the inhabitants of the land must worship the God of the land, the Lord Jesus Christ. The histories of two great nations, told with warning in this sacred volume, indicate that while we must have science, while we must have education, while we must have arms, we must also have righteousness if we are to merit the protection of God.

If the Book of Mormon is true, Joseph Smith was a prophet of God, for he was the instrument in the hands of God in bringing to light this testimony of the divinity of our Lord. . . .

I repeat, if the Book of Mormon is true, the Church is true, for the same authority under which this sacred record came to light is present and manifest among us today. It is a restoration of the Church set up by the Savior in Palestine. It is a restoration of the Church set up by the Savior when he visited this continent as set forth in this sacred record. (*Be Thou an Example* [Salt Lake City: Deseret Book, 1981], pp. 104–5.)

Such has been the power of this great book in the lives of those who have read it prayerfully. I give you my testimony that it is true. That I know by the witness of the Holy Ghost, and that knowledge to me is certain.

Sidney Rigdon did not write it. Oliver Cowdery did not write it. It is not the result of a paranoiac or of a dissociated personality, as some have said. It is not the product of a mythmaker. It is not the result of the environment of a farm boy who grew up in western New York. Joseph Smith did not write it. He, the prophet of this dispensation, translated the writings of prophets of old under the power of God, to testify in our day. (*Be Thou an Example* [Salt Lake City: Deseret Book, 1981], p. 106.)

The ancient record from which [the Book of Mormon] was translated came out of the earth as a voice speaking from the dust. It came as the testimony of generations of men and women who lived their lives upon the earth, who struggled with adversity, who quarreled and fought, who at various times lived the divine law and prospered and at other times forsook their God and went down to destruction. It contains what has been described as the fifth Gospel, a moving testament of the new world concerning the visit of the resurrected Redeemer on the soil of this hemisphere.

The evidence for its truth, for its validity in a world that is prone to demand evidence, lies not in archaeology or anthropology, though these may be helpful to some. It lies not in word research or historical analysis, though these may be confirmatory. The evidence for its truth and validity lies within the covers of the book itself. The test of its truth lies in reading it. It is a book of God. Reasonable men may sincerely question its origin; but those who have read it prayerfully have come to know by a power beyond their natural senses that it is true, that it contains the word of God, that it outlines saving truths of the everlasting gospel, that it came forth by the gift and power of God "to the convincing of the Jew and Gentile that Jesus is the Christ." (Book of Mormon title page.)

It is here. It must be explained. It can be explained only as the translator himself explained its origin. Hand in hand with the Bible, whose companion volume it is, it stands as another witness to a doubting generation that Jesus is the Christ, the Son of the living God. It is an unassailable cornerstone of our faith. ("The Cornerstones of Our Faith," *Ensign*, November 1984, p. 52.)

Without reservation I promise you that if you will prayerfully read the Book of Mormon, regardless of how many times you previously have read it, there will come into your hearts an added measure of the Spirit of the Lord. There will come a strengthened resolution to walk in obedience to his commandments, and there will come a stronger testimony of the living reality of the Son of God. ("The Power of the Book of Mormon," *Ensign*, June 1988, p. 6.)

The Book of Mormon stands as an added testament of Jesus Christ. Through its pages march the testimonies of prophets of the New World. Majestic in its sweep of history, its chapters are filled with the tragedy of war, with divine warnings, and with God-given promises. It speaks as a voice from the dust to a world that needs to listen. ("The Order and Will of God," *Ensign*, January 1989, p. 2.)

May I remind you for a moment of the greatness and of the goodness of this man Mormon. He lived on this American continent in the fourth century after Christ. When he was a boy of ten the historian of the people, whose name was Ammoron, described Mormon as "a sober child, and . . . quick to observe." (Morm. 1:2.) Ammoron gave him a charge that when he reached the age of twenty-four, he was to take custody of the records of the generations who had preceded him.

The years that followed Mormon's childhood were years of terrible bloodshed for his nation, the result of a long and vicious and terrible war between those who were called Nephites and those who were called Lamanites.

Mormon later became the leader of the armies of the Nephites and witnessed the carnage of his people, making it plain to them that their repeated defeats came because they forsook the Lord and He in turn abandoned them. His nation was destroyed with the slaughter of hundreds of thousands. He was one of only twenty-four who survived. As he looked upon the moldering remains of what once had been legions, he cried:

"O ye fair ones, how could ye have departed from the ways of the Lord! O ye fair ones, how could ye have rejected that Jesus, who stood with open arms to receive you!" (Morm. 6:17.)

He wrote to our generation with words of warning and pleading, proclaiming with eloquence his testimony of the resurrected Christ. He warned of calamities to come if we should forsake the ways of the Lord as his own people had done.

Knowing that his own life would soon be brought to an end, as his enemies hunted the survivors, he pleaded for our generation to walk with faith, hope, and charity, declaring: "Charity is the pure love of Christ, and it endureth forever; and whoso is found possessed of it at the last day, it shall be well with him." (Moro. 7:47.)

Such was the goodness, the strength, the power, the faith, the prophetic heart of the prophet-leader Mormon. ("*Mormon Should Mean 'More Good,'*" *Ensign*, November 1990, p. 52.)

[Mormon] was the chief compiler of the book which is called after his name and which has come forth in this period of the world's history as a voice speaking from the dust in testimony of the Lord Jesus Christ.

It has touched for good the lives of millions who have prayerfully read it and pondered its language. May I tell you of one such I recently met in Europe.

He was a businessman, successful in his undertakings. In the course of his travels he met two of our missionaries. They tried to set up an appointment to teach him. He put them off, but finally agreed to listen. He somewhat perfunctorily accepted what they had to say. He became convinced in his mind that they spoke the truth, but he was not moved in his heart.

He decided that he would read the Book of Mormon. He said that he had been a man of the world, never given to crying. But as he read the book, tears coursed his cheeks. It did something to him. He read it again and felt the same emotions. What had been conversion of the mind became conversion of the heart.

His way of life was altered, his perspective changed. He threw himself into the work of the Lord. Today he fills a high and holy calling in the cause he has come to love. ("*Mormon* Should Mean 'More Good,'" *Ensign*, November 1990, p. 52.)

This so-called Book of Mormon, this scripture of the New World, is before us as an added witness of the divinity and reality of the Lord Jesus Christ, of the encompassing beneficence of His atonement, and of His coming forth from the darkness of the grave. Within these covers is found much of the sure word of prophecy concerning Him who should be born of a virgin, the Son of the Almighty God. There is a foretelling of His work among men as a living mortal. There is a declaration of His death, of the lamb without blemish who was to be sacrificed for the sins of the world. And there is an account that is moving and inspiring and true of the visit of the resurrected Christ among living men and women in the western continent. The testimony is here to handle; it is here to be read; it is here to be pondered; it is here to be prayed over with a promise that he who prays shall know by the power of the Holy Ghost of its truth and validity (see Moro. 10:3–5). ("The Greatest Miracle in Human History," *Ensign*, May 1994, p. 72.)

Think of [this] tremendous book of 522 pages, which is being read across the world. More than three million copies of this marvelous record were distributed last year alone. No one, I am satisfied, can prayerfully read the Book of Mormon without coming to a knowledge that it is what it purports to be, and that is another witness of the Lord Jesus Christ speaking out of the dust to those of this generation concerning the Redeemer of the world. (Ricks College Regional Conference, Rexburg, Idaho, October 29, 1995.)

I would like to urge every man and woman . . . and every boy and girl who is old enough to read to again read the Book of Mormon during this coming year. This was written for the convincing of the Jew and the Gentile that Jesus is the Christ. There is nothing we could do of greater importance than to have fortified in our individual lives an unshakable conviction that Jesus is the Christ, the living Son of the living God. That is the purpose of the coming forth of this remarkable and wonderful book. May I suggest that you read it again and take a pencil, a red one if you have one, and put a little check mark every time there is a reference to Jesus Christ in that book. And there will come to you a very real conviction as you do so that this is in very deed another witness for the Lord Jesus Christ. (Corpus Christi Texas Regional Conference, January 7, 1996.)

CHARACTER

I want to make it clear that I am not adverse to some recreation. All work and no play makes Jack a dull boy, and likewise Jill a dull doll. But when it becomes an end in itself, then we are in danger. We cannot expect to refine the substance of character from "the husks of pleasure." ("Cornerstones as Stepping-Stones," BYU Commencement Address, April 20, 1979.)

I plead that you continue to cultivate the companionship and direction of the Holy Spirit, that you look to God as the source of wisdom beyond your own, that you recognize His Divine Son as the fountainhead of those great virtues which are the essence of integrity and character. (BYU Commencement Address, April 23, 1992.)

Beyond your regular vocational duties are responsibilities toward others—toward the community, the state, the nation, society in general, and the Church of which most of you are members. The attention you give to these, the energy you devote to these are of the essence of your character and your virtue. (BYU Management Society, San Diego, California, January 9, 1993.)

CHARITY

See also Love

In your associations one with another, build and strengthen one another. "No man is an island; no man stands alone." We so need help and encouragement and strength, one from another.

On one occasion when the Savior was walking among a crowd, a woman who had been long sick touched his garment. He perceived that strength had gone out of him. The strength that was his had strengthened her. So it may be with each of us. Let me urge you to desist from making cutting remarks one to another. Rather, cultivate the art of complimenting, of strengthening, of encouraging. What wonders we can accomplish when others have faith in us. No leader can long succeed in any society without the confidence of the people. It is so with us in our daily associations. Said the Lord to Peter, "Simon, Simon, behold Satan hath desired to have you, that he might sift you as wheat: But I have prayed for thee, that thy faith fail not: and when thou art converted, strengthen thy brethren" (Luke 22:31–32). Declared Paul, "We then that are strong ought to bear the infirmities of the weak." And then he adds, "and not to please ourselves" (Romans 15:1).

It is a responsibility divinely laid upon us to bear one another's burdens, to strengthen one another, to encourage one another, to lift one another, to look for the good in one another, and to emphasize that good. ("Let Not Your Heart Be Troubled," BYU *Speeches of the Year*, October 29, 1974, p. 271–72.)

Love of God is basic. It is the very foundation of true worship. It puts heart and soul and spirit into our lives. It subdues arrogance and conceit and greed. It leads to love for all of God's creations. It leads to obedience to the second great commandment, love of neighbor. In the world in which we now live, that love of neighbor finds expression not only in Christian acts of charity and kindness to those in need, but in a larger sense includes a sacred regard for the environment in which all men as neighbors across the earth must live. ("A Unique and Wonderful University," *BYU 1988–89 Devotional and Fireside Speeches*, October 11, 1988, p. 51.)

The word *love* is often used in place of the word *charity* in Paul's great declaration. I so read it:

"[Love] never faileth: but whether there be prophecies, they shall fail; whether there be tongues, they shall cease; whether there be knowledge, it shall vanish away. . . .

"And now abideth faith, hope, [love], these three; but the greatest of these is [love]." (1 Cor. 13:8, 13.) . . .

Few of us see the Polar Star anymore. We live in urban centers, and the city lights affect our vision of the wondrous firmament above us. But, as it has been for centuries, the star is there, in its place, its constancy a guide and an anchor. So likewise is love—unyielding, unchanging, "the pure love of Christ," as Moroni declared, "and it endureth forever; and whoso is found possessed of it at the last day, it shall be well with him." (Moro. 7:47.) ("Let Love Be the Lodestar of Your Life," *Ensign*, May 1989, p. 67.)

Last Sunday I attended a sacrament service in one of our university wards, a ward comprised entirely of young married students who are struggling with their educational pursuits as well as with the burdens of family life. Two babies, recently born, were given blessings by their fathers as they were given names to be placed on the rolls of the Church.

I was touched by the prayers of both of these young fathers. One of them, speaking to his newborn son, blessed him that throughout his life he would have a spirit of love for all people regardless of their circumstances or condition. He blessed him that he should practice respect for others regardless of race, religious denomination, or other differences. I know that this young father, a medical student, has carried in his own life, as a faithful member of this Church, love and appreciation and respect for all.

How great a thing is charity, whether it be expressed through the giving of one's substance, the lending of one's strength to lift the burdens of others, or as an expression of kindness and appreciation. (*"Mormon* Should Mean 'More Good,'" *Ensign,* November 1990, p. 54.)

This is the essence of charity—to extend without price a helping, lifting hand to those in need. ("Codes and Covenants," *BYU 1994–95 Devotional and Fireside Speeches,* October 18, 1994, p. 38.)

CHASTITY

See also Morality; Virtue

Petting is simply a step on the road to sexual transgression or immorality. In fact, it is transgression. It is the seeking of physical satisfaction through the invited or forced involvement of another. By the standards of the Church it is unholy, unrighteous, and evil. . . . Petting frequently leads to the most serious kind of immorality. . . . It has done so with thousands. (Youth Fireside Satellite Broadcast, December 5, 1982.)

There is a philosophy among large numbers of people that sex education in our schools is the answer to the terrible problems of teenage pregnancies, abortions, and other grievous matters.

I am not disposed to discuss in this forum the merits or otherwise of sex education in public schools. But in passing, I am inclined to agree with one who was recently quoted in the newspaper *USA Today:* "More sex education in public schools will not reverse the damaging legacy of the sexual revolution unless the clear message is premarital chastity and marital monogamy."

This writer continues: "There are many defects in sex education courses. The philosophy behind them is to ridicule chastity, scoff at fidelity, and glamorize sexual adventurism. They teach there is no such thing as right and wrong. . . .

"Thirty years of advocating sexual liberation has brought raging venereal diseases and rampant teenage pregnancy. . . .

"Most sex education in the public schools morally disarms the students rather than giving them moral sensitivity to help them make the proper sexual choices. . . .

"Sex education fights the modesty and morality endemic to human life" (Tottie Ellis, "Teaching about Sex Endangers Children," 16 Mar. 1987, p. 12A).

There is in each of us that sense of modesty and morality to which this writer refers. . . . The Lord has made it clear, and the experience of centuries has confirmed it, that happiness lies not in immorality, but rather in abstinence. The voice of the Church to which you belong is a voice pleading for virtue. It is a voice pleading for strength to abstain from that which is evil. It is a voice declaring that sexual transgression is sin. It is contrary to the will of the Lord. It is contrary to the teachings of the Church. It is contrary to the happiness and well-being of those who indulge in it.

You should recognize, you *must* recognize, that both experience and divine wisdom dictate virtue and moral cleanliness as the way that leads to strength of character, peace in the heart, and happiness in life. ("Reverence and Morality," *Ensign,* May 1987, pp. 47–48.)

Let parents teach their children the sanctity of sex, that the gift of creating life is sacred, that the impulses that burn within us can be and must be disciplined and restrained if there is to be happiness and peace and goodness. Let there be instilled in the mind of every young man a great salient fact that every young woman is a daughter of our Eternal Father and that in offending her, he not only demonstrates his own weakness, but also offends God. Let him understand that to sire a child brings a responsibility that will last as long as he lives. ("Saving the Nation by Changing Our Homes," BYU Management Society, Washington, D.C., March 5, 1994, p. 9.)

Be clean. "Be ye clean that bear the vessels of the Lord." (D&C 133:5.) That is His injunction to us, young or old. Be clean. "Let virtue garnish thy thoughts unceasingly." Those great words written in the cold and the misery of Liberty Jail come as a great clarion call to us in this day when there is so much of filth and rot and sleaze and trash being peddled. . . . Be clean in thought and word and deed. Then comes the promise: "Then shall thy confidence wax strong in the presence of God; and the doctrine of the priesthood shall distil upon thy soul as the dews from heaven. The Holy Ghost shall be thy constant companion, and thy scepter an unchanging scepter of righteousness and truth; and thy dominion shall be an everlasting dominion, and without compulsory means it shall flow unto thee forever and ever." (D&C 121:45–46.) I do not know of another promise any-where of the magnitude and beauty and wonder of that divinely given promise.

Many years ago President McKay asked me to do something and I did it the best way I knew how to do it. And when it was done I went to report what I had done. He was very kind and generous and gracious in his compliments and expressions of gratitude. As I walked from his apartment back to the Church Administration Building, I said to myself, "What a wonderful thing to stand in confidence before the President of the Church." Then these words came into my mind: "Then shall thy confidence wax strong in the presence of God." What a marvelous thing. Are you and I living our lives in such a way that we could stand, should the moment come at any time, with confidence in the presence of God and give an accounting of our lives and our actions, even our thoughts? (Smithfield/Logan Utah Regional Conference, April 21, 1996.)

We believe in chastity before marriage and total fidelity after marriage. That sums it up. That is the way to happiness in liv-ing. That is the way to satisfaction. It brings peace to the heart and peace to the home. ("'This Thing Was Not Done in a Corner,'" *Ensign,* November 1996, p. 49.)

CHILD SUPPORT

Every man who fails to meet his responsibility to care for those he has fathered may find his standing in the Church in jeopardy, and particularly his eligibility for a temple recommend. Paul wrote to Timothy, "But if any provide not for his own, and specially for those of his own house, he hath denied the faith, and is worse than an infidel." (1 Tim. 5:8.)

There may be extenuating circumstances in some cases, but those cases will be exceptional. We have followed the principle, in cases of men who have been excommunicated for misconduct and who later have desired to return to the Church and to again receive their former blessings, that as an evidence of sincere repentance they must demonstrate that they have been and are meeting those family support payments mandated by law and obligated by the principles of our religion.

The responsibilities of parenthood have been set forth by the Lord and have been emphasized by our leaders from the beginning of the Church. ("Questions and Answers," *Ensign*, November 1985, p. 51.)

Fathers who fail to provide court-mandated support for their children cannot expect the privileges of the House of the Lord. The scriptures are straightforward in their declarations concerning the responsibility of fathers with reference to their children. When divorce occurs and bitterness grows, as it usually does, some men will go to almost any end to escape provision for their care. Where such becomes a violation of that which has been ordered by a court of law, it becomes an act of contempt contrary to the doctrine and teaching of the Church. ("Keeping the Temple Holy," *Ensign*, May 1990, pp. 51–52.)

CHILDREN

See also Family

Children are so very important. I never get over the thought that every man, good or bad, was once a little boy, and that every woman was once a little girl. They have moved in the direction in which they were pointed when they were small. Truly, "As the twig is bent, so the tree is inclined." The time to mold the pattern of virtuous youth and faithful adults is childhood. ("A Friend for Every Child," *Improvement Era*, December 1970, p. 98.)

We took some of our grandchildren to the circus one evening. I was more interested in watching them and many others of their kind than in watching the man on the flying trapeze. I looked at them in wonder as they alternately laughed and stared wide-eyed at the exciting things before them. And I thought of the miracle of children, who become the world's constant renewal of life and purpose. . . .

. . . As we train a new generation, so will the world be in a few years. If you are worried about the future, then look to the upbringing of your children. Wisely did the writer of Proverbs declare, "Train up a child in the way he should go: and when he is old, he will not depart from it." (Proverbs 22:6.) (*Be Thou an Example* [Salt Lake City: Deseret Book, 1981], p. 35.)

Nor let us ever forget the need to respect these, our little ones. Under the revealed word of the Lord, we know they are children of God as we are children of God, deserving of that respect which comes of knowledge of that eternal principle. In fact, the Lord made it clear that unless we develop in our own lives that purity, that lack of guile, that innocence of evil, we cannot enter into his presence. Declared he, "Except ye be converted, and become as little children, ye shall not enter into the kingdom of heaven." (Matthew 18:3.) (*Be Thou an Example* [Salt Lake City: Deseret Book, 1981], p. 39.)

"What are little girls made of? Sugar and spice, and everything nice." So goes the old nursery rhyme. But more importantly, they are the promise of the future. Through them, eventually, must filter the qualities of all of the earlier generations, which will become the bone and the tissue, the minds and the spirits, of the generations yet to be.

To you young girls I say with all of the strength and conviction I can muster, be sweet, be good, be strong and virtuous and wonderful. Somehow I feel that the Lord included you with those of whom he spoke when he said, "Except ye . . . become as little children, ye shall not enter into the kingdom of heaven." (Matt. 18:3.) Channing Pollock, the gifted author and playwright, once wished, through one of his characters, that we might all be born old and gradually grow younger and ever more innocent until at death we have become as little children. ("Live Up to Your Inheritance," *Ensign*, November 1983, p. 81.)

Children are the epitome of innocence, they are the epitome of purity, they are the epitome of love, they are the epitome of hope and gladness in this difficult and troubled world. ("Behold Your Little Ones," Children's Fireside Satellite Broadcast, January 23, 1994.)

In 1988, terrible forest fires raged [in Yellowstone National Park]. Each day the news media brought us graphic reports of the intensity of the fires as they raced over thousands of acres, destroying millions of trees. The flames finally burned out, and people literally mourned over the desolate picture of countless lodgepole pines, their tops burned and the straight, scorched trunks standing like solemn grave markers in a crowded cemetery.

But when we visited there about a month ago, we saw something of captivating interest. The dead pines still stood, but between the burned trees new seedlings have sprung from the ground, millions of them.

Evidently when fire hit the treetops, the pinecones exploded, scattering seed to the ground. There is a new generation of trees now, young and beautiful and filled with promise. The old trees eventually will fall and the new ones will grow tall to create a forest of great beauty and usefulness.

As we drove through the park, I thought of the wonders of nature, of the rhythm of our lives. We grow old, and I am among those who have done so. Our vitality and our powers slacken. But a new generation is at our feet. These are children. These too are sons and daughters of God whose time has come to take their place on earth. They are like the new growth in the park—young, tender, sensitive, beautiful, and full of promise.

As Tagore, the poet of India, once observed, "Every child comes with the message that God is not yet discouraged of man" (Charles L. Wallis, ed., *The Treasure Chest*, New York: Harper and Row, 1965, p. 49).

Children are the promise of the future. They are the future itself. ("Save the Children," *Ensign*, November 1994, p. 52.)

How great is our responsibility, how serious the responsibility of Christian people and men and women of goodwill everywhere to reach out to ease the plight of suffering children, to lift them from the rut of despair in which they walk. . . .

Surely after all of the history we have read, after all of the suffering of which we have been told, after all of the exploitation of which we are aware, we can do more than we are now doing to lift the blight that condemns millions of children to lives that know little of happiness, that are tragically brief, and that are filled with pain.

And we need not travel halfway across the earth to find weeping children. Countless numbers of them cry out in fear and loneliness from the evil consequences of moral transgression, neglect, and abuse. I speak plainly, perhaps indelicately. But I know of no other way to make clear a matter about which I feel so strongly. ("Save the Children," *Ensign*, November 1994, p. 53.)

My plea—and I wish I were more eloquent in voicing it—is a plea to save the children. Too many of them walk with pain and fear, in loneliness and despair. Children need sunlight. They need happiness. They need love and nurture. They need kindness and refreshment and affection. Every home, regardless of the cost of the house, can provide an environment of love which will be an environment of salvation. ("Save the Children," *Ensign*, November 1994, p. 54.)

Children ought to respect their parents. Children are under the mandate of the Lord . . . to "honor thy father and thy mother that thy days may be long upon the land which the Lord thy God giveth thee." Children need to overcome their selfishness and look to their parents for love and understanding and training and wisdom. (*Church News* Interview, June 7, 1995.)

I have here an interesting statement by Elder Orson F. Whitney: "The Prophet Joseph Smith declared—and he never taught more comforting doctrine—that the eternal sealings of faithful parents and the divine promises made to them for valiant service in the Cause of Truth, would save not only themselves, but likewise their posterity. Though some of the sheep may wander, the eye of the Shepherd is upon them, and sooner or later they will feel the tentacles of Divine Providence reaching out after them and drawing them back to the fold. Either in this life or the life to come, they will return. They will have to pay their debt to justice; they will suffer for their sins; and may tread a thorny path; but if it leads them at last, like the penitent Prodigal, to a loving and forgiving father's heart and home, the painful experience will not have been in vain. Pray for your careless and disobedient children; hold on to them with your faith. Hope on, trust on, till you see the salvation of God" (Conference Report, April 1929). If any of you have a child or loved one in that condition, do not give up. Pray for them and love them and reach out to them and help them. (Jordan Utah South Regional Conference, March 2, 1997.)

CHOICE AND ACCOUNTABILITY

I should like to suggest three standards by which to judge each of the decisions that determine the behavior patterns of your lives. These standards are so simple as to appear elementary, but I believe their faithful observance will provide a set of moral imperatives by which to govern without argument or equivocation each of our actions and which will bring unmatched rewards. They are:

1. Does it enrich the mind?
2. Does it discipline and strengthen the body?
3. Does it nourish the spirit?

("Caesar, Circus, or Christ?" *BYU Speeches of the Year,* October 26, 1965, p. 4.)

This, my brethren and sisters, is our divine right—to choose. This is our divine obligation—to choose the right. God give us the strength, the courage, the faith in all our choices to choose that which will enrich the mind, strengthen and discipline the body, nourish the spirit, and thus give us growth and joy in this life and eternal life in the world to come. ("Caesar, Circus, or Christ?" *BYU Speeches of the Year,* October 26, 1965, p. 8.)

Man is God's greatest creation. For him the world was formed. His welfare is the Father's chief concern. But God does not make of man a pawn. He persuades and directs, but never forces. Man is free to choose his own way. There is no predestination in Mormon theology. Free agency is a sacred gift, divinely bestowed. Here is the answer to the old question, "If God loves his children, why does he permit war and strife and kindred evils?" Because he holds inviolable the right given man to choose his own way, between good and evil, between life and destruction. (*What of the Mormons?* pamphlet, 1982, pp. 6–7.)

Mankind has been given agency to choose between right and wrong. Said the prophet Lehi to Jacob:
"Wherefore, men are free according to the flesh; and all things are given them which are expedient unto man. And they are free to choose liberty and eternal life, through the great Mediator of all men, or to choose captivity and death, according to the captivity and power of the devil; for he seeketh that all men might be miserable like unto himself" (2 Nephi 2:27).
I repeat, each of us has a choice between right and wrong. But with that choice there inevitably will follow consequences. Those who choose to violate the commandments of God put themselves at great spiritual and physical jeopardy. The Apostle Paul said, "The wages of sin is death" (Romans 6:23).
Jacob taught, "Remember, to be carnally-minded is death, and to be spiritually-minded is life eternal" (2 Nephi 9:39). ("Reverence and Morality," *Ensign,* May 1987, p. 47.)

Surely, our Father in Heaven loves his sons and daughters. He trusts us. That very trust becomes as an iron rod to which we may cling as we walk the path of immortality. Some stumble and err and violate the trust. They are accountable for what they do. . . .

Trust and accountability are two great words by which we must guide our lives if we are to live beyond ourselves and rise to higher planes of service. ("Trust and Accountability," *BYU 1992–93 Devotional and Fireside Speeches,* October 13, 1992, pp. 25–26.)

The decisions we make, individually and personally, become the fabric of our lives. That fabric will be beautiful or ugly according to the threads of which it is woven. . . . You cannot indulge in any unbecoming behavior without injury to the beauty of the fabric of your lives. Immoral acts of any kind will introduce an ugly thread. Dishonesty of any kind will create a blemish. Foul and profane language will rob the pattern of its beauty.

"Choose the right, when a choice is placed before you" is the call to each of us (*Hymns,* 1985, no. 239). ("This Work Is Concerned with People," *Ensign,* May 1995, p. 53.)

Years ago I worked for one of our railroads. I was in Denver in the office of one of our big railroads working there. I was in charge of head-end traffic—that is, mail, baggage, and express that moved with the passenger trains. One day I got a telephone call from a man who had the same kind of job with another railroad in Newark, New Jersey. He said, "A train has arrived without its baggage car. We have 300 people here who are angry. Their clothes are not here. Their razors are not here. Their makeup is not here. They are all chewing on the station master and are very much upset. What happened to that baggage car?" I phoned Oakland, California, and found that the baggage car had been properly put on the train in Oakland and delivered to our railroad in Salt Lake. It had been taken from Salt Lake to Denver, down to Pueblo, and delivered to the Missouri Pacific to be taken to St. Louis. And in St. Louis it was to have been picked up by the Baltimore & Ohio and taken to Newark, New Jersey. But a thoughtless switchman in the St. Louis yards moved a piece of steel just that far and we discovered that a car that was supposed to be in Newark, New Jersey, was in New Orleans, Louisiana, 1400 miles away. It began with a little thing like that, moving a simple switch. There is a prison in Salt Lake City filled with people who chose the wrong thing, who moved a switch-point in their lives just a little bit and they were soon on the wrong track going to the wrong place.

What will you choose to do? For instance, someone might want you to smoke. Never forget that I told you, don't do it. Say no. That can of beer that somebody wants you to try, don't do it. Don't you ever do it. That drug that someone might want you to use, don't touch it. Stay away from it. It can destroy you. I talked with a school counselor the other day in . . . Utah. He is a counselor to a great school district, and I said, "How many of the young people in your district have tried drugs?" He said, "Fifty percent." And I said, "How many are using them?" He said, "Twenty-five percent." They are losers. They are not winners. . . . They belong to the Future Losers of America Club. . . . Stay away from drugs. I asked him also, "How many of the young people in your school district in high school have tampered with sex?" And he said, "Nearly fifty percent." And I said, "How many get involved right along," and he said again, "Twenty-four or twenty-five percent." They are losers too. They belong to the Future Losers of America Club. . . . They are throwing away their future on some stupid thing of that kind.

Choose the right. I do not have to tell you what that means. You know what that means. Choose the right. Your opportunities are so tremendous, so wonderful. You come on the scene of the world in the greatest age of the history of mankind. Nobody else who has ever lived on this earth has had quite the advantages that you have. . . . Don't become a member of the Future Losers of America. Remember to choose the right in all that you do. (St. George Utah Youth Fireside, January 14, 1996.)

Without acknowledgment of Deity, without recognition of the Almighty as the ruling power of the universe, the all-important element of personal and national accountability shrinks and dies. I am satisfied that this is one of the reasons for the great host of social problems with which we deal these days. Teen pregnancy, abandoned families, failure to recognize the property and rights of others, and many other problems, have resulted, in substantial part at least, from failure to recognize that there is a God to whom someday each of us must give an accounting. ("Preserving Our Trust in God," American Legion Patriotic Religious Service, September 1, 1996.)

I apologize for our lateness. We got up on time. We left the hotel on time. We went to the airport on time. We rose into the sky on time. But after they got up in the air—we were scheduled to fly at 43,000 feet at 600 miles an hour—they noticed that one of the windshield wipers didn't go back into its bracket. That meant that if we flew that high and that fast, it might blow off and hit one of the engines, a jet engine, and ruin that engine. So we circled around over the rivers and forests around Manaus, Brazil, for two hours, getting rid of fuel they had to get rid of before they could land and take care of that wiper blade. The result is that we were two and half hours late when we arrived here. . . .

I've been thinking about that—that little wiper blade set us back two and a half hours. That's the way it is with our lives. We go along and think everything is going just right—this, that, and the other—and then we do some little thing, and it destroys us, it hurts us. It may be we get lazy about going to sacrament meeting and don't go. Before long we're not going at all. Or we get into some moral problem, a small problem that leads to a great disaster. It isn't the big choices of our lives that destroy us. It's the small choices that we make from day to day; they are the things that cause us the real problems and lead to our downfall. . . . You've heard the story of the woman who went to the bishop to get her temple recommend renewed and he asked her if she drank coffee and she said, "Yes, occasionally." She said, "You're not going to let a little cup of coffee keep me out of the temple, are you?" And the bishop said, "You're not going to let a little cup of coffee keep you out of the temple, are you?"

That's the story of that. A little fooling around with this; a little fooling around with that are the things that get us in trouble. (Miami Florida Fireside, November 17, 1996.)

CHRISTMAS

Christmas means giving. The Father gave his Son, and the Son gave his life. Without giving there is no true Christmas, and without sacrifice there is no true worship. There is more to Christmas than neckties, earrings, toys, and all the tinseled stuff of which we make so much.

I recall an experience I heard at a stake conference in Idaho. A farm family in the community had just contracted for the installation of an additional and much-needed room on their home. Three or four days later the father came to the building supply dealer and said, "Will it be all right with you if we cancel the contract? The bishop talked with John about a mission last night. We will need to set this room aside for a while." The building supply dealer responded, "Your son will go on his mission, and he will find the needed room when he returns." Here was the spirit of Christmas—a family sending a boy into the world to teach the gospel, and friends coming to help the family with their problems. . . .

Christmas means giving—and "the gift without the giver is bare." Giving of self; giving of substance; giving of heart and mind and strength in assisting those in need and in spreading the cause of His eternal truth—these are of the very essence of the true spirit of Christmas. ("What Shall I Do Then with Jesus Which Is Called Christ?" *Ensign,* December 1983, p. 3.)

Christmas means compassion and love and, most of all, forgiveness. "Behold the Lamb of God, which taketh away the sin of the world!" (John 1:29.) How poor indeed would be our lives without the influence of his teachings and his matchless example. The lessons of the turning of the other cheek, going the second mile, the return of the prodigal, and scores of other incomparable teachings have filtered down the ages to become the catalyst to bring kindness and mercy out of much of man's inhumanity to man.

Brutality reigns where Christ is banished. Kindness and forbearance govern where Christ is recognized and his teachings are followed.

What shall we do then with Jesus who is called Christ? "He hath shewed thee, O man, what is good; and what doth the Lord require of thee, but to do justly, and to love mercy, and to walk humbly with thy God?" (Micah 6:8.)

"Wherefore, I say unto you, that ye ought to forgive one another; for he that forgiveth not his brother his trespasses standeth condemned before the Lord; for there remaineth in him the greater sin." (D&C 64:9.) ("What Shall I Do Then with Jesus Which Is Called Christ?" *Ensign*, December 1983, p. 4.)

Somehow in the magic of [the Christmas] season, there is less of hate and more of love, there is less of greed and more of giving, there is less of indifference and more of gratitude. If only for a brief season, we are inclined to lay aside our selfishness and reach out to help others. We see this all around us in the generous outpouring of kindness in behalf of those in need and pain and distress. We are more inclined to step beyond the narrow confines of our self-centered routines and reach out to help others less fortunate. ("He Who Redeemed Us," First Presidency Christmas Devotional, Salt Lake Tabernacle, December 3, 1995.)

At the Christmas season, I am grateful beyond power of expression for the plan of salvation, for the gift of the Son of God, who gave His life that we might have eternal life.

Christmas has become something of a travesty with all of its commercialization, when you think of it in terms of its true meaning. And yet with all of that, I am grateful for it. We stand a little taller, we give a little more freely, we act a little more kindly, we reach out a little more to those in distress at this glad season of the year. God be thanked for that touch which comes into our lives at this glorious season. (Los Angeles Temple Workers Christmas Devotional, December 10, 1995.)

What a glorious and wonderful season of year this is. Our hearts change. Our attitudes change. Our way of thinking changes. There is a little more forgiveness in us. A little more of kindness. A little more of love. A little more of patience. A little more of understanding at the Christmas season of the year. What a glorious thing it is that at least once in twelve months we can become a little better than we have been during the remainder of the year. Thanks be to God for the gift of His son, and thanks be to His Son for the gift of His life. How grateful we are at this

Christmas season. (Washington Temple Workers Christmas Devotional, December 1, 1996.)

We were in Jerusalem last year. We went to Shepherd's Field, in the evening after the sun had set, and looked out across those fields to Bethlehem and relived again the timeless and beautiful story of the birth of the Son of God, He who condescended to come to earth, He the Son of the Father, He the Prince of Peace who left His heavenly home to be born into mortality in a simple manger in a vassal state among a hated people. No man who ever walked the earth has touched more lives for greater good than has Jesus of Nazareth. He is our Savior, our Redeemer. He is the Prince of Peace, the Holy One. We love Him. We honor Him. We respect Him. We worship Him. And at this Christmas season, in His holy name, we extend our blessings to people everywhere for peace on earth and good will to men. I like to interpret that as peace on earth and blessings of peace to men of good will. That, I believe, is the essence of the whole thing. How grateful I am for Christmas. How grateful I am for the Son of God, of whom we sing and praise during this season. (Washington Temple Christmas Lighting Ceremony, December 2, 1996.)

Christmas is more than trees and twinkling lights, more than toys and gifts and baubles of a hundred varieties. It is love. It is the love of the Son of God for all mankind. It reaches out beyond our power to comprehend. It is magnificent and beautiful.

It is peace. It is the peace which comforts, which sustains, which blesses all who accept it.

It is faith. It is faith in God and His Eternal Son. It is faith in His wondrous ways and message. It is faith in Him as our Redeemer and our Lord.

We testify of His living reality. We testify of the divinity of His nature. In our times of grateful meditation, we acknowledge His priceless gift to us and pledge our love and faith. This is what Christmas is really about. ("Christmas," First Presidency Christmas Devotional, Salt Lake Tabernacle, December 8, 1996.)

CHURCH AND STATE

See also Politics

We try to follow a very strict course in political matters. We observe the principle of the separation of church and state. We do concern ourselves with matters which we consider of moral consequence and things which might directly affect the Church or our fellow churches. We try to work unitedly with other people of other faiths in a constructive way. We hope we can use our influence for the maintenance and cultivation of the good environment in which we live as a people in these communities. (Press Conference, Salt Lake City, Utah, March 13, 1995.)

We believe in the separation of Church and state. The Church does not endorse any political party or any political candidate, nor does it permit the use of its buildings and facilities for political purposes. We believe that the Church should remain out of politics unless there is a moral question at issue. In the case of a moral issue we would expect to speak out. But, in the matter of everyday political considerations, we try to remain aloof from those as a Church, while at the same time urging our members, as citizens, to exercise their political franchise as individuals. We believe, likewise, that it is in the interest of good government to permit freedom of worship, freedom of religion. Our official statement says, "We believe in worshiping God according to the dictates of conscience, and we allow all men the same privilege, let them worship how, where, or what they may." (Media Luncheon and Press Conference, Tokyo, Japan, May 18, 1996.)

We believe very strongly in the separation between church and state. We become involved in politics only when there is a moral issue at stake. If it is alcohol, if it is gambling, if it is a thing of that kind, we speak out, we exercise our influence. If it is a tax increase, if it is a highway here or there that is before the legislature, we don't bother about it institutionally. Individuals? Yes. We urge all of our people to exercise their constitutional right to be good citizens, to be involved in politics. But, institutionally, the Church moves only when it is a moral issue. (BBC Interview, February 21, 1997.)

CHURCH CALLINGS

We do not seek positions in the Church. I am alarmed, personally, at the number of requests we get from parents and bishops that missionaries be assigned to particular fields of labor. I think this is symptomatic of a growing attitude in the Church. The Lord said, "Ye have not chosen me, but I have chosen you, and ordained you . . ." (John 15:16). It is not the individual's prerogative to select the field to which he will go or the assignment which he will accept in the Church, nor is it his prerogative to casually reject for insignificant reasons a call that may come to him. None of us, I suppose, who heard President Clark in the general conference of April 9, 1951, will ever forget his words. They are worthy of repetition. He said:

"In the service of the Lord it is not where you serve, but how. In the Church of Jesus Christ of Latter-day Saints, one takes the place to which one is duly called, which place one neither seeks nor declines." ("How to Call to Service and How to Release," General Priesthood Board Meeting, December 6, 1967.)

I believe very implicitly in the principle that the names of those who serve in stake capacities should be presented to the high council. There is safety and there is wisdom. [On one occasion] I interviewed a young man who had made application to become a chaplain. We had a letter from his stake president, and I thought he was a likely candidate. He was a very personable young man, but I felt impressed to call the bishop and ask a question or two. I discovered that this young man had been involved in a difficulty in his ward and had been placed on probation for a time and certainly was not worthy to serve in the capacity of a chaplain. I think we cannot be too careful in consulting with others concerning those who are involved in leadership responsibilities. ("How to Call to Service and How to Release," General Priesthood Board Meeting, December 6, 1967.)

You are all familiar with the call of David. Samuel was instructed of the Lord to find a new prophet to replace Saul. The sons of Jesse were brought before Samuel and he looked first upon the handsome and manly older son and said:

"Surely this is the Lord's anointed. But the Lord said: Look not on his countenance, or on the height of his stature: because I have refused him: for the Lord seeth not as a man seeth; for man looketh on the outward appearance, but the Lord looketh on the heart" (1 Samuel 16:6–7).

We need divine inspiration in the calling of those who serve in our Father's kingdom. ("How to Call to Service and How to Release," General Priesthood Board Meeting, December 6, 1967, p. 3.)

Every officer of the Church should have a badge on him, invisible but apparent to his superior officer, "Fragile! Handle with Care." Many people have been unnecessarily injured because of the manner in which they have been released. Of course, releases have to come and they come for various reasons, including ineffectiveness in office. I feel we should not be too prone to release people because they are ineffective. We should make an effort to school them, and only when we are satisfied that they cannot be trained and be made more effective should they be released.

Be wise: I think it good policy to first determine the possibility of another assignment before effecting a release so that it becomes a transfer in the mind of the man and his family and others who may be sensitive. I saw a situation where a man's morale was destroyed and the faith of his family shaken because he was summarily dismissed from service. It need not have been. That man had capabilities that did not suit him for the job that he held, but he had abilities that could have been used in many other places. I think we should make a real effort to determine the possibility of another assignment so that the release becomes a transfer to a new assignment.

The ranking officer should consult with the one to be released. I know of another case where a man heard the first word of his release as it was announced in stake conference, and I think he never went back after that. That was a reflection on his character perhaps, but it need not have happened. He should have been invited into the office and the matter discussed in a positive but quiet, kindly way so that he welcomed the release rather than resented it, and so that he could go home and explain it to his family. He then would have had a great opportunity to teach them a lesson. The officer who must extend releases misses a great opportunity unless he sits down with the individual concerned and discusses the matter with him in a quiet, generous, gracious way.

Express appreciation. There is not a man in the Church who serves in any capacity who does not at least deserve an expression of gratitude. I knew a mission president who took the position that we never thank a man for doing his duty. I feel that any man who serves faithfully deserves thanks. That is the least we can do. ("How to Call to Service and How to Release," General Priesthood Board Meeting, December 6, 1967.)

I am confident that when we make an accounting of our labors to Him who is our Master, we will not be judged by the office we held, but rather, by the good that we did at whatever our level of responsibility. (General Authority Training Meeting, March 28, 1995.)

This church does not belong to its President. Its head is the Lord Jesus Christ, whose name each of us has taken upon ourselves. We are all in this great endeavor together. We are here to assist our Father in His work and His glory, "to bring to pass the immortality and eternal life of man" (Moses 1:39). Your obligation is as serious in your sphere of responsibility as is my obligation in my sphere. No calling in this church is small or of little consequence. All of us in the pursuit of our duty touch the lives of others. To each of us in our respective responsibilities the Lord has said: "Wherefore, be faithful; stand in the office which I have appointed unto you; succor the weak, lift up the hands which hang down, and strengthen the feeble knees" (D&C 81:5).

"And in doing these things thou wilt do the greatest good unto thy fellow beings, and wilt promote the glory of him who is your Lord" (D&C 81:4). . . .

You have as great an opportunity for satisfaction in the performance of your duty as I do in mine. The progress of this work will be determined by our joint efforts. Whatever your calling, it is as fraught with the same kind of opportunity to accomplish good as is mine. What is really important is that this is the work of the Master. Our work is to go about doing good as did He. ("This Is the Work of the Master," *Ensign,* May 1995, p. 71.)

There is no small or inconsequential task, calling, or responsibility in this Church. (Heber City/Springville Utah Regional Conference, priesthood leadership session, May 13, 1995.)

Every one of you who is here tonight has as serious a responsibility in terms of your callings as do I in terms of my calling, for the growth and development and strengthening of this work across the world. And none of us can do a small or mean or shoddy thing without affecting this work because we are part of it. None of us can do an unselfish or outreach type of thing without strengthening the work. (Salt Lake East Millcreek Stake Fiftieth Anniversary Celebration, June 10, 1995.)

Whether it be teaching a class, whether it be serving as a home teacher, whether it be serving as a Church officer, whether it be working as a missionary, serving in the temple or any such thing, it deserves our best effort. There is nothing unimportant about any call in this Church. Every call is important. When we all do our duty working together, the whole Church moves forward in an orderly and wonderful fashion. (Interview with Mike Cannon of *Church News,* Dublin, Ireland, September 1, 1995.)

CHURCH GOVERNMENT

See also Succession to the Presidency

The basic organization of the Church goes back to New Testament times. Its efficiency of operation has often been described as strictly modern. This is not a contradiction.

We maintain that the fundamental organization of The Church of Jesus Christ of Latter-day Saints is the same as that which prevailed in the Church established by the Savior.

Early in his ministry Jesus called twelve men whom he ordained Apostles. To these he gave power to heal the sick, to raise the dead, to minister the ordinances of the gospel. "Freely ye have received, freely give," he enjoined them (Matthew 10:8). Then they were sent forth to the cities of Israel to bear witness of him and his kingdom. Three among them—Peter, James, and John—stand out in the scriptures as the leaders, particularly after the death and resurrection of the Savior.

The Lord also appointed seventy to assist in the work. These he sent out by pairs with authority to speak for him. Success crowned their ministry as becomes evident from the declaration that "the seventy returned again with joy" (Luke 10:17).

Following Jesus' death the work was carried beyond the confines of Israel to the cities of Syria, then to Asia Minor, and later to Greece and Rome. The word was spread with such effect that Paul, some thirty years later, declared that the gospel had been preached to every creature under heaven.

As various branches of the Church were organized, bishops and elders were ordained to preside over them, and other offices in the priesthood were filled. Paul speaks specifically of Apostles and prophets, bishops and elders, evangelists, priests, teachers, deacons, and pastors. He also makes clear the necessity for these various offices in their relationship one with another in furthering their common objective—"For the perfecting of the saints, for the work of the ministry, for the edifying of the body of Christ; Till we all come in the unity of the faith, and of the knowledge of the Son of God, unto a perfect man, unto the measure of the stature of the fulness of Christ" (Ephesians 4:12–13).

The scripture makes clear another important point with reference to these officers of the Church. To his Apostles Jesus said, "Ye have not chosen me, but I have chosen you, and ordained you" (John 15:16). Paul amplifies this thought with the declaration that "no man taketh this honour unto himself, but he that is called of God, as was Aaron" (Hebrews 5:4). During those early years men in the Church were given office, not of their own choosing, but as they were selected and ordained by those who had been given power and authority of the Lord.

Latter-day Saints believe that this same organization with its basic offices has again been restored to the earth, and that men should fill those offices in the same spirit in which they were filled in ancient times. They believe that in this organization lie the keys and means of effective church operation. (*What of the Mormons?* pamphlet, 1982, pp. 21, 23.)

The divine genius of the organization of this work and of calls to leadership is evident. The General Authorities are all individuals, each with his own personality. Each brings to his responsibilities a wide variety of experience and background. When matters come up for discussion in the leading councils of the Church, each is free to express his views. As one observes that interesting process at work, it is fascinating to witness the power of the Holy Spirit influence these men. Initial differences, never sharp but nonetheless perceptible, soften and meld into an expression of unity. ("He Slumbers Not, nor Sleeps," *Ensign*, May 1983, p. 6.)

The holy priesthood carries with it the authority to govern in the affairs of the kingdom of God in the earth. Under the revelations of the Lord, the Church is presided over by three presiding high priests. They are assisted by a council of Twelve Apostles, who in turn are assisted by those of the Seventy. A Presiding Bishopric of three are responsible for temporal affairs under the direction of the Presidency. All of these are priesthood officers. That power divinely given is the authority by which they govern. It is so in the stakes and the wards with presidencies and bishoprics. It is so in the quorums. The auxiliary officers carry forth their work under direction and delegation from the priesthood. Without the priesthood there might be the form of a church, but not the true substance. This is the Church of Jesus Christ, and it is governed by that authority which is after the Order of the Son of God. (Priesthood Restoration Commemoration Fireside, May 15, 1988.)

I thank [Joseph Smith] and love him for the organization of The Church of Jesus Christ of Latter-day Saints. It is a marvel and a miracle under which millions hold office and responsibility in the church and kingdom of God. It is a unique system of ecclesiastical government under which the authority to nominate rests with the presiding officers, but the right to serve is conditioned upon the approval of the membership.

I thank him and the Lord from whom it came for this marvelous organization which is able to function in any land or society, where leadership comes out of the people, where, with few exceptions, the call to serve is but for a season, thereby ensuring a constant renewal of talent, outlook, energy, and spiritual strength. ("As One Who Loves the Prophet," Symposium on the Life and Ministry of the Prophet Joseph Smith, BYU, February 22, 1992.)

This afternoon we followed the customary practice of sustaining Church officers. It may appear as a somewhat perfunctory exercise. But I remind you that it is an act of grave and serious importance, an act required under the revelation of the Lord. . . .

. . . The right to nominate rests with the superior officer or officers at whatever the level. But that nomination must be sustained—that is, accepted and confirmed—by the membership of the Church. The procedure is peculiar to the Lord's church. There is no seeking for office, no jockeying for position, no campaigning to promote one's virtues. Contrast the Lord's way with the way of the world. The Lord's way is quiet, it is a way of peace, it is without fanfare or monetary costs. It is without egotism or vanity or ambition. Under the Lord's plan, those who have responsibility to select officers are governed by one overriding question: "Whom would the Lord have?" There is quiet and thoughtful deliberation. And there is much of prayer to receive the confirmation of the Holy Spirit that the choice is correct. ("God Is at the Helm," *Ensign*, May 1994, p. 53.)

There is an old backyard proverb that says, "Many hands make light work." How true that is with reference to this church. The wonderful system of presidencies and councils makes it possible to spread the load in such a way that none is overburdened, that many are given experience and opportunity, and that if a soldier anywhere in the ranks falters or stumbles, there is another to take his place and march forward. (General Authority Training Meeting, March 28, 1995.)

President of the Church

We shall never be left without a prophet if we will live worthy of one. He does not need to be youthful. He has and will continue to have younger men to travel over the earth in the work of the ministry. He is the presiding high priest, the repository of all of the keys of the holy priesthood, and the voice of revelation from God to his people. ("He Slumbers Not, nor Sleeps," *Ensign*, May 1983, p. 6.)

Some express concern that the President of the Church is likely always to be a rather elderly man, to which my response is, "What a blessing!" The work in this dispensation was first put in place through the instrumentality of the Prophet Joseph Smith. He was at the time young and vigorous, one whose mind was not set in the traditions of his day. His was a youthful mind which the Lord could mold as fresh, moist clay as he initiated his work.

Joseph's successor was relatively young when he was faced with the terrible responsibility of leading an entire people across the wilderness to pioneer a new land.

But the basics of our doctrine are now well in place, and we are firmly established as a people, at least until the Lord should mandate another move. We do not need innovation. We need devotion in adherence to divinely spoken principles. We need loyalty to our leader, whom God has appointed. . . .

To my mind there is something tremendously reassuring in knowing that for the foreseeable future we shall have a President who has been disciplined and schooled, tried and tested, whose fidelity to the work and whose integrity in the cause have been tempered in the forge of service, whose faith has matured, and whose nearness to God has been cultivated over a period of many years. . . .

. . . I shall sustain without reservation him whom the Lord appoints under the process he has established for succession in his kingdom, for I know that this is God's work and that he is watching over it now as he has through the years that have gone before. He makes no mistakes. ("He Slumbers Not, nor Sleeps," *Ensign*, May 1983, pp. 6–7.)

The Church is true. Those who lead it have only one desire, and that is to do the will of the Lord. They seek His direction in all things. There is not a decision of significance affecting the Church and its people that is made without prayerful consideration, going to the fount of all wisdom for direction. Follow the leadership of the Church. God will not let his work be led astray. ("Be Not Deceived," *Ensign*, November 1983, p. 46.)

I want to give you my testimony concerning this work. I have been heavily involved in it for more than a half a century. I have worked with the Presidents of the Church from President Heber J. Grant onward. I have known in a very personal way President Grant, President George Albert Smith, President David O. McKay, President Joseph Fielding Smith, President Harold B. Lee, and President Spencer W. Kimball [and subsequently Presidents Ezra Taft Benson and Howard W. Hunter]. I have known the counselors of all of these men, and I have known the Council of the Twelve during the years of the administration of these Presidents. All of these men have been human. They have had human traits and perhaps some human weaknesses. But over and above all of that, there has been in the life of every one of them an overpowering manifestation of the inspiration of God. Those who have been Presidents have been prophets in a very real way. I have intimately witnessed the spirit of revelation upon them. Each man came to the Presidency after many years of experience as a member of the Council of the Twelve and in other capacities. The Lord refined and polished each one, let him know discouragement and failure, let him experience illness and in some cases deep sorrow. All of this became part of a great refining process, and the effect of that process became beautifully evident in their lives.

My dear friends in the gospel, this is God's work. This is his Church and the Church of his Beloved Son whose name it carries. God will never permit an imposter to stand at its head. He will name his prophets, and he will inspire and direct them. ("Strengthening Each Other," *Ensign*, February 1985, p. 5.)

Some wonder about who is directing the Church. I give you my solemn testimony that inspiration from on high is received and that it is our Father in Heaven and His Beloved Son, the Redeemer of the world, who are guiding and directing this church to bring to pass their eternal purposes in behalf of the sons and daughters of God. ("Rejoice in This Great Era of Temple Building," *Ensign*, November 1985, p. 54.)

I can assure you . . . that I never knowingly moved ahead of my file leader, that I never had any desire to move out ahead of him in Church policy or instruction. I knew that he was the appointed Prophet of the Lord in that day. Even though I, too, had been sustained as a prophet, seer, and revelator, along with my Brethren of the Twelve, I knew also that none of us was the President of the Church. I knew that the Lord prolonged the life of President Kimball for purposes known to the Lord, and I had perfect faith that this prolonging of life was for a reason under the wisdom of Him who has greater wisdom than any man. ("'In . . . Counsellors There Is Safety,'" *Ensign*, November 1990, p. 50.)

I repeat that I have worked with seven Presidents [subsequently nine] of this Church. I have recognized that all have been human. But I have never been concerned over this. They may have had some weaknesses. But this has never troubled me. I know that the God of heaven has used mortal men throughout history to accomplish His divine purposes. They were the very best available to Him, and they were wonderful.

These men whom I have known and with whom I have worked have been totally unselfish in their zeal to build the kingdom of God and bring happiness into the lives of the people. They have been unsparing in giving of themselves to the great work for which each had responsibility in his particular season.

I speak to the priesthood of this Church . . . in gratitude for a prophet to guide us in these latter days. I plead for loyalty to him whom the Lord has called and anointed. I plead for steadfastness in upholding him and giving attention to his teachings. I have said on another occasion at this pulpit that if we have a prophet, we have everything. If we do not have a prophet, we have nothing. We do have a prophet. We have had prophets since the founding of this Church. We shall never be without a prophet if we live worthy of a prophet.

The Lord is watching over this work. This is His kingdom. We are not as sheep without a shepherd. We are not as an army without a leader. ("'Believe His Prophets,'" *Ensign,* May 1992, p. 53.)

A few weeks ago, while returning from a regional conference, we had an experience that remains vivid in my mind. As we approached the airport, the captain came on the public address system and spoke in crisp and authoritative tones: "We have an emergency! Please give me your attention. We have an emergency, and the cabin crew will give you instructions. For your own safety, please do what they ask you to do."

The crew sprang into action. This was the moment for which their training had prepared them. Every one of them knew precisely what to do. All utensils were quickly secured in locked containers.

Passengers were shifted to put strong men at each emergency exit.

We were told to remove our glasses, lower our heads, and firmly grasp our ankles.

A woman with a baby seated immediately behind me was crying. Others could be heard sobbing. Everyone knew that this was not just an exercise, but that it was for real and that it was serious.

A man emerged from the flight deck door. He recognized me and stooped down to say, "I am an off-duty pilot. The primary control system has failed, but I think we are going to be all right. They have managed to get the landing gear down and the flaps down."

Strangely, I felt no fear. In many years of flying, I have had experiences when I *have* known fear. But on this occasion I felt calm. I knew that a redundancy system had been built into the plane to handle just such an emergency and that the crew had been well trained.

I also knew that the effectiveness of that redundancy system would be known in a minute or two when the rubber hit the runway.

That moment came quickly. To the relief of everyone, the plane touched down smoothly, the landing gear held in place, the engines were reversed, and the aircraft was brought to a stop.

. . . The crew was appropriately applauded, and some of us expressed to the Lord our gratitude.

I have reflected on this experience in terms of the Church of which we are members. The head of the Church is the Lord Jesus Christ. It is His Church. But the earthly head is our prophet. Prophets are men who are endowed with a divine calling. Notwithstanding the divinity of that calling, they are human. They are subject to the problems of mortality.

We love and respect and honor and look to the prophet of this day, President Ezra Taft Benson. He has been a great and gifted leader, a man whose voice has rung out in testimony of this work across the world. He holds all the keys of the priesthood on the earth in this day. But he has reached an age where he cannot do many of the things he once did. This does not detract from his calling as a prophet. But it places limitations on his physical activities.

We have seen comparable situations in times past. President Wilford Woodruff grew old in office. So did Presidents Heber J. Grant, David O. McKay, Joseph Fielding Smith, and, more recently, Spencer W. Kimball.

Some people, evidently not knowing the system, worry that because of the President's age, the Church faces a crisis. They seem not to realize that there is a backup system. In the very nature of this system, there is always on board a trained crew, if I may so speak of them. They have been thoroughly schooled in Church procedures. More importantly, they also hold the keys of the eternal priesthood of God. They, too, have been put in place by the Lord.

I hope I will not sound presumptuous in reminding you of the unique and tremendous system of redundancy and backup which the Lord has structured into His kingdom so that without interruption it may go forward, meeting any emergency that might arise and handling every contingency with which it is faced. To me, it is a wondrous and constantly renewing miracle. ("The Church Is on Course," *Ensign,* November 1992, p. 53.)

One cannot come to this sacred office without almost overwhelming feelings of inadequacy. Strengthened resolution to go forward comes from the knowledge that this is the work of God, that He is watching over it, that He will direct us in our efforts if we will be true and faithful, and that our accountability is to Him. (Press Conference, Salt Lake City, Utah, March 13, 1995.)

This morning we all participated in a solemn assembly. That is just what the name indicates. It is a gathering of the membership where every individual stands equal with every other in exercising with soberness and in solemnity his or her right to sustain or not to sustain those who, under the procedures that arise out of the revelations, have been chosen to lead. . . .

Concerning the First Presidency the Lord has said, "Of the Melchizedek Priesthood, three Presiding High Priests, chosen by the body, appointed and ordained to that office, and upheld by the confidence, faith, and prayer of the church" (D&C 107:22).

I emphasize those words, "upheld by the confidence, faith, and prayer of the church."

Your uplifted hands in the solemn assembly this morning became an expression of your willingness and desire to uphold us, your brethren and your servants, with your confidence, faith, and prayer. I am deeply grateful for that expression. . . . This office is not one to be sought after. The right to select rests with the Lord. He is the master of life and death. His is the power to call. His is the power to take away. His is the power to retain. It is all in His hands.

I do not know why in His grand scheme one such as I would find a place. But having this mantle come upon me, I now rededicate whatever I have of strength or time or talent or life to the work of my Master in the service of my brethren and sisters. ("This Work Is Concerned with People," *Ensign,* May 1995, p. 51.)

Mine has been the special privilege to serve as a counselor to three great Presidents. I think I know something of the meaning of heavy responsibility. But with all of that, I have, during these past few days, been overwhelmed with feelings of inadequacy and of total dependency upon the Lord, who is my head and whose church this is, and upon the strength of these good men who are my counselors, my dear Brethren of the Twelve, of the Seventy, and of the Presiding Bishopric, and of the membership of the Church throughout the world. . . .

Years ago I gave a talk on the loneliness of leadership. Now for the first time I realize the full import of that loneliness. I do not know why this mantle has fallen upon my shoulders. I suppose some of you may also wonder. But we are here. ("This Is the Work of the Master," *Ensign*, May 1995, p. 69.)

The First Presidency

I am not here as a substitute for the President of the Church. I am speaking as his second counselor, a responsibility I did not seek but one which I have accepted as a sacred call, in the fulfillment of which I have tried to lift some of the heavy burdens of office from the shoulders of our beloved President and move forward the work of the Lord with diligence. President Kimball is the prophet of the Lord. None other can or will take his place for so long as he lives. ("The Cornerstones of Our Faith," *Ensign*, November 1984, p. 50.)

According to the revelation of the Lord, "of the Melchizedek Priesthood, three Presiding High Priests, chosen by the body, appointed and ordained to that office, and upheld by the confidence, faith, and prayer of the church, form a quorum of the Presidency of the Church." (D&C 107:22.)

This "Presidency of the High Priesthood, after the order of Melchizedek, have a right to officiate in all the offices in the church." (D&C 107:9.)

Further pertaining to this principle, "it is according to the dignity of his office that he [the president] should preside over the council of the church; and it is his privilege to be assisted by two other presidents, appointed after the same manner that he himself was appointed.

"And in case of the absence of one or both of those who are appointed to assist him, he has power to preside over the council without an assistant; and in case he himself is absent, the other presidents have power to preside in his stead, both or either of them." (D&C 102:10–11.)

We who serve as Counselors recognize and know the parameters of our authority and our responsibility. Our only desire is to assist and help our leader with the tremendous burdens of his office. . . .

. . . Where there is not firmly established policy, we have talked with the President and received his approval before taking action. Let it never be said that there has been any disposition to assume authority or to do anything or say anything or teach anything which might be at variance with the wishes of him who has been put in his place by the Lord. We wish to be his loyal servants. We ask no honor for ourselves. We simply desire to do that which needs to be done, when it needs to be done, and according to policies on which the President has expressed himself. ("The Church Is on Course," *Ensign*, November 1992, p. 54.)

The First Presidency and the Council of the Twelve Apostles, called and ordained to hold the keys of the priesthood, have the authority and responsibility to govern the Church, to administer its ordinances, to expound its doctrine, and to establish and maintain its practices. Each man who is ordained an Apostle and sustained a member of the Council of the Twelve is sustained as a prophet, seer, and revelator. . . .

When the President is ill or not able to function fully in all of the duties of his office, his two Counselors together comprise a Quorum of the First Presidency. They carry on with the day-to-day work of the Presidency. In exceptional circumstances, when only one may be able to function, he may act in the authority of the office of the Presidency as set forth in the Doctrine and Covenants, section 102, verses 10–11.

When, on 10 November 1985, President Benson called his two Counselors, it was he himself who was voice in setting them apart, with the members of the Council of the Twelve Apostles also laying their hands upon the heads of the Counselors, each one in turn, as he was set apart. President Benson was at the time in good health, fully able to function in every way.

Furthermore, following this setting apart, he signed with his own hand powers of agency giving each of his Counselors the authority to direct the business of the Church.

Under these specific and plenary delegations of authority, the Counselors in the First Presidency carry on with the regular work of this office. But any major questions of policy, procedures, programs, or doctrine are considered deliberately and prayerfully by the First Presidency and the Twelve together. These two quorums, the Quorum of the First Presidency and the Quorum of the Twelve, meeting together, with every man having total freedom to express himself, consider every major question. . . .

No decision emanates from the deliberations of the First Presidency and the Twelve without total unanimity among all concerned. . . .

I add by way of personal testimony that during the twenty years I served as a member of the Council of the Twelve and during the nearly thirteen years that I have served in the First Presidency, there has never been a major action taken where this procedure was not observed. ("God Is at the Helm," *Ensign,* May 1994, pp. 54, 59.)

With President Hunter's passing, the First Presidency was dissolved. Brother Monson and I, who had served as his counselors, took our places in the Quorum of the Twelve, which became the presiding authority of the Church.

Three weeks ago today all of the living ordained Apostles gathered in a spirit of fasting and prayer in the upper room of the temple. Here we sang a sacred hymn and prayed together. We partook of the sacrament of the Lord's supper, renewing in that sacred, symbolic testament our covenants and our relationship with Him who is our divine Redeemer.

The presidency was then reorganized, following a precedent well established through generations of the past.

There was no campaigning, no contest, no ambition for office. It was quiet, peaceful, simple, and sacred. It was done after the pattern which the Lord Himself had put in place. ("This Is the Work of the Master," *Ensign*, May 1995, p. 69.)

I very much appreciate the wisdom of my counselors. They bring to their callings long years of experience together with a variety of points of view bearing on a particular question. We talk about these things. We reach consensus. There must be unity in the First Presidency. The Lord has made that clear. There must likewise be unity in every other presidency in the Church. (General Authority Training Meeting, October 1, 1996.)

The Council of the Twelve Apostles

I think I feel some sense of the burden of this responsibility to stand as a witness of the Lord Jesus Christ before a world that is reluctant to accept him. "I stand all amazed at the love Jesus offers me." I am subdued by the confidence of the Lord's Prophet in me, and by the expressed love of these, my brethren. . . . I pray for strength; I pray for help; and I pray for the faith and the will to be obedient. I think that I need—and I feel that all of us need—discipline, if this great work is to roll forward as it is ordained to do. (Conference Report, October 1961, pp. 115–16.)

It has always seemed a remarkable thing to me that although the Lord chose twelve Apostles to assist him in the work of the ministry, and to extend it following his death; and that although Paul, who was an Apostle, declared that the Church should be "built upon the foundation of the apostles and prophets, Jesus Christ himself being the chief corner stone" (Eph. 2:20)—notwithstanding all of this, the office of Apostle, and certainly a council of twelve Apostles, is not found to my knowledge in other Christian churches. . . .

The word *apostle*, in its origin, literally means "one sent forth." If that definition were stated to say "one sent forth with certain authority and responsibility," it would properly describe the calling as it was given at the time our Lord walked the earth, and as it has been given in our time. . . .

This same office of apostle was restored to the earth when the Church was reestablished in this dispensation. In the revelation on Church organization received in April of 1830, Joseph Smith was spoken of as one "who was called of God, and ordained an apostle of Jesus Christ, to be the first elder of this church;

"And to Oliver Cowdery, who was also called of God, an apostle of Jesus Christ, to be the second elder of this church, and ordained under his hand." (D&C 20:2–3.) ("Special Witnesses for Christ," *Ensign*, May 1984, p. 50.)

The Three Witnesses to the Book of Mormon—Oliver Cowdery, David Whitmer, and Martin Harris—were given the responsibility of nominating the first members of the Twelve in this dispensation. When they were selected, they were convened in a meeting held in Kirtland on February 27, 1835. Oliver Cowdery served as clerk in that meeting and wrote this in the minutes:

"President Smith proposed the following question: What importance is there attached to the calling of the Twelve Apostles, different from the other callings or officers of the Church?

"After the question was discussed, . . . President Joseph Smith, Jun. gave the following decision:

"They are the Twelve Apostles, who are called to the office of the Traveling High Council, who are to preside over the churches of the Saints, among the Gentiles, where there is no presidency established; and they are to travel and preach among the Gentiles, until the Lord shall command them to go to the Jews. They are to hold the keys of this ministry, to unlock the door of the Kingdom of heaven unto all nations, and to preach the Gospel to every creature. This is the power, authority, and virtue in their apostleship." (*Teachings of the Prophet Joseph Smith*, sel. Joseph Fielding Smith, Salt Lake City: Deseret Book Co., 1938, p. 74.)

As set forth in the further revelations, they are to work under the direction of the First Presidency and to go forth as "special witnesses of the name of Christ in all the world." (D&C 107:23.) ("Special Witnesses for Christ," *Ensign*, May 1984, p. 51.)

I am profoundly grateful to my Brethren of the Council of the Twelve Apostles, who consistently and without exception have met every request and every assignment given them. They have been most supportive. The same holds true for the members of the First Quorum of the Seventy and the Presiding Bishopric. I repeat what I have said before at this pulpit, that there is perfect unity among the Brethren. They are not yes-men. Each is a man of understanding, of conviction, of great proven ability. Each is also a man of humility, with a willingness to subdue all personal considerations and place first the work of the Lord. . . .

. . . Each man is encouraged and is free to give his opinion and express his judgment. It is a most remarkable and wonderful thing to witness how, under the influence of the Holy Spirit, there is a gradual melding of judgment, which invariably leads to a united decision.

No policy of importance, no action of consequence, is taken without consideration in the highest councils of the Church and without unanimity of feeling on the decisions reached. No such action is taken without earnest and sincere prayer and without a plea to the Almighty for guidance and revelation, and, further, without the approval of the President of the Church.

Some wonder about who is directing the Church. I give you my solemn testimony that inspiration from on high is received and that it is our Father in Heaven and His Beloved Son, the Redeemer of the world, who are guiding and directing this church. ("Rejoice in This Great Era of Temple Building," *Ensign,* November 1985, pp. 53–54.)

Now, as I have indicated, there are twelve others on whom have been conferred the keys of the apostleship. They are, as the revelation describes them, "the twelve traveling councilors . . . called to be the Twelve Apostles, or special witnesses of the name of Christ in all the world—thus differing from other officers in the church in the duties of their calling.

"And they form a quorum, equal in authority and power to the three presidents previously mentioned." (D&C 107:23–24.) . . .

I wish now to say a few words about the men who are members of the Quorum of the First Presidency and the Quorum of the Twelve Apostles. I know all of those presently serving. I have known all who have filled these chairs in the last sixty years. I am confident that no one of them ever aspired to office. No one campaigned for it. I think none ever thought himself worthy of it. This is a singular and remarkable thing. . . .

I know each of the Twelve in seniority, from President Howard W. Hunter to Elder Richard G. Scott.

These are my associates in this the work of the Almighty. As I said before, none sought this sacred office. Each was called, and in some instances made serious sacrifice in accepting the call. We pray together. We meet in solemn assembly in the house of the Lord. Periodically, we partake together the sacrament of the Lord's Supper and renew our covenants with Him who is our God, taking upon ourselves anew the name of the Lord of whom we are called to testify. ("The Church Is on Course," *Ensign*, November 1992, pp. 54, 59.)

When a man is ordained to the apostleship and set apart as a member of the Council of the Twelve, he is given the keys of the priesthood of God. Each of the fifteen living men so ordained holds these keys. However, only the President of the Church has the right to exercise them in their fulness. He may delegate the exercise of various of them to one or more of his Brethren. Each has the keys but is authorized to use them only to the degree granted him by the prophet of the Lord. ("The Church Is on Course," *Ensign*, November 1992, p. 54.)

My Brethren of whom I have spoken are Apostles of the Lord Jesus Christ. I bear witness of their integrity. I bear witness of their faith. I bear witness of the voice of inspiration and revelation in their calls. Every one is a man of tested strength. But the greatest of these strengths lies in the acknowledgment that he must have divinely given direction and blessing if he is to perform acceptably.

Now, in conclusion, do you believe this body of men would ever lead this church astray? Remember whose church this is. It carries the name of the Lord Jesus Christ, who stands as its head. His is the power to remove any found remiss in his duty or in teaching that which is not in harmony with His divine will.

I say for each and all that we have no personal agenda. We have only the Lord's agenda. There are those who criticize when we issue a statement of counsel or warning. Please know that our pleadings are not motivated by any selfish desire. Please know that our warnings are not without substance and reason. Please know that the decisions to speak out on various matters are not reached without deliberation, discussion, and prayer. Please know that our only ambition is to help each of you with your problems, your struggles, your families, your lives.

May I say, by way of personal testimony, that for more than a third of a century I have served as a General Authority of this Church. . . . I know how the system works. I know that it is divine in its plan and in its authority. I know that there is no desire to teach anything other than what the Lord would have taught. . . .

When we plead with our people to observe the Sabbath day, to refrain from making it a day of merchandising, we are only repeating that which the Lord declared anciently and which He has confirmed through modern revelation. When we decry gambling, we are only reiterating what has been said by prophets who have gone before. When we urge the strengthening of the foundations of our homes, we are only doing that which will bless the lives of our families. When we urge our people to live the law of tithing, we are only repeating that which the Lord spoke of anciently and confirmed anew in this dispensation for the blessing of His people. When we warn against pornography, immorality, drugs, and such, we are doing only that which prophets have always done.

Ours is the responsibility outlined by Ezekiel: "Son of man, I have made thee a watchman unto the house of Israel: therefore hear the word at my mouth, and give them warning from me." (Ezek. 3:17.)

We have no selfish desire in any of this, other than the wish that our brethren and sisters will be happy, that peace and love will be found in their homes, that they will be blessed by the power of the Almighty in their various undertakings in righteousness. ("The Church Is on Course," *Ensign*, November 1992, pp. 59–60.)

It is important . . . that there be no doubts or concerns about the governance of the Church and the exercise of the prophetic gifts, including the right to inspiration and revelation in administering the affairs and programs of the Church, when the President may be ill or is not able to function fully.

The First Presidency and the Council of the Twelve Apostles, called and ordained to hold the keys of the priesthood, have the authority and responsibility to govern the Church, to administer its ordinances, to expound its doctrine, and to establish and maintain its practices. Each man who is ordained an Apostle and sustained a member of the Council of the Twelve is sustained as a prophet, seer, and revelator. . . . All incumbent members of the Quorum of the First Presidency and of the Council of the Twelve have been the recipients of the keys, rights, and authority pertaining to the holy apostleship. . . .

And now I quote again from the word of the Lord: "And every decision made by either of these quorums must be by the unanimous voice of the same; that is, every member in each quorum must be agreed to its decisions, in order to make their decisions of the same power or validity one with the other" (D&C 107:27).

No decision emanates from the deliberations of the First Presidency and the Twelve without total unanimity among all concerned. At the outset in considering matters, there may be differences of opinion. These are to be expected. These men come from different backgrounds. They are men who think for themselves. But before a final decision is reached, there comes a unanimity of mind and voice.

This is to be expected if the revealed word of the Lord is followed. Again I quote from the revelations:

"The decisions of these quorums, or either of them, are to be made in all righteousness, in holiness, and lowliness of heart, meekness and long suffering, and in faith, and virtue, and knowledge, temperance, patience, godliness, brotherly kindness and charity;

"Because the promise is, if these things abound in them they shall not be unfruitful in the knowledge of the Lord" (D&C 107:30–31).

I add by way of personal testimony that during the twenty years I served as a member of the Council of the Twelve and during the nearly thirteen years that I have served in the First Presidency, there has never been a major action taken where this procedure was not observed. . . . Out of this very process of men speaking their minds has come a sifting and winnowing of ideas and concepts. But I have never observed serious discord or personal enmity among my Brethren. I have, rather, observed a beautiful and remarkable thing—the coming together, under the directing influence of the Holy Spirit and under the power of revelation, of divergent views until there is total harmony and full agreement. . . .

I know of no other governing body of any kind of which this might be said. . . .

. . . The Brethren would not be inclined to do anything which they feel would be out of harmony with the attitude, feelings, and position of their beloved leader, the prophet of the Lord.

It must be recognized that the President, when he became the senior Apostle, had moved up through the ranks of seniority over a period of many years of service in the Quorum of the Twelve. During this time, his Brethren came to know him well. During the years of his ministry, he expressed himself on the many issues that came before that quorum. His view became well known. ("God Is at the Helm," *Ensign,* May 1994, pp. 54, 59.)

I repeat for emphasis that all who have been ordained to the holy apostleship have had bestowed upon them the keys and the authority of this most high and sacred office. In this authority reside the powers of governance of the Church and kingdom of God in the earth. There is order in the exercise of that authority. . . .

. . . Jesus Christ stands at the head of this church which bears His sacred name. He is watching over it. He is guiding it. Standing at the right hand of His Father, He directs this work. His is the prerogative, the power, the option to call men in His way to high and sacred offices and to release them according to His will by calling them home. He is the Master of life and death. I do not worry about the circumstances in which we find ourselves. I accept these circumstances as an expression of His will. I likewise accept the responsibility, acting with my Brethren, to do all we can to move forward this holy work in a spirit of consecration, love, humility, duty, and loyalty.

I assure each of you and the entire world that there is unity and brotherhood with total and united fidelity to one under-girding objective, and that is to build the kingdom of God in the earth. ("God Is at the Helm," *Ensign*, May 1994, p. 59.)

The Seventy

I come now to the Brethren of the Seventy. As you know, we have two Quorums of Seventy who serve as General Authorities with jurisdiction across the Church. The First is comprised of those who serve to age 70. . . . Additionally, we are calling a group of wise and mature men with long experience in the Church and with freedom to go wherever circumstances dictate as members of the Second Quorum of the Seventy. These Brethren will serve for periods of from three to five years. In every sense they will be General Authorities.

We also have a faithful cadre of Brethren serving as Area Authorities. These have been called wherever the Church is organized. They are faithful and devoted men. They are men who love the Church and who have served in many capacities. As we have traveled at home and abroad, we have worked with many of them and have been deeply impressed with their remarkable capacity.

The Lord made provision at a general level for a First Presidency, a Quorum of the Twelve Apostles, Quorums of Seventy, and the Presiding Bishopric. At a local level the revelations speak of stake presidents and bishops. We have had in between the general and local authorities for a period of time the Regional Representatives, now more recently these Area Authorities. We have determined to present to the conference the names of these Area Authorities to be ordained Seventies. They will then have a quorum relationship presided over by the Presidents of the Seventy. They will be known as Area Authority Seventies, to serve for a period of years in a voluntary capacity in the area in which they reside. They are called by the First Presidency and will work under the general direction of the Quorum of the Twelve, the Presidents of the Seventy, and the Area Presidencies in that part of the world in which they live.

They will continue with their present employment, reside in their own homes, and serve on a Church-service basis. Those residing in Europe, Africa, Asia, Australia, and the Pacific will become members of the Third Quorum of the Seventy. Those in Mexico, Central America, and South America will become members of the Fourth Quorum. Those residing in the United States and Canada will become members of the Fifth Quorum. . . .

Consistent with their ordination as Seventies, they become officers of the Church with a specific and definite tie to a quorum. ("May We Be Faithful and True," *Ensign*, May 1997, pp. 5–6.)

Patriarchs

I hope you patriarchs are blessed with the inspiration and revelation of the Lord as you lay your hands upon the people in the fulfillment of that sacred calling as patriarch. What a unique, personal, individual, wonderful thing is a patriarchal blessing spoken by authority of the priesthood and the office and calling of patriarch in the name of the Lord Jesus Christ. (Smithfield/ Logan Utah Regional Conference, priesthood leadership session, April 20, 1996.)

Patriarchs are unique in their calling. They have a special calling, different from all other callings in this Church, and every man and woman who is old enough to understand ought to live worthy to receive the blessings given by a patriarch. (Pittsburgh Pennsylvania Regional Conference, priesthood leadership session, April 27, 1996.)

Stake Presidents

The stake president of course must be the spiritual anchor. He also must be able to manage the complex affairs of the stake, and therefore he must have administrative ability or at least the capacity to learn. On occasion, he stands as a judge of the people and must be a man of wisdom and discernment. But wealth and financial success are not criteria for Church service. I think I speak for all of my brethren when I say that in selecting a man to preside over a stake of Zion there is much of prayer with much of seeking the will of the Lord, and only when that will is recognized is action taken. ("Tithing: An Opportunity to Prove Our Faithfulness," *Ensign*, May 1982, p. 41.)

Bishops

I urge the people of the Church, wherever you may be, when you are faced with problems, first to try to solve those problems yourselves. Think about them, study alternatives available to you, pray about them, and look to the Lord for direction. If you are unable to settle them yourselves, then talk with your bishop or branch president. He is a man of God. . . .

It is so much better that you consult with these your local brethren rather than that you write to the General Authorities of the Church, who, in many instances, will simply refer your query back to your bishop or stake president. Such referral will not come of an unwillingness to take the time to assist those in trouble. It will be prompted by an established procedure in the Church that we should look to our local leaders for counsel, those who know us best. They are entitled to inspiration from the Lord in counseling those for whom they have responsibility.

Even if President Kimball were in good health and vigorous, there is no way that he could deal with all of the personal problems of the people and still carry the tremendous administrative load which is attached to his office. If bishops and stake presidents do not know the answers to problems which come to them, then they may properly write to the Presidency of the Church. That is the order of things, my brethren and sisters, and there is great wisdom in it. ("Live the Gospel," *Ensign,* November 1984, p. 86.)

Every bishop is a man who has been called by the spirit of prophecy and revelation and set apart and ordained by the laying on of hands. Every one of them holds the keys of the presidency of his ward. Each is a high priest, the presiding high priest of his ward. Each carries tremendous responsibilities of stewardship. Each stands as a father to his people.

None receives money for his service. No ward bishop is compensated by the Church for his work as a bishop. ("To the Bishops of the Church," *Ensign,* November 1988, pp. 48–49.)

A young man said to me one day, "Do you belong to a ward and have a bishop?" I replied, "Of course I do." He asked further, "Do you attend tithing settlement with your local ward bishop?" I replied that I do, that I, even though serving as a member of the Presidency of the Church, have an accountability to my local ward bishop just as every other man and woman in this church is accountable either to a bishop or to a branch president.

He was somewhat amazed. I was surprised to think that he would even raise such questions. I thought of the genius of the Lord's work and the wisdom of the organization of His church. I have heard President Benson speak with appreciation for his bishop. I feel a kinship with my bishop. I hope that each of you feels similarly. ("To the Bishops of the Church," *Ensign,* November 1988, p. 48.)

Let me now speak directly to the thousands of bishops who are in attendance tonight. Let me say first that I love you for your integrity and goodness. You *must* be men of integrity. You must stand as examples to the congregations over which you preside. You must stand on higher ground, so that you can lift others. You must be absolutely honest, for you handle the funds of the Lord, the tithes of the people, the offerings that come of their fasting, and the contributions which they make from their own strained resources. How great is your trust as the keepers of the purse of the Lord!

Your goodness must be as an ensign to your people. Your morals must be impeccable. The wiles of the adversary may be held before you because he knows that if he can destroy you, he can injure an entire ward. You must be wise with inspired wisdom in all of your relationships lest someone read into your observed actions some taint of moral sin. You cannot succumb to the temptation to read pornographic literature, to see pornographic films, even in the secrecy of your own chamber to view pornographic videotapes. Your moral strength must be such that if ever you are called upon to sit in judgment on the questionable morals of others, you may do so without personal compromise or embarrassment.

You cannot use your office as bishop to further your own business interests lest through some ensuing financial mishap accusation be placed against you by those who succumbed to your persuasiveness.

You cannot compromise your qualifications to sit as a common judge in Israel. It is a fearsome and awesome responsibility to stand as a judge of the people. . . .

You must be their counselor, their comforter, their anchor and strength in times of sorrow and distress. You must be strong with that strength which comes from the Lord. You must be wise with that wisdom which comes from the Lord. Your door must be open to hear their cries and your back strong to carry their burdens, your heart sensitive to judge their needs, your godly love broad enough and strong enough to encompass even the wrongdoer and the critic. . . .

You stand as a watchman on the tower of the ward over which you preside. ("To the Bishops of the Church," *Ensign*, November 1988, pp. 49–50.)

[The bishop of the ward in which I grew up] served for a quarter of a century. The ward over which he presided had more than 1,100 members, but he seemed to know and love us all. He was our friend, our counselor, our presiding officer, our confidante, our teacher. He knew us boys by our first names and so addressed us. We respectfully addressed him as "Bishop." He was no martinet who ruled with a heavy hand. He could laugh with us. He could sympathize with us. He understood us, and we knew it. We knew also that he loved us. . . .

. . . He was there when I was given a name and a blessing by my good father. He it was who interviewed me and found me worthy of baptism into the Lord's church. He it was who interviewed me and found me worthy to be ordained a deacon. He called me to my first Church responsibility as a member of the presidency of the deacons quorum. He it was who presided over the quorum of priests to which I once belonged. He it was who recommended me to the stake president as worthy to receive the Melchizedek Priesthood. He it was who recommended me to the President of the Church as one worthy to serve as a missionary. He it was who welcomed me home and who subsequently signed my recommend as one worthy to be married in the house of the Lord.

He grew old in the service and died, and it was my honor to speak at his funeral. A great congregation filled the chapel where he had presided for so long. I spoke out of the heart of a boy whom he had befriended and helped, out of the heart of a youth whom he had guided and counseled, out of the experience of an adult whose life he had blessed in many ways. ("To the Bishops of the Church," *Ensign*, November 1988, pp. 49, 51.)

I know that the work is hard at times. There are never enough hours to get it done. The calls are numerous and frequent. You have other things to do. That is true. You must not rob your employer of the time and energy that are rightfully his. You must not rob your family of time which belongs to them. But as most of you have come to know, as you seek for divine guidance, you are blessed with wisdom beyond your own and strength and capacity you did not know you had. It is possible to budget your time so that you neglect neither your employer, your family, nor your flock.

God bless the bishops of The Church of Jesus Christ of Latter-day Saints. You may on occasion be inclined to complain about the burdens of your office. But you also know the joys of your service. ("To the Bishops of the Church," *Ensign*, November 1988, p. 51.)

Without going into technical details of his many responsibilities, may I remind you that a bishop must bring into one personality a remarkable and wonderful set of talents, the like of which he may think he never possessed.

Very quickly and in general terms, a bishop is a manager. He is an executive, directly responsible for all of the programs of the Church in the ward over which he presides. He must know all aspects of these programs. That will require diligent and prayerful study.

He is a father to his people. He must develop the art of listening.

He is a counselor. He is the one to whom the people bring their problems. He is the one who must guide and direct, who must suggest and persuade, who must advise and restrain.

He is a judge who must pass judgment as to worthiness, as to need, as to office, as to eligibility for many things.

Then, whether a bishop wishes to be or not, he is an example. His life and actions will be known to the people. They will become a greater sermon than any he gives from the pulpit.

Finally, he is the spiritual anchor of the entire ward. He must demonstrate, both by example and precept, his nearness to the Lord and the potential within each ward member to seek and live by direction of the Spirit.

No matter how large the Church grows, no matter where its work extends, no matter how many General Authorities are put in place as leaders on a general level, when all is said and done, on a day-to-day basis, the men who will most importantly and most directly affect the faith, the spiritual strength, and the activities of the members of this Church will be the bishops. They cannot do it all themselves. They have counselors to whom they can and must delegate. In so doing, they will bless themselves and their people. (Regional Representatives Seminar, March 30, 1990.)

We are becoming a great global society. But our interest and concern must always be with the individual. Every member of this church is an individual man or woman, boy or girl. Our great responsibility is to see that each is "remembered and nourished by the good word of God" (Moro. 6:4), that each has opportunity for growth and expression and training in the work and ways of the Lord, that none lacks the necessities of life, that the needs of the poor are met, that each member shall have encouragement, training, and opportunity to move forward on the road of immortality and eternal life. This, I submit, is the inspired genius of this the Lord's work. The organization can grow and multiply in numbers, as it surely will. . . . But with all of this there must continue to be an intimate pastoral relationship of every member with a wise and caring bishop or branch president. These are the shepherds of the flock whose responsibility it is to look after the people in relatively small numbers so that none is forgotten, overlooked, or neglected. ("This Work Is Concerned with People," *Ensign*, May 1995, pp. 52–53.)

Everyone has a bishop. I tell you it is a marvelous system and I cannot say enough in tribute to the great bishops of this Church who serve without any compensation except the compensation that comes of the love of the people and the good commendation of the Lord whom they serve. Thank you ever so much, and may you be blessed with inspiration and faith and health and strength and vitality and energy and wisdom beyond your own to do that which the Lord would have you do. (Eugene Oregon Regional Conference, priesthood leadership session, September 14, 1996.)

Presidencies

The Lord, in His infinite wisdom, has created in this church what we call presidencies. Essentially, all quorums and organizations are presided over by a presidency, except the Council of the Twelve Apostles, where there is one president of the Quorum, and the Quorums of the Seventy, where there are seven presidents. I think I can understand why there is no presidency of the Twelve. The Council consists of twelve mature men, each of whom has comparable leadership responsibilities. The number is relatively small. Furthermore, the entire Twelve is a very close-knit body, with every man free to express himself on any matter that comes before the Quorum. Evidently, there is no need for a presidency of three to preside over the remaining nine brethren. All are seasoned by long experience. They are men who have been called with a special calling.

In the case of the Seventy, the number is large and flexible in terms of the number of quorums that might be organized. Each of the presidents, who is called from the First Quorum of Seventy, is co-equal with the others, with one of the seven being denoted as the senior president.

In the case of the priests quorum, the bishop serves as president. But whether it be a bishopric, stake presidency, Aaronic or Melchizedek priesthood quorum presidency, mission presidency, temple presidency, auxiliary organization presidency, Area Presidency, or the First Presidency of the Church, there is a president with counselors. ("'In . . . Counsellors There Is Safety,'" *Ensign*, November 1990, p. 48.)

There are several cardinal principles with reference to counselors. In the first place, the presiding officer selects his own counselors. They are not chosen by others and forced upon him. However, it is necessary in most circumstances that his selections be approved by higher authority. For instance, in the organization of a stake, which occurs under direction of a General Authority [or an Area Authority], a president is carefully and prayerfully chosen. He is then asked to nominate men to serve as his counselors, and it is expected that the General Authority will approve the selection before the men are interviewed.

It is imperative that the president himself select his counselors because theirs must be a compatible relationship. He must have absolute confidence in them. They must have confidence in him. They must work together in a spirit of mutual trust and respect. The counselors are not the president. In certain circumstances, they may act in his behalf, but this is a delegated authority. ("'In . . . Counsellors There Is Safety,'" *Ensign*, November 1990, p. 49.)

I wish to say to you who serve as counselors: Treasure this opportunity and glean from it all that you can. Look for the good in those who lead you. Don't look for their weaknesses. You can find some if you look hard enough. None of us is perfect. There was only one perfect man who ever walked the earth, and He was the Son of God. We all have weaknesses and I guess we all make mistakes and will make mistakes in the future, but look for the virtues, the strengths, the goodness in those with whom you labor, and draw those characteristics into your own lives and make them a part of yourselves, and you will be the richer for it all the days that you live. You have a very precious and wonderful opportunity. (BYU Married Student Stakes Regional Conference, priesthood leadership session, February 10, 1996.)

Every organization in this Church is presided over by a presidency of three, except the Seventies. Otherwise, there are presidents and counselors. Counselors are important. The Lord put them there for a purpose. They are part of a three-legged tripod. You need three members in a presidency. I can tell you that because there was a time when I stood almost alone. I very much appreciate counselors. . . . I can pass a lot of things to them that they can do better than I can do. And that gives me more energy and time to do things that I have to do. That's the way every presidency ought to function. . . .

Use your counselors. Delegate to them. If you overload them, if you wear them out, you can release them and get new ones. But that won't happen. They will grow and become stronger because of the load which you place on their shoulders. And you will be stronger to do that which you alone can do. (Smithfield/ Logan Utah Regional Conference, priesthood leadership session, April 20, 1996.)

Every morning except Monday, the First Presidency meets, when we are in town. I call on President Faust to present his business and we discuss it and make a decision. Then I call on President Monson to present his business and we discuss it and make a decision. Then I present the items which I wish to present and we discuss them and make a decision. We work together and I think it works. You can't be a one-man operation in a presidency. Counselors—what a wonderful thing are counselors. They save you from doing the wrong things, they help you to do the right things, they become a great sounding board in discussions, they are tremendous doers—they can do some things better than you can do yourself. . . . Well, spread the load, brethren. It's the only way you'll get the work done, to spread the load. Spread the burden. Use counselors. (Pittsburgh Pennsylvania Regional Conference, priesthood leadership session, April 27, 1996.)

Disciplinary Councils

Every individual in the Church is free to think as he pleases, but when an individual speaks openly and actively and takes measures to enlist others in opposition to the Church and its programs and doctrines, then we feel there is cause for action. . . . There's a great spirit of tolerance in our church. [We maintain] an earnest desire to work with excommunicated Mormons and bring them back into the fold. (*New York Times* Interview, July 1994.)

We have to discipline people sometimes. I hope we won't forget them. I hope we won't neglect them. I hope that we won't cut them off from the Church to a point where they feel there is no way back. This is a work of redemption. This is a work of salvation. This is a work of reaching out to lift people, to help them find their way through the thicket of life. I want to plead with you, if there be those in your stakes, your wards, who are aggrieved over something, to nurture them while it is still possible. Don't delay. Don't let them feel they are abandoned and forgotten and cast out and cut off. That's so important. I plead with you to reach out to those who are in need of help. (Smithfield/Logan Utah Regional Conference, priesthood leadership session, April 20, 1996.)

Sustaining Leaders

The President of the Church is called by the spirit of revelation acting upon the members of the Quorum of the Twelve Apostles and is chosen from that body of men. However, the selection of this Quorum must be put to a sustaining vote of the membership of the Church. The same principle of common consent applies to all offices. No officer may serve without the consent of those over whom he presides. One of the established orders of business in all conferences is the sustaining of the officers of the organization. (*What of the Mormons?* pamphlet, 1982, p. 24.)

Do we sustain our local and General Authorities? This is not concerned with an exercise in paying homage to those whom the Lord has called to preside. It is a basic question of recognition of the fact that God has called a prophet to stand at the head of His church, that he has called others to work with him on a general level, and that that which they espouse and teach comes of unitedly praying together, pondering together, seeking the will of the Lord, receiving that will, and following it.

Likewise, unless there is loyalty toward the bishop and stake president on a local level, there will be an absence of harmony, there will be suspicion and hesitation to serve with fidelity, there will be that kind of division which is always destructive of faith. Let it ever be remembered that no President of this church, no counselor in the Presidency, no General Authority, no member of a stake presidency or of a bishopric or of an elders quorum presidency is there because he wished to be there and requested the privilege. Each is there because he was "called of God, by prophecy, and by the laying on of hands by those who are in authority, to preach the Gospel and administer in the ordinances thereof." (A of F 5.) ("Keeping the Temple Holy," *Ensign*, May 1990, p. 51.)

The procedure of sustaining is much more than a ritualistic raising of the hand. It is a commitment to uphold, to support, to assist those who have been selected. . . .

Your uplifted hands in the solemn assembly this morning became an expression of your willingness and desire to uphold us, your brethren and your servants, with your confidence, faith, and prayer. ("This Work Is Concerned with People," *Ensign*, May 1995, p. 51.)

CHURCH GROWTH AND PROGRESS

It was my great privilege to attend the Munich area general conference held last month in Germany. It was a tremendous experience to sit in that great Olympic sports hall and look into the faces of 14,000 Latter-day Saints who had gathered from across Europe. Two days before, I had met with the missionaries of the Germany South Mission and had felt something of their discouragement as they labored to find those they might teach. Out of all their efforts there have come only a convert here and another there, and these seem so few. But when I saw that great body of Saints in Munich I saw the fruits of their faith and of the faith of those who had preceded them. I saw a thousand doors knocked on for every man and woman and child present. I saw 999 doors rudely slammed for every one opened. I heard the prayers, the pleadings of missionaries to be led to someone who would accept the truth. I saw those missionaries going up one street and down another in bitter winter weather and the scorching heat of summer. And I witnessed in my mind's eye the lonely struggles of those few who opened their doors—their fasting, their pleadings, their doubts, their faith, weak at first and then strengthening. When I looked over that vast congregation I knew that faith had been rewarded and that, while it had happened ever so slowly, a miracle had come to pass. ("God Shall Give unto You Knowledge by His Holy Spirit," *BYU Speeches of the Year*, September 25, 1973, p. 107.)

The remarkable progress of this church is not so much the result of the requirements of the Church upon its members as it is the result of the conviction in the hearts of those members that this is in very deed the work of God, and that happiness and peace and satisfaction are found in righteous service. (*Be Thou an Example* [Salt Lake City: Deseret Book, 1981], p. 5.)

In 1960 . . . I was given an assignment by the First Presidency to work with the mission presidents, the missionaries, and the Saints in Asia. The Church was weak and small in that part of the earth. The seed had been planted in Japan, Taiwan, and Korea by faithful Latter-day Saints in military service. But it was tiny and unstable. We had no buildings of our own. We met as small groups in rented houses. In winter they were cold and uncomfortable. Converts came into the Church. But some, lacking faith, soon left. However, there remained a residual of strong and wonderful men and women who looked beyond the adversity of the moment. They found their strength in the message, not in the facilities. They have remained faithful to this day, and their numbers have been added to by the tens and tens of thousands.

A few Sundays back we held a regional conference in Tokyo. The spacious hall was filled to capacity. . . . The Spirit of the Lord was there. An attitude of faith filled that vast congregation. For me, who had known those days when we were weak and few in number, it was a miracle to behold, for which I give thanks to the Lord.

We had a similar experience in Hong Kong. . . .

Then in Seoul, Korea, my heart was touched as we entered the largest hall in that great city to find every seat taken by members of The Church of Jesus Christ of Latter-day Saints and their invited guests. A magnificent choir of 320 voices opened with the strains "Oh, how lovely was the morning" ("Joseph Smith's First

Prayer," *Hymns*, 1985, no. 26). It was a moving expression of the first vision of the Prophet Joseph Smith.

I had known South Korea in its days of poverty and reconstruction following the terrible war. When first I went there, we had six missionaries in Seoul and two in Pusan. Some were ill with hepatitis. Today there are four thriving missions in that land, with some six hundred missionaries. Many of the missionaries are sons and daughters of Korea. They include bright and beautiful young women in whose hearts burns the light of faith. They include young men who leave schooling for a season in order to serve missions. These young men are under tremendous pressures because of military requirements as well as educational demands, but they have faith in their hearts.

When first I went to South Korea, there were 2 or 3 tiny branches. Today there are 150 local units of the Church, both wards and branches. Then it was a small, isolated district of the Northern Far East Mission. We had no chapels. Today there are 14 stakes with 47 chapels built and owned and another 52 under lease, with others under construction.

I felt a spirit in that congregation three weeks ago that touched me to the depths of my soul. I saw the sweet fruits of faith. I knew of the early struggles in establishing an unknown church. I knew of the poverty of the people. Now there is strength. There is an undreamed-of measure of prosperity. There is a warm spirit of fellowship. There are families of devoted husbands and wives and good and beautiful children.

These are people I love, and I love them because of their faith. They are intelligent and well educated. They are hardworking and progressive. They are humble and prayerful. They are an example to others across the world. ("Lord, Increase Our Faith," *Ensign*, November 1987, p. 53.)

The progress of the Church in our day is truly astounding. The God of heaven has brought to pass this latter-day miracle, and what we have seen is but a foretaste of greater things yet to come. ("We Have a Work to Do," *Ensign*, February 1988, p. 6.)

This work is concerned with people, each a son or daughter of God. In describing its achievements we speak in terms of numbers, but all of our efforts must be dedicated to the development of the individual. ("This Work Is Concerned with People," *Ensign*, May 1995, p. 53.)

You are part of this great latter-day movement that is going over the earth. Sister Hinckley said we've been in Brazil. We've been in a lot of other places besides Brazil. We went first to Colombia, and then to Peru, then to Bolivia, where we broke ground for a temple in Cochabamba. It was raining terribly, but we had a groundbreaking service there. Then we went to Santiago, Chile, and had a wonderful time there; and then to Buenos Aires, Argentina, where we met with nearly 50,000 people in a great football stadium. From Buenos Aires to Porto Alegre, Brazil, and then to São Paulo, where we had another great crowd of people in a football stadium; and then to Recife . . . [where] we broke ground for a new temple. Then we went to Manaus, over a thousand miles up the Amazon, where the Church is growing. There are three stakes of Zion now. We have 137 stakes in Brazil. Things are moving. Oh, how they are moving down there in South America. The Church is growing in a marvelous and remarkable way. . . .

Brother [Richard G.] Scott speaks Spanish. He's learning Portuguese. He speaks English. That means that he can speak to more than 80 percent of the membership of the Church in their native tongue. Think of it. Marvelous things are happening. This work is spreading over the earth. "This gospel . . . shall be preached in all the world for a witness unto all nations; and then shall the end come" (Matt. 24:14). That is exactly what's happening. We're now in 150 nations, speaking many languages. We have more members outside the United States than we have in the United States. . . . Surely, the work is moving in a grand and marvelous way. (Miami Florida Fireside, November 17, 1996.)

In 1930, on the 100th anniversary of the organization of the Church, one-half of all Latter-day Saints in the world resided in the state of Utah. By 1996 only 17 percent of the membership of the Church resided in Utah, but today we have four times as many members in Utah as we did in 1930. Some of those, incidentally, have moved from California. Last year we had more converts in the state of Utah than we had in all of the United Kingdom. I am told that we are the second largest Christian denomination in California and the seventh largest denomination in the United States. A year ago we passed the point where we have more members of the Church outside the United States than we have in the United States.

We emphasize the importance of education. We maintain the largest private Church-sponsored university in America if not in the world. It is BYU, with an enrollment of more than 27,000 students. We provide religious instruction to some 363,000 more youth in a great worldwide seminary and institute program.

We maintain the largest family history facility in the world. Approximately 70 percent of those who use this facility are not members of the Church. With its great central library and satellite stations throughout the world, it is an ever more popular place for researching one's roots.

We have a very substantial welfare program with farms, dairies, canneries, and other facilities to take care of the poor among us. Additionally, we have given in the past five years $138,000,000 of humanitarian aid to those in distress throughout the world. The vast majority of the recipients of this aid are not of our faith.

We maintain the largest missionary organization of which I am aware, with 55,000 missionaries in the field at their own expense. Most of these are young men who are out for two years.

The Church is growing at a rate of about 4 percent a year. That is a very substantial number on a base of nearly ten million.

We are building from 350 to 400 new meetinghouses each year to accommodate our people. We will break ground this summer for a very large new assembly hall in Salt Lake City. The famous Salt Lake Tabernacle, built under Brigham Young's direction, grows ever smaller as the Church grows ever larger. . . .

In a world of shifting values, or no values whatever, we are working to strengthen the family and build stability in the homes of our people. We think we are succeeding.

We maintain the largest women's organization of which I am aware, with some 3.9 million members. A presidency of strong and able women preside over them, who also serve on various other Church boards and committees.

A vast organization of more than 23,000 congregations is officered by an unpaid ministry, who give of their time to the direction of these congregations.

Our forebears had no government help, no borrowing from banks or other credit institutions. In that tradition The Church of Jesus Christ of Latter-day Saints today stands free of debt because of the faith of the people in the payment of tithes. And so I might go on. . . . (Los Angeles World Affairs Council Meeting, March 6, 1997.)

CHURCH HISTORY AND HERITAGE

See also Pioneers

If New York represented the birthplace of the Church, then Ohio and Missouri represented the places of schooling for the young prophet and his associates. It was a time when the Church was operating in two spheres, hundreds of miles apart. Transportation was most tedious and difficult. There was, of course, no telegraph nor other means of easy communication. It was a time when there was much of bitterness and persecution. It was a time when there was much of apostasy and vile accusations.

But it was also a marvelous and miraculous season, a time of Pentecostal outpouring.

Sixty-two of the revelations found in the Doctrine and Covenants were received in that Ohio period and environment. During that time the Kirtland Temple was constructed, with all of the miraculous incidents that occurred incident to its dedication. Moses, Elias, and Elijah came, bestowing eternal priesthood keys. The Son of God appeared to his servants, who bore testimony of him. The work was strengthened and integrated in a most remarkable manner.

Of that season Orson Pratt wrote: "God was there, his angels were there, the Holy Ghost was in the midst of the people, the visions of the Almighty were opened to the minds of the servants of the living God; the veil was taken from the minds of many; they saw the heavens opened, they beheld the angels of God; they heard the voice of the Lord; and they were filled from the crown of their heads to the soles of their feet with the power and inspiration of the Holy Ghost." (*Journal of Discourses* 18:132.) (Address to Religious Educators, September 14, 1984.)

Out of this earlier episode [the controversy over fraudulent Church history documents] has now arisen another phenomenon. It is described as the writing of a "new history" of the Church as distinguished from the "old history." It represents, among other things, an effort to ferret out every element of folk magic and the occult in the environment in which Joseph Smith lived to explain what he did and why.

I have no doubt there was folk magic practiced in those days. Without question there were superstitions and the superstitious. I suppose there was some of this in the days when the Savior walked the earth. There is even some in this age of so-called enlightenment. For instance, some hotels and business buildings skip the numbering of floor thirteen. Does this mean there is something wrong with the building? Of course not. Or with the builders? No.

Similarly, the fact that there were superstitions among the people in the days of Joseph Smith is no evidence whatever that the Church came of such superstition.

Joseph Smith himself wrote or dictated his history. It is his testimony of what occurred, and he sealed that testimony with his life. It is written in language clear and plain and unmistakable. From an ancient record he translated the Book of Mormon by the gift and power of God. It is here for all to see and handle and read. Those who have read with faith and inquired in prayer have come to a certain knowledge that it is true. The present effort of trying to find some other explanation for the organization of the Church, for the origin of the Book of Mormon, and for the priesthood with its keys and powers will be similar to other anti-Mormon fads which have come and blossomed and faded. Truth will prevail. A knowledge of that truth comes by effort and study, yes. But it comes primarily as a gift from God to those who seek in faith. ("Lord, Increase Our Faith," *Ensign*, November 1987, pp. 52–53.)

I am one who believes in celebrations. I am one who believes in commemorating great events of the past. When we do so we bring to life, as it were, men and women of history who did significant things of which we need reminding. We all need to recognize that a tremendous price has been paid for the freedom we enjoy, the respect we enjoy, the comfort we enjoy as we live in this age of comparative ease and affluence. ("A Declaration to the World," *BYU Studies*, Winter 1987, p. 5.)

Every member of the Church ought to have some understanding of, and familiarity with, the history of this tremendous movement. Without such understanding, it is difficult to sink the roots of faith deep enough that the tree will not topple when false winds of doctrine blow. No man can really appreciate Joseph Smith without reading his history. No one can really understand the tremendous heritage we have, which has been made possible by the sacrifices of the generations who have gone before. Without such understanding, it is not likely that there will be much of gratitude or appreciation. (Church Educational System Conference, June 24, 1989.)

My mind [has] drifted back [to the time when] our people were then in Commerce, Illinois, homeless and destitute, facing the bitter winter that soon followed. They had been driven from Missouri and had fled across the Mississippi seeking asylum in Illinois. Where the river makes a wide bend, they had purchased a tract of land, beautiful in its location, but so swampy that a team could not cross it without becoming mired in mud. This site, with tremendous effort and great sacrifice, was to become Nauvoo, the Beautiful. But in 1839 it was Commerce, a rendezvous for thousands driven from their homes and now homeless. They had left behind the labors of years—houses and barns, churches and public buildings, and hundreds of productive farms. Moreover, they had left loved ones buried beneath the Missouri sod who had been killed by vicious mobocrats. Destitute now, and dispossessed, unable to get redress from Missouri, they determined to petition the president and Congress of the United States. Joseph Smith and Elias Higbee traveled to Washington.

They left Commerce on 20 October 1839, riding in a light horse-drawn buggy. They arrived in Washington five weeks

later. Much of their first day was spent trying to find accommo-
dations they could afford. They noted in a letter to Hyrum Smith:
"We found as cheap boarding as can be had in this city." (*History
of The Church of Jesus Christ of Latter-day Saints*, 4:40.)

Calling upon the president of the United States, Martin Van
Buren, they stated their case. Responded he: "Gentlemen, your
cause is just, but I can do nothing for you. . . . If I take up for you
I shall lose the vote of Missouri." (*History of the Church*, 4:80.)

They then appealed to Congress. In the frustrating weeks
that followed, Joseph returned to Commerce, much of the way
by horseback. Judge Higbee remained to plead their cause, only
finally to be told that Congress would do nothing.

How far the Church had come in the respect and confidence
of public officials between 1839, when Joseph Smith was repudiated in Washington, and 1974, when the Church and its temple
[in Washington, D.C.] were welcomed and honored! . . .

Between those two first and final chapters ran the thread of
a score of other chapters that spoke of the death of Joseph and
Hyrum that sultry day of 27 June 1844; of the sacking of Nauvoo;
of long trains of wagons crossing the river into Iowa Territory; of
the camps in the snows and mud that fateful spring of 1846; of
Winter Quarters on the Missouri, and the black canker, the
fevers, and the plague that decimated their ranks; of the call for
men to join the army, issued by the same government that earlier had been deaf to their pleas; of the grave-marked trail up the
Elkhorn, the Platte, and the Sweetwater, over South Pass, and
thence to Salt Lake Valley; of the tens of thousands who left the
East and England to thread their way over that long trail, some
pulling handcarts and dying in the Wyoming winter; of the endless grubbing of sagebrush in the Utah mountain valleys; of the
digging of miles of ditches to lead water to the thirsty soil; of
decades of hue and cry against us, born of bigotry; of the depri-
vation of rights of citizenship under laws enacted in the same
Washington and enforced by marshals sent out from the seat of
the federal government. Those are among the chapters of our
epic history.

Thanks be to God that those harsh days are past. Thanks be
to those who remained true while walking through those testing
fires. What a price—what a terrible price they paid, of which we

are the beneficiaries. We must never forget it. . . . Thanks be for those who through the virtue of their lives have since earned for this people a new measure of respect. Thanks be for a better day, with greater understanding and with wide and generous appreciation extended to The Church of Jesus Christ of Latter-day Saints. ("A City upon a Hill," *Ensign,* July 1990, pp. 2, 4.)

Nauvoo

I have been to Nauvoo a number of times. I have walked its streets, explored its beautifully restored homes, and contemplated the magnificent temple that once crowned the summit of the hill that rises from the river. I have thought much of my own grandfather, who as a young man lived there and left with the Saints.

Ever since the Prophet named the place Nauvoo, we have spoken of it as Nauvoo the Beautiful. It *is* beautiful. May I mention several aspects of that beauty.

First, Nauvoo is beautiful in its location. One day in June we drove from St. Louis to Carthage. We then took the River Road to Nauvoo. We noted again the great sweeping bend of the Mississippi with the city standing as it were on a peninsula eagerly reaching out, pointing to the West, where the people who lived there would go. . . .

Second, for me Nauvoo is beautiful in its beginnings. It was a place of asylum, a refuge, a safe harbor in a terrible storm. . . .

. . . How inviting is the port, any port that is reached in a storm. How lovely is a place of refuge when there has been oppression and pursuit. How beautiful to the homeless is a home. Nauvoo was beautiful in its beginnings as a place of refuge.

Third, Nauvoo was beautiful in its creation. . . .

Fourth, Nauvoo was even beautiful in its suffering. . . .

Finally, from our viewpoint of almost a century and a half, Nauvoo is beautiful in its death. Notwithstanding tragedy, there is beauty in heroism, there is beauty in faith, there is beauty in devotion to an ideal and a principle. All of these are exemplified in the exodus from Nauvoo. The suffering was indescribable, the disillusionment difficult to bear, the hopelessness overpowering. It is difficult to imagine the emotions that must have been felt when for the last time men, women, and children walked out of those beautiful homes, closed the doors, looked upon the fields they had cultivated and the stature of the trees they had planted, climbed aboard their wagons, and drove down to the river, there to cross and move slowly over the soil of Iowa, looking back now and again at what they were leaving and would never see again. . . .

. . . I am grateful for what Nauvoo does for me, in giving to me a sense of gratitude, a sense of respect, a sense of worship, a sense of love for those who loved the Lord and served him through sunshine and storm. I am grateful for the city by the river—the city which was known as Nauvoo the Beautiful. ("Nauvoo—Sunrise and Sunset on the Mississippi," *BYU Studies* 32 [Winter and Spring 1991]: 19–22.)

Nauvoo was beautiful in its creation. There is no music like the music of industry. This place fairly rang with the cutting and shaping of timber, with the chiseling of stone, with the hammering of hot iron on the anvil, with the surveying and building of streets, the plowing of farmland, the planting and tilling of the soil, the gathering of the harvest. The homes of Nauvoo were beautiful with their salmon-colored brick and their interesting, stepped walls. The Seventies Hall was a structure of graceful lines and a place of learning. The printing plant was an expression of a desire to know what was going on, the Temple an expression of faith, of conviction, concerning the eternity of life and the power of the priesthood of God to reach beyond the veil of death.

I marvel at what those people built during those few short years. There was nothing temporary about it. They built as if they were going to live here for generations. Nauvoo, I submit, was beautiful in its creation.

[It] was even beautiful in its suffering. There can be beauty in suffering when there is faith. There is tragedy, yes; there is sorrow, of course. But there is something sublime in suffering for a great cause. I am not saying that the Saints enjoyed it. It was terrible. But there was something magnificent about the way they held up their heads and kept on going notwithstanding the travail through which they passed, much of that suffering painful and personal. Some of it was similar to the suffering of other peoples on the frontier. I have read the lists of names of those buried in the old Nauvoo cemetery. Many of them were children who died of illnesses now quickly cured through the miracles of modern medicine. Such diseases as whooping cough took a terrible toll. One can sense only in some small degree the sorrow in the loss of a beautiful child after there had already been so many other painful losses. A bronze monument has been erected in the old cemetery. It represents a father and a mother who have buried a child. The monument is beautiful in the sorrow it represents. ("Nauvoo—Sunrise and Sunset on the Mississippi," *BYU Studies* 32 [Winter and Spring 1991]: 19–22.)

Mormon Battalion

The Mormon Battalion hiked for five and a half months without any letup. They left Council Bluffs on the Missouri and went to Fort Leavenworth and came down to San Pedro and turned west and came to Tucson when it was a sleepy little Mexican village of some four or five hundred people with a garrison of Mexican soldiers here. They stayed here about two days, and then they took up their march again west to the Gila River and to the conjunction of that river with the Colorado. Then they went on to California. They had very little water. They drank brackish water, muddy water, in order to slake their thirst. There were times, numerous times, when they were without food. They ate a wild goat, everything from the beard on the front to the little tail on the back and the entrails in between. . . .

I want to hold their example before you. They did not give up. They did not whine. They did not complain. They just kept marching ever westward, ever westward, until they had cut a wagon road from here to the Pacific coast through the most treacherous kind of territory. . . . Their shoes wore out. They wrapped their feet in cloth and animal hides. They had no uniforms. Rather than get uniforms, they sent the money for uniforms to their families. They were paid seven dollars a month for that very arduous travel. They were scouts in a very, very real sense, and I commend to you a reading of their history. (Tucson Arizona Boy Scout Encampment, December 14, 1996.)

The Battalion had traveled all the way from Council Bluffs and they were in very bad condition. They had come without water much of the time. They had gone without food much of the time. When they came here [to Tucson] they replenished their supplies, but they did not last very long.

On Christmas Day they marched eighteen miles up the Gila River and then to where it conjoins with the Colorado River. But they had no water at that time or the next day. Twenty-three of them died in those months. It is a wonder to me that there were not many more. Their doctor was kind of a vicious sort of man who administered calomel and arsenic, the only two medicines he had, and the Battalion men would rather be sick than take those medicines. And when they were sick they just kept pulling, marching ever westward.

On reaching San Diego, Colonel Cooke issued an order which summed up the whole terrible ordeal. He said: "The Lieutenant Colonel commanding, congratulates the battalion on their safe arrival on the shore of the Pacific Ocean, and the conclusion of their march over two thousand miles.

"History may be searched in vain for an equal march of infantry. Half of it has been through a wilderness, where nothing but savages and wild beasts are found, or deserts where, for want of water, there is no living creature. There, with almost hopeless labor, we have dug deep wells, which the future traveler will enjoy. Without a guide who had traversed them we have ventured into trackless tablelands where water was not found for several marches. With crowbar and pick and axe in hand, we have worked our way over mountains, which seemed to defy aught save the wild goat, and hewed a pass through a chasm of living rock more narrow than our wagons. To bring these first wagons to the Pacific, we have preserved the strength of our mules by herding them over large tracts, which you have laboriously guarded without loss. The garrison of our presidios of Sonora concentrated within the walls of Tucson, gave us no pause. We drove them out, with their artillery, but our intercourse with the citizens was unmarked by a single act of injustice. Thus, marching half naked and half fed, and living upon wild animals, we have discovered and made a road of great value to our country." (Robert O. Day, *The Mormon Battalion, the Lord's Faithful*, p. 171.)

They had marched across a trackless wilderness most of the way. They had brought their wagons with them and created a road which became eventually the route of a great interstate highway and a great railway line. It joined east to west, Kansas to California. (Mormon Battalion Monument Dedication, Tucson, Arizona, December 14, 1996.)

In 1846, when they [the Latter-day Saints] left Nauvoo, Illinois, and were struggling across Iowa, strung like beads on a string from the Mississippi to the Missouri, Captain James Allen of the United States Army rode into their camps to recruit a battalion of 500 men to serve in the war with Mexico. Here they were, homeless, on the Iowa prairie. The strength of those 500 men was needed. But Brigham Young told them they should go. They did not know when, if ever, they would see their people again. They marched first to Fort Leavenworth. The officers who enlisted them were surprised that they could sign their names, in contrast with other recruits from the frontier. From Fort Leavenworth began the long and terrible march to San Diego. They finally beheld the Pacific on January 29, 1847, more than six months after leaving their camp at Council Bluffs. . . .

Some of the Battalion were garrisoned in or near San Diego. The others were marched up to Los Angeles, a sleepy little Mexican town, where they built Fort Moore. They were pioneers in the San Diego region. They were pioneers in this Los Angeles region.

When their enlistment was about to expire, their officers tried to persuade them to reenlist. A few did, but the majority wanted to get to their people. In Sacramento some obtained employment with John Sutter. They were sent to Coloma, out on the American River, to build a sawmill. James Marshall was their foreman. It was here that he picked from the tailrace a fleck of gold which set the world on fire. The date of that discovery, January 24, 1848, is recorded in the journal of Henry Bigler, a Battalion man, who wrote: "This date some kind of mettle was found in the tail of the race that looks like goald" (Erwin G. Gudde, *Bigler's Chronicle of The West* [Berkeley: University of California Press, 1962], p. 88).

That journal entry established the date of this historic discovery that changed California forever.

Be it said to the credit of these men, notwithstanding the fact that news of the discovery leaked out, even to the streets of San Francisco, they completed their contract with Sutter.

The story is told that one of them, before getting on his wagon to head for the Salt Lake Valley, took off his trousers, tied the legs, shoveled them full of dirt, panned gold from that dirt, put his trousers back on, climbed on his wagon seat, and headed east (see *Life of a Pioneer, Being the Autobiography of James S. Brown* [Salt Lake City: Geo. Q. Cannon & Sons Co., 1900], pp. 107–9). He would grub sagebrush and live the hard life of a pioneer the remainder of his days. (Los Angeles World Affairs Council Meeting, March 6, 1997.)

CHURCH OF JESUS CHRIST OF LATTER-DAY SAINTS, THE

See also Church Government; Church Growth and Progress; Kingdom of God, Modern-day

When the declaration was made concerning the only true and living Church upon the face of the earth, we were immediately put in a position of loneliness, the loneliness of leadership from which we cannot shrink nor run away and which we must face up to with boldness and courage and ability. Our history is one of being driven, of being winnowed and peeled, of being persecuted and hounded. . . .

I go back to these words of Paul:

"We are troubled on every side, yet not distressed; we are perplexed, but not in despair;

"Persecuted, but not forsaken; cast down, but not destroyed." (2 Corinthians 4:8–9.) ("The Loneliness of Leadership," *BYU Speeches of the Year*, November 4, 1969, p. 4.)

We have basic cornerstones on which this great latter-day church has been established by the Lord and built, "fitly framed together." They are absolutely fundamental to this work, the very foundation, anchors on which it stands. I should like to speak briefly of these four essential cornerstones which anchor The Church of Jesus Christ of Latter-day Saints. I mention first the chief cornerstone, whom we recognize and honor as the Lord Jesus Christ. The second is the vision given the Prophet Joseph Smith when the Father and the Son appeared to him. The third is the Book of Mormon, which speaks as a voice from the dust with the words of ancient prophets declaring the divinity and reality of the Savior of mankind. The fourth is the priesthood with all of its powers and authority, whereby men act in the name of God in administering the affairs of his kingdom. ("The Cornerstones of Our Faith," *Ensign*, November 1984, p. 51.)

[The Church] stands as the creation of the Almighty. It is a shelter from the storms of life. It is a refuge of peace for those in distress. It is a house of succor for those in need. It is the conservator of eternal truth and the teacher of the divine will. It is the true and living Church of the Master. ("The Cornerstones of Our Faith," *Ensign*, November 1984, p. 53.)

I have met with tens of thousands of [Latter-day Saints] in recent months as we have dedicated temples in many parts of the world. There is much faith. There is strong conviction. There is vibrant testimony. There is power and a great residual of spiritual capacity. These are Latter-day Saints in the full meaning of that term. They pray. They rear their families in the nurture and admonition of the Lord. They work in His service, giving generously of their time and means. They reach out to help their fellowmen without selfishness and even at the jeopardy of their own welfare. They labor in the temples without expectation of thanks from those in whose behalf they serve.

. . . We love you. We pray for you and hope that you will pray for us. We are all a part of this great cause, each with a responsibility to make it succeed. We do not need critics standing on the sidelines. We need men of faith and capacity who love the Lord and who work to accomplish His purposes. ("Questions and Answers," *Ensign*, November 1985, p. 52.)

The opening of the British Mission in 1837 was a declaration of a millennial vision. The resurrected Lord had said to His beloved disciples: "Go ye into all the world, and preach the gospel to every creature." (Mark 16:15.)

That was a tremendous charge given to a handful of men who had neither means nor standing before the world to carry out that encompassing mandate! They gave their lives in doing all that they could.

Then John the Revelator in vision "saw another angel fly in the midst of heaven, having the everlasting gospel to preach unto them that dwell on the earth, and to every nation, and kindred, and tongue and people." (Rev. 14:6.)

In these latter days, as Joseph Smith concluded his translation of the Book of Mormon, he arrived at the statement which has become part of the title page and which sets forth the book's purpose—"to show unto the remnant of the House of Israel what great things the Lord hath done for their fathers; and that they may know the covenants of the Lord, that they are not cast off forever—And also to the convincing of the Jew and Gentile that Jesus is the Christ, the Eternal God, manifesting himself unto all nations." (Title Page of the Book of Mormon.)

In the revelation given 1 November 1831, which became section 1 of the Doctrine and Covenants, the Lord said: "Hearken ye people from afar; and ye that are upon the islands of the sea, listen together.

"For verily the voice of the Lord is unto all men, and there is none to escape; and there is no eye that shall not see, neither ear that shall not hear, neither heart that shall not be penetrated. . . .

"And the voice of warning shall be unto all people, by the mouths of my disciples, whom I have chosen in these last days.

"And they shall go forth and none shall stay them, for I the Lord have commanded them." (Vs. 1–2, 4–5.) ("Taking the Gospel to Britain: A Declaration of Vision, Faith, Courage, and Truth," *Ensign,* July 1987, pp. 2, 4.)

I have been in my office up against the stresses that are felt there. This has become a very large church with a tremendous organization. It is now established in more than a hundred nations. There are decisions to be made every day, and some of these are difficult. The guidance of the Lord is sought in all of

these deliberations. The work is demanding, but there is something wonderfully stimulating in the very challenge of it.

It is a marvelous thing to sit where one can see, at least in
some measure, the whole broad encompassing picture of this
great throbbing, viable, growing phenomenon the Lord has
called The Church of Jesus Christ of Latter-day Saints. ("A
Wonderful Summer," *BYU 1989–1990 Devotional and Fireside
Speeches*, September 3, 1989, p. 12.)

I suppose that regardless of our efforts, we may never convert the world to general use of the full and correct name of the
Church. Because of the shortness of the word *Mormon* and the
ease with which it is spoken and written, they will continue to
call us the *Mormons*, the *Mormon* church, and so forth.

They could do worse. More than fifty years ago, when I was
a missionary in England, I said to one of my associates, "How
can we get people, including our own members, to speak of the
Church by its proper name?"

He replied, "You can't. The word *Mormon* is too deeply
ingrained and too easy to say." He went on, "I've quit trying.
While I'm thankful for the privilege of being a follower of Jesus
Christ and a member of the Church which bears His name, I am
not ashamed of the nickname *Mormon*.

"Look," he went on to say, "if there is any name that is totally
honorable in its derivation, it is the name *Mormon*. And so, when
someone asks me about it and what it means, I quietly say—
'*Mormon* means *more good*.'" (The Prophet Joseph Smith first said
this in 1843; see *Times and Seasons*, 4:194; *Teachings of the Prophet
Joseph Smith*, pp. 299–300.)

His statement intrigued me—*Mormon* means "more good." I
knew, of course, that "more good" was not a derivative of the
word *Mormon*. I had studied both Latin and Greek, and I knew
that English is derived in some measure from those two languages and that the words *more good* are not a cognate of the
word *Mormon*. But his was a positive attitude based on an interesting perception. And, as we all know, our lives are guided in
large measure by our perceptions. Ever since, when I have seen
the word *Mormon* used in the media to describe us—in a newspaper or a magazine or book or whatever—there flashes into my

mind his statement, which has become my motto: *Mormon* means "more good."

We may not be able to change the nickname, but we can make it shine with added luster. ("*Mormon* Should Mean 'More Good,'" *Ensign*, November 1990, p. 52.)

God is at the helm. Never doubt it. When we are confronted with opposition, He will open the way when there appears to be no way. Our individual efforts may be humble and appear somewhat insignificant. But the accumulated good works of all, laboring together with a common purpose, will bring to pass great and wondrous accomplishments. The world will be a better place for our united service. . . .

He who is our Savior slumbers not nor sleeps as He watches over this His Kingdom. ("God Is at the Helm," *Ensign*, May 1994, pp. 59–60.)

What a wonderful thing it is to look into the faces of people such as you and know that you pray, that you get on your knees night and morning and pray. . . . You acknowledge the Lord's help and give thanks, ask for forgiveness of your weaknesses, and seek His blessings in righteousness on yourself and others. . . . How wonderful it is that you do live the Word of Wisdom, that you do love your families, that you do pay your tithes and offerings, that you can stand before the Lord with a clear conscience and clean hands. A BBC reporter asked me, in an interview on Monday, a very interesting question. He said to me, "President Hinckley, if the Lord Jesus Christ were to come today, do you think He would be pleased with your church?" I said, "I think He would. Not with everybody. We have problems, of course we do. But I think He would, generally speaking, because I know people, large numbers of them, who are trying to live this gospel and who speak their love for Him constantly in their prayers." If the Lord Jesus Christ were to come today, would He be pleased? I think He would. Thank you for the goodness of your lives. (Nottingham England Fireside, August 30, 1995.)

The greatest safety you have in your lives . . . is your membership in The Church of Jesus Christ of Latter-day Saints.

Cling to the Church and live its principles and I do not hesitate to promise you that your lives will be happy, that your accomplishments will be significant, and that you will have reason to get on your knees and thank the Lord for all He has done for you in giving to you the marvelous and wonderful opportunities that you have. (Vista California Youth Fireside, March 23, 1996.)

What a wonderful thing it is to be a member of a Church with a great heritage, even of suffering as well as of faith. What a wonderful thing to belong to a Church that after 150 years is still reaching out with vigor and vitality to bless the lives of people across the world. I remind you that great is our responsibility . . . and that we cannot slacken or slow down. We live in a world filled with troubles. We live in a world where there is so much of hatred and bitterness. We live in a world where there is so much of enmity and strife. We who are members of this Church have an obligation to reach out and help those in distress wherever they may be and whatever the cause of their suffering. (Grand Encampment Devotional, Council Bluffs, Iowa, July 13, 1996.)

Purpose of the Church

The Church is the great teacher and builder of values. Its precepts are designed to lead men and women along the way of immortality and eternal life, to make their lives more complete, more rich and happy while moving through this vale of tears, and in preparing them for the beauties and wonders of that which lies ahead. Keep faith with the Church. It is true. It is divine. He who stands at its head is the Lord Jesus Christ, the Redeemer of the world. It is the church of the Almighty that carries the name of His divine Son. Its earthly leaders are those who are called of God under a plan that He has put in place. ("To a Man Who Has Done What This Church Expects of Each of Us," *BYU 1995–96 Speeches*, October 17, 1995, p. 52.)

There are so very many people with problems, and our job is to help them. That's why we're here. There's no other reason for our being here when all is said and done. We have to lift and sustain and strengthen people. The Lord is going to hold us accountable for what we do. (Corpus Christi Texas Regional Conference, priesthood leadership session, January 6, 1996.)

The Church is the great reservoir of eternal truth from which we can constantly and freely drink. It is the preserver of standards, the teacher of values. Latch onto those values. Bind them to your hearts. Let them become the lodestar of your lives to guide you as you move forward in the world of which you will become an important part. ("True to the Faith," Salt Lake Valley-Wide Institute Fireside, January 21, 1996.)

When all is said and done, there is one purpose for this Church, and that is to assist our Father in Heaven in bringing to pass the immortality and eternal life of His sons and daughters. The only reason for its being is to build faith in things that are eternal. So many times we get lost in the details of administration that we forget the spirit of the work. (Berlin Germany Regional Conference, priesthood leadership session, June 15, 1996.)

I hope that we will never lose sight of the fact that the purpose of all of our work is to help the sons and daughters of God find their way along the road that leads to immortality and eternal life. It is to have come into their hearts a love for God our Eternal Father, whose children we are. It is to have come into their hearts a solid, certain conviction concerning the place of each of us in the plan of the Almighty, that we are children of God, partakers of a divine birthright, spiritual children, who have come with a touch of divinity within us. All of these administrative things in the Church are important. I want to confirm and endorse and emphasize that. But when all is said and done, our greatest responsibility as leaders in this Church is to increase the knowledge of our people concerning their place as sons and daughters of God, their divine inheritance and their divine, eternal destiny. (Berlin Germany Regional Conference, priesthood leadership session, June 15, 1996.)

I think we stand in this dispensation like the righteous in the days of the cities of the plains when perhaps the Lord might spare the wicked, some of them, because of the righteous. That places upon us a great and significant burden. That's why we are here, to make of ourselves more effective instruments, truer warriors under the direction of the Almighty to save His sons and daughters from those things which will destroy them in time and for eternity unless they turn their lives around. (Eugene Oregon Regional Conference, priesthood leadership session, September 14, 1996.)

Mission of the Church

As we go forward we must never be distracted from the great and compelling triad of responsibility laid upon the Church to, first, carry the gospel of Jesus Christ to the people of the earth; second, to implement that gospel in the lives of the membership of the Church; and, third, to extend through vicarious work its blessings to those who have passed beyond the veil of death. Our mission is "as broad as eternity and as deep as the love of God." ("Five Million Members—A Milestone and Not a Summit," *Ensign*, May 1982, p. 44.)

This work of ours is a great work of redemption. All of us must do more because the consequences can be so remarkable and everlasting. This is our Father's work, and he has laid upon us a divine injunction to seek out and strengthen those in need and those who are weak. As we do so, the homes of our people will be filled with an increased measure of love; the nation, whatever nation it be, will be strengthened by reason of the virtue of such people; and the Church and kingdom of God will roll forward in majesty and power on its divinely appointed mission. ("What This Work Is All About," *Ensign*, November 1982, p. 10.)

The Church has grown consistently stronger because those who have gone before us have pursued a steady course. There are those who would fracture our strength by leading us in the pursuit of objectives which are not pertinent to the central mission of the Church. We are constantly invited, yes, even strongly urged, to get out and march with others for this cause or that cause. There are some causes with which we properly should be involved, which are directly related to the Church, its mission, and the well-being of its people. The determination of these must be left to those who have been called to leadership. Such causes will be few, since we must husband our strength and resources for the far greater obligation to pursue a steady course in building the kingdom of God in the earth.

Our great, basic message to the world is that Jesus is the Christ, the Son of the Living God; that he gave his life as a sacrifice for all mankind; that he rose from the grave that first Easter morning, "the firstfruits of them that slept" (1 Cor. 15:20); that "as in Adam all die, even so in Christ shall all be made alive" (1 Cor. 15:22); that he lives, our resurrected Lord and Master.

As has been said before from this pulpit, he has given us a three-fold mission: first, the teaching of the restored gospel to every nation, kindred, tongue, and people; second, the building of the Saints in their faith and encouraging them in all of their activities to walk in obedience to the commandments of the Lord; and third, the great work of salvation for the dead. This vast mission contemplates all generations of mankind—those who have gone before, all who live upon the earth, and those who will yet be born. It is larger than any race or nation or generation. It encompasses all mankind. It is a cause without parallel. The fruits of its labors are everlasting in their consequences. In the pursuit of that mission we must follow a steady and uncompromising course and never be enticed therefrom. ("He Slumbers Not, nor Sleeps," *Ensign*, May 1983, pp. 7–8.)

Now, I'd like to submit to you that when all is said and done, the work and the mission of this Church is to save. It's just that simple and just that profound . . . to save people. That's the whole purpose of what we are doing. That's why we have home teachers. That's why we have visiting teachers. That's why we have classes. That's why we have sacrament meeting. That's why we build temples, to save the living and the dead. That's our work. "This is my work and my glory—to bring to pass the immortality and eternal life of man" (Moses 1:39). And when all is said and done, that's what it is all about. (Potomac Virginia Regional Conference, priesthood leadership session, April 26, 1997.)

Church Finances

The financial program of the Church—both income and disbursement—is found in sections 119 and 120 of the Doctrine and Covenants. Except for fast offerings and missionary funds, two statements found in these brief revelations constitute the Lord's law of finance and the management program of the fiscal affairs of the Church.

Section 119 simply states that all members "shall pay one-tenth of all their interest [that which is income] annually; and this shall be a standing law unto them forever . . . saith the Lord." (V. 4.)

Then, concerning the disbursement of the money which comes from the tithing, the Lord has said: "Verily, thus saith the Lord, . . . it shall be disposed of by a council, composed of the First Presidency of my Church, and of the bishop and his council, and by my high council; and by mine own voice unto them, saith the Lord." (D&C 120.)

These eighteen men—the Presidency, the Twelve, and the Presiding Bishopric—constitute the Council on the Disposition of the Tithes. What might be regarded as executive committees of this larger council include the Budget Committee and the Appropriations Committee. The expenditure of all Church funds comes under the purview of these bodies.

In the financial operations of the Church, we have observed two basic and fixed principles: One, the Church will live within its means. It will not spend more than it receives. Two, a fixed percentage of the income will be set aside to build reserves against what might be called a possible "rainy day."

For years, the Church has taught its membership the principle of setting aside a reserve of food, as well as money, to take care of emergency needs that might arise. We are only trying to follow the same principle for the Church as a whole.

Some of us, I submit, are old enough to remember vividly the dark times of the Great Depression of the thirties. I hope we shall never see such again. But we know that they are not outside the realm of possibility. We are mindful of the story of Pharaoh's dream of the fat and lean cattle and the full and thin ears of corn. (See Gen. 41.)

How grateful I am to be able to say to the priesthood of this church that the Church in its ecclesiastical operations has no debt. No temple, no meetinghouse, no seminary or institute facility, no welfare facility, no building or property used in the ecclesiastical operations is under mortgage. ("The State of the Church," *Ensign*, May 1991, pp. 53–54.)

"Why is the Church in commercial enterprises?"

Essentially, the business assets which the Church has today are an outgrowth of enterprises which were begun in the pioneer era of our history when we were isolated in the West. When there was no longer a need for a number of these, they were disposed of. The remaining number are relatively few.

I repeat, the combined income from all of these business interests is relatively small and would not keep the Church going for longer than a very brief period. I add, also, that these commercial properties are tax-paying entities who meet their tax obligations under the laws of the areas where they are located. ("The State of the Church," *Ensign*, May 1991, p. 54.)

Criticism of the Church

Joseph F. Smith presided over the Church at a time of great bitterness toward our people. He was the target of vile accusations, of a veritable drumbeat of criticism by editorial writers even in this community. He was lampooned, cartooned, and ridiculed. Listen to his response to those who made sport of demeaning him: "Let them alone. Let them go. Give them the liberty of speech they want. Let them tell their own story and write their own doom." (*Gospel Doctrine*, 5th ed., Salt Lake City: Deseret Book Co., 1939, p. 339.) And then with an outreaching spirit of forgiving and forgetting, he went ahead with the great and positive work of leading the Church forward to new growth and remarkable accomplishments. ("'Of You It Is Required to Forgive,'" *Ensign*, November 1980, p. 62.)

We have those in the Church these days, as there were in Nauvoo, who profess membership but spend much of their time in criticizing, in finding fault, and in looking for defects in the Church, in its leaders, in its programs. They contribute nothing to the building of the kingdom. They rationalize their efforts, trying to justify with pretenses of doing good for the cause, but the result of those efforts is largely only a fragmentation of faith, their own and that of others. ("Dedication of the John Taylor Building," *BYU 1982–83 Fireside and Devotional Speeches,* September 14, 1982, p. 18.)

Do not fear concerning the Church. We have had mentioned in this conference some of our critics. They mock that which is most holy to us. They jest over and hold up to ridicule that which has come by revelation from the Almighty. Any man who tries to find humor at the expense of that which is sacred to another is deeply flawed in character. Shame on those who stoop to such actions in the name of fun and on those who witness and laugh. . . .

. . . There are a few who have taken it upon themselves as their mission to belittle and demean and destroy the faith of the weak, with a badly flawed argument that we are not Christians.

To all of these we have a twofold answer, quietly spoken. The first is this: Would a true follower of Christ, a follower of him who was the epitome of love and mercy and consideration, so seek to injure another?

The second: We ask only that we be judged by our fruits. ("Let Us Go Forward!" *Ensign,* November 1983, pp. 74–75.)

We now seem to have a great host of critics. Some appear intent on trying to destroy us. They belittle that which we call divine.

In their cultivated faultfinding, they see not the majesty of the great onrolling of this cause. They have lost sight of the spark that was kindled in Palmyra which is now lighting fires of faith across the earth, in many lands and in many languages. Wearing the spectacles of humanism, they fail to realize that spiritual promptings, with recognition of the influence of the Holy Ghost, had as much to do with the actions of our forebears as did the processes of the mind. They have failed to realize that religion is as much concerned with the heart as it is with the intellect.

We have those critics who appear to wish to cull out of a vast panorama of information those items which demean and belittle some of the men and women of the past who worked so hard in laying the foundation of this great cause. They find readers of their works who seem to delight in picking up these tidbits, and in chewing them over and relishing them. In so doing they are savoring a pickle, rather than eating a delicious and satisfying dinner of several courses.

We recognize that our forebears were human. They doubtless made mistakes. . . . But the mistakes were minor, when compared with the marvelous work which they accomplished. To highlight the mistakes and gloss over the greater good is to draw a caricature. Caricatures are amusing, but they are often ugly and dishonest. A man may have a blemish on his cheek and still have a face of beauty and strength, but if the blemish is emphasized unduly in relation to his other features, the portrait is lacking in integrity.

There was only one perfect man who ever walked the earth. The Lord has used imperfect people in the process of building his perfect society. If some of them occasionally stumbled, or if their characters may have been slightly flawed in one way or another, the wonder is the greater that they accomplished so much. . . .

I do not fear truth. I welcome it. But I wish all of my facts in their proper context, with emphasis on those elements which explain the great growth and power of this organization. ("Be Not Deceived," *Ensign*, November 1983, p. 46.)

There is an insidious effort going on to try to undermine the Church and destroy its credibility, even among its own members. ("The Miracle Made Possible by Faith," *Ensign*, May 1984, p. 46.)

The Church has a host of critics and an army of enemies. They mock that which is sacred. They demean and belittle that which has come from God. They pander to the desires of others who evidently enjoy seeing that which is sacred made to look funny. I cannot think of anything less in harmony with the spirit of the Christ than this kind of activity.

We are pained by the desecration of that which to us is holy. But we need not fear. This cause is greater than any man. It will outlast all its enemies. We need only go forward by the *power* of faith without fear. ("'God Hath Not Given Us the Spirit of Fear,'" *Ensign*, October 1984, p. 4.)

What about the critics of the Church who have been so vocal of late?
    We have them. We have always had them. They are not as vociferous as they once were. Noisy as they are, they are not as threatening. People ask whether we are fearful of research of our history. My reply to this is no, of course not, provided it is done with balance and integrity. . . .
    When we are called before the bar of God to give an accounting of our performance, I think it unlikely that any of us will be commended for wearing out our lives in an effort to find some morsel of history, incomplete in its context, to cast doubt on the integrity of this work. Rather, I believe we will be examined on what we did to build the kingdom, to bring light and understanding of the eternal truths of the gospel to the eyes and minds of all who are willing to listen, to care for the poor and the needy, and to make of the world a better place as a result of our presence. ("Questions and Answers," *Ensign*, November 1985, p. 52.)

    We are sometimes accused of being narrow and secretive. Nothing could be further from the truth. We have nothing to be ashamed of, nothing to be embarrassed about. Our history, our actions, our programs are not such as to cause us embarrassment when and if they are discussed in the full and true context of the environment and time of their occurrence. ("A Unique and Wonderful University," *BYU 1988–89 Devotional and Fireside Speeches*, October 11, 1988, pp. 49–50).

    We have critics both within and without. Although they are vocal and have access to the media, they are relatively few in number. If we were entirely without criticism, we would be concerned. Our responsibility is not to please the world but, rather, to do the will of the Lord, and from the beginning the divine will so often has been contrary to the ways of the world. ("Bring Up a Child in the Way He Should Go," *Ensign*, November 1993, p. 54.)

    As surely as this is the work of the Lord, there will be opposition. There will be those, perhaps not a few, who with the sophistry of beguiling words and clever design will spread doubt and seek to undermine the foundation on which this cause is established. They will have their brief day in the sun. They may have for a brief season the plaudits of the doubters and the skeptics and the critics. But they will fade and be forgotten as have their kind in the past.

Meanwhile, we shall go forward, regardless of their criticism, aware of but undeterred by their statements and actions. Said the Lord even before the Church was organized:

"Therefore, fear not, little flock; do good; let earth and hell combine against you, for if ye are built upon my rock, they cannot prevail.

"Look unto me in every thought; doubt not, fear not.

"Behold the wounds which pierced my side, and also the prints of the nails in my hands and feet; be faithful, keep my commandments, and ye shall inherit the kingdom of heaven" (D&C 6:34, 36–37). ("God Is at the Helm," *Ensign,* May 1994, p. 60.)

While I am speaking of things that impede our progress as Latter-day Saints, let me mention one other. It is an attitude of being critical about the Church. You are bright, able, and educated young men and women. You have been taught to think critically, to explore, to consider various sides of every question. This is all good. But you can do so without looking for flaws in the Church or its leaders. Keep balance in your studies. I do not say this defensively. So very many people are so very gracious and generous and kind in what they say and write to me. On the other hand, there are a few who evidently thoroughly dislike the Church and seem to thoroughly dislike me. That is their prerogative. I feel no bitterness toward them. I feel only sorrow for them, because I know what the eventual outcome will be.

I have held various offices in this Church since I was called to serve in a deacons quorum presidency at the age of twelve. During the past sixty years I have been in the Administration Building of the Church. Long before I was a General Authority I knew the Presidents of the Church in those days as well as the other General Authorities. I came to know early that they were men, imperfect in some small ways. But I wish to say that I felt they were the best men to be found in this world. They too had critics who spoke evil concerning them. They too had to deal with the writings and talks of malcontents and apostates. But the names of those men are remembered with appreciation and gratitude and respect, while the names of their critics have gone down to oblivion.

As a young man working in the Administration Building, I was asked on one occasion by the President of the Council of the Twelve to take a companion and serve notice of a Church court on a man who had written various books critical of the Church and strongly apostate in their nature. His membership was in a California stake, and the stake president had sent the papers here, where the man was residing at the moment.

My associate and I . . . went to his place of residence. I announced the purpose of our coming. He invited us in and motioned us to seats at the far side of the room away from the door. He stood by the front door so we could not get out until he had time to breathe out his fulminations against us. He was mean and vicious in what he said. He spoke threatening language. Fortunately he did not lay a hand on us. Neither of us was very big. Having completed our mission, we moved toward the door, opened it, and left.

At the time he was alive his writings were read by many who shared his apostate doctrinal views. They were read by many who accepted his charges against certain of the General Authorities. He was false on both counts, but there were those who accepted his writings as true.

He was subsequently excommunicated from the Church, and that only increased his anger. Instead of acknowledging his errors, he lashed out with greater ferocity. And then he suddenly faded. People seemed to have no more interest in him. He has long since passed away. I know of no one who remembers him. . . . I think I am the only one of whom I know who even remembers the man's name.

We have a few of the same kind now. We have had in the past, and will in the future. They are wearing out their lives trying to find fault with this Church. They mine its history for every little negative tidbit. They examine the words of the General Authorities. They may even accord me the dubious honor of examining what I am saying to you tonight. I regret the manner in which they are wasting their time. My heart reaches out to them, and I wish I could persuade them to change their ways, to alter their outlook, and to come back to the Church and apply their talents to the building of the kingdom. But I see little disposition to do so.

I suppose they are enjoying their day in the sun, but their sun will set and they will not be remembered for good.

I remind you that this work has not been moved forward to its present wonderful level by critics. It has been moved forward by men and women of faith, who have done their part, large or small, in expanding it. ("True to the Faith," Salt Lake Valley-Wide Institute Fireside, January 21, 1996.)

This Church came about as a result of intellectual curiosity. We believe in education, and we spend a substantial part of our budget on the education of our young people. We expect them to think. We expect them to investigate. We expect them to use their minds and dig deeply for knowledge in all fields. If we have a motto, it is this, "The glory of God is intelligence." Now, we have been investigated ever since the Church was organized. Scores and scores and scores of people have investigated and written about us. Some of them have worn out their lives doing so. But some of the things in our libraries are of a confidential nature. We have a trust concerning preserving the confidentiality of some of those matters, such as private diaries, but there has been very little of our story that has not been plowed over and plowed over and plowed over. Scores of books have been written and the Church just goes on and on and grows and grows. We don't have anything to be ashamed of in any sense. We have so much to be proud of.

For instance, in December 1995 I was interviewed by Mike Wallace of CBS's *60 Minutes*, who has the reputation of being the toughest reporter on American television. It seems to me he asked about everything. Well, when it all appeared on the air, the program was favorable. He interviewed those with negative perspectives, but I said this to him: "We have only one request, that you judge us by our fruits. Judge us by what this Church is doing, what it is accomplishing across the world. It's a marvelous thing that is happening. It is so positive in its message and so positive in its growth. Of course, we have critics. Of course, we make a mistake now and again. Of course, we fail in some things once in a while. That is to be expected. But, overall, the picture is one of growth, of stability, of strength, of improvement, and of accomplishment." (Media Luncheon and Press Conference, Tokyo, Japan, May 18, 1996.)

Now we have a few blackbirds who like to sit on a telephone pole and sing against us, but they are few and far between, and we don't need to worry about them. We leave them in the hands of the Lord, hoping and praying that they will repent and come back, but we don't need to get too excited—just go forward, keep the faith, live the gospel, build the kingdom. "What e'er thou art, act well thy part" was the motto that President McKay read on a stone in Scotland, and it applies to each of us. (See Conference Report, April 1969, p. 95; or *Improvement Era*, June 1969, p. 30.)

Brethren, let us go forward with faith and enthusiasm and love for the Lord. (Potomac Virginia Regional Conference, priesthood leadership session, April 26, 1997.)

CIVIC RESPONSIBILITY

Leadership in civic and social problems.—Oh, how we need in this day and time men and women who will stand up for decency and truth and honesty and virtue and law and order and all of the other good qualities on which our society is founded. . . .

Now, I want to say to you, and I say it with a plea in my heart, *get involved.* Get involved on the side of righteousness and truth and decency and sobriety and virtue. You, and others like you, are the great hope of this world. God bless you to speak up for truth and decency. I love these marvelous words of Paul to Agrippa when he recounted his experience on the way to Damascus. The Lord spoke unto him and said, when he had fallen to the ground:

"But rise, and stand upon thy feet: for I have appeared unto thee for this purpose, to make thee a minister and a witness. . . .

"To open their eyes, and to turn them from darkness to light, and from the power of Satan unto God. . . ." (Acts 26:16, 18.)

I wish every young man and woman in this church would read and reread those marvelous words from the 26th chapter of Acts—the words of the Lord to Paul who became probably the greatest missionary who ever walked the earth. . . .

The problem with most of us is that we are afraid. We want to do the right thing, but we are troubled by fears and we sit back and the world drifts about us.

I confess to you that by nature I was a very timid boy. When I left to go on a mission my great father said, "I want to give you only one verse of scripture." I think this has become, perhaps, the greatest help of my life, these words of the Lord to the ruler of the synagogue whose daughter was reported dead. And the Lord turned to the ruler of the synagogue and said: "Be not afraid, only believe." (Mark 5:36.)

"Be not afraid, only believe." I commend to you these wonderful words of the Lord as you think of your responsibilities and opportunities. ("Prepare to Lead," BYU *Speeches of the Year,* February 25, 1969, pp. 6–7.)

Following dinner, I picked up the morning paper, which I had not previously read. Thumbing through its pages, my eyes stopped on the theater ads, so many of them an open appeal to witness that which is debauching, that which leads to violence and sex.

I turned to my mail and found a small magazine which lists the television fare for the coming week and saw titles of shows aimed in the same direction. A news magazine lay on my desk. This particular issue was devoted to the rising crime rate, with a graph showing that while the population increased only 11 percent from 1963 to 1973, violent crime had increased a shocking 174 percent. Articles in the magazine spoke of additional billions for increased police forces and larger prisons.

The flood of pornographic filth, the inordinate emphasis on sex and violence are not peculiar to this land. The situation is as bad in Europe and in many other areas. News stories tell of the production in Denmark of a filthy, erotic, and blasphemous movie to be produced on the life of the Son of God. The whole dismal picture indicates a weakening rot seeping into the very fiber of society.

Our legislatures and courts are affected by this wave. Legal restraints against deviant moral behavior are eroding under legislative enactments and court opinions. This is done in the name of freedom of speech, freedom of the press, freedom of choice in so-called personal matters. But the bitter fruit of these so-called freedoms has been enslavement to debauching habits and behavior that leads only to destruction. A prophet, speaking long ago, aptly described the process when he said, "And thus the devil cheateth their souls, and leadeth them away carefully down to hell." (2 Ne. 28:21.)

On the other hand, . . . I am one who believes that the situation is far from hopeless. I am satisfied that there is no need to stand still and let the filth and violence overwhelm us, or to run in despair. The tide, high and menacing as it is, can be turned back if enough of the kind I have mentioned will add their strength to the strength of the few who are now effectively working. I believe the challenge to oppose this evil is one from which members of The Church of Jesus Christ of Latter-day Saints, as citizens, cannot shrink. ("Opposing Evil," *Ensign*, November 1975, p. 38.)

The building of public sentiment begins with a few earnest voices. I am not one to advocate shouting defiantly or shaking fists and issuing threats in the faces of legislators. But I am one who believes that we should earnestly and sincerely and positively express our convictions to those given the heavy responsibility of making and enforcing our laws. The sad fact is that the minority who call for greater liberalization, who peddle and devour pornography, who encourage and feed on licentious display make their voices heard until those in our legislatures may come to believe that what they say represents the will of the majority. We are not likely to get that which we do not speak up for.

Let our voices be heard. I hope they will not be shrill voices, but I hope we shall speak with such conviction that those to whom we speak shall know of the strength of our feeling and the sincerity of our effort. ("Opposing Evil," *Ensign*, November 1975, p. 39.)

Let us not forget that we believe in being benevolent and in doing good to all men. I am convinced that we can teach our children effectively enough that we need not fear that they will lose their faith while being friendly and considerate with those who do not subscribe to the doctrine of this Church. Let us reach out to those in our community who are not of our faith. Let us be good neighbors, kind and generous and gracious. Let us be involved in good community causes. There may be situations where, with serious moral issues involved, we cannot bend on matters of principle. But in such instances we can politely disagree without being disagreeable. We can acknowledge the sincerity of those whose positions we cannot accept. We can speak of principles rather than personalities.

In those causes which enhance the environment of the community, and which are designed for the blessing of all of its citizens, let us step forward and be helpful. An attitude of self-righteousness is unbecoming a Latter-day Saint.

Brethren, teach those for whom you are responsible the importance of good civic manners. Encourage them to become involved, remembering in public deliberations that the quiet voice of substantive reasoning is more persuasive than the noisy, screaming voice of protest. In accepting such responsibilities our people will bless their communities, their families, and the Church. (Regional Representatives Seminar, April 1, 1988.)

CIVILITY AND COURTESY

See also Tolerance

Charity also includes the element of civility toward others. Civility is the root of the word *civilization*. It carries with it the essence of courtesy and politeness and consideration of others. How very much of it we have lost in our contemporary society. The lack of it is seen in the endless barrage of faultfinding and criticism spewed forth by media columnists and commentators. Lack of civility is often the cause of death and injury on the highway. It is the smirk of arrogance worn by many who think themselves superior in intellect, in riches, in station in life. Oh, how we need to cultivate a greater measure of civility in our society.

("Codes and Covenants," *BYU 1994–95 Devotional and Fireside Speeches*, October 18, 1994, p. 38.)

Civility covers a host of matters in the relationships among human beings. Its presence is described in such terms as "good manners" and "good breeding." But everywhere about us we see the opposite. . . .

Crime is essentially an absence of civility. A study sponsored by the National Institute of Justice, the research arm of the Justice Department, concludes that crime costs Americans at least $450 billion a year. Some question the methodology of the study, but surely no one can question the gravity of the problem. An article on this subject points out that another $40 billion could be added, bringing the total annual cost of crime to almost $500 billion. No one can comprehend a figure of that magnitude. But it is interesting to note that the Defense Department's budget for last year was $252 billion, which means that the cost of crime is essentially twice what we spend for the defense of this nation and in giving military assistance to other nations.

It is appalling. It is alarming. And when all is said and done the cost can be attributed almost entirely to human greed, to uncontrolled passion, to a total disregard for the rights of others—in other words, to a lack of civility. As one writer has said, "People might think of a civilized community as one in which there is a refined culture. Not necessarily; first and foremost it is one in which the mass of people subdue their selfish instincts in favor of the common well being" (Royal Bank Letter, May–June 1995). He continues: "In recent years the media have raised boorishness to an art form. The hip heroes of movies today deliver gratuitous put-downs to ridicule and belittle anyone who gets in their way. Bad manners, apparently, make a saleable commodity. Television situation comedies wallow in vulgarity, stand-up comedians base their acts on insults to their audiences, and talk show hosts become rich and famous by snarling at callers and heckling guests." (Ibid.)

All of this speaks of anything but refinement. It speaks of anything but courtesy. It speaks of anything but civility. Rather, it speaks of rudeness and crudeness, and an utter insensitivity to the feelings and rights of others. . . .

Said the Savior to the multitude: "Ye are the salt of the earth: but if the salt have lost his savour, wherewith shall it be salted? it is thenceforth good for nothing, but to be cast out, and to be trodden under foot of men" (Matt. 5:13).

Civility, I submit, is what gives savor to our lives. It is the salt that speaks of good taste, good manners, good breeding. ("Our Fading Civility," BYU Commencement Address, April 25, 1996.)

It is amazing what courtesy will accomplish. It is tragic what a lack of courtesy can bring. We see it every day as we move in the traffic of the cities in which we live. A moment spent in letting someone else get into the line does good for the one who is helped, and it also does good for the one who helps. Something happens inside of us when we are courteous and deferential toward others. It is all part of a refining process, which if persisted in, will change our very natures.

On the other hand, anger over a little traffic problem, with swearing and filthy gestures, demeans those who make them and offends those at whom they are aimed. To practice the kind of self-discipline which can control one's temper in the little things that happen almost every day is an expression of emotional cleanliness. ("'Be Ye Clean,'" *Ensign,* May 1996, p. 49.)

COMMITMENT AND CONVICTION

Herein lies the great strength of this kingdom. It is the conviction, solid and real and personal, that is found in the hearts of millions of Latter-day Saints who live in many lands and who speak a variety of tongues. Each is a part of a great society of believers. ("Special Witnesses for Christ," *Ensign,* May 1984, p. 51.)

I had a letter from a friend in the East the other day. He spoke of a conversation he had had with another member of the Church. He had asked his associate whether he felt close to his Heavenly Father. He replied that he did not feel close. Why not? He said, "Candidly, because I don't want to." Then he went on to say, "If I were close to Heavenly Father, He would probably want some commitment from me, and I am not ready for that."

Think of it—a man who has taken upon himself the name of the Lord in baptism, a man who has renewed his covenants with the Lord in his sacrament meetings, a man who has accepted the priesthood of God and yet has said that if he were close to his Heavenly Father, some commitment might be expected of him, and he was not ready for that.

In this work there must be commitment. There must be devotion. We are engaged in a great eternal struggle that concerns the very souls of the sons and daughters of God. We are not losing. We are winning. We will continue to win if we will be faithful and true. We *can* do it. We *must* do it. We *will* do it. There is nothing the Lord has asked of us that in faith we cannot accomplish. ("The War We Are Winning," *Ensign*, November 1986, p. 44.)

In August of 1852, . . . a special conference was held in the old tabernacle on this square. President Heber C. Kimball opened by saying:

"We have come together today, according to previous appointment, to hold a special conference to transact business, a month earlier than usual, inasmuch as there are elders to be selected to go to the missions of the earth, and they want an earlier start than formerly. . . .

"The missions we will call for during this conference are, generally, not to be very long ones; probably from three to seven years will be as long as any man will be absent from his family."

The clerk then read ninety-eight names of individuals who had been proposed for foreign missions. (*Joseph I. Earl Family History,* p. 1.)

To me it is a thing of wonder that at a time when our people were struggling to gain a foothold in these mountains, they put the spread of the gospel ahead of comfort, security, the well-being of their families, and all other considerations. Across the broad prairie between the mountains of the West and the Missouri and Mississippi rivers there were two bodies of Latter-day Saints moving in opposite directions. Missionaries traveling to the eastern states and Europe passed converts gathering from those lands to the Zion of the West. ("An Ensign to the Nations," *Ensign,* November 1989, p. 53.)

Be strong—in standing for the right. We live in an age of compromise and acquiescence. In situations with which we are daily
confronted, we know what is right, but under pressure from our
peers and the beguiling voices of those who would persuade us,
we capitulate. We compromise. We acquiesce. We give in, and we
are ashamed of ourselves. . . . We must cultivate the strength to
follow our convictions. ("Building Your Tabernacle," *Ensign,*
November 1992, p. 52.)

The time has come for us to stand a little taller, to lift our eyes
and stretch our minds to a greater comprehension and understanding of the grand millennial mission of this The Church of
Jesus Christ of Latter-day Saints. This is a season to be strong. It
is a time to move forward without hesitation, knowing well the
meaning, the breadth, and the importance of our mission. It is a
time to do what is right regardless of the consequences that
might follow. It is a time to be found keeping the commandments. It is a season to reach out with kindness and love to those
in distress and to those who are wandering in darkness and pain.
It is a time to be considerate and good, decent and courteous
toward one another in all of our relationships. In other words, to
become more Christlike.

We have nothing to fear. God is at the helm. He will overrule
for the good of this work. . . .

The little stone which was cut out of the mountain without
hands as seen in Daniel's vision is rolling forth to fill the whole
earth (see Daniel 2:44–45). No force under the heavens can stop it
if we will walk in righteousness and be faithful and true. The
Almighty Himself is at our head. ("This Is the Work of the
Master," *Ensign,* May 1995, p. 71.)

[Alma's] teachings include these words: "Awake and arouse
your faculties, even to an experiment upon my words, and exercise a particle of faith" [Alma 32:27].

. . . Far more of us need to awake and arouse our faculties to
an awareness of the great everlasting truths of the gospel of Jesus
Christ. Each of us can do a little better than we have been doing.
We can be a little more kind. We can be a little more merciful.
We can be a little more forgiving. We can put behind us our

weaknesses of the past, and go forth with new energy and increased resolution to improve the world about us, in our homes, in our places of employment, in our social activities.

We have work to do, you and I, so very much of it. Let us roll up our sleeves and get at it, with a new commitment, putting our trust in the Lord. . . .

The Church needs your strength. It needs your love and loyalty and devotion. It needs a little more of your time and energy. . . .

I am not asking anyone to do so at the expense of your families. The Lord will hold you responsible for your children. But I am suggesting that we spend a little less time in idleness. ("We Have a Work to Do," *Ensign*, May 1995, p. 88.)

There is a tendency on the part of some to become indifferent. There are those who drift off seeking the enticements of the world, forsaking the cause of the Lord. I see others who think it is all right to lower their standards, perhaps in small ways. In this very process they lose the cutting edge of enthusiasm for this work. For instance, they think the violation of the Sabbath is a thing of unimportance. They neglect their meetings. They become critical. They engage in backbiting. Before long they have drifted from the Church.

The Prophet Joseph once declared, "Where doubt is, there faith has no power" (*Lectures on Faith*, Salt Lake City: Deseret Book Co., 1985, p. 46).

I invite any who may have so drifted to come back to the strong and solid moorings of the Church. This is the work of the Almighty. Whether we as individuals go forward will depend on us. But the Church will never fail to move forward. ("Stay the Course—Keep the Faith," *Ensign*, November 1995, p. 72.)

I am humbled, I am overwhelmed, by the confidence and expressions of love which come from the people of this Church. I thank you people who are trying to do the right thing, who pay your tithes, who live the Word of Wisdom, who do your duty to teach and preside and do the little things and the big things that move forward the kingdom of God. You men and women, you boys and girls, you get on your knees and pray. That isn't happening as much as it once did across this land. There isn't a man or woman in this great hall today who doesn't pray. What a remarkable and wonderful thing that is. What a great, sustaining power in the world is one who acknowledges that God is in His heaven and all is right with the world, who goes before the Lord in humility and asks in the name of His Beloved Son that blessings be poured out, not only upon himself or herself but upon others. I heard President Lee say once to a congregation in Europe that "we of this relatively small Church could become the few who would save the world from destruction, as occurred when Abraham bargained with the Lord concerning the cities of the plains." Tremendous is our responsibility and great and marvelous is our opportunity as sons and daughters of God. Every one of us is a child of God. Let us never forget that we are children of God at all times and in all circumstances and in all conditions and in all environments in which we might find ourselves, and that there is never a time or a season or a circumstance when we can let down on our standards. (Smithfield/ Logan Utah Regional Conference, April 21, 1996.)

God bless you, my beloved associates in this great work. We are all in this together. None of us can slip down without taking the whole Church down somewhat. None of us can do better without lifting the whole Church somewhat. You are important. Everyone is important. We are all a part of it. We can do a little better. I pray that we will work at it just a little harder, with a little more devotion, a little more love, a little more prayer, a little more enthusiasm. This is the Savior's work. This is not my church, it is the Savior's church. He stands at the head. We are merely here to do His bidding, to listen to His voice, and try to give expression to it the best way we know how. (Pittsburgh Pennsylvania Regional Conference, priesthood leadership session, April 27, 1996.)

The test of our convictions concerning this work lies in the manner of our living. We meet together as a Church to strengthen one another, to build one another, to increase our resolution to live together as sons and daughters of God should live. As I look into your faces I see strength. I see a love for the

Lord. I see a desire to live the gospel. But we have not reached perfection. We are far from it individually. We have so much yet to do. Let us work at it at all times and in all circumstances. Let us be faithful. Let us never forget who we are. (Copenhagen Denmark Fireside, June 14, 1996.)

You cannot be indifferent to this great cause. You have accepted it. You have entered into sacred covenants. Regardless of what you do in the future with the knowledge you gain from your secular studies, you cannot escape your obligation under the covenant you implicitly made when you were baptized and the covenant which you have renewed each time you have partaken of the sacrament of the Lord's supper.

You cannot simply take for granted this cause, which is the cause of Christ. You cannot simply stand on the sidelines and watch the play between the forces of good and evil. Said Nephi: "They who are not for me are against me, saith our God" (2 Ne. 10:16). Wrote John the Revelator:

"I know thy works, that thou art neither cold nor hot: I would thou wert cold or hot.

"So then because thou art lukewarm, and neither cold nor hot, I will spew thee out of my mouth" (Rev. 3:15–16). . . . I urge you with all the capacity that I have to reach out in a duty that stands beyond the requirements of our everyday lives; that is, to stand strong, even to become a leader in speaking up in behalf of those causes which make our civilization shine and which give comfort and peace to our lives. You can be a leader. You must be a leader, as a member of this Church, in those causes for which this Church stands. Do not let fear overcome your efforts. . . . Cast that fear aside and be valiant in the cause of truth and righteousness and faith. If you now decide that this will become the pattern of your life, you will not have to make that decision again. You will put on "the armour of God," and raise your voice in defense of truth, whatever the circumstances now and in all the years that lie ahead. (See Eph. 6:11.) ("Stand Up for Truth," BYU Devotional Address, September 17, 1996.)

Let every man and woman and child resolve to make the work of the Lord better and stronger and greater than it has ever been before. It is the quality of our lives that makes the difference. It is our resolution to live the gospel of Jesus Christ that makes the difference. This is an individual matter. If we all pray, the Church is so much the stronger. And so it is with every principle of the gospel. Let us be part of this great forward-moving cause that is growing across the entire earth. We cannot stand still, we have to move forward. It is imperative that we do so. The personal conviction that dwells in each of our hearts is the real strength of the Church. Without it, we have very little of anything; with it, we have everything. (Jacksonville Florida West Stake Conference, January 19, 1997.)

I feel like saying, Shape up. We can do better than we are doing. We must do better than we are doing. The world is crowding in on us now. Utah has been discovered. People are coming from all over the nation to live [in Utah], and we must stand tall and be Latter-day Saints in very deed. There is no place for fence-straddlers. "Who's on the Lord's side? Who? Now is the time to show. We ask it fearlessly. Who's on the Lord's side? Who?" (*Hymns*, no. 260.) (Brigham City Utah Regional Conference, February 23, 1997.)

CONSECRATION

See also Sacrifice

I hold in my hand a widow's mite. It was given me in Jerusalem many years ago and I was told that it is genuine. . . . I keep it in my office as a constant reminder of the fearsome responsibility of spending that which comes of the consecrations of the members of the Church. Most of the wonderful, faithful Latter-day Saints who pay their tithing are men and women of modest means. They not only pay their tithing, but they also make many other contributions for the strengthening of this work.

Some time back a small, bent, elderly woman came to my office. For the purpose of this talk I shall call her Mary Olsen, although that is not her name and she would not wish her identity disclosed. She said she had just come over from the temple.

She took from her purse her checkbook. She said that she had been a widow for many years, that life had not been easy for her. She had a great love for the Lord and his Church. She had faithfully paid her tithing all her life. She felt she would not live much longer. Now, she said, she felt she ought to be doing more to help than she had done. In a hand shaky with age, she wrote a check for $5,000. She handed it to me. I noted the address where she lived. It was in a poor neighborhood. I confess that as I looked at that check tears came into my eyes. I have held many larger checks than that in my hands. But as I held the check of this widow woman, I was almost overcome by her faith and the seriousness of the trust that was mine in the expenditure of her consecrated contribution. ("The Widow's Mite," *BYU 1985–86 Devotional and Fireside Speeches,* September 17, 1985, p. 10.)

CONVERSION

See also Missionary Work

Converts are not peas in a pod, they are not automobiles on a production line; they are men and women, sons and daughters of our Father in Heaven, into whose hearts have come the truths of the restored gospel of the Master. Nobody knows, nobody can predict the consequences of those . . . conversions. ("The Consequences of Conversion," Address to BYU Student Body, January 28, 1959, p. 3.)

The other day when I was preparing to leave for a stake conference in Dallas the phone rang, and a man said, "I need a little information. I know a widow who goes out every morning at four o'clock to milk sixty cows to keep her son in the mission field. She has just received a letter from her boy saying that he needs a new overcoat and a pair of shoes, and she doesn't know where to get the money to buy them. Is there some way I can help?"

That procedure, of course, was very easily worked out, but as I traveled to my conference I reflected on the sacrifice of that widow, and of many other parents, to keep sons and daughters in the mission field. On Sunday morning, I rode around the city of Dallas with President and Sister Atkerson. We saw many large and beautiful churches and a magnificent synagogue. People were gathering to these buildings in such numbers that the traffic was blocked in some areas. We then went to our own building where we met six of our missionaries who are laboring in that area.

As I talked with our elders and thought of the sacrifice behind their service, and then thought of the people we had seen going to these other magnificent buildings, the question came into my mind, "Why do we make such efforts at such great cost to come to teach these people who already have so much that is virtuous and good?" . . .

What can we give them that they do not now have? May I just review four or five items which have come to us through the revelation of the Lord and which they can secure from no other source in all this world? . . .

. . . The experience of Joseph Smith in a few moments in the grove on a spring day in 1820, brought more light and knowledge and understanding of the personality and reality and substance of God and his Beloved Son than men had arrived at during centuries of speculation. Notwithstanding the declaration at Jordan at the time of the Savior's baptism when the voice of the Father was heard, and notwithstanding the events on the Mount of Transfiguration when again the voice of the Father was heard, men somehow evidently had been unable to realize the separate entities of the Father and the Son, their relationship and their reality.

I want to say that when we started emphasizing in our missionary program the truth about God as a basic and fundamental and primary principle, and began to encourage those who were willing to listen to get on their knees and ask him . . . concerning the truth of that teaching, we began to get converts in such numbers as we had not had in many, many years.

The second great revelation received in this dispensation was the testimony of another nation, speaking from the dust, of the divinity of the Lord Jesus Christ. . . . When we have been able to get people to read the Book of Mormon prayerfully, we have seen realized in their lives the fulfillment of the words of Moroni that they would know the truth. . . .

Came next the bestowal of the priesthood. . . .

Came next the organization of the Church—the Church of Jesus Christ. . . . There is not [another] church . . . to my knowledge led by prophets who speak as they are moved upon by the Holy Ghost, and apostles who stand as living witnesses to all the world of the divinity of the Lord Jesus Christ.

Came after that the great keys . . . which brought about the opportunity of universal salvation and exaltation. A man said rather smugly one day, "I am saved." I asked, "What about your father?"

He said, "I guess he isn't saved." I said, "Can you believe that in the justice and mercy of God he would make it possible for you to enjoy all the blessings which you claim you have and deny those same blessings to your father and your mother, who gave you all that you have of life and body and mind?" . . .

. . . I have had opportunity to study what causes people to join the Church. I have come to the conclusion that it is testimony, which comes into their hearts of the truth of these great revelations. ("The Cornerstone," *Improvement Era*, June 1960, pp. 425–26.)

If we would improve the world in which we live, we must first improve the lives of the people. Conversion is never a mass process. It is an individual thing. ("The Wonder of Jesus," *Improvement Era*, June 1969, p. 74.)

Discipline imposed for the sake of discipline is repressive. It is not in the spirit of the gospel of Jesus Christ. It is usually enforced by fear, and its results are negative.

But that which is positive, which comes of personal conviction, builds and lifts and strengthens in a marvelous manner. In matters of religion, when a man is motivated by great and powerful convictions of truth, he disciplines himself—not because of demands made upon him by the Church, but because of the knowledge within his heart that God lives; that he is a child of God with an eternal and limitless potential; that there is joy in service and satisfaction in laboring in a great cause. (*Be Thou an Example* [Salt Lake City: Deseret Book, 1981], p. 5.)

A convert is a man, or a woman, or a child. A convert is a living soul into whose life has come new knowledge, light, and understanding.

Converts are those who have been taught and have accepted the restored gospel of Jesus Christ. They are those into whose hearts has come a new faith and into whose minds has come a new understanding. They are those into whose lives has come a new desire to live up to higher standards of behavior. They are those who have come to know a new happiness and an enlarged circle of friends. They are those whose sights have been raised to a new understanding of the eternal purposes of God. ("'The Field Is White Already to Harvest,'" *Ensign*, December 1986, pp. 3–4.)

I met a naval officer from a distant nation, a brilliant young man who had been brought to the United States for advanced training. Some of his associates in the United States Navy, whose behavior had attracted him, shared with him at his request their religious beliefs. He was not a Christian, but he was interested. They told him of the Savior of the world, Jesus Christ, born in Bethlehem, who gave his life for all mankind. They told him of the appearance of God, the Eternal Father, and the resurrected Lord to the boy Joseph Smith. They spoke of modern prophets. They taught him the gospel of the Master. The Spirit touched his heart, and he was baptized.

He was introduced to me just before he was to return to his native land. We spoke of these things, and then I said: "Your people are not Christians. What will happen when you return home a Christian, and, more particularly, a Mormon Christian?"

His face clouded, and he replied, "My family will be disappointed. They may cast me out and regard me as dead. As for my future and my career, all opportunity may be foreclosed against me."

I asked, "Are you willing to pay so great a price for the gospel?"

His dark eyes, moistened by tears, shone from his handsome brown face as he answered, "It's true, isn't it?"

Ashamed at having asked the question, I responded, "Yes, it's true."

To which he replied, "Then what else matters?"

These are questions I should like to leave with you: "It's true, isn't it? Then what else really matters?" ("'It's True, Isn't It?'" *Ensign*, July 1993, p. 2.)

It is the miracle of conversion. It is the great process by which those with responsive hearts listen to the teachings and testimonies of missionaries and change their lives, leaving the past behind them, and moving forward into a new life. There is no miracle quite like it in all the world. (Arlington Hills Ward Sacrament Meeting, Salt Lake City, Utah, June 9, 1996.)

Some individuals have been baptized only, they have not been fellowshipped, and in two or three months they say goodbye. It is so important, my brethren and sisters, to see that they are converted, that they have in their hearts a conviction concerning this great work. It is not a matter of the head only. It is a matter of the heart and its being touched by the Holy Spirit until they know that this work is true, that Joseph Smith was verily a prophet of God, that God lives and that Jesus Christ lives and that they appeared to the boy Joseph Smith, that the Book of Mormon is true, that the priesthood is here with all of its gifts and blessings. I cannot emphasize this too strongly. (Colombia Bogota North, South, and Missionary Training Center Missionary Meeting, November 8, 1996.)

Years ago, when I was running the Missionary Department, we permitted some missionaries to have cars in the United States if their families would furnish them. You never saw such a collection of cars. Well, a father came to see me one day and said he would like to take a car to his son in Los Angeles. He was riding a bicycle and his father was afraid he was going to get killed. So we agreed that he could have a car. He came in after he delivered it to tell me what happened. He drove the car from Salt Lake all the way to Los Angeles. He found where his son lived, knocked on the door, and his son came to the door and said, "Dad, it is good to see you. Are those the keys to the car? Let me have them. We have a baptism in thirty minutes. We need to get to the meetinghouse. There is a little restaurant around the corner. You go around and get something to eat and then you take a taxi to the meeting." The missionaries drove off in the car and the father said to himself, "He is still the same old ingrate he always was." The father decided he would go home.

After he had a little something to eat he felt a little better and decided he would go to the meeting. They were just completing a baptism and having a testimony meeting when he got to the chapel. A man stood up and said, "I am an old man but I have been born today. I am a graduate of three universities but I have learned things that I could never have learned in school. I am so grateful to that missionary right there who taught me the gospel that I do not know how to express my thanks." Then a woman stood up and spoke along the same lines and pointed to the same missionary. This man said, "They were talking about my son and I was on the back row crying like a baby." He said, very thoughtfully, "I left the chapel and threw away the cigarettes that I had in my pocket. I came home and threw the coffee pot into the garbage. I am going to try to live worthy of my boy." I saw that man in the Salt Lake Temple a little over a year later. (Honduras Tegucigalpa Missionary Meeting, January 22, 1997.)

COURAGE

This work requires sacrifice, it requires effort, it means courage to speak out and faith to try. This cause does not need critics; it does not need doubters. It needs men and women of solemn purpose. As Paul wrote to Timothy: " . . . God hath not given us the spirit of fear; but of power, and of love, and of a sound mind. Be not thou therefore ashamed of the testimony of our Lord. . . ." (2 Tim. 1:7–8.)

I would that every member of this church, and every good man throughout the world, would put those words where he might see them every morning as he begins his day. They would give him the courage to speak up, they would give him the faith to try, they would strengthen his conviction of the Lord Jesus Christ.

I believe that miracles would begin to happen over the earth. ("'Be Not Afraid, Only Believe,'" *Improvement Era*, December 1969, p. 99.)

There is no greater courage than the courage of conscience. It is never boisterous or noisy. It is a quiet tempering of the spirit that builds hard steel out of soft iron and gives the will to do whatever must be done to preserve integrity of belief and action. (Utah Mayflower Society Dinner, November 16, 1994.)

COVENANT PEOPLE

It is a tremendously humbling experience to realize that the Melchizedek Priesthood which we hold is after the order of the Son of God, and that we have responsibility and accountability to Him and our Eternal Father for all that we do in exercising the stewardship given us. What I say of myself concerning this matter is equally applicable to all who hold office in this the Church and kingdom of God. It is no simple or unimportant thing to wear the mantle of the holy priesthood in whatever office or at whatever level and in whatever responsibility we might be called to serve. Every member of this church who has entered the waters of baptism has become a party to a sacred covenant. Each time we partake of the sacrament of the Lord's supper, we renew that covenant. We take upon ourselves anew the name of the Lord Jesus Christ and promise to keep His commandments. ("God Is at the Helm," *Ensign*, May 1994, p. 53.)

We are a people who have taken upon us a solemn covenant and the name of the Lord Jesus Christ. Let us strive a little harder to keep the commandments, to live as the Lord has asked us to live. We are His children. He delights in our good behavior and I think He grieves when we misbehave. (St. George Utah Pineview Stake Conference, January 14, 1996.)

We are a covenant people. I have had the feeling that if we could just encourage our people to live by three or four covenants everything else would take care of itself; we would not have to have anything else except to go forward with our program.

The first of these is the covenant of the sacrament, in which we take upon ourselves the name of the Savior and agree to keep His commandments with the promise in His covenant that He will bless us with His spirit. If our people would go to sacrament meeting every week and reflect as they partake of the sacrament on the meaning of the prayers which are offered, . . . if they would listen to the language of those prayers, which were given by revelation, and live by them, we would be a better people, all of us would be. That is the importance of the sacrament meeting. The speakers are incidental. The great thing is that we gather together and partake of the sacrament together. . . .

Second, the covenant of tithing. It is a covenant. "Why have ye robbed me? Bring ye all the tithes into the storehouse . . . and prove me now herewith" (Mal. 3:10). The commandment to us is to pay our tithing. The promise on the other side of that contract, that covenant, is that He will stay the destroyer and open the windows of heaven and pour down blessings that there will not be room enough to receive them. I am one who believes in the literalness of that promise. . . .

Three, the covenants of the temple: Sacrifice, the willingness to sacrifice for this the Lord's work—and inherent in that law of sacrifice is the very essence of the Atonement, the ultimate sacrifice made by the Son of God in behalf of each of us. Consecration, which is associated with it, a willingness to give everything, if need be, to help in the on-rolling of this great work. And a covenant of love and loyalty one to another in the bonds of marriage, fidelity, chastity, morality.

If our people could only learn to live by these covenants, everything else would take care of itself, I am satisfied. We would not have to worry about sacrament meeting attendance. We would not have to worry about willingness to serve missions. We would not have to worry about divorce and the many requests for cancellation of temple sealings. We would not have to worry about any of those things. (Meeting with General Authorities and Wives, April 10, 1996.)

People used to argue as to whether the Chinese were literal descendants of Israel. I do not worry about that. Whether they get their blessings by inherited birthright or by adoption, the end result is the same—they become partakers of the everlasting covenant between Jehovah and Abraham, which extends to all of his posterity, whether by literal descent or by adoption.

Every baptism you perform places someone under covenant, this eternal and everlasting covenant, [which brings] a special relationship with God our Eternal Father and the risen Lord Jesus Christ. Every time we partake of the sacrament we renew that covenant; we take upon ourselves the name of Jesus Christ and contract, as it were, with Him to keep His commandments. He in turn says that His spirit will be with us. That is a covenant, a two-party contract.

The temple is a place of covenants also. In the house of the Lord, as all of you know who have been to a temple, we take upon ourselves covenants and obligations regarding lives of purity and virtue and goodness and truth and unselfishness to others.

We are a covenant people in a special relationship with God our Eternal Father, eternal and everlasting if we live worthy of it. (Hong Kong Missionary Meeting, May 25, 1996.)

We are a covenant people, and that is a very serious matter. When this work was restored and the Lord set forth the purposes for that restoration, He said that one reason for the restoration was that His everlasting covenant might be reestablished. That covenant originally was made between Abraham and Jehovah when the mighty Jehovah made a great and solemn promise to Abraham. He said that his seed should become as the sand upon the seashore, that all nations would be blessed through him. He made this covenant with him, that he would be their God and they would be His people. We hear those words but we do not think of them very seriously. There was established then a relationship that was of eternal consequence in the eternal lives of all who would enter into it. Marvelous are its implications: if we will act as the children of God should act, He will be our God to bless us, to love us, to direct us, to help us.

Now, in this dispensation, that everlasting covenant has been reaffirmed. We, in effect, made that covenant when we were baptized. We became a part of His divine family, as it were. All of God's children are of His family, but in a particular and wonderful way there is a special relationship between God and the children of His covenant. And when we came into the Church, whether by lineage or whether by adoption, we became a part of a covenant people; and each time we partake of the sacrament, not only do we do it in remembrance of the sacrifice of the Son of God, who gave His life for each of us, but there is the added element that we take upon ourselves the name of Jesus Christ and pledge ourselves to keep His commandments and He pledges with us that He will bless us with His Holy Spirit. We are a covenant people, and great are the obligations which go with that covenant. We cannot be ordinary people. We must rise above the crowd. We must stand a little taller. We must be a little better, a little kinder, a little more generous, a little more courteous, a little more thoughtful, a little more outreaching to others. (Copenhagen Denmark Fireside, June 14, 1996.)

COVENANTS

See Baptism; Covenant People; Sacrament; Temple

COVETOUSNESS

See Greed

CRITICISM

See also Church of Jesus Christ of Latter-day Saints, The: Criticism of the Church

I plead for understanding among our people, for a spirit of tolerance toward one another, and for forgiveness. All of us have far too much to do to waste our time and energies in criticism, faultfinding, or the abuse of others. The Lord has commanded this people, saying: "Strengthen your brethren in all your conversation, in all your prayers, in all your exhortations, and in all your doings." This is the commandment, stated unequivocally; and then follows this marvelous promise: "And behold, and lo, I am with you to bless you and deliver you forever." (D&C 108:7–8.) ("Faith: The Essence of True Religion," *Ensign*, November 1981, p. 6.)

None of us is perfect; all of us occasionally make mistakes. There was only one perfect individual who ever walked the earth. Men and women who carry heavy responsibility do not need criticism, they need encouragement. One can disagree with policy without being disagreeable concerning the policymaker. ("'Charity Never Faileth,'" *Ensign*, November 1981, p. 98.)

We live in a society that feeds on criticism. Faultfinding is the substance of columnists and commentators, and there is too much of this among our own people. It is so easy to find fault, and to resist doing so requires much of discipline. . . . The enemy of truth would divide us and cultivate within us attitudes of criticism which, if permitted to prevail, will only deter us in the pursuit of our great divinely given goal. We cannot afford to permit it to happen. We must close ranks and march shoulder to shoulder, the weak helping the strong, those with much assisting those with little. No power on earth can stop this work if we so conduct ourselves. ("Five Million Members—A Milestone and Not a Summit," *Ensign*, May 1982, p. 46.)

I try to read newspapers, two or three a day. I sometimes read the columnists. I occasionally listen to commentators on television and radio. The writers are brilliant. They are men of incisive language, scintillating in expression. They are masters of the written word. But for the most part I find their attitudes negative. Regardless of whom they write about, they seem to look for failings and weaknesses. They are constantly criticizing, seldom praising.

And this spirit is not limited to the columnists and the commentators. Read the letters to the editor. Some of them are filled with venom, written by persons who seem to find no good in the world or in their associates. Criticism, faultfinding, evil speaking—these are of the spirit of our day. From many directions we are told that nowhere is there a man of integrity holding political office. Businessmen are crooks. Utilities are out to rob you. Everywhere is heard the snide remark, the sarcastic gibe, the cutdown of associates. . . . Criticism is the forerunner of divorce, the cultivator of rebellion, sometimes a catalyst that leads to failure. In the Church it sows the seed of inactivity and finally apostasy.

I am asking that we stop seeking out the storms and enjoy more fully the sunlight. I am suggesting that as we go through life we "accentuate the positive." I am asking that we look a little deeper for the good, that we still voices of insult and sarcasm, that we more generously compliment virtue and effort. I am not asking that all criticism be silenced. Growth comes of correction. Strength comes of repentance. Wise is the man who can acknowledge mistakes pointed out by others and change his course.

What I am suggesting is that each of us turn from the negativism that so permeates our society and look for the remarkable good among those with whom we associate, that we speak of one another's virtues more than we speak of one another's faults, that optimism replace pessimism, that our faith exceed our fears. When I was a young man and was prone to speak critically, my father would say: "Cynics do not contribute, skeptics do not create, doubters do not achieve." ("The Continuing Pursuit of Truth," *Ensign,* April 1986, pp. 2, 4.)

There are even those among us whose lives are torn with hate. They lash out at one thing and another, including the Church. They manufacture and spread vile falsehoods behind which there is not a shred of truth. There is nothing new about this, except that there have been those in each generation, including this generation, who appear to be possessed of a sickness that so manifests itself. In such circumstances, we draw comfort from the words of the Master: "Blessed are ye, when men shall revile you, and persecute you, and shall say all manner of evil against you falsely, for my sake." (Matt. 5:11.) ("Let Love Be the Lodestar of Your Life," *Ensign,* May 1989, p. 67.)

DEATH

The mystery of death has been the eminent concern of thoughtful men and women of all ages. The work in the temple, based on the atonement of the Savior of mankind, is the one sure answer to that mystery. It brings light and understanding. It brings hope and assurance. It brings conviction and faith. (Temple Presidents Seminar, August 15, 1989)

At the age of fifty [my mother] developed cancer. [My father] was solicitous of her every need. I recall our family prayers, with his tearful pleadings and our tearful pleadings.

Of course there was no medical insurance then. He would have spent every dollar he owned to help her. He did, in fact, spend very much. He took her to Los Angeles in search of better medical care. But it was to no avail.

That was sixty-two years ago, but I remember with clarity my brokenhearted father as he stepped off the train and greeted his grief-stricken children. We walked solemnly down the station platform to the baggage car, where the casket was unloaded and taken by the mortician. We came to know even more about the tenderness of our father's heart. This has had an effect on me all of my life.

I also came to know something of death—the absolute devastation of children losing their mother—but also of peace without pain, and the certainty that death cannot be the end of the soul. ("Some Lessons I Learned as a Boy," *Ensign*, May 1993, p. 54.)

As mortals we all must die. Death is as much a part of eternal life as is birth. Looked at through mortal eyes, without comprehension of the eternal plan of God, death is a bleak, final, and unrelenting experience described by Shakespeare as "the undiscover'd country from whose bourn no traveller returns" (*Hamlet*, act 3, scene 1, lines 79–80).

But our Eternal Father, whose children we are, made possible a far better thing through the sacrifice of His Only Begotten Son, the Lord Jesus Christ. This had to be. Can anyone believe that the Great Creator would provide for life and growth and achievement only to snuff it all into oblivion in the process of death? Reason says no. Justice demands a better answer. The God of heaven has given one. The Lord Jesus Christ provided it.

His was the ultimate sacrifice, His the sublime victory. ("The Greatest Miracle in Human History," *Ensign*, May 1994, p. 72.)

What a wonderful thing is death, really, when all is said and done. It is the great reliever. It is a majestic, quiet passing on from this life to another life, a better life, I'm satisfied of that. We go to a place where we will not suffer as we have suffered here, but where we will continue to grow, accumulating knowledge and developing and being useful under the plan of the Almighty made possible through the atonement of the Son of God. (Funeral Service for Robert G. Wade, January 3, 1996.)

Death is a part of life. It is a fundamental, basic part of our eternal lives. We can't go on with the great work that lies ahead without stepping over the threshold of death, sorrowful as it is for those who remain. I am satisfied that it is a beautiful experience for those who make that step, who have lived lives of righteousness and faithfulness. (Funeral Service for Harry V. Brooks, February 23, 1996.)

All of us have to deal with death at one time or another, but to have in one's heart a solid conviction concerning the reality of eternal life is to bring a sense of peace in an hour of tragedy that can come from no other source under the heavens. (Plano Texas Regional Conference, March 17, 1996.)

There is nothing more universal than death, and nothing brighter with hope and faith than the assurance of immortality. The abject sorrow that comes with death, the bereavement that follows the passing of a loved one are mitigated only by the certainty of the Resurrection of the Son of God that first Easter morning.

What meaning would life have without the reality of immortality? Otherwise life would become only a dismal journey of "getting and spending," only to end in utter and hopeless oblivion.

"O death, where is thy sting? O grave, where is thy victory?" (1 Cor. 15:55).

The pain of death is swallowed up in the peace of eternal life. Of all the events of the chronicles of humanity, none is of such consequence as this. . . .

Whenever the cold hand of death strikes, there shines through the gloom and the darkness of that hour the triumphant figure of the Lord Jesus Christ, He, the Son of God, who by his matchless and eternal power overcame death. He is the Redeemer of the world. He gave His life for each of us. He took it up again and became the firstfruits of them that slept. He, as King of Kings, stands triumphant above all other kings. He, as the Omnipotent One, stands above all rulers. He is our comfort, our only true comfort, when the dark shroud of earthly night closes about us as the spirit departs the human form. ("This Glorious Easter Morn," *Ensign,* May 1996, p. 67.)

DEBT

See also Self-Reliance; Thrift

Debt can be a terrible thing. It is so easy to incur and so difficult to repay. Borrowed money is had only at a price, and that price can be burdensome. . . .

I hasten to add that borrowing under some circumstances is necessary. Perhaps you need to borrow to complete your education. If you do, see that you pay it back. And do so promptly even at the sacrifice of some comforts that you might otherwise enjoy. You likely will have to borrow in securing a home. But be wise and do not go beyond your ability to pay.

Said President Heber J. Grant: "If there is any one thing that will bring peace and contentment into the human heart and into the family, it is to live within our means, and if there is any one thing that is grinding and discouraging and disheartening, it is to have debts and obligations that one cannot meet."

Ours is such a wasteful generation. The disposal of garbage has become one of the great problems of our time. Part of that comes of wasteful extravagance. Our pioneer forebears lived by the motto: "Fix it up, Wear it out, Make it do, or Do without." (University of Utah Institute of Religion Fireside, May 21, 1989.)

Back in the year 1938, I heard President J. Reuben Clark, Jr., . . . talk about interest. He said: "Interest never sleeps nor sickens nor dies; it never goes to the hospital; it works on Sundays and holidays; it never takes a vacation; it never visits nor travels; it takes no pleasure; it is never laid off work nor discharged from employment; it never works on reduced hours; it never has short crops nor droughts; it never pays taxes; it buys no food; it wears no clothes; it is unhoused and without home and so has no repairs, no replacements, no shingling, plumbing, painting, or whitewashing; it has neither wife, children, father, mother, nor kinfolk to watch over and care for; it has no expense of living; it has neither weddings nor births nor deaths; it has no love, no sympathy; it is as hard and soulless as a granite cliff. Once in debt, interest is your companion every minute of the day and night; you cannot shun it or slip away from it; you cannot dismiss it; it yields neither to entreaties, demands, or orders; and whenever you get in its way or cross its course or fail to meet its demands, it crushes you." (Conference Report, April 1938.)

I wish every family in the Church would copy down those words and read them occasionally as a reminder of the price we pay when we borrow. (University of Utah Institute of Religion Fireside, May 21, 1989.)

Reasonable debt for the purchase of an affordable home and perhaps for a few other necessary things is acceptable. But from where I sit, I see in a very vivid way the terrible tragedies of many who have gone on a binge of borrowing for things they really do not need. ("This I Believe," *BYU 1991–92 Devotional and Fireside Speeches*, March 1, 1992, p. 81.)

The world at that time [the 1920s] was on a reckless pursuit of riches. Then came Black Thursday of November 1929. I was nineteen years of age, a student at the university. I saw the economy crumble. I saw men whom I knew lose everything as their creditors moved against them. I saw much of the trauma and the stress of the times. I thought then, and I have thought since, how so many people might have been saved pain and misery, suffering, embarrassment, and trouble had they listened to the counsel of a prophet concerning personal debt. ("'Believe His Prophets,'" *Ensign*, May 1992, p. 51.)

DISCOURAGEMENT

I have seen President David O. McKay discouraged. I have seen President Joseph Fielding Smith and President Harold B. Lee and President Spencer W. Kimball discouraged. All of us can become discouraged. . . .

It is important to know, when you feel down, that many others do also and that their circumstances are generally much worse than yours. And it's important to know that when one of us is down, it becomes the obligation of his friends to give him a lift. ("Strengthening Each Other," *Ensign*, February 1985, p. 4.)

Those valleys of discouragement make more beautiful the peaks of achievement. (Mexico Veracruz Missionary Meeting, January 27, 1996.)

DISPENSATION OF THE FULNESS OF TIMES

What a great thing it is to be alive in this day and time in the history of the world. No other half-century in all of man's life upon earth can compare with the last fifty years. The things we have seen have been tremendous; and I think it is all part of the opening of this great work of the Lord, this the dispensation of the fulness of times, when everything of all previous dispensations began to gather in one for the blessing of the sons and daughters of God, not only of this generation but of all other generations through the restoration of the priesthood and the powers exercised therein, under which we do work in behalf of those who have passed beyond the veil of death. This is a great time to be alive. (Salt Lake East Millcreek Stake Fiftieth Anniversary Celebration, June 10, 1995.)

In the early days of the Church, as recorded in the first section of the Doctrine and Covenants, . . . the Lord sets forth four great objectives in the creation of this work in this the dispensation of the fulness of times. Why? "That every man might speak in the name of God the Lord, even the Savior of the world; That faith also might increase in the earth; That mine everlasting covenant might be established; That the fulness of my gospel might be proclaimed by the weak and the simple unto the ends of the world, and before kings and rulers. . . . That they might come to understanding" (D&C 1:20–24). (Creation of Canterbury England Stake, August 27, 1995.)

Be thankful to the Almighty for His wonderful blessings upon you. You have all that this great age has to offer in the world and beyond that the marvelous blessings of the restored gospel of Jesus Christ, which has come to earth in this the dispensation of the fulness of times, this great final dispensation when the God of Heaven has reintroduced all of the great truths, blessings, and authority of all past dispensations. (Pittsburgh Pennsylvania Regional Conference, April 28, 1996.)

I believe this is the greatest age in the history of the world. What a wonderful time to be alive. I do not know why I was born at this period of time when there is so much of great opportunity in the world, when we have so much of comfort and health and happiness because of the great progress that has been made in behalf of humanity. I was born eighty-five years ago, in 1910. The life expectancy in the United States at that time was fifty years. Today we live more than seventy-five years, and I have lived for ten years beyond that. What a wonderful blessing are the wonders of science of which we are the beneficiaries.

Then, on top of all of that, the gospel of Jesus Christ has been restored to the earth with all of the blessings associated therewith in this the dispensation of the fulness of times. Paul writing to the Ephesians said that there would come a restoration in the fulness of times when all of God's work of previous dispensations would be restored to the earth. And that is exactly what has happened. It is in Ephesians, the first chapter and tenth verse: "That in the dispensation of the fulness of times he might gather together in one all things in Christ, both which are in heaven, and which are on earth; [even] in him."

This is the dispensation of the fulness of times when God has moved His hand to bring about a restoration of all previous keys, authorities, and blessings of His gospel. How thankful we ought to be. This is a chosen generation. Let us never lose sight of that.

Let us ever be grateful for that. Let us ever live up to that, I humbly pray. (Taipei Taiwan Fireside, May 23, 1996.)

How marvelous to be alive at this time when we are nearing the twenty-first century. And with all of this, the God of heaven has restored His work. . . . This is the great summing-up season of the work of the Lord. This is the day of prophecy fulfilled. (Copenhagen Denmark Fireside, June 14, 1996.)

DIVINE NATURE

Can you imagine a more compelling motivation to worthwhile endeavor than the knowledge that you are a child of God, the Creator of the universe, our all-wise Heavenly Father who expects you to do something with your life and who will give help when help is sought for? ("The Dimension of the Spirit," *Improvement Era*, December 1964, p. 1092.)

The work that goes on in [the temple] sets forth God's eternal purposes with reference to man, God's child and creation. For the most part it is concerned with the family, with each of us as members of God's eternal family and with each of us as members of earthly families. . . .

It affirms that each man and woman born into the world is a child of God, endowed with something of His divine nature. The repetition of these basic and fundamental teachings has a salutary effect upon those who receive them, for as the doctrine is enunciated in language both beautiful and impressive, the participant comes to realize that since every man is a child of a heavenly Father, then each is a member of a divine family and hence every man is his brother. ("Why These Temples?" *Ensign*, August 1974, p. 39.)

Respect for self is the beginning of virtue in men. That man who knows that he is a child of God, created in the image of a divine Father and gifted with a potential for the exercise of great and godlike virtues, will discipline himself against the sordid, lascivious elements to which all are exposed. Said Alma to his son Helaman, "Look to God and live." (Al. 37:47.) ("Opposing Evil," *Ensign*, November 1975, p. 39.)

Man is in reality a child of God. Nothing in the universe is more important than the individual. His spirit was begotten of God; consequently all men are brothers in the literal sense. In the Mormon concept the phrase, "the Fatherhood of God and the brotherhood of man" takes on a new and powerful meaning. (*What of the Mormons?* pamphlet, 1982, p. 6.)

There is a mighty strength that comes of the knowledge that you and I are sons and daughters of God. Within us is something of divinity. One who has this knowledge and permits it to influence his life will not stoop to do a mean or cheap or tawdry thing. ("'God Hath Not Given Us the Spirit of Fear,'" *Ensign*, October 1984, p. 2.)

I believe in myself. I do not mean to say this with egotism or arrogance, but I believe in my capacity and in your capacity to do good, to make some contribution to this society of which we are a part. I believe that I am a child of God endowed with a divine birthright. I believe that there is something of divinity within me and within each of you. I believe that we have a godly inheritance and that it is our responsibility, our obligation, and our opportunity to cultivate and nurture the very best of these qualities within us. I do not have to be a scrub, though my work may be menial. Though my contribution may be small, I can perform it with dignity and offer it with unselfishness. My talents may not be great, but I can use them to bless the lives of others. I can be one who does his work with pride in that which comes from his hand and mind. I can be one who works with respect for my associates, for their opinions, for their beliefs, with appreciation for their problems, and with a desire to help them should they stumble. I believe in the principle that I can make a difference in this world. ("Articles of Belief," Bonneville International Corporation Management Seminar, February 10, 1991.)

You are loved by your Father in Heaven, of whose divine nature you have partaken. And He desires that His Holy Spirit will be near you wherever you go if you will invite it and cultivate it.

There is something of divinity within each of you. You have such tremendous potential with that quality as a part of your inherited nature. Every one of you was endowed by your Father in Heaven with a tremendous capacity to do good in the world. Train your minds and your hands that you may be equipped to serve well in the society of which you are a part. Cultivate the art of being kind, of being thoughtful, of being helpful. Refine within you the quality of mercy which comes as a part of the divine attributes you have inherited.

Some of you may feel that you are not as attractive and beautiful and glamorous as you would like to be. Rise above any such feelings, cultivate the light you have within you, and it will shine through as a radiant expression that will be seen by others.

You need never feel inferior. You need never feel that you were born without talents or without opportunities to give them expression. Cultivate whatever talents you have, and they will grow and refine and become an expression of your true self appreciated by others.

In summary, try a little harder to measure up to the divine within each of you. As Alma said, "Awake and arouse your faculties" (Alma 32:27). ("The Light within You," *Ensign*, May 1995, p. 99.)

Be not faithless, but believe. Believe in what? Believe in God your Eternal Father. Cultivate a knowledge of Him. You can know Him. Any man or woman can gain a testimony of the reality of the living God. Jesus said: He that doeth the will of the Father shall know of the doctrine, "whether it be of God, or whether I speak of myself." (See John 7:16–17.) Believe in God as your Eternal Father. You are His child. You are His child all the time, not just when you are good. You are His child when you are bad. You have within you . . . a portion of divinity that is real and tremendous and marvelous and wonderful.

My great plea is that we all try a little harder to live up to the stature of divinity that is within us. We can do better than we are doing. We can be better than we are. If we would hold before us that image constantly of divine inheritance, of the Fatherhood of

God and the brotherhood of man as realities, we would be a little more tolerant, a little more kindly, a little more outreaching to lift and help and sustain those among us. We would be less prone to stoop to those things which clearly are unbecoming us. We are children of God and we love Him. Act that way a little more. I believe our Father loves us. I believe that with all of my heart. (Smithfield/Logan Utah Regional Conference, April 21, 1996.)

I thank the Lord for the root of the gospel of Jesus Christ. That is where we draw our strength. That is the source of our faith. That is the source of our understanding of things divine. That is the thing which brings purpose to our lives. We are sons and daughters of God our Eternal Father. Did you ever stop to think of what that means, that each of us has something of divinity within ourselves? It does not matter the color of our skin or the color of our hair. Each of us comes into this world with a divine birthright as sons and daughters of God. And as certainly as we are sons and daughters of God, someday we will have to account to Him for the way we lived our lives. Will we be just a beautiful rose for a day or two or will we be planted in the eternal truth of the gospel of Jesus Christ? My brothers and sisters, how thankful I am for the gospel of Jesus Christ into which we can sink our roots and partake of the strength that comes therefrom. Life is purposeful under those circumstances. (Fukuoka Japan Fireside, May 19, 1996.)

DIVORCE

To you who are divorced, please know that we do not look down upon you as failures because a marriage failed. In many, perhaps in most cases you were not responsible for that failure. Furthermore, ours is the obligation not to condemn, but to forgive and forget, to lift and to help. In your hours of desolation, turn to the Lord, who said: "Come unto me, all ye that labour and are heavy laden, and I will give you rest. . . . For my yoke is easy, and my burden is light" (Matthew 11:28, 30).

The Lord will not deny you nor turn you away. The answers to your prayers may not be dramatic; they may not be readily understood or even appreciated. But the time will come when you will know that you have been blessed. For those of you who have children, and struggle to rear them in righteousness, be assured that they will become a blessing and a comfort and a strength to you through all the years to come. (Single Adult Fireside Satellite Broadcast, February 26, 1989.)

Some of you within the sound of my voice could recount family sorrows in your own experience. But among the greatest of tragedies, and I think the most common, is divorce. It has become as a great scourge. The most recent issue of the *World Almanac* says that in the United States during the twelve months ending with March 1990, an estimated 2,423,000 couples married. During this same period, an estimated 1,177,000 couples divorced. (See *The World Almanac and Book of Facts, 1991* [New York: World Almanac, 1990], p. 834.)

This means that in the United States almost one divorce occurred for every two marriages. . . .

Why all of these broken homes? What happens to marriages that begin with sincere love and a desire to be loyal and faithful and true one to another?

There is no simple answer. I acknowledge that. But it appears to me that there are some obvious reasons that account for a very high percentage of these problems. I say this out of experience in dealing with such tragedies. I find selfishness to be the root cause of most of it. . . .

. . . The remedy for most marriage stress is not in divorce. It is in repentance. It is not in separation. It is in simple integrity that leads a man to square up his shoulders and meet his obligations. It is found in the Golden Rule. . . .

There may be now and again a legitimate cause for divorce. I am not one to say that it is never justified. But I say without hesitation that this plague among us, which seems to be growing everywhere, is not of God, but rather is the work of the adversary of righteousness and peace and truth. ("What God Hath Joined Together," *Ensign*, May 1991, pp. 72–74.)

We have wonderful people, but we have too many whose families are falling apart. It is a matter of serious concern. I think it is my most serious concern. I wish to see our people walk in the light of the Lord. That's where they will find their happiness, that's where they will find their progress, that's where they will find their prosperity, in walking the paths which the Lord has laid out for us. (*Church News* Interview, June 7, 1995.)

DOCTRINE AND COVENANTS

The Doctrine and Covenants is unique among our books of scripture. It is the constitution of the Church. While the Doctrine and Covenants includes writings and statements of various origins, it is primarily a book of revelation given through the Prophet of this dispensation.

These revelations open with a thundering declaration of the encompassing purposes of God in the restoration of His great latter-day work:

"Hearken, O ye people of my church, saith the voice of him who dwells on high, and whose eyes are upon all men; yea, verily I say: Hearken ye people from afar; and ye that are upon the islands of the sea, listen together.

"For verily the voice of the Lord is unto all men, and there is none to escape; and there is no eye that shall not see, neither ear that shall not hear, neither heart that shall not be penetrated." (D&C 1:1–2.)

From that majestic opening there unfolds a wondrous doctrinal panorama that comes from the fountain of eternal truth. Some is direct revelation, with the Lord dictating to His prophet. Some is the language of Joseph Smith, written or spoken as he was moved upon by the Holy Ghost. Also included is his narrative of events that occurred in various circumstances. All brought together, they constitute in very substantial measure the doctrine and the practices of The Church of Jesus Christ of Latter-day Saints. ("The Order and Will of God," *Ensign*, January 1989, p. 2.)

I look with wonder at the farm boy of Palmyra. He had very little of schoolbook education. He knew little of the classroom. His opportunity for reading was severely restricted. But as an instrument in the hands of the Almighty, he spoke words that have become the law and the testimony of this great, vital work.

The Doctrine and Covenants is a conduit for the expressions of the Lord to His people.

The variety of matters the book deals with is amazing. They include principles and procedures concerning the governance of the Church. Unique and remarkable rules of health, with promises both physical and spiritual, are set forth. The covenant of the eternal priesthood is described in a manner not found elsewhere in scripture. The privileges and blessings—and the limitations and opportunities—of the three degrees of glory are announced, building on Paul's brief mention of a glory of the sun, and of the moon, and of the stars. Repentance is proclaimed in language clear and compelling. The correct mode of baptism is given. The nature of the Godhead, which has troubled theologians for centuries, is described in language understandable to all. The Lord's law of finance is pronounced, mandating how funds for the operation of the Church are to be acquired and disbursed. Work for the dead is revealed to bless the sons and daughters of God of all generations.

It is evident from reading the Doctrine and Covenants that Joseph Smith had an all-encompassing understanding of the eternal purposes of God. ("The Order and Will of God," *Ensign,* January 1989, p. 4.)

The grand objective of this cause and kingdom comes from an understanding of the remarkable revelations found in the Doctrine and Covenants.

How is the Church to be organized? It is there. What of life beyond the grave and the kingdoms of another world? It is all there. What of the wondrous blessings that may come to women in the Church? You will find it in Section 25. What about the elements of healthful living? Turn to Section 89. How shall the Church be financed? It is clearly set forth. This remarkable book is certainly one of the great evidences of the divinity of Joseph Smith's call as a prophet in this the dispensation of the fulness of times.

Now, as you present the Doctrine and Covenants to those you teach, I hope that you will not spend time in speculative discussion. The revelations are of relatively recent origin. They are not far removed from us in time. The circumstances of their reception are well known. The doctrines are plain and easily understood. Teach them as the word of the Lord revealed in this dispensation. (Church Educational System Conference, June 23, 1989.)

DRUGS

Everyone who partakes of these illicit drugs has on his hands some of the blood of those who have been killed or wounded in the fight to stop the cultivation and exportation of these destructive products. ("The Scourge of Illicit Drugs," *Ensign*, November 1989, p. 50.)

I should like to say a few words on a subject that is much in the public press these days. It is the widespread use of illegal drugs with all of the ramifications associated therewith. . . .

. . . I believe that only when far greater numbers of people conclude within their hearts and minds that the fruits of drug-taking are only sorrow and trouble, remorse, and even death will things change to any significant degree. ("A Plague on the World," *New Era*, July 1990, pp. 4–5.)

I received a letter the other day from a government official who for years has been involved in the fight against illegal drugs. He says: "I know from firsthand knowledge what a scourge illicit narcotics are to this country and others. The drain on the human and monetary resources of the world being caused by this dilemma is inestimable and threatens the very foundations of freedom. I have watched as families dissolved, morals collapsed, and lives were lost, both directly and indirectly due to the effect of drugs." . . .

Some have . . . used as an alibi the fact that drugs are not mentioned in the Word of Wisdom. What a miserable excuse. There is likewise no mention of the hazards of diving into an empty swimming pool or of jumping from an overpass onto the freeway. But who doubts the deadly consequences of such? Common sense would dictate against such behavior.

Regardless of the Word of Wisdom, there is a divinely given reason for avoiding these illegal substances.

I am convinced that their use is an affront to God. He is our Creator. We are made in His image. These remarkable and wonderful bodies are His handiwork. Does anyone think that he can deliberately injure and impair his body without affronting its Creator? We are told again and again that the body is the tabernacle of the spirit. We are told that it is a temple, holy to the Lord. In a time of terrible conflict between the Nephites and the Lamanites, we are told that the Nephites, who had been strong, became "weak, like unto their brethren, the Lamanites, and that the Spirit of the Lord did no more preserve them; yea, it had withdrawn from them because the Spirit of the Lord doth not dwell in unholy temples" (Hel. 4:24). . . .

. . . Can anyone doubt that the taking of these mind- and body-destroying drugs is an act of unholiness? Does anyone think that the Spirit of God can dwell in the temple of the body when that body is defiled by these destructive elements? If any of you are tampering with these things, resolve forthwith, and with the strongest determination of which you are capable, that you will never touch them again. ("A Plague on the World," *New Era*, July 1990, pp. 4–6.)

You cannot afford to tamper with [drugs] in the least. Certainly you must be grateful for your bodies and your minds, the very substance of your mortal lives. Certainly you must know that health is the most precious of assets. Certainly you recognize that, for the years that lie ahead, you will need health of body and clarity of mind if you are to live productively and with the respect of your associates. You would not knowingly break an arm or a leg just for the fun of it. Broken bones will mend and will function again in a normal way. But a mind warped by drugs or a body weakened or distorted by these evil things will not be easily repaired. The drug-induced destruction of self-worth and self-confidence is almost impossible to restore.

To you who may be partaking, I repeat, stop immediately. To you who at any time in the future may be tempted, I urge you to stand your ground. Reflect on the fact that you are a child of God our Eternal Father, endowed with those faculties of body and mind which will help you to take a place that is significant in the world in which you live. Do not throw away your future. Do not jeopardize the well-being of your posterity. ("A Plague on the World," *New Era*, July 1990, pp. 6–7.)

In earlier centuries there were plagues that swept across England and the nations of Europe. They struck like lightning, carrying tens of thousands to their death. This modern drug scourge has become as a plague on the world. But in most cases, the death it brings is not swift, but rather, it follows a long period spent in misery and pain and regret. Unlike the plagues of old, from which there was no known defense, the defense is clear and relatively easy in the case of illicit drugs. It lies in simply refraining from touching them. (National Conference of Christians and Jews Banquet, February 21, 1995.)

Do not become involved in illegal drugs. Do not touch them. Never experiment with them. I plead with you, with every one of you, to shun them as you would poison. . . . A great future is ahead of you. Your lives are radiant with promise. Most of you will someday wish to be married and have children. The use of illegal drugs could place a terrible handicap not only upon you, but also upon your children. I do not hesitate to say that if you tamper with these things, you will regret it. If you discipline yourselves to avoid them, you will have reason to rejoice. ("Stand True and Faithful," *Ensign*, May 1996, p. 92.)

Stay away from drugs! They will destroy you in more ways than one. They will destroy your health. They will destroy your self-respect. They will destroy your character, your honesty, your integrity. They will absolutely destroy you. Stay away from them, is my urgent and humble plea to each of you. You can make it without drugs. (Southern Utah University Institute of Religion Devotional, February 11, 1997.)

EDUCATION

See also Knowledge

Each day we are made increasingly aware of the fact that life is more than science and mathematics, more than history and literature. There is need for another education, without which the substance of our secular learning may lead only to our destruction. I refer to the education of the heart, of the conscience, of the character, of the spirit—these indefinable aspects of our personalities which determine so certainly what we are and what we do in our relationships one with another. (Conference Report, October 1964, p. 116.)

I looked the other day with wonder and affection on a 1916 Model T Ford. It brought back a thousand memories of my childhood, for this was the first automobile we ever owned in our family. It was a thing of wonder when we were children. You today know little of these cars. They had no battery, and the source of electricity was a magneto. At night the intensity of the light depended on the speed of the motor. If the motor were kept running at high speed, the lights were bright. If the motor slowed down, the lights became a sickly yellow.

It is so with our minds. If we keep them sharpened on good literature and uplifting entertainment, development is inevitable. If we starve them with the drivel of miserable shows, cheap literature, beatnik entertainment, they become poor indeed. ("Caesar, Circus, or Christ?" *BYU Speeches of the Year*, October 26, 1965, p. 5.)

Over the years the Church has put vast sums of money into education, secular as well as religious. From the beginning of this work, our leaders have taught us the importance of training.

Be smart. Do not forfeit the schooling that will enhance your future in order to satisfy your desire for immediate, fleeting pleasure. Cultivate the long view of your life. Most of you are going to be around for a good while. ("Four B's for Boys," *Ensign*, November 1981, p. 40.)

Be smart.

By this I do not mean be smart-alecky or anything of that nature. I mean be wise. Be smart about training your minds and hands for the future. Each of you is a member of The Church of Jesus Christ of Latter-day Saints. . . . You have an obligation to make the most of your life. Plan now for all the education you can get, and then work to bring to pass a fulfillment of that plan. . . .

I am not suggesting that all of you should become professional men. What I am suggesting is this: whatever you choose to do, train for it. Qualify yourselves. Take advantage of the experience and learning of those who have gone before you in whatever field you choose. Education is a shortcut to proficiency. It makes it possible to leapfrog over the mistakes of the past. ("Four B's for Boys," *Ensign*, November 1981, p. 40.)

We have in the Church a strong tradition regarding quality education. Over the years we have allocated a substantial part of the Church budget to education, both secular and religious. As a people we have supported public education. Where there is a well-demonstrated need, we should be supportive. Such can become an investment in the lives of our children, our communities, and our nation. However, let it not be supposed that all of the remedies may be found only with increased funding. There is need for a searching analysis of priorities and a careful weighing of costs. Let us be supportive; let us also be prudent concerning the resources of the people. ("Be Not Deceived," *Ensign*, November 1983, p. 45.)

Begin early in exposing children to books. The mother who fails to read to her small children does a disservice to them and a disservice to herself. It takes time, yes, much of it. It takes self-discipline. It takes organizing and budgeting the minutes and hours of the day. But it will never be a bore as you watch young minds come to know characters, expressions, and ideas. Good reading can become a love affair, far more fruitful in long term effects than many other activities in which children use their time. It has been estimated that "the average child on this continent has watched something like 8,000 hours of TV before he or she even starts school." A very large part of that is of questionable value.

Parents, work at the matter of creating an atmosphere in your homes. Let your children be exposed to great minds, great ideas, everlasting truth, and those things which will build and motivate for good.

The Lord has said to this people, "Seek ye out of the best books words of wisdom; seek learning, even by study and also by faith." (D&C 88:118.) I wish to urge every parent within the sound of my voice to try to create within your home an atmosphere of learning and the growth which will come of it. ("The Environment of Our Homes," *Ensign*, June 1985, pp. 4–5.)

When I was a boy we lived in a large old house. One room was called the library. It had a solid table and a good lamp, three or four comfortable chairs with good light, and books in cases that lined the walls. There were many volumes—the acquisitions of my father and mother over a period of many years.

We were never forced to read them, but they were placed where they were handy and where we could get at them whenever we wished.

There was quiet in that room. It was understood that it was a place to study.

There were also magazines—the Church magazines and two or three other good magazines. There were books of history and literature, books on technical subjects, dictionaries, a set of encyclopedias, and an atlas of the world. There was no television, of course, at that time. Radio came along while I was growing up. But there was an environment . . . of learning. I would not have you believe that we were great scholars. But we were exposed to great literature, great ideas from great thinkers, and the language of men and women who thought deeply and wrote beautifully. ("The Environment of Our Homes," *Ensign*, June 1985, p. 4.)

I believe in the pursuit of education. What is education? Reduced to its most simplistic definition it is the training of the mind and the body. What a remarkable thing this is, this process whereby the cumulative knowledge of the centuries has been summarized and filtered so that in a brief period one can learn what was first learned only through long exercises of research, trial, and error. Education is a great conversion process under which abstract knowledge becomes useful and productive activity. It is something that never need stop—no matter how old we grow we can acquire knowledge and use it. We can gather wisdom and profit from it. We can be entertained through the miracle of reading and exposure to the arts—they add to the blessings and fulfillment of living. ("Articles of Belief," Bonneville International Corporation Management Seminar, February 10, 1991.)

As you move forward with your lives, I challenge you never to forget that the schooling of the Spirit is as important, if not more so, that the schooling of the mind. . . .

There is a tendency on the part of some graduates to say, "Now all of that is behind me." No, there is much more ahead than there is behind. We live in a world where knowledge is developing at an ever-accelerating rate. Drink deeply from this ever-springing well of wisdom and human experience. If you should stop now, you will only stunt your intellectual and spiritual growth. Keep everlastingly at it. Read. Read. Read. Read the word of God in sacred books of scripture. Read from the great literature of the ages. Read what is being said in our day and time and what will be said in the future. ("A Three-Point Challenge," BYU Commencement Address, April 27, 1995.)

You young people, the little decisions that you make can so affect your lives. Shall I go to school or not? Shall I continue on with my education? That is a big decision for some of you. Our doctrine suggests . . . that the more education you receive the greater will be your opportunity to serve, and you should never forget that the Lord has placed upon the people of this Church an injunction to learn by study and by faith. That is why this Church operates the largest private university in the nation, if not in the entire world. That is why this Church encourages its young people to get the schooling that will qualify them to take their places in the society in which they will become a part. Make the right decisions. Take a long look. (Pocatello Idaho Biregional Conference, June 4, 1995.)

This is the great day of opportunity for you young people, this marvelous time to be upon the earth. You stand at the summit of all of the past ages. You are exposed to all of the learning of all who have walked the earth, that learning being distilled down into courses where you can acquire knowledge in a relatively short time, that knowledge which men stumbled over in learning through all of the centuries past. Do not sell yourselves short. Do not miss your great opportunity. Get at it, work at it, study hard. (Smithfield/Logan Utah Regional Conference, April 21, 1996.)

Get all the education you can, I wish to say to the young people. Cultivate skills of mind and hands. Education is the key to opportunity. The Lord has placed upon you, as members of this Church, the obligation to study and to learn of things spiritual, yes, but of things temporal also. Acquire all of the education that you can, even if it means great sacrifice while you are young. You will bless the lives of your children. You will bless the Church because you will reflect honor to this work. (Copenhagen Denmark Fireside, June 14, 1996.)

It is not enough just to live, just to survive. There is incumbent upon every member of this Church the mandate of the Lord to equip ourselves to do something worthwhile in society. The Lord has made it very clear in the Doctrine and Covenants that we are to get an education by study and by faith of things under the earth, and on the earth, and above the earth, of the wars and the perplexities of the nations, of the times and the seasons of all things of the earth. (See D&C 88:79.) I want to urge our young people to be hungry for education. You will be doing the will of the Lord as you educate your minds and your hands for future work to make a contribution to the world of which you will be a part. Sacrifice for it, work for it, save for it, plan for it, and do it. (Hailey 1st and 2nd Wards Sacrament Meeting, Sun Valley, Idaho, June 30, 1996.)

Get all the education you can. I repeat, I do not care what you want to be as long as it is honorable. A car mechanic, a brick layer, a plumber, an electrician, a doctor, a lawyer, a merchant, but not a thief. But whatever you are, take the opportunity to train for it and make the best of that opportunity. Society will reward you according to your worth as it perceives that worth. Now is the great day of preparation for each of you. If it means sacrifice, then sacrifice. That sacrifice will become the best investment you have ever made, for you will reap returns from it all the days of your lives. Be smart. Be smart in your studies. Do the very best you can. Maybe you are not an A student. Maybe you are not a B student. Maybe you are not a genius; most of us are not. In fact the vast majority of us are not. I read an article once, long ago, "No More Prodigies Please," in which it set forth the story of a great number of those who are too smart for their own good. I have concluded that the work of the world is done by ordinary people who learned to work in an extraordinary way. You do not have to be a genius to get ahead. Be smart in the way you do things. (Eugene Oregon Regional Conference, September 15, 1996.)

ETERNAL LIFE

I remember standing before the bier of a young man whose life had been bright with hope and promise. He had been an athlete in his high school, and an excellent university student. He was a friendly, affable, brilliant young man. He had gone into the mission field. He and his companion were riding down the highway when a car, coming from the opposite direction, moved into their lane and crashed into them. He died in the hospital an hour later. As I stood at the pulpit and looked into the faces of his father and his mother, there came then into my heart a conviction that I had seldom before felt with such assurance. I knew with certainty, as I looked across that casket, that this young man had not died, but had merely been transferred to another field of labor in the eternal ministry of the Lord.

. . . Let us live with the certain knowledge that some day "we shall be brought to stand before God, knowing even as we know now, and have a bright recollection of all our guilt" (Alma 11:43). Let us live today knowing that we shall live forever. Let us live with the conviction that whatever principle of intelligence and beauty and truth and goodness we make a part of our life here, it will rise with us in the resurrection. ("What Shall I Do Then with Jesus Which Is Called Christ?" *Ensign*, December 1983, p. 4.)

Life is forever. Nearly sixty-one years ago, on a night in July, while serving as a young missionary, I looked out at Lake

Windermere in England. This was the country of Wordsworth. As my eyes went from the lake to the sky in that quiet, lovely place, there passed through my mind the words penned there much earlier:

> *Our birth is but a sleep and a forgetting:*
> *The Soul that rises with us, our life's Star,*
> *Hath had elsewhere its setting,*
> *And cometh from afar:*
> *Not in entire forgetfulness,*
> *And not in utter nakedness,*
> *But trailing clouds of glory do we come*
> *From God, who is our home.*
>
> (WILLIAM WORDSWORTH, "ODE ON
> INTIMATIONS OF IMMORTALITY.")

We are not chance creations in a universe of disorder. We lived before we were born. We were God's sons and daughters who shouted for joy. (See Job 38:7.) We knew our Father; He planned our future. We graduated from that life and matriculated in this. The statement is simple; the implications are profound. Life is a mission, not just the sputtering of a candle between a chance lighting and a gust of wind that blows it out forever. . . .

While here, we have learning to gain, work to do, service to give. We are here with a marvelous inheritance, a divine endowment. How different this world would be if every person realized that all of his actions have eternal consequences. How much more satisfying our years may be if in our accumulation of knowledge, in our relationships with others, in our business affairs, in our courtship and marriage, and in our family rearing, we recognize that we form each day the stuff of which eternity is made. . . . Life is forever. Live each day as if you were going to live eternally, for you surely shall. ("Pillars of Truth," *Ensign,* January 1994, pp. 2, 4.)

We are on the road that leads to immortality and eternal life and today is a part of it. Let us never forget it. (Salt Lake East Millcreek Stake Fiftieth Anniversary Celebration, June 10, 1995.)

Life goes on [after death] because of the atonement of the Son of God. He gave His life so that each of us might have eternal life. (Funeral Service for Margaret "Peggy" Madsen, July 17, 1995.)

Our constant, unwavering objective must be to assist our Father in Heaven in His work and glory, to bring to pass the immortality and eternal life of man. (General Authority Training Meeting, April 2, 1996.)

ETERNAL MARRIAGE

See also Marriage

One of the distinguishing features of The Church of Jesus Christ of Latter-day Saints is a belief in the divine nature of the family as an institution ordained of God. Here center the most sacred of all human relationships. Life is eternal. Love is eternal. And God our Eternal Father designed and has made it possible that our families shall be eternal. ("A Challenge from Vietnam," *Improvement Era*, June 1967, p. 54.)

[May I reflect] on an experience at the time of the prededication showing of the London Temple in 1958. . . .

Those who inspected the building were asked to defer any questions until they had completed the tour. In the evenings I joined the missionaries in talking with those who had questions. As a young couple came down the front steps of the temple, I inquired whether I could help them in any way. The young woman spoke up and said, "Yes. What about this 'marriage for eternity' to which reference was made in one of the rooms?" We sat on a bench under the ancient oak that stood near the gate. The wedding band on her finger indicated that they were married, and the manner in which she gripped her husband's hand evidenced their affection one for another.

"Now to your question," I said. "I suppose you were married by the vicar."

"Yes," she responded, "just three months ago."

"Did you realize that when the vicar pronounced your marriage he also decreed your separation?"

"What do you mean?" she quickly retorted.

"You believe that life is eternal, don't you?"

"Of course," she replied.

I continued, "Can you conceive of eternal life without eternal love? Can either of you envision eternal happiness without the companionship of one another?"

"Of course not," came the ready response.

"But what did the vicar say when he pronounced your marriage? If I remember the language correctly, he said, among other things, 'in sickness and in health, for richer or for poorer, for better or for worse, till death do ye part.' He went as far as he felt his authority would permit him and that was till death separates you. In fact, I think that if you were to question him, he would emphatically deny the existence of marriage and family beyond the grave.

"But," I continued, "the Father of us all, who loves his children and wants the best for them, has provided for a continuation, under proper circumstances, of this most sacred and ennobling of all human relationships, the relationships of marriage and family.

"In that great and moving conversation between the Savior and his apostles, wherein Peter declared, 'Thou art the Christ, the Son of the living God,' and the Lord responded, 'Blessed art thou, Simon Barjona: for flesh and blood hath not revealed it unto thee, but my Father which is in heaven.' The Lord then went on to say to Peter and his associates, 'And I will give unto thee the keys of the kingdom of heaven: and whatsoever thou shalt bind on earth shall be bound in heaven: and whatsoever thou shalt loose on earth shall be loosed in heaven.' (Matt. 16:13–19.)

"In that marvelous bestowal of authority the Lord gave to his apostles the keys of the holy priesthood, whose power reaches beyond life and death into eternity. This same authority has been restored to the earth by those same apostles who held it anciently, even Peter, James, and John." I continued by saying that following the dedication of the temple on the following Sunday, those same keys of the holy priesthood would be exercised in behalf of the men and women who come into this sacred house to solemnize their marriage. They will be joined in a union which death cannot dissolve and time cannot destroy.

Such was my testimony to this young couple in England. Such it is to you today, my dear young friends, and such it is to all the world. Our Father in heaven, who loves his children, desires for them that which will bring them happiness now and in the eternities to come, and there is no greater happiness than is found in the most meaningful of all human relationships—the companionships of husband and wife and parents and children. ("The Marriage That Endures," *Ensign*, May 1974, pp. 22–23.)

Every man who truly loves a woman, and every woman who truly loves a man, hopes and dreams that their companionship will last forever. But marriage is a covenant sealed by authority. If that authority is of the state alone, it will endure only while the state has jurisdiction, and that jurisdiction ends with death. But add to the authority of the state the power of the endowment given by Him who overcame death, and that companionship will endure beyond life if the parties to the marriage live worthy of the promise.

When I was much younger and less brittle, we danced to a song whose words went something like this:

> *Is love like a rose*
> *That blossoms and grows,*
> *Then withers and goes*
> *When summer is gone?*

It was only a dance ballad, but it was a question that has been asked through the centuries by men and women who loved one another and looked beyond today into the future of eternity.

To that question we answer no, and reaffirm that love and marriage under the revealed plan of the Lord are not like the rose that withers with the passing of summer. Rather, they are eternal, as surely as the God of heaven is eternal.

But this gift, precious beyond all others, comes only with a price—with self-discipline, with virtue, with obedience to the commandments of God. ("The Marriage That Endures," *Ensign*, May 1974, p. 23.)

How shortsighted so many of us are, how prone to look only at today without thought for the morrow. But the morrow will surely come, as will also come death and separation. How sweet is the assurance, how comforting is the peace that comes from the knowledge that if we marry right and live right, our relationship will continue, notwithstanding the certainty of death and the passage of time. Men may write love songs and sing them. They may yearn and hope and dream. But all of this will be only a romantic longing unless there is an exercise of authority that transcends the powers of time and death. ("The Marriage That Endures," *Ensign*, May 1974, p. 24.)

Life is eternal. The God of heaven has also made possible eternal love and eternal family relationships.

God bless our dear young people that as they look forward to marriage, they may look not only for rewarding companionship and rich and fruitful family relationships through all of their mortal days, but to an even better estate where love and treasured associations may be felt and known under a promise given of God. (*Be Thou an Example* [Salt Lake City: Deseret Book, 1981], p. 139.)

Marriage, solemnized in the temples of the Church, is performed in the authority of that same holy priesthood, not only for this life, but for the next as well.

The separation of loved ones in death is always fraught with sorrow. It would be fraught with hopelessness if there were not some alternative to the finality of the "until death do thee part" pronouncement in most marriage ceremonies.

It need not be so. Reason would deny that the Father who loves us all would tear asunder the most sacred relationship of all human experience and banish the companionship of marriage by those who love, honor, and respect one another. But there must be rules. There must be compliance. There must be obedience. The way is clear, made so through the exercise of the holy priesthood in these sacred temples. ("Rejoice in This Great Era of Temple Building," *Ensign*, November 1985, p. 60.)

I salute my own beloved companion. It will soon be 60 years that we walked from the Salt Lake Temple as husband and wife, with love for one another. That love has strengthened through all of these years. We have faced many problems during our years of marriage. Somehow, with the blessing of the Lord, we have survived them all.

It is becoming physically harder to stand tall and straight as we did in our younger years. No matter—we still have one another and we still stand together, even though we lean a little. And when the time for separation comes, there will be much of sorrow, but there will also be the comfort that will come from the assurance that she is mine and I am hers for the eternity that lies ahead. ("Women of the Church," *Ensign*, November 1996, p. 70.)

ETERNAL PROGRESSION

The whole design of the gospel is to lead us, onward and upward to greater achievement, even, eventually, to godhood. This great possibility was enunciated by the Prophet Joseph Smith in the King Follet sermon (*see Teachings of the Prophet Joseph Smith*, pp. 342–62) and emphasized by President Lorenzo Snow. It is this grand and incomparable concept: *As God now is, man may become!* (See *The Teachings of Lorenzo Snow*, comp. Clyde J. Williams, Salt Lake City: Bookcraft, 1984, p. 1.) . . .

Today is a part of eternity. . . .

Eternal vigilance is the price of eternal development. ("Don't Drop the Ball," *Ensign*, November 1994, p. 48.)

People sometimes ask me, "What is your favorite verse of scripture?" I tell them that I have many, but among these is one for which I feel a particular love. It is found in the fiftieth section of the Doctrine and Covenants and reads as follows: "And that which doth not edify is not of God, and is darkness.

"That which is of God is light; and he that receiveth light, and continueth in God, receiveth more light; and that light groweth brighter and brighter until the perfect day" (D&C

50:23–24). I ask you to ponder those words: "That which is of God is light; and he that receiveth light, and continueth in God, receiveth more light; and that light groweth brighter and brighter until the perfect day." For me, in those few words there is encompassed the marvelous concept of the eternal plan of God in behalf of His sons and daughters whom He loves. That statement speaks of learning. It speaks of the now and the forever. It speaks of growth and development. It is positive and affirmative and wonderful. ("True to the Faith," Salt Lake Valley-Wide Institute Fireside, January 21, 1996.)

EXAMPLE

All of us, in our various situations, are the result, largely, of the lives that touch ours; and . . . as teachers and officers in the Church we affect for good or ill all who come under our direction according to our diligence in meeting our responsibilities. . . .

. . . Likewise, all of us are largely the products of the lives which touch upon our lives, and today I feel profoundly grateful for all who have touched mine. (Conference Report, April 1958, p. 125.)

A young man came into my office the other day. He was dressed in uniform. He was on his way home from Vietnam. For a year he had walked through the furnace of battle in a hotly contested area along the Laotian border.

I had seen him just before he had left for Asia. Now he had come back, alive—miraculously, as he regarded it—thankful, but depressed in spirit.

He had just arrived at the airport and had a little time before his bus left for the small country town where he had grown up and where some of his family still live. We talked about the war. I noticed the campaign ribbons on his chest, including a citation for outstanding service.

I told him the town band would be out to meet him, that he could go home with pride. He looked up and said, "No, I'm ashamed."

"Ashamed of what?" I asked.

Example   181

"Of what I've done," he replied. "I should have been stronger. I was weak. I gave in, first on little things and then on big ones. Oh, I did nothing that the men all about me were not doing. But I should have done better. My friends back home would have expected better things of me, and had I been stronger I might have helped some of those who, with the right example, would have had the strength to resist."

He lowered his head as we talked, and I saw tears fall from his cheek across the ribbons on his chest.

I tried to reassure him, but he found little comfort. He was a military hero, but he regarded himself as a moral coward.

Not long after that I talked with another young man also recently returned from the war. He too had walked the jungle patrols, his heart pounding with fear. But reluctantly he admitted that the greatest fear he had was the fear of ridicule.

The men of his company laughed at him, taunted him, plastered him with a nickname that troubled him. They told him they were going to force him to do some of the things they reveled in. Then on one occasion when the going was rough, he faced them and quietly said, "Look, I know you think I'm a square. I don't consider myself any better than any of the rest of you. But I grew up in a different way. I grew up in a religious home and a religious town. I went to church on Sundays. We prayed together as a family. I was taught to stay away from these things. It's just that I believe differently. With me it's a matter of religion, and it's kind of a way of respecting my mother and my dad. All of you together might force me toward a compromising situation, but that wouldn't change me, and you wouldn't feel right after you'd done it."

One by one they turned silently away. But during the next few days each came to ask his pardon, and from his example others gained the strength and the will to change their own lives. He taught the gospel to two of them and brought them into the Church. ("'Rise, and Stand upon Thy Feet,'" *Improvement Era*, December 1968, pp. 69–70.)

We recently held an open house in the Arizona Temple. Following a complete renovation of that building, nearly a quarter of a million people saw its beautiful interior. On the first day of the opening, clergymen of other religions were invited as special guests, and hundreds responded. It was my privilege to speak to them and to answer their questions at the conclusion of their tours. I told them that we would be pleased to answer any queries they might have. Many were asked. Among these was one which came from a Protestant minister.

Said he: "I've been all through this building, this temple which carries on its face the name of Jesus Christ, but nowhere have I seen any representation of the cross, the symbol of Christianity. I have noted your buildings elsewhere and likewise find an absence of the cross. Why is this when you say you believe in Jesus Christ?"

I responded: "I do not wish to give offense to any of my Christian brethren who use the cross on the steeples of their cathedrals and at the altars of their chapels, who wear it on their vestments and imprint it on their books and other literature. But for us, the cross is the symbol of the dying Christ, while our message is a declaration of the living Christ."

He then asked: "If you do not use the cross, what is the symbol of your religion?"

I replied that the lives of our people must become the only meaningful expression of our faith and, in fact, therefore, the symbol of our worship. ("The Symbol of Christ," *Ensign*, May 1975, p. 92.)

We cannot hope to influence others in the direction of virtue unless we live lives of virtue. The example of our living will carry a greater influence than will all the preaching in which we might indulge. We cannot expect to lift others unless we stand on higher ground ourselves. ("Opposing Evil," *Ensign*, November 1975, pp. 38–39.)

The most persuasive gospel tract is the exemplary life of a faithful Latter-day Saint. We live in a time when the pressures of life make it so easy and so tempting, in fulfillment of the words of Nephi, to commit "a little sin; yea, lie a little, take the advantage of one because of his words, dig a pit for thy neighbor; . . . turn aside the just for a thing of naught and revile against that which is good." (2 Ne. 28:8, 16.)

Example   183

Said the Savior while speaking on the mount: "Let your light so shine before men, that they may see your good works, and glorify your Father which is in heaven." (Matt. 5:16.)

If we as a people will walk with integrity, will be honest and moral in our actions, will put into our lives the simple and basic and wonderful principle of the Golden Rule, others will be led to inquire and learn. ("Five Million Members—A Milestone and Not a Summit," *Ensign*, May 1982, p. 45.)

"A city that is set on an hill cannot be hid.

"Neither do men light a candle, and put it under a bushel, but on a candlestick; and it giveth light unto all that are in the house.

"Let *your* light so shine before men, that they may see your good works, and glorify your Father which is in heaven." (Matt. 5:14–16; italics added.)

This entire people have become as a city upon a hill which cannot be hid. Sometimes we take offense when one who is a member of the Church is involved in a crime and the public press is quick to say that he is a Mormon. We comment among ourselves that if he had been a member of any other church, no mention would have been made of it.

Yet, is not this very practice an indirect compliment to our people? The world expects something better of us, and when one of our number falters, the press is quick to note it. We have, indeed, become as a city upon a hill for the world to see. . . .

Unless the world alters the course of its present trends (and that is not likely); and if, on the other hand, we continue to follow the teachings of the prophets, we shall increasingly become a peculiar and distinctive people of whom the world will take note. . . . As the integrity of the family crumbles under worldly pressures, our position on the sanctity of the family will become more obvious and even more peculiar in contrast, if we have the faith to maintain that position. ("A City upon a Hill," *Ensign*, July 1990, p. 4.)

We can maintain the integrity of our families if we will follow the counsel of our leaders. . . .

We need not compromise. We must not compromise. The candle that the Lord has lighted in this dispensation can become as a light unto the whole world, and others seeing our good works can be led to glorify our Father in Heaven and emulate in their own lives the examples they have observed in ours.

Beginning with you and me, there can be an entire people who, by the virtue of our lives in our homes, in our vocations, even in our amusements, can become as a city upon a hill to which men may look and learn, and an ensign to the nations from which the people of the earth may gather strength. ("A City upon a Hill," *Ensign,* July 1990, p. 5.)

All of this places upon us of this Church and this generation an incumbent and demanding responsibility to recognize that as we are spoken of as Mormons, we must so live that our example will enhance the perception that *Mormon* can mean in a very real way, "more good." ("*Mormon* Should Mean 'More Good,'" *Ensign,* November 1990, p. 53.)

As His followers, we cannot do a mean or shoddy or ungracious thing without tarnishing His image. Nor can we do a good and gracious and generous act without burnishing more brightly the symbol of Him whose name we have taken upon ourselves.

Our lives must become a symbol of meaningful expression, the symbol of our declaration of our testimony of the living Christ, the Eternal Son of the living God.

It is that simple, my brethren and sisters. It is that profound, and we should never forget it. ("Our One Bright Hope," *Ensign,* April 1994, p. 5.)

My father used to say that more religion is caught than is taught. More is absorbed from those who lead us, from their example, than from their teachings. You must be an example to your people. Be on your guard at all times. A few years ago I boarded a plane in Sydney, Australia. The stewardess came up to me and said, "What would you like to drink?" I said, "I'll have some apple juice." She brought me some apple juice, and as she handed it to me she said, "Elder Hinckley, you'd better have something like apple juice." Now, there I was in Sydney,

Australia. I didn't recognize her. She recognized me. But there is a better reason than that, and that is that we must stand at all times and in all places as examples before our people. (Berlin Germany Regional Conference, priesthood leadership session, June 15, 1996.)

I wish to say that none of us ever need hesitate to speak up for this Church, for its doctrine, for its people, for its divine organization and divinely given responsibility. It is true. It is the work of God. The only things that can ever embarrass this work are acts of disobedience to its doctrine and standards by those of its membership. That places upon each of us a tremendous responsibility. This work will be judged by what the world sees of our behavior. God give us the will to walk with faith, the discipline to do what is right at all times and in all circumstances, the resolution to make of our lives a declaration of this cause before all who see us. ("'This Thing Was Not Done in a Corner,'" *Ensign*, November 1996, p. 51.)

EXCELLENCE

See also Self-Improvement

There is nothing in all the world so satisfying as a task well done. There is no reward so pleasing as that which comes with the mastery of a difficult problem. ("If I Were You, What Would I Do?" *BYU 1983–84 Fireside and Devotional Speeches*, September 20, 1983, p. 9.)

My plea to you is that we constantly take the position that every one of us can do better than we are now doing. We are in a constant search for excellence. That search must be continuous and never ending. It must be consuming and unrelenting. ("Search for Excellence," Bonneville International Corporation Executives, February 6, 1989.)

In this highly competitive world no one can stand still. There must be constant improvement. There must be wrenching thought, there must be frank and at times brutal discussion, there must be unusual effort in the search for excellence. ("Search for Excellence," Bonneville International Corporation Executives, February 6, 1989.)

As a nation we cannot expect to rise to a position of excellence before the world unless there is a foundation of moral and spiritual and ethical strength among our people. (BYU Management Society, San Diego, California, January 9, 1993.)

FAITH

If there is any one thing you and I need in this world it is faith, that dynamic, powerful, marvelous element by which, as Paul declared, the very worlds were framed (Hebrews 11:3). . . . Faith—the kind of faith that moves one to get on his knees and plead with the Lord and then get on his feet and go to work—is an asset beyond compare, even in the acquisition of secular knowledge. I do not minimize the need for study and labor. I would add to these faith and prayer, with the sacred promise that "God shall give unto you knowledge by his Holy Spirit, yea, by the unspeakable gift of the Holy Ghost." ("God Shall Give unto You Knowledge by His Holy Spirit," *BYU Speeches of the Year*, September 25, 1973, p. 109.)

The faith to try leads to direction by the Spirit, and the fruits that flow therefrom are marvelous to behold and experience. A little over a year ago a young woman convert to the Church was called to serve a mission in her homeland, one of the countries of the Far East. Her folks, who were Buddhists, repeatedly insisted that she forsake her mission and her religion and return home. Their demands were so insistent that the mission president last month authorized her to go back and see her family. There she was met by her family, . . . who used every possible means to persuade her to forsake her newly found religion and return to the religion of her forebears. She replied quietly but firmly that she could not deny her faith, that she must heed the call of the Lord rather than follow the counsel of men, even the counsel of her father.

The family, presided over by her uncle, denounced her and expelled her and told her that she could no longer associate with any of them. Then, after further deliberation, the family leaders determined that a mark should be put upon her to remind her of her infidelity to her traditional religion. While the men of the family held her, her father's older brother branded her with three burns in the arm. He told her that this would be a sign to the gods that she had forsaken Buddhism.

With ugly and painful wounds, with a broken heart but a resolute spirit, she returned to her mission. The scars in her flesh will remain to her a sign not of the forsaking of her father's religion but of her unconquerable faith in the gospel of Jesus Christ. Her faith so touched the heart of the father who had denounced her that he came to the mission home and put his arms around her and kissed her and told her that they would never desert her, and there was awakened in him also something of an understanding, faint but real, of the true meaning of the gospel of the Lord. ("God Shall Give unto You Knowledge by His Holy Spirit," BYU *Speeches of the Year*, September 25, 1973, p. 111.)

So certain was [Joseph Smith] of the cause he led, so sure of his divinely given calling, that he placed them above the value of his own life. With prescient knowledge of his forthcoming death, he surrendered himself to those who would deliver him defenseless into the hands of a mob. He sealed his testimony with his life's blood.

It was so with his followers. One will find no evidence, not a scintilla of it, that certitude was the enemy of religion in their lives and actions. Time after time they left their comfortable homes, first in New York, then in Ohio and Missouri, later in Illinois; and even after reaching this valley many left again to plant colonies over a vast area of the West. Why? Because of their faith in the cause of which they were a part. . . .

It is that kind of certitude that has moved this Church forward in the face of persecution, ridicule, sacrifice of fortune, the leaving of loved ones to travel to distant lands to carry the gospel message. That conviction motivates today as it has done from the beginning of this work. Faith in the hearts of millions that this cause is true, that God is our Eternal Father, and that Jesus is the

Christ, must ever be the great motivating force in our lives. ("Faith: The Essence of True Religion," *Ensign*, November 1981, p. 7.)

I am not suggesting that you simply put on rose-colored glasses to make the world about you look rosy. I ask, rather, that you look above and beyond the negative, the critical, the cynical, the doubtful, to the positive and the affirmative.

I carry with me a statement that I took from an article published some years ago on Commander William Robert Anderson, the man who took the submarine *Nautilus* under the North Pole from the waters of the Pacific to the waters of the Atlantic. In his wallet he carried a tattered card with these words: "I believe I am always divinely guided. I believe I will always take the right road. I believe God will always make a way where there is no way."

In a dark and troubled hour the Lord said to those he loved: "Let not your heart be troubled, neither let it be afraid" (John 14:27). ("The Continuing Pursuit of Truth," BYU–Hawaii Commencement Address, June 18, 1983.)

The history of this Church is a history of the expression of . . . faith. It began with a farm boy in the year 1820 when he read that great promise set forth in the Epistle of James:

"If any of you lack wisdom, let him ask of God, that giveth to all men liberally, and upbraideth not; and it shall be given him.

"But let him ask in faith, nothing wavering. For he that wavereth is like a wave of the sea driven with the wind and tossed." (James 1:5–6.)

It was faith, the simple faith of a fourteen-year-old boy, that took him into the woods that spring morning. It was faith that took him to his knees in pleading for understanding. The marvelous fruit of that faith was a vision glorious and beautiful, of which this great work is but the extended shadow.

It was by faith that he kept himself worthy of the remarkable manifestations which followed in bringing to the earth the keys, the authority, the power to reestablish the Church of Jesus Christ in these latter days. It was by faith that this marvelous record of ancient peoples, this testament which we call the Book of Mormon, was brought forth by the gift and power of God "to the convincing of the Jew and Gentile that Jesus is the Christ." It was by faith that a small band of early converts, notwithstanding the very powers of hell brought against them, strengthened and sustained one another, left home and family to spread the word, moved from New York to Ohio and from Ohio to Missouri and from Missouri to Illinois in their search for peace and freedom to worship God according to the dictates of conscience.

It was through the eyes of faith that they saw a city beautiful when first they walked across the swamps of Commerce, Illinois. With the conviction that faith without works is dead, they drained that swampland, they platted a city, they built substantial homes and houses for worship and education and, crowning all, a magnificent temple, then the finest building in all of Illinois.

Again came persecution, with profane and murderous mobs. Their prophet was killed. Their dreams were shattered. Again it was by faith that they pulled themselves together under the pattern he had previously drawn and organized themselves for another exodus.

With tears and aching hearts they left their comfortable homes and their workshops. They looked back upon their sacred temple, and then with faith turned their eyes to the West, to the unknown and to the uncharted, and while the snows of winter fell upon them, they crossed the Mississippi that February of 1846 and plowed their muddy way over the Iowa prairie.

With faith they established Winter Quarters on the Missouri. Hundreds died as plague and dysentery and black canker cut them down. But faith sustained those who survived. They buried their loved ones there on a bluff above the river, and in the spring of 1847 they started west, moving by faith up the Elkhorn and beside the Platte toward the mountains of the West.

It was by faith that Brigham Young looked over this valley, then hot and barren, and declared, "This is the place." Again by faith, four days later, he touched his cane to the ground a few hundred feet east of where I stand and said, "Here will be the temple of our God." The magnificent and sacred house of the Lord to the east of this Tabernacle is a testimony of faith, not only of the faith of those who built it but of the faith of those who now use it in a great selfless labor of love.

Wrote Paul to the Hebrews, "Now faith is the substance of things hoped for, the evidence of things not seen." (Heb. 11:1.) All of the great accomplishments of which I have spoken were once only "the substance of things hoped for, the evidence of things not seen." But with vision, with labor, and with confidence in the power of God working through them, they brought their faith to reality. ("God Grant Us Faith," *Ensign,* November 1983, pp. 52–53.)

Frequently it is not easy to face up to that which is expected of us. Many think they cannot do it. We need a little more faith. We should know that the Lord will not give us commandments beyond our power to observe. He will not ask us to do things for which we lack the capacity. Our problem lies in our fears and in our appetites. ("'Let Us Move This Work Forward,'" *Ensign,* November 1985, p. 83.)

This was a God-given mandate, a millennial mandate. It rested upon a handful of Latter-day Saints living in the farming communities of Kirtland and its environs in the 1830s. They had very little money. At tremendous sacrifice they had constructed a temple as "a house of prayer, a house of fasting, a house of faith, a house of learning, a house of glory, a house of order, a house of God." (D&C 109:8.) With the dedication of that sacred edifice, the power of the adversary began to move through Kirtland, manifesting itself in a spirit of reckless speculation that diverted the minds of many from the things of God to the things of mammon. The United States at that time was gripped by this spirit of speculation, which burst with catastrophic effects in the financial crash of 1837. In Kirtland, people turned against the Prophet Joseph Smith. There was bitterness, and there was greed. The Church was shaken, and a great sifting took place between the faithful and those whose eyes were set upon the things of the world. The problem was compounded by the fact that some members were in Ohio and others were in Missouri, separated by a distance of eight hundred miles and largely without communication.

Here were a people with a millennial vision and a responsibility that encompassed the entire world, but who were embroiled in difficulties sapping the very lifeblood of the Church.

It was in these distressing times, on Sunday, 4 June 1837, that the Prophet Joseph Smith came to Elder Heber C. Kimball of the Quorum of the Twelve while Brother Kimball "was seated in front of the stand, above the sacrament table, on the Melchisedek side of the Temple, in Kirtland, and whispering to [him], said, 'Brother Heber, the Spirit of the Lord has whispered to me: 'Let my servant Heber go to England and proclaim my Gospel, and open the door of salvation to that nation.'" (*History of the Church,* 2:490.)

Imagine, if you will, one man who had very little goods of the world telling another who had practically nothing, having just returned from a mission, that he was to go across the sea to open the work there. Wasn't there enough to be done at home? less faithful might have asked. They were on the frontier of the nation, and the entire membership of the Church probably did not exceed 15,000 people.

But there was a vision in the hearts of these men. It was a millennial vision that the gospel was to be preached to every nation before the end should come. Some work had been done in Canada. But now they were speaking of crossing the sea to the British Isles. One can understand Heber C. Kimball's response. Feeling his weakness he said, "O, Lord, I am a man of stammering tongue, and altogether unfit for such a work; how can I go to preach in that land, which is so famed throughout Christendom for learning, knowledge and piety; the nursery of religion; and to a people whose intelligence is proverbial!" (In Orson F. Whitney, *Life of Heber C. Kimball,* Salt Lake City: Bookcraft, 1945, p. 104.)

The call of Elder Heber C. Kimball and his associates to cross the sea to Britain was a declaration by the Prophet Joseph of the great destiny of this restored work. As I have read of the condition of the Saints in Ohio and Missouri at that time, and of the smallness of their number, I have marveled at the breadth of their vision. From that time forth there has never been a dimming of that vision. . . .

Their response to that call was a magnificent expression of faith. Said Brother Kimball at the time: "The idea of such a mission was almost more than I could bear up under. I was almost ready to sink under the burden which was placed upon me.

"However, all these considerations did not deter me from the path of duty; the moment I understood the will of my Heavenly Father, I felt a determination to go at all hazards, believing that He would support me by His almighty power, and endow me with every qualification that I needed; and although my family was dear to me, and I should have to leave them almost destitute, I felt that the cause of truth, the Gospel of Christ, outweighed every other consideration." (Ibid., p. 104.)

Orson Hyde, Willard Richards, and Joseph Fielding responded with similar faith, and these four were joined in New York by John Goodson, Isaac Russell, and John Snyder, who came forward with comparable faith for that historic and significant undertaking.

Tuesday, June 13, was the scheduled departure date for the four who were to leave Kirtland. One who looked in on the Kimball household that morning described the prayer that was uttered by the father who was leaving and who then, "like the patriarchs, and by virtue of his office, laid his hands upon" the heads of his children "individually, leaving a father's blessing upon them, and commending them to the care and protection of God, while he should be engaged preaching the Gospel in a foreign land. While thus engaged his voice was almost lost in the sobs of those around, who tried in vain to suppress them. The idea of being separated from their protector and father for so long a time was indeed painful. He proceeded, but his heart was too much affected to do so regularly. His emotions were great, and he was obliged to stop at intervals, while the big tears rolled down his cheeks." (Ibid., pp. 108–9.)

Faith? Faith was all they had—faith and courage. They had no money. One of the brethren gave the coatless Heber a coat. One of the women gave him five dollars, with which he paid for passage for himself and Orson Hyde to Buffalo. . . .

What an expression of faith, and what a demonstration of courage! ("Taking the Gospel to Britain: A Declaration of Vision, Faith, Courage, and Truth," *Ensign,* July 1987, pp. 4–5.)

Let me tell you of an experience I had with one of our Area Presidents. We were in a land where, to our knowledge, there was not a member of the Church among the millions of that nation.

There was a man who knew of the Church and desired baptism. He had been a longtime student of the Bible. He belonged to a Christian church but was not satisfied. The thought came into his mind that he should belong to a church that carried the name of the Savior. In an old encyclopedia in a public library, he found listed The Church of Jesus Christ of Latter-day Saints with headquarters in Salt Lake City. He wrote a letter of inquiry and received a response with literature. Other literature followed as he requested it.

When we met him he had read the Book of Mormon again and again. He had read the Doctrine and Covenants and other Church writings. With enthusiasm he had told his friends of his treasured find. He asked to be baptized.

We questioned him. He knew of the priesthood, its orders and its offices. He knew of the various ordinances and the procedures of our meetings.

Did he believe the Book of Mormon to be the word of God? Oh, yes, he knew it to be true. He had read it. He had prayed about it and pondered. He had no doubt of its truth.

Did he believe Joseph Smith to be a prophet of God? Most assuredly. Again, he had studied and prayed. He was convinced of the reality of that glorious vision when God the Eternal Father and His Beloved Son, the resurrected Lord, appeared to the boy Joseph to usher in a new and final dispensation of gospel truth.

The priesthood had been restored with all its gifts and powers. He knew that. Our friend asked for baptism and hoped for the priesthood that he might teach and act with proper authority.

"But," we said, "if we baptize you and then leave, you will be left alone. While there are many Christians in your nation, and freedom of religion is guaranteed under its laws, there are severe restrictions concerning foreigners. There will be no one to teach you and help you. There will be no one on whom you can lean."

He responded, "God will teach me and help me, and He will be my friend and support."

I looked into the eyes of that good man and saw the light of faith. We baptized him under the authority of the holy priesthood. We confirmed him a member of the Church and bestowed upon him the Holy Ghost. We baptized his wife. We conferred upon him the Aaronic Priesthood and ordained him to the office of priest so that under proper direction they might have the sacrament.

We held a sacrament and testimony meeting with them. We embraced them and said good-bye to one another, and tears were in our eyes. They left to return to their home, and we left for responsibilities in other nations.

I shall never forget him. He is poor in the things of the world. But he is educated—a teacher by profession. I know little of his circumstances. But this I know—when we talked with him, the fire of faith burned in his heart, and our own faith was quickened also. . . .

. . . His example has provided a test for me. It is found in the fifth verse of the seventeenth chapter of Luke. Jesus had been teaching his disciples by precept and parable. "And the apostles said unto the Lord, *Increase our faith*" (italics added).

This is my prayer for all of us—"Lord, increase our faith." ("'Lord, Increase Our Faith,'" *Ensign*, November 1987, pp. 51–52.)

As most of you know, in the last four or five years we have passed through an interesting episode in the history of the Church. There came into our hands two letters that were seized upon by the media when we announced them. They were trumpeted across much of the world as documents that would challenge the authenticity of the Church. In announcing them we stated that they really had nothing to do with the essentials of our history. But some few of little faith, who seemingly are always quick to believe the negative, accepted as fact the pronouncements and predictions of the media. . . .

Now, as you know, these letters, together with other documents, have been acknowledged by their forger to be total frauds and part of an evil and devious design which culminated in the murder of two individuals.

I have wondered what those whose faith was shaken have thought since the forger confessed to his evil work.

However, I hasten to add, the vast majority of Church members, all but a very few, paid little attention and went forward with their faithful service, living by a conviction firmly grounded in that knowledge which comes by the power of the Holy Ghost. They knew then and they know now that God watches over this work, that Jesus Christ is the head of this Church, that it is true, and that happiness and growth come of following its precepts and teachings. ("'Lord, Increase Our Faith,'" *Ensign*, November 1987, pp. 51–52.)

Grant us faith to look beyond the problems of the moment to the miracles of the future. Give us faith to pay our tithes and offerings and put our trust in Thee, the Almighty, to open the windows of heaven as Thou hast promised. Give us faith to do what is right and let the consequence follow.

Grant us faith when storms of adversity beat us down and drive us to the ground. In seasons of sickness may our confidence wax strong in the powers of the priesthood. . . .

Lord, when we walk in the valley of the shadow of death, give us faith to smile through our tears, knowing that it is all part of the eternal plan of a loving Father, that as we cross the threshold from this life we enter another more glorious, and that through the atonement of the Son of God all shall rise from the grave and the faithful shall go on to exaltation. ("'Lord, Increase Our Faith,'" *Ensign*, November 1987, pp. 53–54.)

Faith is not a theological platitude. It is a fact of life. Faith can become the very wellspring of purposeful living. There is no more compelling motivation to worthwhile endeavor than the knowledge that we are children of God, the Creator of the universe, our all-wise Heavenly Father! God expects us to do something with our lives, and he will give us help when help is sought. . . .

. . . We were aboard a plane some years ago flying between Honolulu and Los Angeles. It was in the days when only propeller-driven aircraft were available. About midway in the journey one of the motors stopped. There was a decrease in speed, a lowering in altitude, and a certain amount of nervousness among those aboard. The fact of the matter was that much of the power was missing, and the hazards were increased accordingly. Without that power, we could not fly high, fast, and safely.

It is so with our lives when we discount the need for faith and disregard knowledge of the Lord.

Passive acceptance of the Lord is not enough. Vibrant testimony comes of anxious seeking. ("'With All Thy Getting Get Understanding,'" *Ensign*, August 1988, p. 5.)

When I discuss faith, I do not mean it in an abstract sense. I mean it as a living, vital force with recognition of God as our Father and Jesus Christ as our Savior. When we accept this basic premise, there will come an acceptance of their teachings and an obedience which will bring peace and joy in this life and exaltation in the life to come. ("'With All Thy Getting Get Understanding,'" *Ensign*, August 1988, p. 5.)

I repeat what I have said before—when all is said and done, the only real wealth of the Church is in the faith of its people. ("The State of the Church," *Ensign*, May 1991, p. 54.)

The greatest thing we can do for the safety of our nation and to strengthen it is to cultivate within the membership of this Church stronger, ever stronger faith in the Lord Jesus Christ, that our people might walk in righteousness and become an example to all and be as the leaven to leaven the lump. Let us walk in faith and faithfulness. (Vacaville/Santa Rosa California Regional Conference, priesthood leadership session, May 20, 1995.)

Walk by faith. God will open the way. When there is no way, He will open the way. I am satisfied of that. I don't worry about the future of this Church. It is going to roll on with majesty and power. This is the stone which was cut out of the mountain, which rolled forth to fill the whole earth as was seen in Daniel's vision. This is the work of the true and living God, whose power exceeds all other power in the universe. (Vacaville/Santa Rosa California Regional Conference, priesthood leadership session, May 20, 1995.)

Some time ago I read the newspaper report of the remarks of a prominent journalist. He is quoted as having said, "Certitude is the enemy of religion." The words attributed to him have stirred within me much reflection. Certitude, which I define as complete and total assurance, is not the enemy of religion. It is of its very essence.

Certitude is certainty. It is conviction. It is the power of faith that approaches knowledge—yes, that even becomes knowledge. It evokes enthusiasm, and there is no asset comparable to enthusiasm in overcoming opposition, prejudice, and indifference.

Great buildings were never constructed on uncertain foundations. Great causes were never brought to success by vacillating leaders. The gospel was never expounded to the convincing of others without certainty. Faith, which is of the very essence of personal conviction, has always been, and always must be, at the root of religious practice and endeavor. . . .

. . . Theology may be argued over, but personal testimony, coupled with performance, cannot be refuted. ("Faith: The Essence of True Religion," *Ensign*, October 1995, pp. 2–3.)

Following the death of the Savior, would His Apostles have carried on, teaching His doctrine, even giving their lives in the most painful of circumstances, if there were any uncertainty concerning Him whom they represented and whose doctrine they taught? There was no lack of certitude on the part of Paul after he had seen a light and heard a voice while en route to Damascus to persecute the Christians. For more than three decades after that, he devoted his time, his strength, his life to the spreading of the gospel of the resurrected Lord. Without regard for personal comfort or safety, he traveled over the known world of his time, declaring that "neither death, nor life, nor angels, nor principalities, nor powers, nor things present, nor things to come,

"Nor height, nor depth, nor any other creature, shall be able to separate us from the love of God, which is in Christ Jesus our Lord" (Rom. 8:38–39).

Executed in Rome, Paul sealed with his death his final testimony of his conviction of the divine sonship of Jesus Christ. . . .

Would there ever have been a Reformation without the certitude that drove with boldness such giants as Luther, Huss, Zwingli, and others of their kind? ("Faith: The Essence of True Religion," *Ensign,* October 1995, p. 2.)

I wrote these beautiful words as President David O. McKay spoke them to a small group some years ago. Said he:

"As absolute as the certainty that you have in your hearts that tonight will be followed by dawn tomorrow morning, so is my assurance that Jesus Christ is the Savior of mankind, the Light that will dispel the darkness of the world, through the gospel restored by direct revelation to the Prophet Joseph Smith." . . .

It is that kind of certitude that has moved this church forward in the face of persecution, ridicule, sacrifice of fortune, the leaving of loved ones to travel to distant lands to carry the gospel message. That conviction motivates today as it has done from the beginning of this work. Faith in the hearts of millions that this cause is true, that God is our Eternal Father, and that Jesus is the Christ must ever be the great motivating force in our lives. ("Faith: The Essence of True Religion," *Ensign,* October 1995, p. 4.)

I bring to your attention those great words of the Lord to Thomas: "Be not faithless, but believing." This is such a marvelous season of your lives. It is a time not only of positive thinking but sometimes of critical thinking. Let me urge you to not let your critical thinking override your faith. (Ricks College Regional Conference, Rexburg, Idaho, October 29, 1995.)

Faith [is] the great moving power which can change our lives and move us forward on the road of immortality and eternal life. (Pusan Korea Fireside, May 21, 1996.)

Believe in God the Eternal Father. He is the ruler and governor of the universe, and yet we can speak with Him. He has a father's love for His children. He will hear your prayers. I bear testimony of that. I know that is true.

Believe in Jesus Christ, the Savior and Redeemer of the world. It is He who stands at the head of this Church to which you belong. This Church is not mine. It belongs to the Lord Jesus Christ. It bears His holy name. He stands at the head of this great work. He stands to assist us with our problems. He stands to bless us in our time of need.

Believe in the divine calling of the Prophet Joseph Smith. What a wonderful man he was. He was killed while he was still a young man, but in the short years of his life he became the instrument in the hands of the Lord in the restoration of this great and marvelous work.

Believe in the Book of Mormon as the word of God. Study the Book of Mormon. Pray over the Book of Mormon. Let its inspiration come into your lives.

Believe in the Church. It stands as a great anchor in this age of unbelief. It stands as a great repository of faith in this time when people do not believe in things. It is The Church of Jesus Christ which is here to help you, to educate you, to provide social opportunity, to give you the word of the living God.

Believe in yourself as a child of God. Every one of you here, every man, woman, and child, has a divine inheritance. God is your Eternal Father. What a marvelous birthright that is. Do not live beneath it. Stand tall and live the gospel. (Managua Nicaragua Fireside, January 21, 1997.)

FAMILY

See also Children; Family Home Evening; Family Prayer; Fatherhood; Motherhood; Parenting

One of our national magazines carried these words on the cover: "Morality USA. Do we need a new code to solve our crisis of immorality? Have our churches failed? Has money become God? Is sexual morality gone?" (*Look*, September 24, 1963.) I read this provocative article. I have read others of similar tone written by men of government, industry, and education who have expressed themselves with deep concern over the moral crisis that evidently is sweeping across the land.

I am not one to believe that all was good in the long ago, and that all is bad today. I think this is the greatest age the world has known. But I am also confident that there is trouble in the land. . . .

Private and public morality are rooted in the homes of the people. No nation is stronger than its homes. It is in the home that examples of virtue are best caught and lessons of virtue are best taught.

It was said of old, "Except the Lord build the house, they labour in vain that build it." (Psalm 127:1.) ("Except the Lord Build the House," *Improvement Era*, January 1964, p. 32.)

The discipline that is needed in our lives is the discipline that comes from within. Many are crying for more legislation and stricter law enforcement. I do not disparage these as expedients, but I fear they are only expedients. Virtue, integrity, honesty do not come of imposition from without. They are the fruits of good teaching and good example, and that teaching and that example are best followed when they are found in the home. ("Except the Lord Build the House," *Improvement Era*, January 1964, p. 33.)

Fathers and mothers are needed who will rise and stand upon their feet to make of their homes sanctuaries in which children will grow in a spirit of obedience, industry, and fidelity to tested standards of conduct. If our society is coming apart at the seams, it is because the tailor and the seamstress in the home are not producing the kind of stitching that will hold under stress. . . .

I want [my son] to read the great stories of the Old Testament in the very language of the Bible. . . .

I want him to read—along with his science and politics and business—the New Testament, the Gospels with their record of the matchless life of the Son of God. . . .

I want him to read the testament of the New World, the Book of Mormon. . . .

I want my son to have the advantage of faith in the living God. . . .

The home from which [one young man I know] came was
. . . modest, but a good man presided in that home as the father.
He dealt with his wife with kindness, respect, and courtesy. The
mother honored her husband and cast an aura of love about the
home. And the son who left that home carried with him a fiber
in his soul, a fiber that held firm under the tauntings of his associates, whose eyes he opened when he arose and stood on his
feet as a quiet witness of the teachings of his parents. ("'Rise, and
Stand upon Thy Feet,'" *Improvement Era,* December 1968,
pp. 69–70.)

It was said of old that "a soft answer turneth away wrath."
(Prov. 15:1.)

We seldom get into trouble when we speak softly. It is only
when we raise our voices that the sparks fly and tiny molehills
become great mountains of contention. To me there has always
been something significant in the description of the prophet
Elijah's contest with the priests of Baal. The scripture records that
"a great and strong wind rent the mountains, and brake in pieces
the rocks . . . but the Lord was not in the wind: and after the
wind an earthquake; but the Lord was not in the earthquake:

"And after the earthquake a fire; but the Lord was not in the
fire: and after the fire a still small voice." (1 Kings 19:11–12.)

The voice of heaven is a still small voice; likewise, the voice
of domestic peace is a quiet voice.

There is need for a vast amount of discipline in marriage, not
of one's companion, but of one's self.

I know of few more meaningful statements for fathers and
for fathers-to-be than this counsel given by President David O.
McKay. Said he: "A father can do no greater thing for his children
than to let them feel that he loves their mother."

How much greater the peace in the homes of the people, how
much greater the security in the lives of the children, how much
less divorce and separation and misery, how much more gladness and joy and love there would be if husbands and wives
would cultivate the discipline of speaking softly one to another,
and if both would so speak to their children. ("'Except the Lord
Build the House . . . ,'" *Ensign,* June 1971, p. 72.)

A man is in large measure the product of those qualities of mind and body, and even of spirit, bequeathed him by his forebears. ("Harold Bingham Lee: Humility, Benevolence, Loyalty," *Ensign*, February 1974, p. 88.)

Much of the work that goes on within temples is concerned with the family. Basic to an understanding of its meaning is recognition of the fact that even as we existed as children of God before we were born into this world, so also shall we continue to live after death, and the treasured and satisfying relationships of mortality, the most beautiful and meaningful of which are found in the family, may continue in the world to come. ("Why These Temples?" *Ensign*, August 1974, p. 39.)

No nation, no civilization can long endure without strength in the homes of its people. That strength derives from the integrity of those who establish those homes.

No family can have peace, no home can be free from storms of adversity unless that family and that home are built on foundations of morality, fidelity, and mutual respect. There cannot be peace where there is not trust; there cannot be freedom where there is not loyalty. The warm sunlight of love will not rise out of a swamp of immorality. (*From My Generation to Yours, with Love*, pamphlet, 1978, p. 9.)

I recognize that there are parents who, notwithstanding an outpouring of love and a diligent and faithful effort to teach them, see their children grow in a contrary manner and weep while their wayward sons and daughters willfully pursue courses of tragic consequence. For such I have great sympathy, and to them I am wont to quote the words of Ezekiel: "The son shall not bear the iniquity of the father, neither shall the father bear the iniquity of the son." (Ezek. 18:20.) ("'Behold Your Little Ones,'" *Ensign*, November 1978, p. 19.)

The homes of our people have been great homes where there has been love, a spirit of sacrifice, an attitude of respect for one another. There will be need for greater emphasis of these qualities in the future. Selfishness is the canker that drives out peace and love. Selfishness is the root on which grow argument, anger, disrespect, infidelity, and divorce. ("Five Million Members—A Milestone and Not a Summit," *Ensign*, May 1982, p. 45.)

We have been encouraged to strengthen our homes, to fortify the Spirit of the Lord in those homes, to cultivate appreciation and respect and affection one for another. It is a terrible thing that we hear occasionally of child abuse. This is a growing evil across the world. ("Reach Out in Love and Kindness," *Ensign*, November 1982, p. 76.)

"Honour thy father and thy mother: that thy days may be long upon the land which the Lord thy God giveth thee." It is an unusual statement. It is different from all of the other commandments. Each of the other nine is a commandment without a promise. The fifth is a commandment and a promise—the commandment: "Honour thy father and thy mother" and the implied promise ". . . that thy days may be long upon the land which the Lord thy God giveth thee."

To me that is tremendously interesting—and meaningful. Whatever relationship, I first asked myself, is there between honoring one's parents and living long upon the land? Is it likely that we will live longer if we honor father and mother?

I am convinced that Jehovah knew whereof He wrote when His finger traced those words, with that remarkable promise.

Now I recognize that some parents, because of their own manner of living, are scarcely worthy of the honor and respect of their children. This is a tragedy. Fortunately, such cases are very much in the minority.

But even among people of this kind, I think there is scarcely a father or mother who does not wish for a son or daughter the very best that life has to offer. . . .

I recall some years ago a young man who had left home to go into the world. His father had pleaded with him to be careful, to turn away from the siren song of immorality, and said to him that he would rather he would return in a box than with his life tainted by moral transgression. The young man disregarded his father's counsel. Tragedy followed. Marriage ensued, but it was doomed to failure. Divorce occurred with bitterness. That life, so full of hope and bright potential, was blighted and miserable and ended in bleak tragedy.

I repeat, it is interesting that Jehovah, in the case of the fifth commandment, added a promise following the mandate.

I am not here to say that in every case life will be lengthened and its quality improved simply by the process of honoring one's parents. But I do say, and without hesitation, that there is safety, there is protection, there is reward, there is happiness, and satisfaction that come of respect for the counsels of one's parents who wish the very best for every son and daughter. Well did the writer of Proverbs say, "A foolish son is grief to his father, and bitterness to her that bare him." (Proverbs 17:25.) (Address at Dixie College, St. George, Utah, October 9, 1988.)

To those of you who live in troubled homes, may I suggest that you let love become the lodestar of your family life. There is too much of shouting, too much of recrimination, so many tears in the homes of some of our people. Love is the only remedy. It is the very basis of marriage. It can be nurtured and strengthened, or it can be starved and weakened. The power lies within ourselves. Bridle your tempers, husbands. Wives, hold your tongues. Revive the wondrous feeling that brought you to the marriage altar. ("Let Love Be the Lodestar of Your Life," *Ensign*, May 1989, p. 67.)

Every child, with few possible exceptions, is the product of a home, be it good, bad, or indifferent. As children grow through the years, their lives, in large measure, become an extension and a reflection of family teaching. If there is harshness, abuse, uncontrolled anger, disloyalty, the fruits will be certain and discernible, and in all likelihood they will be repeated in the generation that follows. If, on the other hand, there is forbearance, forgiveness, respect, consideration, kindness, mercy, and compassion, the fruits again will be discernible, and they will be eternally rewarding. They will be positive and sweet and wonderful. And as mercy is given and taught by parents, it will be repeated in the lives and actions of the next generation.

I speak to fathers and mothers everywhere with a plea to put harshness behind us, to bridle our anger, to lower our voices, and to deal with mercy and love and respect one toward another in our homes. ("Blessed Are the Merciful," *Ensign*, May 1990, p. 70.)

I recently read an illuminating article on the deterioration of the family in New York City, which is described as a root cause of the severe problems that plague that city and almost every other large city across the world.

The strength of any community lies in the strength of its families. The strength of any nation lies in the strength of its families. Strong family life comes of strong and clear religious understanding of who we are, and why we are here, and of what we may eternally become. Strong family life comes of the perception that each of us is a child of God, born with a divine birthright, and with a great and significant potential. Strong family life comes of parents who love and respect one another, and who love and respect and nurture their children in the ways of the Lord. These are undergirding principles of our teachings as a church. To the degree that we observe these teachings we build strong families whose generations will strengthen the nation.

These are families where there is daily prayer with an acknowledgment of God as our Eternal Father and of our accountability to Him for what we do with our lives. ("*Mormon Should Mean 'More Good*,'" *Ensign*, November 1990, pp. 53–54.)

I believe in the family where there is a husband who regards his companion as his greatest asset and treats her accordingly; where there is a wife who looks upon her husband as her anchor and strength, her comfort and security; where there are children who look to mother and father with respect and gratitude; where there are parents who look upon those children as blessings and find a great and serious and wonderful challenge in their nurture and rearing. The cultivation of such a home requires effort and energy, forgiveness and patience, love and endurance and sacrifice; but it is worth all of these and more. ("This I Believe," *BYU 1991–92 Devotional and Fireside Speeches*, March 1, 1992, p. 80.)

The greatest joys of life are experienced in happy family relationships. The most poignant of sorrows, the most bleak and forlorn feelings of misery come of unhappy family life. ("This I Believe," *BYU 1991–92 Devotional and Fireside Speeches*, March 1, 1992, p. 80.)

"Honour thy father and thy mother: that thy days may be long upon the land which the Lord thy God giveth thee." (Ex. 20:12.) As a boy I came to believe in that divine commandment.

I think it is such a great commandment from the Lord. If it were only observed more widely, there would be far less misery in the homes of the people. Instead of backbiting, accusation, argument, there would be appreciation and respect and quiet love.

My father is long since gone. I have become a father, and a grandfather, and a great-grandfather. The Lord has been very kind. I have experienced my share of disappointments, of failures, of difficulties. But on balance, life has been very good. I have tried to live it with enthusiasm and appreciation. I have known much of happiness, oh, so very much. The root of it all, I believe, was planted in my childhood and nurtured in the home, the school, and the ward in which I grew, where I learned simple but important lessons in living. I cannot be grateful enough.

My heart aches, I grieve, when I see the tragedy of so many broken homes, of homes where husbands do not seem to know how to treat their wives, of homes where children are abused and grow to become the abusers of another generation. None of this tragedy is necessary. I know it is not. The answer to our problems lies in following the simple gospel of Jesus Christ, the Son of God, who brought into the world His Father's love. ("Some Lessons I Learned as a Boy," *Ensign*, May 1993, p. 59.)

When all is said and done, the primary place in building a value system is in the homes of the people. ("Bring Up a Child in the Way He Should Go," *Ensign*, November 1993, p. 59.)

The family is divine. It was instituted by our Heavenly Father. It encompasses the most sacred of all relationships. Only through its organization can the purposes of the Lord be fulfilled. . . .

Most marriages result in children, and most parents seek earnestly to raise righteous progeny. I am satisfied that nothing will assure greater success in the hazardous undertaking of parenthood than a program of family life that comes from the marvelous teaching of the gospel; that the father of the home may be clothed with the priesthood of God; that it is his privilege and obligation as a steward of our Heavenly Father's children to provide for their needs; that he is to govern in the home in the spirit of the priesthood "by persuasion, by long-suffering, by gentleness and meekness, and by love unfeigned" (D&C 121:41–42); that the mother in the home is a daughter of God, a soul of intelligence, devotion, and love who may be clothed with the Spirit of God; that it is her privilege and obligation as a steward of our Heavenly Father's children to nurture those children in their daily needs; that she, in companionship with her husband, is also to teach her children to "understand the doctrine of repentance, faith in Christ the Son of the living God, and of baptism and the gift of the Holy Ghost by the laying on of the hands . . . [and] to pray, and to walk uprightly before the Lord." (D&C 68:25, 28.)

In such a home, parents are loved and not dreaded; they are appreciated and not feared. And children are regarded as gifts of the Lord, to be cared for, nurtured, encouraged, and directed. ("Pillars of Truth," *Ensign,* January 1994, p. 5.)

We are concerned with the quality of family life within so many homes. The home is the seedbed of all true virtue. If proper values are not learned in the home, they are not likely to be learned anywhere. . . .

The family is the basic element of society. It is so important. Good homes produce good people. Good homes become the foundation for the strength of any nation. Good homes are certainly the rock-bottom need of our nation and every nation: homes in which there is a father who stands at the head of the home in love and kindness and who assumes the basic responsibility to provide for his family. And a mother stands as the queen of that home, equally beside her husband, and they have children whom they love and cherish and nourish, and who love them in return. (Press Conference, Salt Lake City, March 13, 1995.)

There is too much selfishness. There is too much of worldliness in our homes. We need to get back to the basics of respect one for another and concern one for another, love and appreciation for one another, working together, worshiping together, and living together as families who love the Lord and look to Him for light and strength and comfort. We need to rear our families in the nurture and admonition of the Lord, as He instructs us to do. (*Church News* Interview, June 7, 1995.)

We are a church which bears testimony of the importance of the family—the father, the mother, the children—and of the fact that we are all children of God our Eternal Father. Parents who bring children into the world have a responsibility to love those children, to nurture them and care for them, to teach them those values which would bless their lives so that they will grow to become good citizens. If there is less trouble in the homes, there will be less trouble in the nations. I want to emphasize that which is already familiar to you, and that is the importance of binding our families together with love and kindness, with appreciation and respect, and with teaching the ways of the Lord so that your children will grow in righteousness and avoid the tragedies which are overcoming so many families across the world. (Veracruz Mexico Regional Conference, January 28, 1996.)

Be true to your parents and your heritage. Regrettably there are a few parents who act in a way that does serious injustice to their children. But these cases are relatively few. No one has a greater interest in your welfare, in your happiness, in your future than do your mothers and fathers. They are of a prior generation. That is true. But they were once the age that you are now. Your problems are not substantially different from what theirs were. If they occasionally place restrictions on you, it is because they see danger down the road. Listen to them. What they ask you to do may not be to your liking. But you will be much happier if you do it. ("Stand True and Faithful," *Ensign*, May 1996, pp. 92–93.)

Why do we have this proclamation on the family now? Because the family is under attack. All across the world families are falling apart. The place to begin to improve society is in the home. Children do, for the most part, what they are taught. We are trying to make the world better by making the family stronger. (Media Luncheon and Press Conference, Tokyo, Japan, May 18, 1996.)

If you want to reform a nation, you begin with families, with parents who teach their children principles and values that are positive and affirmative and will lead them to worthwhile endeavors. ("'This Thing Was Not Done in a Corner,'" *Ensign,* November 1996, p. 49.

Every man ought to regard his wife as a daughter of God, a daughter who is his equal, with whom he walks side by side. Marvelous is that concept that does not place a woman in an inferior position. One great man said a father can do nothing better for his children than to let them see that he loves their mother. Brethren, treat your wives with love and respect and kindness. And, wives, you treat your husbands with love and respect and kindness. And love your children and rear them in the admonition of the Lord, with love and appreciation and respect. They were God's children before they were yours. You don't need to whip them. You don't need to beat them. Let love take its place and you will be a blessed people. (São Paulo Brazil Fireside, November 14, 1996.)

Much of the world is in serious trouble over the disintegration of the family. The family is the basic unit of society. No nation is stronger than the homes of its people. If the current American divorce levels persist, about 50 percent of all marriages contracted in the past fifteen years will end in divorce. Of all marriages contracted in 1995, it is expected that 60 percent will end in divorce.

Lawrence Stone, the noted Princeton University family historian, says: "The scale of marital breakdowns in the West since 1960 has no historical precedent that I know of, and seems unique. . . . There has been nothing like it for the last 2,000 years and probably longer." (Quoted by David Popenoe, "A World without Father," *The Wilson Quarterly*, Spring 1996, p. 13.) You are familiar with the fruits of broken homes. I think the home is the answer to most of our basic social problems, and if we take care of things there, other things will take care of themselves.

We are trying to preserve the traditional family—father, mother, and children—working together in love toward a common goal. In large measure we are succeeding against great odds. (Media Luncheon, Washington, D.C., December 2, 1996.)

FAMILY HISTORY WORK

See also Temple

There are today many genealogical and family history societies in the world. I think they all have come into existence subsequent to the visit of Elijah. One of the oldest and most prestigious is the New England Historic Genealogical Society, organized in 1844. Since then, and in more recent years particularly, there has been a tremendous surge of interest in family history. With that surge, the Family History Department of the Church has grown to be able to handle it.

When the Utah Genealogical Society was organized in 1894, the charter members contributed eleven volumes. That original root stock has grown to a library of 258,000 books. Each month another thousand volumes are added to this collection.

The collection also includes 1.8 million rolls of microfilm to which are added an additional 5,000 rolls monthly. It has become the world's largest collection of family history data.

Only a handful of our people used the modest family history resources of the Church around the turn of the century. How things have changed! During each of the last five years more than 750,000 researchers have used the main library here in Salt Lake City and the more than 2,200 family history centers scattered across the world. Approximately 40 percent of those using the Family History Library and 60 percent of the patrons using local centers are not members of the Church. We offer a tremendous service to those not of our faith.

There is nothing else to compare with this treasury of family history. . . . I feel the Lord has designed that it should be so. This is His church which carries His name, and one of its purposes is to make available to the millions beyond the veil of death the full blessings that lead to eternal life. (Utah Genealogical Society Fireside, November 13, 1994.)

I am confident that the Lord will permit us and direct us to go on building these sacred structures [the temples] as we become worthy of them. One important test of that worthiness will lie in doing the research that becomes the foundation for the major work to be carried on in them. (Utah Genealogical Society Fireside, November 13, 1994.)

FAMILY HOME EVENING

I am grateful that we as a Church have as a basic part of our program the practice of a weekly family home evening. It is a significant thing that in these busy days thousands of families across the world are making an earnest effort to consecrate one evening a week to sing together, to instruct one another in the ways of the Lord, to kneel together in prayer, there to thank the Lord for his mercies and to invoke his blessings upon our lives, our homes, our labors, our land.

I think we little estimate the vast good that will come of this program. I commend it to our people, and I commend it to every parent in the land and say that we stand ready to assist you who may not be of our faith. We shall be happy to send you suggestions and materials on how to conduct a weekly family home evening, and I do not hesitate to promise you that both you and your children will become increasingly grateful for the observance of this practice. It was John who declared: "I have no greater joy than to hear that my children walk in truth." (3 John 4.) This will be your blessing. (Conference Report, October 1965, p. 51.)

In 1915 President Joseph F. Smith asked the people of the Church to have family home evening. My father said we would do so, and so we would warm up the parlor where Mother's grand piano stood and do what the President of the Church had asked.

We were miserable performers as children. We could do all kinds of things together while playing, but for one of us to try to sing a solo before the others was like asking ice cream to stay hard on the kitchen stove. In the beginning, we would laugh and make cute remarks about one another's performance. But our parents persisted. We sang together. We prayed together. We listened quietly while Mother read Bible and Book of Mormon stories. Father told us stories out of his memory. . . .

Out of those simple little meetings, held in the parlor of our old home, came something indescribable and wonderful. Our love for our parents was strengthened. Our love for brothers and sisters was enhanced. Our love for the Lord was increased. An appreciation for simple goodness grew in our hearts. These wonderful things came about because our parents followed the counsel of the President of the Church. I have learned something tremendously significant out of that. ("Some Lessons I Learned as a Boy," *Ensign*, May 1993, p. 54.)

If you have any doubt about the virtue of family home evening, try it. Gather your children about you, teach them, bear testimony to them, read the scriptures together and have a good time together. (Promontory Utah Branch Sacrament Meeting, October 15, 1995.)

I hope, my brothers and sisters, that you are having your family home evenings with your children. You cannot afford to postpone this. The days, the months, and the years pass so quickly, and before long it will be too late. (Veracruz Mexico Fireside, January 28, 1996.)

FAMILY PRAYER

I feel satisfied that there is no adequate substitute for the morning and evening practice of kneeling together—father, mother, and children. This, more than heavy carpets, more than lovely draperies, more than cleverly balanced color schemes, is the thing that will make for better and more beautiful homes.

("The Force of Family Prayer," *Improvement Era,* June 1963, p. 530.)

One cannot ask God to help a neighbor in distress, without feeling motivated to do something oneself. What miracles would happen in the lives of the children of America if they would lay aside their selfishness and lose themselves in the service of others. The seed from which this sheltering and fruitful tree may grow is best planted and nurtured in the daily supplications of the family.

I know of no better way to inculcate love for country than for parents to pray before their children for the land in which we live, invoking the blessings of the Almighty upon it that it may be preserved in liberty and in peace. I know of no better way to build within the hearts of our children a much-needed respect for authority than remembering in the daily supplications of the family the President and the Congress and others who carry the burdens of government. ("Except the Lord Build the House," *Improvement Era,* January 1964, pp. 33, 56.)

All agree that we need a new emphasis on honesty, character, and integrity. All agree that only as we build again into the fiber of our lives the virtues which are the essence of true civilization will the pattern of our times change. The question that confronts us is, *where shall we begin?*

I am satisfied that it must begin with recognition of God as our Eternal Father, of our relationship to him as his children, with communication with him in recognition of his sovereign position, and with daily supplication for his guidance in our affairs.

I submit that a return to the old pattern of prayer, family prayer in the homes of the people, is one of the simple medicines that would check the dread disease that is eroding the fiber of our character. We could not expect a miracle in a day, but in a generation we would have a miracle.

A generation or two ago family prayer in the homes of Christian people throughout the world was as much a part of the day's activity as were the meals. As that practice has diminished, our moral decay has ensued. I fear that as the quality of our housing has improved, the spirit of our homes has deteriorated. ("Except the Lord Build the House," *Improvement Era*, January 1964, p. 33.)

Paul of old declared to Timothy: "This know also, that in the last days perilous times shall come.

"For men shall be lovers of their own selves, . . . blasphemers, disobedient to parents, unthankful, unholy,

"Without natural affection, . . . despisers of those that are good,

"Traitors, heady, highminded, lovers of pleasures more than lovers of God." (2 Tim. 3:1–4.) . . .

. . . Simple as it may sound, I think daily prayer in the homes of the nation would in a generation lift our heads above the flood that evidently is engulfing us. ("Except the Lord Build the House," *Improvement Era*, January 1964, p. 33.)

In 1872 Colonel Thomas L. Kane of Philadelphia visited Utah with his wife and two sons. They traveled by wagon some three hundred miles to the southern part of the state, stopping each night in the homes of the people in the little frontier settlements along the way. Mrs. Kane wrote a series of letters to her father in Philadelphia. In one of them she said: "At every one of the places we stayed on this journey we had prayers immediately after the dinner-supper, and prayers again before breakfast. No one was excused. . . . The Mormons kneel at once, while the head of the household, or an honored guest prays aloud. . . . They spend very little time in ascriptions, but ask for what they need, and thank Him for what He has given. . . . [They] take it for granted that God knows our familiar names and titles, and will ask a blessing on (a particular individual by name). I liked this when I became used to it."

It was so in the pioneer homes across the land. With the faith that came of these daily invocations these people grubbed the sagebrush, led the waters to the parched soil, made the desert blossom as the rose, governed their families in love, lived in peace one with another and with the world, and made their names immortal as they lost themselves in the service of God.

We cannot pray in our public schools, but we can pray in our homes, and in so doing we shall reweave into the character of our children the moral strength which will become the fiber of a better society. "Seek ye the Lord while he may be found." (Isa. 55:6.)

This simple practice, a return to family worship, spreading across the land and over the earth, would in a generation do much to lift the blight that is destroying us. It would restore integrity, mutual respect, and a spirit of thankfulness in the hearts of the people. ("Except the Lord Build the House," *Improvement Era*, January 1964, p. 56.)

I know of nothing that will ease family tensions, that in a subtle way will bring about the respect for parents which leads to obedience, that will affect the spirit of repentance which will largely erase the blight of broken homes, than will praying together, confessing weaknesses together before the Lord, and invoking the blessings of the Lord upon the home and those who dwell there. (*Be Thou an Example* [Salt Lake City: Deseret Book, 1981], p. 32.)

Can we make our homes more beautiful? Yes, through addressing ourselves as families to the source of all true beauty. Can we strengthen our society and make it a better place in which to live? Yes, by strengthening the virtue of our family life through kneeling together and supplicating the Almighty in the name of his Beloved Son. (*Be Thou an Example* [Salt Lake City: Deseret Book, 1981], p. 34.)

Behold your little ones. Pray with them. Pray for them and bless them. The world into which they are moving is a complex and difficult world. They will run into heavy seas of adversity. They will need all the strength and all the faith you can give them while they are yet near you. And they also will need a greater strength that comes of a higher power. They must do more than go along with what they find. They must lift the world, and the only levers they will have are the example of their own lives and the powers of persuasion that will come of their testimonies and their knowledge of the things of God. They will need the help of the Lord. While they are young, pray with them that they may come to know that source of strength which shall then always be available in every hour of need. (*Be Thou an Example* [Salt Lake City: Deseret Book, 1981], p. 40.)

I know of no other practice that will have so salutary an effect upon your lives as will the practice of kneeling together in prayer. The very words, Our Father in Heaven, have a tremendous effect. You cannot speak them with sincerity and with recognition without having some feeling of accountability to God. The little storms that seem to afflict every marriage become of small consequence while kneeling before the Lord and addressing him as a suppliant son and daughter.

Your daily conversations with him will bring peace into your hearts and a joy into your lives that can come from no other source. Your companionship will sweeten through the years. Your love will strengthen. Your appreciation one for another will grow.

Your children will be blessed with a sense of security that comes of living in a home where dwells the Spirit of God. They will know and love parents who respect one another, and a spirit of respect will grow in their own hearts. They will experience the security of kind words quietly spoken. They will be sheltered by a father and mother who, living honestly with God, live honestly with one another and with their fellowmen. They will mature with a sense of appreciation, having heard their parents in prayer express gratitude for blessings great and small. They will grow with faith in the living God. ("Cornerstones of a Happy Home," Husbands and Wives Fireside Satellite Broadcast, January 29, 1984.)

Let every family in this Church have prayer together. Now, it is important to have individual prayer, but it is a wonderful thing to have family prayer. Pray to your Father in Heaven in faith. Pray in the name of the Lord Jesus Christ. You can do nothing better for your children than to have them taking their turn in the family prayer, expressing gratitude for their blessings. If they do that while they are young they will grow with a spirit of thanksgiving in their hearts. (Naha Okinawa Stake and Okinawa Military District Fireside, May 20, 1996.)

If there be any among you who are not having family prayer, let that practice start now, to get on your knees together, if you can possibly do it, every morning and every evening, and speak to the Lord and express your thanks, invoke His blessings upon the needy of the earth, and speak to Him concerning your own well-being. I believe that God our Eternal Father will hear our prayers, and I urge you to have family prayers. Great blessings will come to your children if you will pray together, calling upon the Lord, expressing your thanks and presenting before Him the desire of your hearts. (Buenos Aires Argentina Fireside, November 12, 1996.)

FASTING

I would suppose that on this campus at least 20,000 people have been fasting and that you have accompanied your fasting with earnest prayer. I think that's a most remarkable phenomenon. Most of you, I assume, have fasted and prayed with a purpose—that you might find answers to perplexing personal problems or the needs of others, or that moisture might fall upon these arid western lands. I hope you haven't prayed for snow with the hope that you could go skiing on Sunday.

I believe that the Lord will hear our earnest supplications, if we will back up our fasting and prayers with goodness in our lives. ("Forget Yourself," *BYU Devotional Speeches of the Year,* March 6, 1977, p. 43.)

It is not a burden to refrain from two meals a month and give the value thereof to assist in caring for the poor. It is, rather, a blessing. Not only will physical benefits flow from the observance of this principle, but spiritual values also. Our program of the fast day and the fast offering is so simple and so beautiful that I cannot understand why people everywhere do not take it up. Hearings have recently been held in the Congress of the United States on a proposal to recommend to the president a day of fasting to raise funds for the starving people of Africa. Our own experience last spring was so easy of execution and so tremendously productive that our consecrations have blessed thousands without causing any of us to suffer in the least. ("'Let Us Move This Work Forward,'" *Ensign,* November 1985, p. 85.)

Out of a sense of love for the less fortunate among our own, let us observe the law of the fast, going without a little food— which we do not need—and contributing the value thereof and even more to help those who are in desperate circumstances. ("Let Love Be the Lodestar of Your Life," *Ensign,* May 1989, p. 66.)

FATHERHOOD

See also Family; Parenting

My phone rang one afternoon. The young man on the other end of the line said frantically that he needed to see me. . . . I told him to come and asked my secretary to change [my] other appointments. In a few minutes he walked in, a boy with a hunted and haunted look. His hair was long, his appearance miserable. I invited him to sit and to talk openly and frankly. I assured him of my interest in his problem and of my desire to help him.

He unraveled a story distressing and miserable. He was in serious trouble. He had broken the law, he had been unclean, he had blighted his life. Now in his extremity there had come a realization of the terrible plight in which he found himself. He needed help beyond his own strength, and he pleaded for it. I asked him if his father knew of his difficulties. He replied by saying that he could not talk with his father, that his father hated him.

I happened to know his father, and I know that his father did not hate him. He loved him and mourned and grieved for him, but that father had an uncontrolled temper. Whenever he disciplined his children, he lost control and destroyed both them and himself.

As I looked across the desk at that trembling, broken young man, estranged from a father he considered his enemy, I thought of some great words of revealed truth given through the Prophet Joseph Smith. They set forth in essence the governing spirit of the priesthood, and I believe they apply to the government of our homes. Let me read them to you.

"No power or influence can or ought to be maintained . . . , only by persuasion, by long-suffering, by gentleness and meekness, and by love unfeigned;

"By kindness, and pure knowledge, which shall greatly enlarge the soul without hypocrisy and without guile—"

I believe those marvelous and simple words set forth the spirit in which we should stand as fathers. Do they mean that we should not exercise discipline, that we should not reprove? Listen to these further words:

"Reproving betimes with sharpness [When? While angry or in a fit of temper? No—] when moved upon by the Holy Ghost; and then showing forth afterwards an increase of love toward him whom thou hast reproved, lest he esteem thee to be his enemy;

"That he may know that thy faithfulness is stronger than the cords of death." (D&C 121:41–44.)

This . . . is the key to government in the home directed by the Holy Spirit. ("Feed the Spirit—Nourish the Soul," *Improvement Era*, December 1967, p. 87.)

You men who are husbands and fathers should have had kindled in your hearts tonight . . . a resolve so to conduct yourselves in your homes as to be worthy of the love, the respect, the honor, the companionship of your wives and your children. Holding the priesthood does not give any man the right to domineer over those for whom he should show the greatest of love and the greatest of consideration. Each of us should go home this night with a stronger resolve in our hearts to live worthy of the companionship of those who love us most and whom we should love and honor and respect without reservation. ("The Good and Faithful Servants," *Ensign*, November 1984, p. 48.)

I repeat that plea to all fathers. Yours is the basic and inescapable responsibility to stand as head of the family. That does not carry with it any implication of dictatorship or unrighteous dominion. It carries with it a mandate that fathers provide for the needs of their families. Those needs are more than food, clothing, and shelter. Those needs include righteous direction and the teaching, by example as well as precept, of basic principles of honesty, integrity, service, respect for the rights of others, and an understanding that we are accountable for that which we do in this life, not only to one another but also to the God of heaven, who is our Eternal Father. . . .

. . . With the obligation to beget goes the responsibility to nurture, to protect, to teach, to guide in righteousness and truth. Yours is the power and the responsibility to preside in a home where there is peace and security, love and harmony. ("Bring Up a Child in the Way He Should Go," *Ensign*, November 1993, p. 60.)

It is a tremendous responsibility to be a father in The Church of Jesus Christ of Latter-day Saints. It is a wonderful responsibility to be a man who stands at the head of his family as one who holds the priesthood of God with authority to speak in the name of God. Fathers, are you the kind of father you ought to be? (Anchorage Alaska Regional Conference, June 18, 1995.)

FEAR

Who among us can say that he or she has not felt fear? I know of no one who has been entirely spared. Some, of course, experience fear to a greater degree than do others. Some are able to rise above it quickly, but others are trapped and pulled down by it and even driven to defeat. We suffer from the fear of ridicule, the fear of failure, the fear of loneliness, the fear of ignorance. Some fear the present, some the future. Some carry the burden of sin and would give almost anything to unshackle themselves from those burdens but fear to change their lives. Let us recognize that fear comes not of God, but rather that this gnawing, destructive element comes from the adversary of truth and righteousness. Fear is the antithesis of faith. It is corrosive in its effects, even deadly.

"For God hath not given us the spirit of fear; but of power, and of love, and of a sound mind."

These principles are the great antidotes to the fears that rob us of our strength and sometimes knock us down to defeat. They give us power.

What power? The power of the gospel, the power of truth, the power of faith, the power of the priesthood. ("'God Hath Not Given Us the Spirit of Fear,'" *Ensign*, October 1984, p. 2.)

Is there a missionary who has never felt fear? I know of none. Of course we feel fear now and again. Some are fearful of tracting. Some are fearful of their own capacity. Some are fearful of dogs. Some are fearful of speaking out in declaration of the truth. All of us experience fear now and again. But God has not given us the spirit of fear. That comes from the adversary. When we recognize that, then we can tell the adversary to get behind us, and we can go forward with courage.

God has given us power, and love, and a sound mind. What do these mean? I think they mean the power of our calling, the power of the priesthood, the power of our message; love for the word of the Lord, love for Him whom we serve, and love for those we teach; and a sound mind—the simple sweet beauty of the gospel. (Missionary Training Satellite Broadcast, May 11, 1993.)

When I went on a mission, my father gave me a little card with a verse from the New Testament, the words of the Lord to the centurion servant who brought news concerning the little daughter of the centurion. Those words, "be not afraid, only believe." I commend those words to each of us, my brothers and sisters. You do not need to fear if you are on the side of right. (Oahu Hawaii Regional Conference, February 18, 1996.)

We believe in being true. That means loyal. That means standing up without fear in the face of the storm of criticism that might come against you. (Berlin Germany Regional Conference, June 16, 1996.)

You must be a leader, as a member of this Church, in those causes for which this Church stands. Do not let fear overcome your efforts. . . . The adversary of all truth would put into your heart a reluctance to make an effort. Cast that fear aside and be valiant in the cause of truth and righteousness and faith. If you now decide that this will become the pattern of your life, you will not have to make that decision again. ("Stand Up for Truth," BYU Devotional Address, September 17, 1996.)

So many of us are fearful of what our peers will say, that we will be looked upon with disdain and criticized if we stand for what is right. But I remind you that "wickedness never was happiness" (Alma 41:10). Evil never was happiness. Sin never was happiness. Happiness lies in the power and the love and the sweet simplicity of the gospel of Jesus Christ.

We need not be [afraid]. We need not slink off in a corner, as it were. We need not be ashamed. We have the greatest thing in the world, the gospel of the risen Lord. Paul gives us a mandate: "Be not thou therefore ashamed of the testimony of our Lord" (2 Timothy 1:8). ("Converts and Young Men," *Ensign,* May 1997, p. 49.)

FELLOWSHIPPING

See also Reactivation and Retention

We hear complaints that in high schools where Latter-day Saints are in the majority, those not of our faith feel discriminated against. Most of you will go on missions, we hope all of you. You will learn the importance of friendshipping and fellowshipping. Now is the time to practice these principles, to reach out with appreciation and kindness to others. Many a young man has come into this Church because of the friendship of a high school associate. I earnestly hope that no boy within the sound of my voice will ever do anything to prejudice an associate against the Church or its people. . . .

What I am speaking against is any attitude whatever that demeans, that downgrades, that leads to evil speaking of another. ("Four B's for Boys," *Ensign,* November 1981, p. 41.)

We all look upon one another as brothers and sisters, regardless of the land we call home. We belong to what may be regarded as the greatest society of friends on the face of the earth.

When the emperor of Japan was in the United States some few years ago, I attended a luncheon for him in San Francisco. We sat at a table with three other couples who had had extensive experience in Japan and who had resided there at one time or another while working in government, business, or educational employment. One of the gentlemen said to me, "I have never seen anything like your people. We had many Americans come to Japan while we were there, and most of them experienced a severe cultural adjustment and much loneliness and homesickness. But whenever we had a Mormon family come, they had many instant friends. Members of your church in Japan seemed to know when they were expected and were there to welcome them. They and their children were immediately integrated socially as well as into your religious community. There seemed to be no culture shock and no loneliness. My wife and I talked about it many times."

That is the way it should be. We must be friends. We must love and honor and respect and assist one another. Wherever Latter-day Saints go, they are made welcome, because Latter-day Saints are mutual believers in the divinity of the Lord Jesus Christ and are engaged together in his great cause.

We speak of the fellowship of the Saints. This is and must be a very real thing. We must never permit this spirit of brotherhood and sisterhood to weaken. We must constantly cultivate it. It is an important aspect of the gospel. ("'Fear Not to Do Good,'" *Ensign*, May 1983, pp. 79–80.)

I hope you will develop a spirit of fellowship, a social ease, the capacity to mix and mingle with people wherever you meet them, of low caste or high caste, recognizing their strengths and powers and capacities and goodness. . . .

A vibrant personality that comes of the capacity to listen and learn, that comes of the ability to contribute without boring, that comes of a talent for mingling and mixing with people in a constructive way is something very precious. ("Out of Your Experience Here," *BYU 1990–1991 Devotional and Fireside Speeches,* October 16, 1990, p. 29.)

I received a letter this morning. I think I would like to read it to you. I hope that you will not consider it egotistical for me to do so.

"What a wonderful Conference! Your closing remarks concerning Brigham Young's rescue parties touched our family's heart and we resolved to set out on our rescue mission without delay. We pulled out of the stake center [Sunday afternoon] and headed directly to the humble home of a struggling single parent mother of two who hasn't been out to Church in years (and who has carefully evaded her visiting teachers). We happened to catch her in her driveway, and we told her that you and the bishop had sent us. Her heart was touched. She said that she works at a hospital till 2 A.M. most Sundays. When we asked if we could bring her children to Church with us, she explained that her ten-year-old daughter has no Sunday clothes and that her fourteen-year-old son had felt embarrassed to attend because he felt he didn't fit in. We told the mom we would take care of the needed clothes. We then invited them to Sunday spaghetti dinner that took place thirty minutes later, introduced the boy to our nephew who is in his quorum, and arranged to pick the boy up for Mutual this week. The mom and sister promised to go to Church with us in two weeks when the mom has her Sunday off. (Don't worry, we won't let them forget!)"

That is the whole thing, when all is said and done, to go out and get in our cars and drive from a Church parking lot to someone who has been neglected for a long time and needs a little attention, to lift and cheer and comfort and love and bless. "Inasmuch as ye have done it unto one of the least of these my brethren, ye have done it unto me" (Matt. 25:40). (Meeting with General Authorities and Wives, October 9, 1996.)

FINANCES

See Church of Jesus Christ of Latter-day Saints, The:
Church Finances; Debt; Self-Reliance; Thrift

FIRST VISION

See also Prophets, Latter-day: Joseph Smith

A most remarkable manifestation occurred on a spring morning in the year 1820 when the Father and the Son appeared to the boy Joseph Smith. All of the good we see in the Church today is the fruit of that remarkable visitation, a testimony of which has touched the hearts of millions in many lands. I add my own witness, given me by the Spirit, that the Prophet's description of that marvelous event is true, that God the Eternal Father and the risen Lord Jesus Christ spoke with him on that occasion in a conversation as real and personal and intimate as are our conversations today. (*Be Thou an Example* [Salt Lake City: Deseret Book, 1981], p. 10.)

I thank my Father in Heaven for the testimony I have of the reality of the First Vision. I have stood among the trees where Joseph knelt as a boy, and heard the whisperings of the Spirit that it happened as he said it happened. ("My Testimony," *Ensign*, November 1993, p. 51.)

I read this morning a part of Joseph Smith's testimony of the First Vision. You are all familiar with it. His going into a grove, pleading with the Lord, a light shining above him, and then the appearance of the Father and the Son. I read that testimony and thought of it. I said to myself, "If every one of us knew in our hearts that that statement is true, then we would know that all else which follows it, which came through the restoration of the gospel, is true also." And we would walk and live with greater faithfulness.

Tithing would not be a problem with us. Temple service would not be a problem with us. Keeping the Sabbath day holy would not be a problem with us. We would have no inclination to go to the store and buy things on the Sabbath day. Missionary service would be no problem with us.

All else that follows would be true. We would know it in our hearts if we had a solid, firm, immovable conviction of the truth and validity of that great vision wherein God the Eternal Father and the risen Lord Jesus Christ appeared to the boy Joseph Smith and the Father said, "This is My Beloved Son. Hear Him!" (Joseph Smith History 1:17).

I wish all of you would sit down with your family and read those words again, that testimony of the Prophet Joseph Smith, stated with simplicity, with honesty. Then ask the Lord to put it into your hearts and give you the privilege of a testimony of its truth. And whenever you have any doubt of the practice of this Church, you can reflect on that. If that opening of the curtain of light and knowledge which ushered in this, the dispensation of the fulness of times, is true, then all else which the Prophet taught is true also. (Magna Utah South Stake Conference, October 22, 1995.)

This is where the First Vision occurred. This is the pivotal thing of our story. Every claim that we make concerning divine authority, every truth that we offer concerning the validity of this work, all finds its root in the First Vision of the boy prophet. Without it we would not have anything much to say. This was the great curtain-raiser on the dispensation of the fulness of times, when God promised that He would restore all the power, the gifts, the blessings, of all previous dispensations in one great summing up. (New York Rochester Missionary Meeting, July 12, 1996.)

And then came that most glorious of all manifestations, the manifestation of the Father and the Son to that boy of fourteen years of age, who had gone into the woods in response to the invitation and challenge of James: "If any of you lack wisdom, let him ask of God, that giveth to all men liberally, and upbraideth not; and it shall be given him" (James 1:5). What a great promise! I sometimes wish that Joseph had added, in writing his history, the next verse: "But let him ask in faith, nothing wavering. For he that wavereth is like a wave of the sea driven with the wind and tossed" (James 1:6). There must be faith.

Joseph went in as a boy. I have wondered at times why the Lord would have him go in as a fourteen-year-old boy. Why didn't he wait until he was twenty or thirty or forty, when he would have had the weight of some bit of authority that comes with age? He went in—the Lord permitted it, responded to his inquiry—because he came in perfect trust. There was no doubt in his mind. He said that if anyone needed wisdom, he needed wisdom, and he asked for it with full confidence that something would happen as a result of his prayer.

What did happen, of course, is marvelous and wonderful and quite without compare with anything that had ever happened before. There was the Father, the greatest of all, the God of the universe, and His Beloved Son, the resurrected Redeemer of the world. I do not know how long the conversation took. We do not have all the language, of course. We do not have anything of Joseph's prayer. . . . But Joseph Smith learned in those few minutes, however long or brief, more about the nature of God than all of the learned divines of all time had ever learned. What a remarkable thing it was. (New York Rochester Missionary Meeting, July 12, 1996.)

That becomes the hinge pin on which this whole cause turns. If the First Vision was true, if it actually happened, then the Book of Mormon is true. Then we have the priesthood. Then we have the Church organization and all of the other keys and blessings of authority which we say we have. If the First Vision did not occur, then we are involved in a great sham. It is just that simple. (New York Rochester Missionary Meeting, July 12, 1996.)

Joseph Smith saw the Father and the Son in the Sacred Grove where we stood yesterday. It happened. It was real. If the First Vision occurred, then everything else in connection with the restoration occurred also. That is the great keystone of our faith and our testimony. (Tulsa Oklahoma Youth Conference, July 14, 1996.)

FORGIVENESS

See also Repentance

It becomes us as a grateful people to reach out with a spirit of forgiveness and an attitude of love and compassion toward those whom we have felt may have wronged us.

We have need of this. The whole world has need of it. It is of the very essence of the gospel of Jesus Christ. He taught it. He exemplified it as none other has exemplified it. In the time of his agony on the cross of Calvary, with vile and hateful accusers before him, they who had brought him to this terrible crucifixion, he cried out, "Father, forgive them; for they know not what they do" (Luke 23:34).

None of us is called on to forgive so generously, but each of us is under a divinely spoken obligation to reach out with pardon and mercy. . . .

. . . We see the need for it in the homes of the people, where tiny molehills of misunderstanding are fanned into mountains of argument. We see it among neighbors, where insignificant differences lead to undying bitterness. We see it in business associates who quarrel and refuse to compromise and forgive when, in most instances, if there were a willingness to sit down together and speak quietly one to another, the matter could be resolved to the blessing of all. ("'Of You It Is Required to Forgive,'" *Ensign*, November 1980, p. 61.)

How difficult it is for any of us to forgive those who have injured us. We are all prone to brood on the evil done us. That brooding becomes as a gnawing and destructive canker. Is there a virtue more in need of application in our time than the virtue of forgiving and forgetting? There are those who would look upon this as a sign of weakness. Is it? I submit that it takes neither strength nor intelligence to brood in anger over wrongs suffered, to go through life with a spirit of vindictiveness, to dissipate one's abilities in planning retribution. There is no peace in the nursing of a grudge. There is no happiness in living for the day when you can "get even." ("'Of You It Is Required to Forgive,'" *Ensign*, November 1980, p. 62.)

If there be any within the sound of my voice who have harbored grudges, who have let hatred develop in their hearts one toward another, I ask you to make the effort to turn around. Hatred always fails and bitterness always destroys, but "charity never faileth." (1 Cor 13:8.) ("'Charity Never Faileth,'" *Ensign*, November 1981, p. 98.)

If there be any who nurture in their hearts the poisonous brew of enmity toward another, I plead with you to ask the Lord for strength to forgive. This expression of desire will be of the very substance of your repentance. It may not be easy, and it may not come quickly. But if you will seek it with sincerity and cultivate it, it *will* come. And even though he whom you have forgiven continues to pursue and threaten you, you will know you have done what you could to effect a reconciliation. There will come into your heart a peace otherwise unattainable. That peace will be the peace of Him who said: "For if ye forgive men their trespasses, your heavenly Father will also forgive you: But if you forgive not men their trespasses, neither will your Father forgive your trespasses." (Matthew 6:14–15.) (*Be Thou an Example* [Salt Lake City: Deseret Book, 1981], pp. 50–51.)

Are not the words of Abraham Lincoln beautiful which he spoke out of the tragedy of a terrible civil war: "With malice toward none, with charity for all, . . . let us . . . bind up the nation's wounds." (Second Inaugural Address, March 4, 1865.) . . .

. . . Let us bind up the wounds—oh, the many wounds that have been caused by cutting words, by stubbornly cultivated grievances, by scheming plans to "get even" with those who may have wronged us. We all have a little of this spirit of revenge in us. Fortunately we all have the power to rise above it, if we will "clothe [ourselves] with the bond of charity, as with a mantle, which is the bond of perfectness and peace." (D&C 88:125.)

"To err is human, to forgive divine." (Alexander Pope, *An Essay on Criticism*.) There is no peace in harboring old grudges. There is no peace in reflecting on the pain of old wounds. There is peace only in repentance and forgiveness. This is the sweet peace of the Christ, who said, "Blessed are the peacemakers; for they shall be called the children of God." (Matthew 5:9.) (*Be Thou an Example* [Salt Lake City: Deseret Book, 1981], p. 52.)

"Ye have heard that it hath been said, Thou shalt love thy neighbor, and hate thine enemy.

"But I say unto you, Love your enemies, bless them that curse you, do good to them that hate you, and pray for them which despitefully use you, and persecute you." (Matthew 5:43–44.)

Most of us have not reached that stage of compassion and love and forgiveness. It is not easy. It requires a self-discipline almost greater than we are capable of. But as we try, we come to know that there is a resource of healing, that there is a mighty power of healing in Christ, and that if we are to be His true servants we must not only exercise that healing power in behalf of others, but, perhaps more important, inwardly. ("The Healing Power of Christ," *Ensign*, November 1988, pp. 54, 59.)

"Behold, he who has repented of his sins, the same is forgiven, and I, the Lord, remember them no more." (D&C 58:42.)

So many of us are prone to say we forgive, when in fact we are unwilling to forget. If the Lord is willing to forget the sins of the repentant, then why are so many of us inclined to bring up the past again and again? Here is a great lesson we all need to learn. There is no true forgiveness without forgetting. ("The Order and Will of God," *Ensign*, January 1989, p. 5.)

We come not to judge, to censure, or to renew the passions of the past, but rather to heal and anoint with the balm of peace and love, that balm which comes of the spirit of Jesus Christ our Lord, in whom we all believe and from whom we draw forgiveness and fellowship and healing. (Funeral Service for Rex E. Lee, March 15, 1996.)

Teach our people always to forgive and forget. Get it behind them. We carry the cankering evil of memories of little things that destroy us and destroy our feelings, whereas with just a little turnaround, a little kindness, we could bestow blessings upon people. (Pittsburgh Pennsylvania Regional Conference, priesthood leadership session, April 27, 1996.)

Don't ever feel that you can't be forgiven. Our Father in Heaven loves you. He is your Father. He is your Heavenly Parent. He has great concern for you. He reaches out to you in love and in forgiveness. . . . The Lord has said, "I the Lord will forgive whom I will forgive, but of you it is required to forgive all men" (D&C 64:10). That is a mandate to us. Our Father in Heaven will take care of the forgiveness. You put it behind you. You talk with your bishop. You live in righteousness. You do what is right and things will work out for you. I don't want to see you going around brooding forever about something, some little thing, perhaps, that may have happened, or some serious thing that may have happened. There is hope. There is forgiveness. There is peace for those who follow the right path. (Southern Utah University Institute of Religion Devotional, February 11, 1997.)

FREEDOM

A terrible price has been paid by those who have gone before us, this that we might have the blessings of liberty and peace. I stood not long ago at Valley Forge, where George Washington and his ragged army spent the winter of 1776. As I did so, I thought of a scene from Maxwell Anderson's play in which Washington looks on a little group of his soldiers, shoveling the cold earth over a dead comrade, and says grimly, "This liberty will look easy by and by when nobody dies to get it."

How we need to kindle in the hearts of youth an old-fashioned love of country and a reverence for the land of their birth. But we shall not do it with tawdry political maneuvering and enormous handouts for which nothing is given in return.

Love of country is born of nobler stuff—of the challenge of struggle that makes precious the prize that's earned. ("A Charter for Youth," *Improvement Era*, December 1965, pp. 1124–25.)

We were driven to the Marine base chapel [in DaNang, South Vietnam] where we met with our brethren. I shall never forget that picture or that meeting. What a sight they were! What a wonderful group, these young brethren of ours. We loved them the minute we looked into their eyes. Most of them looked so young. They were dressed in battle fatigues, with mud on their boots. They had come down from the Rock Pile and Marble Mountain along the DMZ, where the fighting has been rough and vicious, and where the smell of cordite and death are in the air. As they entered the chapel, they stacked their M-16 automatic rifles along the two back rows and sat down, many of them with a pistol on the right side and a knife on the left side.

This was district conference in the Northern District of South Vietnam. The program of the services contained the names of three who had been recently killed.

After the meeting we ate from a chow line and then stood about and talked for hours. It was an experience both wonderful and depressing to be so close to these good young men, men who hold and honor the priesthood, men who are valiantly doing their duty as citizens of this country, but who would rather be doing something else. I thought as I talked with them that they ought to be in school, at B.Y.U. or Ricks or at any one of a score of other good institutions, acquiring creative and challenging skills rather than walking fearsome patrols in the dark of the Asian jungle where death comes so quickly and quietly and definitely. These are the boys who ran and laughed and played ball back home, who drove the highways in old jalopies, who danced with lovely girls at the Gold and Green balls, who administered the sacrament on Sunday. These are boys who come from good homes where the linen is clean and showers are hot, who now sweat night and day in this troubled land, who are shot at and who shoot back, who have seen gaping wounds in a buddy's chest and who have killed those who would have killed them. And I thought of the terrible inequality of sacrifice involved in the cause of human liberty. ("Asian Diary," *BYU Speeches of the Year,* January 10, 1967, pp. 6–7.)

Religion and the free exercise thereof, the right to worship God according to one's own conscience—how precious and treasured a boon it is. How necessary that it be safeguarded. Established religion becomes the guardian of the conscience of the people, the teacher of moral values, the defender of belief in the Almighty, the bridge between God and man. No people will live for long in freedom without it. The history of communism, whose founding father declared religion to be the opiate of the people, speaks with harshness and suffering concerning this basic matter.

Congress shall not abridge "the freedom of speech, or of the press; or the right of the people peaceably to assemble, and to petition the government for a redress of grievances."

The history of tyrants is a history of the muzzling of free expression and the denial of assembly. ("The Bill of Rights," Bonneville International Corporation "Gathering of Eagles," June 20, 1991.)

My forebears left there [England] in early times, two of them on the *Mayflower*, another in 1635, whose son became governor of Plymouth Colony, and others who fought in the Revolutionary War, which made of America a separate nation, but still joined together in brotherhood with a common language, a common culture, a common system of justice, a solemn respect for the dignity of man, and above all an attitude that human freedom and liberty are more precious than life itself. (Convocation for Honorary Degrees, BYU, March 5, 1996.)

We went this morning, after our arrival here, to the international cemetery. It's a beautiful place. All of you are familiar with it. I have been there before. It speaks of the price that has been paid for the liberty which we enjoy in this good land. How thankful we ought to be for those who gave their lives for the liberty and freedom which we enjoy. (Pusan Korea Fireside, May 21, 1996.)

My eldest brother lies buried in an American military cemetery in France. As I have stood before the cross that marks his grave, I have thanked the God of heaven for the cause for which he died, for the great and eternal concepts of human dignity, for the precious boon of liberty, for freedom to worship, to speak, to assemble, which, I believe are the gifts of a beneficent providence, codified in the language of our national charter.

("Preserving Our Trust in God," American Legion Patriotic Religious Service, September 1, 1996.)

GAMBLING

I am advised that some twenty-two states in the United States now have state lotteries. Proposals have been placed before Congress for a federal lottery.

There can be no question about the moral ramifications of this practice. A lottery is a form of gambling, regardless of the high-sounding purpose it may be advocated to meet. Lottery fever recently peaked when New York State announced that three winning tickets would split $41 million. People lined up to buy tickets. One winning ticket was held by 21 factory workers, with 778 second-place winners, and 113,000 who received token amounts. That may sound pretty good.

But there were also 35,998,956 losers, each of whom had paid for a chance to win.

The question of lotteries is a moral question. That government now promotes what it once enforced laws against becomes a sad reflection on the deterioration of public and political morality in the nation.

President Brigham Young spoke out against gambling. President Lorenzo Snow spoke against it. President Joseph F. Smith spoke very strongly against it; and, in 1925, President Heber J. Grant and his counselors said, "The Church has been and now is unalterably opposed to gambling in any form." (*Improvement Era*, Sept. 1926, p. 1100.)

Lotteries are advocated as a means of relieving the burden of taxation. That may be a political matter. But a tax by any other name is still a tax, except in this case the burden usually falls on the poor who can least afford to pay it. As an editorial in *USA Today* stated recently: "Lotteries aren't painless—the overwhelming majority of players always lose. The game takes bread and money from the poor. And it is one more temptation for the compulsive gamblers who ruin careers and families with their addiction." (*USA Today*, 26 Aug. 1985.) In this context, it becomes a moral question. ("Questions and Answers," *Ensign*, November 1985, p. 52.)

GATHERING OF ISRAEL

See Missionary Work

GENEALOGY

See Family History Work

GENERAL CONFERENCE

My brethren and sisters, I rejoice with you in the attendance here of bishops and presidents of stakes from foreign lands. This is a great and significant day in the history of the Church, and foretells, I think, the time when these general conferences shall become in reality great parliaments of men gathered from over the world, endowed with the Holy Priesthood, whose only desire is to promote the cause of peace and goodness among the people of the earth. (Conference Report, April 1962, pp. 70–71.)

It's unlikely that we will remember very many of the words that we've heard during the meetings of this conference. But I hope that we shall be able to "hum" the spirit of this conference and that we shall carry with us a great feeling of uplift because of our participation together. It has been a glorious time. The Spirit of the Lord has been with us. We have every reason to be grateful. We have been refreshed in our testimonies and strengthened in our faith.

We have heard sound counsel from the brethren who have spoken to us. Having heard it, I hope we will read it when the proceedings of the conference are published, and again savor to our benefit that which has been said. ("Let Us Go Forward!" *Ensign*, November 1983, p. 74.)

These general conferences each six months are occasions to grow in faith and in love for the Lord and His eternal work. ("'A Prophet's Testimony,'" *Ensign*, May 1993, p. 93.)

My brethren and sisters, it is wonderful that we have the opportunity of meeting together each six months in these great world conferences. We gather from over the earth to bear our testimonies one to another, to hear instruction, to mingle as brethren and sisters. We partake of that sociality which is so pleasant and so important a part of the culture of this great organization. ("As We Gather Together," *Ensign*, November 1995, p. 4.)

GOD THE FATHER

To me it is a significant and marvelous thing that in establishing and opening this dispensation our Father did so with a revelation of himself and of his Son Jesus Christ, as if to say to all the world that he was weary of the attempts of men, earnest though these attempts might have been, to define and describe him. Strange as it seems, we alone, among all the great organizations that worship God, have a true description and a true definition of him. The experience of Joseph Smith in a few moments in the grove on a spring day in 1820, brought more light and knowledge and understanding of the personality and reality and substance of God and his Beloved Son than men had arrived at during centuries of speculation. ("The Cornerstone," *Improvement Era*, June 1960, p. 425.)

God is in form like a man. He is personal. He speaks, and has spoken to man. He is exalted, and by human standards he is all-wise and all-powerful. But he is merciful and kind. He is the father of the spirits of all men, and he has a father's consideration for and interest in his children. His work and his glory lie in their eternal welfare. (*What of the Mormons?* pamphlet, 1982, p. 6.)

The gospel for me is not complex. It is a beautiful and simple pattern, a constant source of strength, a wellspring of faith. The keystone of that doctrine is that God is our Eternal Father and Jesus is the Christ, our living Redeemer. We are sons and daughters of God. He loves us and invites us to love him, showing that love through service to others of his children. His Beloved Son is our Savior, who gave his life on the cross of Calvary as a vicarious sacrifice for the sins of mankind. By the power of his divine Sonship he rose from the grave, becoming "the firstfruits of them that slept" (1 Cor. 15:20), assuring for all a resurrection from the dead and inviting each of us to partake of eternal life according to our obedience to his laws and commandments.

They, that is, the Father and the Son, appeared to the boy Joseph Smith in a most glorious and wonderful manifestation to open this, the dispensation of the fulness of times. (See D&C 112:30.) All of the elements of previous bestowals of divine teaching and authority are now brought together through restoration in a final and everlasting dispensation. ("Five Million Members—A Milestone and Not a Summit," *Ensign*, May 1982, pp. 44–45.)

I believe without equivocation or reservation in God, the Eternal Father. He is my Father, the Father of my spirit, and the Father of the spirits of all men. He is the great Creator, the Ruler of the Universe. He directed the creation of this earth on which we live. In His image man was created. He is personal. He is real. He is individual. He has "a body of flesh and bones as tangible as man's" (D&C 130:22). (*The Father, Son, and Holy Ghost*, booklet [Salt Lake City: Bookcraft, 1988], p. 4.)

Each of us is a dual being of spiritual entity and physical entity. All know of the reality of physical death, when the body dies; and each of us also knows that the spirit lives on as an individual entity, and that at some time, under the divine plan made possible by the sacrifice of the Son of God, the spirit and the body will be reunited. Jesus' declaration that God is a spirit no more denies that he has a body than does the statement that I am a spirit while also having a body.

I do not equate my body with His in its refinement, in its capacity, in its beauty and radiance. His is eternal. Mine is mortal. But that only increases my reverence for Him. I worship Him "in spirit and in truth." I look to Him as my strength. I pray to Him for wisdom beyond my own. I seek to love Him with all my heart, might, mind, and strength. His wisdom is greater than the wisdom of all men. His power is greater than the power of nature, for He is the Creator Omnipotent. His love is greater than the love of any other, for His love encompasses all of His children, and it is His work and His glory to bring to pass the immortality and eternal life of His sons and daughters of all generations (see Moses 1:39). . . .

This is the Almighty of whom I stand in awe and reverence. It is He to whom I look in fear and trembling. It is He whom I worship and unto whom I give honor and praise and glory. He is my Heavenly Father, who has invited me to come unto Him in prayer, to speak with Him, with the promised assurance that He will hear and respond. (*The Father, Son, and Holy Ghost,* booklet [Salt Lake City: Bookcraft, 1988], pp. 5–6.)

God our Eternal Father lives. I know that. I don't understand the wonder of His majesty. I can't comprehend the glory of the Godhead, but I know that He is my Father, notwithstanding all that, and that I can speak with Him in prayer and that He will hear and listen. I know that. (Ketchikan Alaska Fireside, June 22, 1995.)

I want to give you my testimony of this work and I want to say it in such a way that you can remember that I said it. I know this work is true. I know that God our Eternal Father lives. I am thankful for the knowledge that He loves us as His children. I am grateful that I feel in my heart a great love for Him. I know He lives, my Father in Heaven. I can scarcely comprehend the wonder of it all. He who is the Creator and Governor of the universe knows me, knows you, each of you. He loves you; He is concerned for you. (Promontory Utah Branch Sacrament Meeting, October 15, 1995.)

GODHEAD

The Father, the Son, and the Holy Ghost are distinct beings, but they are one in purpose and effort. They are united as one in bringing to pass the grand, divine plan for the salvation and exaltation of the children of God.

In His great, moving prayer in the Garden before His betrayal, Christ pleaded with His Father concerning the Apostles, whom He loved, saying:

"Neither pray I for these alone, but for them also which shall believe on me through their word;

"That they all may be one; as thou, Father, art in me, and I in thee, that they also may be one in us" (John 17:20–21).

It is perfect unity between the Father, the Son, and the Holy Ghost that binds these three into the oneness of the divine Godhead. (*The Father, Son, and Holy Ghost,* booklet [Salt Lake City: Bookcraft, 1988], pp. 12–13.)

"We believe in God the Eternal Father, and in His Son, Jesus Christ, and in the Holy Ghost." People cannot understand why we separate the three members of the Godhead into individuals. We declare to all the world that God, our Eternal Father, is in very deed the ruler of the universe. He is the Almighty. He is the great Creator. He is above all. He is our Father and our God. Somehow He has the capacity to listen and hear and answer when we as individuals pray to Him.

We believe and testify of the Lord Jesus Christ, our Savior and our Redeemer, He who under the direction of His Father was the creator of the earth; He who was the great Jehovah and became the Messiah; He who left His home on high and condescended as the Son of God to come down among men, here to be abused and beaten, reviled, and crucified for the sins of mankind.

We believe in the Holy Ghost as a personage of spirit, who can dwell within us and prompt us and bless us and give us knowledge of things divine. We are a peculiar people in our belief. (Berlin Germany Regional Conference, June 16, 1996.)

Every doctrine of this Church brings with it a feeling of its truth, and the fundamental doctrine above all other doctrine is the doctrine of the godhead. That each of us shall know that God our Eternal Father lives and that Jesus is the Christ . . . that is the great, primary responsibility of each of us; to know that God our Eternal Father lives; to know that Jesus is the Christ; to have that knowledge well up within us as a living fountain of great faith. (São Paulo Brazil Fireside, November 14, 1996.)

GOLDEN RULE

Said Jesus: "Whatsoever ye would that men should do to you, do ye even so to them." (Matt. 7:12.)

May I remind us . . . that if only each of us would reflect occasionally on that Christ-given mandate and make an effort to observe it, this would be a different world. There would be greater happiness in our homes; there would be kinder feelings among our associates; there would be much less of litigation and a greater effort to compose differences. There would be a new measure of love and appreciation and respect.

There would be more generous hearts, more thoughtful consideration and concern, and a greater desire to spread the gospel of peace and to advance the work of salvation among the children of men. ("'Do Ye Even So to Them,'" *Ensign*, December 1991, p. 4.)

I would like to tell you of [one] who lived the Golden Rule. . . . It occurred a few years ago in the winter at O'Hare International Airport, that great and busy place that serves the city of Chicago. On this occasion a severe storm had caused delays and cancellations of flights. The thousands of people stranded or delayed there were impatient and cross and irritable. Among those in trouble was a woman, a young mother standing in a long line at the check-in counter. She had a two-year-old child who was on the dirty floor at her feet. She was pregnant with another child. She was sick and weary to the bone. Her doctor had warned her against bending and picking up anything heavy, so as she moved slowly with the line she pushed her crying and hungry child with her foot. People who saw her made critical and cutting remarks, but none offered to help.

Then a man came toward her and with a smile of kindness on his face said, "You need help. Let me help you." He lifted the dirty, crying child from the floor and held her warmly in his arms. Taking a stick of gum from his pocket, he gave it to the child. Its sweet taste calmed her. He explained to those in the line the woman's need of help, then took her to the head of the line, spoke with the ticket agent, and soon had her checked in. He then found seats where she and her child could be comfortable, chatted for a moment, and disappeared into the crowd without giving his name. She went on her way to her home in Michigan.

Years later there came to the office of the President of the Church a letter which reads as follows:

"Dear President Kimball:

"I am a student at Brigham Young University. I have just returned from my mission in Munich, West Germany. I had a lovely mission and learned much. . . .

"I was sitting in priesthood meeting last week, when a story was told of a loving service which you performed some twenty-one years ago in the Chicago airport. The story told of how you met a young pregnant mother with a . . . screaming child, in . . . distress, waiting in a long line for her tickets. She was threatening miscarriage and therefore couldn't lift her child to comfort her. She had experienced four previous miscarriages, which gave added reason for the doctor's orders not to bend or lift.

"You comforted the crying child and explained the dilemma to the other passengers in line. This act of love took the strain and tension off my mother. I was born a few months later in Flint, Michigan.

"I just want to *thank you* for your love. *Thank you* for your example!"

The world truly would be a different place if each of us frequently and seriously considered our Lord's request: "Whatsoever ye would that men should do to you, do ye even so to them." (Matt. 7:12.) ("'Do Ye Even So to Them,'" *Ensign,* December 1991, p. 5.)

GOSPEL OF JESUS CHRIST

I have thought of the words of Paul to Agrippa when Paul described his experience on the road to Damascus. He saw a light from heaven and heard a voice speaking unto him, and he fell to the ground. And Jesus said, ". . . rise, and stand upon thy feet: for I have appeared unto thee . . . to make thee a minister and a witness . . . ;

"To open their eyes, and to turn them from darkness to light, and from the power of Satan unto God. . . ." (Acts 26:16, 18.)

This is the business of the Church—to open the vision of men to eternal verities, and to prompt them to take a stand for equity and decency, for virtue and sobriety and goodness. ("'Rise, and Stand upon Thy Feet,'" *Improvement Era*, December 1968, p. 68.)

To me the gospel is not a great mass of theological jargon. It is a simple and beautiful and logical thing, with one quiet truth following another in orderly sequence. I do not fret over the mysteries. I do not worry whether the heavenly gates swing or slide. I am only concerned that they open. I am not worried that the Prophet Joseph Smith gave a number of versions of the first vision any more than I am worried that there are four different writers of the gospels in the New Testament, each with his own perceptions, each telling the events to meet his own purpose for writing at the time.

I am more concerned with the fact that God has revealed in this dispensation a great and marvelous and beautiful plan that motivates men and women to love their Creator and their Redeemer, to appreciate and serve one another, to walk in faith on the road that leads to immortality and eternal life. ("'God Hath Not Given Us the Spirit of Fear,'" *Ensign*, October 1984, p. 5.)

I have seen miracles in my time. The greatest miracle of all, I believe, is the transformation that comes into the life of a man or a woman who accepts the restored gospel of Jesus Christ and tries to live it in his or her life. How thankful I am for the wonders of the restored gospel of Jesus Christ. It is indeed a marvelous work and a wonder, which has been brought to pass by the power of the Almighty in behalf of His sons and daughters. We of this season in His work can serve in a work of salvation in behalf of the whole human family, including all the generations of the sons and daughters of God who have lived upon the earth in past centuries. The work is true. (Vacaville/Santa Rosa California Regional Conference, May 21, 1995.)

This work, more than any other, will answer life's perplexing problems and lead the people to walk in paths of safety and happiness. (General Authority Training Meeting, April 2, 1996.)

If there is anything this troubled world needs it is the message of the Lord Jesus Christ. We need it. We do not pay much attention to it. We just read it and read on without paying very much attention to it. We need to do so more deeply and thoughtfully and prayerfully. . . .

There is nothing we can do that is more important than to listen to that which He has spoken. If we are His disciples, there cannot be conflict in our hearts. There cannot be jealousy. There cannot be meanness. There cannot be any of those things. We must stand a little taller, a little higher, and walk in the direction that He has pointed. "Be ye therefore perfect," said He, "even as your Father which is in heaven is perfect" (Matt. 5:48). None of us is perfect. He was the only perfect man to walk the earth. But we are moving toward perfection. (Israel District Fireside, June 21, 1996.)

I have here a letter. It comes from somewhere in Michigan. It states: "Two years ago we met two very special young men. They came due to a phone call I made several months earlier. I called in reply to a television ad for the Book of Mormon. The ad talked about families and of family home evenings. You see, I was concerned about my family. My son was twelve at the time and had just put another youngster in the neighborhood into the emergency room, causing the police to become involved and charges were being prepared. My daughter was hanging around with 'the Future Losers of America.' My wife was very frustrated and scared and so was I. Well, I just got frustrated enough that I didn't know what to do except work harder and ignore it all. Well, this little blue book [speaking of the Book of Mormon] arrived just before I went to go on vacation. I read it out of curiosity as I was raised strictly Baptist. I had heard a lot of things from people about 'those Mormons,' those awful Mormons, and what they believed.

"As I read my 'little blue book,' I began to realize that I had heard a lot of hogwash and more important that I had found something I had looked for all my life. . . .

"When I returned from my vacation, I found two young men at my door. They identified themselves as 'elders' of The Church of Jesus Christ of Latter-day Saints. I let them inside my home with my wife and kids. This was the beginning for me of great things. They were able to prove everything they said out of my King James Version Bible and they did so admirably.

"After about three weeks of grilling the elders, I decided to do something I had never done before. I got on my knees and prayed. Basically I said, 'If this is true, and you want me to be like them, show me.' All I can say is God answers prayers real loud. Within one week I had stopped drinking, smoking, given up coffee and tea and had absolutely no side effects or cravings.

"Then came the big step, telling my mother what I wanted to do. Her reply was a shock to me. It was simply that she and my step-dad knew some 'Mormons' and they and their families had something special, and that if this Church was what I wanted, that was great by her. I was baptized three weeks after meeting the elders. A few weeks later I had the privilege of baptizing my wife and children. Wow!

"The changes from there on in my family's lives were most unbelievable. The influence on my son of the missionaries was wonderful. My daughter immediately began to change her friends and attitudes. This created a total change in my wife as well. And then, last October, my wife and I along with our children were sealed in the temple in Chicago. Wow! Wow! Wow!

"In our brief tenure in the Church, I have been blessed to serve as the Deacon's quorum advisor and Assistant Scoutmaster, and am now in a Melchizedek Priesthood Quorum Presidency, first counselor. My wife is in the presidency of the Primary. My daughter is active in Young Women's and as I write this letter she is packing for girls camp. My son is working on his Eagle Scout award. My parents love this Church and can't tell enough people about the great things it has done for each of us, their children."

These are the wonderful things that bring happiness and gratitude into the lives of people. These become the miracle of Mormonism. (Temple Presidents Seminar, August 22, 1996.)

I want to thank you for living the gospel, for doing what is right, for keeping the commandments and living in faith. I want to thank you for the goodness of your lives. You are the kind of people who keep the Church going. You pay your tithing and your fast offerings, you observe the Word of Wisdom. You try to do the right thing. You have family home evening. You try to help one another. You read the scriptures. You are my kind of people—good people, faithful people. Thank you for being the kind of people you are.

I encourage you to go forward and live the gospel and love the gospel. Make it a part of your lives—this great and glorious thing which has come to us through the providence of the Almighty. Live the gospel. Love the gospel. Read the scriptures. You won't get a testimony of the Book of Mormon unless you read the Book of Mormon. You won't get a testimony of the Doctrine and Covenants unless you read the Doctrine and Covenants. Faith comes of drinking at the fountain of eternal truth. (Salt Lake Sugar House Stake Conference, January 5, 1997.)

The gospel of Jesus Christ is the only thing that will bless the lands of the world. Many people live in poverty and ignorance. They have a long way to go, and the gospel provides a bridge over which they walk, as it were, from their present situation to a brighter future. I remember some years ago being in Mexico. I was at the graduation exercises of the school which we have there. After the exercises, all of the graduates were taken to a hotel for a nice dinner. At our table sat a number of students. I asked each one what he or she was going to do now. I came to a girl who was seated opposite me at the table. I said, "What are you going to do?" She said, "I have been accepted in the medical school of the Mexico National University and have been given a scholarship." That night a dance was held for the graduates, and I went over to look, not to dance. This girl introduced me to her mother and her grandmother. Her grandmother had come out of the bush, as it were. She could not read or write. She had none of these skills. Her daughter, the mother of this girl, could read only a very few words. And now here was this beautiful daughter who had been accepted into the medical school of the Mexico National University. Wonderful things happen to our people as a result of the gospel. When you bring someone into this Church, you do not only bring an individual, you bring generations of people—parents with children, who will become parents of children. That is the story of the gospel of Jesus Christ. (Nicaragua Managua Missionary Meeting, January 21, 1997.)

I hope we are enjoying our work. This isn't a gospel of gloom, it is a gospel of gladness. We ought to be happy in it. We ought to be smiling about it. Oh, there is worry once in a while, but then there is prayer to take care of that. What a great thing the gospel is, when all is said and done. You are responsible for the well-being of somebody else and that makes of you a leader in this great Church. What a marvelous organization this is. I just stand back once in a while and marvel at it all—at the things we are trying to do as a Church to make the world a better place in which to live, a more informed place. We are trying to do a great work, the work of the Savior. (Jordan Utah South Regional Conference, priesthood leadership session, March 1, 1997.)

GRATITUDE

Get on your knees and thank the Lord for his bounties. Cultivate a spirit of thanksgiving for the blessing of life and for the marvelous gifts and privileges you enjoy. The Lord has said, "The meek shall inherit the earth." (See Matt. 5:5.) I cannot escape the interpretation that meekness implies a spirit of gratitude as opposed to an attitude of self-sufficiency, an acknowledgment of a greater power beyond oneself, a recognition of God and an acceptance of his commandments. This is the beginning of wisdom. ("The Dimension of the Spirit," *Improvement Era*, December 1964, p. 1092.)

Gratitude is a divine principle. The Lord has declared through revelation: "Thou shalt thank the Lord thy God in all things. . . .

"And in nothing doth man offend God, or against none is his wrath kindled, save those who confess not his hand in all things." (D&C 59:7, 21.)

Our society is afflicted by a spirit of thoughtless arrogance unbecoming those who have been so magnificently blessed. How grateful we should be for the bounties we enjoy. Absence of gratitude is the mark of the narrow, uneducated mind. It bespeaks a lack of knowledge and the ignorance of self-sufficiency. It expresses itself in ugly egotism and frequently in wanton mischief. We have seen our beaches, our parks, our forests littered with ugly refuse by those who evidently have no appreciation for their beauty. I have driven through thousands of acres of blackened land scourged by a fire evidently set by a careless smoker whose only concern had been the selfish pleasure gained from a cigarette.

Where there is appreciation, there is courtesy, there is concern for the rights and property of others. Without appreciation, there is arrogance and evil.

Where there is gratitude, there is humility, as opposed to pride.

How magnificently we are blessed! How thankful we ought to be! ("'With All Thy Getting Get Understanding,'" *Ensign*, August 1988, pp. 2–3.)

Although I should not have been, I was surprised at something President Kimball said on one occasion. I quote: "I find myself hungering and thirsting for just a word of appreciation or of honest evaluation from my superiors and my peers. I want no praise; I want no flattery; I am seeking only to know if what I gave was acceptable." (*Teachings of Spencer W. Kimball*, p. 489.)

If President Kimball needed a little of that, how much more do these of whom I speak this morning? Perhaps I can say in this company that on one occasion I received a great shock from my mission president. I was his assistant at the time. Some of the Saints in the district had with tremendous effort put on a great program. I suggested to my mission president that we write a letter of thanks to these people for what they had done. His response was, "We do not thank people in the Church for doing their duty."

That was the only thing I ever disagreed with him about. I believe we should thank people. I think that thanks should be genuine and sincere, as it well can be when there is honest effort and dedicated service. (Regional Representatives Seminar, March 31, 1989.)

I stand before you as one who is filled with a tremendous sense of gratitude and thanksgiving. I am thankful for the bedrock of faith on which Latter-day Saints stand and build their lives. I am confident that the Lord loves His people for the goodness of their lives and the generosity of their hearts as they consecrate of their means in the payment of tithes and offerings. I am grateful for the faith of the wealthy who give generously of their abundance. I am equally grateful for the faith of the poor who likewise contribute with a great spirit of consecration. . . .

I am grateful for the promises that He has made to those who walk in faith. . . . I am grateful for the testimonies of legions of Latter-day Saints who bear witness that the Lord has and does keep His promises, to which I add my own testimony. ("Rise to a Larger Vision of the Work," *Ensign*, May 1990, p. 95.)

I believe in beauty. The earth in its pristine beauty is an expression of the nature of its Creator. The language of the opening chapter of Genesis intrigues me. It states that "the earth was without form, and void; and darkness was upon the face of the deep" (Genesis 1:2). I suppose it presented anything but a picture of beauty.

"And God said, Let there be light: and there was light" (Genesis 1:3). And so the Creation continued until "God saw every thing that he had made, and, behold, it was very good" (Genesis 1:31). I interpret that to mean that it was beautiful, for "out of the ground made the Lord God to grow every tree that is pleasant to the sight" (Genesis 2:9).

I believe in the beauty of nature—the flowers, the fruit, the sky, the peaks and the plains from which they rise. I see and believe in the beauty of animals. Is there anything more regal than a magnificent horse—its coat brushed and clean, its head held high, its gait a symphony of motion?

I see and admire beauty in people. I am not so concerned with the look that comes of lotions and creams, of pastes and packs as seen in slick-paper magazines and on television. I am not concerned whether the skin be fair or dark. I have seen beautiful people in a hundred nations through which I have walked. Little children are beautiful everywhere. And so are the aged, whose wrinkled hands and faces speak of struggle and survival. . . .

I believe in beauty—the beauty of God's unspoiled creations, the beauty of his sons and daughters who walk without whimpering, meeting the challenges of each new day. . . .

. . . There is so much of ugliness in the world in which you live. It is found in the scarred earth, the polluted waters, the befouled air. It is expressed in coarse language, in sloppy dress and manners, in immoral behavior that mocks the beauty of virtue and always leaves a scar. But you can rise above this and revel in the beauty to be found with a little effort. ("This I Believe," *BYU 1991–92 Devotional and Fireside Speeches*, March 1, 1992, pp. 77–78.)

I picked up the paper the other evening and read the story of the conquest of smallpox. Once smallpox was a scourge that wiped out thousands, hundreds of thousands, in a miserable death. Smallpox is gone from the earth. There is none today. It is an absolute miracle. It is a miracle. It's all part of this great scientific discovery and the work of dedicated men and women who are using that enlightenment which comes from the divine within them to make life better for all of us. . . .

Last night I picked up a magazine. . . . The cover said, "Who is Jesus?" I read the lead article on "Who is Jesus?" by five great scholars who question the validity of the account in the New Testament, and a sixth who thinks there may be something to it—every one of these a minister of the gospel. We live at a time when people are unwilling to accept the simple narrative of the scripture, the word of the Lord. What a marvelous thing we have. That brief visitation of God the Father and His Beloved Son to the fourteen-year-old boy Joseph brought more light and understanding and knowledge of the nature and divinity of God than all of the studies of all of the religious parliaments of all time. . . . Be grateful. Be thankful. Cultivate a thankful heart, a heart that reaches out with appreciation and respect and gratitude. (Colorado Springs Young Adult Meeting, April 14, 1996.)

Be grateful. How thankful we ought to be. How comfortably we live. How very easy is life compared to what it once was. . . . We have it so easy, so pleasant, so delightful. We ride in cars that are warm in the winter and cool in the summer. What a great season in the history of the world this is in which to be alive and in which to be young. Sometimes I wish that I were as young as you are—and then when I think of what I have been through I am glad I am not. But what a wonderful season to be alive. . . . [We have] the miracles of medicine, the miracles of science, the miracles of communication, transportation, education—what a wonderful time in which to live. Of all of these wondrous, challenging things with which we live, I hope you regard it a blessing to be alive in this great age of the world. . . . I hope you walk with gratitude in your hearts, really. Grateful people are respectful people. Grateful people are courteous people. Grateful people are kindly people. Be grateful. (Smithfield/Logan Utah Regional Conference, April 21, 1996.)

Gratitude is of the very essence of worship—thanksgiving to the God of Heaven, who has given us all that we have that is good.

As you know, I served as a counselor to President Ezra Taft Benson, and I was with him many times when he prayed. He did not ask for very much in his prayers. His prayers were expressions of gratitude. Be thankful. When you walk with gratitude, you do not walk with arrogance and conceit and egotism, you walk with a spirit of thanksgiving that is becoming to you and will bless your lives. Be grateful. Be thankful to the Almighty for His wonderful blessings upon you. You have all that this great age has to offer, and beyond that the marvelous blessings of the restored gospel of Jesus Christ. How lucky can you be. Walk with appreciation and respect for the blessings of life and happiness which you enjoy. (Pittsburgh Pennsylvania Regional Conference, April 28, 1996.)

GREED

"Thou shalt not covet." Is not covetousness—that dishonest, cankering evil—the root of most of the world's sorrows? For what a tawdry price men of avarice barter their lives! . . .

Good men, well-intentioned men of great capacity, trade character for trinkets that turn to wax before their eyes and dreams that become only haunting nightmares. ("An Honest Man—God's Noblest Work," *Ensign*, May 1976, p. 62.)

I want to warn you to be careful of how you measure success. One need only read the daily newspapers to know of case after case of the "Yuppie Generation" whose driving greedy impulses have led to trouble, and serious and abysmal failure. Some of those who once drove about in the fanciest of cars and owned the fanciest of homes are now languishing in prison. They were, without question, men of tremendous capacity and ability. They had good minds, but their very brilliance led to their downfall. . . .

During the past few years, our local papers have carried story after story of able men who began working with integrity and honesty. They lived in reasonable comfort, but they were not satisfied. In their greed to enlarge their own kingdom, they enticed others to invest with them. And the investors, in many cases, were not without the same affliction of greed. They listened to stories of large returns with little effort. Like a dog chasing its own tail, the momentum of the scheme increased until one day there was a collapse. . . .

In one of his great letters to Timothy, Paul wrote: "For the love of money is the root of all evil: which while some coveted after, they have erred from the faith, and pierced themselves through with many sorrows." (1 Tim. 6:10.) You need not look far to see the veritable truth of that great warning. . . .

I think of a friend. He was, and I still think he is, a good man. He had a good home and a good family, and plenty to take care of his needs and the needs of his family. But he became consumed by a yearning for yet greater riches. I think he also was sincere in his desire to help his friends get more. One thing led to another, until when a drop in the economy occurred, he found himself in a trap from which he could not extricate himself. Those who wanted him to make them rich, and who initially professed love for him and admiration for his acumen, have become his violent and hateful accusers. I think it was not the money itself which destroyed them. They could live without it. It was the *love* for money which took hold of them and drove them until they found themselves in difficulty and failure. (University of Utah Institute of Religion Fireside, May 21, 1989.)

I wish every one of you might have some of the good things of life, but I hope your desire will not come of covetousness, which is an evil and gnawing disease. (University of Utah Institute of Religion Fireside, May 21, 1989.)

Let not selfishness canker your relationship. Let not covetousness destroy your happiness. Let not greed, for that which you do not need and cannot get with honesty and integrity, bring you down to ruin and despair. (University of Utah Institute of Religion Fireside, May 21, 1989.)

Of course, we need to earn a living. The Lord told Adam that in the sweat of his face should he eat his bread all the days of his life. It is important that we qualify ourselves to be self-reliant, particularly that every young man at the time of marriage be ready and able to assume the responsibilities of providing for his companion and for the children which may come to that home. . . . This is important. It is wholesome. It is right and proper.

Of course, none of us ever has enough. At least that is what we think. No matter our circumstances, we want to improve them. This, too, is good if it is not carried to an extreme. I am satisfied that the Father of us all does not wish His children to walk in poverty. He wants the best for them. He wants them to have comforts and some of the good things of the earth. . . .

It is when greed takes over, when we covet that which others have, that our affliction begins. And it can be a very sore and painful affliction. (University of Utah Institute of Religion Fireside, May 21, 1989.)

Every one of you wants to be successful.

Successful in what? Successful in earning money, successful in marriage, successful in your own sight and in the eyes of your friends. I wish every one of you great success. But I want to warn you of a trap that can destroy you in your eager search for success.

That trap is greed, human greed. It is that devious, sinister, evil influence that says, "What I have is not enough. I must have more."

When the finger of the Lord wrote the Ten Commandments on the tablets of stone, He gave as the tenth and final commandment: "Thou shalt not covet thy neighbour's house, thou shalt not covet thy neighbour's wife, nor his manservant, nor his maidservant, nor his ox, nor his ass, nor any thing that is thy neighbour's." (Ex. 20:17.)

There have been many changes in this world since that time, but human nature has not changed. When I first read the word "Yuppie," I did not know what it meant. I have since learned that it refers to a generation of young people, mostly young men, and mostly well educated, who with careful design set out on a course to get rich while still young, to drive fancy automobiles, to wear the best of clothing, to have an apartment in New York and a house in the country—all of these, and more. This was the total end for which they lived, and for some the means by which they got there was unimportant in terms of ethics and morality. They coveted that which others had, and selfishness and even greed were all a part of their process of acquisitiveness.

Now, I know that everyone . . . wants to succeed, and I wish that everyone of you might succeed. But I want to warn you to be careful of how you measure success. (University of Utah Institute of Religion Fireside, May 21, 1989.)

What a dismal picture is so often painted of men of greed, who violated every canon of honesty to get a little more when they already had more than they knew how to use. There is the picture of a number of failed savings and loan organizations, whose destruction was caused by selfish men, bringing losses to thousands and increased burdens to every taxpayer in the nation. This is an indication of what happens when people will not stand up and speak out against practices totally dishonest and which lead only to suffering and regret. ("Stand Up for Truth," BYU Devotional Address, September 17, 1996.)

HAPPINESS

Enjoy your work. Be happy. I meet so many people who constantly complain about the burden of their responsibilities. Of course the pressures are great. There is much, too much, to do. There are financial burdens to add to all of these pressures, and with all of this we are prone to complain, frequently at home, often in public. Turn your thinking around. The gospel is good news. Man is that he might have joy. Be happy! Let that happiness shine through your faces and speak through your testimonies. You can expect problems. There may be occasional tragedies. But shining through all of this is the plea of the Lord:

"Come unto me, all ye that labour and are heavy laden, and I will give you rest.

"Take my yoke upon you, and learn of me; for I am meek and lowly in heart; and ye shall find rest unto your souls.

"For my yoke is easy, and my burden is light." (Matthew 11:28–30.)

I enjoy these words of Jenkins Lloyd Jones which I clipped from a column in the *Deseret News* some years ago. . . . Said he:

"Anyone who imagines that bliss is normal is going to waste a lot of time running around shouting that he's been robbed.

"Most putts don't drop. Most beef is tough. Most children grow up to be just people. Most successful marriages require a high degree of mutual toleration. Most jobs are more often dull than otherwise.

"Life is like an old-time rail journey—delays, sidetracks, smoke, dust, cinders, and jolts, interspersed only occasionally by beautiful vistas and thrilling bursts of speed.

"The trick is to thank the Lord for letting you have the ride." (*Deseret News*, 12 June 1973.) ("Four Imperatives for Religious Educators," Church Educational System Address, September 15, 1978, p. 4.)

Enjoy your membership in the Church. Where else in all the world can you find such a society? Enjoy your activity. When I was a missionary in London fifty years ago, my companion and I would shake hands in the morning and say to one another, "Life is good." Life in the service of the Lord is good. It is beautiful. It is rewarding.

Be happy in that which you do. Cultivate a spirit of gladness in your homes. Subdue and overcome all elements of anger, impatience, and unbecoming talk one to another. ("Live the Gospel," *Ensign*, November 1984, p. 86.)

Our people will be a happy people, a blessed people, a people whose shepherd is our Lord, leading us through pastures green and peaceful, if we will walk after His pattern and in His light. ("God Is at the Helm," *Ensign*, May 1994, p. 59.)

Reach out to bless others in all that you do, that, because of your efforts, someone may live a little closer to the Lord and have a little greater happiness in his or her life. That is the end of our existence, when all is said and done: to build happiness in the lives of people, because the thing we teach is the Lord's plan of happiness. (Boston Massachusetts Regional Conference, priesthood leadership session, April 22, 1995.)

If we will live the gospel, if we will put our trust in God, our Eternal Father, if we will do what we are asked to do as members of The Church of Jesus Christ of Latter-day Saints, we will be the happiest and most blessed people on the face of the earth. (Pocatello Idaho Biregional Conference, June 4, 1995.)

Live the gospel. Carry on, carry on, keep the work growing and going. . . . For too many of our people, Church membership becomes a burden instead of a source of happiness. . . . Be happy as you serve. (*Church News* Interview, June 7, 1995.)

I hope you enjoy this work. I really do. Notwithstanding all the problems, this is a work of happiness. This is the good news! This is a work of joy! I hope you can laugh and smile and be happy and rejoice before the Lord over the great opportunity that you have to serve as a leader in carrying forth the work to the world wherever you may be assigned to go. And I'd like to say, concerning that, it doesn't matter where you go. A soul saved in Provo is as valuable as a soul saved in Copenhagen, or anywhere else in the world. We're out to save the sons and daughters of God by teaching them the gospel. Find your happiness doing it. (Mission Presidents Seminar, June 24, 1995.)

Keep the faith. Your happiness lies in following the gospel of Jesus Christ. That's the case with all of us. "Wickedness never was happiness" (Alma 41:10), said Alma to his son Corianton. That's as true as the sunrise in the morning. "Wickedness never was happiness." There is no happiness in doing what's wrong. There is no happiness in sin. There is misery and pain and regret and heartache and suffering. Happiness lies in walking in righteousness. Happiness lies in faithfulness and in righteousness. (Juneau Alaska Fireside, June 18, 1995.)

It is very important to be happy in this work. We have a lot of gloomy people in the Church because they do not understand, I guess, that this is the gospel of happiness. It is something to be happy about, to get excited about. (Temple Recorders Seminar, October 23, 1995.)

I am satisfied that our Father in Heaven likes to see His children happy—not miserable, but happy. I believe He wants to see them enjoy the good things of the earth, obtained in a righteous way. I don't think He likes to see His children in poverty and misery and trouble and wickedness and sin and want. I think He wants to see them happy. (Colorado Springs Young Adult Meeting, April 14, 1996.)

HEAVENLY PARENTS

It was Eliza R. Snow who wrote the words: "Truth is reason; truth eternal / Tells me I've a mother there." (*Hymns*, 1985, no. 292.)

It has been said that the Prophet Joseph Smith made no correction to what Sister Snow had written. Therefore, we have a

Mother in Heaven. Therefore, [some assume] that we may appropriately pray to her.

Logic and reason would certainly suggest that if we have a Father in Heaven, we have a Mother in Heaven. That doctrine rests well with me.

However, in light of the instruction we have received from the Lord Himself, I regard it as inappropriate for anyone in the Church to pray to our Mother in Heaven.

The Lord Jesus Christ set the pattern for our prayers. In the Sermon on the Mount, He declared:

"After this manner therefore pray ye: Our *Father* which art in heaven, Hallowed be thy name." (Matt. 6:9; italics added.)

When the resurrected Lord appeared to the Nephites and taught them, He said: "After this manner therefore pray ye: Our *Father* who art in heaven, hallowed be thy name." (3 Ne. 13:9; italics added.)

While He was among them, He further taught them by example and precept concerning this practice. The record states that "He himself also knelt upon the earth; and behold he prayed unto the *Father,* and the things which he prayed cannot be written, and the multitude did bear record who heard him." (3 Ne. 17:15; italics added.) . . .

And so I might continue with other specific instances from the scripture. Search as I have, I find nowhere in the standard works an account where Jesus prayed other than to His Father in Heaven or where He instructed the people to pray other than to His Father in Heaven.

I have looked in vain for any instance where any President of the Church, from Joseph Smith to Ezra Taft Benson, has offered a prayer to our Mother in Heaven.

I suppose those . . . who use this expression and who try to further its use are well-meaning, but they are misguided. The fact that we do not pray to our Mother in Heaven in no way belittles or denigrates her. . . . . .

. . . None of us can add to or diminish the glory of her of whom we have no revealed knowledge. ("Daughters of God," *Ensign,* November 1991, p. 100.)

HOLY GHOST

See also Revelation

The humanists who criticize the Lord's work, the so-called intellectualists who demean, speak only from ignorance of spiritual manifestation. They have not heard the voice of the Spirit. They have not heard it because they have not sought after it and prepared themselves to be worthy of it. Then, supposing that knowledge comes only of reasoning and of the workings of the mind, they deny that which comes by the power of the Holy Ghost.

The things of God are understood by the Spirit of God. That Spirit is real. To those who have experienced its workings, the knowledge so gained is as real as that which is acquired through the operation of the five senses. I testify of this. And I am confident that most members of the Church can so testify. I urge each of us to continue to cultivate a heart in tune with the Spirit. . . .

Let us not be trapped by the sophistry of the world, which for the most part is negative and which so often bears sour fruit. Let us walk with faith in the future, speaking affirmatively and cultivating an attitude of confidence. ("The Continuing Pursuit of Truth," *Ensign,* April 1986, p. 6.)

The Holy Ghost . . . is a gift, sacred and wonderful, borne by revelation from the third member of the Godhead. I believe in the Holy Ghost as a personage of spirit who occupies a place with the Father and the Son, these three comprising the divine Godhead.

The importance of that place is made clear from the words of the Lord, who said:

"All manner of sin and blasphemy shall be forgiven unto men: but the blasphemy against the Holy Ghost shall not be forgiven unto men.

"And whosoever speaketh a word against the Son of man, it shall be forgiven him: but whosoever speaketh against the Holy Ghost, it shall not be forgiven him, neither in this world, neither in the world to come." (Matthew 12:31–32.) (*The Father, Son, and Holy Ghost,* booklet [Salt Lake City: Bookcraft, 1988], pp. 10–11.)

The Holy Ghost stands as the third member of the Godhead, the Comforter promised by the Savior who would teach His followers all things and bring all things to their remembrance, whatsoever He had said unto them (see John 14:26).

The Holy Ghost is the Testifier of Truth, who can teach men things they cannot teach one another. In those great and challenging words of Moroni, a knowledge of the truth of the Book of Mormon is promised "by the power of the Holy Ghost." Moroni then declares, "And by the power of the Holy Ghost ye may know the truth of all things" (Moroni 10:4–5). (*The Father, Son, and Holy Ghost,* booklet [Salt Lake City: Bookcraft, 1988], p. 11.)

How great a blessing it is to have the ministering influence of a member of the Godhead, having received that gift under the hands of those who act with divine authority. Having received this gift, if we then continue to walk in virtue, we may enjoy the fulfillment of the promise made by the Lord when He said: "The Holy Ghost shall be thy constant companion, and thy scepter an unchanging scepter of righteousness and truth; and thy dominion shall be an everlasting dominion, and without compulsory means it shall flow unto thee forever and ever." (D&C 121:46.) (Priesthood Restoration Commemoration Fireside, May 15, 1988.)

There is no greater blessing that can come into our lives than the gift of the Holy Ghost—the companionship of the Holy Spirit to guide us, protect us, and bless us, to go, as it were, as a pillar before us and a flame to lead us in paths of righteousness and truth. That guiding power of the third member of the Godhead can be ours if we live worthy of it. (Boston Massachusetts Regional Conference, priesthood leadership session, April 22, 1995.)

When I was sustained as a stake president, Elder Harold B. Lee set me apart. I have forgotten nearly everything that he said, but I remember this: He said, "Listen for the whisperings of the Spirit, even in the nighttime; listen for the whisperings of the Spirit and follow them." Those were his words. I believe them.

He told me on one occasion of an incident in which a stake president came to Salt Lake from Florida to make a plea for some families in his stake. A group of them had bought homes, and the contractor or subdivider, or whoever he was, had fleeced them and they were going to lose their homes after spending thousands of dollars. This stake president came and met with the First Presidency and said, "We need help. Can't we get some legal help from the Church?" And Brother Lee said, "If we did it for you, we'd have to do for everybody else, and we can't do that." So the stake president left, disappointed, to return home. Brother Lee told me this himself. The next morning he came to his meeting and said to his counselors, "Brethren, yesterday Harold B. Lee was speaking. Today, the Lord speaks. I have been awake most of the night thinking about this thing. We will send our chief counsel down there to see if something can be done to help these people save their homes." That was done and that was the result. So often we let our own ideas move forward instead of pausing for a minute to try to hear the inspiration of the Lord. (Pittsburgh Pennsylvania Regional Conference, priesthood leadership session, April 27, 1996.)

How do we recognize the promptings of the Spirit? I don't think that's too difficult, really. When all is said and done it is a matter of a feeling we have in our hearts. I am going to read to you some words from Moroni that I think answer this question. They are taken from the seventh chapter beginning with the thirteenth verse.

"But behold, that which is of God inviteth and enticeth to do good continually; wherefore, every thing which inviteth and enticeth to do good, and to love God, and to serve him, is inspired of God.

"For behold, the Spirit of Christ is given to every man [and woman], that he [or she] may know good from evil; wherefore, I show unto you the way to judge; for every thing which inviteth to do good, and to persuade to believe in Christ, is sent forth by the power and gift of Christ; wherefore ye may know with a perfect knowledge it is of God.

"But whatsoever thing persuadeth men to do evil, and believe not in Christ, and deny him, and serve not God, then ye may know with a perfect knowledge that it is of the devil; for after this manner doth the devil work, for he persuadeth no man to do good, no, not one; neither do his angels; neither do they who subject themselves unto him" (Moroni 7:13, 16–17).

That's the test, when all is said and done. Does it persuade one to do good, to rise, to stand tall, to do the right thing, to be kind, to be generous? Then it is of the Spirit of God. If it is dark, sinister, ugly, not good, then you may know that it is of the adversary.

Now, your question: How do we recognize the promptings of the Spirit? You put it to that test. If it invites to do good, it is of God. If it inviteth to do evil, it is of the devil. The Lord is not going to spell out for you, A, B, C, D, E, F. His influence will be felt. And if you are doing the right thing and if you are living the right way, you will know in your heart what the Spirit is saying to you.

You recognize the promptings of the Spirit by the fruits of the Spirit—that which enlighteneth, that which buildeth up, that which is positive and affirmative and uplifting and leads us to better thoughts and better words and better deeds is of the Spirit of God. That which tears us down, which leads us into forbidden paths—that is of the adversary. I think it is just that plain, just that simple. (Southern Utah University Institute of Religion Devotional, February 11, 1997.)

HOME

See Family; Family Home Evening; Family Prayer; Parenting

HOME TEACHING

Many of you are teachers and priests and have home teaching assignments. You have the authority in this service to be teachers of repentance—that is, to encourage those Latter-day Saints for whom you have some responsibility to live the gospel principles more faithfully. A young man who is a priest comes to my home with his father as a home teacher. He has the opportunity and the responsibility to encourage me to live more fully the principles of the restored gospel of Jesus Christ.

The great burden of our work in the ministry of the Lord is to teach repentance, to encourage people to resist sin and to walk uprightly before the Lord. This is the gospel of repentance, and yours is the responsibility and the authority under the priesthood which you hold to teach this gospel of repentance. You recognize, of course, that if you are to do so effectively, your own life must be an example. ("The Priesthood of Aaron," *Ensign,* November 1982, p. 46.)

We were also assigned as home teachers, block teachers as we were then designated.

I recall rather vividly my first assignment. I was to go with one of the high priests of the ward. He called me and made an appointment. I was less than enthusiastic about going with this older man. But on the appointed evening, I put on my best clothes and walked over to his home. I was a boy of fifteen; he was a man I should judge to be about sixty. Timidly I knocked on his door. With a warm welcome he invited me in. He said that we would have prayer before we went out. We went into his bedroom. We kneeled at the side of the bed, and he offered prayer. He thanked the Lord for me to go with him as his companion, and prayed that the Lord would bless me. To you that may sound like a simple thing, but it had an effect upon me.

We visited four or five families that evening, and in each home he called on me for an expression. I have no recollection now of what I said then. But when we had completed our visit in each home, the members of the family shook our hands and spoke words of appreciation to us. The growth that came of that experience may have been small and almost imperceptible. But it became a part of the substance of my life. (Priesthood Restoration Commemoration Fireside, May 6, 1990.)

You have a responsibility, an inescapable responsibility to go out into the homes of the people and teach them the gospel. See that there is no iniquity or backbiting or evil speaking, and build their faith. See that they are getting along temporally. It is a big responsibility. . . . We do not do as well with our home teaching as we ought to. We could do a great deal better than we do. (Anchorage Alaska Regional Conference, priesthood leadership session, June 17, 1995.)

Home teaching isn't a lot of work, it just takes a little faith. (Tacoma Washington Regional Conference, priesthood leadership session, August 19, 1995.)

I hope that home teachers and visiting teachers will experience two things: first, the challenge of the responsibility that is in their great calling, and second, the sweetness of results from their work, particularly with those among us who are less active. I hope that these teachers will get on their knees and pray for direction, and then go to work to bring these wandering prodigals back into the fold of the Church. If home and visiting teachers respond to this challenge, I honestly believe that they will taste the sweet and wonderful feeling which comes of being an instrument in the hands of the Lord in leading someone back into activity in His church and kingdom. (Reception for LDS Congressional Leaders, November 12, 1995.)

Our people need help. They have so many problems—social problems, domestic problems, marital problems—so much of it. We need to help. We need to get home teachers out more among them, to strengthen them, to listen to them, to lift them and encourage them and help them with their complicated lives. (Charlotte North Carolina Regional Conference, priesthood leadership session, February 24, 1996.)

HOMOSEXUALITY

There are those who would have us believe in the validity of what they choose to call same-sex marriage. Our hearts reach out to those who struggle with feelings of affinity for the same gender. We remember you before the Lord, we sympathize with you, we regard you as our brothers and our sisters. However, we cannot condone immoral practices on your part any more than we can condone immoral practices on the part of others. ("Stand

Strong against the Wiles of the World," *Ensign,* November 1995, p. 99.)

All human beings—male and female—are created in the image of God. Each is a beloved spirit son or daughter of heavenly parents, and, as such, each has a divine nature and destiny. Gender is an essential characteristic of individual premortal, mortal, and eternal identity and purpose.

" . . . We declare that God's commandment for His children to multiply and replenish the earth remains in force. We further declare that God has commanded that the sacred powers of procreation are to be employed only between man and woman, lawfully wedded as husband and wife.

"We declare the means by which mortal life is created to be divinely appointed. We affirm the sanctity of life and of its importance in God's eternal plan." ("Stand Strong against the Wiles of the World," *Ensign,* November 1995, p. 101.)

HUMILITY

"O the vainness, and the frailties, and the foolishness of men! When they are learned they think they are wise, and they hearken not unto the counsel of God, for they set it aside, supposing they know of themselves, wherefore, their wisdom is foolishness and it profiteth them not. And they shall perish.

"But to be learned is good if they hearken unto the counsels of God" (2 Nephi 9:28–29).

So declared Jacob, the son of Nephi, long ago.

And Alma, who had been stricken dumb by an angel because of his wicked arrogance, speaking out of that harsh lesson said to his own son, Helaman:

"O, remember, my son, and learn wisdom in thy youth; yea, learn in thy youth to keep the commandments of God. . . .

"Counsel with the Lord in all thy doings, and he will direct thee for good; yea, when thou liest down at night lie down unto the Lord, that he may watch over you in your sleep; and when thou risest in the morning let thy heart be full of thanks unto God" (Alma 37:35, 37).

He concluded by counseling Helaman, "Look to God and live" (Alma 37:47). ("If I Were You, What Would I Do?" *BYU 1983–84 Fireside and Devotional Speeches*, September 20, 1983, pp. 9–10.)

Be humble. Don't be arrogant. The world is full of arrogant people. Oh, how obnoxious they are! How obnoxious is an arrogant man. Girls, isn't that so? And how obnoxious, likewise, is an arrogant girl. (Colorado Springs Young Adult Meeting, April 14, 1996.)

Be humble. There is no place for arrogance with any of us. There is no place for egotism with any of us. There is no place for crass pride. (Smithfield/Logan Utah Regional Conference, April 21, 1996.)

People ask me frequently what is my favorite verse of scripture. I have many and this is one of them, "Be thou humble; and the Lord thy God shall lead thee by the hand, and give thee answer to thy prayers" (D&C 112:10). What a promise to those who walk without arrogance, to those who walk without conceit, to those who walk without egotism, to those who walk humbly. "Be thou humble; and the Lord thy God shall lead thee by the hand, and give thee answer to thy prayers." What a solid and wonderful promise that is. (Japan Tokyo North, Japan Tokyo South, and Japan Sendai Missionary Meeting, May 18, 1996.)

INTEGRITY AND HONESTY

It is not easy to be honest when all about you there are those who are interested only in making "a fast buck." It is not always easy to be temperate when all about you there are those who scoff at sobriety. It is not easy to be industrious when all about you there are those who do not believe in the value of work. It is not easy to be a man of integrity when all about you there are those who will forsake principle for expediency.

. . . There is loneliness—but a man . . . has to live with his conscience. A man has to live with his principles. A man has to live with his convictions. A man has to live with his testimony.

Unless he does so, he is miserable—dreadfully miserable. And while there may be thorns, while there may be disappointment, while there may be trouble and travail, heartache and heartbreak, and desperate loneliness, there will be peace and comfort and strength.

I like these great words of the Lord given to those who would go out and teach this gospel. "I will go before your face. I will be on your right hand and on your left, and my Spirit shall be in your hearts, and mine angels round about you, to bear you up" (D&C 84:88). I think that is a promise to each of us. ("The Loneliness of Leadership," BYU *Speeches of the Year,* November 4, 1969, pp. 5–6.)

Imagine the flood of money that would pour into the offices of government, business, and merchants if all who have filched a little here and there were to return that which they had dishonestly taken.

The cost of every bag of groceries at the supermarket, of every tie or blouse bought at the shopping center, includes for each of us the burden of shoplifting.

How cheaply some men and women sell their good names! I recall the widely publicized case of a prominent public figure who was arrested for taking an item costing less than $5. I do not know whether he was ever convicted in the courts, but his petty misdeed convicted him before the people. In a measure, at least, his foolish act nullified much of the good he had done and was capable of yet doing. ("An Honest Man—God's Noblest Work," *Ensign,* May 1976, p. 60.)

In our childhood we were told the stories of George Washington's confessing to chopping down the cherry tree and Abraham Lincoln's walking a great distance to return a small coin to its rightful owner. But clever debunkers in their unrighteous zeal have destroyed faith in such honesty; the media in all too many cases have paraded before us a veritable procession of deception in its many ugly forms.

What was once controlled by the moral and ethical standards of the people, we now seek to handle by public law. And so the statutes multiply, enforcement agencies consume ever-increasing billions, prison facilities are constantly expanded, but the torrent of dishonesty pours on and grows in volume.

Of course, falsehood is not new. It is as old as man. "The Lord said unto Cain, Where is Abel thy brother? And he said, I know not: Am I my brother's keeper?" (Gen. 4:9.) ("An Honest Man—God's Noblest Work," *Ensign*, May 1976, pp. 60–61.)

How rare a gem, how precious a jewel is the man or woman in whom there is neither guile nor deception nor falsehood! . . .

The appraisal spoken long ago by an English poet is true yet today: "An honest man's the noblest work of God." (Alexander Pope, *An Essay on Man, Epistle III*, line 248.) Where there is honesty, other virtues will follow. . . .

We cannot be less than honest, we cannot be less than true, we cannot be less than virtuous if we are to keep sacred the trust given us. Once it was said among our people that a man's word was as good as his bond. Shall any of us be less reliable, less honest than our forebears?

To those within the sound of my voice who are living this principle, the Lord bless you. Yours is the precious right to hold your heads in the sunlight of truth, unashamed before any man. ("An Honest Man—God's Noblest Work," *Ensign*, May 1976, p. 62.)

Integrity is the very heart of commerce in the world in which we live. . . . Without personal integrity, there can be no confidence. Without confidence there can be no prospect of permanent success.

No nation can either become or remain great if there is an absence of integrity in its citizens. In recent years we have heard much of Watergate, Koreagate, and of other "-gates" in our political society. These are only symptoms of a more general weakening of moral fiber. What a difference there would be in our nation if there were total honesty among our leaders. How much greater would be our appreciation of business if we knew that integrity was the basis for all commercial activity. How much greater would be our confidence in the media if we knew that in all instances events were reported with evenhanded honesty. How much more happiness there would be in the homes of the people if there were total confidence and trust. ("Cornerstones as Stepping-Stones," BYU Commencement Address, April 20, 1979.)

Be fair. As you move onward in your lives, in your university studies and beyond, avoid shady and unfair practices. Clean competition is wholesome; but immoral, dishonest, or unfair practices are reprehensible, and particularly on the part of a Latter-day Saint. ("Four B's for Boys," *Ensign*, November 1981, p. 41.)

On Mount Sinai the finger of the Lord wrote the law on tablets of stone: "Thou shalt not steal." (Exodus 20:15.) There was neither enlargement nor rationalization. And then that declaration was accompanied by three other commandments, the violation of each of which involves dishonesty: "Thou shalt not commit adultery." "Thou shalt not bear false witness." "Thou shalt not covet." (Exodus 20:14, 16–17.) (*Be Thou an Example* [Salt Lake City: Deseret Book, 1981], p. 44.)

Some may regard the quality of character known as honesty to be a most ordinary subject. But I believe it to be the very essence of the gospel. Without honesty, our lives and the fabric of our society will disintegrate into ugliness and chaos. ("We Believe in Being Honest," *Ensign*, October 1990, p. 2.)

I believe that honesty is still the best policy. What a destructive thing is a little dishonesty. It has become a cankering disease in our society. Every insurance adjustor can tell you of the soaring costs of dishonest claims. Cheating in the payment of taxes robs the treasury of millions and places undue burdens on those who pay. Employee theft, padded expense accounts, and similar things bring tremendous losses to business institutions. The institution may be able to stand the loss of money, but the individual cannot afford the loss of self-respect. ("This I Believe," *BYU 1991–92 Devotional and Fireside Speeches*, March 1, 1992, p. 79.)

A letter and an old ash tray came to the office of the Presiding Bishop the other day. The letter reads: "Dear Sir, I stole the enclosed ash tray from your hotel in 1965. After these many years, I want to apologize to you and ask for your forgiveness for my wrong doing. I have enclosed a check that attempts to reimburse you for the ash tray."

The check was in the amount of $26.00, one dollar for each year he had kept the ash tray. I can imagine that during those twenty-six years, each time he tapped his cigarette on the rim of that tray he suffered a twinge of conscience. I do not know that the hotel ever missed the ash tray, but the man who took it missed his peace of mind for more than a quarter of a century and finally ended up paying far more for it than it was worth. Yes, my brethren and sisters, honesty *is* the best policy. ("This I Believe," *BYU 1991–92 Devotional and Fireside Speeches*, March 1, 1992, p. 79.)

Be strong . . . with the strength of simple honesty. How easy it is to "lie a little, take the advantage of one because of his words, dig a pit for thy neighbor" (2 Ne. 28:8). Nephi so describes the people of his day, as he also describes so many of our day. How easy it is for us to say, "We believe in being honest, true, chaste, benevolent" (A of F 1:13). But how difficult for so many to resist the temptation to lie a little, cheat a little, steal a little, bear false witness in speaking gossipy words about others. Rise above it, brethren. Be strong in the simple virtue of honesty. ("Building Your Tabernacle," *Ensign*, November 1992, p. 52.)

Simple honesty is so remarkable a quality. It is of the very essence of integrity. It demands that we be straightforward, unequivocal, in walking the straight and narrow line of what is right and true. It is so easy to cheat. At times it is so enticing to do so. Better a poor grade than a dishonest act. ("To a Man Who Has Done What This Church Expects of Each of Us," *BYU 1995–96 Speeches*, October 17, 1995, p. 53.)

Those of you who read the daily papers must surely recognize that no longer do we seem to care very much about the principles or the behavior of a candidate who runs for political office. We have dishonesty in high offices in the land. How seriously we have fallen.

In all this world there is no substitute for personal integrity. It includes honor. It includes performance. It includes keeping one's word. It includes doing what is right regardless of the circumstances. (Church Educational System Young Adult Fireside, February 2, 1997.)

JESUS CHRIST

Tomorrow is Easter. At sunrise in the morning multitudes will gather on a thousand hills to welcome the dawn of the Easter day and to remind themselves of the story of the Christ, whose resurrection they will commemorate. In language both beautiful and hopeful, preachers of many faiths will recount the story of the empty tomb. To them—and to you—I raise this question: "Do you actually believe it?"

Do you actually believe that Jesus was the Son of God, the literal offspring of the Father?

Do you believe that the voice of God, the Eternal Father, was heard above the waters of Jordan declaring, "This is my beloved Son, in whom I am well pleased"? (Matt. 3:17.)

Do you believe that this same Jesus was the worker of miracles, the healer of the sick, the restorer of the infirm, the giver of life to the dead?

Do you believe that following his death on Calvary's hill and his burial in Joseph's tomb, he came forth alive the third day?

Do you actually believe that he yet lives—real, vital, and personal—and that he will come again as promised by the angels at his ascension?

Do you actually believe these things? If you do, then you are part of a shrinking body of literalists who more and more are being smiled at by philosophers, who more and more are being ridiculed by certain educators, and who more and more are being considered "out of it" by a growing coterie of ministers of religion and influential theologians.

I have recently read a series of provocative writings setting forth the clever reasoning of American, British, and European theologians to "de-myth," as it is called, the story of Jesus of Nazareth. I quote from a capable Protestant layman who writes:

"The most disruptive questions are coming from theologians who . . . are questioning every old concept. They even suggest that maybe the word 'God' should be discarded, since it has become meaningless to so many people.

"Stripped of all else, the question the liberal theologians are asking is the old one that has time and again sundered the Christian church: Who was Jesus?

"The revolutionists . . . turn to the Bible as a source of truth, but their Bible is an expurgated version with embarrassing references to abnormal events edited out. 'De-mythologized,' one says. 'De-literalized,' says another.

"What the new wave casts up is 'religionless' Christianity; a faith grounded on a philosophic system, instead of being suspended precariously from old myths." (*Fortune*, December 1965, p. 173.)

So, in the eyes of these intellectuals, these are myths—the birth of Jesus as the Son of God of whom the angels sang on Judea's plains, the worker of miracles who healed the sick and raised the dead, the Christ resurrected from the grave, the ascension and the promised return.

These modern theologians strip him of his divinity and then wonder why men do not worship him.

These clever scholars have taken from Jesus the mantle of godhood and have left only a man. They have tried to accommodate him to their own narrow thinking. They have robbed him of his divine sonship and taken from the world its rightful King. ("The Miracle That Is Jesus," *Improvement Era*, June 1966, pp. 530–31.)

While seated in front of my television screen watching the funeral of General Eisenhower, I reflected on the wonder of the quiet man of Galilee, whose life and teachings have ever-increasing relevance in our time—as great a relevance, I would like to say, as in the day that he walked the earth.

In response to such a statement as this on another occasion, a straggly haired young intellectual asked, "What relevance? Just what relevance has Jesus for us? Why, he's as out-of-date as the Roman legions who occupied Jerusalem when he was there."

"Relevance?" I replied. "Ask my friends who tearfully watched the body of a beloved child lowered into the grave. Ask my neighbor who lost her husband in an accident. Ask the fathers and mothers of the thousands of good young men who have died in the steaming jungles of Vietnam. He—the risen Lord Jesus Christ—is their only comfort. There is nothing more relevant to the cold, stark fact of death than the assurance of eternal life." . . .

. . . This is the promise of the risen Lord. This is the relevance of Jesus to a world in which all must die. But there is further and more immediate relevance. As he is the conqueror of death, so also is he the master of life. His way is the answer to the troubles of the world in which we live. ("The Wonder of Jesus," *Improvement Era*, June 1969, p. 74.)

On Calvary he was the dying Jesus. From the tomb he emerged the living Christ. The cross had been the bitter fruit of Judas' betrayal, the summary of Peter's denial. The empty tomb now became the testimony of His divinity, the assurance of eternal life, the answer to Job's unanswered question: "If a man die, shall he live again?" (Job 14:14.)

Having died, he might have been forgotten, or, at best, remembered as one of many great teachers whose lives are epitomized in a few lines in the books of history. Now, having been resurrected, he became the Master of Life. ("The Symbol of Christ," *Ensign*, May 1975, p. 94.)

We live in a world of pomp and muscle, of strutting that glorifies jet thrust and far-flying warheads. It is the same kind of strutting that produced the misery of the days of Caesar, Genghis Khan, Napoleon, and Hitler. In this kind of world it is not easy to recognize that—

A babe born in a stable of the village Bethlehem,

A boy reared as a carpenter of Nazareth,

A citizen of a conquered and subdued nation,

A man whose mortal footsteps never went beyond a radius of 150 miles, who never received a school degree, who never spoke from a great pulpit, who never owned a home, who traveled afoot and without purse

Is actually the Creator of heaven and earth and all that in them are. Neither is it easy for many to recognize—

That he is the author of our salvation and his the only name whereby we must be saved,

That he would bring light and understanding of things eternal and divine as none other has ever done.

That his teachings would influence not only the personal behavior of uncounted millions, but would also inspire political systems which dignify and protect the individual, and social truths which foster education and culture.

That his matchless example would become the greatest power for goodness and peace in all the world. ("What Shall I Do Then with Jesus Which Is Called Christ?" *Ensign,* December 1983, p. 3.)

I have looked at majestic mountains rising high against the blue sky and thought of Jesus, the Creator of heaven and earth. I have stood on the sand of an island in the Pacific and watched the dawn rise like thunder—a ball of gold surrounded by clouds of pink and white and purple—and thought of Jesus, the Word by whom all things were made and without whom was not anything made that was made. I have seen a beautiful child—bright-eyed, innocent, loving and trusting—and marveled at the majesty and miracle of creation. What then shall we do with Jesus who is called Christ?

This earth is his creation. When we make it ugly, we offend him. Our bodies are the work of our Creator. When we abuse them, we abuse him. ("What Shall I Do Then with Jesus Which Is Called Christ?" *Ensign,* December 1983, pp. 3–4.)

Every spring the Christian world celebrates Easter in remembrance of the resurrection, when the risen Lord appeared first to Mary Magdalene, and later that day to the ten apostles, Thomas being absent. When the other disciples told Thomas, "We have seen the Lord," he, like so many then and now, said, "Except I shall see in his hands the print of the nails, and put my finger into the print of the nails, and thrust my hand into his side, I will not believe."

Eight days later the apostles were together again, this time Thomas with them. "Then came Jesus, the doors being shut, and stood in the midst, and said, Peace be unto you." Singling out Thomas, He said: "Reach hither thy finger, and behold my hands; and reach hither thy hand, and thrust it into my side; and be not faithless, but believing."

Thomas, astonished and shaken, answered, "My Lord and my God." Then Jesus said to him, "Thomas, because thou hast seen me, thou hast believed: blessed are they that have not seen, and yet have believed." (John 20:25–29.)

Have you not heard others speak as Thomas spoke? "Give us," they say, "the empirical evidence. Prove before our very eyes, and our ears, and our hands, else we will not believe." This is the language of the time in which we live. Thomas the Doubter has become the example of men in all ages who refuse to accept other than that which they can physically prove and explain—as if they could prove love, or faith, or even such physical phenomena as electricity.

To all who may have doubts, I repeat the words given Thomas as he felt the wounded hands of the Lord: "Be not faithless, but believing." Believe in Jesus Christ, the Son of God, the greatest figure of time and eternity. Believe that His matchless life reached back before the world was formed. Believe that He was the Creator of the earth on which we live. Believe that He was Jehovah of the Old Testament, that He was the Messiah of the New Testament, that He died and was resurrected, that He visited these western continents and taught the people here, that He ushered in this final gospel dispensation, and that He lives, the living Son of the living God, our Savior and our Redeemer. ("Be Not Faithless," in *Faith* [Salt Lake City: Deseret Book, 1983], pp. 14–15.)

Absolutely basic to our faith is our testimony of Jesus Christ as the Son of God, who under a divine plan was born in Bethlehem of Judea. He grew in Nazareth as the carpenter's son, within him the elements of both mortality and immortality received, respectively, from his earthly mother and his Heavenly Father. In the course of his brief earthly ministry, he walked the dusty roads of Palestine healing the sick, causing the blind to see, raising the dead, teaching doctrines both transcendent and beautiful. He was, as Isaiah had prophesied, "a man of sorrows, and acquainted with grief." (Isa. 53:3.) He reached out to those whose burdens were heavy and invited them to cast their burdens upon him, declaring, "My yoke is easy, and my burden is light." (Matt. 11:30.) He "went about doing good," and was hated for it. (Acts 10:38.) His enemies came against him. He was seized, tried on spurious charges, convicted to satisfy the cries of the mob, and condemned to die on Calvary's cross.

The nails pierced his hands and feet, and he hung in agony and pain, giving himself a ransom for the sins of all men. He died crying, "Father, forgive them; for they know not what they do." (Luke 23:34.)

He was buried in a borrowed tomb and on the third day rose from the grave. He came forth triumphant, in a victory over death, the firstfruits of all that slept. With his resurrection came the promise to all men that life is everlasting, that even as in Adam all die, in Christ all are made alive. (See 1 Cor. 15:20–22.) Nothing in all of human history equals the wonder, the splendor, the magnitude, or the fruits of the matchless life of the Son of God, who died for each of us. He is our Savior. He is our Redeemer. . . .

He is the chief cornerstone of the church which bears his name, The Church of Jesus Christ of Latter-day Saints. There is no other name given among men whereby we can be saved. (See Acts 4:12.) He is the author of our salvation, the giver of eternal life. (See Heb. 5:9.) There is none to equal him. There never has been. There never will be. Thanks be to God for the gift of his Beloved Son, who gave his life that we might live, and who is the chief, immovable cornerstone of our faith and his church. ("The Cornerstones of Our Faith," *Ensign*, November 1984, pp. 51–52.)

In solemnity, and with understanding of the gravity of that which we say, we add our witness to all the world of the reality of the Resurrection, that this same Jesus who rose from the grave ascended into heaven. We declare that in this dispensation of time He returned to restore to earth the pristine gospel which He had taught while walking among men, that with that restoration has come further certain witness of His reality, and has come also the holy priesthood, given to men, which is exercised in His name. This is our testimony, which we bear in the name of Jesus Christ, and we invite all men to hear and accept it. ("The Victory over Death," *Ensign,* May 1985, p. 53.)

I believe in the Lord Jesus Christ, the Son of the eternal, living God. I believe in Him as the Firstborn of the Father and the Only Begotten of the Father in the flesh. I believe in Him as an individual, separate and distinct from His Father. . . .

I believe that He was born of Mary of the lineage of David as the promised Messiah, that He was in very deed begotten of the Father, and that in His birth was the fulfillment of the great prophetic declaration of Isaiah:

"For unto us a child is born, unto us a son is given: and the government shall be upon his shoulder: and his name shall be called Wonderful, Counsellor, The mighty God, The everlasting Father, The Prince of Peace" (Isaiah 9:6).

I believe that in His mortal life He was the one perfect man to walk the earth. I believe that in His words are to be found that light and truth which, if observed, would save the world and bring exaltation to mankind. I believe that in His priesthood rests divine authority—the power to bless, the power to heal, the power to govern in the earthly affairs of God, the power to bind in the heavens that which is bound upon the earth. . . .

I believe that through His atoning sacrifice, the offering of His life on Calvary's Hill, He expiated the sins of mankind, relieving us from the burden of sin if we will forsake evil and follow Him. I believe in the reality and the power of His resurrection. I believe in the grace of God made manifest through His sacrifice and redemption, and I believe that through His atonement, without any price on our part, each of us is offered the gift of resurrection from the dead. I believe further that through that sacrifice there is extended to every man and woman, every son and daughter of God, the opportunity for eternal life and exaltation in our Father's kingdom, as we hearken and obey His commandments.

None so great has ever walked the earth. None other has made a comparable sacrifice or granted a comparable blessing. He is the Savior and the Redeemer of the world. I believe in Him.

I declare His divinity without equivocation or compromise. I love Him. I speak His name in reverence and wonder. I worship Him as I worship His Father, in spirit and in truth. I thank Him and kneel before His wounded feet and hands and side, amazed at the love He offers me. ("The Father, Son, and Holy Ghost," *Ensign*, November 1986, pp. 50–51.)

Believe in him who was the God of Abraham, Isaac, and Jacob, who was the source of inspiration of all the ancient prophets as they spoke as they were moved upon by the Holy Ghost. . . .

Doubt not, but believe that it was he who was born to earth in a manger when there was no room in the inn. Well did an angel ask a prophet who had foreseen these things in vision: "Knowest thou the condescension of God?" (1 Ne. 11:16.) I suppose none of us can fully understand that—how the great Jehovah should come among men, born in a manger in a vassal state, among a people who would hate him. But at his birth there was an angelic chorus that sang of his glory. There were shepherds who worshipped him. There was a new star in the east. . . .

Believe and know that he was a man of miracles. He who had created the world and governed it as the great Jehovah understood the elements of earth and all the functions of life. Beginning at Cana, where he turned the water into wine, he went on to cause the lame to walk, the blind to see, the dead to return to life—he, the Master Physician, who healed the sick by the authority inherent in him as the Son of God.

He was the comforter of the burdened of his time, and of all the generations who came before and who have come after who have truly believed in him. Said he to each of us:

"Come unto me, all ye that labour and are heavy laden, and I will give you rest.

"Take my yoke upon you, and learn of me; for I am meek and lowly in heart: and ye shall find rest unto your souls.

"For my yoke is easy, and my burden is light." (Matt. 11:28–30.) ("'Be Not Faithless,'" *Ensign*, April 1989, pp. 3–4.)

There is something within all of us that evokes an interest in the lives of the great and famous who have walked the earth. But none other has so affected humankind as has Jesus. . . .

There is none other to compare with Him—in His birthright as the Son of God, in His divinity as the worker of miracles, in His humility in submitting to the torture of His death, in His godhood in bringing to pass His resurrection and the salvation of the human family. More acts of kindness have been done in His name, more words of forgiveness spoken with His love, more deeds of reconciliation performed after His pattern, greater love extended to both friend and enemy by the power of His example than any other in the history of all mankind. He is the author of our salvation. He is the source of the good news of the gospel. He is our hope in our season of desperation, our guide in the wilderness of life through which we walk, our source of comfort and consolation in seasons of distress, our assurance of the eternity of the soul of man. (Message to KIRO Employees, December 16, 1989.)

Jesus Christ is the key figure of our faith. The official name of the Church is The Church of Jesus Christ of Latter-day Saints. We worship Him as Lord and Savior. The Bible is our scripture. We believe that the prophets of the Old Testament who foretold the coming of the Messiah spoke under divine inspiration. We glory in the accounts of Matthew, Mark, Luke, and John, setting forth the events of the birth, ministry, death, and resurrection of the Son of God, the Only Begotten of the Father in the flesh. ("Our One Bright Hope," *Ensign*, April 1994, p. 2.)

We are Christians. No church in the world speaks up with a stronger witness of the divinity of the Lord Jesus Christ as the Son of God and the Redeemer of the world than does this Church, which carries His name—The Church of Jesus Christ of Latter-day Saints. And His gospel is the gospel we teach. And the spirit of love which we exemplify is the spirit in which we try to work. (Interview with Suzanne Evans of BBC Radio 4, August 26, 1995.)

I like to read the Gospel of John. Over sixty years ago my missionary companion and I started reading the Gospel of John which begins with that great opening statement, "In the beginning was the Word, and the Word was with God, and the Word was God." Our reading of the Gospel of John did something to me. And I still love to read the Gospel of John.

"For God so loved the world, that he sent his only begotten son, that whosoever believeth in him should not perish, but have everlasting life" (John 3:16).

"Peace I leave with you, my peace I give unto you: not as the world giveth, give I unto you. Let not your heart be troubled, neither let it be afraid" (John 14:27).

Those are great and marvelous statements that I learned to love in the Gospel of John. We need to do more reading in the scriptures and more dwelling on the Lord Jesus Christ. He must become the foundation of all that we know about the gospel. We must have grow in our hearts and in our minds and in our very souls a knowledge and a conviction of the Son of God and of His atoning sacrifice for each of us. Every leader in this Church ought to carry in his heart a firm and solid conviction of the divinity of the Lord Jesus Christ and His place in the eternal plan of God, our Eternal Father. We need to draw closer to Him, and learn of Him, and love Him, if we are to do our job as we are to do it. "Study to shew thyself approved unto God, a workman that needeth not to be ashamed," wrote Paul to Timothy (2 Timothy 2:15). (Smithfield/Logan Utah Regional Conference, priesthood leadership session, April 20, 1996.)

Can anyone doubt the veracity of [the account of the Risen Lord]? No event of history has been more certainly confirmed. There is the testimony of all who saw and felt and spoke with the Risen Lord. He appeared on two continents in two hemispheres and taught the people before His final ascension. Two sacred volumes, two testaments speak of this most glorious of all events in all of human history. But these are only accounts, the faithless critic says. To which we reply that beyond these is the witness and the testimony, borne by the power of the Holy Ghost, of the truth and validity of this most remarkable event. Through the centuries untold numbers have paid with the sacrifice of their comforts, their fortunes, their very lives for the convictions they carried in their hearts of the reality of the risen, living Lord.

And then comes the ringing testimony of the Prophet of this dispensation that in a wondrous theophany he saw and was spoken to by the Almighty Father and the Risen Son. That vision, glorious beyond description, became the wellspring of this The Church of Jesus Christ of Latter-day Saints, with all the keys, authority, and power found therein, and the sustaining comfort to be found in the testimony of its people. . . .

Towering above all mankind stands Jesus the Christ, the King of glory, the unblemished Messiah, the Lord Emmanuel. In the hour of deepest sorrow we draw hope and peace and certitude from the words of the angel that Easter morning, "He is not here: for he is risen, as he said" (Matt. 28:6). We draw strength from the words of Paul, "As in Adam all die, even so in Christ . . . all [are] made alive" (1 Cor. 15:22).

> *I stand all amazed at the love Jesus offers me,*
> *Confused at the grace that so fully he proffers me.*
> *I tremble to know that for me he was crucified,*
> *That for me, a sinner, he suffered, he bled and died.*
> *Oh, it is wonderful that he should care for me*
> *Enough to die for me!*
> *Oh, it is wonderful, wonderful to me!*
>
> (HYMNS, NO. 193)

He is our King, our Lord, our Master, the living Christ, who stands on the right hand of His Father. He lives! He lives, resplendent and wonderful, the living Son of the living God. ("This Glorious Easter Morn," *Ensign*, May 1996, p. 67.)

We are sometimes accused of not being Christian. Of course we are Christians. We are Christians in the very best sense of that word. We believe in Christ. We teach of Christ. We look to Christ. He is our Redeemer, our Lord, and our Savior. (Berlin Germany Regional Conference, June 16, 1996.)

Sixty-two years ago I was a missionary in London and attended a meeting of the British missionaries, a zone meeting it might have been called. Joseph J. Cannon was the president and he said to the missionaries, "What is the greatest thing we can do for the people of the British Isles?" It was all one mission then. One of them raised his hand and said, "Tell them that the heavens are opened again." "Yes," he said. Another one said, "Tell them that the priesthood is upon the earth." Another one said, "We have a prophet on the earth." "Yes." Another one said, "We have the Book of Mormon," etc., etc. When they had all given their responses, he said, "In my judgment, the greatest thing we can do is to bring to the people of Britain a knowledge concerning Jesus, the Son of God, the Savior and the Redeemer of the world."

The longer I have lived, the more I have come to that conclusion. The greatest thing we can do is to bring to men and women everywhere, first to ourselves and then to those we teach, a living testimony, a vibrant witness of the reality of Jesus as the Son of God, the Redeemer of mankind. (Mission Presidents Seminar, June 23, 1996.)

We carry in our hearts a firm and unshakable conviction of the divine mission of the Lord Jesus Christ. He was the great Jehovah of the Old Testament, the Creator who, under the direction of His Father, made all things and without Him was not anything made that was made (see John 1:3). He was the promised Messiah, who came with healing in His wings. He was the worker of miracles, the great healer, the resurrection and the life. His is the only name under heaven whereby we must be saved. . . .

We honor His birth. But without His death that birth would have been but one more birth. It was the redemption which He worked out in the Garden of Gethsemane and upon the cross of Calvary which made His gift immortal, universal, and everlasting. His was a great atonement for the sins of all mankind. He was the resurrection and the life, the firstfruits of them that slept. Because of Him all men will be raised from the grave.

But beyond this He taught us the way, the truth, and the life. He restored the keys through which we may go on to immortality and eternal life.

We love Him. We honor Him. We thank Him. We worship Him. He has done for each of us and for all mankind that which none other could have done. God be thanked for the gift of His Beloved Son, our Savior, the Redeemer of the world, the Lamb without blemish who was offered as a sacrifice for all mankind. ("Christmas," First Presidency Christmas Devotional, Salt Lake Tabernacle, December 8, 1996.)

"We believe in God, the Eternal Father, and in His Son, Jesus Christ, and in the Holy Ghost" (A of F 1:1). This is our primary declaration of faith. We speak unabashedly of the living reality of the Lord Jesus Christ. We declare without equivocation the fact of His great act of Atonement for all mankind. That act brought assurance of universal resurrection and opened the way to exaltation in our Father's kingdom.

This is the burden of our declaration to the world. It is the substance of our theology. It is the wellspring of our faith. Let no one ever say that we are not Christians. ("Our Testimony to the World," *Ensign*, May 1997, p. 83.)

The Condescension of Christ

Occasionally in times of meditation I reflect on that question posed by the angel in the vision given Nephi: "Knowest thou the condescension of God?" (1 Ne. 11:16). *Condescend* is an interesting word. It means to drop down to a less dignified level and to cast aside the privileges of rank. He was the very Son of God, the child of the Almighty, the creator of the earth under the direction of His divine father. John says that "without him was not any thing made that was made" (John 1:3).

But He willingly and knowingly, as the major participant in the eternal plan of God, set aside every privilege pertaining to His divine sonship and came to earth under the most humble of circumstances. He was born among a conquered people, in a vassal state, into a society where there was much of conflict and bitterness and hate.

He was baptized by John in Jordan, though His life was without sin. He was an example to all of us, saying, "for thus it becometh us to fulfil all righteousness" (Matt. 3:15).

Nephi was shown the course of the Savior's life in vision. He wrote, "I beheld that he went forth ministering unto the people, in power and great glory; and the multitudes were gathered together to hear him; and . . . they cast him out from among them" (1 Ne. 11:28).

"And I beheld multitudes of people who were sick, and who were afflicted with all manner of diseases, and with devils and unclean spirits; and the angel spake and showed all these things unto me. And they were healed by the power of the Lamb of God; and the devils and the unclean spirits were cast out.

". . . and I looked and beheld the Lamb of God, that he was taken by the people; yea the Son of the everlasting God was judged of the world; and I saw and bear record . . . that he was lifted up upon the cross and slain for the sins of the world" (1 Ne. 11:31–33).

How grateful I am, how grateful all of us must be, that He condescended to come to earth and give His life on Calvary's cross for each of us. There is nothing any of us can do to recompense Him fully for what He has done for us, but we can make an earnest effort in this direction by following His divine commandments. ("He Who Redeemed Us," First Presidency Christmas Devotional, Salt Lake Tabernacle, December 3, 1995.)

Believe in His Divine Son, His firstborn, His Only Begotten in the flesh, Jesus the Christ, who condescended to leave His Father on high to be born in a manger under the most humble of circumstances among people in a vassal state, who walked the dusty road of Palestine doing good, healing the sick, blessing and teaching and uplifting and giving strength and hope and faith to those who would listen. Then, in the greatest act of human history, He allowed His quivering flesh to be nailed to the cross and lifted up in an act of atonement for each of us. We cannot comprehend it in all of its meaning, but it is marvelously wonderful. . . . Thanks be to God for the gift of His Son and thanks be to the Lord Jesus Christ for the gift of His life, which makes possible for each of us the blessing of eternal life. Nothing, nothing is of greater significance in all the history of the world than that atoning sacrifice of the Son of God. He was the Son of God. (Smithfield/Logan Utah Regional Conference, April 21, 1996.)

I think of the majesty of the Son of God, the tremendous, quiet, wonderful majesty of the Redeemer of the world, Jesus of Nazareth, He who was born in a manger in Bethlehem of Judea, who, according to the vision of Nephi as recorded in the eleventh chapter of First Nephi, had been the Firstborn of the Father. He who had been chosen, who stood at His Father's side, He who had been Jehovah the Creator of the earth, condescended to come to mortal life in a manger under the humblest of circumstances in this place of so much of bitterness and hatred. I do not know where else he could have been born that would have represented a greater condescension on the part of God. He deigned, as it were, to leave His celestial courts on high to come here, to be reared here as a boy, to walk the dusty roads of this land, to know the temptations of Satan, to be baptized in Jordan's waters to fulfill all righteousness, to become the Master teacher. . . .

I have pondered at great length that vision of Nephi's where it speaks of the condescension of God. It has been going through my mind all the time that I have been here [in Israel]. From the celestial majesty to the dust, as it were, and then the ignominy, the hate, the pain of the cross on Calvary's hill. This is the story of the Son of God, who gave His life for each of us. (Israel District Fireside, June 21, 1996.)

A Testimony of Jesus Christ

[I] know that God lives and that he is the Ruler of the universe, our Father in Heaven; that Jesus Christ, his Only Begotten in the flesh, was born in Bethlehem of Judea as the promised Messiah; that he was the Man of miracles, the one perfect Man who has lived upon the earth; that he was crucified and gave his life as a sacrifice for the sins of all men; that through that great act of atonement, he became the Redeemer of all mankind; that he arose from the grave the third day, thus becoming "the firstfruits of them that slept" (1 Cor. 15:20); that he was seen by many in and about Jerusalem, and in this hemisphere also, who testified that they saw and felt and were instructed by the risen Lord. By the power of the Holy Spirit, which has borne witness to us, we can and do testify of these great, transcendent truths. ("What This Work Is All About," *Ensign*, November 1982, p. 7.)

Let us establish in our lives the habit of reading those things which will strengthen our faith in the Lord Jesus Christ, the Savior of the world. He is the pivotal figure of our theology and our faith. Every Latter-day Saint has the responsibility to know for himself or herself with a certainty beyond doubt that Jesus is the resurrected, living Son of the living God. The Brethren of the Council of the Twelve are advocating that we read a chapter a day of the Gospels—that is, Matthew, Mark, Luke, and John in the Bible; and Third Nephi in the Book of Mormon, particularly beginning with the eleventh chapter of Third Nephi where is found the account of Christ's visit among the Nephites in this hemisphere. I should like to endorse this program and commend it to you and urge you to follow it. ("Fear Not to Do Good," *Ensign,* May 1983, p. 80.)

We who are assembled in this great general conference of The Church of Jesus Christ of Latter-day Saints give our testimony to all the world that Jesus is the Christ, the living Son of the living God; that he came to earth in the meridian of time, the offspring of Deity; that he walked the roads of Palestine, declaring the truths of the eternal gospel, healing the sick, raising the dead, causing the blind to see, and bringing the transcendent messianic message of hope to all who would hear; that he was taken by evil men, condemned, and crucified on Calvary's Hill; that he rose the third day, the firstfruits of them that slept, the conqueror of death, the master of eternal life; that "as in Adam all die, even so in Christ shall all be made alive" (1 Cor. 15:22); that he and his Father, the great Elohim, appeared to the boy Joseph Smith in the spring of 1820, ushering in this, the dispensation of the fulness of times; that he stands at the head of this church which bears his name; that in fulfillment of Isaiah's prophecy, the government of the kingdom of God is upon his shoulder, and his name is "called Wonderful, Counsellor, The mighty God, The everlasting Father, The Prince of Peace." (Isa. 9:6.) ("Special Witnesses for Christ," *Ensign,* May 1984, p. 49.)

I know that I am not the head of this Church. The Lord Jesus Christ is its head. He is its living head. My mission, my chief responsibility, my greatest honor comes in bearing solemn testimony of His living reality. Jesus Christ is the Son of God, who condescended to come into this world of misery, struggle and pain, to touch men's hearts for good, to teach the way of eternal life, and to give Himself as a sacrifice for the sins of all mankind. He is "King of Kings and Lord of Lords, and He shall reign forever and ever" (Handel's *Messiah*). How different, how empty our lives would be without Him. How much truer, how much deeper is our love and appreciation and respect one for another because of Him. How infinite is our opportunity for exaltation made possible through His redeeming love. I bear solemn witness that He lives and stands on the right hand of His Father. ("He Who Redeemed Us," First Presidency Christmas Devotional, Salt Lake Tabernacle, December 3, 1995.)

JOSEPH SMITH

See Prophets, Latter-day: Joseph Smith

JUSTICE AND MERCY

See Mercy

KINDNESS

See also Charity

Joseph Anderson became the oldest living General Authority. He lived to be 102 years of age. He served for many years as personal secretary to President Heber J. Grant. When President Grant was dying, Joseph went up to his home to see him. The President had had a stroke and was in poor condition, but he looked Joseph in the eye and said, "Joseph, you've worked with me for a long time."

Joseph replied, "Yes, President Grant, I have, many years."

President Grant said, "Joseph, have I ever been unkind to you during all these years?"

Joseph said, "No, President Grant, you have never been unkind to me."

And the President said, "I'm glad I have never been unkind to you." The next day President Grant died.

Can those with whom you associate say that you have never been unkind to them? Can they? I hope so. Bless your people with love. (Berlin Germany Regional Conference, priesthood leadership session, June 15, 1996.)

There are so many who have been injured and who need a Good Samaritan to bind up their wounds and help them on their way. A small kindness can bring a great blessing to someone in distress and a sweet feeling to the one who befriends him. (Salt Lake Valley Single Adult Fireside, September 22, 1996.)

KINGDOM OF GOD, MODERN-DAY

See also Church of Jesus Christ of Latter-day Saints, The

I believe in the triumph of the gospel of Jesus Christ and the triumph of the Church and kingdom of God on the earth. . . .

I believe, my friends, that the cause we have the honor to represent is that kingdom which shall stand forever.

I am not engaging in unrealistic dreams when I think of its future, for every day I see the miracle of its strength and of its growing influence in the lives of thousands across the earth. ("Be Not Afraid, Only Believe," *Improvement Era,* December 1969, p. 98.)

Without contention, without argument, without offense, let us pursue a steady course, moving forward to build the kingdom of God. If there is trouble, let us face it calmly. Let us overcome evil with good. This is God's work. It will continue to strengthen over the earth, touching for good the lives of countless thousands whose hearts will respond to the message of truth. No power under heaven can stop it. (Conference Report, April 1970, p. 23.)

In 1845, less than a year after Joseph's death, Parley P. Pratt wrote a summary of the Prophet's work and a statement of our obligation to advance it. These words, poetic in their beauty, are as follows:

"He has organized the kingdom of God.—We will extend its dominion.

"He has restored the fulness of the Gospel.—We will spread it abroad.

"He has kindled up the dawn of a day of glory.—We will bring it to its meridian splendor.

"He was a 'little one,' and became a thousand.—We are a small one, and will become a strong nation.

"In short, he quarried the stone. . . . We will cause it to become a great mountain and fill the whole earth." (*Millennial Star* 5 [March 1845]: 151–52.)

We are seeing the unfolding of that dream. I hope we shall be true and faithful to the sacred trust given us to build this kingdom. Our efforts will not be without sorrow and setbacks. We may expect opposition, both determined and sophisticated. As the work grows, we may expect a strengthening of the efforts of the adversary against it. Our best defense is the quiet offense of allegiance to the teachings which have come to us from those whom we have sustained as prophets of God. (*Be Thou an Example* [Salt Lake City: Deseret Book, 1981], pp. 10–11.)

Recently while wrestling in my mind with a problem I thought to be of serious consequence I went to my knees in prayer. There came into my mind a feeling of peace and the words of the Lord, "Be still and know that I am God." . . .

God is weaving his tapestry according to his own grand design. All flesh is in his hands. It is not our prerogative to counsel him. It is our responsibility and our opportunity to be at peace in our minds and in our hearts, and to know that he is God, that this is his work, and that he will not permit it to fail.

We have no need to fear. We have no need to worry. We have no need to speculate. Our imperative need is to be found doing our duty individually in the callings which have come to us. . . .

The Almighty is blessing his church and his people. He is watching over them. He neither slumbers nor sleeps as he guides, directs, and moves in his own "mysterious way His wonders to perform." (*Hymns*, no. 48.) ("He Slumbers Not, nor Sleeps," *Ensign*, May 1983, p. 6.)

Behind us is a glorious history. It is bespangled with heroism, tenacity to principle, and unflagging fidelity. It is the product of faith. Before us is a great future. It begins today. We cannot pause. We cannot slow down. We cannot slacken our pace or shorten our stride.

In a dark period of our history, when enemies were throwing accusations against the Church, the First Presidency issued a proclamation to the world in which they set forth the dimensions of this work. Said they: "Our motives are not selfish; our purposes not petty and earth-bound; we contemplate the human race—past, present, and yet to come—as immortal beings, for whose salvation it is our mission to labor; and to this work, broad as eternity and deep as the love of God, we devote ourselves, now, and forever" (*Messages of the First Presidency*, comp. James R. Clark, 6 vols. [Salt Lake City: Bookcraft, 1965–75], 26 March 1907, 4:155).

With faith we must go forward toward the fulfillment of that commitment. We must ever keep before us the big picture, while not neglecting the details. That large picture is a portrayal of the whole broad mission of the Church; but it is painted one brush stroke at a time through the lives of all members, the composite of whose activities becomes the Church at work.

Each of us, therefore, is important. Each is a brush stroke, as it were, on the mural of this vast panorama of the kingdom of God. If there are blanks, if there are distortions, if there are off-color areas, then the picture is defective to all who look upon it.

Shall any of us say that with faith we cannot do better than we are now doing?

There is no obstacle too great, no challenge too difficult, that we cannot meet with faith. ("God Grant Us Faith," *Ensign*, November 1983, p. 53.)

The work of the Lord is advancing as much as at any time in its history and ever more rapidly. As individuals we may fail in our part in it, but if we do so God will raise up others to take our places, for he will not permit this work to fail.

We are familiar with stories that the work would fail. When the Book of Mormon came from the press, the crude critics said it would soon be forgotten. When troubles grew in Kirtland, the enemies said the work would fail. When the Saints were driven from Missouri, those who drove them said the Church would soon expire. When the Prophet and Hyrum were killed in Carthage, their murderers said it was the end of this thing. When in February of 1846 the wagons crossed the river into the Iowa winter, the enemies of the Church said that it could not survive. When the Saints found themselves in this lonely valley, with crickets devouring their crops, there were even some of them who thought it was all over.

But the work has gone forward. The Church has never taken a backward step since it was organized in 1830—and it never will. It is the cause of the Master. It is the church of God. It is his work established in this latter day. It is the little stone which was cut out of the mountain without hands, which should roll forth to fill the whole earth. (See Dan. 2:44–45.) ("The Miracle Made Possible by Faith," *Ensign*, May 1984, p. 48.)

The growth of this work has been a constantly unfolding miracle, and what an exciting and wonderful experience it is to be a part of it. Although storms of adversity have raged against it, it continues to move steadily forward along the course which the Almighty has outlined for it. It does so quietly, without great noise and fanfare, touching for good the lives of men and women across the earth. Its mission is not empire building. Its mission is to teach faith and repentance, and to bring truth and gladness to all who will listen and hearken to its message. ("Come and Partake," *Ensign*, May 1986, p. 46.)

Some time ago I noted that a new book, put together by unbelievers as a "history" of the Church, was off the press. I have not read the book, but the conclusion . . . is that the future of the Church is dim. Without wishing to seem impertinent, I should like to ask what the authors know about that future. They know nothing of the prophetic mission of the Church! The future must have looked extremely dim in the 1830s. It must have looked impossible back in those Ohio-Missouri days. But notwithstanding poverty, notwithstanding robbing, notwithstanding murders, notwithstanding confiscation and drivings and disfranchisement forced upon the Saints in the ensuing years, the work moved steadily on. It has continued to go forward. Never before has it been so strong. Never before has it been so widespread. Never before have there been so many in whose hearts has burned an unquenchable knowledge of the truth.

It is the work of the Almighty. It is the work of his Beloved Son, the Lord Jesus Christ. It is the gospel of salvation. Men and women may oppose now, just as others opposed in those days. But the work goes on because it is true and it is divine.

These are the best of times in the history of this work. What a wonderful privilege and great responsibility are ours to be an important part of this latter-day work of God. Do not become sidetracked by the wiles of Satan that seem so rampant in our era. Then as now we have critics. We even have those inside the Church who seem to delight in looking for every element of weakness in the past or the present.

Rather, let us go forward with faith and with the vision of the great and marvelous future that lies ahead as this work grows in strength and gains in momentum. Build faith in the hearts of all those around you. ("Go Forward with Faith," *Ensign*, August 1986, p. 5.)

We are engaged in a great eternal struggle that concerns the very souls of the sons and daughters of God. We are not losing. We are winning. We will continue to win if we will be faithful and true. We *can* do it. We *must* do it. We *will* do it. There is nothing the Lord has asked of us that in faith we cannot accomplish. . . .

The war goes on. It is waged across the world over the issues of agency and compulsion. It is waged by an army of missionaries over the issues of truth and error. It is waged in our own lives, day in and day out, in our homes, in our work, in our school associations; it is waged over questions of love and respect, of loyalty and fidelity, of obedience and integrity. We are all involved in it. . . . We are winning, and the future never looked brighter. ("The War We Are Winning," *Ensign,* November 1986, pp. 44–45.)

"What is the future of the Church?"

The charge laid upon the Church is almost beyond comprehension. While yet upon the earth the Lord declared: "And this gospel of the kingdom shall be preached in all the world for a witness unto all nations; and then shall the end come." (Matt. 24:14.)

Furthermore, the work of the Church is concerned with the eternal welfare of all generations who have lived upon the earth.

No other organization, in my judgment, faces so great a challenge. That challenge, I am confident, will be met by the growing generation and by generations yet to come. To our youth I say . . . great is your responsibility, tremendous is your opportunity.

I am confident that you will be a part of a beautiful pattern of growth and strengthening vitality that will be marvelous to look upon and awesome to experience.

As the Prophet Joseph once said, no man can stop this work from progressing.

Many who are clever and deceitful may try to thwart or destroy it, but none will succeed. ("The State of the Church," *Ensign,* May 1991, p. 54).

We are citizens in the greatest kingdom on earth—a kingdom not directed by the wisdom of men but led by the Lord Jesus Christ. Its presence is real. Its destiny is certain. This is the kingdom of which the prophet Daniel spoke—a stone, as it were, that should be cut out of the mountain without hands and roll forth and fill the earth. (See Dan. 2:34–35.)

No mortal man created this kingdom. It came through revelation from its divine head. And since the nineteenth-century days of its inception, it has gone forth like a rolling snowball gathering mass.

I love the prophetic words from the dedicatory prayer of the Kirtland Temple in which the Prophet Joseph Smith prayed to the Lord "that thy church may come forth out of the wilderness of darkness, and shine forth fair as the moon, clear as the sun, and terrible as an army with banners . . . that thy glory may fill the earth." (D&C 109:73–74.) . . .

Active membership in the Church is as an anchor in the storms of life we all face. The kingdom is here. Cling to this truth. ("Pillars of Truth," *Ensign*, January 1994, pp. 4–5.)

You can't stop the work of the Lord from going forward. You can stop yourself from enjoying its blessings, but you cannot stop the work of the Lord from going forward. This is His work, and regardless of what we do individually, He will find a way to accomplish His eternal purpose. (Vacaville/Santa Rosa California Regional Conference, priesthood leadership session, May 20, 1995.)

What a wonderful thing it is to be part of this growing kingdom of our Lord. There are no political boundaries separating the hearts of the children of God regardless of where they may live. We are all of one great family. ("As We Gather Together," *Ensign*, November 1995, pp. 4–5.)

Our statisticians tell me that if the present trend continues, then sometime in February of 1996 . . . there will be more members of the Church outside the United States than in the United States.

The crossover of that line is a wonderfully significant thing. It represents the fruit of a tremendous outreach. The God of Heaven, whose servants we are, never intended that this should be a narrow, parochial work. . . .

We have not as yet carried the gospel to every nation, kindred, tongue, and people. But we have made great strides. We have gone wherever we are permitted to go. God is at the helm and doors will be opened by His power according to His divine will. Of that I am confident. Of that I am certain.

I cannot understand those of small vision, who regard this work as limited and provincial. They have no expanding view of it. As certainly as there is an Almighty Father in Heaven, as surely as there is His Son, our Divine Redeemer, so certainly is this work destined to reach out to people everywhere. ("Stay the Course—Keep the Faith," *Ensign*, November 1995, pp. 70–71.)

This is an age of pessimism. Ours is a mission of faith. To my brethren and sisters everywhere, I call upon you to reaffirm your faith, to move this work forward across the world. You can make it stronger by the manner in which you live. Let the gospel be your sword and your shield. Each of us is a part of the greatest cause on earth. Its doctrine came of revelation. Its priesthood came of divine bestowal. Another witness has been added to its testimony of the Lord Jesus Christ. . . .

"Brethren, shall we not go on in so great a cause? Go forward and not backward. Courage, brethren; and on, on to the victory!" (D&C 128:22.) So wrote the Prophet Joseph in a psalm of faith.

How glorious is the past of this great cause. It is filled with heroism, courage, boldness, and faith. How wondrous is the present as we move forward to bless the lives of people wherever they will hearken to the message of the servants of the Lord. How magnificent will be the future as the Almighty rolls on His glorious work touching for good all who will accept and live His gospel, and even reaching to the eternal blessing of His sons and daughters of all generations through the selfless work of those whose hearts are filled with love for the Redeemer of the world.

Back in the days of the great Depression, an old sign dangled by one staple from a piece of rusting barbed wire. The owner of the farm had written:

> *Burned out by drought,*
> *Drowned out by flud waters,*
> *Et out by jackrabbits,*
> *Sold out by sheriff,*
> *Still here!*

So it is with us. There have been makers of threats, naysayers, and criers of doom. They have tried in every conceivable way to injure and destroy this church. But we are still here, stronger and more determined to move it forward. To me it is exciting. It is wonderful. I feel like Ammon of old who said: "Now have we not reason to rejoice? Yea, I say unto you, there never were men that had so great reason to rejoice as we, since the world began; yea, and my joy is carried away, even unto boasting in my God; for he has all power, all wisdom, and all understanding" (Alma 26:35.)

I invite every one of you, wherever you may be as members of this church, to stand on your feet and with a song in your heart move forward, living the gospel, loving the Lord, and building the kingdom. ("Stay the Course—Keep the Faith," *Ensign*, November 1995, p. 72.)

This work is growing across the world in a remarkable and wonderful way. The Lord is opening the doors of the nations. He is touching the hearts of the people. The equivalent of 100 new stakes of Zion are coming into the Church each year. This brings with it significant challenges. As has been widely noted, we have passed the line where we now have more members of the Church outside the United States than we have in the United States.

Thank you, my brothers and sisters, for the goodness of your lives. I thank you for your efforts in trying to measure up to the very high standards of this the Lord's Church. Thank you for your faith. Thank you for your sustaining hands and hearts. Thank you for your prayers.

As everyone here knows, there is only one reason for any of us serving. And that is to assist our Father in Heaven in His declared work and glory to bring to pass the immortality and eternal life of His sons and daughters (see Moses 1:39). ("This Glorious Easter Morn," *Ensign*, May 1996, p. 66.)

In the prayer of dedication at the Kirtland Temple, which prayer was received by revelation according to the Prophet, he petitioned the Lord in these words:

"Remember all thy church, O Lord . . . that the kingdom, which thou hast set up without hands, may become a great mountain and fill the whole earth;

"That thy church may come forth out of the wilderness of darkness, and shine forth fair as the moon, clear as the sun, and terrible as an army with banners" (D&C 109:72–73).

We are witnessing the answer to that remarkable pleading. Increasingly the Church is being recognized at home and abroad for what it truly is. There are still those, not a few, who criticize and rebel, who apostatize and lift their voices against this work. We have always had them. They speak their piece as they walk across the stage of life, and then they are soon forgotten. I suppose we always will have them as long as we are trying to do the work of the Lord. The honest in heart will detect that which is true and that which is false. We go forward, marching as an army with banners emblazoned with the everlasting truth. We are a cause that is militant for truth and goodness. We are a body of Christian soldiers "marching as to war, with the cross of Jesus going on before" (*Hymns*, no. 246).

Everywhere we go we see great vitality in this work. There is enthusiasm wherever it is organized. It is the work of the Redeemer. It is the gospel of good news. It is something to be happy and excited about. ("'Remember . . . Thy Church, O Lord,'" *Ensign*, May 1996, p. 83.)

Many of you are descended from pioneers in this Church. They struggled so hard; they paid such a terrible price for their faith. Be true to them and true always to the Church they loved so much. I wish that each of you would remember that tonight you heard me say that this Church is true. Other churches also do much good, but this is the "true and living Church" of the Lord Jesus Christ, whose name it bears. (See D&C 1:30.) Be true to it. Cling to it. If you will do so it will become as an anchor in the midst of a stormy sea. It will be a light to your lives and a foundation upon which to build them. I give you my solemn testimony that this Church will never be led astray. It is in the hands of God, and should any of its leaders ever attempt to lead it astray, His is the power to remove them. He has said that He has restored His work for the last time, "never again to be destroyed nor given to other people" (D&C 138:44; see also Dan. 2:44–45). ("Stand True and Faithful," *Ensign*, May 1996, p. 93.)

I don't know what the system is in the beyond, but I'm satisfied that those beyond are aware of what goes on here. And I think the Prophet Joseph must have tears in his eyes, tears of gratitude and love and appreciation, as he sees the missionaries in these far reaches of the earth. . . .

We're all a part of a great miracle that's occurring. We are not aware of it because every day we go forth, and it's much like every other day; but a great thing is occurring in the spread of this work across the world. It took the Church 100 years to reach a membership of one million people. Now, we are growing at the rate of one million every three and a half years. We're now well past nine million members. We are in 155 nations, we have 51,000 plus missionaries out. The work is on a roll, to use a phrase that some people like to use. There never was a day like this. There never has been a day like this, when this Church stands tall before the world. (Philippines Cebu Missionary Meeting, June 1, 1996.)

The Church is everywhere it seems, almost. You just cannot comprehend the depth and breadth of this work. More than 150 nations now with 9.5 million members and it is only the beginning. We are still pioneers. We are still scratching the surface. This work will go on and on and on.

We don't get the big picture of this glorious Church moving over the earth to bless the lives of all who will receive it. . . . I hope that every one of you will constantly pray to the Lord for His intervening hand that His Spirit might brood over the people of this nation that their hearts may be touched to hear the truth. I believe that if we pray hard enough, and work at it, somehow miracles can come to pass. We can't be satisfied to just go smugly along on our way. We have on our shoulders responsibility for the salvation of the people of this nation. (Copenhagen Denmark Fireside, June 14, 1996.)

The future is ahead. As great things were expected of [the pioneers], so are they of us. We note what they did with what they had. We have so much more, with an overwhelming challenge to go on and build the kingdom of God. There is so much to do. We have a divine mandate to carry the gospel to every nation, kindred, tongue, and people. . . .

We are engaged in a great and consuming crusade for truth and goodness. Fortunately, we live in a season of goodwill. There has come down to us an inheritance of respect and honor to our people. We must grasp the torch and run the race.

Our people are found in positions of responsibility across the world. Their good reputation enhances the work of the Lord. . . .

The little stone envisioned by Daniel is rolling forth in majesty and power. There are some who still scorn. Let us live above it. There are still those who regard us as a peculiar people. Let us accept that as a compliment and go forth showing by the virtue of our lives the strength and goodness of the wonderful thing in which we believe. . . .

With so great an inheritance, we can do no less than our very best. Those who have gone before expect this of us. We have a mandate from the Lord. We have a vision of our cause and purpose. ("'True to the Faith,'" *Ensign*, May 1997, pp. 66–67.)

The Lord is watching over His kingdom. He is inspiring its leadership to care for its ever-growing membership. . . .

We are living in a wonderful season of the work of the Lord. The work is growing ever stronger. It is expanding across the world. Each of us has an important part to play in this great undertaking. People in more than 160 nations, speaking a score of languages and more, worship our Father in Heaven and our Redeemer, His Beloved Son. This is their great work. It is their cause and their kingdom. . . .

May we be faithful and true, doing our duty to move forward the eternal work of the Lord, blessing our Father's children wherever we can touch their lives. ("May We Be Faithful and True," *Ensign*, May 1997, p. 6.)

KNOWLEDGE

See also Education

None of us . . . knows enough. The learning process is an endless process. We must read, we must observe, we must assimilate, and we must ponder that to which we expose our minds. I believe in evolution, not organic evolution, as it is called, but in the evolution of the mind, the heart, and the soul of man. I believe in improvement. I believe in growth. . . .

. . . You cannot afford to stop. You must not rest in your development. . . . There is so much to learn and so little time in which to learn it. I confess I am constantly appalled by the scarcity of my knowledge, and the one resentment I think I carry concerns the many pressing demands which limit the opportunity for reading. As we talk of reading, I should like to add a word concerning that which we absorb not only out of the processes of the mind, but something further which comes by the power of the Spirit. Remember this promise given by revelation: "God shall give unto you knowledge by his Holy Spirit, yea, by the unspeakable gift of the Holy Ghost. . . ." (D&C 121:26.)

Keep on growing, my brothers and sisters, whether you are thirty or whether you are seventy. Your industry in so doing will cause the years to pass faster than you might wish, but they will be filled with a sweet and wonderful zest that will add flavor to your life and power to your teaching. And to all of this you may add the promise that "whatever principle of intelligence we attain unto in this life, it will rise with us in the resurrection." (D&C 130:18.) ("Four Imperatives for Religious Educators," Church Educational System Address, September 15, 1978.)

Brigham Young once declared: "I shall not cease learning while I live, nor when I arrive in the spirit world; but shall there learn with greater facility; and when I again receive my body, I shall learn a thousand times more in a thousand times less time; and then I do not mean to cease learning, but shall still continue my researches" (*Discourses of Brigham Young*, second edition, p. 248).

Immediately to the east of this building is a mountain. Most of you, I am confident, have looked up at that mountain and thought, "If I could just climb to the top it would be interesting to see the valley on the other side." But those of you who have made that climb have discovered that the valley is only a small and rather shallow depression, and that beyond are many other higher mountains to be climbed.

So I hope it will be with you as you leave here today. You will recognize that while your learning experience has been great, there are even greater opportunities and challenges ahead. Add to your store of information, increase your knowledge, continue the great process of learning. Never lose sight of those marvelous words which appear on the logo of this university, words which came of inspiration to a prophet—"The glory of God is intelligence." . . .

During the years of your studies here I know that in the privacy of your bedrooms, and even while in the classroom or the library, you have on occasion pleaded with the source of all true knowledge for inspiration. If you have not come to know God as your Father, your strength, and your helper, then your presence on this campus has been largely in vain.

Again I should like to quote Brigham Young. . . . Said he: "There is no ingenious mind that has ever invented anything beneficial to the human family but what he obtained it from the one Source, whether he knows or believes it or not. There is only one Source whence men obtain wisdom, and that is God, the Fountain of all wisdom; and though men may claim to make their discoveries by their own wisdom, by meditation and reflection, they are indebted to our Father in heaven for all" (Ibid., p. 400). ("Cornerstones as Stepping-Stones," BYU Commencement Address, April 20, 1979.)

There is . . . incumbent upon you, you who are members of The Church of Jesus Christ of Latter-day Saints, the responsibility to observe the commandment to continue to study and to learn. Said the Lord: "Seek ye out of the best books words of wisdom; seek learning, even by study and also by faith" (D&C 88:118).

He further made it clear that our search for truth must be broad, that we are to learn "of things both in heaven and in the earth, and under the earth; things which have been, things which are, things which must shortly come to pass; things which are at home, things which are abroad; the wars and the perplexities of the nations, and the judgments which are on the land; and a knowledge also of countries and of kingdoms" (D&C 88:79).

What a charge has been laid upon us to grow constantly toward eternity. . . . [Ours] must be a ceaseless quest for truth. That truth must include spiritual and religious truth as well as secular. Joseph F. Smith . . . declared: "We believe in all truth, no matter to what subject it may refer. No sect or religious denomination in the world possesses a single principle of truth that we do not accept or that we will reject. We are willing to receive all truth. From whatever source it may come: for truth will stand, truth will endure. No man's faith, no man's religion, no religion in all the world can ever rise above the truth" (Quoted from *Gospel Doctrine Priesthood Course of Study,* 1971, vol. 1, pp. 11–12). ("The Continuing Pursuit of Truth," BYU–Hawaii Commencement Address, June 18, 1983.)

A scholar recently expressed the view that the Church is an enemy of intellectualism. If he meant by intellectualism that branch of philosophy which teaches "the doctrine that knowledge is wholly or chiefly derived from pure reason" and that "reason is the final principle of reality," then, yes, we are opposed to so narrow an interpretation as applicable to religion. (Quotations from the *Random House Dictionary of the English Language,* p. 738.) Such an interpretation excludes the power of the Holy Spirit in speaking to and through man. Of course we believe in the cultivation of the mind. The emphasis in this university in teaching the secular courses here offered is evidence of our advocacy of the cultivation of the mind, but the intellect is not the only source of knowledge. ("The Continuing Pursuit of Truth," BYU–Hawaii Commencement Address, June 18, 1983.)

None of us can assume that he has learned enough. As the door closes on one phase of life, it opens on another, where we must continue to pursue knowledge. Ours ought to be a ceaseless quest for truth. . . . As we go forward with our lives and our search for truth, let us look for the good, the beautiful, the positive. ("The Continuing Pursuit of Truth," BYU–Hawaii Commencement Address, June 18, 1983.)

We are constantly reminded that there is cause for alarm in our nation. It is shocking to read, for instance, that illiteracy is on the rise. Firms that employ large numbers of workers are alarmed over the qualifications of some of those they hire. The Conference Board recently surveyed 163 large companies in a variety of industries. And now I quote, "Nearly 20 percent of surveyed firms say they are having problems finding workers who read well enough for entry-level jobs. Almost 50 percent say that between 15 percent and 35 percent of their current employees are not capable of handling more complex tasks, and 10 percent say that up to half of their current workers do not have the skills needed for promotion. . . . Nearly a quarter of students currently entering high school will not graduate, and those who do will be less literate than their counterparts a decade ago."

That appraisal comes from a recent issue of the *Wall Street Journal* (9 October 1990, p. A2.). . . . One of the reasons for this condition lies in the way in which so many spend much of their time.

I deplore the terrible waste of the intellectual resources of so many people of this nation who devote countless hours watching mindless drivel [on television]. What a wonderful thing it is, on the other hand, to be found submersed . . . in a world of books wherein you can walk with the great minds of all time. Again, in the *Wall Street Journal* was a column written by the former editor of the *Chicago Tribune.* He wrote of certain aspects of television and then asked:

"What is the mystery . . . about a society that has the manners of a rock band, the morals of a soap opera, the decision-making ability of the Simpsons and wants to pay for government with Visa and American Express? Why should we be surprised that our underlying culture is constructed from the ratings-based, give-them-what-they-want, remote-controlled, quick-zap world of commercial television." (Jim Squires, "Television's Civil War," *Wall Street Journal,* 8 October 1990, p. A10.)

This old world needs straightening up. It needs leadership. . . . Georg Wilhelm Friedrich Hegel once made a statement to the effect that those who do not read history will have to repeat it. ("Out of Your Experience Here," *BYU 1990–1991 Devotional and Fireside Speeches,* October 16, 1990, p. 28.)

When all is said and done, we are all students. If the day ever comes when we quit learning, look out. We will just atrophy and die. We all can learn and learn well. (Oahu Hawaii Regional Conference, February 18, 1996.)

There is a great potential within each of us to go on learning. Regardless of our age, unless there be serious illness, we can read, study, drink in the writings of wonderful men and women. Dr. Joshua Liebman once observed:

"The great thing is that as long as we live we have the privilege of growing. We can learn new skills, engage in new kinds of work, devote ourselves to new causes, make new friends. Accepting then the truth that we are capable in some directions and limited in others, that genius is rare, that mediocrity is the portion of most of us, let us remember that we can and must change ourselves. Until the day of our death we can grow. We can tap hidden resources in our makeup" (*Getting the Most Out of Life*, p. 120).

We of this Church have been given a marvelous promise by the Lord Himself. Said He: "That which is of God is light; and he that receiveth light, and continueth in God, receiveth more light; and that light groweth brighter and brighter until the perfect day" (D&C 50:24).

What a remarkable statement that is. It is one of my favorite verses of scripture. It speaks of growth, of development, of the march that leads toward Godhood. It goes hand in hand with these great declarations: "The glory of God is intelligence, or, in other words, light and truth" (D&C 93:36); "If a person gains more knowledge and intelligence in this life through his diligence and obedience than another, he will have so much the advantage in the world to come" (D&C 130:19); and, "whatever principle of intelligence we attain unto in this life, it will rise with us in the resurrection" (D&C 130:18).

What a profound challenge is found in these marvelous statements. We must go on growing. We must continuously learn. It is a divinely given mandate that we go on adding to our knowledge.

We have access to institute classes, extension courses, education weeks, and many other opportunities where, as we study and match our minds with others, we will discover a tremendous reservoir of capacity within ourselves. (Salt Lake Valley Single Adult Fireside, September 22, 1996.)

LANGUAGE

See Profanity

LEADERSHIP

There is a loneliness in all aspects of leadership. . . . It was ever thus. The price of leadership is loneliness. The price of adherence to conscience is loneliness. The price of adherence to principle is loneliness. I think it is inescapable. The Savior of the world was a man who walked in loneliness. I do not know of any statement more underlined with the pathos of loneliness than His statement:

"The foxes have holes, and the birds of the air have nests; but the Son of Man hath not where to lay his head." (Matthew 8:20.)

There is no lonelier picture in history than of the Savior upon the cross, alone, the Redeemer of mankind, the Savior of the world, bringing to pass the atonement, the Son of God suffering for the sins of mankind. As I think of that I reflect on a statement made by Channing Pollock. "Judas with his thirty pieces of silver was a failure. Christ on the cross was the greatest figure of time and eternity."

Joseph Smith likewise was a figure of loneliness. I have a great love for the boy who came out of the woods, who after that experience could never be the same again, who was berated and persecuted and looked down upon. Can you sense the pathos in these words of the boy Prophet?

"For I had seen a vision; I knew it, and I knew that God knew it, and I could not deny it, neither dared I do it; at least I knew that by so doing I would offend God, and come under condemnation." (PGP, Joseph Smith 2:25.)

There are few more sorrowful pictures, not in our history anyway, than of the Prophet being rowed across the Mississippi River by Stephen Markham, knowing that his enemies were after his life, and then there came some of his own who accused him of running away. Hear his response:

"If my life is of no value to my friends, it is of none to myself." (*DHC* 6:549, June 1844.) ("The Loneliness of Leadership," *BYU Speeches of the Year*, November 4, 1969, pp. 3–4.)

As you know, I have served in the Presidency since 1981, a period of almost 14 years now. I have served as a counselor to three great Presidents. I have been exposed to the duties and responsibilities of the Presidency and for a good while found myself almost alone. But I have come to learn in the last few days that one can carry the responsibility of the Presidency without experiencing the awesome breadth and depth and length of the responsibility of the office of President.

I have received many expressions of friendship and brotherhood and support, and I have discovered, even to my surprise, that with all of this there is an interesting loneliness that comes with this office. That may sound strange. It is strange. But it is real. One feels compelled to go to one's knees and plead with the Lord for direction and guidance, for strength and capacity. (General Authority Training Meeting, March 28, 1995.)

I love these great words of Alma, where he talks about the things of the Spirit and says, "Behold, I say unto you they are made known unto me by the Holy Spirit of God. Behold, I have fasted and prayed many days that I might know these things of myself. And now I do know of myself that they are true; for the Lord God hath made them manifest unto me by his Holy Spirit; and this is the spirit of revelation which is in me." (Alma 5:46.) Ask the Lord to lead you by His quiet voice in the things you ought to do as leaders in this Church. You have a great responsibility for the well-being, even the salvation of others. You are very important in this Church. The kind of help you really need won't come from the handbook, though you need to know the handbook; but you'll get the best help from private and thoughtful communion with the Lord. We all need to quietly and calmly reflect on the things of God. (Smithfield/Logan Utah Regional Conference, priesthood leadership session, April 20, 1996.)

I don't know whether you are butchers or bakers or college professors or doctors or lawyers or brick masons, or whatever, but you come of the rank and file of the Church. We all do. We are not born to it in the sense that we inherit it. We are developed, trained, polished, refined, blessed as we serve in the great capacities to which we have been called. And I'd like to suggest that there is no mean or small or unimportant responsibility in the work of the Lord.

Leadership. I copied this down some years ago, words from General Mark W. Clark, "All nations seek it constantly because it is the key to greatness, sometimes to survival . . . the electric and the elusive quality known as leadership. Where does juvenile delinquency begin? In leaderless families. Where do slums fester? In leaderless cities. Which armies falter? Which political parties fail? Poorly led ones. Contrary to the old saying that leaders are born not made, the art of leading can be taught and it can be mastered" (General Mark W. Clark, quoted in Thomas Jefferson Research Center Bulletin, No. 23, December 1967).

If anyone doubts that, he only need look across this Church to see where the butcher and the baker and the candlestick maker are nurtured to become men of great leadership in the Church. I stand back in reverent respect for the bishops of this Church and what they do. To use an old phrase, that's where the rubber hits the road, at the ward level. . . . That's where authority touches people, in the office of bishop. And as I see their devotion and the wisdom and the inspiration and the consecration of bishops, I thank the Lord for these marvelous men—thousands upon thousands of them now—and they are just the same in Pittsburgh as they are in Salt Lake City; and they are just the same in Salt Lake City as they are in Tokyo; and they are just the same in Seoul, Korea, or in Stockholm, Sweden, or Manchester, England, or Mexico City, or Veracruz, or Caracas, Venezuela, or Guayaquil, Ecuador. Wherever you go, as the man accepts the call, the Lord magnifies the man. And so it is with the other offices in this Church. (Pittsburgh Pennsylvania Regional Conference, April 27, 1996.)

I copied these words from Peter Drucker, a long time ago, but I've never found anything any better. "Executive ability," said he, "seems to have little correlation with intelligence, imagination, or brilliance." That's a great comfort to me. I hope it is to you.

"The good executive," he said, "(1) practices conservation of time, (2) has his eye fixed on new developments, (3) builds on the strengths of his colleagues, (4) starves the problems and feeds the opportunities."

It's so easy to feed the problems and starve the opportunities. I spend a good part of every day dealing with problems; in fact, it seems to me that every letter that comes in and everybody who comes in has a problem. We have many problems in this Church, many of them. Some of them are on two feet, a good many of them are, walking around causing trouble, doing what they shouldn't do. And then somebody writes a letter to the First Presidency. We should be able to rise above the problems. We have them. Of course we have them. But it's a great thing to rise above the problems and get the big picture of this, the Church and kingdom of God, restored to earth in the dispensation of the fulness of times, to go forth across the world to change the lives of men and women. (Pittsburgh Pennsylvania Regional Conference, April 27, 1996.)

I recently reread a statement given on [the BYU] campus years ago by Charles H. Malik, then Secretary General of the United Nations. He said:

"I respect all men, and it is from disrespect for none that I say there are no great leaders in the world today. In fact, greatness itself is laughed to scorn. You should not be great today—you should sink yourself into the herd, you should not be distinguished from the crowd, you should simply be one of the many.

"The commanding voice is lacking. The voice which speaks little, but which when it speaks, speaks with compelling moral authority—this kind of voice is not congenial to this age. The age flattens and levels down every distinction into drab uniformity. Respect for the high, the noble, the great, the rare, the specimen that appears once every hundred or every thousand years, is gone. Respect at all is gone! If you ask whom and what people do respect, the answer is literally nobody and nothing. This is simply an unrespecting age—it is the age of utter mediocrity. To become a leader today, even a mediocre leader, is a most uphill grade. You are constantly and in every way and from every side pulled down. One wonders who of those living today will be remembered a thousand years from now—the way we remember with such profound respect Plato, and Aristotle, and Christ, and Paul, and Augustine, and Aquinas."

He concludes: "If you believe in prayer, my friends, and I know you do, then pray that God send great leaders, especially great leaders of the spirit" (*BYU Studies,* Vol. 16, No. 4, p. 543).

It is in harmony with that profound and sobering statement that I wish to say a few words to you today. You are good. But it is not enough just to be good. You must be good for something. You must contribute good to the world. The world must be a better place for your presence. And the good that is in you must be spread to others.

I do not suppose that any of us here this day will be remembered a thousand years from now. I do not suppose that we will be remembered a century from now.

But in this world so filled with problems, so constantly threatened by dark and evil challenges, you can and must rise above mediocrity, above indifference. You can become involved and speak with a strong voice for that which is right. ("Stand Up for Truth," BYU Devotional Address, September 17, 1996.)

Newspaper reporters ask me what is the greatest problem facing the Church today. I reply that it is growth. That is our most serious problem, and if you must have a problem, what a wonderful problem it is.

This growth entails two major responsibilities: (1) the training of leadership; and (2) the building of houses of worship in which the people can meet.

It does not matter the background of those who come into the Church. We must have leaders wherever they are. We must take what we have and train them. Some of them will not be very well educated. They may not appear to be very smart. But with humility and prayer and the help of the Lord, they can succeed. I can commend to them Peter Drucker's recipe:

The good executive practices conservation of time. Time is really all that we have. And every individual has an equal portion of it. The trick is to get more out of what is available to us. A man who knows how to control his time has won half the battle. . . .

Two, he has his eye fixed on new developments. Every leader must keep current. He must read. He must study. In the Church he must know the scriptures and the handbook. He must read the bulletins. He must keep his eye fixed on new developments. If he does not he will soon find himself lagging behind and the work will suffer.

Three, he builds on the strengths of his colleagues. No man can do it alone. Every executive, every manager, every leader must have around him a body of trusted colleagues. If they do what they ought to do, they will make him successful, and they will become successful along with him. He will develop a great team whose accomplishments will be remarkable. It is thus in the Church. Every bishop, every branch president throughout the world has two counselors. They are his assistants, his aides, his Joshuas to hold up his hands while the battle rages. All of you are familiar, of course, with the organization of the Church. You are involved in it. In every ward beneath the level of the bishopric is at least a score of very able and devoted and loyal people, both men and women. People of other faiths ask how we do it without a paid ministry. The answer is simple. We divide the burden of responsibility.

When I was first made a stake president, we had two very large and worrisome projects. The first was to build a stake center. In those days we raised 50 percent of the money and handled the contracting, architectural services, and other things ourselves. The second consuming project was a large welfare farm.

I said to my first counselor, who was a builder, "You take care of the new building. This will be your responsibility. I will come and drive some nails and do what I can, but the construction of this stake center is your responsibility." He did it. He did it much better than I could have done it. That stake center is still one of the finest in the Church.

To the second I said, "The stake farm is your responsibility. If I get a phone call in the middle of the night that our cows are in the neighbor's corn, I will simply ask the caller to get in touch with you and I will go back to sleep."

It worked that way. These two men did the work, and I received the credit. I submit that this is good management.

The good executive builds on the strengths of his colleagues.

Four, he starves the problems and feeds the opportunities. What a great concept that is.

Yesterday I was in meetings all day beginning at 7:30 in the morning and concluding very late in the afternoon. We dealt with one vexatious problem after another. I said to myself, "How can you keep this up? Constantly dealing with problems of this kind will eat you up."

Then I thought of Peter Drucker's statement. I said to myself, "Deal with the problems as wisely as you can. Make your decisions. You may be right, you may be wrong. Hopefully you will be right because you have prayed earnestly over the matter and you have discussed it with your associates. But once made, put these decisions behind you and do not worry about them. Turn around, stand tall, put your head up, and look forward to the marvelous opportunities that you have." (BYU Management Society Awards Dinner, April 17, 1997.)

In your ministry as leaders in this Church, brethren, bless the people. Lift them. Encourage them. Help them. There are so many in distress. They have so many troubles, so many problems. . . . We receive thousands of letters in the Office of the First Presidency from people who live all over this world, in spite of all of our efforts to get them to see their bishops instead of writing to the First Presidency. But they have problems, many of them, and they need help, and they need encouragement, and they need listening to, and that's our great opportunity to bless them.

Bless them with leadership. "For if the trumpet give an uncertain sound, who shall prepare himself to the battle?" (1 Cor. 14:8). Yours is the opportunity to blow the trumpet with a certain sound. You are leaders. Every man here is a leader because you are responsible for the well-being of others. That makes of you a leader. Lead the people. Lead them with boldness. Lead them with faith. Get on your knees and pray to the Lord and lead the people with faith. They will follow where you go as their leaders. God bless you in so doing.

Lead them with doctrine. "Search the scriptures; for in them ye think ye have eternal life; and they are they which testify of me" (John 5:39). Teach out of the word of God the doctrine of the kingdom which will save them and bless them and help them and lift them. Teach them the scriptures. Lead them with the scriptures.

Bless them with responsibility. Give them something to do. . . . I talked the other day with a man who's been in the stake presidency, who's been in the bishopric, who presided over a mission, who's been a regional representative, and he doesn't have a thing to do, except to sit home with his sick wife and nurse and tend her. He is almost destroyed because he has nothing to reach out to, no responsibility in this kingdom. Bless them with responsibility, brethren. They long for it. They hunger for it, and they need it.

Bless them with example. My father used to say that "more religion is caught than is taught." I believe that. This is a contagious thing. . . . Teach them with example. Let your example be such that they can follow it. Brethren, there's no place in your lives, there is no place in your lives for any element of infidelity or immorality, or the reading of pornography, or anything of that kind. You just cannot afford to touch it. . . .

Treat your wives with kindness. You will never have a greater asset in all of this world than the woman with whom you joined hands over the altar in the temple and to whom you pledged your love and loyalty and devotion for time and all eternity. . . . Be an example to your people of those who walk the path of faith. God bless you as leaders to set an example before your people.

Bless those you lead. May their lives be richer for their experience with you under your leadership. I am so grateful, as I look back, at the privilege that has been mine to work with great men since I was a very young man, even when I was on a mission. My mission president was a member of the Council of the Twelve, a great and good man, and ever since then, it has been my privilege to work with great men who have blessed my life in a very real sense. I am here today because of the munificent effect that others have had upon my life. I know that. I've been blessed, and as long as I live, I'd like to bless the lives of others. (Potomac Virginia Regional Conference, priesthood leadership session, April 26, 1997.)

LITERACY

See also Education

You know that your children will read. They will read books and they will read magazines and newspapers. Cultivate within them a taste for the best. While they are very young, read to them the great stories which have become immortal because of the virtues they teach. Expose them to good books. Let there be a corner somewhere in your house, be it ever so small, where they will see at least a few books of the kind upon which great minds have been nourished. ("Opposing Evil," *Ensign,* November 1975, p. 39.)

The older I grow, the more thankful I feel to my parents in providing for us, in the home in which we were reared, good things to read. We had a library in that home with more than a thousand volumes. In those days, of course, we had no television, and radio was not even available during most of those earlier years. I do not wish to convey the idea that as children we read extensively in our father's books. But they provided an environment. We saw our father and mother read, and they read to us. It did something of an indefinable nature. It gave us a familiarity with good books. We felt at home and at ease with them. They were not strangers to us. They were as friends, willing to give to us if we were willing to make a little effort. . . .

As I look back upon my high school and university days, I am amazed that we had so little exposure to what we call today pornography and obscenity. Perhaps ours was a sheltered society, but it was a wonderful environment in which to grow.

Unfortunately, we live now in a sex-saturated society. Pornography comes at us from all sides: in the theater, in books and magazines, in newspaper advertising, in television in its various forms, and in some instances from radio.

There is no way to blank it out entirely. But we can do something to offset its corrosive influence. We can expose our children to good reading. Let them grow with good books and good Church magazines around them. . . .

Years ago I read that Emerson was once asked which of all the books he had read had most affected his life. His response was that he could no more remember the books he had read than he could remember the meals he had eaten, but they had made him. All of us are the products of the elements to which we are exposed. ("Tithing: An Opportunity to Prove Our Faithfulness," *Ensign*, May 1982, p. 42.)

Now a great new project is to be undertaken. It is a practical and much-needed part of this 150th anniversary celebration [of the Relief Society]. But its consequences will go on and on and be felt in the lives of generations yet to come. It is a program to teach those who suffer from functional illiteracy. It is designed to bring light into the lives of those who can neither read nor write.

This lack of literacy skills is far more common than many believe. In some areas of the world 75 percent are unable to read or write. Illiteracy's effects are tragic. Those who are its victims are denied the opportunity to become acquainted with history and the great minds of the past. They cannot read the daily newspaper. They cannot understand the word of God set forth in the immortal scripture. For them there is little light of ages past, and only diminished knowledge of the vast and intriguing world of which they are a part. The darkness that surrounds them, the bleak shadow of illiteracy, condemns them to poverty, hunger, and ignorance. Theirs is only half a world, a world in which they are literally blinded from much of that which goes on about them. Now there is to be provided a means to open the doors of communication and let in the light of understanding. Women old and young, in various nations, will be taught by their sisters to read and write. Imagine, if you can, the potential of this inspired program. Who dare dream of its consequences? ("'Ambitious to Do Good,'" *Ensign*, March 1992, p. 6.)

I have done a little study on literacy in the world. A billion of the five billion people on earth cannot read or write. A substantial portion—at least 10 percent and probably closer to 15 percent—of the people in America cannot read or write, right here in this nation. We have slipped from first to fifth place among the nations of the world in our competitive ability. How can you expect otherwise when so many people can't read a simple set of instructions in front of them? I read a while ago that 99 percent of the accidents in India are caused by truck drivers and taxi drivers who can't read "stop" and "go." What a tragedy—what a stark, miserable, and dark tragedy. To not be able to read, to understand, to write—what a tragedy. We can help to lift this curse. Things can be brought to pass to change this intolerable condition. ("Our Philosophy," Bonneville International Corporation "Gathering of Eagles," June 25, 1992.)

I feel sorry for parents who do not read to their young children. I feel sorry for children who do not learn the wonders to be found in good books. How stimulating an experience it is to get into the mind of a great thinker as he expresses himself with language cultivated and polished concerning great and important issues. I read once that Thomas Jefferson grew up on the magnificent phrases of the King James Bible. . . .

A man sent me a book the other day. He is a doctor of philosophy in one of our great universities. He told me that reading that book had become a great experience in his life.

I have now read it. It is the story of a boy in Paris who in an accident was blinded at the age of eight. It is an account of how when darkness surrounded him there came a new light into his life. When he was 16 or 17, the Germans conquered France and hordes of German soldiers marched into Paris. The Vichy government was formed by those who were traitors to the great traditions of a proud and strong nation. This blind boy, a brilliant student, organized a resistance group. He and his associates ran a clandestine operation in getting information and circulating it with a little newspaper printed on a duplicator. Their effort grew until they were distributing more than 250,000 copies an issue. Then he was betrayed, arrested, and sent to Buchenwald. Here, in filth and despair, he lived with similar victims. He could not see, but there was a light within that rose above the tragedy of his circumstances. He survived as a leader among those in that foul camp. The little newspaper he started became a great newspaper, the *France-Soir*. I read that book and was lifted and strengthened and, if I may say so, purified just a little by the story of that remarkable young man. ("Saving the Nation by

Changing Our Homes," BYU Management Society, Washington, D.C., March 5, 1994.)

I love books. I grew up in a home where we had a library. My father and mother had a room set aside as a library with bookcases all around the room and more than 1,000 books on them. I still have my father's set of the Harvard Classics. I was preparing to speak a few days ago and went to the Harvard Classics to look through George Washington's inaugural address. I picked the volume up in my hand and held it there and thought to myself, "What a marvelous thing is a book. What a marvelous thing is a book, an extraordinary thing, these sheets of paper that are bound together, upon which are set forth the great thoughts of great and good and wise men and women to which we can refer as occasion demands."

There is something wonderful about a good book. I have a computer in my study but I am still a stranger to it. And I am afraid I ever will be. I putter around with it, but it and I do not get along very well. That is why I am so grateful for books. I know how to handle them, how to deal with them, how to use them, I hope.

I am so grateful for libraries. I have been in some of the great libraries of the world. . . . There is something sacred, I think, about a great library because it represents the preservation of the wisdom, the learning, the pondering, of men and women of all of the ages accumulated together under one roof to which we can have access as our needs require. (Harold B. Lee Library Expansion Groundbreaking Ceremony, September 20, 1996.)

Not long ago I was at the great Vatican Library at the Vatican in Rome and it was a most inspirational experience to see those old illuminated texts, hundreds and hundreds of years old, that had been preserved for the blessing of mankind. I once studied in the British Museum, the great national library of Britian, great tall stacks of books, hundreds and hundreds and hundreds of thousands of them.

I love libraries. I love books. There is something wonderful about a book. You can pick it up. You can heft it. You can read it. You can set it down. You can think of what you have read. It does something for you. You can share great minds and great actions and great undertakings in the pages of a book. (Howard W. Hunter Law Library Dedication, BYU, March 21, 1997.)

LOVE

See also Charity

Our young friends of the psychedelic crowd clamor for love as the solution to the world's problems. Their expression may sound genuine, but their coin is counterfeit. Too often the love of which they speak is at best only hollow mummery; at worst it deteriorates into a lascivious eroticism. On the other hand, the love of Jesus was a thing of courage so much needed in our time. It was the love that embraced all men as the children of God; it was the love that turned the other cheek; it was the love spoken from the cross in undying words, "Father, forgive them; for they know not what they do." (Luke 23:34.) (Conference Report, April 1969, p. 61.)

We must be more diligent and effective as we pursue a steady course in instructing and perfecting the lives of our own people. We must hold to first principles. We must prioritize our teachings to emphasize that which is of the greatest worth.

"Then one of them, which was a lawyer, asked him a question, tempting him, and saying,

"Master, which is the great commandment in the law?

"Jesus said unto him, Thou shalt love the Lord thy God with all thy heart, and with all thy soul, and with all thy mind.

"This is the first and great commandment.

"And the second is like unto it, Thou shalt love thy neighbour as thyself.

"On these two commandments hang all the law and the prophets." (Matt. 22:35–40.)

This must be the foundation of our instruction: love of God and love for and service to others—neighbors, family, and all with whom we have association. That which we teach must be constantly gauged against these two standards established by the Lord. If we shall do so, this work will continue to roll forward. ("He Slumbers Not, nor Sleeps," *Ensign*, May 1983, p. 8.)

When I was a little boy, we children traded paper hearts at school on Valentine's Day. At night we dropped them at the doors of our friends, stamping on the porch and then running in the dark to hide.

Almost without exception those valentines had printed on their face, "I love you." I have since come to know that love is more than a paper heart. Love is of the very essence of life. It is the pot of gold at the end of the rainbow. Yet it is more than the end of the rainbow. Love is at the beginning also, and from it springs the beauty that arches across the sky on a stormy day. Love is the security for which children weep, the yearning of youth, the adhesive that binds marriage, and the lubricant that prevents devastating friction in the home; it is the peace of old age, the sunlight of hope shining through death. How rich are those who enjoy it in their associations with family, friends, church, and neighbors.

I am one who believes that love, like faith, is a gift of God. ("And the Greatest of These Is Love," *Ensign*, March 1984, p. 3.)

This principle of love is the basic essence of the gospel of Jesus Christ. Without love of God and love of neighbor there is little else to commend the gospel to us as a way of life. ("And the Greatest of These Is Love," *Ensign*, March 1984, p. 5.)

Love is the only force that can erase the differences between people, that can bridge chasms of bitterness. I recall these lines:

> *He drew a circle that shut me out —*
> *Heretic, rebel, a thing to flout.*
> *But Love and I had the wit to win:*
> *We drew a circle that took him in.*
> (EDWIN MARKHAM, "OUTWITTED.")

He who most beautifully taught this everlasting truth was the Son of God, the one perfect exemplar and teacher of love. His coming to earth was an expression of his Father's love.

"For God so loved the world, that he gave his only begotten Son, that whosoever believeth in him should not perish, but have everlasting life.

"For God sent not his Son into the world to condemn the world; but that the world through him might be saved." (John 3:16–17.) . . .

As we look with love and gratitude to God, as we serve him with an eye single to his glory, there goes from us the darkness of sin, the darkness of selfishness, the darkness of pride. There will come an increased love for our Eternal Father and for his Beloved Son, our Savior and our Redeemer. There will come a greater sense of service toward our fellowmen, less of thinking of self and more of reaching out to others. ("And the Greatest of These Is Love," *Ensign*, March 1984, p. 5.)

I have seen time and again that love of God can bridge the chasm of fear. Love for the Church can also lift one above doubt. I have told university students of my collegiate experience more than fifty years ago. . . .

Young people of college age are inclined to be a little critical and cynical anyway, but that attitude was compounded in the 1930s by the cynicism of the times. It was easy to wonder about many things, to question things in life, in the world, in the Church, in aspects of the gospel. But it was also a season of gladness and a season of love. Behind such thoughts, there was for me an underlying foundation of love that came from great parents and a good family, a wonderful bishop, devoted and faithful teachers, and the scriptures to read and ponder.

Although in our youth we had trouble understanding many things, there was in our hearts something of a love for God and his great work that carried us above any doubts and fears. We loved the Lord and we loved good and honorable friends. From such love we drew great strength.

How great and magnificent is the *power of love* to overcome fear and doubt, worry and discouragement. ("'God Hath Not Given Us the Spirit of Fear,'" *Ensign*, October 1984, pp. 4–5.)

Love of God is basic. It is the very foundation of true worship. It puts heart and soul and spirit into our lives. It subdues arrogance and conceit and greed. It leads to love for all of God's creations. It leads to obedience to the second great commandment, love of neighbor. . . .

. . . [Love] is of the very essence of our faith and must be in the structure of all of our thinking. ("A Unique and Wonderful University," *BYU 1988–89 Devotional and Fireside Speeches*, October 11, 1988, p. 51.)

Love is like the Polar Star. In a changing world, it is a constant. It is of the very essence of the gospel. It is the security of the home. It is the safeguard of community life. It is a beacon of hope in a world of distress. ("Let Love Be the Lodestar of Your Life, *Ensign*, May 1989, p. 66.)

To love the Lord is not just counsel; it is not just well-wishing. It is a commandment. It is the first and great commandment incumbent upon each of us because love of God is the root from which spring all other types of love; love of God is the root of all virtue, of all goodness, of all strength of character, of all fidelity to do right. Love the Lord your God, and love His Son, and be ever grateful for their love for us. Whenever other love fades, there will be that shining, transcendent, everlasting love of God for each of us and the love of His Son, who gave His life for us. (Ricks College Regional Conference, Rexburg, Idaho, October 29, 1995.)

When I was a missionary in England sixty years ago, we held street meetings at a corner around from Trafalgar Square, and right across the street was a beautiful statue of an English girl. On that statue were engraved the words, "Brussels Dawn, 1918" and the words, "Patriotism is not enough, I must have love for all men." Edith Cavell was shot by the German conquerors in Brussels as an English spy, although she was there working as a nurse doing Christian good. But, ever since sixty years ago when I held street meetings on that corner and looked across at that statue and read those words, the word "Brussels" has had added meaning in my life. "Patriotism is not enough, I must have love for all men." (Belgium Brussels Missionary Meeting, June 12, 1996.)

LOYALTY

Stand up for loyalty, to your associates, to your heritage, to your good name, to the Church of which you are a part. How marvelous a quality is loyalty. There is no substitute for it. It comes of an inner strength. . . .

In this world, almost without exception, we must work together as teams. It is so obvious to all of us that those on the football field or the basketball court must work together with loyalty one to another if they are to win. It is so in life with each of us. We work as teams, and there must be loyalty among us.

William Manchester, as a young Marine, fought through the terrible battle of Okinawa. He was savagely wounded, but lived to return to fight again in the hellish fire of the Shuri Line, where thousands on each side perished. Years later, as a grown and mature man, and an accomplished writer, he returned to Okinawa and walked over its once battle-scarred ridges. Reflecting on those earlier brutish days, he wrote:

"Men, I now knew, do not fight for flag or country, for the Marine Corps or glory or any other abstraction. They fight for one another. Any man in combat who lacks comrades who will die for him, or for whom he is willing to die, is not a man at all. He is truly damned." (*Goodbye Darkness: A Memoir of the Pacific War,* p. 391.) Be loyal to those with whom you work in the battles of life. "A house divided against itself cannot stand." (See Mark 3:25.) ("Stand Up for Truth," BYU Devotional Address, September 17, 1996.)

Be loyal to the Church. Stand tall for it. Defend it. Speak no evil against it. It is the work of God. He who ridicules it or defames it offends Him whose church it is. It carries the sacred name of the Lord Jesus Christ. ("Stand Up for Truth," BYU Devotional Address, September 17, 1996.)

The pioneers were loyal. They were loyal to one another. They were loyal to the Church. They were loyal to the nation of which they were a part and which, in a sense, had betrayed them. I quote from a recent article that appeared in the *Church News:*

"Heber McBride, then 13 years old, traveled to the Salt Lake Valley in the Martin Handcart Company in 1856 with his parents, Robert and Margaret, and four brothers and sisters.

"The following incident, found in his memoirs, occurred one day after the company crossed the North Platte River, just west of the present-day Casper, Wyoming.

"'That evening as we crossed the Platte River for the last time it was very cold. The next morning there was about six inches of snow on the ground, then what we had to suffer can never be told. Father was very bad and could hardly sit up in the tent. . . . I managed to get Father in one of the wagons. That was the last we ever saw of him alive. . . .

"'[That evening] the snow was getting very deep and my sister and me had to pitch our tent and get some wood, but there were plenty of dry willows. After we had made mother as comfortable as possible, we went to find father, but the wind was blowing the snow so hard we could not see anything. . . . We did not find father that night.

"'The next morning the snow was about eighteen inches deep and awful cold. While my sister was preparing our little bite of breakfast I went to look for father, and found him under the wagon with snow all over him and he was stiff and dead. I felt as though my heart would burst as I sat down with him in the snow and took his hand in mine and cried, 'Oh, Father, Father.'

"'There we were, away from everything, away out on the plains with hardly anything to eat or wear, and father dead and mother sick; a widow with five children and hardly able to live from day to day. After I had my cry out I went back to the tent and told mother and the children. To try to write my feelings is out of the question.

"'We were not the only family called upon to mourn the loss of a father that morning, for there were thirteen men dead in camp.

"'The men that were able to do anything cleared off the snow and made a fire and thawed the ground and dug a hole and buried all in one grave. I can assure you that the men had no heart to do more than they had to do.'" (Memoirs of Heber McBride, October 1856; *Church News*, December 28, 1996.)

In those terrible, terrible circumstances they were loyal to one another. When they were sick they nursed one another. When they died, the whole company worked together to bury them. . . . Loyalty to one another and loyalty to the Church marked their actions.

God be thanked for their great and noble example to each of us. My brethren and sisters, we must be loyal. We cannot be found on the sidelines carping and criticizing and finding fault with one another. We must help one another with each other's burdens. We must share the sorrows of one another. We must rejoice with one another in their victories. We must be loyal to the Church against all its enemies. (Church Educational System Young Adult Fireside, February 2, 1997.)

MARRIAGE

See also Eternal Marriage

Under the gospel plan marriage is a companionship, with equality between the partners. We walk side by side with respect, appreciation, and love one for another. There can be nothing of inferiority or superiority between the husband and wife in the plan of the Lord. I am satisfied that our Father in Heaven loves his daughters as much as he loves his sons, and any man who demeans or belittles his wife affronts her Father in Heaven.

If husbands and wives would only give greater emphasis to the virtues that are to be found in one another and less to the faults, there would be fewer broken hearts, fewer tears, fewer divorces, and much more happiness in the homes of our people. ("If I Were You, What Would I Do?" *BYU 1983–84 Fireside and Devotional Speeches*, September 20, 1983, p. 10.)

It is difficult for me to understand the tragic accounts of troubled marriages that come to me. They speak of abuse. They speak of dictatorial attitudes, and of some husbands who are bullies in their own homes. They speak of violations of trust, and of broken covenants. They speak of divorce and tears and heartache. Only the other day a letter came to my desk from a woman who wrote at length of her troubles. In a spirit of desperation she asked: "Does a woman have any promise of some day being a first class member of the human race? Will she always be a piece of chattel wrapped in a chuddar acting only by the permission of the man who stands at her head?" (A chuddar, incidentally, is a very simple shawl worn by women in India.) She then continued: "To me the answers to these questions are no longer important, but I have daughters. If it is possible for a woman to look forward to an eternity of anything other than being barefoot and pregnant, I would like to be able to teach them this."

There is bitter tragedy in the lines of that letter. I fear there are many others who may feel that way. The situation is tragic because it is so extremely different from what our Father in heaven would have for his daughters. Behind this woman's words I see the picture of a wife who is discouraged, starved for appreciation, ready to give up, and not knowing which way to turn. I see a husband who has defaulted on his sacred obligations, one who is calloused in his feelings, warped in his perceptions, denying through his manner of living the very essence of the gospel of Jesus Christ. I do not doubt that there has been fault on her part as well as his, but I am inclined to think that his is the more serious.

To men within the sound of my voice, wherever you may be, I say, if you are guilty of demeaning behavior toward your wife, if you are prone to dictate and exercise authority over her, if you are selfish and brutal in your actions in the home, then, stop it! Repent! Repent now while you have the opportunity to do so.

To you wives who are constantly complaining, and see only the dark side of life, and feel that you are unloved and unwanted, look into your own hearts and minds. If there is something wrong, turn about. Put a smile on your faces. Make yourselves attractive. Brighten your outlook. You deny yourselves happiness and court misery if you constantly complain and do nothing to rectify your own faults. Rise above the shrill clamor over rights and prerogatives and walk in the quiet dignity of a daughter of God. . . .

The time is now for husbands and wives who may have offended one another to ask forgiveness and resolve to cultivate respect and affection one for another, standing before the Creator as sons and daughters worthy of His smile upon us. ("Cornerstones of a Happy Home," Husbands and Wives Fireside Satellite Broadcast, January 29, 1984.)

God our Eternal Father ordained that we should be companions. That implies equality. Marriage is a joint venture. Of course, there are hazards and problems, but these are secondary to the greater opportunities and greater satisfactions that come of sublimating selfish interests to the good of the partnership.

Some years ago I clipped from the *Deseret News* a column by Jenkins Lloyd Jones, who said in part: "There seems to be a superstition among many thousands of our young who hold hands . . . that marriage is a cottage surrounded by perpetual hollyhocks, to which a perpetually young and handsome husband comes home to a perpetually young and beautiful wife. When the hollyhocks wither and boredom and bills appear, the divorce courts are jammed. . . . ("Big Rock Candy Mountains," Deseret News, 12 June 1973, A4).

The trick, my brethren and sisters, is to enjoy the journey, traveling hand in hand, in sunshine and storm, as companions who love one another. ("Cornerstones of a Happy Home," Husbands and Wives Fireside Satellite Broadcast, January 29, 1984.)

I hear so many complaints from men and women that they cannot communicate with one another. Perhaps I am naive, but I do not understand this. Communication is essentially a matter of conversation. They must have communicated when they were courting. Can they not continue to speak together after marriage? Can they not discuss with one another in an open and frank and candid and happy way their interests, their problems, their challenges, their desires? It seems to me that communication is largely a matter of talking with one another.

But let that talk be quiet, for quiet talk is the language of love. It is the language of peace. It is the language of God. . . . The voice of heaven is a still small voice. The voice of peace in the home is a quiet voice. ("Cornerstones of a Happy Home,"

Husbands and Wives Fireside Satellite Broadcast, January 29, 1984.)

I have never forgotten my father's tenderness toward my mother. She died when she was fifty, a relatively young woman. During the months of her illness he was constantly solicitous for her comfort. But this attitude was not expressed only after she became ill. It had been evident to us, their children, throughout our lives. In the happy home of our childhood, we knew—and that came of a feeling and not of any declaration—that they loved, respected, and honored one another. What a blessing that image has been. When we were children we felt a certain security because of it. As we grew older our thoughts and our actions were colored by that remembered example. ("Cornerstones of a Happy Home," Husbands and Wives Fireside Satellite Broadcast, January 29, 1984.)

I have long felt that happiness in marriage is not so much a matter of romance as it is an anxious concern for the comfort and well-being of one's companion. That involves a willingness to overlook weaknesses and mistakes.

One man has said, "Love is not blind—it sees more, not less. But because it sees more, it is willing to see less" (Julius Gordon, *Treasure Chest*, ed. Charles L. Wallis [New York: Harper and Row, 1965], p. 168). . . .

Unfortunately, some women want to remake their husbands after their own design. Some husbands regard it as their prerogative to compel their wives to fit their standards of what they think to be the ideal. It never works. It only leads to contention, misunderstanding, and sorrow. ("Cornerstones of a Happy Home," Husbands and Wives Fireside Satellite Broadcast, January 29, 1984.)

No man can please his Heavenly Father who fails to respect the daughters of God. No man can please his Heavenly Father who fails to magnify his wife and companion, and nurture and build and strengthen and share with her.

It has been a wonderful thing to see Sister Kimball in her relationship to President Kimball. She is a woman of learning, a woman who reads much, a woman who is constantly refining her talents, a woman who loves the Lord and serves in His kingdom—a woman who supports and sustains, loves and encourages her husband and their children. And he, throughout his married life, has encouraged and sustained her, has relied upon her, has shared with her in times of sorrow and rejoicing, in seasons of stress and ease, in sickness and in health. They have worked together, they have prayed together, they have sorrowed together, they have stood side by side in a relationship that becomes an example to the entire Church. He has never lost sight of that boyhood resolution to do that which would please his Heavenly Father.

Wife abuse is totally inconsistent with the gospel of Jesus Christ. Child abuse is an affront to our Father in Heaven. As President Harold B. Lee was wont to remind us, the greatest work that any of us will ever do will be within the walls of our own homes. A father who wishes to please his Heavenly Father will govern his family in a spirit of example and love. ("To Please Our Heavenly Father," *Ensign*, May 1985, p. 49.)

I am satisfied that God our Eternal Father does not love His daughters less than He loves His sons. Under the gospel plan the wife walks neither ahead nor behind her husband, but at his side in a true companionship before the Lord.

I see my own companion of fifty-two years. Is her contribution less acceptable before the Lord than is mine? I am satisfied it is not. She has walked quietly at my side, sustained me in my responsibilities, reared and blessed our children, served in many capacities in the Church, and spread an unmitigated measure of cheer and goodness wherever she has gone. The older I grow the more I appreciate—yes, the more I love—this little woman with whom I knelt at the altar in the house of the Lord more than half a century ago.

I wish with all of my heart that every marriage might be a happy marriage. I wish that every marriage might be an eternal partnership. I believe that wish can be realized if there is a willingness to make the effort to bring it to pass. ("Rise to the Stature of the Divine within You," *Ensign*, November 1989, p. 97.)

How wonderful a thing is marriage under the plan of our Eternal Father, a plan provided in His divine wisdom for the happiness and security of His children and the continuity of the race.

He is our Creator, and He designed marriage from the beginning. At the time of Eve's creation, "Adam said, This is now bone of my bones, and flesh of my flesh: . . .

"Therefore shall a man leave his father and his mother, and shall cleave unto his wife: and they shall be one flesh." (Gen. 2:23–24.) Paul wrote to the Corinthian Saints, "Neither is the man without the woman, neither the woman without the man, in the Lord." (1 Cor. 11:11.) . . .

Surely no one reading the scriptures, both ancient and modern, can doubt the divine concept of marriage. The sweetest feelings of life, the most generous and satisfying impulses of the human heart, find expression in a marriage that stands pure and unsullied above the evil of the world.

Such a marriage, I believe, is the desire—the hoped-for, the longed-for, the prayed-for desire—of men and women everywhere. ("What God Hath Joined Together," *Ensign*, May 1991, p. 71.)

Regretfully, there is all too much misery among some of the marrieds. I believe this need not be. I believe that where the gospel of Jesus Christ is lived—where there is unselfishness and mutual respect and kindness and forgiveness, there can be happiness and love and eternal life in the most sacred of all human relationships. (Ellen Pucell Unthank Monument Dedication, Cedar City, Utah, August 3, 1991.)

My brethren, you who have had conferred upon you the priesthood of God, you know, as I know, that there is no enduring happiness, that there is no lasting peace in the heart, no tranquility in the home, without the companionship of a good woman. Our wives are not our inferiors.

Some men who are evidently unable to gain respect by the goodness of their lives use as justification for their actions the statement that Eve was told that Adam should rule over her. How much sadness, how much tragedy, how much heartbreak has been caused through centuries of time by weak men who have used that as a scriptural warrant for atrocious behavior! They do not recognize that the same account indicates that Eve was given as a helpmeet to Adam. The facts are that they stood side by side in the garden. They were expelled from the garden together, and they worked together, side by side, in gaining their bread by the sweat of their brows. ("Our Solemn Responsibilities," *Ensign*, November 1991, p. 51.)

May I be personal for a moment? I sat at dinner across the table from my wife the other evening. It was fifty-five years ago that we were married in the Salt Lake Temple. The wondrous aura of young womanhood was upon her. She was beautiful, and I was bewitched. Now, for more than half a century, we have walked together through much of storm as well as sunshine. Today neither of us stands as tall as we once did. As I looked at her across the table, I noted a few wrinkles in her face and hands. But are they less beautiful than before? No, in fact, they are more so. Those wrinkles have a beauty of their own, and inherent in their very presence is something that speaks reassuringly of strength and integrity and a love that runs more deeply and quietly than ever before. ("This I Believe," *BYU 1991–92 Devotional and Fireside Speeches*, March 1, 1992, p. 78.)

We knew that our father loved our mother. . . . I have no recollection of ever hearing him speak unkindly to her or of her. He encouraged her in her individual Church activities and in neighborhood and civic responsibilities. She had much of native talent, and he encouraged her to use it. Her comfort was his constant concern. We looked upon them as equals, companions who worked together and loved and appreciated one another as they loved us.

She likewise encouraged him, did everything in the world to make him happy. ("Some Lessons I Learned as a Boy," *Ensign*, May 1993, p. 54.)

The most important decision of life is the decision concerning your companion. Choose prayerfully. And when you are married, be fiercely loyal one to another. Selfishness is the great destroyer of happy family life. I have this one suggestion to offer. If you will make your first concern the comfort, the well-being, and the happiness of your companion, sublimating any personal concern to that loftier goal, you will be happy, and your marriage will go on through eternity. ("A Three-Point Challenge," BYU Commencement Address, April 27, 1995.)

Of all of the difficult and discouraging responsibilities I have, the most difficult and the most discouraging is handling cancellation of sealings. Most of those requests come from women—women who on their marriage day were in the house of the Lord, in each case with the young man she loved. And then as the years passed there was argument, anger, losing temper, throwing a chair across the room and other such foolish and unnecessary things, until all love was gone and hatred had taken its place. Now, having run their course, there comes a request for a cancellation of a temple sealing. You can trace it all to selfishness, thinking of oneself instead of one's companion. . . . Any man who will make his wife's comfort his first concern will stay in love with her throughout their lives and through the eternity yet to come. (Anchorage Alaska Regional Conference, June 18, 1995.)

You men who hold the priesthood, be good husbands. There are a lot of bad husbands, as a lot of women can testify. Let me read you a letter I received the other day.

"Dear President Hinckley, my husband is a righteous priesthood holder. That is the highest compliment I can pay him. When he is around it is as though the Savior himself is directing us. He is kind and gentle, always finding ways to help me and the children. He has always been the one who gets up with the children during the night. He has never raised his voice or hand to me and has been a big help during my various health problems. Although we have had our difference of opinion, we have never had an argument and I know it is because he is so careful in the way he communicates with me. He guides us through family Book of Mormon study and prayers and has now instigated a few minutes of gospel study together in the evening after the children are in bed. He is just the best man that could ever be. I feel it is an honor to be married in the temple to such a man. We are happy and in love and life is good."

Isn't that a great letter? It is so simple that a wayfaring man, though he were a fool, could not misunderstand it. Brethren, don't lose your temper. Anger is a corrosive thing that destroys, breaks hearts, destroys peace and happiness and brings sadness and regret. Curb your anger. Wives, support your husbands. Don't be resentful if they are busy in the Church. Just be glad you know where they are, and support them and help them. They aren't the great big heroes that some of you may think. They need a little encouragement now and again, a little kindness, a little love, a little goodness in the way of support from you. (Birmingham England Fireside, August 29, 1995.)

I believe that it should be the blessing of every child to be born into a home where that child is welcomed, nurtured, loved, and blessed with parents, a father and a mother, who live with loyalty to one another and to their children. . . . Stand strong against the wiles of the world. The creators of our entertainment, the purveyors of much of our literature, would have you believe otherwise. The accumulated wisdom of centuries declares with clarity and certainty that the greater happiness, the greater security, the greater peace of mind, the deeper reservoirs of love are experienced only by those who walk according to time-tested standards of virtue before marriage and total fidelity within marriage. ("Stand Strong against the Wiles of the World," *Ensign*, November 1995, p. 99.)

Your wives are indispensable to your eternal progress. I hope you will never forget that. There are a few men in this Church, I'm glad there are not very many, but there are a few, who think they are superior to their wives. They better realize that they will not be able to achieve the highest degree of glory in the celestial kingdom without their wives standing at their side equally with them. Brethren, they are daughters of God. Treat them as such. (Veracruz Mexico Regional Conference, priesthood leadership session, January 27, 1996.)

We were married fifty-nine years ago and we are still at it. We went to the Salt Lake Temple and there we were sealed for time and eternity, and it has been a good life. We have had our ups and downs. We were once taller than we are now. We once walked a little faster. We could even dance. We do not do it anymore. She would tell you we have not done it since the day we were married. But we have had a good life. The weather of the last two days has reminded me of it. Storms then sunshine, good things and bad things, happy days and sad days, and life that has been good, really, wonderful. . . . She is now the grandmother of twenty-five grandchildren and twelve greatgrandchildren, and they all call her "Grandma" and love her. It is interesting that when our children call home, our grown sons, one is a stake president and the other a member of a high council, they never want to talk with me. If I answer the phone they say, "Is Mother there?" They have been saying that all their lives and it has been wonderful, really wonderful. I am so grateful for this dear little woman who has been my companion, my sweetheart, my love, the mother of my children, and the only one in the world who can tell me what to do and I do it, and have been doing it for a very, very long time. As a matter of fact, she doesn't hesitate to tell me. If I go down the wrong track somewhere just one step, she pulls me back, and has done all these many, many years. (Smithfield/Logan Utah Regional Conference, April 21, 1996.)

I wish you could read some of the letters that come from heartbroken women who weep and mourn because of the thoughtless and mean and, in many cases, evil husbands. I want to say to you men that the greatest asset you will ever have in time or eternity is the woman with whom you joined hands over the altar in the house of the Lord, and there in the presence of God, angels, and witnesses, pledged your love and loyalty and affection, one to another for time and all eternity. All of your other assets can disappear, and will do. You won't take five cents to heaven with you, not five cents. But, if you are the kind of man you ought to be, you will take her. Maybe it's the other way around—maybe she'll take you. Treat your wives with respect and kindness. (Pittsburgh Pennsylvania Regional Conference, priesthood leadership session, April 27, 1996.)

MEDIA

See also Television

I regret to say that journalism has changed in recent years. There was a time when it was a cardinal rule of reporting that editorializing was kept out of the news columns. The reporter was to present the "who, why, what, when, where" of the story without his personal opinions or judgments. Now, in both broadcast and print media, news reporting is saturated with opinion. There is a certain amount of arrogance in this. It presumes that the reporter is more knowledgeable than the listener. All too often this simply is not the case. ("Keep Faith," Bonneville International Corporation Senior Management Seminar, March 7, 1993.)

We are constantly fed a steady and sour diet of pessimism, faultfinding, evil speaking one of another. Read the newspaper columnists. Listen to the radio and television commentators. The writers of our news columns are brilliant, the commentators on the electronic media are masters, but they seem unable to deal with balanced truth, notwithstanding their protests to the contrary. The negative becomes the stuff of headlines and long broadsides that in many cases are a caricature of the facts and a distortion of the truth—at least the whole truth. This spirit of negativism seems to hang as a cloud over the land. (Utah Mayflower Society Dinner, November 16, 1994.)

Months ago I was invited to be interviewed by Mike Wallace, a tough senior reporter for the CBS *60 Minutes* program, which is broadcast across America to more than 20 million listeners each week.

I recognized that if I were to appear, critics and detractors of the Church would also be invited to participate. I knew we could not expect that the program would be entirely positive for us.

On the other hand, I felt that it offered the opportunity to present some affirmative aspects of our culture and message to many millions of people. I concluded that it was better to lean into the stiff wind of opportunity than to simply hunker down and do nothing. It has been an interesting experience. The program's crews have photographed hours of eyeball-to-eyeball interview, if you'll pardon that expression, dialogue, and formal talks in various settings. They have interviewed other members of the Church, as well as our critics. From all of this I assume they have distilled a presentation of about a quarter of an hour.

We have no idea what the outcome will be—that is, I don't. We will discover this this evening when it is aired in this valley. If it turns out to be favorable, I will be grateful. Otherwise, I pledge I'll never get my foot in that kind of trap again. ("'Remember . . . Thy Church, O Lord,'" *Ensign*, May 1996, p. 83.)

I have great respect for the media. I have had much to do with newspapers and radio and television over a period of many years, and I admire the media. (Press Conference, Seoul, Korea, May 22, 1996.)

Two of our Brethren were recently in Washington and called on three or four people of national prominence back there. Among those they met was the man who speaks for the motion-picture industry and now for the television industry on morality in the media. He said, in essence, to our Brethren, "We do what we can, but it is a well nigh impossible task to change the moral perspective of the media, writers, and programmers. There is only one force in America with enough clout to turn this thing around, and that is the Mormon Church." What a tremendous compliment that is. (BYU 1970–72 Class Reunion, October 11, 1996.)

As I have gone about the world, I have had opportunity for interviews with representatives of the media. This is always a worrisome undertaking because one never knows what will be asked. These reporters are men and women of great capacity, who know how to ask questions that come at you like a javelin.

It is not exactly an enjoyable experience, but it represents an opportunity to tell the world something of our story. As Paul said to Festus and Agrippa, "This thing was not done in a corner" (Acts 26:26).

We have something that this world needs to hear about, and these interviews afford an opportunity to give voice to that. ("'This Thing Was Not Done in a Corner,'" *Ensign*, November 1996, p. 48.)

MEDITATION

See also Prayer; Reverence

We need the Spirit of the Lord in our lives more. We live in a very mad world when all is said and done. The pressures are tremendous. We fly at high speeds. We drive at high speeds. We program ourselves. I guess I'm the only one in the Church who doesn't have a daytimer; but, I have a secretary and he has a daytimer. But there is hardly time to reflect and think and pause and meditate. I daresay that most of those in this room today have not taken an hour in the last year to just sit down quietly, each man to himself, as a son of God, reflecting upon his place in this world, upon his destiny, upon his capacity to do good, upon his mission to make some changes for good. We need to. I recall so vividly President McKay in his old age in a meeting with his counselors and the Twelve saying, "Brethren, we need to take more time to meditate, to think quietly." (Smithfield/Logan Utah Regional Conference, priesthood leadership session, April 20, 1996.)

President McKay used to tell the story of General Gordon. . . . He was leading a military campaign in the Sudan, a British general. He had a custom every morning of going into his tent and leaving his handkerchief out in front of the tent door. And everybody under his command knew that as long as that handkerchief was there on the ground, General Gordon was inside communing with his God, talking things over in prayer and trying to get inspiration. When he was through, he came out and picked up his handkerchief and things began to happen.

President McKay said to us once, to the Brethren of the Twelve, "Brethren, we need to meditate more. We're so busy doing little things. We need to meditate more." I believe, my brethren, that we need to. And I suggest to you that fast day, a week from Sunday, you arrange an hour all to yourself. You say to your wife, "I want to be alone for an hour." Just think. Just meditate on your responsibilities and your relationships. (Pittsburgh Pennsylvania Regional Conference, priesthood leadership session, April 27, 1996.)

I'm going to make a suggestion to each of you. On the next fast day, take occasion and arrange your affairs in such a way that you can be by yourself, maybe under a tree in the backyard, maybe in the locked bedroom of your home, where you can think. Read the scriptures and think of sacred things and think of yourself. Your attitude toward your wife—are you the kind of husband you ought to be, considerate, kind, generous, or are you a bully, an abuser? You cannot be a good servant of the Lord if there isn't peace in your heart concerning your companion. . . . Your attitude toward your children: Are you rearing them in an atmosphere of love, or are you the kind of man who thinks he has to deal out punishment all the time? I'm one who believes that it isn't necessary in rearing children to beat them. I'm one who believes that they will respond to love and appreciation. Think, under those circumstances, of your personal integrity—are you a man of honesty; are you a man who deals honestly with others? Say to yourselves, I must stand a little taller and be a little better. Try it, will you? Find a place where next fast day you can spend an hour with yourselves quietly thinking of what you can do to make yourselves more worthy of the sacred call which you have. (Berlin Germany Regional Conference, priesthood leadership session, June 15, 1996.)

MELCHIZEDEK PRIESTHOOD

See Priesthood: Melchizedek Priesthood

MERCY

I spoke one day with a young mother, a single parent who had been abandoned by her husband. With only meager skills, she was trying to make a living for her children. Broken and discouraged, she said, with tears in her eyes, "It's a rough world out there. It's a jungle without mercy."

How godlike a quality is mercy. It cannot be legislated. It must come from the heart. It must be stirred up from within. It is part of the endowment each of us receives as a son or daughter of God and partaker of a divine birthright. I plead for an effort among all of us to give greater expression and wider latitude to this instinct which lies within us. I am convinced that there comes a time, possibly many times, within our lives when we might cry out for mercy on the part of others. How can we expect it unless we have been merciful ourselves? ("Blessed Are the Merciful," *Ensign*, May 1990, p. 68.)

I plead for a stronger spirit of compassion in all of our relationships, a stronger element of mercy, for the promise is sure that if we are merciful we shall obtain mercy.

Along with you I have observed in recent months a wondrous, almost unbelievable, change in some of the nations of the earth. Dictators have fallen, and the voices of the people are heard again with a new song of freedom.

I watched on television the summary trial given one who had been a merciless despot. Now in the moment of his extremity he wished for mercy on the part of his accusers. I know nothing of the court system under which he and his wife were tried. I know only that the hearing was short, the judgment death, and the execution quick and final. There had been no mercy shown through long years of oppression, harsh and unrelenting; and now in this hour of bitter culmination none was extended.

Mercy is of the very essence of the gospel of Jesus Christ. The degree to which each of us is able to extend it becomes an expression of the reality of our discipleship under Him who is our Lord and Master. ("Blessed Are the Merciful," *Ensign*, May 1990, pp. 68–69.)

I remind you that it was He who said, "Whosoever shall smite thee on thy right cheek, turn to him the other also." (Matt. 5:39.)

It was He who said, "And if any man will sue thee at the law, and take away thy coat, let him have thy cloke also." (Matt. 5:40.)

It was He who said, "And whosoever shall compel thee to go a mile, go with him twain." (Matt. 5:41.)

It was He who said, "Give to him that asketh thee, and from him that would borrow of thee turn not thou away." (Matt. 5:42.)

It was He who said to the woman taken in sin:

"Where are those thine accusers? hath no man condemned thee? . . .

"Neither do I condemn thee: go, and sin no more." (John 8:10–11.)

It was He who, while hanging on the cross in dreadful agony, cried out, "Father, forgive them; for they know not what they do." (Luke 23:34.)

He, the Son of the everlasting Father, was the epitome of mercy. His ministry was one of compassion toward the poor, the sick, the oppressed, the victims of injustice and man's inhumanity to man. His sacrifice on the cross was an unparalleled act of mercy in behalf of all humanity.

How great a thing is mercy. Most often it is quiet and unassuming. It receives few headlines. It is the antithesis of vengeance and hatred, of greed and offensive egotism. ("Blessed Are the Merciful," *Ensign,* May 1990, p. 69.)

Of all the wars that have afflicted the United States, none was so costly in suffering and death, none so filled with venom and hatred as was the American Civil War. There are few more touching scenes in history than that of April 9, 1865, at Appomattox, Virginia, when General Robert E. Lee surrendered to General Ulysses S. Grant. General Grant wrote a brief statement of terms under which the soldiers of the South were free to return to their homes with their personal sidearms, their private horses and baggage.

There was no recrimination, no demand for reparations, no apologies required or punishment given. This has gone down in the chronicles of war as a great and magnificent act of mercy.

In the story of our own people there stands out the example of Brigham Young's attitude toward the Indians. His declaration that it was "better to feed them than to fight them" evidenced not only the innate mercy of his nature, but the greater wisdom inherent in a compassionate attitude toward the less fortunate. ("Blessed Are the Merciful," *Ensign,* May 1990, p. 69.)

Let us be more merciful. Let us get the arrogance out of our lives, the conceit, the egotism. Let us be more compassionate, gentler, filled with forbearance and patience and a greater measure of respect one for another. In so doing, our very example will cause others to be more merciful, and we shall have greater claim upon the mercy of God who in His love will be generous toward us.

"For behold, are we not all beggars? Do we not all depend upon the same Being, even God, for all the substance which we have, for both food and raiment, and for gold, and for silver, and for all the riches which we have of every kind? . . .

"And now, if God, who has created you, on whom you are dependent for your lives and for all that ye have and are, doth grant unto you whatsoever ye ask that is right, . . . O then, how ye ought to impart of the substance that ye have one to another." (Mosiah 4:19, 21.) . . .

I am confident that a time will come for each of us when, whether because of sickness or infirmity, of poverty or distress, of oppressive measures against us by man or nature, we shall wish for mercy. And if, through our lives, we have granted mercy to others, we shall obtain it for ourselves. ("Blessed Are the Merciful," *Ensign,* May 1990, p. 70.)

There is need for compassion toward many of the victims of drugs. Whenever we help one to find a better way, our effort becomes an act of mercy with a grateful response rather than an act of punishment followed by resentment.

The plight of the homeless is a repudiation of the greatness of our nation. I commend most warmly those who with a compelling spirit of kindness reach out to those in distress. ("Blessed Are the Merciful," *Ensign,* May 1990, p. 70.)

Be strong, my brethren, in the quality of mercy. It is easy to be a bully in one's home, in one's business, in one's speech and acts. This sick world so cries out for kindness and love and mercy. These virtues become an expression of strength rather than weakness on the part of any holder of the priesthood of God. ("Building Your Tabernacle," *Ensign,* November 1992, p. 52.)

MINISTERING

See also Fellowshipping; Home Teaching; Love;
Reactivation and Retention; Service

God would have us do His work, and do it with energy and cheerfulness. That work, as He has defined it, is to ". . . succor the weak, lift up the hands which hang down, and strengthen the feeble knees" (D&C 81:5).

It is to minister to those in need. It is to comfort the bereaved. It is to visit the widow and the fatherless in their affliction. It is to feed the needy, to clothe the naked, to shelter those who have not a roof over their heads. It is to do as the Master did, to "go about doing good." (Single Adult Fireside Satellite Broadcast, February 26, 1989.)

President Lee told us on more than one occasion to survey large fields and cultivate small ones. He was saying that we must know the big picture and then assiduously work on the particular niche assigned to each of us, and that in doing so we concentrate on the needs of the individual.

This work is concerned with people, each a son or daughter of God. ("This Work Is Concerned with People," *Ensign,* May 1995, p. 53.)

Bless them with love. Let them know that you love them. It's so important. You are not generals running an army. You are servants of God, ministering to His people. Bless them with love. (Berlin Germany Regional Conference, priesthood leadership session, June 15, 1996.)

MIRACLES

How wondrous a creation is a child! Is there a greater miracle than human birth? ("Behold Your Little Ones," Children's Fireside Satellite Broadcast, January 23, 1994.)

I have seen miracles in my time, my brothers and sisters. The greatest miracle of all, I believe, is the transformation that comes into the life of a man or a woman who accepts the restored gospel of Jesus Christ and tries to live it in his or her life. (Vacaville/Santa Rosa California Regional Conference, May 21, 1995.)

If you move with faith, keeping in touch with Him and building around you people of faith, you can accomplish anything. I believe that with all my heart. I have seen miracle after miracle after miracle across this world. I once thought that the best people in the world are in East Millcreek [where I presided as stake president] and I still believe that. But there are millions of others just like you wherever you go in Hong Kong, Korea, Taiwan, Bangkok, Singapore, Bombay, Sydney, Edinburgh, Wellington, Christchurch, Nuku'alofa, São Paulo, Buenos Aires, Santiago, Lima, Stockholm, Copenhagen, London, Birmingham, everywhere there are wonderful people in this Church. This is an age of miracles. We are part of a miracle as this work moves across the world in fulfillment of the great destiny which the Lord has set for us. (Salt Lake East Millcreek Stake Fiftieth Anniversary Celebration, June 10, 1995.)

I love the missionaries of this Church. I have been one and I have worked with them and I love them. And I mean that. To me it is an ever-refreshing miracle that a boy from a dusty little town like Parowan and a girl from a dusty little town like Vacaville could come out into the world and touch people's hearts and change their lives. It is a miracle. (Washington D.C. North and South Missionary Meeting, November 12, 1995.)

Every one of you knows this gospel is true. Every one of you knows that God lives. Every one of you knows that Jesus is the

Christ. Every one of you knows that Joseph Smith was a prophet. Every one of you knows that the Book of Mormon is true. That's a miracle in and of itself. (McAllen Texas Regional Conference, January 7, 1996.)

After this month there will be more Latter-day Saints outside the United States than in the United States. We are in more than 150 nations.

The spread of the Book of Mormon is a miracle. Think of what Joseph Smith and Martin Harris must have thought when they saw that first edition of the Book of Mormon coming off the press. It is a miracle to think that someday in our time the distribution of that book will have reached a figure of seventy to eighty million.

Things are happening. You walk your little trail each day and you do not have the great vision of this work perhaps because you are a small part of it but a very important part of it. When you see the overall picture of what is happening, with 100 new stakes created last year through the efforts of such as you, it is a miracle. (Hawaii Honolulu Missionary Meeting, February 17, 1996.)

This is a work of miracles. Miracles are performed in the lives of the missionaries. Your presence here is really a miracle. This is a nation in which only about 1 percent of the people are Christians, but here we have a great, growing organization now, more than a thousand missionaries in Japan; about a hundred thousand members of the Church in Japan; three hundred congregations of Latter-day Saints in Japan. I've seen the miracle of the whole thing since I started coming here thirty-six years ago. In those days we did not own a chapel; we did not have a building of our own except a little run-down place up on the north island, not a single building did we own in all of Asia.

When I see the strength of the Church here today, and go into stake centers and beautiful houses of worship and think of those smelly, cold, drafty little old houses in which we used to meet, I know that a miracle has taken place. It is wonderful. What a marvelous thing that each of you can be a part of this great miracle that's taking place in this good land, this nation of Japan, which is one of the great nations of the earth, among these very able and wonderful people. (Japan Tokyo North, Japan Tokyo South, and Japan Sendai Missionary Meeting, May 18, 1996.)

President Jay Quealy was seriously injured while he was presiding here. He went over to see what time the missionaries were getting up on the island and it was raining and he foolishly rode a scooter, which they were permitted to do in those days. He got on a road where there was some pea gravel and skidded right into a police van. Of all the vehicles to hit, he picked the worst one he could have done. It threw him right up over the hood and into the windshield. He broke both legs, an arm, and some ribs.

I came over here then to look after the mission for a time. He says (I do not say this) that when I administered to him I said that he would walk again on his natural legs and be unimpaired in his work. The doctors said he had gangrene in his legs and they would have to take them off. He said, "No, I won't let you take them off. I was given a promise by a servant of the Lord that I would walk again with my natural legs."

Now, I do not remember that, but he did and spoke of it. The nurses, wonderful Chinese nurses, massaged his legs and the gangrene miraculously cleared and until the time of his death he walked on his natural legs. I have seen miracles here by the power of the priesthood and by the power of faith. (Hong Kong Missionary Meeting, May 25, 1996.)

I had an uncle come here, Alonzo A. Hinckley, way back in the early days. He later became a member of the Council of the Twelve. He spoke of the miracle, the great difficulty in learning this language and of his pleas with the Lord to help him, to loosen his tongue so that he could speak to the people words of testimony and truth. Suddenly, just out of the clear blue, he sat in a meeting and understood what was being said and then was called upon to speak and spoke with clarity to the people. A miracle. This is a land of miracles and, as has been said, this is a work of miracles. (Netherlands Amsterdam Missionary Meeting, June 13, 1996.)

It is nice to be back in Berlin. I came here first in 1935, when I completed my mission. . . . The last time was for the dedication of the beautiful temple in Freiberg. This was a different city then. This was a different nation then. There was an atmosphere of tension and fear and oppression and the ugly wall.

A miracle has come to pass. What a wondrous miracle—there is now freedom to come and go as you please and gather in this great hall this morning from areas that were once in the East and once in the West, as faithful Latter-day Saints united together. (Berlin Germany Regional Conference, June 16, 1996.)

The history of this Church is replete with miracles of healing. I know that. I am confident of that. I recall once when I arrived in Hong Kong I was asked if I would visit a woman in the hospital whose doctors had told her she was going blind and would lose her sight within a week. She asked if we would administer to her and we did so, and she states that she was miraculously healed. I have a painting in my home that she gave me which says on the back of it, "To Gordon B. Hinckley in grateful appreciation for the miracle of saving my sight." I said to her, "I didn't save your sight. Of course, the Lord saved your sight. Thank Him and be grateful to Him." (Mission Presidents Seminar, June 23, 1996.)

MISSIONARY SERVICE, FULL-TIME

See also Missionary Work

We are deeply grateful for the opportunities of radio and television, and the generosity of the public press, all of which help to build a favorable atmosphere in which to teach the gospel. But I am confident that the time will never come when we shall not need vigorous men and women of faith to go into the world as missionaries for this cause. We have never found, and I think we never shall find, an adequate substitute for the situation in which two wholesome young men meet with a family, reason with them, teach them, testify to them, and pray with them. We shall always need missionaries. (Conference Report, April 1959, pp. 119–20.)

Cultivate in our homes a proper attitude toward missionary service. We enjoy the blessings we so greatly treasure because of those who have gone before us. Out of a sense of appreciation, out of simple gratitude, we should make an effort to extend these same blessings to others. Our young people have an obligation to prepare themselves for missionary service.

We should also build the attitude that there is nothing of a vacation, nothing of a holiday in this great missionary service. It is hard, and at times discouraging, work. Last year our missionaries averaged sixty-seven hours a week in actual proselyting effort. Let those who contemplate missions realize that they will work as they have never worked before, and that they may expect such joy as they have not previously known.

. . . Foster training for missionary service. One of the great compliments paid the Savior was that he taught as one having authority. The missionary who knows scripture and can quote it speaks with the voice of authority. It is not essential to memorize five hundred citations, nor even three hundred. Fifty well chosen verses of scripture will become a remarkably effective tool in the hands of a missionary. May I suggest that in our family night gatherings we make it a project to memorize one scripture citation a week pertinent to this work. At the conclusion of a year our children will have on their lips a fund of scripture which will remain with them throughout their lives.

. . . Make financial preparation. Missionary work, like everything else, has become more costly. . . . A little at a time, systematically saved, will assure our children that the necessary means will be available when a missionary call comes. (Conference Report, April 1959, p. 120.)

To our young men I would like to say, prepare yourselves, not only financially as you have been urged to do, but also intellectually and morally and spiritually. Study languages. This gospel is not for the people of America only. This gospel is for the people of the earth, and we have incumbent upon us the obligation to learn to speak their tongues. If you be called to a foreign language mission, you will be better equipped if you have studied the language. If called to an English-speaking mission, you will understand your own language better.

Live for the opportunity when you may go out as a servant of the Lord and an ambassador of eternal truth to the people of the world. "And this gospel of the kingdom shall be preached in all the world for a witness unto all nations; and then shall the end come." (Matt. 24:14.) This is our commission, and this is our obligation spoken anciently and reaffirmed in modern revelation. (Conference Report, April 1962, p. 73.)

Is it not a miracle in itself that in this day of doubt and disbelief young men, thousands of them, with lives to live and careers to build, spend two years in the service of the Lord, laboring constantly and even willing to fast and pray in behalf of those to whom they seek to teach a better life? I know of no experience more refreshing than to be with them and feel of their spirit. If any of you who are listening this day should have two of them come to your door, I hope that you will welcome them and hear them. They will restore your faith in youth. They will quicken your faith in the Lord. They will lead you to a joy you have never previously known. (Conference Report, October 1969, pp. 114–15.)

I know that our young men are under a great obligation to qualify themselves through education to fill positions of responsibility in the world. Their time is precious. But I do not hesitate to promise that the time spent in faithful and devoted service as a missionary, declaring the Master, will only add to their qualifications for positions of responsibility in the future. Regardless of the vocation they choose to pursue, they will be better qualified in their powers of expression, in their habits of industry, in the value they place on training, in the integrity of their lives, and in their recognition of a higher source of strength and power than that which lies within their native capacity. ("He Slumbers Not, nor Sleeps," *Ensign*, May 1983, p. 8.)

Every man or woman who goes forth in [missionary] service blesses the lives of all he teaches. Furthermore, his or her own life is enriched by this selfless labor. Who has not witnessed the miracle of a missionary who has grown in a wondrous way while engaged in the work of the Master?

Priesthood leaders and fathers and mothers should begin while a boy is very young to point him in the direction of missionary service. ("The Miracle Made Possible by Faith," *Ensign*, May 1984, p. 46.)

Every young man seeking to please his Heavenly Father would be willing and anxious to give approximately a tithe of his life at the age of nineteen or twenty to go into the world to preach the gospel. He would save his money for this; he would plan his life's program around it; he would keep himself physically, mentally, and morally alert, as well as spiritually strong, to be prepared for this great and sacred responsibility.

While in the mission field he would be "anxiously engaged" in the work of the Lord (see D&C 58:27), willing to give freely of his time, his talents, his strengths, and his substance to bless the lives of others. He would guard against wasting his time or diminishing his effectiveness through engaging in activities that might in any way be out of harmony with his great and sacred call. ("To Please Our Heavenly Father," *Ensign*, May 1985, p. 49.)

[At the time I entered the mission field] it was the time of the worst economic depression in the history of the world. Unemployment in this area [Salt Lake City] was about 35 percent, and most of the unemployed were husbands and fathers. . . . Very few missionaries were going into the field at that time. We send out as many in a week now as then went during the entire year. I received my bachelor's degree and planned on somehow attending graduate school. Then the bishop came with what seemed to me a shocking suggestion. He spoke of a mission. I was called to go to England which, at that time, was the most expensive mission in the world. The cost per month was the equivalent of what would be about $500 now.

We discovered that my mother, who had passed away, had established a small savings account to be available for this purpose. I had a savings account in a different place, but the bank in which I had mine had failed. There was then no government insurance program to cover its failure as there is now. My father, a man of great faith and love, supplied the necessary means, with all of the family cooperating at a sacrifice. As I look back upon it, I see all of it as a miracle. Somehow the money was there every month.

The work in the field was not easy. It was difficult and discouraging. But what a wonderful experience it was. In retrospect, I recognize that I was probably a selfish young man when I arrived in Britain. What a blessing it became to set aside my own selfish interests to the greater interests of the work of the Lord. I had the association of tremendous young men and women. They have become treasured friends whom I have known and loved now for more than half a century. ("The Question of a Mission," *Ensign*, May 1986, p. 40.)

There may be a few young men in this vast audience tonight who may be wondering, ever so seriously, whether they should go on missions. There may be a scarcity of money. There may be compelling plans for education. There may be that wonderful girl you love and feel you cannot leave. You say to yourself, "The choice is mine."

That is true. But before you make a decision against a mission, count your blessings, my dear friend. Think of all the great and marvelous things you have—your very life, your health, your parents, your home, the girl you love. Are they not all gifts from a generous Heavenly Father? Did you really earn them alone, independent of His blessing? No, the lives of all of us are in His hands. All of the previous things that are ours come from Him who is the giver of every good gift.

. . . I am saying that out of a spirit of appreciation and gratitude, and a sense of duty, you ought to make whatever adjustment is necessary to give a little of your time—as little as two years—consecrating your strength, your means, your talents to the work of sharing with others the gospel, which is the source of so much of the good that you have.

I promise that if you will do so, you will come to know that what appears today to be a sacrifice will prove instead to be the greatest investment that you will ever make. . . .

The Church needs you. The Lord needs you. The world needs you. . . . There are many out there who need exactly what you have to offer. They are not easy to find, but they will not be found unless there are those who are prepared and willing to seek them out. ("The Question of a Mission," *Ensign,* May 1986, pp. 40–41.)

How profoundly grateful I am for the experience of [my] mission. I touched the lives of a few who have, over the years, expressed appreciation. That has been important. But I have never been greatly concerned over the number of baptisms that I had or that other missionaries had. My satisfaction has come from the assurance that I did what the Lord wanted me to do and that I was an instrument in His hands for the accomplishment of His purposes. In the course of that experience, there became riveted into my very being a conviction and knowledge that this is in very deed the true and living work of God, restored through a prophet for the blessing of all who will accept it and live its principles. ("The Question of a Mission," *Ensign,* May 1986, p. 40.)

It follows that if we have *more missionaries,* there will be *more converts.* It also follows that if missionaries are *better prepared,* they will be *more effective.* . . .

I am one who believes that missionary work is primarily a priesthood responsibility. While many young women perform a tremendous service in the field, some more effectively than the elders, the basic responsibility lies with our young men. We must point our young men toward missionary service earlier, and we must prepare them better. . . .

If we are to increase substantially the number of missionaries, we must begin the preparation process early. That process begins with parents. I wish to discuss four phases of preparation for missionary service: (1) spiritual preparation; (2) mental preparation; (3) social preparation; (4) financial preparation.

A missionary's *spiritual preparation* will be strengthened by better family home evenings, by improved teaching in the Aaronic Priesthood and auxiliary organizations, by attendance at seminary and institute, by going to the temple to be baptized in behalf of the dead, by encouragement to read the Book of Mormon. . . .

Mental preparation. Bishoprics need to be diligent and prayerful as they conduct personal interviews with boys, beginning when the boys are deacons. Let bishoprics give encouragement in the direction of missionary service. . . .

Social preparation. Let us teach our young people with counsel and love the importance of keeping themselves clean and worthy to represent the Lord as His ambassadors before the world. Let us encourage wholesome social activities, and let our youth learn the great art of getting along with others. . . .

Financial preparation. Missions have become costly. . . . The time to start saving is when boys are very young. . . .

We urge adherence to the rule of missionary support which has been in effect from the beginnings of the Church—namely, that it is the responsibility of the individual and the family to provide support for the missionary. This must be encouraged, even though there may necessarily be some delay in departure. Better that a young man delay his mission for a year and earn money toward his support than that he rely entirely on others.

But because of economic conditions in some lands, it is not possible for some young men and women to serve without some financial help. Wards and quorums should then help to the extent possible. ("'The Field Is White Already to Harvest,'" *Ensign,* December 1986, pp. 4–6.)

In missionary work, as in all else, preparation precedes power. Encouragement to prepare while still very young can make a tremendous difference. (Regional Representatives Seminar, April 1987.)

I, like Heber C. Kimball and his associates ninety-six years earlier, was sent to Preston [as a missionary].

That was my first assignment and my first field of labor. I became as familiar with the places they knew and the streets they walked as they had been nearly a century earlier. My companion and I walked up and down the same road where they had seen that banner, "Truth Will Prevail." . . .

I feel especially fortunate to have been sent to Preston as my initial assignment. Not only did I labor there, but I labored in the surrounding towns where those first missionaries taught the gospel. I was not as effective as were they. When they first arrived, there evidently was little or no prejudice against them.

When I arrived, it seemed that everyone was prejudiced against us.

I was not well when I arrived. Those first few weeks, because of illness and the opposition which we felt, I was discouraged. I wrote a letter home to my good father and said that I felt I was wasting my time and his money. He was my father and my stake president, and he was a wise and inspired man. He wrote a very short letter to me which said, "Dear Gordon, I have your recent letter. I have only one suggestion: forget yourself and go to work." Earlier that morning in our scripture class my companion and I had read these words of the Lord: "Whosoever will save his life shall lose it; but whosoever shall lose his life for my sake and the gospel's, the same shall save it." (Mark 8:35.)

Those words of the Master, followed by my father's letter with his counsel to forget myself and go to work, went into my very being. With my father's letter in hand, I went into our bedroom in the house at 15 Wadham Road, where we lived, and got on my knees and made a pledge with the Lord. I covenanted that I would try to forget myself and lose myself in His service.

That July day in 1933 was my day of decision. A new light came into my life and a new joy into my heart. The fog of England seemed to lift, and I saw the sunlight. I had a rich and wonderful mission experience, for which I shall ever be grateful, laboring in Preston where the work began and in other places where it had moved forward, including the great city of London, where I served the larger part of my mission. ("Taking the Gospel to Britain: A Declaration of Vision, Faith, Courage, and Truth," *Ensign*, July 1987, pp. 6–7.)

The SS *Manhattan* on which I traveled to England docked at Plymouth the night of 1 July 1933. The three of us missionaries aboard took the boat train to London, arriving late at night. The next day I was assigned to go to Preston, Lancashire, the same city to which the first Latter-day Saint missionaries had gone ninety years earlier to open the work in the British Isles.

After what seemed like a long, lonely train ride, I met my companion at the station, and he took me to our "digs," a short distance from Vauxhall Chapel where the first LDS missionary sermon had been preached in 1837.

My companion then announced that we would go into town and hold a street meeting. I was terrified. Following supper, we walked to the marketplace. There we sang a hymn and offered prayer. Then he called on me to speak. A crowd gathered. They looked menacing to me. The world was then in the bottom of the Depression, and Lancashire had been particularly hard-hit. The people were poor. They wore wooden clogs on their feet. Their dress reflected the hard times in which they lived. They were difficult to understand; I was a westerner from the United States, and they spoke with a Lancashire dialect.

In the months that followed, I came to know them and to love them. I walked during those months where Heber C. Kimball and his pioneer missionary associates had once walked while laying the foundation for The Church of Jesus Christ of Latter-day Saints in the British Isles. Vauxhall Chapel, where they first spoke; the River Ribble, where the first baptisms took place; the location of the old cock pit and the Temperance Hall where they preached; and the obelisk in the marketplace all became familiar to me.

After five months in Lancashire, I was transferred to the European Mission office in London, where I worked as assistant to Elder Joseph F. Merrill of the Council of the Twelve, who presided over the missions in Europe. London was a great and interesting and challenging city. Each Sunday, weather permitting, the two of us in the European office would join missionaries from the British Mission office in holding street meetings in Hyde Park and other public areas. In addition to our office duties, we also tracted. We likewise taught in the branches, which were then small and weak.

Missionaries then in Britain were few. It was a time of severe economic difficulties across the world, and money was scarce. Relatively few went on missions. At one time there were only sixty-five of us in all of the British Isles.

Those mission experiences provided a great undergirding for my life. There were many faithful and wonderful Latter-day Saints in Britain whom I came to know and love for the strength of their testimonies in the face of opposition, and for their great, unwavering loyalty to the cause to which they had given their allegiance. I came to know and respect the strong and sturdy people of Britain. I came to know the rich beauty of England—its hills and its meadowlands, its vast, teeming cities, its literature, its art, its science. I have since learned also to love Scotland, Ireland, and Wales. As a young man engaged in a sacred work, I came to know, to a degree unrealized before, my Father in Heaven and my Savior, the Redeemer of the world, the Lord Jesus Christ.

I am grateful for that wonderful season of my life when I did the best I knew how to teach the gospel and build the kingdom. ("Taking the Gospel to Britain: A Declaration of Vision, Faith, Courage, and Truth," *Ensign*, July 1987, p. 9.)

Let me tell you of a recent experience. We were in the city of Bacolod on the island of Negros Occidente, in the Republic of the Philippines. There, to my great surprise, I met a man I had not seen in years.

The weather was steamy hot, as it always is in Bacolod. . . . My friend was in a short-sleeved white shirt with dark trousers, his shoes shined. His beautiful wife, Marva, was beside him. I said, "Victor Jex, what are you doing here?"

He smiled and replied, "We're doing the Lord's work. . . . We're missionaries."

"Where do you live?"

"In a little house in Iloilo on the island of Panay. We came over on the ferry for the conference."

I thought of when I had last seen them. It was a few years ago. They then lived in a beautiful home in Scarsdale, New York. He was a widely recognized and honored chemist, with a doctorate in chemical engineering. He worked for one of the big multinational companies headquartered in New York. He was credited with putting together the chemical ingredients of a product now sold around the world, the name of which is known to millions of people and the profit from which has run into many millions of dollars for his company.

He was well paid and highly respected.

He was also the president of the Yorktown stake of The Church of Jesus Christ of Latter-day Saints. He had under his direction a corps of church workers who served faithfully in their local wards, many of whom commuted each day to and from

New York City, where they held high and responsible positions in some of the great corporations of America. He was their church leader.

Now he was retired. He and his wife had sold their beautiful home, had given their children what furniture they wanted, and donated the rest to others. They had disposed of their cars and everything except their clothing, the family photographs, and their family history records. They had made themselves available to the Lord and His Church to go wherever they might be sent at their own expense. They were now in the Philippines Bacolod Mission, working among the wonderful, friendly, brown-skinned people of the area. Unemployment is high in this region, and there is much of misery. But wherever Elder and Sister Jex go, they touch for good the lives of those among whom they serve.

They are there to heal the suffering people, to teach the gospel of Christ, to give encouragement and strength and hope and faith. They are there to heal wounds of misunderstanding and contention. They are there to bless the sick and to help those with diseased bodies and frustrated minds. . . . They are living humbly among the poor, down at the level of the people, but standing straight and tall to lift with strong hands.

This former New York executive and his charming companion are in the service of the Savior, giving their full time, their resources, and their love to bless with healing the lives of many who are discouraged and need help. ("The Healing Power of Christ," *Ensign*, November 1988, p. 52.)

You will be remembered in prayer this morning in hundreds of homes. People are praying for you, you know that. You can't do less than your best when people are praying for you. Of course the work is not easy. It's hard. . . . But He has given us the power, the power of our message, the power of our call, the power of our priesthood and of love for the people. (Boston Massachusetts Regional Conference, missionary meeting, April 23, 1995.)

You are part of a great miracle that's occurring over the earth. I never get over the fact that what we are doing is in very deed a remarkable miracle: to send out young men and young women into a world that is unreceptive, generally, to their message, and to teach that world and to have one here and another there give attention. (Mission Presidents Seminar, June 24, 1995.)

The missionary program is the great, vibrant, pulsating thing that keeps this Church growing and moving and going forward across the world. It is a miracle. It is a miracle beyond the comprehension of most of us. We are from Dan to Beersheba and far beyond in a wonderful, great effort. Between forty-eight and fifty thousand missionaries. Behind every one of them lie a mother's prayers, a father's faith, and the love of the people of this Church and the blessing of the Lord upon these His chosen servants. There is nothing like it. . . .

They are out there as servants of the Lord to dedicate all they have of strength and wisdom and means and time to the building of the kingdom of God. Why do they do it? Because they know in their hearts that it's true. And that's the strength of the Church. It isn't in these buildings, it isn't at BYU, it isn't in Temple Square. It is in the hearts of the people, individuals, who can stand and say, as I believe everyone in this congregation can stand and say, "This is the work of God. He lives. Jesus is our Redeemer. They appeared to the boy Joseph. It happened in the grove. The Book of Mormon has come forth as a witness to the world of the living reality of the Son of God, and the priesthood and the Church are upon the earth. We are his servants and his ministers." (East Millcreek 12th Ward Sacrament Meeting, July 2, 1995.)

I was recently in London, England, and there we held a meeting with the missionaries serving in that area. Representatives of the British Broadcasting Corporation filmed part of the service. They are preparing a documentary of our missionary work in the British Isles.

Prior to this I had been interviewed by a representative of the BBC Radio Worldwide Service. He had seen the missionaries and noted their youthful appearance. He asked me, "How do you expect people to listen to these callow youth?"

In case some of you do not know the meaning of *callow*, it means immature, inexperienced, lacking sophistication.

I replied to the reporter with a smile, "Callow youth? It is with these missionaries today as it was with Timothy in the days of Paul. It was Paul who wrote to his young companion, saying, 'Let no man despise thy youth; but be thou an example of the believers, in word, in conversation, in charity, in spirit, in faith, in purity' (1 Tim. 4:12).

"The remarkable thing is that people do receive them and listen to them. They are wholesome. They are bright, they are alert, they are upstanding. They are clean looking, and people quickly develop confidence in them." . . .

"Callow youth?" Yes, they are lacking in sophistication. What a great blessing this is. They carry no element of deception. They speak with no element of sophistry. They speak out of their hearts, with personal conviction. Each is a servant of the living God, an ambassador of the Lord Jesus Christ. Their power comes not of their learning in the things of the world. Their power comes of faith, and prayer, and humility. As we have been reminded, the work is not easy. It has never been easy. Long ago Jeremiah said that the Lord would gather His people one of a city and two of a family and bring them to Zion and feed them with pastors after His own heart (see Jer. 3:14–15). In terms of the individual missionary, the harvest is not great in most instances, but in the aggregate it becomes tremendous. ("Of Missions, Temples, and Stewardship," *Ensign*, November 1995, p. 51.)

I throw out a challenge to every young man. . . . Prepare yourself now to be worthy to serve the Lord as a full-time missionary. He has said, "If ye are prepared ye shall not fear" (D&C 38:30). Prepare to consecrate two years of your lives to this sacred service. That will in effect constitute a tithe on the first twenty years of your lives. . . . I promise you that the time you spend in the mission field, if those years are spent in dedicated service, will yield a greater return on investment than any other two years of your lives. You will come to know what dedication and consecration mean. You will develop powers of persuasion which will bless your entire life. Your timidity, your fears, your shyness will gradually disappear as you go forth with boldness and conviction. You will learn to work with others, to develop a spirit of teamwork. The cankering evil of selfishness will be supplanted by a sense of service to others. You will draw nearer to the Lord than you likely will in any other set of circumstances. You will come to know that without His help you are indeed weak and simple, but that with His help you can accomplish miracles.

You will establish habits of industry. You will develop a talent for the establishment of goals of effort. You will learn to work with singleness of purpose. What a tremendous foundation all of this will become for you in your later educational efforts and your life's work. Two years will not be time lost. It will be skills gained. . . .

And above and beyond all of this will come that sweet peace in your heart that you have served your Lord faithfully and well. Your service will become an expression of gratitude to your Heavenly Father.

You will come to know your Redeemer as your greatest friend in time or eternity. . . .

If you serve a mission faithfully and well, you will be a better husband, you will be a better father, you will be a better student, a better worker in your chosen vocation. Love is of the essence of this missionary work. Selflessness is of its very nature. Self-discipline is its requirement. Prayer opens its reservoir of power. ("Of Missions, Temples, and Stewardship," *Ensign*, November 1995, pp. 51–52.)

You are making a sacrifice, but it is not a sacrifice because you will get more than you give up, you will gain more than you give, and it will prove to be an investment with tremendous returns. It will prove to be a blessing instead of a sacrifice. No one who ever served this work as a missionary, who gave his or her best efforts, need worry about making a sacrifice because there will come blessings into the life of that individual for as long as he or she lives. I have not the slightest doubt about that. (Hawaii Honolulu Missionary Meeting, February 17, 1996.)

Go forward. Do your work. It's so very, very important. You have on your narrow shoulders the responsibility of teaching the gospel to a world that doesn't want it. At least they think they don't want it because they haven't tasted of it. And for many,

many of those people you are the only knowledge they will ever have of this Church. It is so very important, therefore, that you make a good appearance. Someday someone might well say, "Well, yes, I met two of your missionaries years ago and I've been thinking about it ever since then. Come in and tell me what you have to offer." Go forward with faith and without fear. (Pennsylvania Pittsburgh Missionary Meeting, April 27, 1996.)

Every one of you is so important to this cause. Without you the Church would not grow; it would just go along in a static way and finally it would fade and dwindle and die here. You are what keeps it alive with a constant infusion of new blood, of converts who come into the Church who bring with them their strengths. You are so very, very, very important. Do not ever think that what you are doing is not important. It is so very, very important. You may not bring very many converts into the Church during your mission. I do not care about that so long as you try, so long as you work hard. If you will work hard, the matter of converts will take care of itself. I am satisfied of that. Give it your very best. (Korea Pusan and Korea Taejon Missionary Meeting, May 21, 1996.)

Every time you bring a convert into this Church you bless a life. Not one life, if he or she remains faithful, but many lives. For that which you do becomes the work of generations yet to come. All of us here are the fruits of missionary work—our fathers, our grandfathers, our great-grandfathers who accepted the testimony of missionaries and came into the Church. We are the beneficiaries. I never look at missionaries that I do not feel inclined to say, you never can foretell the consequences of that which you do in this service. (Hong Kong Missionary Meeting, May 25, 1996.)

This is a great time in your lives. This is a wonderful season in your lives. This is a unique and different time in your lives. This is a time when you have opportunities that you will never have again as long as you live—the opportunity of spending your full time in the service of the Lord without any thought of money. You know you are going to have enough to get by on, not too much, I hope, but enough to get by on. You don't have to worry about a job. You don't have to worry about school. You don't have to worry about social life. There is no need to worry about Mary whom you left behind. Suppose she does marry somebody else while you are away? Get on your knees and thank the Lord and ask Him to bless her. You'll find somebody that's better suited to you. Your tastes will be changed. (Philippines Manila/Quezon City Missionary Meeting, May 31, 1996.)

Temptation is everywhere. It's everywhere in this world. There are those who would like to entrap the missionaries if they could. Each of you has a companion. Why? Well, for one reason the Savior said, "In the mouths of two or three witnesses shall [all things] be established." (Matthew 18:16.) Another is for your mutual protection, so that you can protect one another. When you are together, it isn't likely that both of you will go wrong. One of you might be tempted. The other will pull him up and straighten him out and give him strength to resist. Subtle are the ways of the world. Clever are the designs of the adversary. Be careful. You want to go home in honor. Don't step into tragedy. Transgression never was happiness. Sin never was happiness. Evil never was happiness. (Philippines Manila/Quezon City Missionary Meeting, May 31, 1996.)

I'm going to read two or three statements from what I regard as the greatest missionary letters ever written. They were written by Paul to his young companion, Timothy. In 1 Timothy, the fourth chapter, the twelfth verse, Paul wrote: "Let no man despise thy youth." People look at you and say, "What are you doing as a minister of the gospel? What do you know about it, you young men and women?" That's what they think. Here you are, nineteen, twenty, twenty-one. Not educated—they look upon you as being not educated—as youth. "Let no man despise thy youth"—Timothy was a young man, like you—"but be thou an example of the believers in word, in conversation, in charity, in spirit, in faith, in purity." What he is saying is that if you reflect in your lives the elements of the gospel, people will look beyond your youth as in the faces of men and women who are believers in word, in their conversation, in their acts of love and charity, in spirit, their attitude, in faith, in purity.

Skipping to the fourteenth verse, "Neglect not the gift that is in thee which was given thee by prophecy with the laying on of the hands of the presbytery." Timothy was called just the way you were, by the spirit of prophecy with the laying on of the hands of the presbytery. Who are the presbytery? The elders of the Church who set you apart, in most cases your stake presidents. . . .

Skip down to verse sixteen. "Take heed unto thyself, and unto the doctrine, continue in them, for in doing this thou shalt both save thyself and them that hear thee." That's what happens when you go out and teach others: you save them. You are an instrument in the hands of the Lord in saving them, but you also save yourselves. You come home a different young man from what you were when you came into the field. And, if you remember what you learned in the mission field, you will be faithful all of your life. Those are the words of Paul to Timothy and they are the words from me to you.

Let me add one or two other things. The fifth chapter, twenty-second verse, reads: "Keep thyself pure." Paul put it just that plainly and just that simply. "Keep thyself pure." Every one of you knows what that means. I remember thirty years ago being in Taiwan when a missionary destroyed himself because he became involved in immorality. He was excommunicated from the Church. I have been trying to find him ever since. I don't know what's happened to him. I guess he's out of the Church. I guess his children are out of the Church. He's old enough to have grandchildren; I suppose probably they are out of the Church because of the foolish thing which he did. "Keep thyself pure." There is no substitute for purity. What was it that Sir Galahad said? "My strength is as the strength of ten, because my heart is pure." What was it the Lord said? "Let virtue garnish thy thoughts unceasingly." That's the commandment of the Lord through modern revelation. (Spain Madrid Missionary Meeting, June 11, 1996.)

You will shed more tears when you leave to go home than you shed when you left home to come here. . . .

What a great love develops in our hearts for the people among whom we serve as missionaries. It was my privilege to serve in the British Isles sixty years ago. I love the people because I worked among them. You have that great privilege here, coming to know these people.

The nation of Argentina once ordered all of our missionaries out and it was a very, very serious thing. I went to Washington to meet with the Argentine Ambassador to the United States. Brother Richard Scott, who was then the mission president in Argentina, came up and met with us. Brother Robert Barker, who had entrée to many people in Washington, opened the door and we called on the Ambassador. He was as cold as ice. All that we said didn't touch him. He remained adamant. He wouldn't give in on any concession. Brother Scott had with him a book showing all of his missionaries, and he handed the book to me. I said, "Mr. Ambassador," as I opened it, "these are the young men and women that we are talking about. They will come home from your country when they have completed their missions. They will go on to school. They will become people of substance.They will become people of influence. Argentina will never have better friends anywhere in this world than these young men and women who have served in your country as missionaries of The Church of Jesus Christ of Latter-day Saints. They will dream of getting married and taking their brides back to Argentina. They may not be able to afford it, but they'll never get over the idea of going back to Argentina. They will always have a warm place in their hearts for your land and people. I believe that they are blessing your nation, and I believe that they will be your friends forever."

He said, "Well, I'll see what I can do." And miraculously the order was lifted and missionaries were given their visas and permitted to continue to go there. (Spain Madrid Missionary Meeting, June 11, 1996.)

You don't know how much good you can do; you can't foresee the results of the effort you put in. Years ago, President Charles A. Callis, then a member of the Quorum of the Twelve, but who previously was president of the Southern States Mission for twenty-five years, told me this story. He said that he had a missionary in the southern states who came in to get his release at the conclusion of his mission. His mission president said to him, "Have you had a good mission?"

He said, "No."

"How is that?"

"Well, I haven't had any results from my work. I have wasted my time and my father's money. It's been a waste of time."

Brother Callis said, "Haven't you baptized anyone?"

He said, "I baptized only one person during the two years that I have been here. That was a twelve-year-old boy up in the back hollows of Tennessee."

He went home with a sense of failure. Brother Callis said, "I decided to follow that boy who had been baptized. I wanted to know what became of him. The next time I went up into that area I looked him up. He had put on shoes (he'd never worn shoes before), he'd put on a shirt (he'd never had a shirt before), he was the clerk of the little branch Sunday School."

Brother Callis said, "I followed him through the years. He became the Sunday School Superintendent, and he eventually became the branch president. He married. He moved off the little tenant farm on which he and his parents before him had lived and got a piece of ground of his own and made it fruitful. He became the district president. He sold that piece of ground in Tennessee and moved to Idaho and bought a farm along the Snake River and prospered there. His children grew. They went on missions. They came home. They had children of their own who went on missions."

Brother Callis continued, "I've just spent a week up in Idaho looking up every member of that family that I could find and talking to them about their missionary service. I discovered that, as the result of the baptism of that one little boy in the back hollows of Tennessee by a missionary who thought he had failed, more than 1,100 people have come into the Church."

You never can foretell the consequences of your work, my beloved brethren and sisters, when you serve as missionaries.

Now, the Lord has said something about that. He said, "Be not weary in well-doing, for ye are laying the foundation of a great work. And out of small things proceedeth that which is great. Behold, the Lord requireth the heart and a willing mind"

(D&C 64:33–34). That's what it takes: the heart and a willing mind. These are the words of the Lord. You are laying the foundation of a great work, and the power lies within you to accomplish it. (Belgium Brussels Missionary Meeting, June 12, 1996.)

"Behold how great is your calling" (D&C 112:33). How great is your calling! You are not sent here to take pictures. You are not sent here to play. You are sent here to find and teach. That's our opportunity, our challenge, and our responsibility. You'll never rise higher in all your lives than you will do while you are in the mission field. That may sound like a strange thing. I said that once in Argentina many years ago, and about ten years later I received a letter from a young man who said, "When I was on a mission in Argentina, you came there and you put a hex on me. I haven't been able to lift it. I have been no good ever since. I failed in school, I failed in my work, I failed in my marriage." I didn't put a hex on him. I simply told him that he would never stand taller, never rise higher, than while in the service of the Lord, and his subsequent life demonstrated that.

This is the great day of your opportunity to establish within yourselves habits of work that will bless you throughout your lives. Said the Lord, "And if your eye be single to my glory, your whole bodies shall be filled with light, and there shall be no darkness in you." (D&C 88:67.) If you concentrate on the work of the Lord, if you give it everything you have, your whole body shall be filled with light, and there shall be no darkness in you. Gone will be the darkness of sin. Gone will be the darkness of laziness. Gone will be all of these negative things. That's the word of the Lord to you and to me. (Belgium Brussels Missionary Meeting, June 12, 1996.)

You are His messengers. You are ambassadors of the Lord Jesus Christ. Never forget that. You do not have the responsibility only to go out and give missionary lessons—that is, you do not have that alone. You are ambassadors of Jesus Christ. He has given you His right, His power, His authority to teach people the truth that will save them, that will turn their lives around and give them opportunity and growth. Will you please see that every convert who comes into the Church while you are here on this mission is so taught that he or she will grow in faith and that a year after baptism he or she will be ready to get a temple recommend, and as soon as the temple is completed will be eligible to go to the house of the Lord? (Bolivia Cochabamba Missionary Meeting, November 10, 1996.)

In the early days of the Church, John Taylor was called to go to France to open the work there. There had not been missionaries in the great nation of France, and this was what he said in 1849: "I am engaged in my Master's business; I am a minister of Jehovah to proclaim His will to the nations. I go to unlock the door of life to a mighty nation, to publish to millions the principles of life, light, and truth, intelligence and salvation, to burst their fetters, liberate the oppressed, reclaim the wandering, correct their views, improve their morals, save them from degradation, ruin and misery, and lead them to light, life, truth and celestial glory" (*Life of John Taylor*, p. 208).

It is the same today. You missionaries are here in your Master's business. You are ministers of Jehovah to proclaim His will to the nations. You have come to unlock the door to a mighty nation, to publish to millions the principles of truth and salvation. How tremendous is your calling! You are going to be here for less than two years; the sister missionaries, less than eighteen months. Make the most of it while you are here. You can't afford to sleep longer than is needful. You have a great work to do, and if you don't do it, who will? Don't waste your time, please. You are here to do the work of the Lord. He needs your help. On your narrow shoulders rests this work. Your testimony will make the difference between those who accept the gospel and those who do not. (Brazil Porto Alegre Missionary Meeting, November 13, 1996.)

When you go home, you may wish to take some gifts. Everyone likes to shop. I don't know why. Let me suggest ten gifts to take home with you on that day when you are released from this labor and go back to your loved ones.

1. A knowledge of and love of God our Eternal Father and His Son the Lord Jesus Christ. "And this is life eternal, that they might know thee the only true God, and Jesus Christ, whom

thou hast sent" (John 17:3). Make that your number-one gift to carry home with you from the mission field.

2. A knowledge and love for the scriptures, the word of the Lord. You read them. Continue to read them when you get home. Read the Book of Mormon the rest of your life. You will be inspired. You will retain the memories of your mission. And you will prepare yourselves for any opportunities that might come your way.

3. An increased love for parents. You are no longer the care-less young men and women you were. You have learned to appreciate and love your parents. Tell them so.

4. A love for the people among whom you labor.

5. An appreciation for hard work. Nothing happens unless we work. You never will plow a field by turning it over in your mind. You have to get out and take hold of the plow and go to work. Work is what makes things happen. You won't accomplish anything by sitting in your apartments thinking of all the nice people to whom you would like to teach the gospel.

6. The assurance that the inspiration of the Holy Spirit is available to each of us when we live for it. Listen for the whisperings of the Spirit and follow those whisperings.

7. An understanding of teamwork. You can't do it alone. Every one of you has a companion. Don't look for his faults; he has plenty of them. Look for his virtues and try to bring those virtues into your life.

8. The value of personal virtue. There is no room for evil thoughts in your lives while you are here. They will destroy you if you persist in them. Dismiss them. Stay away from them. Pray to the Lord for strength to rise above them.

9. The faith to act.

10. The humility to pray. There is power greater than any of us that is available to us. The Lord will bless us. He will guide us. He will magnify us. He will lead us to those who will accept the truth. He will protect us if we will listen to the still small voice and follow it. (Guatemala City Central, North, and South Missionary Meeting, January 24, 1997.)

These missionaries are a miracle—these young men and young women. What happens to them when the gospel really comes into their lives, when they lose themselves in the service of others? Something begins to shine through that is bright and beautiful and wonderful and tremendous. Let's give every boy the opportunity of a mission whom we possibly can, who is worthy to go and whose health is such that he can go. Let's not make those who can't go because of health reasons feel inferior, or that they have no place in this kingdom, but let us see, if we possibly can, that all those who are able to go have that great and marvelous opportunity. . . .

There is nothing that builds solid faith for the present and the future like serving a mission. How grateful I am for the mission which I was on more than sixty years ago. I think I was a fairly faithful young man in this Church, but going on a mission did something for me. I don't know how to define it, but it did something that has value every day of my life. I would like to see every boy have the opportunity of a mission. (Brigham City Utah Regional Conference, priesthood leadership session, February 22, 1997.)

Prepare now to go on a mission. It will not be a burden. It will not be a waste of time. It will be a great opportunity and a great challenge. It will do something for you that nothing else will do for you. It will sharpen your skills. It will train you in leadership. It will bring testimony and conviction into your heart. You will bless the lives of others as you bless your own. It will bring you nearer to God and to His Divine Son as you bear witness and testimony of Him. Your knowledge of the gospel will strengthen and deepen. Your love for your fellowman will increase. Your fears will fade as you stand boldly in testimony of the truth. ("Converts and Young Men," *Ensign*, May 1997, p. 50.)

MISSIONARY WORK

See also Conversion; Fellowshipping; Missionary
Service, Full-Time; Reactivation and Retention

I believe . . . with all my heart that the field is white ready to harvest. . . . I think the answer to an increased number of converts does not lie particularly in our methods—effective as those methods are. Rather, I think we are living in the day of the ful-fillment of the word of the Lord given through the Prophet Joel, and repeated by Moroni in his first visitation to the Prophet Joseph.

"And it shall come to pass afterward, that I will pour out my Spirit upon all flesh. . . ." (Joel 2:28.)

. . . Great and magnificent as is the work of the . . . mission-aries who have been set apart, I am convinced that we have a far greater force for teaching the gospel to the world in the mem-bership of the Church—"every man a missionary"—as has been said here so convincingly tonight. "Every man a missionary!" (Conference Report, April 1961, pp. 87–88.)

I think every member of the Church has the capacity to teach the gospel to nonmembers. I was told the other day of a crippled woman, homebound, who spends her days in a wheelchair, who has been the means of bringing thirty-seven people into the Church. . . . We need an awareness, an everyday awareness of the great power that we have to do this thing.

Second, a desire. I think many of us realize that we could do it, but we lack the desire. Let every man single out another, a friend. Let him get on his knees and pray to the Lord to help him bring that man into the Church. I am as satisfied as I am of any-thing that with that kind of prayerful, conscientious, directed effort, there isn't a man in this Church who could not convert another. . . .

Third, the faith to try. It is so simple. . . . This is not complex. It is simple. We have in the Northern Far East Mission of the Church today a beautiful and capable Japanese girl, born in Honolulu. I said to her, "Were your folks members of the Church?" "No, they were Buddhists." "How is it then that you are here?" She said, "I had a high school friend who took me to Mutual once a week and then gave me a tract to read." That girl went on to the University of Hawaii and then to Illinois Wesleyan University, from which school she was graduated. Today she is a missionary in Japan. ("Ready to Harvest," *Improvement Era,* July 1961, p. 508.)

It is an inspiring experience . . . to witness the manner in which the Lord is weaving the tapestry of his grand design in those foreign parts of the earth. He is gathering his children there as elsewhere—"one of a city and two of a family." He is remembering the promises made of old as he works among those who have seen so much of poverty and misery and evil and oppression. He is answering the prayers of those who have gone before, and who struggled to establish a foothold for the gospel in those distant places. . . .

. . . The work is becoming very much enlarged. It does require a commensurate accumulation of men and means. It requires an expansion of mind and energy, ability and perseverance. Let us prepare ourselves more diligently for the great assignment which God has laid upon us to carry this work to the children of the earth wherever we may be permitted to go. (Conference Report, April 1962, p . 71, 73.)

I am at least superficially acquainted with some of the problems encountered by our missionaries incident to our carrying out the program of the Church where there are marked differences between our culture and the cultures of the people of those lands. But I feel these differences are of minor importance in comparison with the great burden of our responsibility to teach the gospel of the Master and that alone. . . .

The Spirit of the Lord will overcome the effect of any differences in culture or other situations between a missionary and those he teaches. The Lord himself made the process clear. . . .

Now even greater challenges lie ahead for the future. One cannot think of . . . China, . . . India, the vast populations of Russia and the Middle East without wondering how it can ever be accomplished. It will be accomplished, for the Lord has given us a mandate. If we will put forth our efforts, he will open the way. ("Things Are Getting Better," *BYU Devotional Speeches of the Year,* April 8, 1976, pp. 87, 90, 91.)

Within the space of that twenty years preceding his death, Joseph Smith set in motion a program for carrying the gospel to the nations of the earth. I marvel at the boldness with which he moved. Even in the infant days of the Church, in times of dark adversity, men were called to leave homes and families, to cross the sea, to proclaim the restoration of the gospel of Jesus Christ. His mind, his vision encompassed the entire earth. ("Joseph the Seer," *Ensign*, May 1977, p. 65.)

In recent months I have had the opportunity of traveling in the People's Republic of China and in the nations of eastern Europe, including Russia. My heart has been touched by the warmth of good people wherever I have gone. All are children of our Father in Heaven. True, there are vast chasms of political and ideological differences. But innately people are the same. They are all sons and daughters of God. They have within their hearts basically the same longings. Husbands love their wives, and wives their husbands. Parents love their children, and children their parents. Their minds respond to the same truths if they are given opportunity to hear them. Speaking of the people generally, they desire peace and not war. They desire brotherhood and not conflict. They desire truth and not propaganda. Ours is a great and compelling responsibility, to teach the everlasting gospel to the peoples of the earth. Many gates are now closed against us. But I am convinced that the Lord in his own time will open them, provided we constantly seek and pray for such openings and are prepared to take advantage of them. I do not know specifically the time frame of the Lord's work, but I do know that we must be anxiously engaged. ("Faith: The Essence of True Religion," *Ensign*, November 1981, pp. 5–6.)

During the twenty years and more that I have served as a General Authority, I have seen in a very personal and intimate way a miraculous opening and strengthening of the work in some of the great nations of Asia. We now have well over a hundred thousand members with strong wards and stakes in lands where only twenty-five years ago we scarcely dreamed of entering. The Lord, moving in his mysterious way, has unlocked those doors and touched the hearts of the people. That process is at work today in other lands. I am convinced of this, although the progress may appear almost imperceptible. ("Faith: The Essence of True Religion," *Ensign*, November 1981, p. 6.)

We have so much to do in this world to spread the influence of this gospel. Let us go forth on our assigned mission. We feel the compulsion of the Lord's mandate to teach the gospel to every nation, kindred, tongue, and people. (See D&C 133:37.) We hope that in so doing we shall not offend, but rather that we shall do so with graciousness and in that spirit of love which was of the very essence of him of whom we testify. ("Reach Out in Love and Kindness," *Ensign,* November 1982, p. 77.)

We all need to be reminded to share the gospel with our associates. I emphasize the word *share.* I like it. I deprecate the use of what might be perceived as force and pressure upon those who live among us. I think it unnecessary. Neighborliness and exemplary living of the gospel of Jesus Christ, with an awareness of opportunity to quietly and graciously lead them in the direction of the Church, will accomplish much more, and will be resisted less and appreciated more by those we seek to help. ("The Miracle Made Possible by Faith," *Ensign,* May 1984, p. 46.)

I am convinced that there are many, many thousands . . . who, with warmth and welcome, can be led to the eternal truths of the restored gospel of Jesus Christ. They are looking for something better than they have. They must be friendshipped. They must be fellowshipped. They must be made to feel comfortable and at home, so they can observe in the lives of the members of the Church those virtues they wish for themselves. . . .

The world is our responsibility. We cannot evade it. I think of the words of Jacob in the Book of Mormon, who with his brother Joseph had been consecrated a priest and teacher unto the people:

"And we did magnify our office unto the Lord, taking upon us the responsibility, answering the sins of the people upon our own heads if we did not teach them the word of God with all diligence." (Jacob 1:19.) ("The Question of a Mission," *Ensign,* May 1986, p. 42.)

I vividly recall the great and moving experience it was to participate in [the dedication of the Guatemala City Temple].

In ten dedicatory sessions, thousands of wonderful people joined in presenting this sacred house to God our Eternal Father and His Beloved Son Jesus Christ. Those familiar with the people estimated that more than 75 percent of those who were there were descendants of Father Lehi.

What an inspiration it was to look into their faces—handsome men and beautiful women with lovely children. Yet behind their stoic expressions, I felt I could see, almost in vision, generations of their forebears—the glorious days of their strength and goodness when they knew and worshipped the Christ, and then the tragic, miserable years, reaching through many generations, when, having rejected Him, their blood ran from the wounds of conflict, and they lived in pain, filth, poverty, and oppression.

Hundreds of those who came to the dedicatory services lived in the mountains and jungles of Guatemala and other areas of Central America. They came because their lives have been touched by faithful missionaries who have walked from humble home to humble home and told these people of their forebears and read to them from their own forgotten testament of Christ. They have been touched by the power of the Holy Spirit. The scales of darkness have slowly but surely fallen from their eyes. . . . It is a latter-day miracle, a wonderful thing to behold. How did it happen? How did it all come to be?

One need look no further than to the many missionaries who have labored in that part of the world, who in obedience to the Lord accepted a call from His prophet to serve a mission. ("Giving Ourselves to the Service of the Lord," *Ensign*, March 1987, p. 2.)

You will recall that Alma gave up the judgment seat so that he might have time and strength for a greater work: "And this he did that he himself might go forth among his people . . . that he might preach the word of God unto them, to stir them up in remembrance of their duty, and that he might pull down, by the word of God, all the pride and craftiness and all the contentions which were among his people, seeing no way that he might reclaim them save it were in bearing down in pure testimony against them." (Alma 4:19.)

For this same reason, the world today needs the power of pure testimony. It needs the gospel of Jesus Christ, and if the world is to hear that gospel, there must be messengers to teach it. ("There Must Be Messengers," *Ensign*, October 1987, p. 2.)

One cannot think of the hundreds of millions who have never heard of this work without wondering how our charge to teach all mankind can ever be accomplished. There are nations where we presently cannot legally go. We honor and obey the laws of these nations. But if we will be both alert and patient, the Lord will open the way in the appropriate season. His is the timetable. ("We Have a Work to Do," *Ensign*, February 1988, p. 6.)

I wish to invite members of the Church to consider anew the great mandate given by the Lord to all who desire to be known as his disciples. It is a mandate we cannot dodge, and one from which we cannot shrink. That mandate is to teach the gospel to the nations and peoples of the earth.

This was the final charge given by the Lord following his resurrection and before his ascension. It was repeated at the opening of this dispensation. Following the organization of the first Quorum of the Twelve in 1835, Oliver Cowdery, Counselor in the First Presidency, delivered a "charge" to these men. That statement has become something of a charter for all members of the Twelve who have succeeded that first group. In that charge is the following counsel:

"Be zealous to save souls. The soul of one man is as precious as the soul of another. . . . The Gospel must roll forth, and it will until it fills the whole earth. . . . You have a work to do that no other men can do; you must proclaim the Gospel in its simplicity and purity; and we commend you to God and the word of His grace." (*History of the Church*, 2:196–98.)

Subsequent to that counsel, the Lord gave the revelation known as Doctrine and Covenants section 112, which was directed to the Twelve. In it are these words:

"Contend thou, therefore, morning by morning; and day after day let thy warning voice go forth; and when the night cometh let not the inhabitants of the earth slumber, because of thy speech. . . .

"And I will be with you; and in whatsoever place ye shall proclaim my name an effectual door shall be opened unto you, that they may receive my word." (D&C 112:5, 19.) ("We Have a Work to Do," *Ensign,* February 1988, p. 2.)

Years ago I was asked whether the missionary lessons we use in the Orient are substantially different from those we use in Christian countries. I responded that we use essentially the same lessons because we teach the same kind of people whose hearts are touched by the same eternal truths. I stated further that the people of Asia are children of God, just as are the people of America, and because we have all come of the same parentage, we respond to the same truth. The fact that one's skin may be of a slightly different color, that one's eyes may have a slightly different set, that one may wear a different type of clothing does not in any sense make of him or her a different kind of individual. Men and women the world over respond to the same stimuli in essentially the same way. They seek warmth when they are cold; they know the same kinds of pain; they experience sadness, and they know joy. And everywhere, people look to a superior power. They may call him by various names, and they may describe him in various ways; but they are aware of his being and look to him for strength beyond their own.

When differences—either with our neighbors or in other cultures—seem to stand as hurdles as we seek to share the gospel, quiet courtesy usually removes these hurdles. As we keep the Lord's commandment to introduce others to the gospel, I testify that the Spirit of the Lord helps overcome the differences between him who is teaching and him who is being taught. ("We Have a Work to Do," *Ensign,* February 1988, pp. 5–6.)

I am satisfied that the most effective means each of us has in our calling to share the gospel is the Spirit of the Lord. We have all seen it in others. As we do the Lord's work, we have also sensed it in ourselves. On such occasions, superficial differences between us and those we teach seem to fall like scales from our eyes. (See 2 Nephi 30:6.) A warmth of kinship and understanding emerges which is marvelous to behold. We literally understand one another, and we literally are edified and rejoice together. ("We Have a Work to Do," *Ensign,* February 1988, p. 6.)

We can never hold within ourselves the great blessings of light and truth which have come to us from the Almighty. Ours is an obligation, a serious responsibility to carry to the world not only the secular truth we acquire . . . but also the great good news of the gospel of Jesus Christ. Ours is truly a message of hope and reconciliation. It is a word of hope for all mankind, a beacon of eternal truth to which men may look as they lift their eyes and souls to their Creator and in the process come to recognize their common brotherhood. That sense of brotherhood must bring reconciliation among those who differ and argue over their differences. ("A Unique and Wonderful University," *BYU 1988–89 Devotional and Fireside Speeches,* October 11, 1988, p. 51.)

This sick world cries out for healing. Christ, the Son of God, was the Master Healer, and he has shown us the way. It is his message of peace and reconciliation that we teach. His is the gospel of charity and peace and love. Ours is a mission of understanding, ours is a mission of teaching, ours is a mission of reconciliation. It is accomplished in substantial measure through our great missionary program. That program is essentially concerned with carrying a message of hope and reconciliation to a needy world. ("A Unique and Wonderful University," *BYU 1988–89 Devotional and Fireside Speeches,* October 11, 1988, p. 51.)

Missionary work is concerned with searching and winnowing and gleaning and teaching with love and kindness. (Mission Presidents Seminar, June 22, 1994.)

You never can foretell the consequences of that which you do when you talk about the Church with another. This work is nothing of which we need be ashamed. It is something in which we can take great pride. The problem is that most of us are filled with fear. . . . Try it. Taste the sweet and wonderful joy of sharing your testimony of this work with others. (Anchorage Alaska Regional Conference, June 18, 1995.)

I wish I could awaken in the heart of every man, woman, boy, and girl here this morning the great consuming desire to share the gospel with others. If you do that you live better, you try to make your lives more exemplary because you know that those you teach will not believe unless you back up what you say by the goodness of your lives. Nobody can foretell the consequences of that which you do when you teach the gospel to another. (Anchorage Alaska Regional Conference, June 18, 1995.)

Missionary work is a work of love and trust, and it has to be done on that basis. (Mission Presidents Seminar, June 24, 1995.)

Be a part of this great process which constantly adds to the vitality of the Church. Every time a new member comes into the Church, something happens. There is an infusion of strength and faith and testimony that is wonderful. Think of what this Church would be without the missionary program. Think of it! I think this is the greatest age in the history of the world. I think this is the greatest time in the history of the Church. I believe that. I think there will be greater times in the future. We are growing ever and ever stronger. (Washington D.C. North and South Missionary Meeting, November 12, 1995.)

In behalf of the missionaries who are here, I want to plead with the Saints to do all that you possibly can to provide referrals whom they might teach. You will be happy if you do so. Everyone that you see come into the Church because of your effort will bring happiness into your lives. I make that as a promise to each of you. (Pusan Korea Fireside, May 21, 1996.)

What a responsibility we have. The whole fate of the world depends on us, according to the revelations of the Almighty. We cannot waste time. We cannot be unrighteous in our living. We cannot let our thoughts dwell on immoral things. We have to be the very best that we can be, you and I, because the very relationship of God our Eternal Father to His children on the earth depends on their accepting what we have come to teach according to His magnificent word. (Taiwan Taipei Missionary Meeting, May 24, 1996.)

What we are after are men and women with faith, who will rear families of faith, who will have grandchildren of faith, who will have great-grandchildren of faith and thus build the kingdom of God. (Taiwan Taipei Missionary Meeting, May 24, 1996.)

Don't be gloomy. Even if you are not happy, put a smile on your face. This is the gospel of good news, this is a message of joy, this is the thing of which the angels sang when they sang of the birth of the Son of God. This is a work of eternal salvation; this is something to be happy and excited about. You won't get anywhere if you go with a frown on your face. Put a smile on your face when you meet somebody, no matter where it is—at a door, on the street, in the Metro, whatever. "Let thy heart be of good cheer," said the Lord. "Contend thou, therefore, morning by morning; and day after day let thy warning voice go forth; and when the night cometh let not the inhabitants of the earth slumber, because of thy speech" or the lack of thy speech (D&C 112:4–5). The Lord is saying, "Keep at it. Keep at it. You have to keep going. You can't stop. You just have to keep going, even in the face of discouragement." (Belgium Brussels Missionary Meeting, June 12, 1996.)

Be friendly. You have to make a friend before you make a convert. Conversion follows friendship. The opportunity to teach follows friendship. (Belgium Brussels Missionary Meeting, June 12, 1996.)

You stake missionaries . . . can do such a wonderful thing. You can stimulate people of your ward to refer to the missionaries their friends who will listen to the gospel. I remember well, I was in Denver, Colorado, many years ago, in a meeting like this. A bishop spoke. He had been a branch president somewhere in a little town in Colorado and he said the mission president gave them a challenge that every member of the branch, within a month's time, could develop a contact who could be taught by the full-time missionaries. There he was, the branch president. He couldn't think of anybody who might be taught. Among the members of his branch, one man said, "I have someone," another man said, "I have someone," another man said, "I have someone." But the branch president didn't have anybody. It got to be the 28th day of the month and he didn't have anybody. It got to be the 29th day of the month, he didn't have anybody. He fasted. He pleaded with the Lord to bless him to find someone to teach. It got to be the 30th of the month, and he went out to lunch. He had been fasting that morning, but decided he would go out for lunch. And when he came back a little early, someone else got on the elevator, a man who worked four or five desks away. And he said, "Jones, while the two of us are together here alone, before everybody comes back from lunch, I want to ask you something. I've noticed you're a little different. You do things in a different way. You don't smoke. You don't drink. You don't even drink coffee. What is it?"

He said he told him, "I'm a member of The Church of Jesus Christ of Latter-day Saints," and that those things were proscribed by his religion.

He said, "How can I learn about your Church?"

He said, "Tears came to my eyes. There, on the last day of the month, the Lord had answered my prayers. He let me worry for thirty days. He let me humble myself until I was desperate almost, because I wanted to do my part as president of the branch. And on the thirtieth day, when I had fasted and prayed and pleaded, He brought someone to me. That man," he said, "joined the Church with his family."

Now, you who are stake missionaries, that's your great opportunity—to find those who can be taught by these full-time missionaries, and to urge the people of your wards and branches to find people who can be taught. (Denmark Copenhagen Missionary Meeting, June 14, 1996.)

I had an interesting letter the other day from a young man who is in a stake presidency and has served as a bishop. Some years ago his parents were flying across the Atlantic on the same plane that I was. When they served breakfast I leaned over the aisle and said, "Where are you from?" The man said he was from

New Jersey. "Where are you from," he asked in return. "Salt Lake City." "I thought so," he said. "Are you a Mormon? I noticed that you had more orange juice than anyone else on the plane." We talked and he told me that he had three sons. He was then living on the Isle of Wight in England, where he had to go in order to qualify for an inheritance from his grandfather. But he had three sons, all American citizens, and he wanted the eldest to go to a forestry school in the United States. I told him that Utah State University was a great forestry school, and the upshot of our conversation was that they brought him there and put him in school. He did not like forestry, but he joined the Church. It was my pleasure to perform his sealing in the Salt Lake Temple. His brother came along. He was in the Army Air Corps. He called me one day and told me he was being transferred to Korea. I told him someone would be there to meet him, and then called the mission president in Seoul. This boy also joined the Church. The third boy came along and said, "You got the other two, but you're not going to get me." Well, I ultimately performed his marriage in the Salt Lake Temple. The father became so angry that he had a stroke and died from it, with a curse on his lips against me for having done what I had to his three sons. Well, long after that I was at a stake conference in the Salt Lake Valley, and I noticed a woman in the back of the hall. It was the mother of these three boys. She came up to the stand to tell me that she had been baptized into the Church and had her husband's work done in the temple. And they all silently hoped and prayed that he would accept the gospel. This is a great family. Missionaries have gone out from those families as a result of one small conversation on a plane. All I am trying to say is that we can all do missionary work. If we have a mind to do it, we can do it. (Jacksonville Florida West Stake Conference, January 19, 1997.)

MORALITY

See also Chastity; Values; Virtue

We do not need a new moral standard in our modern society. The laws of God have not been abrogated. They were not given to one generation to be laid aside by another. Their disregard can result only in trouble, misery, and insecurity as witness the fruits of the erosion of morality among us. Their application is the way of life and peace and progress. ("Except the Lord Build the House," *Improvement Era*, January 1964, p. 56.)

Rationalization and equivocation will not erase the cankering scar that blights the self-respect of a young man who takes that virtue which he can never replace. Self-justification will never mend the heart of a young woman who has drifted into moral tragedy. ("The Dimension of the Spirit," *Improvement Era*, December 1964, p. 1092.)

Can anything be more false or dishonest than gratification of passion without acceptance of responsibility?

I have seen in Korea the tragic aftermath of war in the thousands of orphans born of Korean mothers and soldier fathers. They have been abandoned, creatures of sorrow, unwanted, the flotsam of a miserable tide of immorality. . . .

Men are prone to gloat over their immoral conquests. What a cheap and sullied victory. There is no conquest in such. It is only self-deception and a miserable fraud. The only conquest that brings satisfaction is the conquest of self. It was said of old that "he that governeth himself is greater than he that taketh a city." (*From My Generation to Yours, with Love*, pamphlet, 1978, pp. 5–6.)

Self-discipline was never easy. I do not doubt that it is more difficult today. We live in a sex-saturated world. Notwithstanding the conclusions of a government commission, which I am happy to say has been widely repudiated, I am convinced that many of our youth, and many older but no less gullible, are victims of the persuasive elements with which they are surrounded—the pornographic literature which has become a $500 million a year business in this country alone, seductive movies that excite and give sanction to promiscuity, dress standards that invite familiarity, judicial decisions that destroy legal restraint, parents who often unwittingly push the children they love toward situations they later regret.

A wise writer has observed that "a new religion is emerging throughout the world, a religion in which the body is the supreme object of worship to the exclusion of all other aspects of existence. The pursuit of its pleasures has grown into a cult; . . . for its ritual no efforts are spared. We have bartered holiness for convenience, . . . wisdom for information, joy for pleasure, tradition for fashion" (Abraham Heschel, *The Insecurity of Freedom* [New York: Farrar, Straus and Giroux, 1966], p. 200).

Nakedness has become the hallmark of much public entertainment. It reaches beyond this into the realm of sadistic perversion. As one seasoned New York critic remarked, "It's not only the nudity; it's the crudity."

Can there be any reasonable doubt that in sowing the wind of pornography, we are reaping the whirlwind of decay? (*From My Generation to Yours, with Love,* pamphlet, 1978, pp. 7–8.)

Is there a valid case for virtue? It is the only way to freedom from regret. The peace of conscience which flows therefrom is the only personal peace that is not counterfeit. (*From My Generation to Yours, with Love,* pamphlet, 1978, p. 9.)

We live in a time when the world considers virtue lightly. You . . . cannot consider it lightly. For a Latter-day Saint, loss of virtue inevitably means loss of self-respect, loss of respect for her with whom he transgresses, loss of discipline in managing one's mind and body, and loss of integrity as a holder of the priesthood. Of course there is repentance, and of course there is forgiveness. But there will also be heartache and regret and disappointment. There may likewise be cast a cloud upon your opportunity for future service in the Church.

I am not asking you to be prudish. I am asking you to be virtuous, and I think there is a vast difference between the two.

Be clean. Watch what you read. No good and much harm can come of reading pornographic magazines and other such literature. They will only stimulate within you thoughts that will weaken your discipline of yourself. No good will come of going to movies that are designed to take from you your money and give you in exchange only weakened wills and base desires. ("Four B's for Boys," *Ensign,* November 1981, p. 41.)

I recall a very troubling conversation I had years ago with a young man in a South American airport, where we were both delayed by late planes.

His hair was long and his face bearded, his glasses large and round. Sandals were on his feet, and his clothing such as to give the appearance of total indifference to any standard of style.

He was earnest and evidently sincere. He was educated and thoughtful, a graduate of a great North American university. Without employment and sustained by his father, he was traveling through South America.

What was he after in life? I asked. "Peace—and freedom" was his immediate response. Did he use drugs? Yes, they were one of his means to obtain the peace and freedom he sought. Discussion of drugs led to discussion of morals. He talked matter-of-factly about the new morality that gave so much more freedom than any previous generation had ever known.

He had learned in our opening introductions that I was a church-man; and he let me know, in something of a condescending way, that the morality of my generation was a joke. Then with earnestness he asked how I could honestly defend personal virtue and moral chastity. I shocked him a little when I declared that *his* freedom was a delusion, that *his* peace was a fraud, and that I would tell him why.

I have thought much of that discussion and others like it that I have held over the years. Today there are persons numbered in the millions who, in a search for freedom from moral restraint and peace from submerged conscience, have opened a floodgate of practices that enslave and debauch. These practices, if left unchecked, will not only destroy these individuals but also the nations of which they are a part.

I remember thinking of this freedom and this peace when I faced a young man and a young woman across the desk of my office. He was handsome, tall, and manly. She was a beautiful girl, an excellent student, sensitive and perceptive.

The girl sobbed, and tears fell from the eyes of the young man. They were freshmen at a university. They were to be married the next week, but not in the kind of wedding of which they had dreamed. They had planned *that* to come three years in the future, following graduation.

Now they found themselves in a situation that both regretted and for which neither was prepared. Shattered were their dreams of schooling, the years of preparation they knew each needed for the competitive world that lay ahead. Rather, they would now have to establish a home, he to become the breadwinner at the best figure his meager skills could command.

The young man looked up through his tears. "We were sold short," he said.

"We've cheated one another," she responded. "We've cheated one another and the parents who love us—and we've cheated ourselves. We were betrayed. We fell for the rubbish that virtue is hypocrisy; and we've found that the new morality, the idea that sin is only in one's mind, is a booby trap that's destroyed us."

They spoke of a thousand thoughts that had crossed their minds in the fearful days and the anxious nights of the past few weeks. Should she seek an abortion? The temptation was there in the frightening contemplation of the ordeal that lay ahead. No, never, she had concluded. Life is sacred under any circumstance. How could she ever live with herself if she took measures to destroy the gift of life even under these conditions?

Perhaps she could go to some place where she was not known, they thought, and he could go on with his schooling. The child could be placed for adoption. There were excellent organizations that could assist in such a program, and there were good families anxious for children. But they had dismissed that thought. He would never leave her to face her trial alone. He was responsible, and he would meet that responsibility even though it blighted the future of which he had dreamed.

. . . My heart ached as I watched them, bereft and sobbing. Here was tragedy. Here was heartbreak. Here was entrapment. Here was bondage.

They had been told of freedom, that evil was only a thing of the mind. But they found they had lost their freedom. Nor had they known peace. They had bartered their peace and their freedom—the freedom to marry when they chose to marry, the freedom to secure the education of which they had dreamed, and, more important, the peace of self-respect. . . .

Can there be peace in the heart of any person, can there be freedom in the life of one who has been left only misery as the bitter fruit of indulgence? ("In Search of Peace and Freedom," *Ensign,* August 1989, pp. 2–5.)

We need to read more history. Nations and civilizations have flowered, then died, poisoned by their own moral sickness. As one commentator has remarked, Rome perished before the Goths poured over its walls. "But it was not that the walls were low. It was that Rome itself was low." (*U.S. News & World Report,* May 28, 1962, p. 90.)

As with the bud, so with the blossom. Youth is the seedtime for the future flowering of family life. No nation, no civilization can long endure without strength in the homes and lives of its people. . . .

To hope for peace and love and gladness out of promiscuity is to hope for that which will never come. To wish for freedom out of immorality is to wish for something that cannot be. ("In Search of Peace and Freedom," *Ensign,* August 1989, pp. 5–6.)

One need not, of course, read statistics to recognize a moral decay that seems to be going on all about us. It is evident in the easy breakup of marriages, in widespread infidelity, in the growth of youth gangs, in the increased use of drugs and the epidemic spread of AIDS, and in a growing disregard for the lives and property of others. It is seen in the defacement of private and public property with graffiti, which destroys beauty and is an insult to art. It is expressed in the language of the gutter, which is brought into our homes.

The endless sex and violence on network TV, the trash of so many motion pictures, the magnified sensuality found in much of modern literature, the emphasis on sex education, a widespread breakdown of law and order—all are manifestations of this decay. ("Bring Up a Child in the Way He Should Go," *Ensign,* November 1993, p. 59.)

There are storms blowing around you. There is the clever exploitation of sex and violence to be seen on television, through videotapes, salacious magazines, long-distance telephone services, and even the Internet.

My plea to you, my dear associates in this work, is to distance yourselves from these things. You can turn the dial on the TV set. You can shun like a plague the renting or acquisition of videotapes designed to titillate and lead you into regrettable paths. Only the producer profits from such things. The buyer or the renter never does. . . .

I do not ask that you be prudes. I ask only that you choose the right. Members of the Mike Wallace team spoke with a few students like you when they were here. These were both young men and young women. The reporters told me that the students said that it was easy to turn down a cigarette. There was no problem in refusing beer. The lines were clearly drawn on these things. But sex was a different matter. It was harder to tell where to draw the line.

I replied, "Those students know where to draw the line. They do not have to have that defined in clinical detail. They know when they are on slippery ground." . . . It is all a matter of self-discipline. Of course you know what is right and what is wrong. You have been trained from your childhood in these matters. When you find yourself slipping in the direction of that which you know is wrong, it may be difficult to stop and turn around. But it can be done. It has been done by hundreds of thousands, millions just like you who experience the same emotional appeals that you experience.

The Lord has said, "Let virtue garnish thy thoughts unceasingly" (D&C 121:45).

That is a commandment. He has repeated it in numerous ways. We cannot violate that commandment without paying a price, sometimes a terrible price. Likewise if we exercise self-discipline, calling into play the mighty power of individual will, accompanied by an invitation of the Spirit of the Lord, happiness will be the result. ("True to the Faith," Salt Lake Valley-Wide Institute Fireside, January 21, 1996.)

Virtue—there is nothing more precious in all this world than virtue. Now, if there are any of you here who may have stepped over the line and transgressed and think that all is lost, let me say to you that all is not lost. The principle of repentance is the first principle of the gospel after faith in the Lord Jesus Christ. You can repent and you can put the past behind you and, as it were, clean the slate, rub those marks off the chalkboard, and go forward with your lives. If there is anything of that kind in the past, talk in confidence with your bishop and get it straightened out and move forward with cleanliness. Be clean. There is nothing more beautiful in this world than a beautiful young woman who is clean in thought and word and deed, nor anything more handsome or attractive than a young man of similar character. (San Diego California Youth Fireside, March 23, 1996.)

It seems as if the whole world has become obsessed with sex. In a very beguiling and alluring way, it is thrown at you constantly. You are exposed to it on television, in magazines and books, in videos, even in music. Turn your back on it. Shun it. I know that is easy to say, and difficult to do. But each time that you do so, it will be so much the easier the next time. What a wonderful thing it will be if someday you can stand before the Lord and say, "I am clean." ("'Be Ye Clean,'" *Ensign,* May 1996, p. 48.)

John Engler, governor of Michigan, recently said, "The wisdom of the ages reveals that our moral compass cannot ultimately come from Lansing or from any other state capital, any more than it can come from the nation's capital, or Hollywood, or the United Nations, or some abstract liberal conception of the 'Village.' It comes from deep within us—it comes from our character, which is forged in our families and our faith and tempered in the arena of decision making and action." (*Imprimis,* August 1996, Vol. 25, No. 8, p. 4.)

I encourage you . . . to speak up for moral standards in a world where filth, sleaze, pornography, and their whole evil brood are sweeping over us as a flood. In the first place, none of us can afford to be partakers of this rubbish. Not one of us, neither I nor any one of you, can become involved with such things as sleazy videotapes, suggestive television programs, debasing movies, sensual magazines, so-called "900 numbers," or the kind of filth that evidently can be picked up now on the Internet.

Avoid them like the plague, for they are a serious and deadly disease.

Lend your strength to the crusade against illegal drugs. Their use, particularly among youth, has doubled in the last four years. Think of it! Doubled since 1992. (See "Survey Predicts Big Jump in Teen-Age Drug Use," *Salt Lake Tribune*, pp. 1, 5.) Where are we going? Lives are blighted, careers are destroyed, even the next generation is injured, in many cases beyond repair, when young people take up drugs and develop an addiction.

You can reach out to prevent a foolhardy decision on the part of a boy or girl. Your interest, your caring attitude, and your voice may make the difference between life and death in a very literal sense.

Stand up for integrity in your business, in your profession, in your home, in the society of which you are a part.

Again, it is not enough that you retreat to your private cloister and pursue only your special private interests. Your strong voice is needed. The weight of your stance may be enough to tip the scales in the direction of truth. ("Stand Up for Truth," BYU Devotional Address, September 17, 1996.)

MORTALITY

See also Plan of Salvation

All of us are here as part of a divine plan made by a loving Father who is concerned with our immortality and eternal life. The mortal sphere in which we live is preparatory to that which will follow when we return to dwell with God our Father, provided we live worthy of that glorious privilege. ("Daughters of God," *Ensign*, November 1991, p. 99.)

This earthly state is a season of testing and opportunity. It is a period in which to prepare for the next life. . . . The lives we live today are part of a great eternal journey. Men and women are children of God. There is something of divinity in each of us. We have been endowed with divine qualities and instincts, and we have been sent here "for a wise and glorious purpose." ("Why I Am a Member of The Church of Jesus Christ of Latter-day Saints," Foreword to book by Dr. Matthew Naythons, March 22, 1995.)

If mortality were the only consequence of our birth, there would be no real meaning in our lives. It would simply mean that we slave our days through, educate ourselves through this and that and the other, to have it all snuffed out in oblivion at the time of death. (Boston Massachusetts Regional Conference, priesthood leadership session, April 22, 1995.)

This stage of mortality is only a stage in the grand march of our lives on the road to immortality and eternal life. (Vernal Temple Groundbreaking Ceremony, May 13, 1995.)

This life is a time of testing, a time of trials, a time of education. It is a time of gaining experience, a time of trying to qualify for things that lie ahead. (*Church News* Interview, June 7, 1995.)

This is what it is all about: putting our lives in order to make something worthwhile of what the Lord has given us, this wonderful, precious thing of life, of being on the earth at this greatest of all seasons in human history. (Vista California Youth Fireside, March 23, 1996.)

MOTHERHOOD

See also Family; Parenting

The true strength that is America's, the true strength of any nation, lies in those qualities of character that have been acquired for the most part by children taught in the quiet, simple, everyday manner of mothers. What Jean Paul Richter once declared of fathers is even more true of mothers—and I paraphrase it just a little to make the point—"What a mother says to her children is not heard by the world, but it will be heard by posterity."

A mother I know had experienced a rough day with her two little boys and a score of other problems. She was weary when her husband returned in the evening. Then something else went wrong, and in desperation she cried out, "I quit." To which her four-year-old responded, "You can't quit. You're the mother." (Salt Lake Exchange Club Mother's Day Program, May 11, 1977.)

Women for the most part see their greatest fulfillment, their greatest happiness in home and family. God planted within women something divine that expresses itself in quiet strength, in refinement, in peace, in goodness, in virtue, in truth, in love. And all of these remarkable qualities find their truest and most satisfying expression in motherhood.

Said Thomas Wolfe: "There is no spectacle on earth more appealing than that of a beautiful woman in the act of cooking dinner for someone she loves." Or, to which I might add, cuddling a baby, or leading a child in prayer, or counseling a strong young son or daughter, or comforting a tired companion.

God bless you, mothers. When all the victories and defeats of men's efforts are tallied, when the dust of life's battles begins to settle, when all for which we labor so hard in this world of conquest fades before our eyes, you will be there, you must be there, as the strength for a new generation, the ever-improving onward movement of the race. (Salt Lake Exchange Club Mother's Day Program, May 11, 1977.)

To you women who find it necessary to work when you would rather be at home, may I speak briefly. I know that there are many of you who find yourselves in this situation. Some of you have been abandoned and are divorced, with children to care for. Some of you are widows with dependent families. I honor you and respect you for your integrity and spirit of self-reliance. I pray that the Lord will bless you with strength and great capacity, for you need both. You have the responsibilities of both breadwinner and homemaker. I know that it is difficult. I know that it is discouraging. I pray that the Lord will bless you with a special wisdom and the remarkable talent needed to provide your children with time and companionship and love and with that special direction which only a mother can give. I pray also that he will bless you with help, unstintingly given, from family, friends, and the Church, which will lift some of the burden from your shoulders and help you in your times of extremity.

We sense, at least in some small degree, the loneliness you must occasionally feel and the frustrations you must experience as you try to cope with problems that sometimes seem beyond your capacity to handle. . . .

Now to others who work when it is not necessary and who, while doing so, leave children to the care of those who often are only poor substitutes, I offer a word of caution. Do not follow a practice which will bring you later regret. If the purpose of your daily employment is simply to get money for a boat or a fancy automobile or some other desirable but unnecessary thing, and in the process you lose the companionship of your children and the opportunity to rear them, you may find that you have lost the substance while grasping at the shadow. ("Live Up to Your Inheritance," *Ensign*, November 1983, p. 83.)

Nearly sixty years have gone since my mother passed away. At the time I was a university student. I have forgotten much of what I was studying then, but the memories of those last months of my mother's life remain ever green, as do the memories of earlier years. I hope she knew that I loved her. I did not say so very often. Like most boys, it was not easy for me to speak those words.

She died in the early harvest season of her life. Her youngest child was ten, old enough that Mother had come into a freedom she had not known for many years. She was on a journey in Europe when she felt the pain that frightened her. Six months later she was gone.

I recall the gray November day of her funeral. We put on a front of bravery and fought back the tears. But inside, the wounds were deep and painful. That experience, at a sensitive season of my life, has, I hope, given me a deeper understanding of all who lose a mother.

I was called on a mission shortly after that. It was in the depths of the Great Depression. Few missionaries were called at the time because of distressing financial circumstances all over the world. I had saved a few dollars, my brother worked and contributed generously, and my father carried the major burden.

But something else made it all possible. We discovered that my mother, with prescient foresight, had nurtured a savings account with the small coins she received in change when buying groceries. This money provided the balance needed for my expenses in what was then the costliest mission in the world.

For me, the money I received was sacred. I felt it had been consecrated not so much for me as for the Lord. I hope I was careful in its expenditure.

I experienced times of discouragement on my mission, as does every missionary. On an occasion or two, when the clouds were particularly dark, I felt in a very real but indescribable way the protecting, guiding, encouraging influence of my mother. She seemed very close. I tried then, as I have tried since, to so conduct my life and perform my duty as to bring honor to her name. I am the first to concede that I may not always have done so, and the thought of living beneath my mother's expectations has been painful, and has afforded a discipline that otherwise might have been lacking. (*The Wondrous Power of a Mother,* booklet [Salt Lake City: Deseret Book, 1989], pp. 1–2.)

It is my opinion that the very situation of an ever-increasing number of mothers out of the home and in the workplace is a root cause of many of the problems of delinquency, drugs, and gangs, both male and female. Why then do women leave families to work? A recently published newspaper article pointed out some of the problems family heads face which dictate this move. . . . Not only are we exacting a terrible slice of income for taxes and family-required goods and services, but concomitantly we are exacting a terrible price in the weakening of the family which occurs when a mother absents herself from the home each working day while latchkey children wait for her return. When she does return, too often she is tired and under such stress and frustration that in all too many cases she cannot give to her children the attention and the affection which they so much crave and need. (Belle S. Spafford Conference on Women, February 23, 1990.)

Let every mother realize that she has no greater blessing than the children which have come to her as a gift from the Almighty;

that she has no greater mission than to rear them in light and truth, and understanding and love; that she will have no greater happiness than to see them grow into young men and women who respect principles of virtue, who walk free from the stain of immorality and from the shame of delinquency. . . .

I remind mothers everywhere of the sanctity of your calling. No other can adequately take your place. No responsibility is greater, no obligation more binding than that you rear in love and peace and integrity those whom you have brought into the world. ("Bring Up a Child in the Way He Should Go," *Ensign,* November 1993, p. 60.)

In this age when more and more women are turning to daily work, how tremendous it is once in a while to just stop and recognize that the greatest job that any woman will ever do will be in nurturing and teaching and living and encouraging and rearing her children in righteousness and truth. There is no other thing that will compare with that, regardless of what she does. I hope that the women of the Church will not slight their greatest responsibility in favor of a lesser responsibility. To the mothers of this Church, as the years pass you will become increasingly grateful for that which you did in molding the lives of your children in the direction of righteousness and goodness and integrity and faith.

As I sat in the Tabernacle at the last conference and was sustained by the people of this Church, there came before me in my mind's eye, the picture of my mother when I was a little boy. I am grateful that I have the opportunity in my old age to bring honor to her name. How grateful I am for mothers! (Heber City/Springville Utah Regional Conference, May 14, 1995.)

It's been the mothers who have been the great carriers and purveyors of faith throughout the history of this Church. I believe that with all my heart. (Heber City/Springville Utah Regional Conference, May 14, 1995.)

Strengthen your families. Build faith in those for whom you are responsible. You women, some of you may have to work. I hope you will never forget that when all is said and done, your greatest responsibility is to those to whom you have given life. There is no responsibility more encompassing or more important than that responsibility. "All thy children shall be taught of the Lord; and great shall be the peace of thy children" (Isaiah 54:13). You mothers, read to your children. Read the scriptures to your children. You may not think they understand. They won't understand everything you read. But they will develop within themselves a feeling, an attitude, a spirit that will be wonderful. And I don't hesitate to promise you that the day will come, if you nurture your children and love and teach in righteousness, you will get on your knees with tears in your eyes and thank the Lord for His blessing to you. (Nottingham England Fireside, August 30, 1995.)

To you wives and mothers who work to maintain stable homes where there is an environment of love and respect and appreciation I say, the Lord bless you. Regardless of your circumstances, walk with faith. Rear your children in light and truth. Teach them to pray while they are young. Read to them from the scriptures even though they may not understand all that you read. Teach them to pay their tithes and offerings on the first money they ever receive. Let this practice become a habit in their lives. Teach your sons to honor womanhood. Teach your daughters to walk in virtue. Accept responsibility in the Church, and trust in the Lord to make you equal to any call you may receive. Your example will set a pattern for your children. Reach out in love to those in distress and need. . . .

It is the home which produces the nursery stock of new generations. I hope that you mothers will realize that when all is said and done, you have no more compelling responsibility, nor any laden with greater rewards, than the nurture you give your children in an environment of security, peace, companionship, love, and motivation to grow and do well. ("Stand Strong against the Wiles of the World," *Ensign*, November 1995, p. 99.)

The more surely you rear your children in the ways of the gospel of Jesus Christ, with love and high expectation, the more likely that there will be peace in their lives.

Set an example for them. That will mean more than all the teaching you can give them. Do not overindulge them. Let them grow up with respect for and understanding of the meaning of labor, of working and contributing to the home and its surroundings, with some way of earning some of their own expense money. Let your sons save for missions, and encourage them to prepare themselves, not only financially, but spiritually and in an attitude to go out to serve the Lord without selfishness of any kind. I do not hesitate to promise that if you will do so, you will have reason to count your blessings. . . .

May the Lord bless you, my beloved sisters. You are the guardians of the hearth. You are the bearers of the children. You are they who nurture them and establish within them the habits of their lives. No other work reaches so close to divinity as does the nurturing of the sons and daughters of God. ("Stand Strong against the Wiles of the World," *Ensign*, November 1995, pp. 99–101.)

Some years ago President Benson delivered a message to the women of the Church. He encouraged them to leave their employment and give their individual time to their children. I sustain the position which he took.

Nevertheless, I recognize, as he recognized, that there are some women (it has become very many in fact) who have to work to provide for the needs of their families. To you I say, do the very best you can. I hope that if you are employed full-time you are doing it to ensure that basic needs are met and not simply to indulge a taste for an elaborate home, fancy cars, and other luxuries. The greatest job that any mother will ever do will be in nurturing, teaching, lifting, encouraging, and rearing her children in righteousness and truth. None other can adequately take her place.

It is well-nigh impossible to be a full-time homemaker and a full-time employee. I know how some of you struggle with decisions concerning this matter. I repeat, do the very best you can. You know your circumstances, and I know that you are deeply concerned for the welfare of your children. Each of you has a bishop who will counsel with you and assist you. If you feel you need to speak with an understanding woman, do not hesitate to get in touch with your Relief Society president.

To the mothers of this Church . . . I want to say that as the years pass you will become increasingly grateful for that which you did in molding the lives of your children in the direction of righteousness and goodness, integrity and faith. That is most likely to happen if you can spend adequate time with them. ("Women of the Church," *Ensign*, November 1996, p. 69.)

Sister Hinckley and I were married sixty years ago. I do not know how we had the nerve to do it. We had practically nothing. It was during the Depression. I was earning $165 a month. . . . We have now been married for six decades. That is a long time. Her middle name is Endurance. . . . The years have come and gone, and we have grown older. Our lives have been rich and rewarding. They have also been marked by seasons of sorrow and sickness, of saying no to things we could not afford, of foregoing some of the luxuries. . . .

The Lord has been so very kind to us. Through the years doors have been opened before us in a miraculous way. . . .

How magnificently and munificently we have been blessed of the Lord. My heart is full of gratitude beyond my power to express. Furthermore, my heart reaches out to those who have been less fortunate. There are so many who carry such heavy burdens. There are so many women who cry out in distress for help in their time of loneliness and need. This world can be a brutal place, and there are so many young mothers who fight their way through the jungle of the world in an effort to provide for their children and themselves.

I know that many of your circumstances are different from what our circumstances were, and so I do not criticize you. I think most of you are trying to do the very best you can in your circumstances.

It is you who bear and nurture your children. It is you who comfort them and sustain them, who listen to them and counsel them wisely. You are the ones who teach them to pray and trust in the Lord. It is you who guide them in the schooling they receive which will prepare them to take their places in society. It is you who keep them close to the Church and who nourish their faith.

Most of you and your associates who are married are now employed outside the home. That is a statistical fact. You feel you must do this if you are to provide a home, music lessons, and other rather costly and consuming things. Again, I do not criticize you. I wish that it were otherwise. I wish every mother could be at home. I recognize that this is not possible. But I warn against too fancy a home with too large a mortgage, perhaps with a boat and such costly things in the driveway. I simply say that there is nothing in all this world which will bring you greater satisfaction, as the years pass ever so quickly, than seeing your children grow in faith, confidence, freedom from the enslaving elements around us. You will be a very important part of what happens to them. None can adequately substitute for you as mothers.

Weigh your options carefully. Be careful, lest you find yourself trading your birthright for a mess of pottage. (BYU Women's Conference Address, May 1, 1997.)

MUSIC

Let there be music in the home. If you have teenagers who have their own recordings, you will be prone to describe the sound as something other than music. Let them occasionally hear something better. Expose them to it. It will speak for itself. More of appreciation will come than you may think. It may not be spoken, but it will be felt, and its influence will become increasingly manifest as the years pass. (*Be Thou an Example* [Salt Lake City: Deseret Book, 1981], p. 56.)

Emma [Smith] was instructed to make a collection of hymns for the Church, and it is interesting that this counsel came only three months after the Church was organized. In connection with that call the Lord made a remarkable declaration which is often quoted among us: "For my soul delighteth in the song of the heart; yea, the song of the righteous is a prayer unto me, and it shall be answered with a blessing upon their heads." (V. 12.)

As this gifted chorus has sung to us tonight, those words have gone through my mind. The song of the righteous is a prayer unto God, and it shall be answered with a blessing upon their heads. ("'If Thou Art Faithful,'" *Ensign*, November 1984, p. 91.)

Music, of course, is an important factor. Our buildings for the most part are equipped with organs, which when properly played can add much to the worship atmosphere of the service. The singing of hymns and the rendition of selections from the great sacred oratorios by ward choirs all enhance the spirit of worship. ("Reverence and Morality," *Ensign*, May 1987, p. 45.)

We recognize the universal power of music to touch the hearts of men and women everywhere and in all generations—to inspire and encourage, to sustain and lift, to comfort and bring peace. ("60 Years of Radio Broadcasting," Tabernacle Choir Broadcast and Program, July 16, 1989.)

The Tabernacle Choir's offerings on radio and television, in motion pictures, and on records have brought its music to millions. No medium has touched the lives of so many for so long as has the weekly CBS radio broadcast of *Music and the Spoken Word*. Here these gifted singers have shared the great choral works of the master composers of all ages. They have presented inspirational music from Broadway, motion pictures, and the immortal folk melodies and patriotic songs of many people. They have lifted their voices in anthems of praise and thanksgiving unto God our Eternal Father and His Beloved Son. ("60 Years of Radio Broadcasting," Tabernacle Choir Broadcast and Program, July 16, 1989.)

Enjoy music. Not the kind that rocks and rolls, but the music of the masters, the music that has lived through the centuries, the music that has lifted people. If you do not have a taste for it, listen to it thoughtfully. If you do not like it the first time, listen to it again and keep listening. It will be something like going to the temple. The more often you go, the more beautiful will be the experience. (Ellen Pucell Unthank Monument Dedication, Cedar City, Utah, August 3, 1991.)

The words of the great missionary hymn "I'll Go Where You Want Me to Go" are not original with us. They were written by one not of our faith, a woman by the name of Mary Brown. But we have adopted it, and I guess we sing it more frequently than any other group of people in the entire world. Let me take a moment and tell you how we came to sing it.

In 1896, three missionaries were called to labor in St. Louis. They were George D. Pyper, who later became General Superintendent of the Church Sunday Schools; B. H. Roberts, who became one of the First Council of the Seventy and an assistant historian of the Church; and Melvin J. Ballard, who became a member of the Council of the Twelve Apostles.

The work was slow and difficult. The people were unresponsive. Elders Pyper and Roberts were released to return home, and Elder Ballard was left. It was an extremely discouraging and difficult situation, more so because he had left his young wife at home.

In that season of dark discouragement, Elder Ballard came across the words of this hymn. He read them again and again. They brought comfort and strength into his heart. They changed his attitude. They lifted him and gave him the incentive to work with greater faith and diligence.

They were set to music by Carrie E. Rounsefell, and Brother Ballard later sang them with a beautiful and melodious voice wherever he went. He subsequently became chairman of the Church Music Committee, and included the song in the Church hymnbook. It has been continued in all subsequent editions. It has become one of our great missionary hymns, a song of personal dedication.

Let me tell you of another experience with that hymn. Sister Hinckley and I were in Hong Kong thirty years ago. At that time I had responsibility for the work in Asia. While touring the various missions, we held testimony and instruction meetings with the missionaries. . . .

In one of these meetings in Hong Kong a sister missionary bore her testimony. As I recall, she was from New Zealand. She said that one day she and her companion were tracting in the rain. They were working in what was called a resettlement area of Hong Kong. Here the government had built multistory blocks of apartments, very plain and drab, with small units where were housed refugees from the mainland of China.

They had gone all day without an opportunity to teach. It was about 4:30 in the afternoon, and they were wet and tired and discouraged. They faced the prospect of going into another of those resettlement flats and climbing the long flights of stairs—there were no elevators. As they stood in the street facing another high-rise apartment building, she said to her junior companion, "We've done enough for today. Let's go home and get warm and dry." They started down the road where they could catch the bus.

She said, "As we began to walk toward the bus stop, the hymn, 'I'll Go Where You Want Me to Go,' came into my mind. I could not understand why. The last time I had heard it was at my farewell many months before. Now it would not leave me. Both the words and the tune continually raced through my mind. Finally, I grabbed the sleeve of my companion's raincoat and said, 'We've got to back. I don't know why. But we have to go back.'

"We retraced our steps. We climbed the stairs to the sixth floor of that drab apartment building. There was only one lighted room on that floor. We knocked on the door. We were welcomed in. We taught a lesson. We were invited back. We have taught the other lessons since then. And last week this wonderful Chinese family of five, the father and the mother and three children whom we found and taught in that apartment, were baptized and became members of The Church of Jesus Christ of Latter-day Saints."

That sister and her companion were in tune with the guiding spirit of the Lord. That spirit expressed itself in the unspoken words and unsung music of that hymn. They were obedient to the promptings of that spirit and returned and reaped a harvest, sweet and beautiful and eternal in its consequences.

I would like to suggest that if you have not already done so, you learn to sing this hymn. You do not have to sing it aloud. But when you are discouraged, when the going seems rough, when you think of home and wish you might be there, sing to yourself these great and simple words:

> *It may not be on the mountain height*
> *Or over the stormy sea,*
> *It may not be at the battle's front*
> *My Lord will have need of me.*
> *But if, by a still, small voice he calls*
> *To paths that I do not know,*
> *I'll answer, dear Lord, with my hand in thine:*
> *I'll go where you want me to go.*
> *I'll go where you want me to go, dear Lord,*
> *Over mountain or plain or sea;*
> *I'll say what you want me to say, dear Lord;*
> *I'll be what you want me to be.*
> (*HYMNS*, NO. 270)

("Carry the Message," Missionary Satellite Broadcast, November 26, 1991.)

I believe in the beauty of good music and art, of pleasing architecture, and of good literature untainted by profanity or verbal filth. ("This I Believe," *BYU 1991–92 Devotional and Fireside Speeches*, March 1, 1992, p. 78.)

I have in my home a reasonably good sound system. I do not use it frequently, but now and again, I sit quietly in the semidarkness and listen for an hour or so to music that has endured through the centuries because of its remarkable qualities. I listened the other evening to Beethoven's Concerto for the Violin and marveled that such a thing could come out of the mind of a man. The composer, I suppose, was very much like the rest of us. I do not know how tall he was or how broad he was or how much he weighed. I assume that he got hungry, felt pain, and had most of the problems that we all have, and maybe some that we do not have. But out of the genius of that mind came a tremendous blending to create rare and magnificent masterpieces of music. (General Authority Training Meeting, September 29, 1992.)

"Praise to the man who communed with Jehovah, Jesus anointed that prophet and seer. Blessed to open the last dispensation, kings shall extol him and nations revere." I never hear that song sung that I do not think of my experience as a newly ordained deacon when I was twelve years of age. Stake priesthood meeting where I lived was held on Monday evening—that was before Monday evening was set aside as family home evening. My father, who was in the stake presidency, said, "Well, we will go to stake priesthood meeting tonight." I did not want to go. I was a typical twelve-year-old boy. Why would I want to go to priesthood meeting on Monday night? He said, "Come on," and I went. He went to the stand when we got to the old Tenth Ward in Salt Lake and I was a reluctant conscript sitting on the back row. The opening song was "Praise to the Man." The men stood, in that great hall filled with men. Many of them were immigrants from Europe, converts to the Church—Germans, Swedes, Norwegians, Danes—and in the heart of every man was a conviction of the truth of this work and of the divine calling of the Prophet Joseph Smith. They sang out until it seemed to me as a boy that the whole building rang with their music. As I listened to that song, I had an impression that has never left that Joseph Smith was indeed a prophet of God. (St. George Utah Pineview Stake Conference, January 14, 1996.)

We are so greatly blessed with dedicated musicians in the Church. They add so substantially to the spirit of the conference. . . .

I wish to say a particular word about this Tabernacle Choir. . . . I came across a letter written by Wilford W. Woodruff and his counselors, George Q. Cannon and Joseph F. Smith, under date of 11 February 1895, 101 years ago. It was addressed to the choir at that time. It reads:

"We desire to see this choir not only maintain the high reputation it has earned at home and abroad, but become the highest exponent of the 'Divine Art' in all the land; and the worthy head, example and leader of all other choirs and musical bodies in the Church, inspiring musicians and poets with purest sentiment and song and harmony, until its light shall shine forth to the world undimmed, and nations shall be charmed by its music."

The letter goes on: "This choir is and should be a great auxiliary to the cause of Zion. By means of its perfection in the glorious realm of song, it may unstop the ears of thousands now deaf to the truth, soften their stony hearts, and inspire precious souls with a love for that which is divine. Thus removing prejudice, dispelling ignorance and shedding forth the precious light of heaven to tens of thousands who have been, and are still, misled concerning us" (in James R. Clark, comp., *Messages of the First Presidency of The Church of Jesus Christ of Latter-day Saints,* 6 vols. [1965–75], 3:267–68).

Such has been the responsibility resting upon this choir for more than a century. Personnel changes have occurred through the years, but the quality of performance has only improved. This choir is one of the great treasures of the Church. I think it is one of the great treasures of America. I regard it as the outstanding choir in all the world. May it continue its great mission of providing lofty and inspiring music at home and abroad. I thank, in behalf of the entire Church, the officers, directors, organists, and members of this dedicated body of talented and gifted musicians who give so generously of their time. ("'Remember . . . Thy Church, O Lord,'" *Ensign,* May 1996, pp. 82–83.)

MYSTERIES

"For God hath not given us the spirit of fear; but of power, and of love, and of a sound mind." [2 Timothy 1:7.] . . . Of a sound mind. I think that refers to the simplicity of the gospel. It isn't all tangled up in mysteries. It is simple and straightforward and beautiful. (England London South Missionary Meeting, August 26, 1995.)

Nobody has all the answers to everything—no one in this life. We do have mysteries that we do not fully comprehend. Don't argue over them. Don't spend your time talking about those things; they can lead to argument. (Korea Seoul and Korea Seoul West Missionary Meeting, May 22, 1996.)

You don't need to worry about the mysteries. It doesn't matter whether the pearly gates swing or slide, the important thing is that they open. Don't worry about the mysteries. (Spain Madrid Missionary Meeting, June 11, 1996.)

OBEDIENCE

I recall sitting in this Tabernacle when I was fourteen or fifteen—up in the balcony right behind the clock—and hearing President Heber J. Grant tell of his experience in reading the Book of Mormon when he was a boy. He spoke of Nephi and of the great influence he had upon his life. And then, with a voice ringing with a conviction that I shall never forget, he quoted those great words of Nephi: "I will go and do the things which the Lord hath commanded, for I know that the Lord giveth no commandments unto the children of men, save he shall prepare a way for them that they may accomplish the thing which he commandeth them." (1 Ne. 3:7.)

There came into my young heart on that occasion a resolution to try to do what the Lord has commanded. ("'If Ye Be Willing and Obedient,'" *Ensign*, December 1971, p. 123.)

I give you my witness that the leaders of this church will never ask us to do anything that we cannot perform with the help of the Lord. We may feel inadequate. That which we are asked to do may not be to our liking or fit in with our ideas. But if we will try with faith and prayer and resolution, we can accomplish it.

I give you my testimony that the happiness of the Latter-day Saints, the peace of the Latter-day Saints, the progress of the Latter-day Saints, the prosperity of the Latter-day Saints, and the eternal salvation and exaltation of this people lie in walking in obedience to the counsels of the priesthood of God. ("'If Ye Be Willing and Obedient,'" *Ensign*, December 1971, p. 125.)

Does God help those who seek him? Yes, but all blessings are predicated upon obedience to law. Man must therefore live up to divine principles to claim the blessings of God. Only those who seek him and seek to do his will have claim upon him. (*What of the Mormons?* pamphlet, 1982, pp. 6–7.)

Some time ago I stood in Trafalgar Square in London and looked up at the statue of Lord Nelson. At the base of the column are his words uttered on the morning of the Battle of Trafalgar: "England expects every man to do his duty." Lord Nelson was killed on that historic day in 1805, as were many others; but England was saved as a nation, and Britain became an empire.

The image of duty and obedience has been seriously tarnished since that time. This condition is not exactly new; it is as old as human history. Isaiah declared to ancient Israel:

"If ye be willing and obedient, ye shall eat the good of the land:

"But if ye refuse and rebel, ye shall be devoured with the sword: for the mouth of the Lord hath spoken it" (Isa. 1:19–20). ("If Ye Be Willing and Obedient," *Ensign*, July 1995, p. 2.)

The assignments given us or the lots we receive in life may be difficult. Surely many a latter-day pioneer must have felt that way—or some who pioneer today for the Lord in challenging circumstances. Naaman the leper came with his horses and with his chariot, with his gifts and his gold, to the prophet Elisha to be cured. And Elisha, without seeing him, sent a messenger saying, "Go and wash in Jordan seven times, and thy flesh shall come again to thee, and thou shalt be clean" (see 2 Kings 5:1–10).

But Naaman, the proud captain of the Syrian host, was insulted at so distasteful a thing and went away. Only when his servants pleaded with him was he humbled enough to return. And the record says, "Then went he down, and dipped himself seven times in Jordan, according to the saying of the man of God: and his flesh came again like unto the flesh of a little child, and he was clean" (see vs. 11–14).

Sometimes it is the very assignment we would avoid that gives us a great blessing. ("If Ye Be Willing and Obedient," *Ensign*, July 1995, p. 4.)

Years ago I was on a mission in England. I had been called to labor in the European Mission office in London under President Joseph F. Merrill of the Council of the Twelve, then president of the European Mission. One day three or four of the London papers carried reviews of a reprint of an old book, snide and ugly in tone, indicating that the book was a history of the Mormons. President Merrill said to me, "I want you to go down to the publisher and protest this." I looked at him and was about to say, "Surely not me." But I meekly said, "Yes, sir."

I do not hesitate to say that I was frightened. I went to my room and felt something as I think Moses must have felt when the Lord asked him to go and see Pharaoh. I offered a prayer. My stomach was churning as I walked over . . . to get the underground train to Fleet Street. I found the office of the president and presented my card to the receptionist. She took it into the inner office and soon returned to say that the president was too busy to see me. I replied that I had come five thousand miles and that I would wait. During the next hour she made two or three trips to his office; then finally he invited me in. I shall never forget the picture when I entered. He was smoking a long cigar with a look that seemed to say, "Don't bother me."

I held in my hand the reviews. I do not recall what I said after that. Another power seemed to be speaking through me. At first he was defensive and even belligerent. Then he began to soften. He concluded by promising to do something. Within an hour word went out to every book dealer in England to return the books to the publisher. At great expense he printed and tipped in the front of each volume a statement to the effect that the book was not to be considered as history, but only as fiction, and that no offense was intended against the respected Mormon people. Years later he granted another favor of substantial worth to the Church, and each year until the time of his death I received a Christmas card from him.

I came to know that when we try in faith to walk in obedience to the requests of the priesthood, the Lord opens the way, even when there appears to be no way. ("If Ye Be Willing and Obedient," *Ensign,* July 1995, pp. 4–5.)

Those who live the Word of Wisdom know the truth of the Word of Wisdom. Those who engage in missionary service know the divine wisdom behind that service. Those who are making an effort to strengthen their families in obedience to the call of the Lord know that they reap the blessings of doing so. Those who engage in temple work know the truth of that work, its divine and eternal implications. Those who pay their tithing know the divine promise underlying that great law, the law of finance for the Church. Those who keep the Sabbath know the divine wisdom which provided for the Sabbath day. . . .

I have been interviewed by many reporters. The one thing they say is, "Now what is going to be your theme during your presidency?" I simply say, "The same theme which I have heard repeated in this Church by the presidents of the Church and the apostles for as far back as I can remember: Simply live the gospel, and every one who does so will receive in his heart a conviction of the truth of that which he lives." (Tacoma Washington Regional Conference, August 20, 1995.)

The religion of which you are a part is seven days a week, it isn't just Sunday; it isn't the block plan, it isn't just three hours in Church; it isn't just the time you spend in seminary, it's all the time—twenty-four hours a day, seven days a week, 365 days a year. (Parowan Utah Youth Fireside, January 13, 1996.)

I want to say a few words about what the Church expects of you Latter-day Saints, what it expects you would do with your lives.

1. It expects that you will go on learning, that you will develop and grow, that you will learn the gospel and put it into your lives, that you will make your lives productive in righteousness. This is your obligation as a member of the Church.

2. It expects that each of you will have a testimony of the living reality of God our Eternal Father and His Son, the Lord Jesus Christ. This is the beginning of all wisdom. It is the beginning of all faith. It is your duty and your obligation to acquire that knowledge. It is the only knowledge which will bring you salvation. Jesus said, "If any man will do his will, he shall know of the doctrine" (John 7:17), and that is the way you acquire a testimony—by doing the will of the Father.

3. The Word of Wisdom. All of us can live the Word of Wisdom. No liquor. No tobacco. No tea or coffee. None of those things. It isn't hard and it brings a tremendous reward. Since 1833 our people have been living it, and we have been blessed with health in our navel and marrow in our bones, to run and

not be weary and to walk and not faint, and to be blessed of the Lord with knowledge, even great treasures of knowledge of the things of God our Eternal Father (see D&C 89).

4. Tithing. The law of tithing is a law designed to bless us. It does not take from us, it adds to us. It is not so much a matter of money as it is a matter of faith, and great are the promises of the Lord to those who live honestly with Him in the payment of their tithes and their offerings.

5. Moral cleanliness. Cleanliness before the Lord in matters of morality and virtue and purity. There is so much of pornography in the world. There is so much of evil, enticing evil, in the world. Shun it, my brothers and sisters. Avoid it. . . .

6. Family relationships. Fathers, are we the kind of husbands we ought to be? Do we treat our wives with kindness and respect? They are our companions and our partners. You will never get into the celestial kingdom alone. If you get there, you will walk hand in hand with your wife as your partner and your companion. Let there not be any swearing, let there not be any shouting, let there be kindness and respect. And you wives, have respect for your husbands and help them in their priesthood obligations. Fathers and mothers, respect your children. They are children of God, sons and daughters of God. They are His. You don't need to try to bring them up by whipping them and beating them. Let love prevail between you and your children. . . .

7. Sacrament meeting attendance. I simply want to repeat the importance of your going to your sacrament meetings and of there partaking of the sacrament of the Lord's Supper in renewing the covenants that you have made with Him.

8. Likewise, family home evening. Gather your children around you. Teach them the gospel. Let it become a thing of importance in their lives.

9. Finally—prayer. Pray over the food which you eat; thank the Lord for it and ask Him to bless it. Have your individual prayers. Have your family prayers. The Lord will bless you. (Manaus Brazil Fireside, November 16, 1996.)

Brigham Young once said that "every principle of the gospel carries with it a conviction of its truth to those who live it." I believe that with all my heart. The Word of Wisdom carries with it a conviction of its truth to those who live it. What a marvelous thing it is. Four hundred thousand people die each year as a result of tobacco. You cannot live the Word of Wisdom, you cannot observe it, without recognizing the hand of the Lord in this marvelous thing which we call the Word of Wisdom, which is the only law of health anywhere under the heavens that carries with it a divine promise concerning those who observe it and live it. And that conviction comes into our hearts of its truth and divinity as we live it.

It is so with tithing. You do not have to preach tithing to a man who pays his tithing. He knows it is a divine law. It is the Lord's law of finance. It is the Lord's law to take care of His Church. Everyone who lives it knows of its truth and divinity. You do not have to preach temple work to those who go to the temple. They know it is divine. "Every principle carries with it a conviction of its truth to those who live it." Thank the Lord for this wonderful restored gospel. Thank the Lord that somehow you and I have become participants in and partakers of its great blessings. What a marvelous and wonderful thing it is! (Jacksonville Florida West Stake Conference, January 19, 1997.)

I am pleased to see many people here who are the sons and daughters of Father Lehi. I think if he could look down upon this vast audience there would be tears in his eyes, tears of gratitude and appreciation. What a great lesson we have to learn from the people of the Book of Mormon. We are reminded in the Book of Mormon of the time when the people were great and wonderful and prospered in the land. Mormon records: "They were once a delightsome people, and they had Christ for their shepherd; yea, they were led even by God the Father. But now, behold, they are led about by Satan, even as chaff is driven before the wind, or as a vessel is tossed about upon the waves, without sail or anchor, or without anything wherewith to steer her; and even as she is, so are they. And behold, the Lord hath reserved their blessings, which they might have received in the land, for the Gentiles who shall possess the land" (Mormon 5:17–19).

The whole story of the Book of Mormon is a story that speaks of the people who, when they were righteous, when they worshipped Jesus Christ, prospered in the land and were richly and abundantly blessed of the Lord; and when they sinned and went astray and forgot their God, they fell into misery and war and trouble. Your safety, your peace, your prosperity lie in obedience to the commandments of the Almighty. . . .

We are all part of a great conflict that is going on. This conflict has been going on since the war in heaven. It is the conflict between good and evil. It is endless. We shall never know the end of it in our lifetime. We must be strong. We must be faithful. We must be true. We must stand up for that which is right as members of The Church of Jesus Christ of Latter-day Saints. God help us to do what is right. (Guatemala City Guatemala North and South Regional Conference, January 26, 1997.)

OPPOSITION

See also Church of Jesus Christ of
Latter-day Saints, The: Criticism of the Church; Criticism

On the desk in my home I have a small metal box. It is about twelve inches square and half as high. On its face are six knobs and two dials. Now and again, when I have an hour, it becomes my plaything. It is a shortwave radio. Turning the knobs, I listen to London, Washington, Tokyo, Peking, Moscow, Havana, and other great capitals of the world.

The voices I hear are persuasive, seductive, fascinating, and confusing. Speaking across the earth, they are part of a mighty battle that is being waged for the minds of men. They are aimed at persuasion in political philosophy. There are voices of democracy competing with voices of communism, and each is winning converts according to the discernment and the judgment of listeners. The stakes are high, the weapons are sophisticated, the methods are clever.

There is a comparable battle being waged for the faith of men, but the lines are not always so clearly drawn, for even among the forces of Christianity there are those who would destroy the divinity of the Christ in whose name they speak. They might be disregarded if their voices were not so seductive, if their influence were not so far-reaching, if their reasoning were not so subtle. (*Be Thou an Example* [Salt Lake City: Deseret Book, 1981], p. 79.)

There is [a] war that has gone on since before the world was created and which is likely to continue for a long time yet to come. John the Revelator speaks of that struggle:

"And there was war in heaven: Michael and his angels fought against the dragon; and the dragon fought and his angels,

"And prevailed not; neither was their place found any more in heaven.

"And the great dragon was cast out, that old serpent, called the Devil, and Satan, which deceiveth the whole world: he was cast out into the earth, and his angels were cast out with him" (Revelation 12:7–9).

That war, so bitter, so intense, has gone on, and it has never ceased. It is the war between truth and error, between agency and compulsion, between the followers of Christ and those who have denied Him. His enemies have used every stratagem in that conflict. They've indulged in lying and deceit. They've employed money and wealth. They've tricked the minds of men. They've murdered and destroyed and engaged in every other unholy and impure practice to thwart the work of Christ.

It began in the earth when Cain slew Abel. The Old Testament is replete with accounts of the same eternal struggle.

It found expression in the vile accusations against the Man of Galilee, the Christ, who healed the sick and lifted men's hearts and hopes, He who taught the gospel of peace. His enemies, motivated by that evil power, seized Him, tortured Him, nailed Him to the cross, and spoke in mockery against Him. But by the power of His godhood, He overcame the death His enemies had inflicted and through His sacrifice brought salvation from death to all men. ("The War We Are Winning," *Ensign*, November 1986, pp. 42–43.)

The adversary has never stopped trying. Ninety years ago, in the October conference of 1896, President Wilford Woodruff, then an aged man, standing where I stand in this tabernacle, said:

"There are two powers on the earth and in the midst of the inhabitants of the earth—the power of God and the power of the devil. In our history we have had some very peculiar experiences. When God has had a people on the earth, it matters not in what age, Lucifer, the son of the morning, and the millions of fallen spirits that were cast out of heaven have warred against God, against Christ, against the work of God, and against the people of God. And they are not backward in doing it in our day and generation. Whenever the Lord set His hand to perform any work, those powers labored to overthrow it." (*Deseret Evening News*, 17 October 1896).

President Woodruff knew whereof he spoke. He had then only recently passed through those difficult and perilous days when the government of the nation had come against our people, determined to destroy them. The buildings on this Temple Square, this tabernacle in which we meet tonight and the temple then under construction, were escheated to the federal government. Many citizens were disfranchised. But in faith they moved forward. They kept going. They put their trust in the Almighty, and He revealed unto them the path they should follow. In faith they accepted that revelation and walked in obedience. ("The War We Are Winning," *Ensign*, November 1986, p. 43.)

Of course, we have a lot of people across the world who oppose us and oppose us viciously, and all kinds of false stories are raised and circulated concerning us in an effort to undermine this work. That is to be expected. If we did not have some opposition, I would worry. I think that we must be aware of the fact that the adversary recognizes the truth of this work and that he will do everything he can to deter it, to hinder it, to impede its progress. He is very clever and industrious about it. (Anchorage Alaska Regional Conference, priesthood leadership session, June 17, 1995.)

Do we still have opposition? Yes, some. We always will have. The adversary will always attack this work and do what he can to hinder it. If you have any doubt about the truth of this work, you take notice of the efforts of the adversary to injure it and try to destroy it. (Creation of Canterbury England Stake, August 27, 1995.)

OPTIMISM

I stand here today as an optimist concerning the work of the Lord. I cannot believe that God has established his work in the earth to have it fail. I cannot believe that it is getting weaker. I know that it is getting stronger. I realize, of course, that we are beset with many tragic problems. I am a newspaper reader, and I have seen a good deal of this earth. I have seen its rot and smelled its filth. I have been in areas where war rages and hate smolders in the hearts of people. I have seen the appalling poverty that hovers over many lands. I have seen the oppression of those in bondage and the brutality of their overlords. . . . I have watched with alarm the crumbling morals of our society.

And yet I am an optimist. I have a simple and solemn faith that right will triumph and that truth will prevail. ("'Be Not Afraid, Only Believe,'" *Improvement Era*, December 1969, pp. 97–98.)

Of course there are times of sorrow. Of course there are hours of concern and anxiety. We all worry. But the Lord has told us to lift our hearts and rejoice. I see so many people . . . who seem never to see the sunshine, but who constantly walk with storms under cloudy skies. Cultivate an attitude of happiness. Cultivate a spirit of optimism. Walk with faith, rejoicing in the beauties of nature, in the goodness of those you love, in the testimony which you carry in your heart concerning things divine. ("'If Thou Art Faithful,'" *Ensign*, November 1984, p. 92.)

Spare yourselves from the indulgence of self-pity. It is always self-defeating. Subdue the negative and emphasize the positive. ("Ten Gifts from the Lord," *Ensign*, November 1985, p. 86.)

Looking at the dark side of things always leads to a spirit of pessimism which so often leads to defeat. . . .

I have little doubt that many of us are troubled with fears concerning ourselves. We are in a period of stress across the world. There are occasionally hard days for each of us. Do not despair. Do not give up. Look for the sunlight through the clouds. Opportunities will eventually open to you. Do not let the prophets of gloom endanger your possibilities. ("The Continuing Pursuit of Truth," *Ensign*, April 1986, p. 4.)

A distinguished Protestant minister called on us the other day. In the course of our conversation he asked, "How do you feel about things?"

I replied, "I feel very optimistic. Things are happening in the world that are salutary and good. There are wars, yes. There is conflict, yes. But there also is much of peace among the nations of the earth. Something of tremendous significance is happening in the USSR and the People's Republic of China. There is growing freedom of expression and activity. A new openness is developing. I feel the spirit of Christ is brooding over the nations of the earth.

"Of course there are problems, many and serious. We sorrow over the plague of drugs with its bitter harvest. We deplore the terrible scourge of pornography. We grieve over the wicked flood of immorality and abortion. We are concerned with the epidemic of infidelity, of divorce and broken homes. We are disturbed over the plight of the homeless and over stark hunger in many parts of the earth.

"But the remarkable thing is that so many people care. More than at any time in the history of the world, I believe, there are men and women by the tens of thousands who are reaching out with their strength and their substance to help those in distress. Modern science and medicine are doing wonders to alleviate pain and prolong life. There is greater fulfillment in the lives of millions.

"Concerning our own work—that is, the work of this church—I feel even more optimistic. We are growing stronger. I hope our people are growing better. I think they are. There is increased activity, increased devotion, increased faithfulness."

I told him that two or three weeks earlier I was in an area where the percentage of members regularly attending their Sunday meetings was 70 to 75 percent. I think that is wonderful. In fact, I believe it is unique. . . .

I concluded by saying, "I repeat, I feel optimistic—guardedly so, yes, because of the extent of evil in the world. But, on the basis of what I see, goodness is gaining, and the work of the Lord is growing in strength and power." ("Let Love Be the Lodestar of Your Life," *Ensign*, May 1989, p. 65.)

I see so many good people everywhere—and there's so much good in them. And the world is good. Wonderful things are happening in this world. This is the greatest age in the history of the earth. . . .

We have every reason to be optimistic. Tragedy is around, yes. Problems everywhere, yes. But look at Nauvoo. Look at what they built here in seven years and then left. But what did they do? Did they lie down and die? No! They went to work! They moved halfway across this continent and turned the soil of a desert and made it blossom as the rose. On that foundation this church has grown into a great worldwide organization affecting for good the lives of people in more than 140 nations. You can't, you don't, build out of pessimism or cynicism. You look with optimism, work with faith, and things happen. (*New York Times* Interview, 1995.)

I feel so optimistic about this Church, so very, very optimistic. . . . What tremendous things we are doing because of the faithfulness of the people, the building of these chapels across the earth, the building of temples—the tremendous work that is going forward and the effect that it is having upon individuals as it increases in numbers. It's true. Be happy about it. Be affirmative about it. Don't look for its weaknesses. Magnify its strengths and build on those and don't be critical of people. Find their virtues—they have some—and build on those. You will be very happy if you do. (Vacaville/Santa Rosa California Regional Conference, priesthood leadership session, May 20, 1995.)

Let us go forward in this glorious work. How exciting and wonderful it is. I do not know how anybody can feel gloomy for very long who is a member of this Church. Do you feel gloomy? Lift your eyes. Stand on your feet. Say a few words of appreciation and love to the Lord. Be positive. Think of what great things are occurring as the Lord brings to pass His eternal purposes. This is a day of prophecy fulfilled . . . this great day in the history of this Church. This is the day which has been spoken of by those who have gone before us. Let us live worthy of our birthright. Keep the faith. Nurture your testimonies. Walk in righteousness and the Lord will bless you and prosper you and you will be a happy and wonderful people. (Sandy Utah Cottonwood Creek Stake Conference, December 3, 1995.)

I have been reading a book—Robert Bork's *Slouching Towards Gomorrah*—in which he speaks of what is happening in the United States. I do not like to read it. It makes one feel hopeless, helpless almost. I put it aside and try to get a positive, upbeat look at things. You cannot blink at the fact that there are problems in this land and in every other country in the world that are very serious. . . . We have a great message to give to the world, a message of hope, a message of assurance that all is not lost, that there is so much of good in the world. We invite people to come and join and become a part of that great good. (Public Affairs Luncheon, November 5, 1996.)

ORDER

I have occasion to go about the Church a good deal, and I feel proud of our buildings and grounds. It has been a long time since I have seen one that I felt needed attention. The grounds are well kept, the grass is mowed, the shrubs pruned. They carry a message to the entire community that our people have an appreciation for the orderly and the beautiful. (Regional Representatives Seminar, April 1, 1988.)

[As a boy] I attended the Hamilton School, which was a big three-story building. . . .

We dressed neatly for school, and no unkempt appearance was tolerated. The boys wore a shirt and a tie and short trousers. We wore long black stockings that reached from the foot to above the knee. They were made of cotton, and they wore out quickly, and they had to be darned frequently. We learned how to darn because it was unthinkable to go to school with a hole in your stocking.

We learned a lesson on the importance of personal neatness and tidiness, and that has blessed my life ever since. ("Some Lessons I Learned as a Boy," *Ensign*, May 1993, pp. 52–53.)

I am thankful for the system of governance of this great cause. What a miracle it is, this system which the Lord set up. . . . The orderliness with which change takes place in this Church is a miracle to behold. There is no vying for office. There is no campaigning for positions. There is no seeking a vote. There is a quiet, solemn, beautiful way. (Vacaville/Santa Rosa California Regional Conference, May 21, 1995.)

I can learn the requirements of my office. I hope everybody here knows something about the handbook. It is a manual of procedures in the Church. It is important to have order in the Church across the world, because we work according to a pattern. (Anchorage Alaska Regional Conference, priesthood leadership session, June 17, 1995.)

Question: Now, the organization is a large one, and you have that in common with the Roman Catholic Church, the Anglican Church, and so on, so in a sense the question could be directed at them. However, you are here, so I will direct it at you. If Jesus Christ were to come back today, then, and see this enormous, almost corporation, do you think He would feel at ease in it, it being run almost like a business?

President Hinckley: Well, it's being run with efficiency. We are not comparing it to a business. We are trying to do our work in the most efficient way that we can, to get the greatest result out of the effort and the resources we put in. I think if He were to come back, He would be pleased. Order is the first law of heaven, and I think He would be happy to see what is going on. I earnestly hope He would be. What we are doing, we are trying to do as followers of the Lord, as those who place in their lives a love of God and a love for fellowmen. (Interview with Trevor Barnes, BBC World Service, August 28, 1995.)

Nauvoo was a beautiful city, beautiful in its setting in a bend of the river reaching out like a peninsula pointing to the west, where the Saints would eventually go. It was beautiful in its creation, as with industry and careful planning they structured an orderly city. It was not established or built in ragtag fashion, as were so many cities on the frontier of America in those days. (Kanesville Tabernacle Dedication, July 13, 1996.)

I want to read, just for a moment or two, three or four verses from this great revelation which came to Brigham Young in January of 1847 at Winter Quarters on the Missouri. Said he, "Let all the people of The Church of Jesus Christ of Latter-day Saints, and those who journey with them, be organized into companies, with a covenant and promise to keep all the commandments and statutes of the Lord our God." Let me remind you that we are still pioneering in this Church. We are reaching out across the world. We are now established in more than 150 nations with a membership of 9,700,000. We are pioneering still. Let us in our efforts go forward with a covenant and promise to keep all the commandments and statutes of the Lord our God. "Let the companies be organized with captains of hundreds, captains of fifties, and captains of ten, with a president and his two counselors at their head, under the direction of the Twelve Apostles." This was an organized movement. It wasn't a rag-tail kind of exodus from Illinois into Iowa. It was not a disorganized movement from here west. There was organization which was strictly observed and which led to order in the camps. "And this shall be our covenant—that we will walk in all of the ordinances of the Lord." Get this. "Let each company bear an equal proportion, according to the dividend of their property, in taking the poor, the widows, the fatherless, and the families of those who have gone into the army, that the cries of the widow and the fatherless come not up into the ears of the Lord against this people." They were to take care of one another, to assist the unfortunate, to see that all moved to their Zion in the west. (Grand Encampment Devotional, Council Bluffs, Iowa, July 13, 1996.)

ORDINANCES

See Baptism; Temple

PARENTING

See also Family; Fatherhood; Motherhood

Good homes are not easily created or maintained. They require discipline, not so much of children as of self. They require respect for others, that respect which comes best from acceptance of the revealed word of the Lord concerning the purpose of life, of the importance and sacred nature of the family, and recognition of each member of the family as a child of God. . . .

There will be a growing trend in [the] future to leave to others the tasks of rearing children, while more and more mothers work to get a few more dollars to buy a few more baubles. If the present trend continues, babysitting will become the concern and one of the multitudinous functions of government. (Today a babysitter is a teenager who is expected to act like an adult while the adults go out and act like teenagers.) I recognize that it is necessary for some mothers unfortunately to have to work and leave their children. But in the future, a growing number will do so, not out of necessity but because they enjoy the glamour of outside employment more than the somewhat colorless tasks of homemaking. . . .

There is no supervision like a good mother's supervision. Every child is entitled to grow up in a home where there is warm and secure companionship, where there is love in the family relationship, where appreciation one for another is taught and exemplified, and where God is acknowledged and His peace and blessings invoked before the family altar.

The preservation of the family will be one of the great and serious challenges facing you in the future into which you move. ("Conquer or Be Conquered," BYU Commencement Address, August 19, 1966.)

A better tomorrow begins with the training of a better generation. This places upon parents the responsibility to do a more effective work in the rearing of children. The home is the cradle of virtue, the place where character is formed and habits are established. ("Opposing Evil," *Ensign,* November 1975, p. 39.)

When I met one of my childhood friends the other day, there came a train of memories of the neighborhood in which we grew up. It was a microcosm of the world, with many varieties of people. They were a close-knit group, and I think we knew them all. I think, also, we loved them all—that is, except for one man. I must make a confession: I detested that man. I have since repented of that emotion, but as I look back, I can sense again the intensity of my feeling. His young boys were our friends, but he was my enemy. Why this strong antipathy? Because he whipped his children with strap or stick or whatever came to hand as his vicious anger flared on the slightest provocation.

Perhaps it was because of the home in which I lived, where there was a father who, by some quiet magic, was able to discipline his family without the use of any instrument of punishment, though on occasion they may have deserved it. ("'Behold Your Little Ones,'" *Ensign,* November 1978, p. 18.)

E. T. Sullivan once wrote these interesting words: "When God wants a great work done in the world or a great wrong righted, he goes about it in a very unusual way. He doesn't stir up his earthquakes or send forth his thunderbolts. Instead, he has a helpless baby born, perhaps in a simple home out of some obscure mother. And then God puts the idea into the mother's heart, and she puts it into the baby's mind. And then God waits. The greatest forces in the world are not the earthquakes and the thunderbolts. The greatest forces in the world are babies." (*The Treasure Chest,* p. 53.)

And those babies, I should like to add, will become forces for good or ill, depending in large measure on how they are reared. . . .

If I may be pardoned for suggesting the obvious, I do so only because the obvious is not observed in so many instances. The obvious includes four imperatives with reference to children:

Love them, Teach them, Respect them, Pray with them and for them. ("'Behold Your Little Ones,'" *Ensign*, November 1978, p. 18.)

There is need for discipline with families. But discipline with severity, discipline with cruelty, inevitably leads not to correction, but rather to resentment and bitterness. It cures nothing and only aggravates the problem. It is self-defeating. The Lord, in setting forth the spirit of governance in his church has also set forth the spirit of governance in the home in these great words of revelation:

"No power or influence can or ought to be maintained . . . , only by persuasion, by long-suffering, by gentleness and meekness, and by love unfeigned;

"Reproving betimes with sharpness, when moved upon by the Holy Ghost; and then showing forth afterwards an increase of love toward him whom thou hast reproved, lest he esteem thee to be his enemy;

"That he may know that thy faithfulness is stronger than the cords of death." (D&C 121:41, 43–44.)

Behold your little ones and teach them. I need not remind you that your example will do more than anything else in impressing upon their minds a pattern of life. It is always interesting to meet the children of old friends and to find in another generation the ways of their fathers and mothers. ("'Behold Your Little Ones,'" *Ensign*, November 1978, p. 19.)

How much more beautiful would be the world and the society in which we live if every father looked upon his children as the most precious of his assets, if he led them by the power of his example in kindness and love, and if in times of stress he blessed them by the authority of the holy priesthood; and if every mother regarded her children as the jewels of her life, as gifts from the God of heaven who is their Eternal Father, and brought them up with true affection in the wisdom and admonition of the Lord. ("'Behold Your Little Ones,'" *Ensign*, November 1978, p. 20.)

How beautiful is that home where lives a man of godly manner, who loves those for whose nurture he is responsible, who stands before them as an example of integrity and goodness, who teaches industry and loyalty, not spoiling his children by indulging their every wish, but rather setting before them a pattern of work and service which will underpin their lives forever. How fortunate is the man whose wife radiates a spirit of love, of compassion, of order, of quiet beneficence, whose children show appreciation one for another, who honor and respect their parents, who counsel with them and take counsel from them. Such home life is within the reach of all who have cultivated in their hearts a resolution to do that which will please their Father in Heaven. ("To Please Our Heavenly Father," *Ensign*, May 1985, p. 50.)

When little problems occur, as they inevitably will, restrain yourself. Call to mind the wisdom of the ancient proverb: "A soft answer turneth away wrath." (Prov. 15:1.)

There is no discipline in all the world like the discipline of love. It has a magic all its own. ("The Environment of Our Homes," *Ensign*, June 1985, p. 6.)

Not long after we were married, we built our first home. We had very little money. I did much of the work myself. It would be called "sweat equity" today. The landscaping was entirely my responsibility. The first of many trees that I planted was a thornless honey locust. Envisioning the day when its filtered shade would assist in cooling the house in the summertime, I put it in a place at the corner where the wind from the canyon to the east blew the hardest. I dug a hole, put in the bare root, put soil around it, poured on water, and largely forgot it. It was only a wisp of a tree, perhaps three-quarters of an inch in diameter. It was so supple that I could bend it with ease in any direction. I paid little attention to it as the years passed.

Then one winter day, when the tree was barren of leaves, I chanced to look out the window at it. I noticed that it was leaning to the west, misshapen and out of balance. I could scarcely believe it. I went out and braced myself against it as if to push it upright. But the trunk was now nearly a foot in diameter. My strength was as nothing against it. I took from my toolshed a block and tackle. Attaching one end to the tree and another to a well-set post, I pulled the rope. The pulleys moved a little, and the trunk of the tree trembled slightly. But that was all. It seemed to say, "You can't straighten me. It's too late. I've grown this way because of your neglect, and I will not bend."

Finally in desperation I took my saw and cut off the great heavy branch on the west side. The saw left an ugly scar, more than eight inches across. I stepped back and surveyed what I had done. I had cut off the major part of the tree, leaving only one branch growing skyward.

More than half a century has passed since I planted that tree. My daughter and her family live there now. The other day I looked again at the tree. It is large. Its shape is better. It is a great asset to the home. But how serious was the trauma of its youth and how brutal the treatment I used to straighten it.

When it was first planted, a piece of string would have held it in place against the forces of the wind. I could have and should have supplied that string with ever so little effort. But I did not, and it bent to the forces that came against it.

I have seen a similar thing, many times, in children whose lives I have observed. The parents who brought them into the world seem almost to have abdicated their responsibility. The results have been tragic. A few simple anchors would have given them the strength to withstand the forces that have shaped their lives. Now it appears it is too late. ("Bring Up a Child in the Way He Should Go," *Ensign*, November 1993, p. 59.)

There is nothing any of us can do that will have greater long-time benefit than to rekindle wherever possible the spirit of the homes in which we grew up. We lived in the city during the school season when I was a boy. We lived on a farm during the summer. On that farm we had an apple orchard and a peach orchard, and various other fruit trees. When we were in our early teens, my brother and I were taught the art of pruning trees. Each holiday and Saturday in February and March, while snow was still on the ground, we would go out to the farm. We attended demonstrations put on by the agricultural college. I think we learned something about pruning as it was taught in those days. We learned, for instance, that you could prune a peach tree in February and in large measure determine the kind of fruit you would pick in September. The idea was to prune in such a way that the developing fruit would be exposed to air and sunlight, uncrowded as it occupied its place on the branch of the tree.

The same principle applies to children. There is an old and true proverb which states, "As the twig is bent, so the tree is inclined." . . .

Children are like trees. When they are young, their lives can be shaped and directed, usually with ever so little effort. Said the writer of Proverbs: "Train up a child in the way he should go: and when he is old, he will not depart from it" (Proverbs 22:6). That training finds its roots in the home. ("Saving the Nation by Changing Our Homes," BYU Management Society, Washington, D.C., March 5, 1994.)

Of all the joys of life, none other equals that of happy parenthood. Of all the responsibilities with which we struggle, none other is so serious. To rear children in an atmosphere of love, security, and faith is the most rewarding of all challenges. The good result from such efforts becomes life's most satisfying compensation.

President Joseph F. Smith said on one occasion: "After all, to do well those things which God ordained to be the common lot of all mankind, is the truest greatness. To be a successful father or a successful mother is greater than to be a successful general or a successful statesman. One is universal and eternal greatness, the other is ephemeral." (*Gospel Doctrine*, Salt Lake City: Deseret Book Co., 1939, p. 285.)

I am satisfied that no other experiences of life draw us nearer to heaven than those that exist between happy parents and happy children. ("Save the Children," *Ensign*, November 1994, p. 54.)

You parents, love your children. Cherish them. They are so precious. They are so very, very important. They are the future. You need more than your own wisdom in rearing them. You need the help of the Lord. Pray for that help and follow the inspiration which you receive. ("The Fabric of Faith and Testimony," *Ensign*, November 1995, p. 89.)

Never forget that these little ones are the sons and daughters of God and that yours is a custodial relationship to them, that He was a parent before you were parents and that He has not relinquished His parental rights or interest in these His little ones. Now, love them, take care of them. Fathers, control your tempers, now and in all the years to come. Mothers, control your voices, keep them down. Rear your children in love, in the nurture and admonition of the Lord. Take care of your little ones, welcome them into your homes, and nurture and love them with all of your hearts. They may do, in the years that come, some things you would not want them to do, but be patient, be patient. You have not failed as long as you have tried. Never forget that. (Salt Lake University 3rd Stake Conference, November 3, 1996.)

Do not beat your children. I do not think children have to be severely punished. I was blessed with a good father and a good mother. I can never remember their laying a hand on me or any of their other children. We probably deserved it, but they did not do it. They sat us down and talked with us. That was enough. I do not think you need to beat your children. How precious they are. Bring them up in the nurture and admonition of the Lord. (El Salvador San Salvador Fireside, January 23, 1997.)

PATRIARCHAL BLESSINGS

I had a patriarchal blessing when I was a little boy, eleven years of age. A convert to the Church who had come from England, who was our patriarch, laid his hands upon my head and gave me a blessing. I think I never read that blessing until I was on the boat coming over to England in 1933. I took it out of my trunk and read it carefully, and I read it every now and again while I was on my mission in England.

I don't want to tell you everything in that blessing, but that man spoke with a prophetic voice. He said, among other things, that I would lift my voice in testimony of the truth in the nations of the earth. When I was released from my mission, I spoke in London in a testimony meeting in the Battersea Town Hall. The next Sunday I spoke in Berlin. The next Sunday I spoke in Paris. The next Sunday I spoke in Washington, D. C. I came home tired and weak and thin and weary, . . . and I said, "I've had it. I've traveled as far as I want to travel. I never want to travel again." And I thought I had fulfilled that blessing. I had spoken in four of the great capitals of the world—London, Berlin, Paris, and Washington, D. C. I thought I had fulfilled that part of that blessing.

I say with gratitude and in a spirit of testimony . . . that it has since been my privilege, out of the providence and goodness of the Lord, to bear testimony of this work and of the divine calling of the Prophet Joseph Smith in all of the lands of Asia—nearly, at least—Japan, Korea, Thailand, Taiwan, the Philippines, Hong Kong, Vietnam, Burma, Malaysia, India, Indonesia, Singapore, what have you. I have testified in Australia, New Zealand, the islands of the Pacific, the nations of Europe, all of the nations of South America, and all of the nations of the Orient in testimony of the divinity of this work. (Hyde Park Chapel Rededication, August 27, 1995.)

What a blessing to receive a patriarchal blessing! Encourage your people to live worthy—not to go to the patriarch in terms of a soothsayer or a fortune-teller or anything of that kind, but as one who has, as President Kimball put it, a spirit of prophecy concerning that individual. (Corpus Christi Texas Regional Conference, priesthood leadership session, January 6, 1996.)

I hope that we are encouraging those who are mature enough to understand the importance of a patriarchal blessing to receive one. I count my patriarchal blessing as one of the great sacred things of my life. A patriarchal blessing is a unique and sacred and personal and wonderful thing that may be given to every member of this Church who lives worthy of it. I hope, brethren, that you men of the bishoprics, particularly, are counseling your people concerning this. (Smithfield/Logan Utah Regional Conference, priesthood leadership session, April 20, 1996.)

I hope we encourage our people to live worthy to receive a patriarchal blessing, and to make the effort to get one. It's a rare privilege to have a patriarchal blessing. It's unique from all other things in this world. There is nothing like it, to have a man speak on an individual basis and pronounce blessings in authority of the Holy Priesthood. (Pittsburgh Pennsylvania Regional Conference, priesthood leadership session, April 27, 1996.)

I want to repeat that those blessings are sacred. They are not to be bandied about. They are not to be spoken of. (Pittsburgh Pennsylvania Regional Conference, priesthood leadership session, April 27, 1996.)

PEACE

See also War

It has been said that old men make wars and young men fight them. Unless you of this generation master the bitter forces of hate that periodically engulf mankind, there can be little doubt that the world will be destroyed. Politically the old concept of a balance of power has been replaced by a balance of terror. But terror will not long preserve peace. Only as men's hearts change can lasting peace come to the world. ("Conquer or Be Conquered," BYU Commencement Address, August 19, 1966.)

I am satisfied that a man cannot do well in his work unless there is peace in his home. You recall that when the Prophet Joseph was translating the Book of Mormon, he quarreled with his wife and discovered that "the gift and power of God" left him. Brethren, be true to your wives. Wives, keep faith with your husbands. Parents, admire and respect your children. Without peace and mutual respect in your homes, there will be neither peace nor proficiency in your labors. ("Keep Faith," Address to BYU Faculty and Staff, August 29, 1972.)

I would that the healing power of Christ might spread over the earth and be diffused through our society and into our homes, that it might cure men's hearts of the evil and adverse elements of greed and hate and conflict. I believe it could happen. I believe it must happen. If the lamb is to lie down with the lion, then peace must overcome conflict, healing must mend injury. ("The Healing Power of Christ," *Ensign*, November 1988, p. 59.)

The temple must ever be a place of peace, a refuge from the turmoil of the world. All of us live in something of a jungle, if I may use that expression. We long for peace and quiet; we hunger for an opportunity to meditate and reflect on things spiritual and eternal in their nature. There must be no atmosphere of frenzy or hurry in the house of the Lord. It is to be a house of order. There must be an atmosphere that constantly proclaims, "Holiness to the Lord."

We are dealing with the things of eternity. We need not rush. Of course there are ordinances to be performed. But this can be done in a manner that speaks of peace and the quiet assurance which dwells in the heart when there is an absence of pressure. (Temple Presidents Seminar, August 15, 1989.)

It was twelve years ago that Voyager left planet earth to undertake a journey of 4.4 billion miles, traveling at 61,000 miles an hour, which led with precision to that celestial orb we call the planet Neptune.

Now Voyager goes on, out into outer space, to the edge of the universe.

Did you watch it? Did you experience the awesome feeling that I did? Did you wonder why, if man can do such remarkable things, he cannot live together in peace with his brothers on this earth? Did you stop and reflect on the wonders of the human mind when that mind devotes itself to constructive rather than destructive things? Why do we spend our personal resources in conflict and acquisitiveness, in litigation and name-calling, when we are capable of things so much greater and more wonderful? ("A Wonderful Summer," *BYU 1989–1990 Devotional and Fireside Speeches*, September 3, 1989, p. 13.)

I have thought many times that war among the nations would cease if the women of the world were united in standing for peace. (Belle S. Spafford Conference on Women, February 23, 1990.)

I want to say that we of this Church deplore violence in any form or of any nature as a protest against the legal processes under which we live. There are peaceable ways to settle questionable matters, through the legislative process or the judicial process, and violence of any kind is out of order and is to be condemned, and it is contrary to the word and will of the Lord. We believe in honoring, obeying and sustaining the law. We have little sympathy for those who in various parts of the world engage in terrorist activities to the destruction of life and property. (Boston Massachusetts Regional Conference, April 23, 1995.)

Do you long for peace in your heart and an opportunity to commune with the Lord and meditate upon His way? Go to the House of the Lord and there feel of His spirit and commune with Him, and you will know a peace that you will find nowhere else. (Wandsworth England Stake Conference, August 27, 1995.)

The gospel of Jesus Christ is the only element that will destroy the hatred that exists among people. If they will bring this gospel into their lives and recognize the fatherhood of God and the brotherhood of man and the effects of the atonement of Christ, there will be a far greater measure of peace in the world. We will not have peace until that happens more generally. That is why we are here, brothers and sisters, you and I. That is the objective of our work—to teach the gospel of the Lord Jesus Christ and touch the hearts of people so that they can look upon one another as brothers and sisters, as children of our Father in Heaven. (Solihull England Church Employee Devotional, August 30, 1995.)

I could not wish for you anything more than that happiness which comes of being at peace in your hearts and at peace with the Lord. (Ricks College Regional Conference, Rexburg, Idaho, October 29, 1995.)

Where shall I go for peace in this world of rush and stress? Where shall I go for peace? There is only one place to go for peace, and that's in the gospel of the Lord Jesus Christ. When I was a youth, I attended a conference at which the man who spoke, a General Authority, said that the gospel has the answer to all of life's problems. I was a university student in that doubting, critical age, and I said, "He must be kidding. How can the gospel have the answer to all of life's problems?" I want to say that I did have faith, I was reared in a good home, but I still had, at that age of my life, a critical attitude about a lot of things. And I said "How can that be?" But I have discovered it's true—my brothers and sisters, it is true. (Plano Texas Regional Conference, March 17, 1996.)

Our entire aim is to teach the gospel of Jesus Christ, which is the gospel of peace among people. Our voice is a voice of peace to the entire world. We speak the words of Jesus Christ, who said, "Peace I give unto you." (Media Luncheon and Press Conference, Tokyo, Japan, May 18, 1996.)

PEER PRESSURE

We must stand a cut above our peers in that which we do. It is not enough to be a part of the herd. We can and must be out in front. ("Search for Excellence," Bonneville International Corporation Executives, February 6, 1989.)

You have here the opportunity for a wonderful social life. Each of you is one of a great congregation of friends. What an exhilarating thing to be involved every day with bright and personable and good associates. ("Out of Your Experience Here," *BYU 1990–1991 Devotional and Fireside Speeches,* October 16, 1990, p. 26.)

[The year I] enrolled in junior high school . . . the building could not accommodate all the students, and so our class of the seventh grade was sent back to the Hamilton School.

We were insulted. We were furious. We'd spent six unhappy years in that building, and we felt we deserved something better. The boys of the class all met after school. We decided we wouldn't tolerate this kind of treatment. We were determined we'd go on strike.

The next day we did not show up. . . . We just wandered about and wasted the day.

The next morning, the principal, Mr. Stearns, was at the front door of the school to greet us. His demeanor matched his name. He said some pretty straightforward things and then told us that we could not come back to school until we brought a note from our parents. That was my first experience with a lockout. Striking, he said, was not the way to settle a problem. We were expected to be responsible citizens, and if we had a complaint, we could come to the principal's office and discuss it.

There was only one thing to do, and that was to go home and get the note.

I remember walking sheepishly into the house. My mother asked what was wrong. I told her. I said that I needed a note. She wrote a note. It was very brief. It was the most stinging rebuke she ever gave me. It read as follows:

"Dear Mr. Stearns, Please excuse Gordon's absence yesterday. His action was simply an impulse to follow the crowd."

She signed it and handed it to me.

I walked back over to school and got there about the same time a few other boys did. We all handed our notes to Mr. Stearns. I do not know whether he read them, but I have never forgotten my mother's note. Though I had been an active party to the action we had taken, I resolved then and there that I would never do anything on the basis of simply following the crowd. I determined then and there that I would make my own decisions on the basis of their merits and my standards and not be pushed in one direction or another by those around me.

That decision has blessed my life many times, sometimes in very uncomfortable circumstances. It has kept me from doing some things which, if indulged in, could at worst have resulted in serious injury and trouble, and at best would have cost me my self-respect. ("Some Lessons I Learned as a Boy," *Ensign,* May 1993, p. 53.)

I want to say to you, look for your friends among members of the Church. Band together and strengthen one another. And when the time of temptation comes, you will have someone to lean on, someone to bless you and give you strength when you need it. That is what this Church is for, so that we can help one another in our times of weakness to stand on our feet, tall and straight and true and good. (Eugene Oregon Regional Conference, September 15, 1996.)

Mingle together as opportunity affords. It is important that we do so. We need others to talk with, to share our feelings with, with whom to share our faith. Cultivate friends. Begin by being a good friend to others. (Salt Lake Valley Single Adult Fireside, September 22, 1996.)

President Kimball used to tell the story of his boyhood. Some of his friends were not doing the right thing. They were doing a little stealing. They were violating the Word of Wisdom. Spencer Kimball, seeing what was going on in their lives, went to his room and got on his knees and told the Lord, as a fourteen-year-old boy, that he would not do those things. And having once made that decision, he never had to make it again. (Santiago Chile Fireside, November 11, 1996.)

PERFECTION

Said the Savior to his disciples, "Be ye therefore perfect, even as your Father which is in heaven is perfect." (Matt. 5:48.)

This is the commandment which is before us. Regrettably we have not reached perfection. We have a great distance to go. We must cultivate the faith to reform our lives, commencing where we are weak and moving on from there in our work of self-correction, thus gradually and consistently growing in strength to live more nearly as we should.

With faith we can rise above those negative elements in our lives which constantly pull us down. With effort we can develop the capacity to subdue those impulses which lead to degrading and evil actions.

With faith we can school our appetites. ("God Grant Us Faith," *Ensign*, November 1983, p. 53.)

I certainly make no pretense of being perfect, nor do any of my brethren. There was only one perfect man who ever walked the earth. The Lord has used imperfect people in the process of building His perfect society. If some of them occasionally stumble, or if their characters may have been slightly flawed in one way or another, the wonder is the greater that they accomplished so much. ("Optimism in the Face of Opposition," Los Angeles Institute Student Fireside, February 10, 1990.)

Marvelous is the chronicle that began with the singing of angels at Bethlehem and ended on Golgotha's cruel cross. There is no other life to compare with His life. He was the one perfect man to walk the earth, the paragon of excellence, the singular example of perfection. ("Jesus Christ," First Presidency Christmas Devotional, Salt Lake Tabernacle, December 4, 1994.)

What good people we have in this Church. I marvel at the strength of the work. We haven't reached perfection; we are far from it. But there is much of goodness and tremendous strength in the work, and it comes from the strength in the hearts of the individual members of the Church. (Heber City/Springville Utah Regional Conference, priesthood leadership session, May 13, 1995.)

PERSPECTIVE

I urge you to see the big picture and cease worrying about the little blemishes. Abraham Lincoln was a gangling figure of a man, with a long and craggy face. There were many who looked only at the imperfections of his countenance. There were others who joked over the way he walked, and kept their eyes so low that they never saw the true greatness of the man. That enlarged view came only to those who saw the whole character—body, mind, and spirit—as he stood at the head of a divided nation in its darkest hour, lacing it together "with malice toward none, with charity for all, with firmness in the right as God" gave him to see the right. (Second Inaugural Address.)

Of course, there are aberrations in our history. There are blemishes to be found, if searched for, in the lives of all men, including our leaders past and present. But these are only incidental to the magnitude of their service and to the greatness of their contributions.

Keep before you the big picture, for this cause is as large as all mankind and as broad as all eternity. This is the church and kingdom of God. It requires the strength, the loyalty, the faith of all if it is to roll forward to bless the lives of our Father's children over the earth. ("Five Million Members—A Milestone and Not a Summit," *Ensign*, May 1982, p. 46.)

How different is life when there is no assurance of eternity. When we know that this earthly estate is but one station along the road to immortality and eternal life, things take on an entirely different perspective. (Temple Presidents Seminar, August 15, 1989.)

Sometimes in our day, as we walk our narrow paths and fill our little niches of responsibility, we lose sight of the grand picture. When I was a small boy, draft horses were common. An important part of the harness was the bridle. On the bridle were blinders, one on each side. They were so placed that the horse could see only straight ahead and not to either side. They were designed to keep him from becoming frightened or distracted and to keep his attention on the road at his feet.

Some of us do our work as if we had blinders on our eyes. We see only our own little narrow track. We catch nothing of the broader vision. . . .

President Harold B. Lee once said from this pulpit, quoting an unknown writer, "Survey large fields and cultivate small ones."

My interpretation of that statement is that we ought to recognize something of the breadth and depth and height—grand and wonderful, large and all-encompassing—of the program of the Lord, and then work with diligence to meet our responsibility for our assigned portion of that program.

Each of us has a small field to cultivate. While so doing, we must never lose sight of the greater picture, the large composite of the divine destiny of this work. It was given us by God our Eternal Father, and each of us has a part to play in the weaving of its magnificent tapestry. ("An Ensign to the Nations," *Ensign*, November 1989, pp. 52–53.)

I think the perspective of our leaders who have gone beyond may be somewhat different from what it was here. I think that when we get up there we shall look at this work from a somewhat different perspective. We will not be greatly concerned with buildings and budgets. We will not be greatly concerned with reports and statistics. We will not be concerned with handbooks, with their many rulings and regulations. We will be concerned with men and women and children. We will be concerned with their happiness, with their growth and progress and their onward marching toward the resplendent goal of eventual Godhood. We will be concerned, as I feel we ought to be more so here, with "faith in the Lord Jesus Christ; repentance; baptism by immersion for the remission of sins; and the laying on of hands for the gift of the Holy Ghost" that we might be instructed and enlightened and inspired as we walk the great journey of eternal life. (General Authority Training Meeting, September 27, 1994.)

We've got to have a little humor in our lives. You had better take seriously that which should be taken seriously but, at the same time, we can bring in a touch of humor now and again. If the time ever comes when we can't smile at ourselves, it will be a sad time. (Interview with Mike Cannon of *Church News*, Dublin, Ireland, September 1, 1995.)

PHYSICAL BODY

See also Mortality

Have you ever contemplated the wonder of yourself—the eyes with which you see, the ears with which you hear, the voice with which you speak? No camera ever built can ever compare with the human eye. No method of communication ever devised can compare with the voice and the ear. No pump ever built will run as long or as efficiently as the human heart. What a remarkable thing each of us is. We can think by day and dream by night. We can speak and hear and smell and feel. Look at your finger. The most skillful attempt to reproduce it mechanically has brought only a crude approximation. The next time you use your fingers, look at them and sense the wonder of it.

Not long ago I sat in Symphony Hall in Salt Lake listening to a concert. I was in a position to see the fingers of the performers in the orchestra. Everyone, whether playing the strings, the percussion instruments, the brass, all involve the use of fingers. One does not have to use one's fingers to sing, but beyond that there would be little of musical harmony without the action of trained fingers.

I believe the human body to be the creation of divinity. George Gallup once observed, "I could prove God statistically. Take the human body alone—the chance that all the functions of the individual would just happen is a statistical monstrosity." ("Articles of Belief," Bonneville International Corporation Management Seminar, February 10, 1991.)

Our bodies are sacred. They were created in the image of God. They are marvelous, the crowning creation of Deity. . . . The ear and the brain constitute a miracle. The capacity to pick up sound waves and convert them into language is almost beyond imagination. . . . These, with others of our parts and organs, represent the divine, omnipotent genius of God, who is our Eternal Father. I cannot understand why anyone would knowingly wish to injure his body. And yet it happens around us every day as men and boys drink alcoholic beverages and use illegal drugs. What a scourge these are. For a little temporary lift they take into their systems that which robs them of self-control, becomes habit-forming, is terribly expensive, enslaves, and yields no good. ("'Be Ye Clean,'" *Ensign,* May 1996, p. 48.)

PIONEERS

See also Church History and Heritage

On July 24, 1847, the pioneer company of our people came into this valley. . . . The next day, Sabbath services were held. . . . The next morning they divided into groups to explore their surroundings.

Brigham Young, Wilford Woodruff, and a handful of their associates hiked from their campground a little to the south of us, on past the ground where we are, and up the hill to the north of us. They climbed a dome-shaped peak, President Young having difficulty because of his recent illness.

When the Brethren stood on the summit, they looked over this valley to the south of them. It was largely barren, except for the willows and rushes that grew along the streams that carried water from the mountains to the lake. There was no building of any kind, but Brigham Young had said the previous Saturday, "This is the place."

The summit where they stood was named Ensign Peak out of reference to these great prophetic words of Isaiah: "And he [speaking of God] will lift up an ensign to the nations from far, and will hiss unto them from the end of the earth: and, behold, they shall come with speed swiftly." (Isa. 5:26.)

"And he shall set up an ensign for the nations, and shall assemble the outcasts of Israel, and gather together the dispersed of Judah from the four corners of the earth." (Isa. 11:12.)

There is some evidence to indicate that Wilford Woodruff took from his pocket a bandanna handkerchief and waved it as an ensign or a standard to the nations, that from this place should go the word of the Lord, and to this place should come the people of the earth. . . .

How foolish, someone might have said, had he heard these men that July morning of 1847. They did not look like statesmen with great dreams. They did not look like rulers poring over maps and planning an empire. They were exiles, driven from their fair city on the Mississippi into this desert region of the West. But they were possessed of a vision drawn from the scriptures and words of revelation.

I marvel at the foresight of that little group. It was both auda-cious and bold. It was almost unbelievable. . . . These prophets, dressed in old, travel-worn clothes, standing in boots they had worn for more than a thousand miles from Nauvoo to this val-ley, spoke of a millennial vision. They spoke out of a prophetic view of the marvelous destiny of this cause. They came down from that peak that day and went to work to bring reality to their dream. ("An Ensign to the Nations," *Ensign*, November 1989, pp. 51–52.)

It is imperative that the people of this community, of this state, and of the entire West be reminded of the labors and the sacrifices of those who, at so great a cost, laid the foundations of that which we enjoy today. An awareness of history establishes the very foundation of the better aspects of our culture. . . .

There have been many movements of epic proportions in the history of mankind that are worthy of remembrance and which we cannot afford to forget. But the migration to this valley before the coming of the railroad is of so vast a scope, involving so many people, and entailing so much of human suffering and sacrifice, that it must ever occupy a unique place in the annals of human history. It has all of the elements of a great epic—persecution, flight into the wilderness, hope, vision, sickness, the unrelenting cruelty of the elements, deaths numbering in the thousands, and final triumph through unspeakable courage and labor. We must never forget those who have gone before. We must never take lightly the price they paid. It is a story not only for the members of the Church of which they were members; it is a story for all the world and for all generations. (Days of '47 Pioneer Luncheon, Salt Lake City, Utah, July 24, 1995.)

Brigham Young knew they could not stay [in Nauvoo]. They determined to move west, to a faraway place where, as Joseph Smith had said, "the devil cannot dig us out." On February 4, 1846, wagons rolled down Parley's Street to the river. Here they were ferried across and began to roll over the soil of Iowa. The weather subsequently turned bitter cold. The river froze; they crossed on the ice. Once they said good-bye to Nauvoo, they consigned themselves to the elements of nature and to the mercy of God.

When the ground thawed, it was mud—deep and treacherous mud. Wagons sank to their axles, and teams had to be doubled and tripled to move them. They cut a road where none had been before.

Finally reaching the Grand Encampment on the Missouri, they built hundreds of shelters, some very crude and others more comfortable. It was anything to get out of the treacherous weather.

All during that winter of 1846 in those frontier establishments, forges roared and anvils rang with the making of wagons. My own grandfather, barely out of his teens, became an expert blacksmith and wagon builder. No vocation was more useful in those days than that of the ability to shape iron. He would later build his own wagon and with his young wife and baby and his brother set off for the West. Somewhere on that long journey, his wife sickened and died and his brother died on the same day. He buried them both, tearfully said good-bye, tenderly picked up his child, and marched on to the valley of the Great Salt Lake.

In the spring of 1847, the wagons of the first company pulled out of Winter Quarters and headed west. Generally they followed a route along the north side of the Platte River. Those going to California and Oregon followed a route on the south side. The road of the Mormons later became the right-of-way of the Union Pacific Railroad and the transcontinental highway.

As we all know, on July 24, 1847, after 111 days, they emerged from the mountain canyon into the Salt Lake Valley. Brigham Young declared, "This is the right place."

I stand in reverent awe of that statement. They might have gone on to California or Oregon, where the soil had been tested, where there was ample water, where there was a more equable climate. Jim Bridger had warned them against trying to grow crops in the Salt Lake Valley. Sam Brannan had pleaded with Brigham to go on to California. Now they looked across the barren valley, with its saline waters shimmering in the July sun to the west. No plow had ever broken the sun-baked soil. Here stood Brigham Young, 46 years of age, telling his people this was the right place. They had never planted a crop or known a harvest. They knew nothing of the seasons. Thousands of their numbers were coming behind them, and there would yet be tens of thousands. They accepted Brigham Young's prophetic statement.

Homes soon began to spring from the desert soil. Trees were planted, and the miracle is that they grew. Construction of a new temple was begun, a task that was to last unremittingly for 40 years. From that 1847 beginning to the coming of the railroad in 1869, they came by the tens of thousands to their Zion in the mountains. Nauvoo was evacuated. Its temple was burned by an arsonist, and its walls later fell in a storm. ("'True to the Faith,'" *Ensign*, May 1997, pp. 65–66.)

Faith of the Pioneers

Every man and woman in this church knows something of the price paid by our forebears for their faith. I was again reminded of this when I recently read the narrative of my wife's grandmother. I think I would like to share a few words from that story of a 13-year-old girl. She tells of her childhood in Brighton, that delightful city on the south coast of England, where the soft, green hills of Sussex roll down to the sea.

It was there that her family were baptized. Their conversion came naturally because the Spirit whispered in their hearts that it was true. But there were critical relatives and neighbors and even mobs to deride and inflame others against them. It took courage, that rare quality described as moral courage, to stand up and be counted, to be baptized and recognized as a Mormon.

The family traveled to Liverpool, where with some 900 others they boarded the sailing vessel *Horizon.*

As the wind caught the sails, they sang, "Farewell, My Native Land, Farewell." After six weeks at sea—to cover the distance covered today by a jet plane in six hours—they landed at Boston and then traveled by steam train to Iowa City, for fitting out.

There they purchased two yoke of oxen, one yoke of cows, a wagon, and a tent. They were assigned to travel with and assist one of the handcart companies.

Here at Iowa City also occurred their first tragedy. Their youngest child, less than two years of age, suffering from exposure, died and was buried in a grave never again visited by a member of the family.

Now let me give you the very words of this 13-year-old girl as I read a few lines from her story:

"We traveled from 15 to 25 miles a day . . . till we got to the Platte River. . . . We caught up with the handcart companies that day. We watched them cross the river. There were great lumps of ice floating down the river. It was bitter cold. The next morning there were fourteen dead. . . . We went back to camp and had our prayers, [and] . . . sang 'Come, Come Ye Saints, No Toil Nor Labor Fear.' I wondered what made my mother cry [that night]. . . . The next morning my little sister was born. It was the 23rd of September. We named her Edith. She lived six weeks and died. . . . [She was buried at the last crossing of the Sweetwater.]

"[We ran into heavy snow. I became lost in the snow.] My feet and legs were frozen. . . . The men rubbed me with snow. They put my feet in a bucket of water. The pain was terrible. . . .

"When we arrived at Devil's Gate it was bitter cold. We left many of our things there. . . . My brother James . . . was as well as he ever was when he went to bed [that night]. In the morning he was dead. . . .

"My feet were frozen; also my brother's and my sister's. It was nothing but snow [snow everywhere and the bitter Wyoming wind]. We could not drive the pegs in our tents. . . . We did not know what would become of us. [Then] one night a man came to our camp and told us . . . Brigham Young had sent men and teams to help us. . . . We sang songs, some danced and some cried. . . .

"My mother had never got well. . . . She died between the Little and Big Mountains. . . . She was 43 years of age. . . .

"We arrived in Salt Lake City nine o'clock at night the 11th of December 1856. Three out of the four that were living were frozen. My mother was dead in the wagon. . . .

"Early next morning Brigham Young came. . . . When he saw our condition, our feet frozen and our mother dead, tears rolled down his cheeks. . . .

"The doctor amputated my toes . . . [while] the sisters were dressing mother for her grave. . . . When my feet were fixed they [carried] . . . us in to see our mother for the last time. Oh, how did we stand it? That afternoon she was buried. . . .

"I have thought often of my mother's words before we left England. 'Polly, I want to go to Zion while my children are small, so they can be raised in the Gospel of Christ, for I know this is the true church.'" (Life of Mary Ann Goble Pay.)

Thus conclude portions of the narrative of a 13-year-old girl.

I conclude with this question: Should we be surprised if we are called upon to endure a little criticism, to make some small sacrifice for our faith, when our forebears paid so great a price for theirs? ("Contend Not with Others, But Pursue a Steady Course," *Improvement Era,* June 1970, pp. 40–41.)

The pioneers regarded their coming west as a blessing divinely given. Said Brigham Young on one occasion: "I do not wish men to understand I had anything to do with our being moved here, that was the providence of the Almighty; it was the power of God that wrought out salvation for this people, I never could have devised such a plan." (*Discourses of Brigham Young,* ed. John A. Widtsoe, Salt Lake City: Deseret Book Co., 1954, p. 480.)

The power that moved our forebears was the power of faith in God. It was the same power which made possible the exodus from Egypt, the passage through the Red Sea, the long journey through the wilderness, and the establishment of Israel in the Promised Land.

It was by this power that our forebears left Nauvoo and the beautiful lands of the Mississippi to travel to the shores of the Great Salt Lake. To me, it is a thing of never-ending wonder that Brigham Young and his associates had the faith to move to the mountain valleys of Utah. Of course, there were others who traversed the continent, but for the most part they were small groups. The movement of our people involved an exodus of many thousands to a land which others thought barren and unproductive. Nevertheless, they went west, putting their trust in God that he would rebuke the sterility of the soil and temper the climate that they might be sustained and grow and become a mighty people in the midst of the Rocky Mountains in order to send from its bastions the word of truth everywhere. ("The Faith of the Pioneers," *Ensign*, July 1984, p. 5.)

We need so very, very much a strong burning of that faith in the living God and in his living, resurrected Son, for this was the great, moving faith of our forebears.

Theirs was a vision, transcendent and overriding all other considerations. When they came west they were a thousand miles, a thousand tedious miles, from the nearest settlements to the east and eight hundred miles from those to the west. A personal and individual recognition of God their Eternal Father to whom they could look in faith was of the very essence of their strength. They believed in that great scriptural mandate: "Look to God and live." (Alma 37:47.) With faith they sought to do his will. With faith they read and accepted divine teaching. With faith they labored until they dropped, always with a conviction that there would be an accounting to him who was their Father and their God.

Brigham Young's words concerning his own death and burial are worth noting. After giving instructions concerning where he should be buried, he said, "There let my earthly house or tabernacle rest in peace, and have a good sleep, until the morning of the first resurrection; no crying or mourning with anyone *as I have done my work faithfully and in good faith.*" (cited in Preston Nibley, *Brigham Young: The Man and His Work,* Salt Lake City: Deseret Book Co., 1936, p. 537; italics added.)

As we reflect on those who have gone before us, and as we consider our present labors for the good of ourselves and others, would that we all might say each day, "I am doing my work faithfully and in good faith." ("The Faith of the Pioneers," *Ensign*, July 1984, p. 6.)

After the Saints went West, even though they were faced with the tremendous tasks of subduing the wilderness and building a commonwealth, they did not slacken their efforts to carry the gospel to the nations of the earth. In the conference held in 1852, men were called from the congregation to go not only to the lands of Europe, but to China and Siam. It is stirring to note that in those pioneering days, missionaries were sent to

India, where today, after a long lapse, we are again planting gospel seeds.

I marvel at the boldness—rather, I prefer to characterize it as the *faith*—of the leaders and members of the Church in that pioneering era to stretch their relatively small membership and their thin resources so far in carrying the gospel to distant lands. One cannot read Elder Parley P. Pratt's account of his travels to Chile without recognizing with gratitude the courage and the faith of those early missionaries, who took with such seriousness the Lord's charge to carry the gospel to the nations of the earth.

Their long journeys across the seas were made under extremely adverse circumstances. When they stepped ashore, there was neither friend nor companion to meet them. They had no briefing concerning the conditions they were to meet, no knowledge of the languages of the people among whom they were to labor. Many of them sickened as their bodies struggled to adapt to the food and other circumstances of living. But they were filled with a sense of mission, commanded by a charge to take the gospel of salvation to the peoples of the earth. The cultures they encountered created challenges for them, but these were only incidental to their larger responsibilities. ("We Have a Work to Do," *Ensign*, February 1988, p. 4.)

I stood the other day on the old docks of Liverpool, England. There was practically no activity the Friday morning when we were there. But once this was a veritable beehive. During the 1800s, tens of thousands of our people walked over the same stone paving on which we walked. They came from across the British Isles and from the lands of Europe, converts to the Church. They came with testimony on their lips and faith in their hearts. Was it difficult to leave their homes and step into the unknown of a new world? Of course it was. But they did it with optimism and enthusiasm. They boarded sailing vessels. They knew the crossing at best was hazardous. They soon found out that for the most part it was miserable. . . . They endured storms, disease, sickness. Many died on the way and were buried at sea. It was an arduous and fearsome journey. They had doubts, yes. But their faith rose above those doubts. Their optimism rose above their fears. They had their dream of Zion, and they were on their way to fulfill it. . . .

I can scarcely comprehend the magnitude of Brigham Young's faith in leading thousands of people into the wilderness. He had never seen this country, except as he had seen it in vision. It was an act of boldness almost beyond comprehension. For him their coming here was all part of the grand pattern of the growth and destiny of this work. To those who followed him it was the pursuit of a great dream. ("Stay the Course—Keep the Faith," *Ensign*, November 1995, p. 72.)

Why did they do it? They did it because of their faith. They counted the costs. They knew they would be heavy. They knew they were facing extreme hazards. I stood on the Liverpool docks a while ago, from which place they left to come here. They gathered from Scandinavia and Britain and assembled there and boarded their ships and came across the seas in sailing vessels. They traveled up the Mississippi or from Boston to Iowa City, where they were fitted out. They went on to Winter Quarters and made the long march to this valley. They knew that many of them would die along the way. More than 4,000 of them did die, gave their lives as a testimony of their belief in the cause which they had undertaken. (Interview with Lee Groberg for PBS Documentary "Trail of Hope," November 4, 1996.)

Did [the pioneers] ever become discouraged? Of course they did. I quote now from James Brown, this remarkable experience and prophecy:

"The winter of 1848–49 was quite cold. Many people had their feet badly frozen. . . . As the days grew warmer the gold fever attacked many so that they prepared to go to California. Some said they would go only to have a place for the rest of us; for they thought Brigham Young too smart a man to try to establish a civilized colony in such a God-forsaken country as they called the Salt Lake Valley. . . .

"It was at this time of gloom that President Young stood before the whole people, and said, in substance:

"'Some have asked me about going. I have told them that God has appointed this place for the gathering of His Saints, and you will do better right here than you will by going to the gold mines. Some have thought they would go there and get fitted out and come back, but I told them to stop here and get fitted out. Those who stop here and are faithful to God and his people will make more money and get richer than you that run after the God of this world; and I promise you in the name of the Lord that many of you that go thinking you will get rich and come back, will wish you had never gone away from here, and will long to come back, but you will not be able to do so. Some of you will come back, but your friends who remain here will have to help you. . . .

"'We have been kicked out of the frying pan and into the fire, out of the fire into the middle of the floor, and here we are and here we will stay. God has shown me that this is the spot to locate His people, and here is where they will prosper; He will rebuke the elements for the good of His saints. He will rebuke the frost and the sterility of the soil, and the land shall become fruitful. Brethren, go to now, and plant out your fruit seeds. . . .

"'We shall build a city and a temple to the Most High God in this place. We will extend our settlements to the east and west, to the north and south, and we will build towns and cities by the hundreds, and thousands of the Saints will gather in from the nations of the earth.

"'This will become the great highway of the nations. Kings and emperors and the noble and wise of the earth will visit us here, while the wicked and ungodly will envy us our comfortable homes and possessions.

"'Take courage, brethren. I can stand in my door and see where there is untold millions of the rich treasures of the earth— gold and silver. But the time has not come for the saints to dig gold. . . . For if the mines are open first, we are a thousand miles from any base of supplies and the people would rush in here in such great numbers that they would breed a famine. . . . People would starve to death with barrels of gold. . . .

"'It is our duty to preach the gospel, gather Israel, pay our tithing and build temples. The worst fear that I have about this people is that they will get rich in this country, forget God and His people, wax fat, and kick themselves out of the Church and go to hell. [That is a quotation!] This people will stand mobbing, robbing, poverty, and all manner of persecution, and be true. But my greater fear for them is that they cannot stand wealth; and yet they have to be tried with riches, for they will become the richest people on this earth.'" (Autobiography of James Brown, pp. 119–23, cited by Preston Nibley, *Brigham Young, the Man and His Work,* Deseret News Press, 1936, pp. 127–28.) I would like to say that we are a very rich and blessed people.

Notwithstanding the temptation to go to the California gold fields where the entire world seemed to be rushing, the people accepted their leader's words. They stayed here and grubbed the sagebrush and made their way. Brigham Young's prophecy has been fulfilled. This is now a great and beautiful and fertile area. It has become the crossroads of the West. Thousands and tens of thousands and hundreds of thousands pass this way constantly. We in the Office of the First Presidency are called upon day after day and week after week to meet the great of the earth.

Faith was the guiding principle in those difficult days. Faith is the guiding principle which we must follow today. From this valley we have now spread across the nation, and across much of the earth. We can change our place of residence, but we must never change the principles which guide us. There must be faith as a predominant factor in our lives as it was in the lives of those who have gone before us. (Church Educational System Young Adult Fireside, February 2, 1997.)

Am I an impractical idealist concerning the pioneers? No. There were exceptions here and there, but by and large they were a noble and wonderful people who walked in faith, who lived with loyalty, who were industrious, and who worked with integrity.

Shining above all of their principles and ideals was their solemn and wonderful belief in the Lord Jesus Christ as their Savior and their Redeemer. They knew Him. He walked with them on that long march to the Elkhorn, up the Platte, beside the Sweetwater, over the Continental Divide, and down through the dry and desert country to this valley of the Great Salt Lake. He was their friend. They offered their prayers in His name. They sang to His glory. With humble appreciation they spoke of His great atoning sacrifice. They put their faith in Him.

"And should we die before our journey's through, Happy day! All is well! We then are free from toil and sorrow, too; With the just we shall dwell!" (*Hymns*, no. 30.) Such was their belief. Death was tragic for those left behind. But they knew there would be another day, a day of happy reunions. "But if our lives are spared again to see the Saints their rest obtain, Oh, how we'll make this chorus swell—All is well! All is well!"

What a wonderful people they were. There is nothing like their great effort in all of history. There have been other great migrations. There have been many great causes for which men have given their lives. But in our time, within the span of our memory, stand these noble pioneers. God bless their memory to our good. When the way seems hard, when we are discouraged, thinking all is lost, we can turn to them and see how much worse was their condition. When we wonder about the future, we can look to them and their great example of faith. (Church Educational System Young Adult Fireside, February 2, 1997.)

Heritage of the Pioneers

The notes of this talk were prepared last night while we were riding a plane 600 miles an hour between New York and Salt Lake. We left Kennedy Airport at six in the evening, rose faster than any bird could ever fly to an elevation of 35,000 feet, passed over the great cities of the East, and landed in Chicago an hour and forty-five minutes later. After a brief pause, we headed west again, out into the blackness of the night, across the great Mississippi lowlands, and then over the vast prairies, relentlessly driven by the great jet engines, flying at 39,000 feet to take advantage of a tail wind that carried us to Salt Lake from Chicago in less than two and a half hours from takeoff to touch-down. The air was smooth, the seats were comfortable. . . .

Many of you have had similar experiences. This kind of everyday miracle has become commonplace to us. Like so many other marvelous things, we take it for granted.

We passed over Des Moines, skirted Omaha, and flew high over the rivers beside which a century ago our forefathers drove their oxen, traveling fifteen miles a day.

In my mind's eye I saw below the long wagon trains, dust rising with each turn of the huge, wooden-spoked wheels. I saw the wagons circled in the evening, the oxen turned out to feed and water, the burdensome preparation of coarse food eaten with thanksgiving, the nursing of the sick, the burial of the dead among those who were leaving persecution to lay the foundation for all that we enjoy.

In imagination I saw my own grandfather. . . . He, with his young bride, started across Iowa, then followed the long trail up the Elkhorn and the North Platte in the direction of Fort Laramie. His wife grew pale and sick and died. With his own hands he chopped a tree beside the trail, made a coffin, dug a grave, left his sweetheart in a place he never again visited, and carried a three-month-old baby to the Salt Lake Valley.

I thought of him last night as we flew smoothly more than seven hundred miles over Nebraska and Wyoming, and reached in my case, took out my Bible, and turned to Joshua, chapter 24, and read these words of the Lord given to an ungrateful Israel:

"And I have given you a land for which ye did not labour, and cities which ye built not, and ye dwell in them; of the vineyards and oliveyards which ye planted not do ye eat." (Joshua 24:13.)

I thought of how appropriately that might be applied to our own generation. You and I live in a marvelous land for which we have not labored, and we dwell in cities which we built not and eat of vineyards which we have not planted. How thankful we ought to be for the magnificent blessings we enjoy. Our society is afflicted by a spirit of thoughtless arrogance unbecoming those who have been blessed so generously. ("How Lucky Can You Be!" *BYU Speeches of the Year,* October 13, 1964, pp. 2–3.)

It is good to look to the past to gain appreciation for the present and perspective for the future. It is good to look upon the virtues of those who have gone before, to gain strength for whatever lies ahead. It is good to reflect upon the work of those who labored so hard and gained so little in this world, but out of whose dreams and early plans, so well nurtured, has come a great harvest of which we are the beneficiaries. Their tremendous example can become a compelling motivation for us all, for each of us is a pioneer in his own life, often in his own family, and many of us pioneer daily in trying to establish a gospel foothold in distant parts of the world. . . .

In the environment in which many of us live, there is need for reminders of lessons learned in the past. In our times of abundance, it is good occasionally to be taken back to earlier days, to have our minds refocused on the struggles of the early Latter-day Saints, to remind us of the necessity for labor if the earth is to be made to yield, of the importance of faith in God if there is to be lasting achievement, and of the need to recognize that many of the so-called old values are worthy of present application.

Oh, how much is faith needed in each of our lives—faith in ourselves, faith in our associates, and faith in the living God. ("The Faith of the Pioneers," *Ensign,* July 1984, p. 3.)

One hundred and thirty-seven years ago the pioneers entered Salt Lake Valley. They had traveled from the Missouri River, taking three months to cover the distance we cover in two hours by airplane. With faith in their capacity to do what needed doing, they set to work. Theirs was a philosophy of self-reliance. There was no government to assist them. They had natural resources, it is true. But they had to dig them out and fashion them. Their workmanship is a miracle to me. They had little more than their bare hands. Their tools were simple and relatively crude in comparison with ours. Of machinery they had little, and for the most part it was self-improvised. But they had skills, patiently learned, in masonry, the working of wood, the making and application of plaster, the setting of glass. The quality of their craftsmanship is not excelled in our time. In many respects, it is not equaled. Those who look upon it today are quick to agree that it was inspired. . . .

I walked through that temple the other day. There was renewed in my mind a tremendous appreciation for its remarkable beauty and for the capacity of its builders. ("The Faith of the Pioneers," *Ensign,* July 1984, pp. 3–4.)

[Loyal holders of the priesthood] have carried forward this work from the beginning. They were present in the home of Peter Whitmer when the Church was organized. They were among the few who stood by the Prophet in the troubled days of the New York period of the Church. They readily left Kirtland to serve missions wherever they were asked to go, at the call of the Prophet.

They made the long march with Zion's Camp, the eight-hundred-mile journey from Ohio to western Missouri. They stood by the Prophet in Liberty Jail. Peeled and driven, they staggered with the destitute Saints across the bottomlands of the Mississippi and into Quincy, Illinois.

They drained the swamps of Commerce to create Nauvoo the Beautiful. They erected the magnificent house of the Lord on the hill above the river. They were with Joseph at Carthage. They mourned his death and rallied to the leadership of the Twelve. With mobs at their backs they abandoned their homes and temple and faced the Iowa winter. Some of them marched the long, long road with the Mormon Battalion to San Diego and then back to the valley of the Great Salt Lake.

Others followed the Elkhorn and the Platte on to Scottsbluff, Independence Rock, South Pass, and down into this valley. Here they grubbed sagebrush; fought crickets; labored and prayed; built homes, churches, and temples to their God.

Through all of this long odyssey there were those who were not loyal, some few who were traitors, who were betrayers, but they were a small minority. Honor be to those who stood firm, and to their wives who worked beside them. ("The Good and Faithful Servants," *Ensign*, November 1984, p. 49.)

I have a copy of a statement written years ago by James H. McClintock, who was Arizona State Historian. This is what he wrote concerning the pioneering of our people in outlying settlements: "First of the Mormon faith on the western slopes of the continent was a settlement at San Francisco from the ship *Brooklyn*. They landed July 31, 1846, to found the first English-speaking community of California, theretofore Mexican. These Mormons established the farming community of New Helvetia in the San Joaquin Valley the same fall, while men from the Mormon Battalion, January 24, 1848, participated in the discovery of gold at Sutter's Fort. They also were pioneers in southern California where, in 1851, several hundred families of the faith settled at San Bernardino. The first Anglo-Saxon settlement within the boundaries of the present state of Colorado was at Pueblo, November 15, 1846, by Captain James Brown and about 150 men and women a part of the Mormon Battalion. The first American settlement in Nevada was one of Mormons in the Carson Valley of Genoa in 1851. In Wyoming, as early as 1854, was a Mormon settlement at Green River near Fort Bridger known as Fort Supply. In Idaho, too, preeminence is claimed by virtue of a Mormon settlement at Fort Limhi on the Salmon River in 1855, and at Franklin and Cache Valley in 1860. In Arizona there were the early settlements on the Muddy and the Virgin. The first permanent Anglo-Saxon agricultural settlement in Arizona, that of Beaver Dams, now known as Littlefield on the Virgin, was founded at least as early as the fall of 1864." He then concludes with these words: "It must be acknowledged that the Mormons were wilderness breakers of high quality. They not only broke it but they kept it broken. And instead of the gin mill and the gambling hell as cornerstones of their progress and as examples to the natives of the white men's superiority, they planted orchards, gardens, farms, schoolhouses, and peaceful homes."

Every one of us ought to be very proud of those who have gone before us to lay the foundations of this work in this part of the West. Every one of us ought to be very thankful for those who preceded us to make it possible for us to live so comfortably in our time. God be thanked for the Mormon pioneers. (Cove Fort Fireside and Centennial Wagon Train Celebration, June 24, 1996.)

What a miracle has come to pass! How richly blessed we are! How kind the Lord has been to us, my brethren and sisters! What a wonderful thing to have an inheritance of great history, and the heritage that comes from people who valued their faith more than they valued their lives. I don't know how many were buried in [Council Bluffs]. Across the river at Winter Quarters, there were some 600 of the 6,000 who died on the trail between there and the Salt Lake Valley before the coming of the railroad. In addition to that there were frequent burials along the Mississippi River and along the Missouri, as converts to the Church coming from England and Europe came across the sea and then up the Mississippi and Missouri, many of them the victims of cholera, a terrible disease that attacked with great suddenness. People would be as well as anything in the morning and be dead before nightfall. Thanks to the blessing of modern medicine, those things are all behind us. We are so richly blessed, and there ought to be in our hearts a great, overpowering sense of gratitude toward those who laid the foundations for all that we have today. (Grand Encampment Devotional, Council Bluffs, Iowa, July 13, 1996.)

This is the 150th anniversary of the coming of the Mormon pioneers to the Salt Lake Valley. We will have many great celebrations in Salt Lake City. We will remember with pageantry and many other things that great act of faith when our people came to the valleys of the mountains, a place not looked upon with favor by any who knew of it. But there they planted themselves in that valley and from there they spread to establish many other communities. Today we are the beneficiaries of their great faith. From their establishment in the mountains have gone forth the blessings of this restored gospel to the peoples of the earth. . . . Be grateful for the gospel. Be grateful for the Prophet Joseph Smith. Be grateful for the pioneers. Be grateful for the Church in this day. . . . Life is not so hard for us in this day. We get along much better. We have the gospel without paying a big price for it. Let us resolve to live it. (Panama City Panama Fireside, January 20, 1997.)

They were travel-worn, these pioneers. It had taken 111 days to bring them from Winter Quarters to the Salt Lake Valley. They were tired. Their clothes were worn. Their animals were jaded. The weather was hot and dry, the hot weather of July. But here they were, looking down the years, and dreaming a millennial dream, a grand dream of Zion.

You are familiar with their story. You are the fruit of all of their planning and of all of their labors. Whether you have pioneer ancestry or came into the Church only yesterday, you are a part of this whole grand picture of which those men dreamed. Theirs was a tremendous undertaking. Ours is a great continuing responsibility. They laid the foundation. Ours is the duty to build on it. They marked the path and led the way. Ours is the obligation to enlarge and broaden and strengthen that path until it encompasses the whole earth.

What a marvelous thing it is to have a great heritage. . . . What a grand thing to know that there are those who have gone before and laid out the way we should walk, teaching those great eternal principles which must be the guiding stars of our lives and of those who come after us. We today can follow their example. (Church Educational System Young Adult Fireside, February 2, 1997.)

PLAN OF SALVATION

Man is an eternal being. As an individual of spiritual substance, he lived before coming to earth. . . .

Life upon the earth in a mortal body is but another step in a great, eternal march. Here we have opportunity for experience, for improvement, for growth. And on the basis of what we believe here we shall continue to live and grow in the life beyond the grave.

In the life to come we shall not be arbitrarily divided into two fixed groups—inhabitants of heaven and hell. Jesus stated, "In my Father's house are many mansions." There will be various grades and stations. There will be activity and learning. We shall know each other there as we know each other here. Our individuality will be retained. "Whatever principle of intelligence we attain unto in this life, it will rise with us in the resurrection." "The glory of God is intelligence." These are Mormon aphorisms. Life is purposeful. It is progressive. It leads to Godhood.

There is nothing of reincarnation, nothing of Nirvana, nothing of a static heaven, nor a hell of hot flame in Latter-day Saint philosophy. Heaven lies in the growth that comes of improvement and achievement. It is the place where will be those who have achieved this goal by obedience to the commandments of God. (*What of the Mormons?* pamphlet, 1982, pp. 7–8.)

I thank the Prophet Joseph and love him for the doctrine of salvation which was revealed through him. Through the grace of

God all men will be privileged to rise from the dead, a gift freely given and made possible through the atoning sacrifice of the Lord Jesus Christ. Beyond this, all who walk in obedience to the teachings and commandments of the gospel may go on, even to exaltation. There are various kingdoms and principalities in the life beyond, named and described in the incomparable divine revelations which came through him. I thank him and love him for all of this. I love him for the assurance, certain and unequivocal, of life after death in a realm of activity and growth, in contrast with a condition of static and unfruitful ecstasy as others have taught. How grateful I am for the grandeur of his vision of eternity. I thank him for the assurance that, "mingling with Gods, he can plan for his brethren." . . .

I thank him and love him for the light and understanding he brought to the world concerning the purpose of life—that mortality is a step in an eternal journey, that we lived before we came here, that there was design in our coming, that we are sons and daughters of God our Eternal Father with a divine and wonderful birthright, that we are here to be tested and to grow, that, as one man has said, "Life is a mission and not a career," that death is a step across the threshold into another realm as real and as purposeful as this. Infinite is our opportunity to grow toward Godhood under the plan of our Eternal Father and His Beloved Son. ("As One Who Loves the Prophet," Symposium on the Life and Ministry of the Prophet Joseph Smith, BYU, February 22, 1992.)

I think we must never lose sight of our Father's transcendent declaration: "For behold, this is my work and my glory—to bring to pass the immortality and eternal life of man" (Moses 1:39).

When all is said and done, this is the purpose of our being, to assist our Father in the accomplishment of His work and His glory. For this reason He sent His Son into the world to take upon himself the sins of the world, to offer his life in a wondrous atonement for those sins, to suffer and die upon the cross in a supreme sacrifice for the blessing of all mankind, to come forth triumphant from the tomb as the master of life and death, of mortality and immortality.

For this purpose the gospel was restored in this dispensation, that knowledge, hidden from before the foundation of the earth, might come from the heavens to open the eyes of mankind and to lift their minds to an understanding of their potential as sons and daughters of God.

For this purpose was the Book of Mormon translated and brought forth, speaking as a voice from the dust in declaration of the eternal purposes of the Almighty and in testimony of His beloved Son, the Savior and Redeemer of mankind.

For this purpose was the priesthood restored, that men might receive those ordinances which will permit them to pass by the angels and the gods as they go forward on their eternal and celestial journey of salvation and exaltation.

For this purpose was the Church organized as the great conservator of these eternal truths, as the means of providing activity that will lead to growth and understanding and knowledge of the everlasting purposes of God, as the conveyor of a program of teaching the world the truths that will save them from their sins; as the unique institution which binds and gives opportunity for its members to socialize together as those of common understanding and love; as the builder of sacred houses in which instruction may be given, in which ordinances of eternal consequence may be performed, in which covenants are entered into, and in which is done that work which will free from bondage those in the beyond who cannot move forward without those ordinances which were designed to be given in the environment of mortality.

These are the truths, beautiful in design, grand in their concept, glorious and wonderful when understood, which will save people. (General Authority Training Meeting, September 27, 1994.)

The work of the Lord is a work of salvation. For whom? Through the grace of our Eternal Father and without any effort on the part of the beneficiaries, the atoning sacrifice of the Son of God has made it possible for all to rise from the dead. And beyond this, by virtue of that divine sacrifice, and through His grace and goodness, opportunities for eternal life may be opened to all through personal or vicarious service. (Utah Genealogical Society Fireside, November 13, 1994.)

We do not succeed, I believe, until the Spirit of the Lord reaches down into the heart of the people and touches them with that conviction that Jesus is the Christ, the Son of God, the Firstborn of the Father, the Only Begotten in the flesh, He who gave His life for each of us. I can't comprehend, in terms of eternities and the blessings of eternities, the magnitude of the Atonement, but I can sense it and appreciate it in a measure at least, and the older I grow—and I am getting pretty ancient—the more certain I feel that when all is said and done, that is the key to everything else. That is the heart of the eternal plan of salvation. We lived before we came here. We are here for a purpose. We shall live after we die, and all of it is a part of eternity, and the key to everlasting life is the atonement wrought by the Savior. (England Birmingham Missionary Meeting, August 29, 1995.)

The fact of all life is that it is eternal. That's the great, salient truth. We have come into the world for a purpose, under a divine plan, and when we conclude this life we will go on to something that will be better, if we live worthy of it. And that great eternal course which we may follow is made possible through the sacrifice of the Son of God. (Charlotte North Carolina Regional Conference, priesthood leadership session, February 24, 1996.)

You know what life is for, what it's about, that you're part of an eternal plan, that you lived with purpose before you came to this life, that this life is a mission and not just a career, and that we will step over the veil someday but keep on going and growing. I don't know of anybody in the world who has the concept of the meaning of life that we have as a result of the restoration of the gospel of Jesus Christ. (San Diego California Young Adult Fireside, March 24, 1996.)

POLITICS

See also Church and State; Civic Responsibility

Now a word on politics. This is an election year, and there are many strong and strident voices incident to political campaigning. It's a wholesome and wonderful system that we have under which people are free to express themselves in electing those who shall represent them in the councils of government. I would hope that those concerned would address themselves to issues and not to personalities. The issues ought to be discussed freely, openly, candidly, and forcefully. But, I repeat, I would hope that there would be an avoidance of demeaning personalities. ("Reach Out in Love and Kindness," *Ensign*, November 1982, p. 77.)

I am confident that so long as we have more politicians than statesmen, we shall have problems. ("Be Positive," Young Single Adult Fireside, BYU Marriott Center, March 6, 1994.)

Question: As you know, some skeptics will say that major changes in Church policy have come from political pressures, not necessarily as revelations from God. For example, the business of ending polygamy: the skeptics will say, it wasn't because it was a revelation, it was because Utah wanted to become a state and they couldn't become a state unless they banned polygamy.

President Hinckley: Well, one of the purposes of a prophet is to seek the wisdom and the will of the Lord and to teach his people accordingly. It was the case with Moses when he led the children of Israel out of Egypt. It was the case for the Old Testament prophets when people were faced with oppression and trouble and difficulty. That is the purpose of a prophet, to give answers to people to the dilemmas in which they find themselves. That is what happens. That is what we see happen. Is it a matter of expediency, political expediency? No. Inspired guidance. Yes.

Question: Well, then I think you have already given me the answer. I was going to ask: To what degree is Church policy dictated or helped along by politics?

President Hinckley: Well, we believe in honoring, obeying, and sustaining the law. If we should find ourselves in a situation where we had to make a choice, we would seek guidance on that matter. That could be a very difficult thing to handle, what we might construe as a divine pattern of doing something vis-à-vis some piece of legislation. We would seek the guidance of the Lord and act accordingly. (Interview with Mike Wallace of *60 Minutes*, March 10, 1996.)

Question: I am sure you have had experiences where politicians try to win your favor or approval, probably here in the state of Utah, considering 70 percent of the people in the state are Mormons. Do the politicians here try to win your approval, knowing that you are the head of the very powerful Mormon Church?

President Hinckley: That is the business of politicians, to win, to get approval. Yes, of course, they want to gain our approval, but we maintain a hands-off policy in terms of the Church advocating this party or that party, this candidate or that candidate. (Interview with ABS-CBN Television, Philippines, April 30, 1996.)

We are in the midst of a political campaign in this nation. As usual, we are being saturated with claims and counter claims. Anyone who has lived as long as I have has heard again and again the sweet talk that leads to victory but seems never to be realized thereafter. It is imperative that good people, men and women of principle, be involved in the political process—otherwise we abdicate power to those whose designs are almost entirely selfish. ("Stand Up for Truth," BYU Devotional Address, September 17, 1996.)

POLYGAMY

To many people Mormonism has meant one thing only—polygamy. This has been the subject of lurid tales in all parts of the world. Once such stories were extremely popular. But as the facts have come to be known, such writings have largely disappeared.

The truth of the matter is this: Mormonism claims to be a restoration of God's work in all previous dispensations. The Old Testament teaches that the patriarchs—those men favored of God in ancient times—had more than one wife under divine sanction. In the course of the development of the Church in the nineteenth century, it was revealed to the leader of the Church that such a practice of marriage again should be entered into.

The announcement of this doctrine was a severe shock. Most of the converts to Mormonism were of Puritan New England stock. Shortly after Brigham Young heard of the doctrine he saw a funeral cortege passing down the street, and he is reported to have said that he would gladly trade places with the man in the coffin rather than face this doctrine.

Nevertheless, the leaders of the Church accepted it as a commandment from God. It was not an easy thing to do. Only those whose characters were of the highest, and who had proved themselves capable of maintaining more than one family, were permitted so to marry. Never at any time were more than a small percentage of the families of the Church polygamous. The practice was regarded strictly as a religious principle.

In the late Eighties, Congress passed various measures prohibiting the practice, and when the Supreme Court declared the law constitutional, the Church indicated its willingness to comply. Consistently it could do nothing else in view of its basic teaching on the necessity for obedience to the law of the land. That was in 1890. (*What of the Mormons?* pamphlet, 1982, pp. 10–11.)

POOR

See also Welfare

In remembering together before the Lord the poor, the needy, and the oppressed, there is developed, unconsciously but realistically, a love for others above self, a respect for others, a desire to serve the needs of others. One cannot ask God to help a neighbor in distress without feeling motivated to do something oneself toward helping that neighbor. (Conference Report, April 1963, p. 127.)

I heard a man of prominence say the other day, "I have amended the language of my prayers. Instead of saying, 'Bless the poor and the sick and the needy,' I now say, 'Father, show me how to help the poor and the sick and the needy, and give me resolution to do so.'" ("'And the Greatest of These Is Love,'" *BYU Devotional Speeches of the Year*, February 14, 1978, p. 24.)

If every member of this Church observed the fast and contributed generously, the poor and the needy—not only of the Church, but many others as well—would be blessed and provided for. Every giver would be blessed in body and spirit, and the hungry would be fed, the naked clothed according to need. (Belle S. Spafford Conference on Women, February 23, 1990.)

The plight of the homeless is a repudiation of the greatness of our nation. I commend most warmly those who with a compelling spirit of kindness reach out to those in distress, regardless of whom they might be, to help and assist, to feed and provide for, to nurture and to bless. As these extend mercy, I am confident that the God of heaven will bless them, and their posterity after them, with His own mercy. I am satisfied that these who impart so generously will not lack in their own store, but that there will be food on their tables and a roof over their heads. One cannot be merciful to others without receiving a harvest of mercy in return. ("Blessed Are the Merciful," *Ensign*, May 1990, p. 70.)

I don't know how long ago it was that I first came to Mexico, but it was many years ago, and for the most part the people were poor, with little opportunity for education—struggling, really, to stay alive. And then I came down to dedicate the Mexico Temple and the Saints had gathered from all over the nation. I was in the temple president's office, and I could look out the window at the people who were lined up to come into the temple, but they couldn't see me. And there was every one, clean, bright-looking, polished, a card in one hand and a handkerchief in the other, to come to the house of the Lord and participate in the dedication of that sacred temple. That, to me, is the miracle of Mormonism in Mexico. (Mexico Veracruz Missionary Meeting, January 27, 1996.)

We must take care of the poor. Said the Lord, "The poor ye have with you always." (See Mark 14:7; John 12:8.) There have always been poor and I guess there always will be poor until the Millennium. We must take care of them and we must have the facilities to do so. But we must be very careful not to overinstitutionalize that care. We must not shift the burden that we ought to carry in our own hearts of spreading kindness and love and help to others, to the institution, which at best, is impersonal.

I do not want you to get any idea that I am saying we should not have the welfare program. We must have it. It is a part of the Lord's plan and the good it does is vast and incalculable. But I think there is a tendency among us to say, "Oh, the Church will take care of that. I pay my fast offering. Let the Church take care of that." We need as individuals, I think, to reach down and extend a helping hand without notice, without thanks, without expectation of anything in return, to give of that with which the Lord has so generously blessed us. (General Authority Training Meeting, April 2, 1996.)

Question: Many people, sadly, living in this country live in poverty with few employment opportunities, poor housing, sickness, and great unhappiness. What hope can you give to those who are suffering?

President Hinckley: Well, I hope that their circumstances will improve. We are trying to help. We're extending a great deal of humanitarian aid across the world. We've distributed a good deal of aid here. There is suffering everywhere. There is so much of suffering in so many areas of the world. It is tragic. I believe our Heavenly Father must grieve over the plight of so many of His children. Much of that results from the selfishness of others. We think that the answer to all of these problems lies in the gospel of Jesus Christ and in the application of the Golden Rule, "Whatsoever ye would that men should do to you, do ye even so to them" (Matt. 7:12). If that were practiced more generally, there would be less of misery in the world. (Interview with David Fuster, Public Affairs, Philippines, May 30, 1996.)

I would hope that the economy would increase here for the blessing of the people. I do not think that our Father in Heaven likes His people to be hungry and miserable and poor. I think our Father in Heaven loves His children and wishes for them to have the good things of life so long as they will keep the faith. And He would wish to bless them, I believe, and we will pray that His beneficent hand will come upon this land for the blessing of the people. (Philippines Manila/Quezon City Missionary Meeting, May 31, 1996.)

PORNOGRAPHY

There are those among us who would succumb to evil things and to the wiles of the adversary. I would like to say a word about pornography. It is a growing, vile, and evil thing. It is on our motion picture screens, it comes into the homes of the people on television receivers, it is on newsstands, it reaches out in other ways to entrap and beguile and destroy those who are enticed to partake of it. I am satisfied . . . that no Latter-day Saint can with impunity afford to witness or read or partake of this growing evil in any way. God help us and bless us with the self-discipline to resist and abstain and flee from, if necessary, this pernicious and growing thing which would destroy us. ("Reach Out in Love and Kindness," *Ensign*, November 1982, p. 76.)

Pornography is printed and pictorial material designed to excite us and attract us into areas that will only bring regret. It is enticing in its appeal. It plays on the instincts that lie within all of us, God-given instincts placed within us for his great purposes. Pornography is a tool of the devil to twist those instincts to forbidden ends. It most often involves beautiful young women and handsome young men. The purpose of its creation is to put dollars in the pockets of its creators. The result of its use is to warp the minds and excite the passions of those who fall into its trap. It brings billions to its creators. It leads to heartache and pain and regret for those who indulge in it.

It is found in magazines that can be bought at most newsstands, in theaters showing R- and X-rated movies, and on our television screens in our homes.

It is made wonderfully attractive. . . . I remember interviewing a young man who had been excommunicated from the Church because of serious moral transgression. He was a successful young lawyer with a promising future. I asked him how he got into the trap that finally caught him and almost destroyed him.

He said it began with reading pornographic magazines and then going to pornographic shows. From this he was led deeper into the rapids until his whole family life capsized in trouble, dishonor, and heartbreak. (Youth Fireside Satellite Broadcast, December 5, 1982.)

There is an ever-growing plague of pornography swirling about us. The producers and purveyors of smut are assiduously working a mine that yields them many millions in profit. Some of their products are artfully beguiling. They are designed to titillate and stimulate the baser instincts. Many a man who has partaken of forbidden fruit and then discovered that he has destroyed his marriage, lost his self-respect, and broken his companion's heart, has come to realize that the booby-trapped jungle trail he has followed began with the reading or viewing of pornographic material. Some who would not think of taking a sip of liquor or of smoking a cigarette, have rationalized indulgence in pornography. Such have warped values totally unbecoming one who has been ordained to the priesthood of God.

Portrayals of sexual perversion, violence, and bestiality become increasingly available for those who succumb to their lures. As this happens, religious activities are likely to become less attractive because the two do not mix any more than oil and water mix.

A thought-provoking study was recently published in *Public Opinion* magazine. It has been commented upon by many writers. John Dart, religion editor for the *Los Angeles Times*, wrote a column last February in which he said:

"A survey of influential television writers and executives in Hollywood has shown that they are far less religious than the general public and 'diverge sharply from traditional values' on such issues as abortion, homosexual rights and extramarital sex. . . . While nearly all of the 104 Hollywood professionals interviewed had a religious background, 45 percent now say they have no religion, and of the other 55 percent only 7 percent say they attend a religious service as much as once a month.

"'This group has had a major role in shaping the shows whose themes and stars have become staples in our popular culture.' . . .

"Eighty percent of the respondents said they did not regard homosexual relations as wrong, and 51 percent did not deem adultery as wrong. Of the 49 percent who called extramarital affairs wrong, only 17 percent felt that way strongly, the study said. Nearly all—97 percent—favored the right of a woman to choose an abortion, 91 percent holding that view strongly.

"By contrast, other surveys have indicated that 85 percent of Americans consider adultery wrong, 71 percent regard homosexual activity wrong and nearly three-fourths of the public wants abortion limited to certain hard cases or banned altogether." (*Los Angeles Times*, 19 Feb. 1983, part 2, page 5.)

These are the people who, through the medium of entertainment, are educating us in the direction of their own standards, which in many cases are diametrically opposed to the standards of the gospel. Even beyond these, who produce for public television and cable, are the hard-core pornographers who seductively reach out to ensnare those gullible enough and those so weak in their discipline of self that they spend money to buy these lascivious products. ("Be Not Deceived," *Ensign*, November 1983, pp. 45–46.)

How many otherwise good men squander their strength and dissipate their will and literally destroy their lives because they have not the power of self-discipline. Let me read to you from a letter I received from a man ashamed to sign his name. He writes:

"I am a 35-year-old male and am a convert to the Church of more than ten years. For most of my adult life I have been addicted to pornography. I am ashamed to admit this. My addiction is as real as that of an alcoholic or a drug addict.

"I was first introduced to this material as a child. I was molested by an older male cousin and pornography was used to attract my interest. I am convinced that this exposure at an early age to sex and pornography is at the root of my addiction today. I think it is ironic that those who support the business of pornography say that it is a matter of freedom of expression. I have no freedom. I have lost my free agency because I have been unable to overcome this. It is a trap for me, and I can't seem to get out of it. Please, please, please, plead with the brethren of the Church to not only avoid but eliminate the sources of pornographic material in their lives. . . .

"Finally, President Hinckley, please pray for me and others in the Church who may be like me to have the courage and strength to overcome this terrible affliction."

Brethren, there is neither happiness nor peace to be gained from surrendering to the weakness of indulging in these things which degrade and destroy. ("Building Your Tabernacle," *Ensign,* November 1992, pp. 51–52.)

Pity the poor man or boy of low purpose and weak ambition who, after a day of work, finishes his evening meal and then turns to the television screen for the rest of the evening to watch pornographic videotapes or sleazy late-night programs. . . .

Do you wish to help Satan score? There is no surer way than to become engulfed in the tide of pornography that is sweeping over us. If we succumb to it, it destroys us, body and mind and soul. ("Don't Drop the Ball," *Ensign,* November 1994, p. 48.)

Stay away from pornography! Avoid it as you would a terrible disease. It is a consuming disease. It is addictive. It gets hold of men and grasps them until they can scarcely let go. . . . These magazines, these video tapes, these late-night programs, you don't need them. They will just hurt you, they won't help you. They will destroy you, if you persist in looking at them. (Heber City/Springville Utah Regional Conference, priesthood leadership session, May 13, 1995.)

Recognize pornography for what it is—a vicious brew of slime and sleaze, the partaking of which only leads to misery, degradation, and regret. This Church expects you who have taken upon yourselves the name of the Lord Jesus Christ to walk in the sunlight of virtue and enjoy the strength, the freedom, the lift that comes from so doing. ("To a Man Who Has Done What This Church Expects of Each of Us," *BYU 1995–96 Speeches,* October 17, 1995, p. 53.)

You don't have to read sleazy literature of any kind. It will not help you. It will only injure you. Years ago I had responsibility for our work in Asia. I visited Okinawa many times when there were American servicemen stationed there in large numbers. Some of them had cars, and I noted that most of those cars were badly rusted. There were holes in the fenders. There were holes in the side panels. Whatever paint was left was dull. All of this was the result of corrosive ocean salt which was carried by the wind and which ate through the metal. That is the way pornography is. This sleazy filth is like corrosive salt. It will eat through your armor if you expose yourselves to it.

I cannot emphasize this too strongly. The makers and marketers of this slimy stuff grow wealthy while the character of their customers decays. Stay away from it. Stand above it. It becomes addictive. It will destroy those who become its slaves. ("True to the Faith," Salt Lake Valley-Wide Institute Fireside, January 21, 1996.)

Pornography is everywhere. According to *U. S. News and World Report,* Los Angeles has become the pornography capital of the world. They spin the stuff out of there and grow rich in the process while they impoverish and destroy those who become its users. You as faithful members of the Church are not immune to this. This material is titillating, it is made to look attractive. But leave it alone! Get away from it! Avoid it! It is sleazy filth. It is rot that will do no good. You cannot afford to watch videotapes of this kind of trash. You cannot afford to read magazines that are designed to destroy you. Avoid pornography like the plague. It is just as deadly, perhaps even more so. The plague will destroy the body. Pornography will destroy the body and the soul. Stay away from it! It is a great disease that is sweeping over the country and over the entire world. Avoid it. I repeat, avoid it! (Jordan Utah South Regional Conference, priesthood leadership session, March 1, 1997.)

PRAYER

See also Family Prayer

Speak with your Eternal Father in the name of his Beloved Son. "Behold," he says, "I stand at the door, and knock; if any man hear my voice, and open the door, I will come in to him, and will sup with him, and he with me." (Rev. 3:20.)

This is his invitation, and the promise is sure. It is unlikely that you will hear voices from heaven, but there will come a heaven-sent assurance, peaceful and certain. (Conference Report, April 1966, p. 87.)

While speaking of prayers, may I express appreciation to the members of the Church throughout the world for your prayers in behalf of all of the General Authorities. We recognize the great and sacred trust reposed in us. We are aware of our inadequacies and of the need for divine help in carrying forward the great work that must be done if this cause is to roll on to its promised destiny. ("What This Work Is All About," *Ensign,* November 1982, p. 7.)

I remember being in Europe a number of years ago at the time tanks were rolling down the streets of a great city, and students were being slaughtered with machine-gun fire. I stood that December day in the railroad station in Berne, Switzerland. At eleven o'clock in the morning, every church bell in Switzerland began to ring, and at the conclusion of that ringing, every vehicle stopped—every car on the highway, every bus, every railroad train. The great, cavernous railway station became deathly still. I looked out the front door across the plaza. Men working on the hotel opposite stood on the scaffolding with bared heads. Every bicycle stopped. Every man and woman and child dismounted and stood with bared, bowed heads. Then, after three minutes of prayerful silence, trucks, great convoys of them, began to roll from Geneva and Berne and Basel and Zurich toward the suffering nation to the east, laden with supplies—food, clothing, and medicine. The gates of Switzerland were thrown open to refugees.

As I stood there that December morning, I marveled at the miraculous contrast of the oppressive power mowing down students in one nation and the spirit of a Christian people in another who bowed their heads in prayer and reverence, then rolled up their sleeves to provide succor and salvation. ("'What Shall I Do Then with Jesus Which Is Called Christ?'" *Ensign,* December 1983, pp. 4–5.)

Twice blessed is the child who, while he or she is so young as perhaps to be unable to comprehend the words, can nevertheless feel the spirit of prayer as a loving mother or a kind father helps with a few words of prayer at bedtime. Fortunate, indeed, are the boys and girls, including those in their teens, in whose homes there is the practice of morning and evening family prayer.

I know of no better way to develop a spirit of appreciation in children than for all of the members of the family to kneel to thank the Lord for his blessings. Such humble expression will do wonders to build within the hearts of children a recognition of the fact that God is the source of the precious gifts we have.

I know of no better way to cultivate a desire to do what is right than to humbly ask for forgiveness from him whose right it is to forgive, and to ask for strength to live above weakness.

What a wonderful thing it is to remember before the Lord those who are sick and in sorrow, those who are hungry and destitute, those who are lonely and afraid, those who are in bondage and sore distress. When such prayers are uttered in sincerity, there will follow a greater desire to reach out to those in need.

There will be increased respect and love for the bishop, for the stake president, for the President of the Church when they are remembered in the prayers of the family.

It is a significant thing to teach children how to pray concerning their own needs and righteous desires. As members of the family kneel together in supplication to the Almighty and speak with him of their needs, there will distill into the hearts of children a natural inclination in times of distress and extremity to turn to God as their Father and their friend.

Let prayer, night and morning, as a family and as individuals, become a practice in which children grow while yet young. It will bless their lives forever. No parent in this Church can afford to neglect it. ("The Environment of Our Homes," *Ensign,* June 1985, p. 6.)

There is something in the very posture of kneeling that contradicts the attitudes described by Paul: "proud . . . heady, high-minded."

. . . There is something in the act of addressing Deity that offsets a tendency toward blasphemy and toward becoming lovers of pleasure more than lovers of God.

The inclination to be unholy, as Paul described it, to be unthankful, is erased as together family members thank the Lord for life and peace and all they have. ("The Blessings of Family Prayer," *Ensign,* February 1991, p. 4.)

I believe in prayer, that prayer which is the practice of those who have been called to leadership in this Church and which brings forth inspiration and revelation from God for the blessing of his church and people. I believe in prayer, the precious and wonderful privilege given each of us for our individual guidance, comfort, and peace. ("This I Believe," *BYU 1991–92 Devotional and Fireside Speeches,* March 1, 1992, p. 83.)

Of all the great and wonderful and inspiring promises I have read, the most reassuring to me are the words of the Savior: "Ask, and it shall be given you; seek, and ye shall find; knock, and it shall be opened unto you." (Matt. 7:7.) . . . Let us never forget to pray. God lives. He is near. He is real. He is our Father. He is accessible to us. ("Pillars of Truth," *Ensign,* January 1994, p. 2.)

I recall a story of a Latter-day Saint boy in military service. He was the only Latter-day Saint in his barracks, and he soon wearied of the jibes of his associates. One day when the going was particularly rough, he finally agreed to go into town with the crowd. But as they entered the town, there came before his mind's eye a picture. He saw the kitchen of his home. It was supper time. There was his family, kneeling at the kitchen chairs—his father, mother, two sisters, and a small brother. The little brother was praying, and he was asking our Heavenly Father to look after his brother in the military.

That mental picture did it. The young man turned away from the crowd. The prayer of that little brother, of that family, brought clarity of mind and courage to that Latter-day Saint youth. ("Pillars of Truth," *Ensign,* January 1994, p. 2.)

God, our Eternal Father, lives. He is the Creator and Ruler of the universe and yet He is our Father. He is the Almighty and is above all. He can be reached in prayer. . . . Does He hear a child's prayer? Of course He does. Does He answer it? Of course He does. Not always as we might wish, but He answers. He hears and answers. (Jackson Wyoming 1st, 2nd, and 3rd Wards Combined Sacrament Meeting, July 16, 1995.)

Brethren and sisters, I know that you are a praying people. That is a wonderful thing in this day and time when the practice of prayer has slipped from many lives. To call upon the Lord for wisdom beyond our own, for strength to do what we ought to do, for comfort and consolation, and for the expression of gratitude is a significant and wonderful thing. ("The Fabric of Faith and Testimony," *Ensign,* November 1995, p. 89.)

Be prayerful. You can't do it alone. You know that. You cannot make it alone and do your best. You need the help of the Lord . . . and the marvelous thing is that you have the opportunity to pray, with the expectation that your prayers will be heard and answered. . . . The marvelous thing about prayer is that it is personal, it's individual, it's something that no one else gets into, in terms of your speaking with your Father in Heaven in the name of the Lord Jesus Christ. Be prayerful. Ask the Lord to forgive your sins. As the Lord for help. Ask the Lord to bless you. Ask the Lord to help you realize your righteous ambitions. . . . Ask the Lord for all of the important things that mean so much to you in your lives. He stands ready to help. Don't ever forget it. (Colorado Springs Young Adult Meeting, April 14, 1996.)

I can call on the Lord for help as a leader in this Church. I know we do it, but we need to do it a little more earnestly.

Nothing helps so much as putting a matter in the hands of the Lord. . . . I don't hesitate to say that I have had prayers answered. I know that. I could not deny it. We need to pray for guidance in this difficult age. . . . Prayer is a marvelous and miraculous resource, the most marvelous and miraculous resource we have available to us. The marvelous thing is you don't have to be a genius to pray. He will listen to the voice of the most humble.

I always remember two young men who served in my mission. One was a superstar. He was educated. He was bright. He was quick. He was a little arrogant. We had another who was a sign painter. He came from a sign shop with very little education, but he knew his inadequacies and he relied on the Lord. When he prayed, you knew he was talking with the Lord. It wasn't a rote thing, it was a conversation and that young man accomplished wonders while the other young man went through the motions. The power that was in the one and the absence of power in the other was so apparent. Call upon the Lord. He has extended the invitation, and He will answer. (Smithfield/Logan Utah Regional Conference, priesthood leadership session, April 20, 1996.)

Believe in prayer and the power of prayer. Pray to the Lord with the expectation of answers. I suppose there is not a man or woman in this entire congregation today who doesn't pray. I hope that is so. The trouble with most of our prayers is that we give them as if we were picking up the telephone and ordering groceries—we place our order and hang up. We need to meditate, contemplate, think of what we are praying about and for and then speak to the Lord as one man speaketh to another. "Come now, and let us reason together, saith the Lord" (Isa. 1:18). That is the invitation. Believe in the power of prayer—it is real, it is wonderful, it is tremendous. (Smithfield/Logan Utah Regional Conference, April 21, 1996.)

Be prayerful. You won't make it on your own. You need the help of your Father in Heaven who loves you and wants you to succeed and be happy. (Smithfield/Logan Utah Regional Conference, April 21, 1996.)

Prayer unlocks the powers of heaven in our behalf. Prayer is the great gift which our Eternal Father has given us by which we may approach Him and speak with Him in the name of the Lord Jesus Christ. Be prayerful. You cannot make it alone. You cannot reach your potential alone. You need the help of the Lord. (Pittsburgh Pennsylvania Regional Conference, April 28, 1996.)

PREPAREDNESS, PERSONAL

"If ye are prepared ye shall not fear." (D&C 38:30.)

This brief statement is a promise wonderful and sure. It carries a message for all of us—for the youth who wonders about education, for the head of a household who has responsibility for a family, for the business or professional man, for the teacher or the speaker, for the church officer. All of us occasionally face responsibilities that bring with them a sense of fear. Where there is adequate preparation, there need be no fear. Such is the promise of the Lord. ("The Order and Will of God," *Ensign,* January 1989, p. 5.)

There are seasons in our lives, seasons when we can prepare and work, when the sun shines and the air is warm. And there are other seasons when the storms of life would beat upon us and destroy us if they could. Summer is the time for preparation against the harshness of winter. (Varsity Scouts, Arapahoe District, Denver Area Council, July 17, 1993.)

Bishop [James] Baker has told me that you have a theme that you are working on: "Prepare Ye the Way of the Lord," that great statement from Isaiah which was repeated by John the Baptist, "The voice of one crying in the wilderness, Prepare ye the way of the Lord, [and] make his paths straight" (Matt. 3:3). I would like to paraphrase that a little to this: Prepare ye to follow the way of the Lord. That is what this church is all about—to help us to prepare to follow the way of the Lord, to walk in obedience to His commandments, to get into our lives the spirit of His work, to come to know Him and to love Him, and to seek to do His will. Prepare ye to follow the way of the Lord. (Eagle Gate 7th Ward Sacrament Meeting, September 17, 1995.)

I hope you do the very best you can to prepare yourselves to make a significant contribution to the society of which you will become a part. Your knowledge, your integrity, your standards of workmanship and honesty as you live your future lives will reflect honor to the good name of this the Lord's church. ("True to the Faith," Salt Lake Valley-Wide Institute Fireside, January 21, 1996.)

I don't care what you plan to do as your life's vocation, but prepare yourselves. Get the best education you can. Qualify yourselves in the best way you know how. It's part of a mandate from the Lord that you train yourselves. (Colorado Springs Young Adult Meeting, April 14, 1996.)

Someday every one of you is going to have to defend this Church, to explain it to others. Now is the time to prepare, now is the time when you can remember things. When you get to be my age, what you hear goes in one ear and out the other. When you are young you can remember things. This is the great day of preparation in your lives, so that as the years pass you will remain steadfast and true and be happy. (Denver Colorado Willow Creek Youth Meeting, April 14, 1996.)

PRIESTHOOD

See also Church Government

Priesthood Keys

In that great and moving conversation between the Savior and his apostles, wherein Peter declared, "Thou art the Christ, the Son of the living God," and the Lord responded, "Blessed art thou, Simon Barjona: for flesh and blood hath not revealed it unto thee, but my Father which is in heaven." The Lord then went on to say to Peter and his associates, "And I will give unto thee the keys of the kingdom of heaven: and whatsoever thou shalt bind on earth shall be bound in heaven: and whatsoever thou shalt loose on earth shall be loosed in heaven." (Matt. 16:13–19.)

In that marvelous bestowal of authority the Lord gave to his apostles the keys of the holy priesthood, whose power reaches beyond life and death into eternity. This same authority has been restored to the earth by those same apostles who held it anciently, even Peter, James, and John. ("The Marriage That Endures," *Ensign*, May 1974, p. 23.)

We have been, this afternoon just before we came here, to the Church of the Apostles . . . where is found the original *Christus* statue by Thorvaldsen. It was the statue in this church here in Copenhagen which was copied in marble in Italy and which is on Temple Square in Salt Lake City. It is beautiful. . . . And then on either side of that beautiful chapel are the carved figures of the Apostles, [including] Peter, with the keys in his hand. I don't think the people who have responsibility for that church understand the significance of those keys, but for us they are real, they are genuine. . . . Those are the eternal keys of the priesthood which have been restored under the hands of Peter, James, and John, and also, Moses, Elias, and Elijah, the great keys of the dispensation of the fulness of times, the keys which have the fulness of the priesthood in them. They are the keys of the fulness of the priesthood as the Lord uses the word in the 124th section of the Doctrine and Covenants—those keys which are exercised in the House of the Lord. (Denmark Copenhagen Missionary Meeting, June 14, 1996.)

Priesthood Authority

The next phrase to which I bring your attention denotes the authority in which John spoke. Said he, "in the name of Messiah." None of us exercises this priesthood in the power or authority which we have naturally within ourselves. Always in the exercise of the priesthood we do it in the authority of Messiah. ("The Priesthood of Aaron," *Ensign*, November 1982, p. 45.)

[Priesthood] authority was given to men anciently, the lesser authority to the sons of Aaron to administer in things temporal as well as in some sacred ecclesiastical ordinances. The higher priesthood was given by the Lord himself to his Apostles. . . .

In its full restoration, it involved the coming of John the Baptist, the forerunner of Christ, whose head was taken to satisfy the whims of a wicked woman, and of Peter, James, and John, they who faithfully walked with the Master before his death and proclaimed his resurrection and divinity following his death. It involved Moses, Elias, and Elijah, each bringing priesthood keys to complete the work of restoring all of the acts and ordinances of previous dispensations in this the great, final dispensation of the fulness of times.

The priesthood is here. It has been conferred upon us. We act in that authority. We speak as sons of God in the name of Jesus Christ and as holders of this divinely given endowment. We know, for we have seen, the power of this priesthood. We have seen the sick healed, the lame made to walk, and the coming of light and knowledge and understanding to those who have been in darkness.

Paul wrote concerning the priesthood: "No man taketh this honour unto himself, but he that is called of God, as was Aaron." (Heb. 5:4.) We have not acquired it through purchase or bargain. The Lord has given it to men who are considered worthy to receive it, regardless of station in life, the color of their skin, or the nation in which they live. It is the power and the authority to govern in the affairs of the kingdom of God. It is given only by ordination by the laying on of hands by those in authority to do so. The qualification for eligibility is obedience to the commandments of God.

There is no power on the earth like it. Its authority extends beyond life, through the veil of death, to the eternities ahead. It is everlasting in its consequences. ("The Cornerstones of Our Faith," *Ensign*, November 1984, pp. 52–53.)

What is this remarkable gift and power which has come to us with no price other than our personal worthiness? The Prophet Joseph Smith described it on one occasion in these words: "The Priesthood is an everlasting principle, and existed with God from eternity, without beginning of days or end of years" (*History of the Church*, 3:386).

It is veritably the power of the Almighty given to man to act in His name and in His stead. It is a delegation of divine authority, different from all other powers and authorities on the face of the earth. It was restored to man by resurrected beings who held it anciently. There can be no question concerning its authority and validity. Without it there could be a church in name only, lacking authority to administer in the things of God. With it, nothing is impossible in carrying forward the work of the kingdom of God. It is divine in its nature. It is both temporal and eternal in its authority. It is the only power on the earth which reaches beyond the veil of death. . . .

It includes the right to receive the things of God. It carries the responsibility to instruct. It holds the authority to govern. It grants the power to bless. (Priesthood Restoration Commemoration Fireside, May 15, 1988.)

Without the priesthood there might be the form of a church, but not the true substance. ("Priesthood Restoration," *Ensign*, October 1988, p. 72.)

I thank my Eternal Father for the restoration of the holy priesthood, that "every man might speak in the name of God the Lord, even the Savior of the world" (D&C 1:20). I have seen the beauty and wonder of that priesthood in the governance of this remarkable church. I have felt its power flow through me to the blessing and the healing of the sick. I have seen the ennoblement it has given to humble men who have been called to great and serious responsibility. I have seen it as they have spoken with power and authority from on high as if the voice of God were speaking through them. ("My Testimony," *Ensign*, November 1993, p. 52.)

I hope every man in this congregation is trying a little harder to live worthy of the marvelous gift which he has in holding the Priesthood after the Order of the Son of God, the holy Melchizedek Priesthood which carries with it the power to bless and the power to govern in the affairs of the kingdom of God. (Boston Massachusetts Regional Conference, April 23, 1995.)

God has blessed us, above all other people who have gone before us, with light and knowledge, with truth and understanding. We are a royal priesthood. Every worthy man in this Church is eligible to receive the priesthood of God, but his life must be in harmony with the principles of the gospel. The Lord has said that one of His purposes in restoring the gospel was so that every man might speak in the name of God the Lord, even the Savior of the world. We are, in very deed, a royal priesthood. We do not receive the priesthood on the basis of wealth or standing in the community. We receive it on the basis of personal worthiness, and every man is a potential priesthood holder. If there is any man here tonight who does not hold the priesthood of God, let him from this day forward put his life in order, live up to the high standards of the gospel, and make himself worthy to receive His royal priesthood, to act in the name of God, to speak in His holy name in accomplishing His great and singular purposes. (Buenos Aires Argentina Fireside, November 12, 1996.)

Sealing Power

I never confer the sealing authority upon a good man that I do not think of the profound importance of that priesthood power. It is the only authority on the entire earth which reaches beyond the veil of death. It is divine in its nature. It is eternal in its consequences. It is a part of the plan of God our Eternal Father to bless the lives of His sons and daughters of all generations. (Temple Presidents Seminar, August 23, 1988.)

In its ultimate expression the holy priesthood carries with it the authority to seal on the earth and have that sealing effective in the heavens. It is unique and wonderful. It is the authority exercised in the temples of God. It concerns both the living and the dead. It is of the very essence of eternity. It is divine power bestowed by the Almighty as a part of His great plan for the immortality and eternal life of man. ("Priesthood Restoration," *Ensign*, October 1988, p. 72.)

I thank him and love him [Joseph Smith] for the sealing power of the holy priesthood that makes possible and certain the continuance of the family through eternity. I have said many times that if nothing else came out of all of the sorrow and travail and pain of the restoration than the sealing power of the holy priesthood to bind together families forever, it would have been worth all that it has cost. ("As One Who Loves the Prophet," Symposium on the Life and Ministry of the Prophet Joseph Smith, BYU, February 22, 1992.)

I conferred the sealing power on a man Friday. I never do that but I do not think of the wonderful authority that is there conferred. There is nothing else like it. It is the only power on the earth that reaches beyond the veil of death. It comes of that act and promise which the Lord Himself gave to His chosen Apostles when he said, "And I will give unto thee the keys of the kingdom of heaven: and whatsoever thou shalt bind on earth shall be bound in heaven" (Matt. 16:19). And we, as mortal men, those who are qualified to seal in the house of the Lord, have that marvelous and remarkable and unique authority to reach beyond the veil of death in a work that is efficacious there just as surely as it is efficacious here. This is one of the great signs of the divinity of this work. (Salt Lake Temple Workers Devotional, June 11, 1995.)

Priesthood Responsibility
See also Home Teaching

The time has come for all of us who have been ordained to either the Aaronic or the Melchizedek Priesthood, and to any of the offices therein, to reflect upon our lives, to assess our shortcomings, and to repent of those matters of conduct which are at variance with the high and holy commission we have received. . . .

No man, young or old . . . who has been . . . ordained, can regard lightly that which he holds. He is in partnership with God and has resting upon him a solid and sacred obligation so to live as one worthy to speak and act in the name of God as his qualified representative. ("Priesthood Restoration Honored," *Ensign*, July 1983, p. 76.)

The priesthood is not a passive thing. It is an active power. It is ours to enjoy to exercise for the blessing of others, to magnify by the manner of our lives, and to advance the cause of the

Almighty. No man is entitled to feel that he is magnifying his priesthood who is dishonest, who cheats or lies or steals. No boy is honoring his priesthood if he is immoral, or if he abuses his body which is the temple of his spirit, by the use of tobacco or liquor or those drugs which are forbidden by the law. ("Priesthood Restoration Honored," *Ensign,* July 1983, p. 76.)

No man, be he youth or elder, is living up to the standards of the priesthood who demeans or degrades womanhood, who fails to accord that measure of respect to the daughters of God which our Father in heaven would have them receive. No man or boy can truly regard himself as worthy of this great and holy power, this bestowal of authority to act for God in his behalf, who takes unrighteous advantage of another, or who would take from another his good name by the spreading of vicious gossip or rumor, or who fails to reach out a helping hand to those in distress. ("Priesthood Restoration Honored," *Ensign,* July 1983, p. 76.)

Brethren, the war goes on. It is as it was in the beginning. . . . The victims who fall are as precious as those who have fallen in the past. It is an ongoing battle. We of the priesthood are all part of the army of the Lord. We must be united. An army that is disorganized will not be victorious. It is imperative that we close ranks, that we march together as one. We cannot have division among us and expect victory. We cannot have disloyalty and expect unity. We cannot be unclean and expect the help of the Almighty.

You boys who are here, you deacons, teachers, and priests, are all a part of this. The Lord has laid upon you in your priesthood offices the duty to preach the gospel, to teach the truth, to encourage the weak to be strong, to "invite all to come unto Christ" (D&C 20:59).

You cannot afford to partake of things that will weaken your minds and your bodies. These include cocaine, "crack," alcohol, tobacco. You cannot be involved in immoral activity. You cannot do these things and be valiant as warriors in the cause of the Lord in the great, everlasting contest that goes on for the souls of our Father's children.

You men of the Melchizedek Priesthood, you cannot be unfaithful or untrue to your wives, to your families, to your priesthood responsibilities if you are to be valiant in moving the work of the Lord forward in this great battle for truth and salvation. You cannot be dishonest and unscrupulous in your business affairs without tarnishing your armor. ("The War We Are Winning," *Ensign,* November 1986, p. 44.)

To every officer, to every teacher in this Church who acts in a priesthood office, there comes the sacred responsibility of magnifying that priesthood calling. Each of us is responsible for the welfare and the growth and development of others. We do not live only unto ourselves. If we are to magnify our callings, we cannot live only unto ourselves. As we serve with diligence, as we teach with faith and testimony, as we lift and strengthen and build convictions of righteousness in those whose lives we touch, we magnify our priesthood. To live only unto ourselves, on the other hand, to serve grudgingly, to give less than our best effort to our duty, diminishes our priesthood just as looking through the wrong lenses of binoculars reduces the image and makes more distant the object. . . .

We magnify our priesthood and enlarge our calling when we serve with diligence and enthusiasm in those responsibilities to which we are called by proper authority. I emphasize the words, "diligence and enthusiasm." This work has not reached its present stature through indifference on the part of those who have labored in its behalf. The Lord needs men, both young and old, who will carry the banners of His kingdom with positive strength and determined purpose. . . .

We magnify our calling, we enlarge the potential of our priesthood when we reach out to those in distress and give strength to those who falter. ("Magnify Your Calling," *Ensign,* May 1989, pp. 47–49.)

There is upon the earth at this time the very power to act in the name of God. And every man who has been ordained an elder in this Church has received that divine authority. I hope, my brethren, I hope with all my heart, that you are the kind of men you ought to be to hold the priesthood of God. There is no room in your lives for pornography, for immorality, for anything of that kind. Get it out of your lives. Get rid of it. Don't let it be a part of you. Are you the kind of a man who is kind and gracious to your wife? You are a part of a royal priesthood. You need to live that part at all times and in all circumstances. Don't abuse your children. Don't beat them. Don't whip them. Rear them in love and they will return that love to you. You are a royal priesthood. (Miami Florida Fireside, November 17, 1996.)

Priesthood Blessings
See also Patriarchal Blessings

I stand reverently before a father who in the authority of the holy priesthood lays his hands upon the head of a son or daughter at a time of serious decision and in the name of the Lord and under the direction of the Holy Spirit gives a father's blessing. ("'Behold Your Little Ones,'" *Ensign*, November 1978, p. 20.)

We in the Church recognize that the fulfillment of all blessings given under authority of the priesthood is conditioned upon two things: one, the worthiness and faithfulness of the recipient, and, two, the overriding will and wisdom of God. ("The Joseph Smith III Document and the Keys of the Kingdom," *Ensign*, May 1981, p. 20.)

The priesthood includes the power to bless the sick. Is there anyone within my hearing who has not exercised or felt that divine power? Can any of us have any doubt concerning its efficacy? We could tell of miracles, sacred and wonderful, that we have witnessed within our own experience. Declared James of old: "Is any sick among you? let him call for the elders of the church; and let them pray over him, anointing him with oil in the name of the Lord: And the prayer of faith shall save the sick, and the Lord shall raise him up" (James 5:14–15). (Priesthood Restoration Commemoration Fireside, May 15, 1988.)

That power to heal the sick is still among us. It is the power of the priesthood of God. It is the authority held by the elders of this Church.

We welcome and praise and utilize the marvelous procedures of modern medicine which have done so much to alleviate human suffering and lengthen human life. All of us are
indebted to the dedicated men and women of science and medicine who have conquered so much of disease, who have mitigated pain, who have stayed the hand of death. I cannot say
enough of gratitude for them.

Yet they are the first to admit the limitations of their knowledge and the imperfection of their skills in dealing with many
matters of life and death. The mighty Creator of the heavens and
the earth and all that in them are has given to His servants a
divine power that sometimes transcends all the powers and
knowledge of men. I venture to say that there is scarcely a faithful elder within the sound of my voice who could not recount
instances in which this healing power has been made manifest
in behalf of the sick. It is the healing power of Christ. ("The
Healing Power of Christ," *Ensign,* November 1988, p. 54.)

I want to speak a little about blessing the people, placing our
hands upon their heads and blessing them. Brethren, how great
is our opportunity, how tremendous our responsibility, to live
worthy to be, as it were, a conduit between the powers of heaven
and those upon the earth on whose heads we lay our hands. I
suppose every man here who holds the Melchizedek Priesthood
has had the opportunity to bless. And I suppose that, when
called on to do so, he has prayed within his heart that he might
be a worthy instrument to bestow a blessing upon the heads of
those who come in faith. Bless the people when you set them
apart and under other circumstances, in times of sickness. You
fathers bless your children. Lay your hands upon their heads
and bless them. You cannot do a greater thing for them. My
eldest daughter is now a woman in her fifties. She was recently
appointed to a very responsible position. She was the only
woman in a large organization, all of the other directors were
men, and they had elected her as chairman of that body. She
called me and said, as she had said when she was a little girl,
"Will you give me a blessing?" I want to say that it was a very
touching and emotional experience for me. Her husband could
have given her a blessing. He's a good bishop. Maybe he had.

But she called her father and asked if he would give her a blessing. And when I was through and she stood, and we embraced one another, the tears were rolling down her cheeks and they were rolling down mine. Oh, brethren, what a marvelous thing it is that the Almighty has given us, the power and the opportunity to bless those whom we love. And how important that we live in such a way as to be worthy of the use of that power. Bless those you love. (Berlin Germany Regional Conference, priesthood leadership session, June 15, 1996.)

Aaronic Priesthood

I should like to tell you of three eighteen-year-old boys. In 1856 more than a thousand of our people, some of them perhaps your forebears, found themselves in serious trouble while crossing the plains to this valley. Because of a series of unfortunate circumstances, they were late in getting started. They ran into snow and bitter cold in the highlands of Wyoming. Their situation was desperate, with deaths occurring every day.

President Young learned of their condition as the October general conference was about to begin. He immediately called for teams, wagons, drivers, and supplies to leave to rescue the bereft Saints. When the rescue team reached the Martin Company, there were too few wagons to carry the suffering people. The rescuers had to insist that the carts keep moving.

When they reached the Sweetwater River on November 3, chunks of ice were floating in the freezing water. After all these people had been through, and in their weakened condition, that river seemed impossible to cross. It looked like stepping into death itself to move into the freezing stream. Men who once had been strong sat on the frozen ground and wept, as did the women and children. Many simply could not face that ordeal.

And now I quote from the record: "Three eighteen-year-old boys belonging to the relief party came to the rescue, and to the astonishment of all who saw, carried nearly every member of the ill-fated handcart company across the snowbound stream. The strain was so terrible, and the exposure so great, that in later years all the boys died from the effects of it. When President Brigham Young heard of this heroic act, he wept like a child, and later declared publicly, 'that act alone will ensure C. Allen

Huntington, George W. Grant, and David P. Kimball an ever-lasting salvation in the Celestial Kingdom of God, worlds without end.'" (Solomon F. Kimball, *Improvement Era*, Feb. 1914, p. 288.)

Mark you, these boys were eighteen years of age at the time. And, because of the program then in effect, they likely were holders of the Aaronic Priesthood. Great was their heroism, sacred the sacrifice they made of health and eventually of life itself to save the lives of those they helped.

They are part of the heritage that lies behind you of the Aaronic Priesthood. Be true, my young brethren, to that great inheritance. ("Four B's for Boys," *Ensign*, November 1981, p. 42.)

Have you ever realized that in the holding and exercise of this priesthood you are a fellow servant with John the Baptist, the very man who, while he was alive, baptized Jesus, the Savior of the world and the Son of God, in the waters of the River Jordan? It is interesting to me that John spoke to Joseph and Oliver, when they were both young men and when they were not highly regarded by people of the world, as his fellow servants. He did not speak down to them as a king might speak to one of his subjects. He did not speak down to them as a judge might speak to an individual on trial before him. He did not speak down to them as a university president or a high school principal might speak to his students. Rather, he who was a resurrected being addressed these young men as his fellow servants. To me there is something wonderful in this. It speaks of the true spirit of the great and magnificent brotherhood of which we are all a part, the priesthood of God. We are all servants together, regardless of our position in the Church or in the world, regardless of wealth or lack of it, regardless of the color of our skin—we are all servants together. . . .

That should mean something to each of us. It does not demean us or put us down in any way. It elevates all of us as fellow servants of the Lord in the responsibility of carrying on the work of the ministry in his Church. ("The Priesthood of Aaron," *Ensign*, November 1982, pp. 44–45.)

Then John the Baptist, in his bestowal of this authority, spoke concerning the powers of this priesthood. He said, among other things, that it "holds the keys of the ministering of angels."

When Wilford Woodruff, a man who had lived many years and had many experiences, was the President of the Church, he said to the boys of the Aaronic Priesthood: "I desire to impress upon you the fact that it does not make any difference whether a man is a Priest or an Apostle, if he magnifies his calling. A Priest holds the keys of the ministering of angels," said he. "Never in my life, as an Apostle, as a Seventy, or as an Elder, have I ever had more of the protection of the Lord than while holding the office of a Priest." (*Millennial Star*, 53:629.)

Think of it, my dear young brethren. This priesthood which you hold carries with it the keys of the ministering of angels. That means, as I interpret it, that if you live worthy of the priesthood, you have the right to receive and enjoy the very power of heavenly beings to guide you, to protect you, to bless you. What boy, if he is thoughtful, would not welcome this remarkable blessing? ("The Priesthood of Aaron," *Ensign*, November 1982, p. 45.)

The occasion was a Sunday afternoon, on February 28, 1897. The place was this Tabernacle. It was in commemoration of President Woodruff's ninetieth birthday. This great building was filled to capacity with all seats occupied and the aisles packed in every part of the building, such as we are not permitted to do now. It is estimated there were more than ten thousand young people present—a vast congregation of young men your age and young women of the same age. President Woodruff, who was then weak in body and whose voice was not strong, stood at the pulpit where I stand and said, particularly to the young men present, these words:

"I have passed through the periods of boyhood, early manhood and old age. I cannot expect to tarry a great while longer with you, but I want to give you a few words of counsel. You occupy a position in the Church and Kingdom of God and have received the power of the holy priesthood. The God of heaven has appointed you and called you forth in this day and generation. I want you to look at this. Young men listen to the counsel of your brethren. Live near to God; pray while young; learn to pray; learn to cultivate the Holy Spirit of God; link it to you and it will become a spirit of revelation unto you, inasmuch as you nourish it. . . ."

He went on to say: "God in heaven has willed to spare me to see this day. He has given me power to reject every testimony and reject every example that leads to evil. I say to you . . . do not use tobacco, liquor, or any of these things that destroy the body and mind, but honor Him and you will have a mission upon your heads that the world knows not of. May God bless you. Amen." (*Wilford Woodruff: Fourth President of The Church of Jesus Christ of Latter-day Saints,* prepared for publication by Matthias F. Cowley, Salt Lake City: Deseret News, 1909, pp. 602–3.)

I echo that great counsel of President Wilford Woodruff as I testify to you young men this night that God our Eternal Father lives and that Jesus Christ is his Beloved Son. . . .

God bless the young men of the Aaronic Priesthood, that they may walk in the dignity of the sacred and marvelous calling and authority that has been conferred upon them through the mercy and goodness of the God of heaven. ("The Priesthood of Aaron," *Ensign,* November 1982, pp. 46–47.)

The young men of the Aaronic Priesthood should be trained to know that the sacrament which they administer is sacred and holy unto the Lord. Encouragement and training should be given to see that the prayers are spoken plainly and in a spirit of communion with our Father in Heaven. The priest at the sacrament table places all in the congregation under sacred covenant. The offering of the prayer is not a ritual to be thoughtlessly spoken. It is, rather, the voicing of an obligation and a promise. Cleanliness of hands, as well as purity of heart, should be taught to the priests who officiate at the sacrament table. ("Reverence and Morality," *Ensign,* May 1987, p. 46.)

When you, as a priest, kneel at the sacrament table and offer up the prayer, which came by revelation, you place the entire congregation under covenant with the Lord. Is this a small thing?

It is a most important and remarkable thing. ("The Aaronic Priesthood—a Gift from God," *Ensign*, May 1988, p. 46.)

This Aaronic Priesthood, bestowed by John the Baptist, also includes the keys of baptism by immersion for the remission of sins. It is one thing to repent. It is another to have our sins remitted or forgiven. The power to bring this about is found in the Aaronic Priesthood. ("The Aaronic Priesthood—a Gift from God," *Ensign*, May 1988, p. 46.)

In the large ward in which I grew up, there were five quorums of deacons. Each was presided over by a presidency of three boys. My first responsibility in the Church, the first office I ever held, was counselor to the boy who presided over our deacons quorum. Our good bishop called me in and talked with me about this calling. I was tremendously impressed. I was worried and concerned. I was by nature, believe it or not, a rather shy and backward boy, and I think this call to serve as a counselor in a deacons quorum was of as much concern to me, in terms of my age and experience, as is my present responsibility in terms of my age and experience. ("'In . . . Counsellors There Is Safety,'" *Ensign*, November 1990, p. 49.)

You young men, you *are* a royal priesthood. Do you ever pause to think of the wonder of it? You have had hands placed upon your heads to receive that same priesthood exercised by John who baptized Jesus of Nazareth. With worthiness in your lives, you may enjoy the comforting, protecting, guiding influence of ministering angels. No individual of earthly royalty has a blessing as great. Live for it. Be worthy of it, is my plea to each of you. ("'A Chosen Generation,'" *Ensign*, May 1992, pp. 70–71.)

Melchizedek Priesthood

The Melchizedek Priesthood carries with it the authority to bestow the Holy Ghost. How great a blessing it is to have the ministering influence of a member of the Godhead, having received that gift under the hands of those who acted with divine authority. (Priesthood Restoration Commemoration Fireside, May 15, 1988.)

This holy Melchizedek Priesthood carries with it the power to bless with prophecy, to comfort, to sustain, to direct. We have patriarchs in our midst who, under the authority that they hold, declare lineage and pronounce blessings for our guidance. These blessings may become as an anchor to which we may hold to keep us steady through the storms of life. ("Priesthood Restoration," *Ensign*, October 1988, p. 72.)

I thank him [Joseph Smith] for the Melchizedek Priesthood with all of its powers, keys, and authority. It is the divine power of the Almighty conferred upon man to act in His name and in His stead. It is efficacious in life, and its authority reaches beyond the veil of death. It is the only power on the earth that may be exercised by man to seal and bind for eternity as well as for time. How remarkable and precious a boon it is. ("As One Who Loves the Prophet," Symposium on the Life and Ministry of the Prophet Joseph Smith, BYU, February 22, 1992.)

How magnificent a figure, how royal a character is a man who has been ordained to that priesthood which is called Melchizedek after the great high priest of Salem, who walks with dignity and yet with humility before his God, who lives with respect and appreciation for his associates, who turns his back upon the temptations of the adversary, who becomes a true patriarch in his home, a man of kindness and love, who recognizes his wife as his companion and a daughter of God, and his children as those for whom he has a God-given responsibility to nurture and lead in righteousness and truth. Such a man need never hang his head in shame. He lives without regret. Men may speak of him as they will, but he knows that God knows his heart and that it is pure and unsullied. ("Only upon Principles of Righteousness," Priesthood Restoration Commemoration Fireside, May 3, 1992.)

What a marvelous blessing that every man who holds the Melchizedek Priesthood can lay his hands upon the heads of his wife and his children when they need a blessing. And to the women I wish to say this: Great is your blessing in the priesthood which your husbands hold. Every man who lives and honors the priesthood will be a better husband, will be a better father, will be a better man. How wonderful that in the restoration of the work of the Lord, one of the great purposes was that every man might speak in the name of God the Lord, even the Savior of the world. (Pusan Korea Fireside, May 21, 1996.)

"A royal priesthood." That's a very descriptive term. This is the priesthood of the King of kings, it is a royal priesthood of the Lord Jesus Christ, it is the priesthood after the order of the Son of God, called Melchizedek to avoid the too frequent use of His name, but it is His priesthood. It is the power by which the earth was formed and it has been bestowed upon us, brethren. Are we worthy of it? (Copenhagen Denmark Fireside, June 14, 1996.)

Priesthood Quorums

I should like to tell you of an experience I had many years ago while serving as a stake president. I received a telephone call from a bishop who reported that a husband and wife in his ward were seeking a divorce. Having gone beyond all limits of prudence in installment buying, they now argued endlessly over money matters.

The husband in his employment faced the constant threat of garnishment of wages, and the wife refused to remain at home because of the harassment of bill collectors. Furthermore, they soon would be without a home because they had received notice of foreclosure. In their mutual frustration, he shouted at her for being a poor manager, and she at him for being a poor provider.

The bishop reported that he had taken care of their emergency needs, and that he had counseled with them at length in an effort to restore the love and respect they once had known. He had reached the point where he felt he had done all he could to help them.

I asked whether the man belonged to a priesthood quorum. The bishop replied that he was an elder. That evening the quorum presidency responded to a call to meet with the bishop. On a confidential basis the problem was outlined. Then the quorum presidency suggested the names of a committee who might work with the family. As I recall, the committee included a lawyer, a credit manager, and an accountant, all members of that quorum.

The couple was then called in and asked whether they would be willing to put their financial affairs in the hands of these brethren. They broke into tears at this sign of help with the burden they had found too heavy to bear themselves.

The men nominated for the committee were then approached and each agreed to serve. What they discovered was a dismal picture indeed. Obligated monthly payments totaled almost twice the monthly income. But these men were accustomed to dealing with problems of this kind. They analyzed the situation thoroughly.

They found, for instance, two cars where one could do at the price of a little inconvenience. There were other things that could be dispensed with.

Then, with the facts before them, they called on the various creditors. They did what the beleaguered husband could not do for himself. They spoke the language of the creditors, and worked out a plan of payment with each. They gave the creditors the assurance that they had control of the assets of the family, and with this assurance and the evident expertise of the committee, the creditors were willing to go along.

While in the process of managing the family's affairs, the committee effectively taught principles of budgeting, financial responsibility, and money management. The problem was not cured in a day. It required many months. But miracles happened. A new and satisfying discipline came into the lives of the husband and wife. The creditors received their just due. The home was saved, and—most important—love and peace returned to that home.

I have recalled this experience to emphasize a principle. That principle was defined by President J. Reuben Clark many years ago:

"The priesthood quorums in their extending of relief have not the obligation prescribed to the bishop. But the relationship of the priesthood, [and] the spirit of lofty unselfish brotherhood which it carries with it, do require that they individually and as quorums exert their utmost means of power to rehabilitate, spiritually and temporally, their erring and unfortunate brethren. . . ." (J. Reuben Clark, Jr., "Bishops and Relief Society," July 9, 1941, pp. 17–18.) . . .

I am satisfied, my brethren, that there is enough of expertise, of knowledge, of strength, of concern in every priesthood quorum to assist the troubled members of that quorum if these resources are properly administered. ("Welfare Responsibilities of the Priesthood Quorums," *Ensign*, November 1977, pp. 84–86.)

It was Kuan Tzu, a Chinese philosopher, who said, "If you give a man a fish, he will have a single meal; if you teach him how to fish, he will eat all his life." This, as I see it, illustrates the principle of Welfare Services. It is the responsibility of the bishop to give emergency help to see that neither the individual nor his family suffers. It is the obligation of the priesthood quorum to set in motion those forces and facilities which will equip the needy member to provide on a continuing basis for himself and his family.

In the words of President Harold B. Lee, spoken many years ago, "All priesthood quorums are 'commanded' [by the Lord] to marshall their forces and, under the spirit and power of the Priesthood, to see to it that every person who is in distress is assisted by his quorum to become self-sustaining." (*Improvement Era*, October 1937, p. 634.)

I am confident that the Lord intended that a priesthood quorum should be far more than a class in theology on Sunday mornings. Of course, the building of spirituality and the strengthening of testimony through effective gospel teaching is an important priesthood responsibility. But this is only a segment of the quorum function. Each quorum must be a working brotherhood for every member if its purpose is to be realized. ("Welfare Responsibilities of the Priesthood Quorums," *Ensign*, November 1977, p. 86.)

I recall a quorum officer in our stake who was an employee of a businessman who was a member of that quorum. The businessman was the quorum president's employer for forty hours a week. It was this same quorum president who called on and assigned the businessman, his boss, to go to the stake farm at five o'clock in the morning to hoe beets. And be it said to the credit of both that each respected the other in his position. They were working brothers in a great fraternity. ("Welfare Responsibilities of the Priesthood Quorums," *Ensign*, November 1977, p. 86.)

It will be a marvelous day, my brethren—it will be a day of fulfillment of the purposes of the Lord—when our priesthood quorums become an anchor of strength to every man belonging thereto, when each such man may appropriately be able to say, "I am a member of a priesthood quorum of The Church of Jesus Christ of Latter-day Saints. I stand ready to assist my brethren in all of their needs, as I am confident they stand ready to assist me in mine. Working together, we shall grow spiritually as covenant sons of God. Working together, we can stand, without embarrassment and without fear, against every wind of adversity that might blow, be it economic, social, or spiritual." ("Welfare Responsibilities of the Priesthood Quorums," *Ensign*, November 1977, p. 86.)

Brethren, you who hold the priesthood in this great kingdom, I know of no better place to find fellowship and good friends than among the quorums of the Church. Where on earth should there be a better association than in a quorum, each of whose members is ordained to act in the name of the Lord, dedicated to help one another, and whose officers are set apart to this purpose under divine authority?

Brethren, the quorums of the Church need your talents, your loyalty, your devotion; and each man needs the fellowship and blessings that come of quorum activity in the kingdom of God. ("Pillars of Truth," *Ensign*, January 1994, p. 4.)

PRIESTHOOD, REVELATION ON

In a revelation given in 1831, which has become Section 1 of the Doctrine and Covenants and is known as the preface to that book of revelation, the Lord set forth one of the great purposes for the restoration of the gospel in this the dispensation of the fulness of times. He said that, among other reasons, the gospel was restored so that "every man might speak in the name of God the Lord, even the Savior of the world." (V. 20.)

It does not say that every man *shall* speak in the name of God the Lord. The meaning is that every man *may* speak, provided he is worthy and receives the priesthood.

But for many years during the history of the Church, the priesthood was withheld from many worthy men because of their lineage. Then, in June of 1978, a remarkable and wonderful thing occurred. The president of the Church, the prophet of the Lord at the time, Spencer W. Kimball, announced a revelation under which *every* worthy man could, under proper circumstances, receive the eternal priesthood with authority to act in the name of God.

I was not present when John the Baptist conferred the Aaronic Priesthood. I was not present when Peter, James, and John conferred the Melchizedek Priesthood. But I was present and was a participant and a witness to what occurred on Thursday, June 1, 1978. My memory is clear concerning the events of that day. . . .

Each first Thursday of the month is a day for fasting and the bearing of testimony by the General Authorities of the Church. So many of the Brethren are absent from home on the first Sunday of the month because of assignments to stake conferences that we hold our monthly testimony meeting in an upper room of the Salt Lake Temple the first Thursday of the month. The Thursday of which I speak was June 1, 1978. We heard testimonies from some of the brethren, and we partook of the sacrament of the Lord's Supper.

It was a wonderfully spiritual meeting, as are all such meetings in these holy precincts and under these circumstances. Then the members of the First Quorum of the Seventy and the Presiding Bishopric were excused, while there remained the president of the Church, his two Counselors, and ten members of the Council of the Twelve—two being absent, one in South America and the other in the hospital.

The question of extending the blessings of the priesthood to blacks had been on the minds of many of the Brethren over a period of years. It had repeatedly been brought up by Presidents of the Church. It had become a matter of particular concern to President Spencer W. Kimball.

Over a considerable period of time he had prayed concerning this serious and difficult question. He had spent many hours in that upper room in the temple by himself in prayer and meditation.

On this occasion he raised the question before his Brethren—his counselors and the Apostles. Following this discussion we joined in prayer in the most sacred of circumstances. President Kimball himself was voice in that prayer. I do not recall the exact words that he spoke. But I do recall my own feelings and the nature of the expressions of my Brethren. There was a hallowed and sanctified atmosphere in the room. For me, it felt as if a conduit opened between the heavenly throne and the kneeling, pleading prophet of God who was joined by his Brethren. The Spirit of God was there. And by the power of the Holy Ghost there came to that prophet an assurance that the thing for which he prayed was right, that the time had come, and that now the wondrous blessings of the priesthood should be extended to worthy men everywhere regardless of lineage.

Every man in that circle, by the power of the Holy Ghost, knew the same thing.

It was a quiet and sublime occasion.

There was not the sound "as of a rushing mighty wind," there were not "cloven tongues like as of fire" (Acts 2:2–3) as there had been on the Day of Pentecost. But there was a Pentecostal spirit, for the Holy Ghost was there.

No voice audible to our physical ears was heard. But the voice of the Spirit whispered with a certainty into our minds and our very souls.

It was for us, at least for me personally, as I imagine it was with Enos, who said concerning his remarkable experience, "And while I was thus struggling in the spirit, behold, the voice of the Lord came into my mind." (Enos 1:10.)

So it was on that memorable June 1, 1978. We left that meeting subdued and reverent and joyful. Not one of us who was present on that occasion was ever quite the same after that. Nor has the Church been quite the same. ("Priesthood Restoration," *Ensign,* October 1988, pp. 69–70.)

PRIORITIES

See also Balance

Let the pulpits of all churches ring with righteousness. Let people everywhere bow in reverence before the Almighty who is our one true strength. Let us look inward and adjust our priorities and standards. Let us look outward in the spirit of the Golden Rule. If we will do so in significant numbers across the land, something marvelous will begin to happen. (Freedom Festival Address, Provo, Utah, June 26, 1988.)

Safeguard against abuse, keep out of your homes the filthiness of the world which can lead to such abuse, cultivate the good and the beautiful, the uplifting and the ennobling, those refining and divine elements which in the last analysis become the essential difference between man and the animals. If these elements are neglected in the search for dollars, then the homes of the people, and also the nation of which they are the foundation, will be poor indeed. (Belle S. Spafford Conference on Women, February 23, 1990.)

I remember when the New Zealand Temple was dedicated. I attended a testimony meeting of some of the Saints who had come from Australia. A man from Perth, on the far side of Australia, bore his testimony and said, "We didn't have the means to get here. We lived in Perth. We had to cross all of Australia, almost as far as it is from San Francisco to New York, and then cross the Tasman Sea and come to New Zealand. We couldn't afford it. We had nothing but a little furniture and some dishes and an automobile. We rented the little home in which we lived." And he said, "I sat down one evening to our evening meal and looked across the table at my beautiful wife and our three children and I said to myself, 'You cannot afford not to go. You can sell your dishes. You can sell your furniture. You can sell your car. Somehow the Lord will help you to replace them. But if you should ever fail in your opportunity to bind to you these, your beloved companion and children, you would be poor indeed through all eternity.'" He said, "We sold our furniture.

We sold our dishes. We sold our car. We sold everything we had and came here. If the Lord will bless me with strength, somehow I will make it up." (Salt Lake Temple Workers Devotional, June 11, 1995.)

There is much of beauty about [the people of the world], but without the root that finds itself in faith and conviction concerning God and the risen Lord, there isn't much of real substance when it comes to a crisis or a showdown of some kind. Seek for the real things, not the artificial. Seek for the everlasting truths, not the passing whim. Seek for the eternal things of God, not for that which is here today and gone tomorrow. Look to God and live, as the scripture enjoins us. (Plano Texas Regional Conference, March 17, 1996.)

PROFANITY

Conversations I have had with school principals and students lead me to the same conclusion—that even among *our* young people, there is an evil and growing habit of profanity and the use of foul and filthy language. I do not hesitate to say that it is wrong, seriously wrong, for any young man ordained to the priesthood of God to be guilty of such. The taking of the Lord's name in vain is a most serious matter. . . .

In our dialogues with others we must be an example of the believer. Conversation is the substance of friendly social activity. It can be happy. It can be light. It can be earnest. It can be funny. But it must not be salty, or uncouth, or foul if one is in sincerity a believer in Christ. . . .

It is a tragic and unnecessary thing that boys and girls use foul language. It is inexcusable for a girl so to speak. It is likewise serious for the boy who holds the priesthood. This practice is totally unacceptable for one authorized to speak in the name of God. To blaspheme His holy name or to speak in language that is debauched is offensive to God and man.

The man or the boy who must resort to such language immediately says that he is poverty-ridden in his vocabulary. He does not enjoy sufficient richness of expression to be able to speak effectively without swearing or using foul words. ("Take Not the Name of God in Vain," *Ensign*, November 1987, pp. 45, 47–48.)

I once worked with a group of railroad men who seemed to pride themselves on the use of profanity. They tried to make an art of it. I recall handing a written instruction to a switchman. It was his job to take care of the matter as instructed, but he thought it inconvenient that he should have to do so at that time. On reading the order, he flew into a tantrum. He was a fifty-year-old man, but he acted like a spoiled child. He threw his cap on the ground and jumped on it and let forth such a string of expletives as to seem to cause the air to turn blue around him. Every third or fourth word was the name of Deity spoken in vain.

I thought, how childish can a grown man be? The very idea of a man acting and speaking like that was totally repugnant. I could never again give him my full respect. ("Take Not the Name of God in Vain," *Ensign*, November 1987, p. 46.)

When I was a small boy in the first grade, I experienced what I thought was a rather tough day at school. I came home, walked in the house, threw my book on the kitchen table, and let forth an expletive that included the name of the Lord.

My mother was shocked. She told me quietly, but firmly, how wrong I was. She told me that I could not have words of that kind coming out of my mouth. She led me by the hand into the bathroom, where she took from the shelf a clean washcloth, put it under the faucet, and then generously coated it with soap. She said, "We'll have to wash out your mouth." She told me to open it, and I did so reluctantly. Then she rubbed the soapy washcloth around my tongue and teeth. I sputtered and fumed and felt like swearing again, but I didn't. I rinsed and rinsed my mouth, but it was a long while before the soapy taste was gone. In fact, whenever I think of that experience, I can still taste the soap. The lesson was worthwhile. I think I can say that I have tried to avoid using the name of the Lord in vain since that day. I am grateful for that lesson. ("Take Not the Name of God in Vain," *Ensign*, November 1987, p. 46.)

President George Q. Cannon, who served long and faithfully as a Counselor in the First Presidency, said on one occasion:

"Do angels take the Lord's name in vain? The idea is so ridiculous that we scarcely like to ask the question. . . . How dare we do that which angels dare not do? Is it possible for us to argue that that which is forbidden in heaven is praiseworthy on earth? . . .

"Though we are sure no boy can tell us any advantage that can arise from the abuse of God's holy name, yet we can tell him many evils that arise therefrom. To begin," Brother Cannon said, "it is unnecessary and consequently foolish; it lessens our respect for holy things and leads us into the society of the wicked; it brings upon us the disrespect of the good who avoid us; it leads us to other sins, for he who is willing to abuse his Creator is not ashamed to defraud his fellow creature; and also by so doing we directly and knowingly break one of the most direct of God's commandments" (*Juvenile Instructor*, 27 Sept. 1873, p. 156). . . .

. . . Stay out of the gutter in your conversation. Foul talk defiles the man who speaks it. ("Take Not the Name of God in Vain," *Ensign*, November 1987, pp. 46–47.)

Paul, perhaps the greatest missionary of all time, wrote to Timothy, his young associate in the ministry . . ."Be thou an example *in word*." He is speaking here of language. . . . He is saying that coarse and lewd words are incompatible with one's calling as a believer in Christ. ("Take Not the Name of God in Vain," *Ensign*, November 1987, p. 47.)

You can't use that filthy, dirty language that's so common in the high schools and other schools—you can't do it, if you believe you're a child of God, without betraying your birthright. (Parowan Utah Youth Fireside, January 13, 1996.)

Cultivate the art of conversation. It is a tremendous asset. For me there is nothing more delightful than to listen in on the conversation of a group of bright and happy young people such as you. Their dialogue is witty. It is scintillating. It sparkles and is punctuated by laughing even when dealing with serious subjects. But, I repeat, it is not necessary in conversation to profane the name of Deity or to use salty and salacious language of any kind. And let me add that there is plenty of humor in the world without resorting to what we speak of as dirty jokes. I challenge each of you to avoid all such. During the coming week as you talk with friends and associates, see if you can do so without speaking any words that you might regret having said. ("True to the Faith," Salt Lake Valley-Wide Institute Fireside, January 21, 1996.)

Be clean in language. There is so much of filthy, sleazy talk these days. I spoke to the young women about it. I speak to you also. It tells others that your vocabulary is so extremely limited that you cannot express yourselves without reaching down into the gutter for words. Dirty talk is unbecoming any man who holds the priesthood, be he young or old.

Nor can you as a priesthood holder take the name of the Lord in vain. Said Jehovah to the children of Israel, "Thou shalt not take the name of the Lord thy God in vain; for the Lord will not hold him guiltless that taketh his name in vain" (Ex. 20:7).

That commandment, engraved by the finger of the Lord, is as binding upon us as it was upon those to whom it was originally given. The Lord has said in modern revelation, "Remember that that which cometh from above is sacred, and must be spoken with care, and by constraint of the Spirit" (D&C 63:64).

A filthy mind expresses itself in filthy and profane language. A clean mind expresses itself in language that is positive and uplifting and in deeds that bring happiness into the heart. ("'Be Ye Clean,'" *Ensign*, May 1996, p. 48.)

PROPHETS

It is true that man's essential nature does not change, and that principles laid down centuries ago by the prophets are as applicable today as they were when they were first enunciated; but the world evidently knows not how to apply them. Today that application needs the direction of the Almighty as certainly as when Jehovah spoke to Enoch and Moses and Isaiah and Elijah.

"For the prophecy came not in old time by the will of man: but holy men of God spake as they were moved by the Holy Ghost." (2 Pet. 1:21.) And prophecy, which is revelation, comes not now, nor will it come in the future, by the will of man, but only as men of God speak as they are moved upon by that same spirit.

How poverty-ridden is our world in the wisdom of living one with another. The stresses, the strains, the tensions in human relationships, the wars and rumors of wars that constantly afflict us all become evidence that " . . . the wisdom of the wise has failed and the understanding of the prudent is hid." (See Isa. 29:14.) Religion, to be effective, must be a vital and timely force in the lives of men. . . .

Israel today has a prophet, and we give our witness to the world that the channel of communication is open between God and his appointed servant. ("'The Heavens Are Not Stayed,'" *Improvement Era*, June 1964, p. 477.)

We have just sung a great hymn, "We thank thee, O God, for a prophet, to guide us in these latter days." We sing many of the hymns written by men of other churches—"Onward Christian Soldiers," and many hymns such as that. And other churches sing some of our hymns, but this is one hymn, perhaps "Joseph Smith's First Prayer" being another, peculiar to us alone. No other people on earth can with propriety sing this marvelous hymn of gratitude which was written by an English convert, a man who had never seen the prophet of whom he wrote, but who out of the spirit of testimony which he felt in his heart, penned these marvelous words. How grateful I am for that expression of gratitude. (Idaho Falls 26th and 29th Ward Building Dedication, February 14, 1965.)

Twelve years ago, in company with the mission president from Hong Kong, it was my opportunity to initiate the work in the Philippines. On April 28, 1961, we held a meeting that will never be forgotten by those of us who were present. We had no hall then in which to meet. We made a request of the United States Embassy for permission to meet on the beautiful porch of the marble memorial in the American military cemetery at Fort

McKinley on the outskirts of Manila. We convened at 6:30 in the morning. In that hallowed and sacred place, where are remembered the tragedies of war, we commenced the work of teaching the gospel of peace.

We called upon the only native Filipino member we had been able to locate. He recounted a story which I have never forgotten.

When he was a boy he found in a garbage can an old tattered copy of the *Reader's Digest*. It contained a condensation of a book giving the story of the Mormon people. It spoke of Joseph Smith and described him as a prophet. The word *prophet* did something to that boy. Could there actually be a prophet upon the earth? he wondered. The magazine was lost, but concern over the presence of a living prophet never left him during the long, dark years of war and oppression when the Philippines were occupied. Finally the forces of liberation came, and with them the reopening of Clark Air Base. David Lagman found employment there. His supervisor, he learned, was a Mormon, an Air Force officer. He wanted to ask him if he believed in a prophet, but was afraid to do so. Finally, after much inner turmoil, he mustered the courage to inquire.

"Are you a Mormon, sir?" the young man asked. "Yes, I am," was the forthright reply. "Do you believe in a prophet, do you have a prophet in your church?" came the anxious question.

"We do have a prophet, a living prophet, who presides in this church and who teaches the will of the Lord."

David asked the officer to tell him more, and out of that teaching came his baptism. He was the first native elder ordained in the Philippines. ("'We Thank Thee, O God, for a Prophet,'" *Ensign*, January 1974, p. 122.)

How thankful we ought to be . . . how thankful we are, for a prophet to counsel us in words of divine wisdom as we walk our paths in these complex and difficult times. The solid assurance we carry in our hearts, the conviction that God will make his will known to his children through his recognized servant is the real basis of our faith and activity. We either have a prophet or we have nothing: and having a prophet, we have everything. . . .

Could any people have a greater blessing than to have standing at their head one who receives and teaches the will of God concerning them? We need not look far in the world to know that "the wisdom of the wise has perished and that the understanding of the prudent has come to naught." That wisdom for which the world should seek is the wisdom which comes from God. The only understanding that will save the world is divine understanding. . . .

As one to whom the spirit has borne witness, I testify of his prophetic calling, and add my voice to the voices of our people over the earth, "We thank thee, O God, for a prophet to guide us in these latter days." I am grateful. I am satisfied that the peace and the progress and the prosperity of this people lie in doing the will of the Lord as that will is articulated by [the prophet]. ("'We Thank Thee, O God, for a Prophet,'" *Ensign,* January 1974, pp. 122–25.)

I am profoundly grateful . . . not only for Joseph Smith as the prophet who served as an instrument in the hands of the Almighty in restoring this work, but also for all of those who have followed him. A study of their lives will reveal the manner in which the Lord has chosen them, has refined them, and has molded them to his eternal purposes. Joseph Smith declared on one occasion: "I am like a huge, rough stone rolling down from a high mountain: . . . with all hell knocking off a corner here and a corner there, and thus I will become a smooth and polished shaft in the quiver of the Almighty."

He was hated and persecuted. He was driven and imprisoned. He was abused and beaten. And as you read his history, you see the evolution of which he spoke. There developed a power in his life. There came a refinement. There grew a love for others which even overcame his own love for life. The corners of that rough stone *were* knocked off, and he became a polished shaft in the hand of the Almighty.

It has been so with those who have succeeded him. Through long years of dedicated service, they have been refined and winnowed and chastened and molded for the purposes of the Almighty. Could anyone doubt this after reading the lives of such men as Brigham Young, Wilford Woodruff, and Joseph F.

Smith? The Lord subdued their hearts and refined their natures to prepare them for the great and sacred responsibility later thrust upon them. ("'We Thank Thee, O God, for a Prophet,'" *Ensign*, January 1974, p. 124.)

PROPHETS, LATTER-DAY

Joseph Smith
See also First Vision

An acquaintance said to me one day: "I admire your church very much. I think I could accept everything about it—except Joseph Smith." To which I responded: "That statement is a contradiction. If you accept the revelation, you must accept the revelator. . . ."

The remarkable organization of the Church, which has received much attention, was framed by him as he was directed by revelation, and no modification or adaptation of that organization is ever considered without searching the revelations set forth by the Prophet. ("Joseph the Seer," *Ensign*, May 1977, p. 64.)

It is a constantly recurring mystery to me how some people speak with admiration for the Church and its work, while at the same time disdaining him through whom, as a servant of the Lord, came the framework of all that the Church is, of all that it teaches, and of all that it stands for. They would pluck the fruit from the tree while cutting off the root from which it grows. ("Joseph the Seer," *Ensign*, May 1977, p. 64.)

Anyone who has any doubt about Joseph Smith's powers of leadership need only look at the men who were attracted to him. They did not come for wealth. They did not come for political power. They were not drawn by dreams of military conquest. His offering to them was none of these; rather, it concerned only salvation through faith in the Lord Jesus Christ. It involved persecution with its pains and losses, long and lonely missions, separation from family and friends, and in many cases death itself. ("'Praise to the Man,'" *BYU Devotional Speeches of the Year*, November 4, 1979, p. 205.)

This gospel dispensation, of which we are the beneficiaries, opened with a glorious vision in which the Father and the Son appeared to the boy Joseph Smith. Having had that experience, the boy recounted it to one of the preachers of the community. He treated the account "with great contempt, saying it was all of the devil, that there were no such things as visions or revelations in these days." (JS–H 1:21.)

Others took up the cry against him. He became the object of severe persecution. But, he said, and note these words: "I had actually seen a light, and in the midst of that light I saw two Personages, and they did in reality speak to me; and though I was hated and persecuted for saying that I had seen a vision, yet it was true; and while they were persecuting me, reviling me, and speaking all manner of evil against me falsely for so saying, I was led to say in my heart: Why persecute me for telling the truth? I have actually seen a vision; and who am I that I can withstand God, or why does the world think to make me deny what I have actually seen? For I had seen a vision; I knew it, and I knew that God knew it, and I could not deny it, neither dared I do it." (JS–H 1:25.)

There is no lack of certitude in that statement. For Joseph Smith that experience was as real as the warmth of the sun at noonday. He never flagged nor wavered in his conviction. Listen to his later testimony of the risen Lord:

"And now, after the many testimonies which have been given of him, this is the testimony, last of all, which we give of him: That he lives!

"For we saw him, even on the right hand of God; and we heard the voice bearing record that he is the Only Begotten of the Father—

"That by him, and through him, and of him, the worlds are and were created, and the inhabitants thereof are begotten sons and daughters unto God." (D&C 76:22–24.)

So certain was he of the cause he led, so sure of his divinely given calling, that he placed them above the value of his own life. With prescient knowledge of his forthcoming death, he surrendered himself to those who would deliver him defenseless into the hands of a mob. He sealed his testimony with his life's blood.

It was so with his followers. One will find no evidence, not a scintilla of it, that certitude was the enemy of religion in their lives and actions. ("Faith: The Essence of True Religion," *Ensign*, November 1981, pp. 6–7.)

Great was the Prophet Joseph Smith's vision. It encompassed all the peoples of mankind, wherever they live, and all generations who have walked the earth and passed on. How can anyone, past or present, speak against him except out of ignorance? They have not tasted of his words; they have not pondered about him, nor prayed about him. As one who has done these things, I add my own words of testimony that he was and is a prophet of God, raised up as an instrument in the hands of the Almighty to usher in a new and final gospel dispensation. ("'Praise to the Man,'" *Ensign*, August 1983, p. 6.)

This was also the season—those seven years between 1831 and 1838—of harsh and unrelenting persecution. Enemies threatened to knock down the walls of the [Kirtland] temple. Philastus Hurlburt was excommunicated and in bitterness set in motion the Spaulding manuscript story of the origin of the Book of Mormon with all of the mischief that for years followed that concoction; the Kirtland bank failed; the Prophet and Sidney Rigdon were taken from their homes, dragged through the cold of a March night, tarred and feathered, and left for dead. In addition to all of this, troubles equally as serious were being experienced in Missouri, the other center of the Church.

I have frequently reflected on how the Prophet Joseph Smith must have felt at those times. He was directly or indirectly responsible for all of the misery and suffering that occurred. Did doubt occasionally assail his mind? I find the exact opposite in the revelations that came through him during that period.

While sitting in the John Johnson home in Hiram, Ohio, I reflected on some of the words of section 1 of the Doctrine and Covenants. . . . Section 1 was given as a revelation at Hiram on 1 November 1831 as a preface to the forthcoming publication of . . . what has now become our Doctrine and Covenants.

We need to get a picture in our minds of the setting. Here was the leader of a little group of people in Ohio, numbering at the time perhaps three hundred, scattered through frontier communities where there was much bitterness and hatred. But with vision both prophetic and bold he declared in the name of the Lord:

"Verily the voice of the Lord is unto all men, and there is none to escape; and there is no eye that shall not see, neither ear that shall not hear, neither heart that shall not be penetrated.

"And the rebellious shall be pierced with much sorrow. . . .

"And the voice of warning shall be unto all people, by the mouths of my disciples, whom I have chosen in these last days.

"And they shall go forth and none shall stay them, for I the Lord have commanded them." (D&C 1:2–5.)

Later in that same revelation, received in the humble Johnson home in the village of Hiram, there were set forth the grand objectives of this great latter-day work—

1. "That every man might speak in the name of God the Lord, even the Savior of the world."

2. "That faith also might increase in the earth."

3. "That mine everlasting covenant might be established."

4. "That the fulness of my gospel might be proclaimed by the weak and the simple unto the ends of the world, and before kings and rulers . . . that they might come to understanding." (See D&C 1:20–24.)

These are truly remarkable objectives. It was not a country pastor who spoke these words. It was a prophet of the living God setting forth the depth and breadth and length of this great restored kingdom that was to go over the earth. In that remarkable revelation, the truth of the Book of Mormon was declared and the validity of the revelations was affirmed. Bold as were these declarations, there was no apology. ("Go Forward with Faith," *Ensign*, August 1986, pp. 4–5.)

What is . . . this of which I speak? It is the lengthened shadow of the hand of God. It is the lengthened shadow of a mighty prophet, Joseph Smith, who was called and ordained to open this, the dispensation of the fulness of times spoken of in the scriptures. His numerous critics, now as in the past, spend their lives in trying to explain him on some basis other than the one which he gave.

Of what credibility, I ask, is their estimate in comparison with the opinions of those who were at his side in laying the foundations of this ever-growing, ever-strengthening cause? . . .

Said [Brigham Young] concerning this leader:

"Who can justly say aught against Joseph Smith? I was as well acquainted with him as any man. I do not believe that his father and mother knew him any better than I did. I do not think that a man lives on the earth that knew him any better than I did; and I am bold to say that, Jesus Christ excepted, no better man ever lived or does live upon this earth. I am his witness." (*Discourses of Brigham Young*, sel. John A. Widtsoe, Salt Lake City: Deseret Book Co., 1941, p. 459.)

John Taylor was a gifted and educated Englishman, a lay preacher of the gospel, a man of recognized intelligence. Said he:

"I was acquainted with Joseph Smith for years. I traveled with him; I have been with him in public and in private; I have associated with him in councils of all kinds; I have listened hundreds of times to his public teachings, and his advice to his friends and associates of a more private nature. . . . I was with him living and with him when he died; when he was murdered in Carthage jail by a ruthless mob with their faces painted black. I was there and was myself wounded in my body. I have seen him under all these various circumstances, and I testify before God, angels and men that he was a good, honorable, and virtuous man, that his private and public character was irreproachable, and that he lived and died a man of God" (in Ezra C. Dalby, "Joseph Smith, Prophet of God," ms., talk delivered 12 December 1926, Salt Lake City, p. 13). . . .

Orson Pratt, a man with a sharp and incisive mind, said:

"In 1830 I became intimately acquainted with the Prophet Joseph Smith, and continued intimately acquainted with him until the day of his death. I had the great privilege . . . of boarding . . . at his house, so that I not only knew him as a public teacher, but as a private citizen, and as a husband and father. I witnessed his earnest and humble devotions, both morning and evening in his family. I heard the words of eternal life flow from his lips, nourishing and soothing and comforting his family, neighbors and friends. I saw his countenance lighted up as the inspiration of the Holy Ghost rested upon him, dictating the great and most precious revelations now printed for our guide. . . .

"I knew that he was a man of God. It was not a matter of opinion with me, for I received a testimony from the heavens concerning that matter" (in Ezra C. Dalby, p. 14). ("The Lengthened Shadow of the Hand of God," *Ensign*, May 1987, pp. 53–54.)

This Book of Mormon, which [Joseph Smith] brought forth by the power and inspiration of the Almighty, this remarkable thing alone would be more than enough to guarantee his place in history forever. Add to this the marvelous revelations that came by the power of God through him, and we have a prophet whose stature looms above all his insignificant detractors, as a sainted giant looking down on a crowd of pygmies. . . .

Is it any wonder that this work moves on from nation to nation, from people to people? Is it any wonder that it grows in strength and numbers, in influence and interest, notwithstanding its critics and naysayers? It is the work of God restored to the earth through a prophet. ("The Lengthened Shadow of the Hand of God," *Ensign*, May 1987, pp. 54, 59.)

It was said in other circumstances that the blood of the martyrs has become the seed of the Church. Yes, and no. The blood of the Prophet Joseph has sealed the testimony of the truth of this work. But the true seed of the Church is found in the revelations which came through a veritable cloud of witnesses to him whom we honor as revelator, as seer, and as prophet of the Lord Jesus in whose name he served and died. (Carthage Jail Dedication, June 27, 1989, p. 16.)

When in June of 1844 [Joseph] crossed the Mississippi to Montrose to escape his enemies, he told Steven Markham that if he was taken again he would be "massacred." He was young, then, only 38 and a few months. He was at the zenith of his ministry. Nauvoo was then a place of industry and growth. In only five years it had risen from the swamps to become perhaps the most impressive city in all of the state of Illinois. He was loved by his people and, in turn, he loved them. . . . A magnificent temple was rising on the hill to the east up the slope from the river. This was the prime time of his life, but there were a few who spoke of cowardice in running away. When he heard this, he said, "If my life is of no value to my friends, it is of none to myself."

He returned to Nauvoo. He was arrested under false charges. As he gazed upon the city while being escorted to Carthage, he said, "This is the loveliest place and the best people under the heavens."

While en route to his rendezvous with death he said, "I am going like a lamb to the slaughter . . . and it shall be said of me, 'He was murdered in cold blood!'"

I love him for the brooding sorrow of those last hours in the old jail. John Taylor sang, "A Poor Wayfaring Man of Grief." Then, at Joseph's request, he sang it again. . . . Then came the vile, cursing, angry mob. Shots were fired and the Prophet fell from the window. It was the afternoon of June 27, 1844.

John Taylor, who had been wounded when Joseph and Hyrum were killed, wrote their epitaph: "Joseph Smith, the Prophet and Seer of the Lord," he said, "has done more, save Jesus only, for the salvation of men in this world, than any other man that ever lived in it. In the short space of twenty years, he has brought forth the Book of Mormon, which he translated by the gift and power of God, and has been the means of publishing it on two continents; has sent the fulness of the everlasting gospel, which it contained, to the four corners of the earth; has brought forth the revelations and commandments which compose this book of Doctrine and Covenants, and many other wise documents and instructions for the benefit of the children of men; gathered many thousands of the Latter-day Saints, founded a great city, and left a fame and name that cannot be slain. He lived great, and he died great in the eyes of God and his people; and like most of the Lord's anointed in ancient times, has sealed his mission and his works with his own blood; and so has his brother Hyrum. In life they were not divided, and in death they were not separated!" (D&C 135:3.) . . .

Of the events of that tragic June 27th, Governor Thomas Ford of Illinois wrote, "Thus fell Joe Smith, the most successful imposter in modern times; a man who, though ignorant and

coarse, had some great natural parts which fitted him for temporary success, but which were so obscured and counteracted by
the inherent corruption and vices of his nature that he never
could succeed in establishing a system of policy which looked
to permanent success in the future." (*History of Illinois*, vol. II,
p. 213.)

The man who wrote that appraisal died six years later, practically bankrupt, leaving five orphan children to the mercy of
others. Both he and his wife, who had died three months earlier,
were buried at public expense. He is remembered for little more
than his association with the death of the Prophet Joseph.

I like to compare his appraisal with the prophetic statement
given by Moroni when he appeared to the boy Joseph the night
of September 21, 1823. On that occasion the angel said "that God
had a work for me to do; and that my name should be had for
good and evil among all nations, kindreds, and tongues, or that
it should be both good and evil spoken of among all people."
(JS–H 1:33.) ("As One Who Loves the Prophet," Symposium on
the Life and Ministry of the Prophet Joseph Smith, BYU,
February 22, 1992.)

Some years ago in company with the Rochester stake president, the Cumorah mission president, and a Regional Representative, I went to the Sacred Grove early in the morning of a
spring Sabbath day. . . . We prayed together in that quiet and hallowed place, and there came into my heart at that time a conviction that what the Prophet described actually happened in 1820
here amidst the trees.

I have climbed the slopes of the Hill Cumorah. I have walked
the banks of the Susquehanna River. I have been to Kirtland, to
Independence, Liberty, Far West, Adam-ondi-Ahman, Nauvoo,
and Carthage. While I have never met Joseph Smith, I think I
have come to know him, at least in some small measure.

I know that he was foreordained to a mighty work to serve
as an instrument of the Almighty in bringing to pass a restoration of the work of God of all previous dispensations of time. I
have read the Book of Mormon, again and again. I know that he
did not write it out of his own capacity. I know that he was a
translator who by the gift and power of God brought forth this

great testament of the new world. I know that it is true, that it is powerful, that it is a witness to the nations of the Divine Redeemer of mankind, the Living Son of the Living God. . . .

I worship the God of heaven who is my Eternal Father. I worship the Lord Jesus Christ who is my Savior and my Redeemer. I do not worship the Prophet Joseph Smith, but I reverence and love this great seer through whom the miracle of this gospel has been restored. I am now growing old, and I know that in the natural course of events before many years, I will step across the threshold to stand before my Maker and my Lord and give an accounting of my life. And I hope that I shall have the opportunity of embracing the Prophet Joseph Smith and of thanking him and of speaking of my love for him. ("As One Who Loves the Prophet," Symposium on the Life and Ministry of the Prophet Joseph Smith, BYU, February 22, 1992.)

We sing a hymn in this Church that is peculiar to us, "We thank thee, O God, for a prophet to guide us in these latter days" (*Hymns*, 1985, no. 19).

I have not spoken face to face with all of the prophets of this dispensation. I was not acquainted with the Prophet Joseph Smith, nor did I ever hear him speak. My grandfather, who as a young man lived in Nauvoo, did hear him and testified of his divine calling as the great prophet of this dispensation. But I feel I have come to know the Prophet Joseph Smith.

I have read and believed his testimony of his great first vision in which he conversed with the Father and the Son. I have pondered the wonder of that as I have stood in the grove where he prayed, and in that environment, by the power of the Spirit, I have received a witness that it happened as he said it happened.

I have read the Book of Mormon, which he translated by the gift and power of God. By the power of the Holy Ghost I have received a testimony and a witness of the divine origin of this sacred record. Joseph Smith did not write it of his own capacity.

I have seen with my own eyes the power of the priesthood which came to him under the hands of those who held it anciently. I have studied his life and measured his words. I have pondered the circumstances of his death, and I have come to know him—at least in some degree, at least enough that I can stand before you and testify that he was a prophet called and ordained to stand as God's instrument in this great work of restoration. ("'Believe His Prophets,'" *Ensign*, May 1992, pp. 50–51.)

I think of the great words of section 122 of the Doctrine and Covenants, written when the Prophet was in Liberty Jail, after spending five months of that terrible, bitter winter in a dungeon cell. He cried out to the Lord in an hour of stress: "O God, where art thou?" (D&C 121:1.)

And among the words which came in response to that cry were these: "The ends of the earth shall inquire after thy name, and fools shall have thee in derision, and hell shall rage against thee;

"While the pure in heart, and the wise, and the noble, and the virtuous, shall seek counsel, and authority, and blessings constantly from under thy hand.

"And thy people shall never be turned against thee by the testimony of traitors." (D&C 122:1–3.)

This is another day of fulfillment for that prophecy, my brothers and sisters. I love the Prophet Joseph Smith. I love the Prophet Joseph Smith!

I bear testimony of the divinity of his calling. There is not a shadow of doubt in my mind of the fact that he was called of God. I know that the conversation which took place in the grove was as intimate and as real and as personal as is my conversation with you this night. I know that. I thank the Prophet for his testimony, for his work, for his life, for his sacrifice, for his witness of the living reality of God our Eternal Father and the risen Lord Jesus Christ. ("A Tour of the Joseph Smith Memorial Building," *Ensign*, September 1993, p. 38.)

I bear solemn testimony of the divinity of his call, of the magnitude of his accomplishments, of the virtue of his life, and of the security of his place among the great and honored of the Almighty in all generations of time. ("In Memory of Joseph Smith," Martyrdom Commemoration Satellite Broadcast, Carthage, Illinois, June 26, 1994.)

This is June 26th. One-hundred and fifty years ago, June 26th was on a Wednesday. That morning Governor Thomas Ford of Illinois, who had come to Carthage, visited Joseph Smith in the jail. He and the Prophet talked for about an hour. Out on the streets of the town more than a thousand men belonging to various military units were lazily spending the day, venting their hatred for the Mormons as they talked in groups. The target of that hatred was Joseph Smith, the Mormon Prophet.

That morning he told the governor of the danger surrounding him. The governor dismissed this. He said he was going to Nauvoo the next day and promised that if he did so, he would take Joseph with him. He repeated that pledge when he left that morning.

In the afternoon, the constable arrived at the jail accompanied by men of the Carthage Grays. The prisoners were marched to the courthouse in public humiliation. There, after an hour of debate over legal matters, the court adjourned until noon the next day. Joseph and Hyrum were returned to the jail. The weather was sultry and hot and miserable.

The next morning, Dan Jones, who had spent the night in the jail with Joseph and Hyrum and others, left. He talked with Frank Worrel, one of the Carthage Grays. He reported that Worrel said: "We have had too much trouble to bring old Joe here to let him ever escape alive, and unless you want to die with him, you had better leave before sundown. . . . You'll see that I can prophesy better than old Joe, for neither he nor his brother, nor anyone who will remain with them will see the sunset today."

Dan Jones reported this to Governor Ford, who responded that he was "unnecessarily alarmed."

At 10:30 that morning, Governor Ford and his troops left for Nauvoo, leaving those in the jail behind at the mercy of the mob militia. As the afternoon of that sultry day wore on, the Prophet asked John Taylor to sing: "A Poor Wayfaring Man of Grief." He sang all seven verses, and Joseph asked him to sing them again. Elder Taylor replied that he did not feel like doing so, but at Hyrum's importuning he repeated the song.

The jailer suggested about 5 o'clock that the four of them in the jail—Joseph Smith, Hyrum Smith, Willard Richards, and

John Taylor—might be safer if they went into the cell. Joseph indicated that they would do so after supper.

A few minutes later, a noise was heard outside, followed by a cry of surrender. Then came two or three gunshots.

Willard Richards looked out the window and saw a large group of men with painted faces. The mob ran up the steep stairs and began firing. The prisoners pushed the door shut and then tried to knock down the guns sticking through the door. John Taylor used Stephen Markham's large hickory cane, and Willard Richards used John Taylor's cane. A bullet fired through the door hit Hyrum on the left side of the nose. He fell back saying, "I am a dead man!" Another ball, coming through the window, hit him in the back almost simultaneously. Two other balls hit him as he fell. Joseph cried, "Oh dear, Brother Hyrum!" John Taylor was then hit. One of the balls struck his watch. It stopped at 5:16.

One or two balls then hit Joseph. He jumped to the window, paused for a moment, cried, "Oh Lord, my God," then fell out the window, his body resting against the curb of the well.

It was all over. Joseph was dead. Hyrum was dead. John Taylor was wounded. Willard Richards miraculously escaped.

Thus ended the long odyssey that had taken Joseph Smith within a period of 38 years from his birth on December 23rd, 1805, in Sharon, Windsor County, Vermont; to western New York; to northern Pennsylvania; to Kirtland, Ohio; to Missouri— first to Independence and eventually to Far West—and then to Liberty Jail; from there to Quincy, Illinois; to Nauvoo; and on to Carthage. . . .

Those sad days are gone. But the glorious work, begun by him who was killed at Carthage, has grown in a miraculous and wonderful way. . . . This marvelous work, which has sprung from the prophetic calling of the boy of Palmyra, has "come forth out of the wilderness of darkness," and is shining "forth fair as the moon, clear as the sun, and terrible as an army with banners," as the Prophet prayed it would. (D&C 109:73.) . . .

We pause in reverence here this evening. We reflect on the miracle of the life begun in the green hills of Vermont and ended here in the jail of Carthage. That life was not long, less than 39 years. But the fruits of that life have been something almost beyond comprehension.

This great cause of The Church of Jesus Christ has been more precious than life itself to thousands upon thousands who have died in its service. Witnesses have gone into the world by the hundreds of thousands to bear testimony of Joseph Smith's calling as a prophet of God. The holy priesthood restored through him has fallen as a mantle upon uncounted numbers of men of integrity and virtue who have been clothed with this divine power. The Book of Mormon is going across the earth as Another Testament of the Lord Jesus Christ. This vast organization, with its very many facets, is blessing the lives of all who will hearken to its message.

To quote a truism uttered long ago and in different circumstances, "the blood of the martyrs has become the seed of the Church." The testimonies which were sealed here in these very precincts, that hot and sultry day 150 years ago now nurture the faith of people around the world.

God bless the memory of Joseph Smith who died here. With gratitude and love we sing all across this Church the words of his friend, W. W. Phelps:

> *Great is his glory and endless his priesthood.*
> *Ever and ever the keys he will hold.*
> *Faithful and true, he will enter his kingdom,*
> *Crowned in the midst of the prophets of old.*
> (*HYMNS*, NO. 27)

("In Memory of Joseph Smith," Martyrdom Commemoration Satellite Broadcast, Carthage, Illinois, June 26, 1994.)

I did not know much about Joseph Smith when I was twelve, but I had a feeling in my heart. Since then I have come to know Joseph Smith. I have read his experiences. I have read his testimony. I have read the Book of Mormon. I have seen the organization of this marvelous Church. I have seen the power of the priesthood. And I think I know Joseph Smith. . . . He is God's prophet in the restoration of the gospel in this, the dispensation of the fulness of times. If we can only get that into our hearts, then we will know that this is truly the work of God. (Lima Peru Fireside, November 9, 1996.)

I wish to express appreciation for the birth of the Prophet Joseph Smith. . . .

How great indeed is our debt to him. His life began in Vermont and ended in Illinois, and marvelous were the things that happened between that simple beginning and that tragic ending. It was he who brought us a true knowledge of God the Eternal Father and His Risen Son, the Lord Jesus Christ. During the short time of his great vision he learned more concerning the nature of Deity than all of those who through centuries had argued that matter in learned councils and scholarly forums. He brought us this marvelous book, the Book of Mormon, as another witness for the living reality of the Son of God. To him, from those who held it anciently, came the priesthood, the power, the gift, the authority, the keys to speak and act in the name of God. He gave us the organization of the Church and its great and sacred mission. Through him were restored the keys of the holy temples, that men and women might enter into eternal covenants with God, and that the great work for the dead might be accomplished to open the way for eternal blessings.

He was the instrument in the hands of the Almighty. He was the servant acting under the direction of the Lord Jesus Christ in bringing to pass this great latter-day work.

We stand in reverence before him. He is the great prophet of this dispensation. He stands at the head of this great and mighty work which is spreading across the earth. He is our prophet, our revelator, our seer, our friend. Let us not forget him. . . . God be thanked for the Prophet Joseph. ("Christmas," First Presidency Christmas Devotional, Salt Lake Tabernacle, December 8, 1996.)

Brigham Young

I stand in awe at Brigham Young's boldness to lead people out of the security, as it were, the comfort of Nauvoo, to move into a wilderness, thousands upon thousands of them. It wasn't just a migration of a little handful; there were thousands of them and more were coming all the time from the British Isles and from the lands of Europe. To move them to a place they had never seen in reality, a place where a crop had never been grown. They had no idea of the conditions of the soil. They had no idea of the conditions of the seasons or when the frost would come. It was a most bold thing, a thing of tremendous courage to say, "Brothers and sisters, let's go. Let's move west into a wilderness." When they reached that wilderness there were those who said, "Let's go on to California. This is no place to establish a colony." And Brigham Young said, "No. This is where we will settle and God will rebuke the sterility of the soil and the frost and we will plow and plant and crops will mature and the fruit trees will bloom and bear fruit" ("Centennial Message from the First Presidency, July 1947," *Messages of the First Presidency*, Vol. 6, p. 265). Was he a prophet? There isn't the slightest doubt in my mind that he was a prophet. Was he a man of vision? There isn't the slightest doubt in my mind that he had a heavenly vision. There can be no doubt that he was a man of tremendous purpose and tremendous faith and tremendous courage. (Grand Encampment Devotional, Council Bluffs, Iowa, July 13, 1996.)

Brigham Young was a tremendous leader. There is no question about it. He had been through the fires of adversity, and when he came West he came as the leader of a great people. He had a tremendous vision. He not only looked to the establishment of this community of Salt Lake City, but reached north and south and east and west to establish some three or four or five hundred other communities. He was an empire builder with a tremendous vision. He was, to say the least, a great leader whose figure will loom ever larger on the landscape of American history. (Interview with Lee Groberg for PBS Documentary "Trail of Hope," November 4, 1996.)

I stand in absolute awe of Brigham Young, the leader of that first pioneer company. I happen to occupy the office which has come down from him, and know at least in some small measure the enormity of the challenges which faced him.

With the death of Joseph Smith in 1844, Brigham Young, as President of the Quorum of the Twelve Apostles, stepped forth to lead the Church. Our people then lived in the finest city in Illinois, so acknowledged by Governor Edgar the other day. Nauvoo was larger than Chicago at the time. Solid brick homes lined the streets. On a spot that looks down across the town and then over the Mississippi into Iowa, Joseph Smith had begun a temple. Brigham Young completed it. It was then the finest structure in Illinois. He finished it although he knew they would have to leave it. The mobs were at their doors. They could not live in peace. They determined to go west.

They threaded their way on this long journey. They met Jim Bridger along the way. He had seen this valley. He warned them against it as a place to live.

Sam Brannan, who had brought some of the Saints around the Cape and up to Yerba Buena, now San Francisco, came east to meet Brigham Young and pleaded with him not to stop here but to go on to California.

When they came through Emigration Canyon and he looked out over this valley it was not a promising sight. The salty lake was in the west. The canyon streams emptied into it. The soil was hard and baked under the July sun. No plow had ever broken this soil. These people knew nothing of the climate. They knew nothing of its rainfall or snowpack. They knew nothing of when the frost came. They knew nothing whatever about it. Yet here was Brigham Young, 46 years old, leading a pioneer company to this valley which was to be followed by thousands and thousands of others.

He said, "This is the right place."

It took courage, it took faith, it took vision to bring the thousands who resided in Nauvoo, and yet other thousands who were coming from England and Europe.

The first company arrived on Saturday. They worshiped on Sunday. On Monday they climbed Ensign Peak. The canyon streams were diverted onto the dry soil and the ground was plowed. They planted their potatoes in order to save their seed. They hoped for a crop. That crop the next year was slim and small, but it helped.

Here they were a thousand miles from the nearest settlement to the east and nearly 800 miles from the nearest settlement to the west.

If they were to eat they had to grow it. If they were to clothe themselves they had to produce wool and cotton. If they needed machinery or tools they had to make them. From here they spread out going north and south, east and west, to establish more than 350 other communities.

That achievement alone marked Brigham Young as a tremendous colonizer. What he did in that migration and what he did thereafter, to use a modern term, makes of him a chief executive officer of extraordinary vision and accomplishment.

They laid out this city with its streets running to the cardinal points—streets 132 feet wide with ten-acre blocks. They built homes. They planted trees, and the miracle is that they grew. They established a woolen mill. He sent people down to St. George on a cotton mission. There was a crusade to produce silk. Mulberry trees were planted all up and down the territory to give food to the silkworms who produced the silk which was spun and made into clothing.

I bow in reverent respect before President Young as an architect. He conceived and designed the Salt Lake Temple. I live in an apartment that faces down the mall toward the temple. I have looked at that great building in fair weather and foul, in the daytime and at night. I marvel at it. I really do.

His was the concept of the great Tabernacle. What a remarkable building it is. For 120 years it has served the people of this community very well. As I have sat under the great domed roof, I have said to myself, "What a remarkable thing this building is."

I have been working with the architects on the new assembly building we are going to erect. I have a great appreciation for architects. But above them all stands Brigham Young, painter and glazier, carpenter and wood worker. We will build a great new building. It will be constructed to the seismic code. It will be large and commodious. It will be the result of well-trained architects and engineers, of experts on sound and structural details. But it will not be the kind of extraordinary structure we find in the Salt Lake Temple. His was the prominent part in building almost every industry that had a root in those early days, including the transcontinental railroad. (Rotary Club Luncheon, Salt Lake City, Utah, April 22, 1997.)

John Taylor

John Taylor was a remarkable man, whose life and example we ought to study more. He was a man of principle, and integrity, and fidelity. . . . [He] and his wife were baptized into the Church in 1836 through the labors of Parley Pratt who said,

"The people there drank in truth as water, and loved it as they loved life." (*PPP*, p. 152.) Thereafter, until the day of his death, John Taylor, the convert, was an unflinching and powerful exponent of the truths which had come into his life and which had taken possession of all his loyalties. He selected as his motto, "The kingdom of God or nothing." . . .

John Taylor said on one occasion: "I do not believe in a religion that cannot have all my affections; but, in a religion for which I can both live and die. I would rather have God for my friend than all other influences and powers." (*Truth Restored*, p. 140.)

He believed this. He lived it. He advocated it by his example. He was a man of absolute fidelity and loyalty to him whom he accepted as his leader. . . .

In the dark and troubled days of Nauvoo, when a number of those who had been close to the Prophet turned against him, John Taylor was one who remained at his side with absolute loyalty. There were traitors in those days, men who clandestinely connived against the Prophet. There was another group, the members of which professed belief but who spent much time criticizing and finding fault rather than holding the work together and building the kingdom. Selfishness and pride, and a lust for power and attention, took possession of them. All this dissention reached its climax on the tragic day of June 27, 1844, when Joseph and Hyrum Smith were killed by the mob in Carthage Jail. There were two good men with them in that jail at that time. One was Willard Richards, who miraculously escaped injury; and the other was John Taylor, who was savagely wounded, four balls having entered his body from the pistols of the mob. The watch which he carried in his pocket stopped the one which likely would have taken his life. He would have given that life. Concerning his coming into the Church he had said: "I expected when I came into this Church, that I should be persecuted and proscribed. I expected that the people would be persecuted. But I believed that God had spoken, that the eternal principles of truth had been revealed, and that God had a work to accomplish which was in opposition to the ideas, views, and notions of men, and I did not know but it would cost me my life before I got through. . . .

"Was there anything surprising in all this? No. If they killed Jesus in former times, would not the same feeling and influence bring about the same results in these times? I had counted the cost when I first started out, and stood prepared to meet it." (*Journal of Discourses* 25:91–92, February 10, 1884.)

It was he who wrote what we now have as section 135 of the Doctrine and Covenants concerning the death of Joseph Smith, saying: "Joseph Smith, the Prophet and Seer of the Lord, has done more, save Jesus only, for the salvation of men in this world, than any other man that ever lived in it. . . . He lived great, and he died great in the eyes of God and his people; and like most of the Lord's anointed in ancient times, has sealed his mission and his works with his own blood; and so has his brother Hyrum." (D&C 135:3.)

It was that kind of loyalty to his leader, it was that kind of fidelity to the cause to which he had given his life, that sustained that cause and kept it moving forward in the dark and troubled days that lay ahead. John Taylor's faith in those difficult times was unmistakable. Listen to his words on the position of the Church in that fateful year of 1844: "The idea of the church being disorganized and broken up because of the Prophet and the Patriarch being slain is preposterous. This church has the seeds of immortality in its midst. It is not of man, nor by man—it is the offspring of Deity. It is organized after the pattern of heavenly beings, through the principles of revelation; by the opening of the heavens, by the ministering of angels, and the revelations of Jehovah. It is not affected by the death of one or two, or fifty individuals. . . . Times and seasons may change, revolution may succeed revolution, thrones may be cast down, and empires be dissolved, earthquakes may rend the earth from centre to circumference, the mountains may be hurled out of their places, and the mighty ocean be moved from its bed; but amidst the crash of worlds and the crack of matter, truth, eternal truth must remain unchanged, and those principles which God has revealed to his Saints be unscathed amidst the warring elements, and remain as firm as the throne of Jehovah." (*Times and Seasons* 5:744, December 15, 1844.) ("Dedication of the John Taylor Building," *BYU 1982–83 Fireside and Devotional Speeches*, September 14, 1982, pp. 17–18.)

Joseph F. Smith

I wish to begin this evening by reading a dream which President Joseph F. Smith had as a young man. As some of you know, President Joseph F. Smith was the sixth President of the Church. He served from 1901 to 1918, a period of seventeen years. . . .

At the age of eleven, this fatherless lad drove an ox team with his mother across the plains to this valley. At the age of fifteen, he was called on a mission to Hawaii. He made his way to San Francisco and there worked in a shingle mill to earn enough money to get to the islands.

Hawaii was not a tourist center then. It was peopled largely by the native Hawaiians. They were, for the most part, poor but generous with what they had. He learned to speak their language and to love them. He never lost his love for the Hawaiian people, nor did they for him. I give you this as background for the dream which he had when he was serving there as a very young man. I quote his words:

"I was very much oppressed, once, [when I was] on a mission. I was almost naked and entirely friendless, except the friendship of a poor, benighted . . . people. I felt as if I was so debased in my condition of poverty, lack of intelligence and knowledge, just a boy, that I hardly dared look a . . . man in the face.

"While in that condition I dreamed [one night] that I was on a journey, and I was impressed that I ought to hurry—hurry with all my might, for fear I might be too late. I rushed on my way as fast as I possibly could, and I was only conscious of having just a little bundle, a handkerchief with a small bundle wrapped in it. I did not realize just what it was, when I was hurrying as fast as I could; but finally I came to a wonderful mansion. . . . I thought I knew that was my destination. As I passed towards it, as fast as I could, I saw a notice, 'Bath.' I turned aside quickly and went into the bath and washed myself clean. I opened up this little bundle that I had, and there was a pair of white, clean garments, a thing I had not seen for a long time, because the people I was with did not think very much of making things exceedingly clean. But my garments were clean, and I put them on. Then I rushed to what appeared to be a great opening, or door. I knocked and the door opened, and the man who stood there was the Prophet Joseph Smith. He looked at me a little reprovingly, and the first words he said: 'Joseph, you are late.' Yet I took confidence and replied:

"'Yes, but I am clean—I am clean!'

"He clasped my hand and drew me in, then closed the great door. I felt his hand just as tangible as I ever felt the hand of man. I knew him, and when I entered I saw my father, and Brigham [Young] and Heber [C. Kimball], and Willard [Richards], and other good men that I had known, standing in a row. I looked as if it were across this valley, and it seemed to be filled with a vast multitude of people, but on the stage were all the people that I had known. My mother was there, and she sat with a child in her lap; and I could name over as many as I remember of their names, who sat there, who seemed to be among the chosen, among the exalted. . . .

"[When I had this dream] I was alone on a mat, away up in the mountains of Hawaii—no one was with me. But in this vision I pressed my hand up against the Prophet, and I saw a smile cross his countenance. . . .

"When I awoke that morning I was a man, although only a boy. There was not anything in the world that I feared [after that]. I could meet any man or woman or child and look them in the face, feeling in my soul that I was a man every whit. That vision, that manifestation and witness that I enjoyed at that time has made me what I am, if I am anything that is good, or clean, or upright before the Lord, if there is anything good in me. That has helped me out in every trial and through every difficulty" (*Gospel Doctrine*, 5th ed. [1939], 542–43).

The core of that meaningful dream is found in the reproof given by Joseph Smith to young Joseph F. Said the Prophet, "Joseph, you are late."

Replied Joseph F., "Yes, but I am clean—I am clean!"

The result of that dream was that a boy was changed into a man. His declaration "I am clean" gave him self-assurance and courage in facing anyone or any situation. He received the strength that comes from a clear conscience fortified by the approbation of the Prophet Joseph. (*"'Be Ye Clean,'" Ensign,* May 1996, pp. 46–47.)

Heber J. Grant

I heard President Grant on several occasions before I met him. As teenage boys, my brother and I came to this Tabernacle at conference when there was room for anybody who wished to come. As boys are wont to do, we sat in the balcony at the very far end of the building. To me it was always impressive when this tall man stood to speak. Some kind of electricity passed through my boyish frame. His voice rang out in testimony of the Book of Mormon. When he said it was true, I knew it was true. He spoke with great power on the Word of Wisdom and, without hesitation, promised blessings to the people if they would observe it. I have often thought of the human misery, the pain that has resulted from the smoking of cigarettes, the poverty that has resulted from the drinking of liquor which might have been avoided had his prophetic counsel been followed.

He spoke on the law of tithing. I can still hear his great testimony of this principle. He spoke of the fast offering and said, as I remember him from my boyhood days, that if all the world would observe this simple principle, which came as a revelation from God, the needs of the poor over the earth would be met without taxing the people for welfare purposes.

He warned against the enslavement of personal debt. The world at that time was on a reckless pursuit of riches. Then came Black Thursday of November 1929. I was nineteen years of age, a student at the university. I saw the economy crumble. I saw men whom I knew lose everything as their creditors moved against them. I saw much of the trauma and the stress of the times. I thought then, and I have thought since, how so many people might have been saved pain and misery, suffering, embarrassment, and trouble had they listened to the counsel of a prophet concerning personal debt. (*"'Believe His Prophets,'" Ensign,* May 1992, p. 51.)

George Albert Smith

George Albert Smith succeeded Heber J. Grant as President and prophet. The terrible Second World War came to a close during his presidency. Our people, as well as others in Europe, were starving in the aftermath of that war. President Smith went to see the president of the United States, Harry Truman. He asked for transportation to get foodstuffs and clothing to those in need. President Truman asked President Smith where he would get these resources. President Smith replied that the Church operated production projects under a welfare program and that women of the Relief Society had saved wheat. The shelves of our storehouses were well stocked, and our granaries were filled. This had come of the prophetic foresight of Church leaders.

The government promised transportation, and Elder Ezra Taft Benson of the Council of the Twelve was sent to Europe to look after the distribution of the commodities which were shipped to Germany.

I was among those who worked nights at Welfare Square here in Salt Lake City loading commodities onto rail cars which moved the food to the port from which it was shipped across the sea. During the time of the Swiss Temple dedication, when many of the Saints of Germany came to the temple, I heard some of them, with tears running down their cheeks, speak with appreciation for that food which had saved their lives.

President Smith used to talk of a line which we must not cross. One side was the Lord's, the other the adversary's. President Smith would say to us, "Stay on the Lord's side of the line." He frequently reminded us: "We are all our Father's children. We must love people into doing what's right." He was the epitome of love. ("'Believe His Prophets,'" *Ensign*, May 1992, pp. 51–52.)

David O. McKay

President David O. McKay was a tall and handsome man, physically robust, he loved the contest, his mind was scintillating and his wit delightful. His was a buoyant personality, he was always encouraging, lifting up, seeing the bright side of things, and challenging others to move forward.

On one occasion he submitted to a lengthy interview from an internationally renowned writer who had interviewed the great and famous of the world. President McKay's secretary told me that when this man came out of the President's office after a long question and answer session, he said to her, "Today, for the first time in my life, I have talked with a prophet. I have spoken with a most remarkable man, who will stand out always in my mind as one who is preeminent among the many with whom I have spoken over the years and across the world. I have had an unusual and wonderful experience for which I am grateful."

No one could be in President McKay's presence for long without being impressed with the remarkable strength of his personality. He was a giant among men, impressive in appearance and noble in character, a true prince. As I worked under his direction on a number of projects, I constantly marveled at the depth of his insight, at the breadth of his understanding, his great powers of expression, and his untiring pursuit of his objectives.

He was a man who stood in reverence before the Almighty as the author of all truth. He was a true disciple of Jesus of Nazareth. Without selfish consideration, he consecrated his time to the service of his Lord and Master, and in bringing hope, renewal, and faith to all with whom he mingled. . . .

He enjoyed life. He revered learning. He knew how to fight for victory. He loved young people who reached out to gain knowledge. He saw no limitations on what they could accomplish when they were guided and persuaded by dedicated teachers and coaches. Yes, he was indeed a remarkable man, a unique character, a dedicated and wonderfully happy and good leader among people. I loved him; I shall always love him as a man who could stand as an example before the entire world. (David O. McKay Events Center Dedication, Utah Valley State College, April 22, 1995.)

He was a man of gracious ways. He was a man who loved the refining things of life, the arts. He could recite from the classics. You will find as you read his sermons that he would frequently recite from Shakespeare and the great figures of English literature. That training came of his training to be an educator. His first profession was that of a teacher, and he was a very able teacher throughout his life in his great work in the Sunday School organization of the Church, in his great work in the Church Educational System. He was the one who had the vision of the Church College of Hawaii, as it was then known, which became the Hawaii Campus of BYU.

He was a man of vision. He was a man of faith. He was a man with tremendous powers of expression. He was a man who had confidence in young people and saw in them their possibilities. He could look above their little idiosyncracies to the possibility of the boy or the girl in the future. He had a nurturing spirit about him that was tremendous and wonderful.

He looked every bit the part of a prophet. . . . He was just a very thoughtful, kind, gracious man. [He had a] bright, scintillating personality. He loved humor—good, clean, wholesome humor—he knew how to listen to it and knew how to tell it. But his great power was to lift people. I can see him in my mind's eye now at the pulpit, tall and stately, lifting his hands to that vast congregation as he spoke words that inspired and lifted and made everyone there want to live a little better as a Latter-day Saint. (Interview with Glenn Anderson of BYU Media Services, October 7, 1996.)

Joseph Fielding Smith

Joseph Fielding Smith . . . became President of the Church and the prophet of the Lord. Some thought he spoke harshly in the tone of a prophet of the Old Testament. He did speak straightforwardly and without equivocation. Such is the mission of a prophet. But it was my experience that he was a man of great kindness who grieved over the unwillingness of so many to follow the commandments of the Lord.

He used three great words that I can never forget—"true and faithful." In his public addresses, in his private conversation, in his prayers to the Lord, he pleaded that we might be true and faithful. Those who followed his counsel have tasted the sweet fruit of obedience. Those who have scoffed have known something of the bitterness that comes of a denial of truth. ("'Believe His Prophets,'" *Ensign*, May 1992, p. 52.)

I think I shall speak again [in the hereafter] with President Joseph Fielding Smith. I expect that he will repeat those same words that he used so many times on earth: "Brother Hinckley, have you been true and faithful?" On one occasion, long before I was a General Authority, I was doing some historical research. He was then the Church Historian and Recorder, and I went into his office to ask him a question. He answered my question. He had been wrestling with a response to an apostate who had published a book designed to injure the Church. He talked about that apostate, and then he said to me something I have never before spoken of in public. He said, looking me in the eye: "I want you to be true and faithful. I want to help you to be true and faithful and to be an effectual instrument in the hands of the Lord in advancing His work."

I hope I will be able to say to President Smith, "President, I have tried to be true and faithful. I have kept my sacred covenants. I may not have been very effective, but I have worked to the best of my ability, in whatever my calling, to do my part to build the kingdom." I can see his characteristic quizzical smile as he says, "Thank you." (General Authority Training Meeting, September 27, 1994.)

Harold B. Lee

Ours was the rare privilege of traveling with President and Sister [Harold B.] Lee many thousands of miles in the British Isles, in Europe, in Israel, and in other lands. No one could have that experience without coming to know that here was a humble man—a man without arrogance, void of officiousness, never haughty or noisy or offensive. . . .

In 1972 we walked together in the Holy Land. In a quiet corner in Bethlehem we read together the account of the coming to earth of the Only Begotten of the Father, the mighty Jehovah. . . .

We dipped our hands in the waters of Jordan and thought of that Perfect One who was there baptized that he might fulfill all righteousness. We stood in Capernaum and reflected on the miracles of his ministry. . . .

We left the city walls and saw the hill on which stood a lonely cross where the Son of God was sacrificed for the sins of the world. We gathered at the Garden Tomb, in a meeting which will never be forgotten by those present. Here President Lee expressed his feeling that here, indeed, was placed the body of the crucified Lord, and that here occurred the miracle of miracles when the stone was rolled away. ("Harold Bingham Lee: Humility, Benevolence, Loyalty," *Ensign*, February 1974, p. 89.)

Harold B. Lee . . . was a man I loved. During the short tenure of his presidency, I traveled in Europe with him on two different occasions. Those were wonderful days when we talked together. I was his junior companion on those journeys, and he spoke out of his great heart about many things. He warned against the neglect of families. He told us that the greatest work any of us would ever do would be within the walls of our own homes. He told us to survey large fields and cultivate small ones. In so saying, he wanted us to get the great, broad picture of this work, and then with faithfulness take care of our own individual responsibility in it. He had come out of humble circumstances and carried in his heart a great sensitivity for the poor. He was the first managing director of the welfare program as it was established in 1936, and taught its principles across the Church. He extended to me a call to serve as a stake president and set me apart in that office. I still remember some of the things he said in that blessing. Said he: "Be sensitive to the promptings of the Spirit. Be slow to censure and quick to encourage." I commend that counsel to each of you. It came from a living prophet of God. ("'Believe His Prophets,'" *Ensign*, May 1992, p. 52.)

Spencer W. Kimball

What a magnificent example he has been for all of us. He has given impetus to this work in a remarkable way. The whole Church has quickened its pace and lengthened its stride in response to his clarion call. He has been a prophet to us, a prophet whose vision and revelation have reached out to the people of the entire earth. ("He Slumbers Not, nor Sleeps," *Ensign*, May 1983, p. 5.)

I speak a few words of personal testimony of President Spencer W. Kimball. For forty-two years he served as Apostle and prophet. His moving example of sincere humility, his outreaching love for people, his quiet and earnest declarations of faith have touched all of us. The majesty of his life was found in its simplicity. There was never any of the ostentatious, the boastful, the proud evident in his character. Yet there was an excellence that shone like gold. He was a man from whose life the husk of mediocrity had been winnowed by the hand of God. I loved him with that love which men in the service of the Lord come to feel and know. ("Come and Partake," *Ensign,* May 1986, p. 46.)

This kindly man, short of stature, was so diligent, so energetic, so determined to overcome any handicap, that even the quality of his injured voice actually became an asset. When he stood to speak, we all listened. Who can ever forget his great, moving statement: "So much depends upon our willingness to make up our minds, collectively and individually, that present levels of performance are not acceptable unto [us] or . . . the Lord. In saying that, I am not calling for flashy, temporary differences in our performance levels, but a quiet resolve . . . to do a better job, to lengthen our stride." (*The Teachings of Spencer W. Kimball,* ed. Edward L. Kimball, Salt Lake City: Bookcraft, 1982, p. 174.)

That call to lengthen our stride went across the entire Church. Many took it to heart and worked with greater enthusiasm and dedication. As they did so, they were blessed in their lives. How great is my debt, and is yours also, to this kindly man of gentle ways and prophetic leadership. ("'Believe His Prophets,'" *Ensign,* May 1992, p. 52.)

Ezra Taft Benson

We commemorated President Benson's ninetieth birthday last August fourth with a great celebration in this Tabernacle, which was carried to the Church across the nation and even to some foreign areas. His life has been rich and wonderful and marvelous. His service has been tremendous and unceasing. His love for the people has been deep and magnificent.

I know that he would have me express in his behalf his deep love for each of you, for you members of the Church throughout the world wherever you may be. Likewise, he would extend that love to those who are not members of the Church, for he stands as a prophet of the Lord Jesus Christ, extending in his life and in his authority as that prophet all of the love which the Lord would have his children receive. ("A Word of Benediction," *Ensign*, November 1989, p. 85.)

President Ezra Taft Benson was ordained and set apart to his high and holy calling immediately following the death of President Kimball. Could anyone doubt his qualifications for this responsibility? Over the years in public and Church affairs, he had moved with ease among the great of the earth. Since the days of his childhood, he has carried in his heart a deep and unmovable conviction concerning the divinity of this work. He has exercised the authority of the apostleship in his ministry among the nations. He has spoken prophetically and wonderfully on many things, but his most oft-repeated message to the people of the Church has been, "Read the Book of Mormon."

Why? Because he knows that the reading of this sacred testament will bring us closer to God and that there is no greater need among us than this. ("'Believe His Prophets,'" *Ensign*, May 1992, pp. 52–53.)

But with all that he did, with all the honors accorded him at home and abroad, with his pleasure in mingling with people wherever he went, his greatest interest and his truest love, beyond his own family, was The Church of Jesus Christ of Latter-day Saints, its people, and its interests throughout the world.

He treasured above all other calls and responsibilities the holy Apostleship, a call extended when he was forty-four years of age by President Heber J. Grant. He knew the meaning of that call. He recognized the responsibilities inherent in it. With the energy of his boyhood farm experiences, he labored at it. He traveled across the world teaching righteousness, building faith, bearing witness in unequivocal terms. . . .

For more than thirty-two years I sat in councils with him— in the Council of the Twelve Apostles and in the Council of the First Presidency. I have been the beneficiary of his kindness and deferential manner. I have been blessed by his wisdom. I have seen the spirit of prophecy rest upon him. I have knelt with him and heard him pray.

His prayers were always interesting. Almost without exception, they consisted for the most part of expressions of thanks. He asked for very little. He expressed gratitude for very much.

He thanked the Lord for life, for family, for the gospel, for faith, for sunlight and rain, the bounties of nature, and the freedom-loving instincts of man. He thanked the Lord for friends and associates. He expressed love for the Savior and gratitude for His atoning sacrifice. He thanked the Lord for the opportunity to serve the people.

Service was of his nature. His life became a fulfillment of the declaration of the Master: "He that findeth his life shall lose it: and he that loseth his life for my sake shall find it" (Matt. 10:39).

Like the Master whom he served, he "went about doing good" (Acts 10:38). At the height of his career he was a powerful speaker. An excellent student of the gospel, he spoke with a powerful conviction and a great sense of mission. The sermons he delivered from this pulpit dealt with a great variety of subjects. He covered the whole broad gamut of the gospel. No one could question his love for his Redeemer. He bore strong and convincing testimony of a certain knowledge that the Son of God gave His life for the sins of mankind and that through His atoning sacrifice all may be raised from the dead.

He spoke of the beauty of the gospel plan under which all who walk in obedience to its principles may attain eternal life and exaltation. On many occasions he voiced, with great emotion, his hope and prayer that among his own posterity there would be no vacant chairs on the other side.

As has been indicated, the Book of Mormon was his love. He read it. He quoted it in his teachings. His voice rang out in eloquent warning of the fate that could overtake this nation unless the people of the land walk in righteousness and serve the God of the Land, who is Jesus Christ. As holder of the keys of the priesthood, restored in this dispensation, he blessed the people he loved. He honored the sacred office to which he had been called. ("Farewell to a Prophet," *Ensign,* July 1994, pp. 39–40.)

Howard W. Hunter

Much has been said about his kindness, his thoughtfulness, his courtesy to others. It is all true. He surrendered himself to the pattern of the Lord whom he loved. He was a quiet and thought-ful man. But he also could be aroused to voice strong and wise opinions. For twenty years I sat next to him in the Council of the Twelve, from the time I was ordained to the apostleship in 1961 until I was called into the Presidency in 1981. The meetings at which I sat at his elbow could be counted in the hundreds. I have seen him in all of his moods, his times of reflection, and in the speaking of his opinions. . . .

Brother Hunter was kind and gentle. But he also could be strong and persuasive in his statements. As has been said, he was trained in the law. He knew how to present a matter. He laid out the various premises in orderly fashion. He moved from these to his conclusion. When he spoke we all listened. His suggestions most often prevailed. But when they were not accepted, he had the flexibility to withdraw his advocacy, to accept the decision of the President of the Church, his prophet, and to thereafter go throughout the Church furthering with conviction the conclusion that was reached and the program determined upon. ("A Prophet Polished and Refined," *Ensign*, April 1995, pp. 33–34.)

REACTIVATION AND RETENTION

See also Fellowshipping

I am satisfied that there are thousands across the world who in their loneliness and hunger for truth are crying out for help. . . . And in addition to these there is another group who are members of the Church in name, but who have left, and who now in their hearts long to return, but do not know how and are too timid to try. . . .

To you, my brethren and sisters, who have taken your spiri-tual inheritance and left, and now find an emptiness in your lives, the way is open for your return. . . .

If you will take the first timid step to return, you will find open arms to greet you and warm friends to make you welcome.

I think I know why some of you left. You were offended by a thoughtless individual who injured you, and you mistook his actions as representative of the Church. Or you may have moved from an area where you were known to an area where you were largely alone, and there grew up with only little knowledge of the Church.

Or you may have been drawn to other company or habits which you felt were incompatible with association in the Church. Or you may have felt yourself wiser in the wisdom of the world than those of your Church associates, and with some air of disdain, withdrawn yourself from their company.

I am not here to dwell on the reasons. I hope you will not. Put the past behind you. ("Everything to Gain—Nothing to Lose," *Ensign*, November 1976, pp. 95–96.)

The way of the gospel is a simple way. Some of the requirements may appear to you as elementary and unnecessary. Do not spurn them. Humble yourselves and walk in obedience. I promise that the results that follow will be marvelous to behold and satisfying to experience. . . .

There is everything to gain and nothing to lose. Come back, my friends. There is more of peace to be found in the Church than you have known in a long while. There are many whose friendship you will come to enjoy. ("Everything to Gain—Nothing to Lose," *Ensign*, November 1976, p. 96.)

One Sunday I found myself in a California city for a stake conference. My name and picture had been in the local newspaper. The phone rang at the stake center as the stake president and I entered the building that morning. The call was for me, and the caller identified himself. He wanted to see me. I excused myself from the meeting I was to have held early that morning and asked the stake president to carry on with it. I had something more important to do.

He came, this friend of mine, timidly and somewhat fearfully. He had been away for a long time. We embraced as brothers long separated. At first the conversation was awkward, but it soon warmed as we discussed together days spent in England many years ago. There were tears in the eyes of this strong man as he spoke of the Church of which he had once been so effective a part, and then told of the long, empty years that had followed. He dwelt upon them as a man speaks of nightmares. When he had described those wasted years, we talked of his returning. He thought it would be difficult, that it would be embarrassing, but he agreed to try.

I had a letter from him not long ago. He said, "I'm back. I'm back, and how wonderful it feels to be home again." ("Everything to Gain—Nothing to Lose," *Ensign,* November 1976, p. 97.)

May I go back to Peter who denied the Lord and wept. Recognizing his error, repenting of his weakness, he turned about and became a mighty voice in bearing witness of the risen Lord. He, the senior apostle, dedicated the remainder of his life to testifying of the mission, the death, and the resurrection of Jesus Christ, the living Son of the living God. He preached the moving sermon on the day of Pentecost when the multitude were touched in their hearts by the power of the Holy Ghost. In the authority of the priesthood received from his Master, he, with John, healed the lame man, the miracle that brought on persecution. He fearlessly spoke for his brethren when they were arraigned before the Sanhedrin. His was the vision that led to carrying the gospel to the Gentiles. (See Acts 2–4, 10.)

He suffered chains and prison and a terrible martyr's death as a witness of Him who had called him from his nets to become a fisher of men (see Matt. 4:19). He remained faithful and true to the great and compelling trust given when the resurrected Lord in his final instructions to the eleven apostles charged them to go "and teach all nations, baptizing them in the name of the Father, and of the Son, and of the Holy Ghost" (Matt. 28:19). And he it was who, with James and John, came back to earth in this dispensation to restore the holy priesthood, under which divine authority the Church of Jesus Christ was organized in these latter days and under which same authority it now functions. These mighty works and many more unmentioned were done by Peter who once had denied and sorrowed, and then rose above that remorse to carry forward the work of the Savior following his ascension and to participate in the restoration of that work in this dispensation.

Now, if there be any within the sound of my voice today who by word or act have denied the faith, I pray that you may draw comfort and resolution from the example of Peter who, though he had walked daily with Jesus, in an hour of extremity denied both the Lord and the testimony which he carried in his own heart. But he rose above this, and became a mighty defender and a powerful advocate. So too, there is a way for you to turn about, and add your strength and faith to the strength and faith of others in building the kingdom of God. ("And Peter Went Out and Wept Bitterly," *Ensign,* May 1979, pp. 66–67.)

There sits in this hall today a man who grew up with love for the Church. But when he became involved in his business career, obsessed with ambition he began in effect to deny the faith. The manner of his living became almost a repudiation of his loyalty. Then fortunately, before he had gone too far, he heard the whisperings of the still, small voice. There came a saving sense of remorse. He turned around, and today he stands as the president of a great stake of Zion, while also serving as a senior officer in one of the leading industrial corporations of the nation and of the world.

My beloved brethren and sisters who may also have drifted, the Church needs you, and you need the Church. You will find many ears that will listen with understanding. There will be many hands to help you find your way back. There will be hearts to warm your own. There will be tears, not of bitterness but of rejoicing. ("And Peter Went Out and Wept Bitterly," *Ensign,* May 1979, p. 67.)

I should like to read portions of a letter that came to my desk. I have changed the names to preserve anonymity and have somewhat abbreviated it, paraphrasing a few words in the process. The letter reads:

"Dear President Hinckley,

"When I met you in the elevator at the hospital I had the urge to write you and tell you of some of the things that have happened to me.

"When I was sixteen or seventeen I cared nothing for the Church and would not have anything to do with it. But a bishop who was concerned about me came over to see me and asked me to help build some scenery for a road show production, and of course I told him no.

"Well, about ten days went by, and the bishop came back to ask me to build the scenery, and again I told him no. But then he went on to explain that he had asked others, and they had told him that they didn't know how. He indicated that I was needed. I finally gave in and proceeded to build the scenery.

"When I got it done, I said, 'There is your scenery,' and decided I had done my part. But the bishop insisted that they needed me on the stage to move the scenery and make sure it got put up right and that it got moved carefully as the road show moved from ward to ward. So I finally gave in again.

"That bishop kept me busy for quite a while, and pretty soon I was involved and enjoying it. He then moved from our area and we got a new bishop, and he picked up the challenge and kept after me.

"Bishop Smith had asked me to go on a mission, but I was undecided on that, and when Bishop Sorensen was put in, he asked me also, and I finally decided that I would go.

"Well, the bishop and I went to tell Mom and Dad about my decision. They told the bishop they couldn't pay for it. Dad told the bishop that if I was really sincere about going that I should work and save, and pay for the mission myself.

"My eyesight was not the greatest, as you know, and when I went places I had to be taken. When I became sixteen, I wanted to drive a car more than anything, and Dad took me to several eye doctors, all with the same result. The vision in my right eye was 20/800, and the vision in my left eye was 20/50, and I had an astigmatism. So earning enough money to go on a mission was not an easy task. I worked in the sign shop at a department store for six to eight months to save some money. The bishop finally felt it was time for me to go, and we went to talk to my parents again. I had a thousand dollars saved, and the bishop told my Dad that the elders quorum would support me for the rest. Dad sat there for a while and said if anybody was going to support his son, he would. I filled out my papers and got my call in May of 1961. . . .

"I have held many positions in the Church: chorister, Senior Aaronic Adviser, everything in the elders quorum, Assistant Ward Clerk, Seventies President, Executive Secretary, and now I am a counselor in the bishopric. . . .

"Now for the most amazing piece of news ever. Two years ago in June, I went to a new eye doctor who examined my eyes and asked me what restrictions I had on my driver's license. I told him that didn't have a license. He said that my eyesight was probably acceptable.

"I sat there in shock, and my wife said, 'Does this mean he could get a driver's license?' The doctor said, 'I don't see why not.' The next day my wife had me signed up for a driver education course, and after I finished it I went to get my license and they checked my eyes. The doctor had written a note explaining my eye problem, and that maybe I should not drive at night. The examiner put the letters up and I read them right off. He went to talk to his supervisor, and came back and approved my license with only a minor restriction.

"President Hinckley, the Lord has blessed me more than I can ever deserve. People say how lucky I am that my eyes have improved so much, but I know that it is the Lord's doing. I feel it is because I have tried to serve the Lord and do what I can to build up his kingdom here on the earth. I am sure there are times he is disappointed in me, and I'm sure he should be. But I will try to do my best and be worthy of his blessings upon me and my family."

He concludes with appreciation and testimony and signs his name. I have taken your time to read this somewhat lengthy letter because I feel it tells so simply and yet so eloquently what this work is all about.

Under the sacred and compelling trust we have as members of the Church of Jesus Christ, ours is a work of redemption, of lifting and saving those who need help. Ours is a task of raising the sights of those of our people who fail to realize the great potential that lies within them. ("What This Work Is All About," *Ensign,* November 1982, pp. 7–8.)

Here is a great key to reactivation of many of those who have fallen by the wayside. Each has a talent that can be employed. It is the task of leaders to match those talents with needs, and then to offer a challenge. ("What This Work Is All About," *Ensign,* November 1982, p. 8.)

I recognize that there are many in this vast congregation who have not had the opportunity of temple marriage, whose husbands may not be members of the Church or may not have qualified themselves to go to the house of the Lord. To you I wish to say, be patient, be prayerful. Stifle your tendency to criticize. Live the kind of life in your home that will cause your companion to see in you that goodness, that virtue, and that strength which come of the gospel.

I remember a family I knew fifty years ago. The wife was a devoted member of the Church. The husband was not a member. He smoked and drank. She hoped and she prayed. She lived for the day when his heart might be touched by the Spirit of the Lord. Years passed one after another into more than a decade. Her example was one of goodness and gladness and faith. After many years he began to soften. He saw what the Church did for her and for their children. He turned around. He humbled himself. He was baptized. He has since served as a quorum president and a bishop, as a missionary, and as a worker in the temple.

You have not failed until you have quit trying, and please remember that your example in your home will be a more persuasive sermon than will any other kind of preachment. ("Live Up to Your Inheritance," *Ensign*, November 1983, p. 82.)

I wish to mention something I have spoken on in many gatherings. It is concerned with the disheartening losses we experience among converts to the Church, as well as among the ranks of the membership generally. I feel so much of it is unnecessary. . . . I have something of a slogan that I commend to you: "Save the convert. Restore the dropout."

I want to emphasize that there is a very positive and wonderful net growth in the Church. Generally speaking there is greater activity than we have experienced in more than half a century, notwithstanding the fact that we are reaching out into distant areas of the world. We have every reason to feel encouraged. But any convert whose faith grows cold is a tragedy. Any member who falls into inactivity is a matter for serious concern. The Lord left the ninety and nine to find the lost sheep. His concern for the dropout was so serious that He made it the theme of one of His great lessons. We cannot let down. We must constantly keep Church officers and the membership aware of the tremendous obligation to fellowship in a very real and warm and wonderful way those who come into the Church as converts, and to reach out with love to those who for one reason or another step into the shadows of inactivity. There is ample evidence that it can be done where there is a will to do it. (Regional Representatives Seminar, March 31, 1989.)

I want to give you a threefold key for holding on to converts. It's very simple. Love them. Challenge them. Thank them. . . . Let them know of your interest in them. Put your arms around them. Let them feel the warmth of your interest and concern. Challenge them. Give them something to do. They will not grow strong in the faith without exercise. Faith and testimony are like the muscles of my arm. If I use those muscles and nourish them, they grow stronger. If I put my arm in a sling and leave it there, it becomes weak and ineffective, and so it is with testimonies.

Now, some of you say they are not ready to assume responsibility. But none of us was ready when the call came. I can say that of myself. Do you think I was ready for this great and sacred calling? I felt overwhelmed. I felt inadequate. I still feel overwhelmed. I still feel inadequate. But I am trying to go forward, seeking the blessing of the Lord and trying to do His will and hoping and praying that my service will be acceptable to him. The first responsibility I had in this Church was a counselor to a deacons quorum president when I was twelve years of age. I didn't feel adequate. I felt overwhelmed. But I tried, just as you do, and after that came other responsibilities. Never a feeling of adequacy, but always a feeling of gratitude and a willingness to try.

Thank them. We are pretty slow in this Church sometimes to thank people for the service which they give. Everyone welcomes a word of appreciation.

Love them. Challenge them with responsibility. Overlook their mistakes if they make them and gently and graciously teach them. (Berlin Germany Regional Conference, priesthood leadership session, June 15, 1996.)

It is a difficult thing for one who has lived in the world and partaken of the world's ways to come into this Church. We do things in a different way and these people need help. They need companionship. They need love. They need direction. They need kindness when they make a mistake. They need to learn about this Church. They need to have things to do. I make a plea to you . . . an urgent plea to put your arms around these converts and welcome them into the Church. There is no need to lose them. We do not need to lose the converts to this Church if we will be as anxiously engaged in assisting them with their problems as the missionaries were in teaching them the gospel. And that places upon you and upon me a very serious and a very compelling burden. (Palm Springs California Regional Conference, February 9, 1997.)

It was the Savior who left the ninety and nine to go out and find the one. Now we are obsessed with the ninety and nine, and we are not very much concerned with the one. But the ninety and nine will go along pretty well. They don't need a lot of attention. I don't mean to suggest that you not do your duty toward them, but it is the one that we need to help. Let's work at it. Let us do something about these people and those who are cold in their faith. They are worth saving and bringing back. Do you know who they are? Have you identified them? Start with that step. And then put them to work. No man or woman will grow in this Church unless he or she is busy and has something to do. (Jordan Utah South Regional Conference, priesthood leadership session, March 1, 1997.)

With the ever-increasing number of converts, we must make an increasingly substantial effort to assist them as they find their way. Every one of them needs three things: a friend, a responsibility, and nurturing with the "good word of God" (Moro. 6:4). It is our duty and opportunity to provide these things.

To illustrate, I think I would like to share with you one of my failures. I suppose some people think I have never experienced failure. I have. Let me tell you of one such instance.

Sixty-three years ago, while serving as a missionary in the British Isles, my companion and I taught, and it was my pleasure to baptize, a young man. He was well educated. He was refined. He was studious. I was so proud of this gifted young man who had come into the Church. I felt he had all of the qualifications someday to become a leader among our people.

He was in the course of making the big adjustment from convert to member. For a short period before I was released, mine was the opportunity to be his friend. Then I was released to return home. He was given a small responsibility in the branch in London. He knew nothing of what was expected of him. He made a mistake. The head of the organization where he served was a man I can best describe as being short on love and strong on criticism. In a rather unmerciful way, he went after my friend who had made the simple mistake.

The young man left our rented hall that night smarting and hurt by his superior officer. He said to himself, "If that is the kind of people they are, then I am not going back."

He drifted into inactivity. The years passed. . . .

When I was in England again, I tried desperately to find him. . . . I came home and finally, after a long search, was able to track him down.

I wrote to him. He responded but with no mention of the gospel.

When next I was in London, I again searched for him. The day I was to leave, I found him. I called him, and we met in the underground station. He threw his arms around me as I did around him. I had very little time before I had to catch my plane, but we talked briefly and with what I think was a true regard for one another. He gave me another embrace before I left. I determined that I would never lose track of him again. . . .

The years passed. I grew older as did he. He retired from his work and moved to Switzerland. On one occasion when I was in Switzerland, I went out of my way to find the village where he lived. We spent the better part of the day together—he, his wife, my wife, and myself. We had a wonderful time, but it was evident that the fire of faith had long since died. I tried every way I knew, but I could not find a way to rekindle it. I continued my correspondence. I sent him books, magazines, recordings of the Tabernacle Choir, and other things for which he expressed appreciation.

He died a few months ago. His wife wrote me to inform me of this. She said, "You were the best friend he ever had."

Tears coursed my cheeks when I read that letter. I knew I had failed. Perhaps if I had been there to pick him up when he was first knocked down, he might have made a different thing of his life. I think I could have helped him then. I think I could have dressed the wound from which he suffered. I have only one comfort: I tried. I have only one sorrow: I failed.

The challenge now is greater than it has ever been because the number of converts is greater than we have ever before known. . . . Every convert is precious. Every convert is a son or daughter of God. Every convert is a great and serious responsibility. . . .

In a recent press interview I was asked, "What brings you the greatest satisfaction as you see the work of the Church today?"

My response: "The most satisfying experience I have is to see what this gospel does for people. It gives them a new outlook on life. It gives them a perspective that they have never felt before. It raises their sights to things noble and divine. Something happens to them that is miraculous to behold. They look to Christ and come alive."

. . . Your friendly ways are needed. Your sense of responsibility is needed. The Savior of all mankind left the ninety and nine to find the one lost. That one who was lost need not have become lost. But if he is out there somewhere in the shadows, and if it means leaving the ninety and nine, we must do so to find him. ("Converts and Young Men," *Ensign,* May 1997, pp. 47–48.)

RELIEF SOCIETY

I know that many of you out there feel lonely at times. Some of you girls find that there are only two or three Latter-day Saints in the large schools which you attend. You women who work may find yourselves the only member of the Church at your places of employment. You who are widows and some who have been divorced may feel that you are alone. The numbers who are participating in this meeting tonight should give you the assurance that you are not alone. You [in Relief Society] are part of the greatest sisterhood on earth. ("Live Up to Your Inheritance," *Ensign,* November 1983, p. 81.)

The Relief Society of the Church . . . has as its motto Charity Never Faileth. Innumerable are the deeds of these remarkable and wonderful and unselfish women in succoring those in distress, in binding up the wounds of those who have been hurt, in giving cheer and comfort to those in distress, in feeding the hungry and clothing the naked, and in lifting up those who have fallen and giving them strength and encouragement and the will to go forward. ("*Mormon* Should Mean 'More Good,'" *Ensign,* November 1990, p. 54.)

The growth of the Relief Society from twenty members, when it was organized on 17 March 1842 in the frontier city of Nauvoo, to more than three million 150 years later, with members in communities large and small across the world, is a saga both extraordinary and remarkable. While all who qualify as members do not participate, the very large number who are active is most impressive. ("Ambitious to Do Good," *Ensign,* March 1992, p. 2.)

Who can gauge the miraculous effects upon the lives of millions of women whose knowledge has been increased, whose vision has been extended, whose lives have been broadened, and whose understanding of the things of God has been enriched by reason of countless lessons effectively taught and learned in meetings of the Relief Society?

Who can measure the joy that has come into the lives of these women as they have mingled together, socializing in the atmosphere of the ward or branch, enriching the lives of one another through companionships that have been sweet and treasured?

Who, even in the wildest stretch of imagination, can fathom the uncountable acts of charity that have been performed, the food that has been put on barren tables, the faith that has been nurtured in desperate hours of illness, the wounds that have been bound up, the pains that have been ameliorated by loving hands and quiet and reassuring words, the comfort that has been extended in times of death and consequent loneliness? . . .

Following the exodus from Nauvoo, the formal Relief Society organization disintegrated while the Saints were crossing the plains. But the impetus and the spirit of the work continued. The sick were nursed, children were born, and mothers and babies were cared for during the long and difficult trek. The dead were dressed and buried by kind and gentle hands along the entire length of that trail from the Mississippi River to Winter Quarters and to the valley of the Great Salt Lake.

In 1866 Brigham Young called Eliza R. Snow to serve as president of the Relief Society and gave her a mandate to see that an organization was established in every ward and branch of the Church. This has since been the policy. Wherever the Church has gone, the organization of a Relief Society in each branch has been basic.

No one could possibly calculate the projects that have been undertaken and completed by local Relief Societies. No one could possibly estimate the good that has come into the lives of the women belonging to these organizations and those whom they have benefited through their good works. ("Ambitious to Do Good," *Ensign*, March 1992, pp. 4–5.)

God bless the Relief Society of The Church of Jesus Christ of Latter-day Saints. May the spirit of love which has motivated its members for a century and a half continue to grow and be felt over the world. May their works of charity touch for good the lives of uncounted numbers wherever they find expression. And may light and understanding, learning and knowledge, and eternal truth grace the lives of generations of women yet to come, throughout the nations of the earth, because of this singular and divinely established institution. ("Ambitious to Do Good," *Ensign*, March 1992, p. 6.)

The elements from which the Relief Society grew predate its organization. Those elements include the natural instincts of women to reach out to assist in promoting the common good, to help those in distress, and to improve their own minds and talents.

During the construction of the Kirtland Temple the women were called upon to grind their china into small particles to be mixed with the plaster used on the walls of the temple, which would catch the light of the sun and the moon and reflect that light to beautify the appearance of the building.

In those times, when there was very little of money but an abundance of faith, the workmen gave of their strength and resources to the construction of the Lord's house. The women supplied them with food, the best they could prepare. Edward W. Tullidge reported that while the women were sewing the temple veils, Joseph Smith, observing them, said, "Well, sisters, you are always on hand. The sisters are always first and foremost in all good works. Mary was first at the resurrection; and the sisters now are the first to work on the inside of the temple." (Edward W. Tullidge, *The Women of Mormondom*, Salt Lake City: Photo Lithographic Reprint, 1957, p. 76.)

Again in Nauvoo, when the temple was under construction, a few women joined together to make shirts for the workmen. It was out of these circumstances that twenty of them gathered on Thursday, 17 March 1842, in the upper room of the Prophet's store.

On that occasion Joseph Smith organized them and said that this "society of sisters might provoke the brethren to good works in looking to the wants of the poor—searching after objects of charity, and in administering to their wants—to assist by correcting the morals and strengthening the virtues of the community." (Minutes of the Female Relief Society of Nauvoo, 17 Mar. 1842, p. 13.)

From that modest beginning has grown what I regard as the largest and most effective organization of its kind in all the world. At that first meeting, when Emma H. Smith was elected president, she said that "each member should be ambitious to do good." (Ibid.) . . .

It was at a subsequent meeting of the society, held on 28 April 1842, that the Prophet, speaking as a prophet, declared: "This Society is to get instruction through the order which God has established—through the medium of those appointed to lead—and I now turn the key to you in the name of God, and this Society shall rejoice, and knowledge and intelligence shall flow down from this time—this is the beginning of better days to this Society." (Minutes, 28 April 1842; spelling standardized.)

That prophetic statement has stood as a charter through a century and a half of the Relief Society of The Church of Jesus Christ of Latter-day Saints. ("Ambitious to Do Good," *Ensign*, March 1992, pp. 2, 4.)

Lucy Mack Smith, mother of the Prophet, in speaking to the sisters in Nauvoo, said, "We must cherish one another, watch over one another, comfort one another and gain instruction that we may all sit down in heaven together." (Minutes, 24 March 1842.) The history of [Relief Society] has shown that women of the Church have not had to wait to sit together in heaven to taste the sweet fruit of the kind of activities she described. They have experienced much of heaven on earth as in life they have cherished one another, comforted one another, and instructed one another. ("Ambitious to Do Good," *Ensign*, March 1992, pp. 4–5.)

If you want to find a group of happy women, go visit one of these Relief Society meetings any time. See what they are doing. You will find a group of happy women learning and working together. (Edelman Public Relations Luncheon, Harvard Club, New York, November 13, 1995.)

Women have a tremendous place in this Church. They have their own organization. It was started in 1842 by the Prophet Joseph Smith, called the Relief Society, because its initial purpose was to administer help to those in need. It has grown to be the largest women's organization in the world, with a membership of more than three million. They have their own officers, their own presidency, their own board. That reaches down to the smallest unit of the Church everywhere in the world. (Interview with Mike Wallace of *60 Minutes*, December 18, 1995.)

REPENTANCE

If there be any here who have . . . sinned, there is repentance and there is forgiveness, provided there is "godly sorrow." (See 2 Cor. 7:10.) All is not lost. Each of you has a bishop, who has been ordained and set apart under the authority of the holy priesthood and who, in the exercise of his office, is entitled to the inspiration of the Lord. He is a man of experience, he is a man of understanding, he is a man who carries in his heart a love for the youth of his ward. He is a servant of God who understands his obligation of confidentiality and who will help you with your problem. Do not be afraid to talk with him. ("Be Not Deceived," *Ensign,* November 1983, p. 45.)

John the Baptist went on to say to Joseph Smith and Oliver Cowdery that this priesthood, which he bestowed upon them, included the keys of the gospel of repentance. What a marvelous and wonderful thing this is! It is our privilege, yours and mine, as those who hold this priesthood, to repent of evil with the expectation that we will be forgiven if we live worthy of the forgiveness of the Lord. Furthermore, it is our privilege to preach repentance, as the Lord has made clear in section 20 of the Doctrine and Covenants. He there sets forth the duties of deacons, teachers, and priests. It is their responsibility to watch over the Church and see that there is no iniquity and to invite all to come unto Christ. That involves repentance from sin and obedience to the principles and laws of the gospel. ("The Aaronic Priesthood—a Gift from God," *Ensign,* May 1988, p. 46.)

Eternal vigilance is the price of eternal development. Occasionally we may stumble. I thank the Lord for the great principle of repentance and forgiveness. When we drop the ball, when we make a mistake, there is held out to us the word of the Lord that he will forgive our sins and remember them no more against us. But somehow we are prone to remember them against ourselves. ("Don't Drop the Ball," *Ensign,* November 1994, p. 48.)

When I was a boy living here in Salt Lake City, most homes were heated with coal stoves. Black smoke belched forth from almost every chimney. As winter came to a close, black soot and grime were everywhere, both inside and outside of the house. There was a ritual through which we passed each year, not a very pleasant one, as we viewed it. It involved every member of the family. It was known as spring cleaning. When the weather warmed after the long winter, a week or so was designated as cleanup time. It was usually when there was a holiday and included two Saturdays. My mother ran the show. All of the curtains were taken down and laundered. Then they were carefully ironed. The windows were washed inside and out, and oh, what a job that was in that big two-story house. Wallpaper was on all of the walls, and father would bring home numerous cans of wallpaper cleaner. It was like bread dough, but it was a pretty pink in color when the container was opened. It had an interesting smell, a pleasant refreshing kind of smell. We all pitched in. We would knead some of the cleaning dough in our hands, climb a ladder, and begin on the high ceiling, and then work down the walls. The dough was soon black from the dirt it lifted from the paper. It was a terrible task, very tiring, but the results were like magic. We would stand back and compare the dirty surface with the clean surface. It was amazing to us how much better the clean walls looked.

All of the carpets were taken up and dragged out to the backyard, where they were hung over the clothesline, one by one. Each of us boys would have what we called a carpet beater, a device made of light steel rods with a wooden handle. As we beat the carpet, the dust would fly, and we would have to keep going until there was no dust left. We detested that work. But when all of it was done, and everything was back in place, the result was wonderful. The house was clean, our spirits renewed. The whole world looked better.

This is what some of us need to do with our lives. Isaiah said:

"Wash you, make you clean; put away the evil of your doings from before mine eyes; cease to do evil;

"Learn to do well. . . .

"Come now, and let us reason together, saith the Lord: though your sins be as scarlet, they shall be as white as snow; though they be red like crimson, they shall be as wool" (Isa. 1:16–18).

"Be ye clean that bear the vessels of the Lord" (D&C 133:5). Thus has He spoken to us in modern revelation. Be clean in body. Be clean in mind. Be clean in language. Be clean in dress and manner. ("Be Ye Clean," *Ensign*, May 1996, pp. 47–48.)

If any of you has stepped over the line, please do not think all is lost. The Lord reaches out to help you, and there are many willing hands in the Church also who will help you. Put evil behind you. Pray about the situation, talk with your parents if you can, and talk with your bishop. You will find that he will listen and do so with confidentiality. He will help you. We all stand ready to help you.

Repentance is one of the first principles of the gospel. Forgiveness is a mark of divinity. There is hope for you. Your lives are ahead, and they can be filled with happiness, even though the past may have been marred by sin. This is a work of saving and assisting people with their problems. This is the purpose of the gospel.

This is the time, this is the very hour, to repent of any evil in the past, to ask for forgiveness, to stand a little taller and then to go forward with confidence and faith. ("Stand True and Faithful," *Ensign*, May 1996, p. 94.)

RESTORATION OF THE GOSPEL

See also Dispensation of the Fulness of Times; First Vision

The year was 1820, the season spring. The boy with questions walked into the grove of his father's farm. There, finding himself alone, he pleaded in prayer for that wisdom which James promised would be given liberally to those who ask of God in faith. (See James 1:5.) There, in circumstances which he has described in much detail, he beheld the Father and the Son, the great God of the universe and the risen Lord, both of whom spoke to him.

This transcendent experience opened the marvelous work of restoration. It lifted the curtain on the long-promised dispensation of the fulness of times.

For more than a century and a half, enemies, critics, and some would-be scholars have worn out their lives trying to disprove the validity of that vision. Of course they cannot understand it. The things of God are understood by the Spirit of God. There had been nothing of comparable magnitude since the Son of God walked the earth in mortality. Without it as a foundation stone for our faith and organization, we have nothing. With it, we have everything.

Much has been written, much will be written, in an effort to explain it away. The finite mind cannot comprehend it. But the testimony of the Holy Spirit, experienced by countless numbers of people all through the years since it happened, bears witness that it is true, that it happened as Joseph Smith said it happened, that it was as real as the sunrise over Palmyra, that it is an essential foundation stone, a cornerstone, without which the Church could not be "fitly framed together." ("The Cornerstones of Our Faith," *Ensign,* November 1984, p. 52.)

You and I are experiencing the profound and wonderful blessings of the dispensation of the fulness of times. In this day and time there have been restored to the earth all of the principles, powers, blessings, and keys of all previous dispensations. By certain and clear and unequivocal revelation there has come knowledge of the living reality of God our Eternal Father and His Beloved Son, the Savior and Redeemer of the world. ("'A Chosen Generation,'" *Ensign,* May 1992, p. 70.)

This is The Church of Jesus Christ of Latter-day Saints, the only true and living church upon the face of the whole earth. A minister said to me one time, "It is egotistical to say that." I said, "I didn't say that. The Lord said it. I am only quoting." This is The Church of Jesus Christ of Latter-day Saints. We can and we must recognize the good in other churches and in other people. We can disagree without being disagreeable. We must be tolerant. We must work with others who are engaged in good causes to bring about good results. But we must never lose sight of the fact that the God of heaven brought forth this work in this the Dispensation of the Fulness of Times, that His true church might be upon the earth. And with it came the restoration of the holy priesthood, under the hands of John the Baptist, who came to earth a resurrected being and brought the keys of the Aaronic Priesthood, including the keys of the ministering of angels. Following that, the Melchizedek Priesthood was restored under the hands of Peter, James, and John. This was followed by the bestowal of various authority under the hands of Moses and

Elias and Elijah. There is nothing like it anywhere. This is not a reformation. This is a restoration of that church which was set up by the Savior. This is the handiwork of the God of heaven and His Beloved Son. (Anchorage Alaska Regional Conference, June 18, 1995.)

I like to reflect now and again on the purposes of the bringing forth of this work, as the Lord set those purposes forth in the first section of the Doctrine and Covenants: "That every man might speak in the name of God the Lord, even the Savior of the world; That faith also might increase in the earth; That mine everlasting covenant might be established; That the fulness of my gospel might be proclaimed by the weak and the simple unto the ends of the world, and before kings and rulers. . . . that they might come to understanding." (D&C 1:20–24.)

We are among "the weak and the simple." We are not very professional, most of us, in this work. We're ordinary people with ordinary capacities, who have been given an extraordinary assignment—to teach the gospel to the world, which will save the world, if people of the world will hearken unto the message we have to give.

And to see what's taking place! Ten years ago we never would have dreamed that we'd be in some of the places we're in today. To think we'd have missionaries and congregations in Russia and Latvia and Albania and Mongolia, places of that kind! Most of us never knew that there was such a city on the whole face of the earth as Ulaanbaatar. (Mission Presidents Seminar, June 24, 1995.)

Some years ago I had an assignment to the Rochester Stake conference. I said on Saturday to the stake president and the regional representative and the mission president: "Tomorrow is Sunday. Let's get up very early in the morning and go to the Sacred Grove." It was in the springtime. Nobody was there. It had been raining during the night. Little drops of rain were on the small leaves. We went into the Grove, four of us, and we joined in prayer. I did not hear a voice. I think none of us heard a voice. But there came into my mind a conviction which has never left me of the reality, so certain that I could not deny, that it happened here. It happened as Joseph said it happened. He was visited by the Father and the Son—the great God of the Universe, the Creator of the universe, the greatest of all and the Redeemer of the world, He who had been the great Jehovah and who became the mighty Messiah, He who became the first fruits of them that slept, through whose suffering and sacrifice salvation is made available to all men and women—visited the boy Joseph there and conversed with him. I am grateful for that knowledge. I am grateful for that testimony. I am confident that as Joseph says in his history, it is a true account, I know it is. I see the wonder of this Church. I see it every day as it moves across the world. You cannot build strength on falsehood. You cannot build conviction on imagination. The basis of this great thing which we have, the restored gospel of the Lord Jesus Christ and the Church, which was organized under divine authority, find their roots in that vision which occurred in the grove not far from here. (New York Rochester Missionary Meeting, July 12, 1996.)

RESURRECTION

Men are born, they live for an hour of glory, and die. Most throughout their lives are teased by various hopes; and among all the hopes of men in all ages of time, none is so great as the hope of immortality.

The empty tomb that first Easter morning brought the most comforting assurance that can come into man's heart. This was the affirmative answer to the ageless question raised by Job, "If a man die, shall he live again?" (Job 14:14.) . . .

" . . . [but] those that die in me shall not taste of death, for it shall be sweet unto them" (D&C 42:45–46). . . .

This is the promise of the risen Lord. This is the relevance of Jesus to a world in which all must die. But there is further and more immediate relevance. As he is the conqueror of death, so also is he the master of life. His way is the answer to the troubles of the world in which we live. (Conference Report, April 1969, pp. 59–60.)

"If a man die, shall he live again?" (Job 14:14.) This is the great universal question framed by Job. He spoke what every other living man or woman has pondered. The Christ alone, of all the millions who up to that time had walked the earth, was the first to emerge from the grave triumphant, a living soul complete in spirit and body. He became "the firstfruits of them that slept." (1 Cor. 15:20.) Were greater words ever spoken than those of the angel that first resurrection morn—"Why seek ye the living among the dead?" (Luke 24:5.) "He is not here: for he is risen, as he said." (Matt. 28:6.)

His death sealed the testimony of His love for all mankind. His resurrection opened the gates of salvation to the sons and daughters of God of all generations. . . .

All of us will die. But that will not be the end. Just as He in the spirit world taught those who once had been disobedient in the days of Noah and were capable of being taught, even so shall each of us continue as individual personalities capable of learning and teaching and other activities. And just as He took up His body and came forth from the tomb, even so shall all of us enjoy a reunion of body and spirit to become living souls in the day of our own resurrection. ("The Victory over Death," *Ensign*, May 1985, pp. 52–53.)

I penned these lines some years ago while seated in the funeral service of a friend:

> *What is this thing that men call death,*
> *This quiet passing in the night?*
> *'Tis not the end, but genesis*
> *Of better worlds and greater light.*
>
> *O God, touch Thou my aching heart,*
> *And calm my troubled, haunting fears.*
> *Let hope and faith, transcendent, pure,*
> *Give strength and peace beyond my tears.*
>
> *There is no death, but only change*
> *With recompense for victory won;*
> *The gift of Him who loved all men,*
> *The Son of God, the Holy One.*

("The Empty Tomb Bore Testimony," *Ensign*, May 1988, p. 66.)

Can you imagine what a wonderful experience it must have been for Joseph Smith and Oliver Cowdery when John the Baptist spoke to them? Here was a man who had lived upon the earth more than 1800 years earlier. Now he was speaking to two young men while he held his hands upon their heads. His was a resurrected body. Theirs were mortal bodies. They felt his hands, the materiality of them, and understood the words which he spoke. This tells us that resurrected beings are tangible, that they can move and act, that they can speak and be understood. (Priesthood Restoration Commemoration Fireside, May 15, 1988.)

Just as the Savior's resurrection from the dead was the great summation of His life, so is service in the temple a tangible assurance that if a man die he shall live again, and in that future life he will have opportunity to grow toward exaltation. (Temple Presidents Seminar, August 15, 1989.)

Of all the victories in human history, none is so great, none so universal in its effect, none so everlasting in its consequences as the victory of the crucified Lord, who came forth in the resurrection that first Easter morning. ("The Son of God," *Ensign*, December 1992, p. 2.)

We are here for a purpose. We shall live after we die, and all of it is a part of eternity, and the key to everlasting life is the atonement wrought by the Savior. Through His crucifixion, His death on the cross, the giving of His life came the resurrection. As Paul said, "For as in Adam all die, even so in Christ shall all be made alive." (1 Corinthians 15:22.) He was the firstfruits of the resurrection, and beyond that great, marvelous gift which has come through the grace of God without any effort on our part, there has come an enlarged gift that leads to eternal life and exaltation in our Father's kingdom. (England Birmingham Missionary Meeting, August 29, 1995.)

I thank the Lord for the assurance that has come to us of the immortality of the soul. We have walked around old churchyards where are buried the dead who died long ago. Someday they will rise in the resurrection, with a renewal of body and spirit under the plan of the Almighty, made possible by the atonement of the Lord Jesus Christ. What a wonderful thing that is! We do not need to feel dour. We ought to rejoice. (Nottingham England Fireside, August 30, 1995.)

None of us fully understands the Atonement. I think it is beyond the comprehension of any man, but we know something of it, and we know that as a result of it all will be resurrected from the grave, and that those who walk in obedience to His commandments will be given the opportunity of going on to eternal exaltation. Nothing can compare with that. All of us are going to die someday, but that won't be the end. We'll go on living because Christ broke the bands of death for each of us. (San Diego California Young Adult Fireside, March 24, 1996.)

REVELATION

See also Holy Ghost

Fundamental in Mormon theology is the principle of modern revelation. . . . Christians and Jews generally maintain that God revealed himself and directed chosen men in ancient times. Mormonism maintains that the need for divine guidance is as great in our modern, complex world as it was in the comparatively simple times of the Hebrews. It is true that fundamental truths set forth in the Old and New Testaments are as binding in our day as in the day they were pronounced. Yet our daily life poses problems unknown centuries ago. Moreover, some of the teachings of the Bible have been interpreted in so many different ways because the record is not clear, that many thoughtful people know not what to believe.

If God spoke anciently, is it unreasonable to believe that he can speak in our time? What man would think to deny God the right to express himself?

In essence, Mormonism claims to be a modern revelation of old principles divinely pronounced with new emphasis and completeness in our day. (*What of the Mormons?* pamphlet, 1982, p. 9.)

"We believe all that God has revealed, all that He does now reveal, and we believe that He will yet reveal many great and important things pertaining to the Kingdom of God." (Article of Faith 9.)

This statement from the Prophet Joseph Smith is the creed, the guide, the foundation of the faith of all members of The Church of Jesus Christ of Latter-day Saints.

God is the one sure source of truth. He is the fount of all inspiration. It is from him that the world must receive direction if peace is to come to the earth and if goodwill is to prevail among men. This earth is his creation. We are his children. Out of the love he bears for us, he will guide us if we will seek, listen, and obey. "Surely the Lord God will do nothing, but he revealeth his secrets unto his servants the prophets." (Amos 3:7.) (*Be Thou an Example* [Salt Lake City: Deseret Book, 1981], p. 92.)

Somebody asked Brother Widtsoe once, "When are we going to have another revelation? How is it that we haven't had any revelations since the Doctrine and Covenants was compiled? How long has it been since we've had a revelation?" Brother Widtsoe replied, "Oh, about last Thursday." Now, that's the way it goes. Each Thursday, when we are at home, the First Presidency and the Twelve meet in the temple, in those sacred hallowed precincts, and we pray together and discuss certain matters together, and the spirit of revelation comes upon those present. I know. I have seen it. I was there that June day in 1978 when President Kimball received revelation, surrounded by members of the Twelve, of whom I was one at the time. This is the work of God. This is His almighty work. No man can stop or hinder it. It will go on and continue to grow and bless the lives of people across the earth. (Ketchikan Alaska Fireside, June 22, 1995.)

I remember a mission presidents seminar we had many years ago. We brought the mission presidents in from the world, and we had a testimony meeting at the close. One mission president told this story: "I dreamed one night that one of my missionaries off in a distant place was in deep mud. It was up to his shoulders. He was sinking to his chin. And I awakened, and I couldn't get that graphic picture out of my mind. I went downstairs, awakened my assistants, and said, 'There's something wrong with Elder so-and-so, out in such-and-such a place. I want you to get dressed right now and drive there and see what's wrong.' It was a six-hour drive, but they did as I asked. When they arrived, they found this missionary in serious moral difficulty. Not so far gone that he would have to be sent home, but approaching that."

Listen to the whisperings of the Spirit. Brother Harold B. Lee set me apart, when he was a member of the Twelve, as a stake president. I remember only one thing he said: "Listen for the whisperings of the Spirit in the middle of the night, and respond to those whisperings." I don't know why revelation comes sometimes in the night, but it does. It comes in the day as well, of course. But listen to the whisperings of the Spirit, the gift of revelation, to which you are entitled. (Mission Presidents Seminar, June 24, 1995.)

We believe all that has been revealed. We believe in all that is now revealed. We believe the Lord will yet reveal many great and important things. Now we have a great body of revelation which guides us in the everyday conduct of the affairs of the Church. Situations arise where we feel we need guidance. When those conditions happen, we discuss the matter, pray about it, perhaps fast about it, and go to the Lord about it. It is like the experience recounted by Elijah, who needed help on a problem and went to the Lord, and a great wind occurred and the Lord was not in the wind. Then an earthquake, and the Lord was not in the earthquake. Then a fire, and the Lord was not in the fire. And then a still, small voice. That is the way it works. (Interview with Mike Scheartl of *Fox Network News*, December 11, 1996.)

REVERENCE

See also Meditation; Sabbath Day

Socializing is an important aspect of our program as a Church. We encourage the cultivation of friends with happy conversations among our people. However, these should take place in the foyer, and when we enter the chapel we should understand that we are in sacred precincts. All of us are familiar with the account in Exodus of the Lord's appearance to Moses at the burning bush. When the Lord called, Moses answered, "Here am I" (Exodus 3:4).

And the Lord said, "Draw not nigh hither: put off thy shoes from off thy feet, for the place whereon thou standest is holy ground" (v. 5).

We do not ask our people to remove their shoes when they come into the chapel. But all who come into the Lord's house should have a feeling that they are walking and standing on holy ground and that it becomes them to deport themselves accordingly. ("Reverence and Morality," *Ensign*, May 1987, pp. 45–46.)

When I was a missionary in London, England, . . . we held our meetings in the Battersea town hall, which we rented. The floors were hard, and we sat on chairs. Every time a chair moved there was a noise. But this was not the worst aspect of the situation. Far worse was the noisy socializing of the members of the branch.

On one occasion we invited a family whom we had met while tracting. With great expectation we as missionaries stood by the door to welcome them. There was the usual convivial spirit in the hall, with the members talking noisily one with another. When this family came into the room, they quietly moved toward some chairs, knelt for a moment, and closed their eyes in a word of prayer. They then sat in an attitude of reverence amidst all the commotion.

Frankly, I was embarrassed. They had come to what they regarded as a worship service, and they behaved themselves accordingly.

At the close of the meeting they left quietly, and when we next met they spoke of their disappointment in what they had experienced. I have never forgotten that.

I invite you brethren of the priesthood, wherever you may be, and particularly you members of bishoprics, to begin an earnest effort to cultivate a more beautiful spirit of worship in our sacrament meetings and an attitude of increased reverence generally in our Church buildings. ("Reverence and Morality," *Ensign*, May 1987, p. 45.)

We need to strengthen our sacrament meetings and make them hours of worship in very deed. Cultivate a spirit of reverence, an attitude in which people come into the chapel and are quiet and reverent and thoughtful. There is too much noise. We are a sociable people, but I wish we would not keep it up so loudly in the chapel. (Pittsburgh Pennsylvania Regional Conference, priesthood leadership session, April 27, 1996.)

I hope, brethren and sisters, that we will do all we can to cultivate a spirit of reverence always in the House of the Lord. I regret to say that we have so little of it in our meetinghouses. There is little of it even in the homes of the people. The temple is the one place to which our people can go, many of them carrying very heavy burdens, and feel a quiet and wonderful spirit of communion with our Father in Heaven. (Temple Presidents Seminar, August 22, 1996.)

RIGHTEOUSNESS

See Morality; Standards; Values

SABBATH DAY

See also Sacrament; Sacrament Meeting

On July 24, 1847, the pioneer company of our people came into this valley. An advance group had arrived a day or two earlier. Brigham Young arrived on Saturday. The next day, Sabbath services were held both in the morning and in the afternoon. There was no hall of any kind in which to meet. I suppose that in the blistering heat of that July Sunday they sat on the tongues of their wagons and leaned against the wheels while the Brethren spoke. The season was late, and they were faced with a gargantuan and immediate task if they were to grow seed for the next season. But President Young pleaded with them not to violate the Sabbath then or in the future. ("An Ensign to the Nations," *Ensign*, November 1989, p. 51.)

Keep the Sabbath Day holy. It is a sad thing to me to see stores open on the Sabbath Day. But we do not need to shop on the Sabbath. Nobody needs to shop on the Sabbath. You can buy enough meat on Saturday to get through Sunday. You can buy enough milk on Saturday to get through Sunday. The bread will not get unduly stale when it is bought on Saturday to be used on Sunday. You certainly do not need to buy clothing on Sunday nor furniture nor anything of that kind. Keep the Sabbath day holy. What a blessing is the Lord's day. (Nottingham England Fireside, August 30, 1995.)

If you have any doubt about the wisdom, the divinity of observing the Sabbath Day, . . . stay home and gather your family about you, teach them the gospel, enjoy yourselves together on the Sabbath Day, come to your meetings, participate. You will know that the principle of the Sabbath is a true principle which brings with it great blessings. (Promontory Utah Branch Sacrament Meeting, October 15, 1995.)

The Sabbath is such a precious thing. It represents the great culmination of the work of Jehovah in the creation of the earth and all that is found therein. When that was completed He looked upon it and saw that it was good and He rested on the Sabbath day. Now, I make a plea to our people to refrain from shopping on Sunday. You may say, "The little bit that I do doesn't make a bit of difference." It makes all the difference in the world to you and to your children who will see your example. (Charlotte North Carolina Regional Conference, priesthood leadership session, February 24, 1996.)

The Lord wrote concerning the sanctity of the Sabbath when His finger touched the tablets of stone on Sinai: Keep the Sabbath day holy. And that commandment has been reiterated in modern times as set forth in the fifty-ninth section of the Doctrine and Covenants. Let us be a Sabbath-keeping people. Now I do not want to be prudish. I do not want you to lock your children in the house and read the Bible all afternoon to them. Be wise. Be careful. But make that day a day when you can sit down with your families and talk about sacred and good things. "Keep the Sabbath holy," saith the Lord to all people and particularly to this people. (Smithfield/Logan Utah Regional Conference, priesthood leadership session, April 20, 1996.)

Let us not let down our standards. Keep the boats at home on Sunday. You do not need to shop for your groceries on Sunday, or your furniture, or your automobiles. There are six days of the week and the Lord will bless those who keep His commandments. (Smithfield/Logan Utah Regional Conference, priesthood leadership session, April 20, 1996.)

It appalls me to see Latter-day Saints who shop on Sunday. I cannot understand how they can go in the face of the direct word of the Lord that "thou shalt keep the Sabbath day holy." Shopping is not a part of keeping the Sabbath day holy. . . . On the first Sabbath in the Salt Lake Valley, Brigham Young said, "We will not work on Sunday, for those who do will lose five times as much as they gain." I believe God will honor and bless and magnify and be quick to help those who try to keep His commandments. The commandment on the Sabbath Day is the longest of the Ten Commandments. The Lord was very specific about it, very detailed about it. I can't help but believe that the merchants would not be open on Sunday if we did not patronize their stores. Therefore, that responsibility rests upon our shoulders. I hope you will not shop on Sunday. (Jordan Utah South Regional Conference, March 2, 1997.)

SACRAMENT

We *can* attend our sacrament meetings, there to partake of the emblems of the sacrifice of our Savior. As we do so, we will renew our covenants and be reminded of sacred obligations falling upon those who have taken upon themselves the name of the Lord. ("'Let Us Move This Work Forward,'" *Ensign*, November 1985, p. 85.)

That great and important sacrament was instituted by the Savior himself shortly before His crucifixion. It was He who first gave to those He loved the emblems of His flesh and blood and commanded that all should partake of them in remembrance of Him and as a token of a covenant between God and man. ("The Aaronic Priesthood—a Gift from God," *Ensign*, May 1988, p. 46.)

The sacrament and the partaking of these emblems is the very heart of our sabbath worship. It includes a renewal of covenants with God. It carries with it a promise of His Holy Spirit to be with us. It is a blessing without peer to be enjoyed by all and made possible by the authority given to worthy young men. (Priesthood Restoration Commemoration Fireside, May 15, 1988.)

I am confident the Savior trusts us, and yet he asks that we renew our covenants with him frequently and before one another by partaking of the sacrament, the emblems of his suffering in our behalf. ("Trust and Accountability," *BYU 1992–93 Devotional and Fireside Speeches*, October 13, 1992, p. 25.)

As we partake of the sacrament we all stand on a level plane before the Lord. Each is accountable for what he does as he renews his covenants with the Lord in that magnificent and beautiful and simple ordinance of the gospel which carries with it such tremendous meaning. I am grateful for this opportunity. (Eagle Gate 7th Ward Sacrament Meeting, September 17, 1995.)

I feel in my heart that if every member of the Church would resolve within himself or herself that they would partake of the sacrament every week, if possible, we would have greater spirituality and we would have fewer defaults, as it were, among our membership. (Meeting with General Authorities and Wives, October 9, 1996.)

I like occasionally to open the New Testament and read of the Last Supper. I think I can envision in my mind the gathering together of the Twelve in the Upper Room. I think maybe they came in very happily, very jauntily. They were all brethren and they probably shook hands with one another and said, "How are you doing, Peter? How are things going, John?" and a few such things as that. But I think when the Lord came in He was sober and quiet and thoughtful and sad. He knew what was coming. They could not seem to understand it. But He knew what was coming, that He would have to give His life in pain and terrible, unspeakable suffering if He were to accomplish the mission outlined by His Father for the redemption of mankind. And when they had been seated, He was exceedingly sorrowful because He said unto them: " . . . one of you shall betray me. . . . and began every one of them to say unto him, Lord, is it I? And he answered and said, He that dippeth his hand with me in the dish, the same shall betray me.

"The Son of man goeth as it is written of him: but woe unto that man by whom the Son of man is betrayed! it had been good for that man if he had not been born. Then Judas, which betrayed him, answered and said, Master, is it I? He said unto him, Thou hast said.

"And as they were eating, Jesus took bread, and blessed it, and brake it, and gave it to the disciples, and said, Take, eat; this is my body. And he took the cup, and gave thanks, and gave it to them, saying, Drink ye all of it; For this is my blood of the new testament, which is shed for many for the remission of sins. But I say unto you, I will not drink henceforth of this fruit of the vine, until that day when I drink it new with you in my Father's kingdom. And when they had sung an hymn, they went out into the mount of Olives" (Matt. 26:21–30). (Meeting with General Authorities and Wives, October 9, 1996.)

SACRAMENT MEETING

I have been in many inspirational meetings in my life, in many places, but I think I have never been in a more inspirational meeting than one I attended in Korea . . . as part of a military retreat at the Eighth Army Retreat Center on the outskirts of Seoul. The bread of the sacrament was administered that morning by a tall captain of infantry on whose chest were many campaign ribbons. He had been ordained a priest only that morning. He had joined the Church while serving in Korea as a result of the actions of his associates. As he knelt at the sacrament table, he gave, with a quiver in his voice, that solemn and beautiful and simple prayer. Somehow the Spirit of the Lord went through that old Quonset-hut chapel in a marvelous and touching manner. When I opened my eyes, every man in that hall was weeping. I am frank to confess I was weeping too. After that, as each of the sixty-one men present bore his testimony, there was an outpouring of the Spirit of the Lord that was marvelous to experience. These were men of war who spoke the gospel of peace— colonels and majors and captains and lieutenants, sergeants and pfc's—faithful men and among them, a handful of investigators who had come to learn and who were marvelously taught. ("Lest We Forget," *BYU Speeches of the Year*, November 10, 1970, p. 4.)

The sacrament meeting is not a time for entertainment; it is not a time for telling stories unrelated to the gospel. Rather, it is time in which to grow spiritually and in which to increase our understanding of the marvelous revelations of the Lord concerning his eternal plan and of himself as our Savior and our Redeemer.

It is in our sacrament meetings that we should be testifying of the Lord and teaching of his life and ways, and particularly of his redeeming sacrifice. ("The Priesthood of Aaron," *Ensign*, November 1982, p. 47.)

Every sacrament meeting ought to be a spiritual feast. It ought to be a time for meditation and introspection, a time for singing songs of praise to the Lord, a time for renewing one's covenants with him and our Eternal Father, and a time for hearing the word of the Lord with reverence and appreciation.

I plead with you who are responsible for these meetings that you strive a little more diligently to program them in such a manner that each sacrament meeting will become a time for spiritual refreshening. I plead with all of you who participate in these meetings, and I include with some emphasis you boys, to see that there is cultivated a spirit of reverence in these sacred gatherings.

It is not easy to keep oneself unspotted from the world. Each of us needs all the help he can get. The Lord has given us direction in how to achieve this. ("The Priesthood of Aaron," *Ensign*, November 1982, p. 47.)

Why do we go to sacrament meeting? We go, of course, to renew our covenants in partaking of the sacrament. This is the most important element of these meetings. And we also go to be instructed, to meditate upon the things of God, and to worship the Lord in spirit and in truth. We go because of the commandment of the Lord, who said in revelation:

"Thou shalt offer a sacrifice unto the Lord thy God in righteousness, even that of a broken heart and a contrite spirit. And that thou mayest more fully keep thyself unspotted from the world, thou shalt go to the house of prayer and offer up thy sacraments upon my holy day; For verily this is a day appointed unto you to rest from your labors, and to pay thy devotions unto the Most High." (D&C 59:8–10.)

We need, every one of us needs, to pause from the hectic pace of our lives and to reflect upon things sacred and divine. ("Reverence and Morality," *Ensign*, May 1987, p. 45.)

Sacrament meeting ought to be a time of spiritual refreshment for our people, when, on Sunday, they gather to partake of the sacrament and renew their covenants with the Lord. They should rethink the contract which exists between them and the Lord under which we take upon ourselves His name and agree to keep His commandments and He, in turn, promises that His Spirit will be with us. If we could bring about the consummation of that covenant in the lives of our people with a renewal each week, what a marvelous thing it would be. Let us encourage a spirit of reverence in sacrament meeting and as bishops and counselors in bishoprics, responsible for what goes on, let us see that all that is done is in harmony with the purpose of that meeting. It should be a time when together we meet to renew our faith, our covenants, our obligations, our loyalty, our love, our willingness to take upon ourselves the name of the Lord Jesus Christ and keep His commandments. (Pittsburgh Pennsylvania Regional Conference, priesthood leadership session, April 27, 1996.)

Bless [your people] with doctrine. See that the doctrines of the kingdom are taught in the meetings of your wards. "Search the scriptures," said the Lord, "for in them ye think ye have eternal life: and they are they which testify of me" (John 5:39.) Every sermon given in a sacrament meeting ought to contain some words of scripture. This is the great source of our doctrine. Bless them with doctrine. (Guatemala City Guatemala North and South Regional Conference, priesthood leadership session, January 25, 1997.)

SACRIFICE

See also Consecration

Sacrifice is the very essence of religion; it is the keystone of happy home life, the basis of true friendship, the foundation of peaceful community living, of sound relations among people and nations. . . .

Without sacrifice there is no true worship of God. I become increasingly convinced of that every day. "The Father gave his Son, and the Son gave his life," and we do not worship unless we give—give of our substance, give of our time, give of our strength, give of our talent, give of our faith, give of our testimonies. ("Without Sacrifice There Is No True Worship," *BYU Speeches of the Year,* October 17, 1962, p. 4.)

A religion which requires devotion, which asks for sacrifice, which demands discipline, also enjoys the loyalty of its membership and the interest and respect of others.

It was ever thus. The Savior did not equivocate when he said to Nicodemus: "Except a man be born of the water and of the Spirit, he cannot enter into the kingdom of God." (John 3:5.) There were no exceptions. There was no permissiveness in complying with the rule. It was so in other matters of which he spoke.

Paul never hedged nor quibbled when setting forth the requirements of the gospel of Jesus Christ. It is so today. The Lord himself declared that "strait is the gate and narrow is the way." Any system dealing with the eternal consequences of human behavior must set guidelines and adhere to them, and no system can long command the loyalties of men that does not expect of them certain measures of discipline, and particularly of self-discipline. The cost in comfort may be great. The sacrifice may be real. But this very demanding reality is the substance of which character and strength and nobility come.

Permissiveness never produced greatness. Integrity, loyalty, and strength are virtues whose sinews are developed through the struggles that go on within a man as he practices self-discipline under the demands of divinely spoken truth. (*Be Thou an Example* [Salt Lake City: Deseret Book, 1981], pp. 4–5.)

Over the past years it has been my responsibility to extend calls to scores of men, their wives, and their families to leave all behind and go into the mission field. Those with whom we shall speak in coming months will respond in the same way that those in the past have responded. They will, in effect, say, "Of course, I am ready to go whenever and wherever the Lord calls."

They and their wives will gather their children around them. There will be tears as the children think of leaving their schools and their friends. The family will kneel together in prayer, and when they arise from their knees, although their eyes will be moist, they will say in unison, "We'll go where you want us to go, dear Lord; we'll do what you want us to do." (See *Hymns*, 1985, no. 270.)

I confess that at times I feel reluctant to ask people to do things in the Church because I know they will respond without hesitation. And I know also that those responses will entail great sacrifice. But I know this also, in the case of mission presidents and their families, there will be more tears shed when they leave the mission field to return home than will be shed when they leave home to go into the field. It is so with temple presidents and with many others who are called by the Church to leave their homes to serve in the harvest field of the world.

In all of my experience I have never had anyone turn down such a call. There have been a few who, when I have inquired concerning their circumstances, we have felt that they should not go, at least at that time. But even in those cases a strange thing happens. Once a man has been talked with concerning such an assignment, even though a call was not extended, he never seems to get over it. Before long he is writing a letter or telephoning to say that he is ready to go.

Someone occasionally says that there was so much of sacrifice in the early days of the Church, but there is no sacrifice today. The observer goes on to say that in pioneer days people were willing to lay their fortunes and even their lives on the altar. "What has happened to the spirit of consecration?" some of these ask. I should like to say with great emphasis that this spirit is still very much among us. I have discovered that no sacrifice is too great for faithful Latter-day Saints. ("'Let Us Move This Work Forward,'" *Ensign*, November 1985, p. 84.)

The growth statistics of the Church are impressive and gratifying. They call to mind a broadcast in recent years when the head of the National Council of Churches was interviewed, and he spoke of the declining membership of some of the larger well-known religious bodies, and also of the accelerating growth of others. He gave as the reason for the decline: "Because they have become permissive; they allow just anybody to become members or remain members. They don't insist on any rigorous requirements of belief or of contributions." He pointed out, on the other hand, that those groups which require sacrifice of time and effort and means are enjoying vigorous growth.

He then went on to say: "The fastest growing church [of] over a million members in this country is the Mormon Church, the Latter-day Saints, with headquarters in Salt Lake City, which is growing at five percent a year, [and] that's a very rapid increase."

This is a most striking commentary, and one that should concern every thoughtful man and woman. One thing that it says is that a religion which requires devotion, which asks for sacrifice, which demands discipline, also enjoys the loyalty of its membership and the interest and respect of others. ("'It's True, Isn't It?'" *Ensign*, July 1993, pp. 2–4.)

It is not a sacrifice to live the gospel of Jesus Christ. It is never a sacrifice when you get back more than you give. It is an investment. And the living of the gospel of Jesus Christ becomes a greater investment than any of which we know because its dividends are eternal and everlasting. (Tacoma Washington Regional Conference, August 20, 1995.)

SALVATION FOR THE DEAD

See also Family History Work; Priesthood: Sealing Power; Temple

The salvation of the Lord applies to every man, woman, and child on the face of the earth. The exaltation of our Father's family rests upon the completion of required ordinances, if all are to move forward on the road that leads to immortality and eternal life. The determination of accurate family history records, and the work that follows in the temples, are basic in this vast undertaking which the Lord has placed upon our shoulders. (Phoenix Arizona North/West Regional Conference, January 13, 1991.)

I have been tremendously impressed with the priority which the Lord has given this work.

The great promise of this work, the work of turning the hearts of the children to their fathers that their fathers might be fully redeemed, was given before the Book of Mormon plates were received, before the Aaronic or Melchizedek Priesthood were restored, before the Church was organized.

The actual keys of this work were not restored until 1836, after the dedication of the Kirtland Temple, when Moses, Elias, and Elijah appeared and bestowed the keys which each held. But the priority of this work, emphasizing the importance of it, was established that night in 1823, thirteen years earlier.

It is interesting to observe that it was following the restoration of these keys that there commenced a growing interest in family history. The spirit of Elijah, as we speak of it, began to rest upon people, impelling them to look for their ancestral roots. In 1844, the New England Historic Genealogical Society was organized. It was the first of its kind in America, and has continued as a strong and viable organization. It was followed by many others, as millions of people looked back to their fathers. Most have regarded their work as a matter of curiosity. But there has been a purpose in it, unknown to many, but plainly evident to us. It concerns the very redemption of the dead. It is concerned with their eternal welfare and their progress along the road that leads to immortality and eternal life.

In that process there must be a twofold effort—the research needed to establish the identity of these individuals, and the administration of ordinances by vicarious agents working in their behalf. The first is concerned with family history research, the second with temple activity. Family research would serve no other purpose than the satisfaction of curiosity if the temple work did not follow. Likewise, only a portion of the purpose of temples would be met if there were not family history research.

Ordinances for the living, of course, could go forward. But the Lord would be a respecter of persons, discriminating in favor of a few, unless there were means by which the opportunities for these ordinances could be extended to all. (Jordan River Temple Workers Christmas Devotional, November 27, 1994.)

It is interesting to me that, of the very many churches in the world, this Church is unique and alone in declaring the necessity of the administration of these ordinances in behalf of those who did not receive them in mortality. (Jordan River Temple Workers Christmas Devotional, November 27, 1994.)

What a blessing family history research and temple work are in behalf of the dead. A man once said to me, "I'm saved," in a rather boisterous tone. And I said, "What about your father and your grandfather and your great-grandfather?" He said, "I guess they've gone to hell." And I said, "Are you more deserving of the blessings of the Savior of the world than those who gave you life, and through whom your inheritance has come, of mind and body and spirit? Can there be a just God who is not a respecter of persons who would deny the one group that which has been given freely to another?" (Birmingham England Fireside, August 29, 1995.)

I don't know where in all the world, except for the restored gospel of Jesus Christ, it is possible to give the saving ordinances of the gospel to those beyond the veil of death. At the London Temple I conferred the sealing authority on eight worthy men, who will have the power to bind in the heavens that which is bound upon the earth. It is the only authority that I know of that reaches beyond the veil of death. It is wonderful, unique, and tremendous. (Liverpool England Fireside, August 31, 1995.)

SCOUTING

I became a Boy Scout. We did not have the Cub Scout program then, and a boy had to be twelve to be a Scout. This was 1922, only nine years after the Church adopted the Scout program. I lived in a very large ward by today's standards. There were more than eleven hundred people in that ward. We had a large troop, and we met in the cultural hall of the old First Ward. We made a lot of noise. The floors were of hardwood; the walls were hard and smooth, and the sound bounced around them. Our Scoutmaster had a whistle which he blew frequently to get order.

I filled out an application and paid the fifty-cent registration fee, which seemed like a lot of money at the time. I learned the Scout motto: "Be Prepared." I learned the Scout slogan: "Do a Good Turn Daily." I learned the Scout Oath . . .

I learned the Scout Law . . . And when we recited the law, one of the boys always added, "A Scout is hungry." I think it was literally true. He came from a very large family, and getting enough to eat was always a challenge. ("The Aaronic Priesthood—a Gift from God," *Ensign,* May 1988, p. 44.)

I am glad to be able to pay my respects to you who move the great Scouting program along. We would not have the kind of gang problems we have if there were more boys enrolled in Scouting, because the spirit of Scouting and the spirit of gang life are contradictory one to another. This program builds boys, builds their futures, leads them on the right path so they can make something of their lives, whereas the other kind of behavior leads to tragedy and difficulty and problems unnumbered. Every man or woman who helps a boy along the road of life not only does a great thing for him but does a great thing for society as a whole. (Scout-O-Rama Breakfast, Salt Lake City, Utah, May 4, 1996.)

I am very proud of the record of the church which I represent in terms of the sponsorship of Scouting. My father was a member of the committee of three who went to New York and made a study of the Scout program. The record shows that he made the motion that the Church adopt the program of the Boy Scouts of America as the activity program for boys in the LDS Church. (Scout-O-Rama Breakfast, Salt Lake City, Utah, May 4, 1996.)

I want to make a remark or two on the Scout oath, which I think is such a tremendous thing and which I learned as a boy: "On my honor I will do my best to do my duty to God and my country and to obey the Scout law; to help other people at all times; to keep myself physically strong, mentally awake, and morally straight."

There is so much of filthy talk by boys and girls in junior high and high school. There is so much of immoral filth around us. We who are Scouts must stand tall and stand above all of this. We cannot afford to get involved in the use of drugs. To do so would become a repudiation of those great words of the Scout oath: " . . . to keep myself physically strong, mentally awake, and morally straight." . . . I would like to say that if every boy in America knew and were to observe the Scout oath throughout his life, we would do away with most of the prisons and jails in this country. If only every young man were to pledge and keep that pledge throughout his life to keep himself "physically strong, mentally awake, and morally straight."

"To help other people at all times." Never forget that you have an obligation to do a good turn daily. Start that habit now, and it will remain with you throughout your lives if you will impress it upon your hearts.

To do your duty to God and this great country of which each of us is a citizen—what a wonderful pledge that is.

Finally, "On my honor I will do my best." Karl G. Maeser, who was the founding father of Brigham Young University, said this about his word of honor: "You may put me in a prison with walls so high and so thick and perhaps somehow, some way I could get out. But put my feet on the floor and draw a chalk line around me and place me on my honor not to step over the chalk line. I would die before I would try to do so." That is the meaning of honor. "On my honor I will do my best." If each of us, my dear fellow Scouts, would live up to those few words throughout our lives, "On my honor I will do my best," whether it be in school, in our social life, in our business life, in our professional life, whatever it might be—if we will do our very best, success and happiness will be ours. (Boy Scout Jamboral, Fillmore, Utah, September 27, 1996.)

SCRIPTURES

See also Book of Mormon; Doctrine and Covenants

I promise you that if you will read the words of that writing which we call scripture, there will come into your heart an understanding and a warmth that will be pleasing to experience. "Search the scriptures; for in them ye think ye have eternal life: and they are they which testify of me." (John 5:39.) Read, for instance, the Gospel of John from its beginning to its end. Let the Lord speak for himself to you, and his words will come with a quiet conviction that will make the words of his critics meaningless. Read also the testament of the New World, the Book of Mormon, brought forth as a witness "that Jesus is the Christ, the Eternal God, manifesting himself unto all nations." (Book of Mormon title page.) ("The Miracle That Is Jesus," *Improvement Era*, June 1966, p. 531.)

God has not left us in ignorance to walk in darkness. His word, spoken both anciently and in our generation, is available to all to read, to ponder, and to accept. There are many books among us and many preachers, and I find virtue in the words of all. But the truest source of divine wisdom is the word of the Lord in these sacred volumes, the standard works of the Church. Here is found the doctrine to which we must hold fast if this work is to roll forth to its divinely charted destiny. ("Five Million Members—A Milestone and Not a Summit," *Ensign*, May 1982, p. 45.)

We *can* read the scriptures, ponder their meaning, and develop familiarity with them for our everlasting blessing. We can do so in our family home evenings, and as we do there will grow within our children a love for the Lord and His holy word. ("'Let Us Move This Work Forward,'" *Ensign,* November 1985, p. 85.)

Even though some of you may be fully occupied with families and have little time for other things at this stage of your lives, you can enlarge your minds and broaden your understanding through the reading of good books. . . . How marvelous a thing is a good book! How stimulating to read and share with a great writer thoughts that build and strengthen and broaden one's horizon! You may think you are too busy. Ten or fifteen minutes a day with the scriptures, and particularly with the Book of Mormon, can give you marvelous understanding of the great eternal truths which have been preserved by the power of the Almighty for the blessing of His children. As you read of the life and teaching of the Lord Jesus Christ, you will draw closer to Him who is the author of our salvation. ("Rise to the Stature of the Divine within You," *Ensign,* November 1989, p. 97.)

I believe in the sacred writings of the past. Our books of scripture, which have lived through the centuries, set forth the basis of our civil law, of our societal relationships, of our family responsibilities, and, most important, contain the divinely given teachings, principles, and commandments by which to set the course of our lives. They enunciate the relentless law of the harvest: "As ye sow, so shall ye reap" (see D&C 6:33). They spell out a law of accountability under which we must someday give a report of our labors, our activities, and our words to the God of Heaven, who has granted us the privilege of life with all of its joys, with all of its opportunities, and with all of its challenges. ("This I Believe," *BYU 1991–92 Devotional and Fireside Speeches,* March 1, 1992, p. 82.)

I am grateful for emphasis on reading the scriptures. I hope that for you this will become something far more enjoyable than a duty; that, rather, it will become a love affair with the word of God. I promise you that as you read, your minds will be enlightened and your spirits will be lifted. At first it may seem tedious, but that will change into a wondrous experience with thoughts and words of things divine. ("The Light within You," *Ensign*, May 1995, p. 99.)

The more we read of history, and particularly of sacred history, . . . the more we can establish a pattern by which to guide our own lives which will lead us into productive living. He has set the way. That's the road to progress, and whether it be in matters of theology or day-to-day living as part of the society in which we live, the principles which are set forth in the scriptures become principles which can make for happiness and understanding, lofty ideals by which to guide our lives, and the faith by which to move through the problems which we will inevitably confront as we go forward with our lives. (*Church News* Interview, June 7, 1995.)

Take time in a methodical way to read the Book of Mormon. Read the "fifth gospel," 3 Nephi, beginning with the 11th chapter. Then read the entire Book of Mormon to fortify all of that. Then read the other gospels. They will give you things that will be as treasures to you in your life and will bring to you a greater understanding of the Savior of the world. (Ricks College Regional Conference, Rexburg, Idaho, October 29, 1995.)

When all is said and done, the test of the doctrine lies in the standard works of the Church. These have been accepted in conference and assembled as our doctrinal standards. (General Authority Training Meeting, October 1, 1996.)

SEALING POWER

See Priesthood: Sealing Power

SECOND COMING OF CHRIST

Among the things I know and of which I am sure is the fact that [the Savior] will come again. I hope that all of you have seen the beautiful and impressive mural on the east wall of the lobby of the Church Office Building in which is portrayed the resurrected Lord giving final instruction to eleven of his apostles. At that time he charged them concerning their future responsibility to take the gospel to every nation, kindred, tongue, and people.

"And when he had spoken these things, while they beheld, he was taken up; and a cloud received him out of their sight.

"And while they looked steadfastly toward heaven as he went up, behold, two men stood by them in white apparel;

"Which also said, Ye men of Galilee, why stand ye gazing up into heaven? this same Jesus, which is taken up from you into heaven, shall so come in like manner as ye have seen him go" (Acts 1:9–11).

I know likewise that when he shall come the second time he shall come in glory, in contrast with the way he came in the meridian of time. The first time, he who had been the great Jehovah, the Creator of the earth and the God who spoke to the prophets of old, condescended to come as a babe born in a manger in Bethlehem of Judea. He walked the dusty roads of Palestine, "a man of sorrows, and acquainted with grief" (Isaiah 53:3). He yielded himself into the hands of wicked men and was crucified on Golgotha's hill.

Now, in this dispensation, the Lord has declared that "the time is soon at hand that he shall come in a cloud, with power and great glory" (D&C 34:7). ("'We Need Not Fear His Coming,'" *BYU Devotional Speeches of the Year*, March 25, 1979, pp. 81–82.)

Some years ago one of our brethren spoke of the payment of tithing as "fire insurance." That statement evoked laughter. Nonetheless, the word of the Lord is clear that those who do not keep the commandments and observe the laws of God shall be burned at the time of his coming. For that shall be a day of judgment and a day of sifting, a day of separating the good from the evil. I would venture a personal opinion that no event has occurred in all the history of the earth as dreadful as will be the day of the Second Coming—no event as fraught with the destructive forces of nature, as consequential for the nations of the earth, as terrible for the wicked, or as wonderful for the righteous.

It will be a time of great and terrible fears, of cataclysmic upheavals of nature, of weeping and wailing, of repentance too late, and of crying out unto the Lord for mercy. But for those who in that judgment are found acceptable, it will be a day for thanksgiving, for the Lord shall come with his angels, and the apostles who were with him in life, and those who have been resurrected. Further, the graves of the righteous will be opened and they shall come forth. Then will begin the great Millennium, a period of a thousand years when Satan shall be bound and the Lord shall reign over his people. Can you imagine the wonder and the beauty of that era when the adversary shall not have influence? Think of his pull upon you now and reflect on the peace of that time when you will be free from such influence. There will be quiet and goodness where now there is contention and evil. ("'We Need Not Fear His Coming,'" *BYU Devotional Speeches of the Year*, March 25, 1979, pp. 82–83.)

Certainly there is no point in speculating concerning the day and the hour. Let us rather live each day so that if the Lord does come while we yet are upon the earth we shall be worthy of that change which will occur as in the twinkling of an eye and under which we shall be changed from mortal to immortal beings. And if we should die before he comes, then—if our lives have conformed to his teachings—we shall arise in that resurrection morning and be partakers of the marvelous experiences designed for those who shall live and work with the Savior in that promised Millennium. We need not fear the day of his coming; the very purpose of the Church is to provide the incentive and the opportunity for us to conduct our lives in such a way that those who are members of the kingdom of God will become members of the kingdom of heaven when he establishes that kingdom on the earth. ("'We Need Not Fear His Coming,'" *BYU Devotional Speeches of the Year*, March 25, 1979, p. 83.)

The God of heaven has ordained that day. The prophets of all dispensations have spoken of it. We know not when it will come, but its dawning is certain. (*Be Thou an Example* [Salt Lake City: Deseret Book, 1981], p. 16.)

I don't know when the Savior will come. I'm ready for Him. I hope it isn't too long in this evil-filled world. I do not know. "Come, O thou King of Kings"; I can sing that with conviction. But I don't know. Neither do the angels in heaven. None of us knows. (Ireland Dublin Missionary Meeting, September 1, 1995.)

SELF-DISCIPLINE

Discipline imposed for the sake of discipline is repressive. It is not in the spirit of the gospel of Jesus Christ. It is usually enforced by fear, and its results are negative.

But that which is positive, which comes of personal conviction, builds and lifts and strengthens in a marvelous manner. In matters of religion, when a man is motivated by great and powerful convictions of truth, then he disciplines himself, not because of demands made upon him by the Church but because of the knowledge within his heart that God lives; that he is a child of God with an eternal and limitless potential; that there is joy in service and satisfaction in laboring in a great cause. . . . When an individual has that witness and testimony, the requirements of the Church become challenges rather than burdens. ("The True Strength of the Church," *Ensign*, July 1973, p. 48.)

I should like to take you, for a moment, back to that most dreadful night in and about Jerusalem when the Last Supper was concluded. Jesus and his disciples left the city and went over to the Mount of Olives. Knowing that his terrible ordeal was at hand, he spoke with those he loved. And he said to them: "All ye shall be offended [that is, shall fall away] because of me this night. . . .

"Peter answered and said unto him, Though all men shall be offended because of thee, yet will I never be offended.

"Jesus said unto him, Verily I say unto thee, That this night, before the cock crow, thou shalt deny me thrice.

"Peter said unto him, Though I should die with thee, yet will I not deny thee." (Matt. 26:31, 33–36.)

There followed shortly thereafter the terrible agony in the Garden of Gethsemane, and then the betrayal. As the procession moved to the court of Caiaphas, "Peter followed . . . unto the high priest's palace, and went in, and sat with the servants, to see the end" (Matt. 26:58).

While the mockery of that trial was going on and Jesus' accusers spit on him, and buffeted him, and smote him with the palms of their hands, a damsel, seeing Peter, said: "Thou also wast with Jesus of Galilee.

"But he denied before them all, saying, I know not what thou sayest.

"And when he was gone out into the porch, another maid saw him, and said unto them that were there, This fellow was also with Jesus of Nazareth.

"And again he denied with an oath, I do not know the man.

"And after a while came unto him they that stood by, and said to Peter, Surely thou also art one of them; for thy speech bewrayeth thee.

"Then began he to curse and to swear, saying, I know not the man. And immediately the cock crew.

"And Peter remembered the word of Jesus, which said unto him, Before the cock crow, thou shalt deny me thrice. *And he went out, and wept bitterly.*" (Matt. 26:69–75; italics added.)

What pathos there is in those words! Peter, affirming his loyalty, his determination, his resolution, said that he would never deny. But the fear of men came upon him and the weakness of his flesh overtook him, and under the pressure of accusation, his resolution crumbled. Then, recognizing his wrong and weakness, "he went out, and wept."

As I have read this account my heart goes out to Peter. So many of us are so much like him. We pledge our loyalty; we affirm our determination to be of good courage; we declare, sometimes even publicly, that come what may we will do the right thing, that we will stand for the right cause, that we will be true to ourselves and to others.

Then the pressures begin to build. Sometimes these are social pressures. Sometimes they are personal appetites. Sometimes they are false ambitions. There is a weakening of the will. There is a softening of discipline. There is capitulation. And then there is remorse, self-accusation, and bitter tears of regret.

One of the great tragedies we witness almost daily is the tragedy of men of high aim and low achievement. Their motives are noble. Their proclaimed ambition is praiseworthy. Their capacity is great. But their discipline is weak. ("And Peter Went Out and Wept Bitterly," *Ensign*, May 1979, p. 65.)

Mental control must be stronger than physical appetites or desires of the flesh. As thoughts are brought into complete harmony with revealed truth, actions will then become appropriate.

The timeless proverb is as true now as when it was first spoken: "For as he thinketh in his heart, so is he" (Proverbs 23:7).

Each of us, with discipline and effort, has the capacity to control our thoughts and our actions. This is part of the process of developing spiritual, physical, and emotional maturity. ("Reverence and Morality," *Ensign*, May 1987, p. 47.)

The only conquest that brings satisfaction is the conquest of self. It was said of old that he who governs himself is greater than he who takes a city. ("In Search of Peace and Freedom," *Ensign*, August 1989, p. 5.)

I'd like to tell you a baseball story. . . . The event of which I speak occurred in the World Series of 1912. It was an eight-game series because one of the games was called at midpoint because of darkness. Playing fields were not electrically lighted at that time. It was the last game and the score was tied 1–1. The Boston Red Sox were at bat, the New York Giants in the field. A Boston batter knocked a high-arching fly. Two New York players ran for it. Fred Snodgrass at center field signaled to his associate that he would take it. He came squarely under the ball, which fell into his glove. It went right through his hand and fell to the ground. A howl went up in the stands. The roaring fans couldn't believe it. Snodgrass had dropped the ball. He had caught hundreds of fly balls before. But now, at this crucial moment, he dropped the ball.

. . . The Boston Red Sox won the series.

Snodgrass came back the following season and played brilliant ball for nine more years. He lived to be eighty-six years of age, dying in 1974. But after that one slip, for sixty-two years when he was introduced to anybody, the expected response was, "Oh, yes, you're the one who dropped the ball." . . .

This phenomenon is not peculiar to sports. It happens every day in life.

There is the student who thinks he is doing well enough, and then under the stress of the final exam, flunks out.

There is the driver who all of his life has had a flawless record and then in a moment of carelessness is involved in a tragic accident.

There is the trusted employee whose performance has been excellent, and then he succumbs to the temptation to steal a little from his employer. A mark is placed upon him which never seems to entirely disappear.

There is the life lived with decency—and then comes the destructive, ever-haunting, one-time moral letdown.

There is the outburst of anger that suddenly destroys a long-cherished relationship.

There is the little sin that somehow grows and eventually leads to separation from the Church.

In all of these, someone dropped the ball. He had the self-confidence, possibly even the arrogance, to think that he didn't really have to try, that he could make it with only half an effort. But the ball passed through his hands and hit the ground, and he gave away the game. . . .

It all points up the need to be constantly alert. It points up the importance of unrelenting self-discipline. It indicates the necessity of constantly building our strength against temptation. It warns us against the misuse of our time, especially our idle time. ("Don't Drop the Ball," *Ensign*, November 1994, pp. 46–47.)

SELF-IMPROVEMENT

Train yourselves to make a contribution to the society in which you will live. There is an essence of the divine in the improvement of the mind. ("Rise to the Stature of the Divine within You," *Ensign*, November 1989, p. 96.)

So many of us begin strong and then flatten out. So many of us climb to a plateau and then drift. John W. Gardner once wrote, "If one defines the term 'dropout' to mean a person who has given up serious effort to meet his responsibilities, then every business office, government agency, golf club and university faculty would yield its quota." ("The Recovery of Confidence," *Readers Digest,* October 1971, p. 127.)

Commenting on what Shelley described as "the contagion of the world's slow stain," Channing Pollock once said, "We begin with a banner inscribed 'Excelsior,' and gradually the dust of battle obliterates everything but the second syllable."

So many players in the game of life get to first base. Some reach second. A handful make third. But how few there are who get home and score.

My wife clipped these words from an editorial in one of our national magazines some years ago. Said the writer:

"Above all, let's cut out the rotten excuse that we are 'only human,' that we are entitled to some daily quota of error or indifference. Only human? This is the ultimate insult.

"Remember that man's greatness does not lie in perfection, but in striving for it. Once we don't give a damn, we have lost everything." (*Better Homes and Gardens,* July 1971.) . . .

My beloved associates, keep faith with the best that is in you. Your example is so important to those who sit at your feet. Your own constant self-improvement will become as a polar star to them. They will remember longer what they saw in you than what they heard from you. Your attitude, your point of view can make such a tremendous difference. ("Keep Faith," Bonneville International Corporation Senior Management Seminar, March 7, 1993.)

We have a job to do. We have a lot of work to do and it's all concerned with improvement, with betterment, with making people better. As President McKay used to say, "Of making bad men good and good men better." That's our job: to improve people. (Vacaville/Santa Rosa California Regional Conference, priesthood leadership session, May 20, 1995.)

We are all in it together, all of us, and we have a great work to do. Every teacher can be a better teacher than he or she is today. Every officer can be a better officer than he or she is today. Every father can be a better father, every mother can be a better mother, every husband can be a better husband, every wife a better wife, every child a better child. We are on the road that leads to immortality and eternal life and today is a part of it. Let us never forget it. (Salt Lake East Millcreek Stake Fiftieth Anniversary Celebration, June 10, 1995.)

There is need for constant improvement in all of our lives. There is need occasionally to leave the noise and the tumult of the world and step within the walls of a sacred house of God, there to feel His spirit in an environment of holiness and peace. ("Of Missions, Temples, and Stewardship," *Ensign,* November 1995, p. 53.)

Thank you for the goodness of your lives. You try to live the gospel. You haven't reached perfection—none of us has; it will be a long time before we do—but we are working in that direction, hopefully. And, hopefully, we're making some progress in our own individual lives. I hope that every man here can feel that something's happened to make him a little better today than he was yesterday, a little kinder, a little more gracious, a little more generous, a little more honest in purpose and word and deed, a little stronger for the right, a little stronger to resist the wrong. (Corpus Christi Texas Regional Conference, priesthood leadership session, January 6, 1996.)

Shape up. I say that to myself constantly. Shape up. Stand a little taller. Be a little better, a little stronger, a little more thoughtful, a little humbler, a little more prayerful, that you may be worthy of the guidance of the Lord and of His wonderful blessings. (Smithfield/Logan Utah Regional Conference, priesthood leadership session, April 20, 1996.)

SELFISHNESS

Selfishness is the basis of our troubles, on this campus and in this community and in this nation and in the world—a vicious preoccupation with our own comforts, with the satisfaction of our own appetites, with worship of what Paul Tillich calls the "Idol of Security." ("Without Sacrifice There Is No True Worship," *BYU Speeches of the Year*, October 17, 1962, p. 3.)

Selfishness is the cause of most of the domestic problems that afflict so many homes of our nation. I do not have the statistics at hand; your sociologists do. But I know that the divorce rate of America is a tragic disgrace that hangs over this land. I sat for hours the other day, listening to two people who had been divorced but who said they still loved one another. First I talked to the husband. He sobbed and sobbed for his wife and then talked about what a terrible woman she was. Then I talked to the wife. She cried over her husband, and then talked of what a stingy man he was. After I had listened to them individually, I brought them together and said to them, "There is only one thing wrong with you. You're just too miserably selfish. You are unwilling to sacrifice for one another. You are unwilling to lay aside your own little comforts in order to accommodate one another." ("Without Sacrifice There Is No True Worship," *BYU Speeches of the Year*, October 17, 1962, p. 5.)

So many in the game of life get to first base, or second, or even third, but then fail to score. They are inclined to live unto themselves, denying their generous instincts, grasping for possessions and in their self-centered, uninspired living, sharing neither talent nor faith with others. Of them the Lord has said: "And this shall be your lamentation in the day of visitation, and of judgment, and of indignation: The harvest is past, the summer is ended, and my soul is not saved!" (D&C 56:16). ("And Peter Went Out and Wept Bitterly," *Ensign*, May 1979, p. 66.)

The antidote for selfishness is service, a reaching out to those about us—those in the home and those beyond the walls of the home. A child who grows in a home where there is a selfish, grasping father is likely to develop those tendencies in his own life. On the other hand, a child who sees his father and mother forgo comforts for themselves as they reach out to those in distress, will likely follow the same pattern when he or she grows to maturity. ("The Environment of Our Homes," *Ensign*, June 1985, p. 4.)

I speak of conflicts, quarrels, arguments which are a debilitating disease particularly afflicting families. If there be such problems in the homes of any within the sound of my voice, I encourage you to invite the healing power of Christ. To those to whom He spoke on the Mount, Jesus said: "Ye have heard that it hath been said, An eye for an eye, and a tooth for a tooth:

"But I say unto you, That ye resist not evil: but whosoever shall smite thee on thy right cheek, turn to him the other also. . . .

"And whosoever shall compel thee to go a mile, go with him twain." (Matt. 5:38–41.)

The application of this principle, difficult to live but wondrous in its curative powers, would have a miraculous effect on our troubled homes. It is selfishness which is in the cause of most of our misery. It is as a cankering disease. The healing power of Christ, found in the doctrine of going the second mile, would do wonders to still argument and accusation, fault-finding and evil speaking. ("The Healing Power of Christ," *Ensign*, November 1988, p. 54.)

SELF-RELIANCE

See also Self-Discipline; Welfare; Work

We can more fully care for our own who may be in need rather than pass the burden to government and thereby preserve the independence and dignity of those who must have and are entitled to help. ("A City Set Upon a Hill," *Ensign*, November 1974, p. 100.)

We feel the need to emphasize with greater clarity the obligation for members of the Church to become more independent and self-reliant, to increase personal and family responsibility, to cultivate spiritual growth, and to be more fully involved in Christian service. (Regional Representatives Seminar, April 1, 1983.)

I read with great interest a talk recently given by Margaret Thatcher, Prime Minister of Britain. She addressed the general assembly of the Church of Scotland. She spoke on self-reliance and personal responsibility as an expression of Christian principle. Among other things she said: "Any set of social and economic arrangements which is not founded on the acceptance of individual responsibility will do nothing but harm. We are all responsible for our own actions. We cannot blame society if we disobey the law." (Freedom Festival Address, Provo, Utah, June 26, 1988.)

A spirit of self-reliance was built into those who worked the soil. There were no government farm programs then, no subsidies of any kind. The vagaries of the seasons had to be accepted. Killing frosts, unseasonal storms, wind, and drought were all accepted as the risks of life against which there was no available insurance. Storage against a day of want was a necessity, else there would be hunger. The one constant resource against the risks of life was prayer, prayer to our eternal, loving Father, the Almighty God of the universe. ("Farewell to a Prophet," *Ensign*, July 1994, p. 38.)

We teach emphatically the importance of self-reliance, the importance of education, of equipping our people so they can earn a living; the importance of saving and being prudent in the management of their affairs; the importance of setting something aside, a reserve, to take care of their needs if there should come a rainy day in their lives. And it's amazing how many follow that teaching. That's basic with us. (Interview with Suzanne Evans of BBC Radio 4, August 26, 1995.)

Question: Why are members of the Church expected to keep a year's supply of food, clothing, and fuel?

President Hinckley: We teach self-reliance as a principle of life, that we ought to provide for ourselves and take care of our own needs. And so we encourage our people to have something, to plan ahead, keep a little food on hand, to establish a savings account, if possible, against a rainy day. Catastrophes come to people sometimes when least expected—unemployment, sickness, things of that kind. The individual, as we teach, ought to do for himself all that he can do for himself. (Interview with Mike Wallace of *60 Minutes*, December 18, 1995.)

Self-reliance in the family was very important to them [the early settlers of Utah]. There were no government aid programs in those days. You either did it yourself or you didn't get it. The Church, of course, stepped in in times of dire need to help people. It is still willing to do so. But people were self-reliant. There were no handouts of any kind. They grew it themselves. They had to or they starved. Well, I repeat, the Church would step in to help them, but every family knew that it was their responsibility to provide for themselves if there was any way in the world for them to do so. And it was only when they had exhausted their resources that they could look to others, to the Church. (Interview with KJZZ-TV, Dean May and Larry Miller, March 20, 1996.)

My wife's grandfather, George Paxman, was a young finish carpenter who, while hanging those very heavy east doors of the Manti Temple, suffered a strangulated hernia. He was in terrible pain. They took him to Nephi in a wagon; then they put him on the old train and took him to Provo. After suffering several days in terrible pain, he died. And his widow was young, she was twenty-two, I think, at the time. She lived to a ripe old age, reared her children, educated them, made her way sewing—she was a fine seamstress. She paid her way. It was all part of the tradition to practice a spirit of self-reliance. We have lost much of that these days, much of it, unfortunately. (Interview with KJZZ-TV, Dean May and Larry Miller, March 20, 1996.)

SERVICE

The Lord declared: "He that findeth his life shall lose it: and he that loseth his life for my sake shall find it." (Matt. 10:39.)

These words have something more than a cold theological meaning. They are a statement of a law of life—that as we lose ourselves in a great cause we find ourselves—and there is no greater cause than that of the Master. (Conference Report, April 1966, p. 87.)

The cause of Christ does not need your doubts; it needs your strength and time and talents; and as you exercise these in service, your faith will grow and your doubts will wane. ("The Miracle That Is Jesus," *Improvement Era*, June 1966, p. 531.)

A night or two ago I received a phone call from an officer just returned from Vietnam. He had hoped to be here today. I was with him during the time we were there. I heard him speak of his reluctance to go to Asia. It was not easy to leave his wife and seven children, including triplet sons three years of age. "But," he said, "I resolved I would give the Air Force the best I had, and I would try to help my brethren in the Church."

He went on to say quietly but earnestly, "I think I have done a better work here than I have ever done before in my life."

I can bear witness to the great good he has done. Not only has he been highly honored by his government and by the government of South Vietnam; his good example and his faithful service under difficult circumstances have brought religious activity into the lives of hundreds of men. I have heard many of these testify of the vast good that has come to them, of the great strength they have gained from such activity in the Church.

To young people everywhere I should like to say that you need the Church, and the Church needs you. . . .

I have seen backward men become giants as they served in the work of the Lord. The cause of Christ does not need critics; it needs workers. ("A Challenge from Vietnam," *Improvement Era*, June 1967, p. 54.)

Last Sunday morning I was in the home of a stake president in a small Idaho town. Before the morning prayer, the family read together a few verses of scripture. Among these were some of the words of Jesus as recorded in John 12:24: "Verily, verily, I say unto you, Except a corn of wheat fall into the ground and die, it abideth alone: but if it die, it bringeth forth much fruit." No doubt He was referring to his own forthcoming death, declaring that except he die his mission in life would be largely in vain. But I see in this a further meaning. It seems to me that he is saying to each of us that unless we lose ourselves in the service of others our lives are largely lived to no real purpose, for he went on to say, "He that loveth his life shall lose it; and he that hateth his life in this world shall keep it unto life eternal" (John 12:25). Or, as recorded in Luke, "Whosoever shall seek to save his life shall lose it; and whosoever shall lose his life shall preserve it" (Luke 17:33). In other words, he who lives only unto himself withers and dies, while he who forgets himself in the service of others grows and blossoms in this life and in eternity.

That morning in stake conference the president with whom I had stayed was released after thirteen years of faithful service. There was a great outpouring of love and appreciation, not because of this man's wealth, not because of his stature in the business community, but because of the great service he had unselfishly given. Without thought of personal interest, he had driven tens of thousands of miles in all kinds of weather. He had spent literally thousands of hours in the interest of others. He had neglected his personal affairs to assist those who needed his help. And in so doing he had come alive, and had become great in the eyes of those he had served.

A new president was installed that morning, and there were many who were proud and happy concerning him; but most proud and most happy was a little man who sat at the stake clerk's table, a rural mail carrier by profession. He it was who, twelve years ago, had with quiet, patient labor persuaded his totally inactive neighbor to come back into activity. It would have been so much easier to have let that indifferent neighbor go his own way, and it would have been so much easier for the mail carrier to have lived his own quiet life. But he had put aside his personal interests in the interest of another; and that other, last

Sunday, became the honored and respected leader of a great stake of Zion. As the people sustained their new president, the little man at the clerk's table wept tears of gratitude. . . . Phillips Brooks once made this significant observation: "How carefully most men creep into nameless graves, while now and again one or two forget themselves into immortality." ("Forget Yourself," *BYU Devotional Speeches of the Year*, March 6, 1977, pp. 43–44.)

One able thinker . . . said that every great institution is but the lengthened shadow of a great man. I have thought . . . of the status of our work in Korea, where today we have two strong missions and a strong stake of Zion. All of this is the lengthened shadow of Dr. Kim and the two young men who taught him the gospel while he was a student at Cornell University—Oliver Wayman and Don C. Wood. They stirred within their associate student an interest in reading the Book of Mormon. Their interest in him, their activities with him were entirely separate from the reasons for their being at Cornell. Each of the three was there working on an advanced degree that could have consumed every minute of his waking time, but they took the time to teach and to learn; and when the Korean Ph.D. returned to his native land, he took with him his love for the Book of Mormon and for the Church whose services he had attended in Ithaca, New York. American servicemen involved in the Korean War had also shared the gospel with some of their associates, and the presence of Dr. Kim, man of learning and man of responsibility in the nation of Korea, became a catalyst that led to the establishment of the work, including the sending of missionaries from Japan. Dr. Kim is dead, but the work lives on in splendor, touching for eternal good an ever-increasing number of lives in the "Land of the Morning Calm." ("Forget Yourself," *BYU Devotional Speeches of the Year*, March 6, 1977, p. 46.)

Generally speaking, the most miserable people I know are those who are obsessed with themselves; the happiest people I know are those who lose themselves in the service of others. . . . By and large, I have come to see that if we complain about life, it is because we are thinking only of ourselves.

For many years there was a sign on the wall of a shoe repair shop I patronized. It read, "I complained because I had no shoes until I saw a man who had no feet." The most effective medicine for the sickness of self-pity is to lose ourselves in the service of others. ("'Whosoever Will Save His Life,'" *Ensign*, August 1982, p. 5.)

When the history of the work in the Philippines is written, it must include the story of Sister Maxine Grimm, a girl from Tooele, Utah, who served with the Red Cross in the Pacific campaign of the Second World War. She married an American army officer, and after the war they established their home in Manila. She did much to teach the gospel to others; she pleaded that missionaries be sent. Her husband had legal work done and did many other things to make it possible for the missionaries to come. It would have been much easier for them to have simply gone along their way, making money and enjoying the fruits of it; but Sister Grimm was unceasing in her efforts and in her pleas.

At the time, I had responsibility for the work in Asia and I carried her pleas to the First Presidency, who, in 1961, authorized the extension of formal missionary work to that land. In May 1961 we held a meeting in the Philippines to begin the work. We had no place to meet and received permission from the American Embassy to do so at the American Military Cemetery on the outskirts of Manila.

There, where are solemnly remembered the sacrifices of more than 50,000 men who gave their lives in the cause of freedom, we gathered together at 6:30 in the morning. Sister Grimm played a little portable organ she had carried through the campaigns of the Pacific War, and we sang the songs of Zion in a strange land. We bore testimony together and invoked the blessings of heaven on what we were to begin there. Present was one native Filipino member of the Church.

That was the beginning of something marvelous, the commencement of a miracle. The rest is history, discouraging at times and glorious at others. I was there for the area conference held several years ago with President Spencer W. Kimball and others. Some 18,000 members of the Church were assembled in the great

Araneta Coliseum, the largest indoor meeting place in the Republic.

I wept as I thought of the earlier years, and I remember with appreciation the woman who largely forgot her own interests as she relentlessly pursued her dream of the day when the Church would be strong in the land in which she then lived, bringing happiness of a kind previously unknown to thousands of wonderful people. ("'Whosoever Will Save His Life,'" *Ensign*, August 1982, p. 6.)

Who is my neighbor? To answer this, we need only read the moving parable of the good samaritan, or the word of the Lord concerning the day of judgment when the King shall "say unto them on his right hand, Come ye blessed of my Father, inherit the kingdom prepared for you from the foundation of the world:

"For I was an hungred, and ye gave me meat: I was thirsty, and ye gave me drink: I was a stranger, and ye took me in:

"Naked, and ye clothed me: I was sick, and ye visited me: I was in prison, and ye came unto me.

"Then shall the righteous answer him, saying, Lord, when saw we thee an hungred, and fed thee? or thirsty, and gave thee drink?

"When saw we thee a stranger, and took thee in? or naked, and clothed thee?

"Or when saw we thee sick, or in prison, and came unto thee?

"And the King shall answer and say unto them, Verily I say unto you, Inasmuch as ye have done it unto one of the least of these my brethren, ye have done it unto me." (Matt. 25:34–40.)

The greatest challenge we face in our hurried, self-centered lives is to follow this counsel of the Master. Years ago I read the story of a young woman who went into a rural area as a schoolteacher. Among those in her class was a girl who had failed before and who was failing again. The student could not read. She came from a family without means to take her to a larger city for examination to determine whether she had a problem that could be remedied. Sensing that the difficulty might lie with the girl's eyes, the young teacher arranged to take the student, at the teacher's own expense, to have her eyes tested. A deficiency was discovered that could be corrected with glasses. Soon an entire new world opened to the student. For the first time in her life, she saw clearly the words before her. The salary of that country schoolteacher was meager, but out of the little she had, she made an investment that completely changed the life of a failing student, and in doing so she found a new dimension in her own life.

Every returned missionary can recount experiences of losing oneself in the service of others and finding that to be the most rewarding experience of his or her life. ("And the Greatest of These Is Love," *Ensign*, March 1984, pp. 4–5.)

Our pioneer forebears worked together for the common good. I am profoundly grateful for the essence of that spirit of helpfulness which has come down through the generations and which has been so evident in the troubles Latter-day Saints experience in time of disaster and difficulty. The mayor of Salt Lake City told me that when the Salt Lake City flood situation became serious one Sunday afternoon in 1983 that he called a stake president. Within a very short time 4,000 volunteers showed up. The story of such mutual helpfulness caught the attention of many individuals and publications across the nation. Latter-day Saints, working together with their neighbors of other faiths, have labored with one another in times of distress and have been heralded on radio and television, in newspapers and magazines. Writers have treated it as if it were a new and unique phenomenon. It is not new, although it may be unique in this time. I noticed with interest the quoted comment of a Federal Relief official who said that those sent to Utah to offer government aid had received far fewer calls than they had anticipated. The fact is that many people simply said resolutely, as their forebears before them might have said, "We will work together and do what we need to do to restore our homes and farms." May God bless all who work unitedly with such faith and love and appreciation one for another in times of difficulty. ("The Faith of the Pioneers," *Ensign*, July 1984, pp. 4–5.)

One who seeks to please his Heavenly Father will serve the needs of our Father's kingdom. This Church is a part of His divine plan. It is the kingdom of God in the earth. Its work is important. Its work is necessary to the accomplishment of the eternal purposes of our Father. If each of us is to please our Father in Heaven, we must be responsive to the needs of His kingdom. We must be willing to work wherever we are called to work and to develop our talents so that our work will be more effective in reaching out to those who are not members of the Church or those who are inactive in the Church. We must be diligent in carrying forward the great work of salvation for the dead and in every other way giving of our strength and talent and substance to move forward and strengthen the Church. This may involve some sacrifice, yes, but with every sacrifice comes a blessing.

Mine has been the privilege these past two or three months of interviewing and extending calls to fifty-eight men to serve as mission presidents. What a gratifying and inspiring experience this has been. Each of these men is one who is carrying substantial responsibility in business or professional service, who has many concerns and interests demanding attention. But without exception, in every case, the response has been, "If I can help the work of the Lord, that is what I want to do. If the Lord is extending a call, I am ready to leave." Sometimes after such interviews, tears have welled in my eyes as I have reflected on the great faith of so many who, at the call of the Church, are willing to set aside every other interest out of a desire to please our Heavenly Father.

The remarkable and wonderful thing is that although they give up much to go, as everyone can testify when he returns home, they gain so very much that is unique and wonderful. They all come back saying there is no experience like it, and they would not trade it for any other on earth. It is so with any service we do as an expression of love for our Father in Heaven. ("To Please Our Heavenly Father," *Ensign*, May 1985, pp. 50–51.)

Let me tell of [a man] I met in Guatemala. He is John O'Donnal, [then] president of the Guatemala City Temple. He stood before a congregation and with a voice choked with emotion told his story.

As a young man he was graduated from the University of Arizona with a degree in agricultural science. He was employed by the U.S. Department of Agriculture and was sent to

Guatemala to work on a project to develop the growth of natural rubber trees to meet a critical need when war was engulfing the world.

As I remember his words, he said: "I was twenty-four years of age and unmarried when I came to Guatemala forty-three years ago. I had been reared with a love for the Savior and His teachings. In the course of my work here, I walked day after day through these mountains and jungles among the native peoples of this land. I came to know them and to love them, and as I saw the poverty and darkness in which they lived, I wept for them. They were the purest people I had ever known, but they were without the light of the gospel. I cried to the Lord concerning them. I knew that their one sure hope lay in obtaining a knowledge of and a love for Jesus Christ, and in receiving the record of their forebears, which testifies of Him.

"In time I fell in love with a beautiful girl in whose veins flowed English and Spanish blood and also the blood of Lehi, Laman, and Samuel. We were married. . . .

"In 1946 and again in 1947 I traveled to Salt Lake City and pleaded with the President of the Church to send missionaries. Finally, in September 1947, the mission president and his counselors brought four elders to our house. The next day we drove onto a mountain where together we had the sacrament, and the mission president dedicated the land for the preaching of the restored gospel.

"My wife was the first native of Central America baptized into The Church of Jesus Christ of Latter-day Saints. Today she stands at my side as the matron of this beautiful temple."

He continued: "In 1956 I was in a serious accident and was taken to the hospital for major surgery. My life hung in the balance, and in those circumstances I had a remarkable experience. The Lord showed me that a temple would be built in this land.

"Also, I was informed by a power beyond the power of man that my life would be spared but that my life would not be my own."

His life has not been his own. As a scientist and administrator, he established and operated a large rubber plantation and operated for a short period a tire factory for one of the great rubber companies in the United States. But he did still yet a far more significant thing. In the spirit of the Master, he went about doing good. He worked sharing the gospel among the native peoples of Guatemala. For more than forty years he has lived with them, has spoken their language, has sorrowed with them in their sorrows, has taught them the everlasting gospel, and has been a quiet, unassuming, but magnificent pioneer in the development of the work of the Lord in that land.

When he walked the jungle trails alone, he was the only member of the Church in all that land. Today there are more than forty-four thousand of them. He nurtured the first little branch. Today there are twelve stakes of Zion in Guatemala and many more in the surrounding nations of Central America. . . .

John O'Donnal was told when the veil between life and death was thin that his life would be spared but that his life would not be his own. How true that must be for each of us. None of us may rightly say that his life is his own. Our lives are a gift from God, and when we leave this life may not be according to our wish. Truthfully, our days are numbered not by ourselves, but according to the will of God. ("Giving Ourselves to the Service of the Lord," *Ensign*, March 1987, pp. 4–5.)

Of all people, we must surely realize that there can be no true worship of Him who is the Christ without giving of ourselves. Why are missionaries happy? Because they lose themselves in the service of others.

Why are those who labor in the temples happy? Because their labor of love is in very deed harmonious with the great vicarious work of the Savior of mankind. They neither ask for nor expect thanks for what they do. For the most part, they know nothing more than the name of him or her in whose behalf they labor.

Sadly, many of us use our lives as if they were our own. It is true that ours is the choice to waste our lives if we wish. But that becomes a betrayal of a great and sacred trust. ("Giving Ourselves to the Service of the Lord," *Ensign*, March 1987, p. 5.)

The best antidote I know for worry is work. The best medicine for despair is service. The best cure for weariness is the challenge of helping someone who is even more tired. (Single Adult Fireside Satellite Broadcast, February 26, 1989.)

Let love be the Polar Star of our lives in reaching out to those who need our strength. There are many among us who lie alone in pain. Medicine helps, but kind words can bring to pass miracles. Many there are who walk in frightening circumstances, fearful and unable to cope. There are good bishops and Relief Society officers who are available to help, but these cannot do it all. Each of us can and must be anxiously engaged. ("Let Love Be the Lodestar of Your Life," *Ensign*, May 1989, pp. 66–67.)

The people of this . . . Church have given generously of their resources to help those in need. My mind goes back to one Sunday, a few years ago, when the Presidency of the Church asked that our people fast for two meals and consecrate the equivalent value, and more, to help the homeless and hungry in areas of Africa where we had no members, but where there was much of famine and suffering.

On Monday morning the money began to come in. There were hundreds of dollars, and then thousands of dollars, then hundreds of thousands of dollars, and then millions of dollars. These consecrated funds became the means of saving many who otherwise might have starved.

We do not boast of this. I simply mention it in furtherance of my theme that *Mormon* can and for many does mean "more good." ("*Mormon* Should Mean 'More Good,'" *Ensign*, November 1990, p. 54.)

What a therapeutic and wonderful thing it is for a man or woman to set aside all consideration of personal gain and reach out with strength and energy and purpose to help the unfortunate, to improve the community, to clean up the environment, and to beautify our surroundings. ("This I Believe," *BYU 1991–92 Devotional and Fireside Speeches*, March 1, 1992, p. 79.)

No person who is a member of this church and has taken upon himself the covenants incident to membership can reasonably expect the blessings of the Lord upon his efforts unless being willing to bear his share of the burden of the Lord's king-dom. . . .

While riding on an airplane, I picked up a magazine and read a description of the moral bankruptcy into which the world is falling. The author gave as the dominant reason for this decay an attitude that is characterized by the question, What's in it for me?

Brothers and sisters, you will never be happy if you go through life thinking only of yourself. Get lost in the best cause in the world—the cause of the Lord. ("Pillars of Truth," *Ensign*, January 1994, pp. 6–7.)

Do you want to be happy? Forget yourself and get lost in this great cause. Lend your efforts to helping people. Cultivate a spirit of forgiveness in your heart against any who might have offended you. Look to the Lord and live and work to lift and serve His sons and daughters. You will come to know a happi-ness that you have never known before if you will do that. I do not care how old you are, how young you are, whatever. You can lift people and help them. Heaven knows there are so very, very, very many people in this world who need help. Oh, so very, very many. Let's get the cankering, selfish attitude out of our lives, my brothers and sisters, and stand a little taller and reach a little higher in the service of others. As Browning said, "A man's reach should exceed his grasp." Stand taller, stand higher, lift those with feeble knees, hold up the arms of those that hang down. Live the gospel of Jesus Christ. Forget yourself. (Liverpool England Fireside, August 31, 1995.)

I hope you are enjoying your work and service. I know that it is demanding. I know that it is strenuous. But what a tremen-dous opportunity we all have. What better thing could we be doing? How could we better spend our time? We are dealing with the very fiber of eternity. We are dealing with the salvation and exaltation of our Father's children. We get weary. Yes. So what? We may get sick in the service. In all likelihood, we will recover. "And should we die before our journey's through, Happy day! All is well! We then are free from toil and sorrow, too; with the just we shall dwell!" (*Hymns*, no. 30.) What more could we ask for? (General Authority Training Meeting, October 1, 1996.)

We have some of our own who cry out in pain and suffering and loneliness and fear. Ours is a great and solemn duty to reach out and help them, to lift them, to feed them if they are hungry, to nurture their spirits if they thirst for truth and righteousness. ("'Reach with a Rescuing Hand,'" *Ensign*, November 1996, p. 86.)

When I was a stake president, we had an elders quorum that was doing nothing. . . . It wasn't going anywhere. We came to the conclusion we would have to reorganize that elders quorum; and after prayer and consideration, I called a man into the stake office. I talked with him and told him we would like him to serve as president of the elders quorum. He said, "I can't do that. I couldn't possibly do that. I don't have it in me to do that." He said, "I'm a convert to the Church. I was an orphan boy born down in Alabama. The only thing I learned to do while I was there was to make brooms of corn straw. I work in a garage downtown, a dealership, fixing cars. I'm not qualified to be president of the elders quorum." And I said, "Well, you are called to be president of the elders quorum." He sat and put his head down in his hands and cried, and then stood up and said, "I'll do my best." He selected two counselors who were intellectual superiors in many ways. But he had a remarkable knack. Things began to happen in that elders quorum. He let his counselors deal with the professors who belonged to that quorum. He went out among the slackers, among those who had quit coming. He knew their language. He knew how to talk to them, and they responded. He built a wonderful quorum of elders and has since gone on to other responsibilities. Work. Give your people something to do. Faith withers with idleness. Put them to work. (Brigham City Utah Regional Conference, priesthood leadership session, February 22, 1997.)

Brigham Young and a handful of others are remembered from our pioneer history. But what of the unsung, the unheralded, the unrecognized who lived the gospel, loved the Lord, and did their daily work without fanfare or applause? Will their eternal reward be any less? I think not.

So it is with us. We each make our own contribution, and that contribution adds up to the building of the cause. Your contribution is as acceptable as ours. Jesus said, "If any man desire to be first, the same shall be last of all, and servant of all" (Mark 9:35).

Brethren and sisters, we're all part of one great family. Each has a duty, each has a mission to perform. And when we pass on, it will be reward enough if we can say to our beloved Master, "I have fought a good fight, I have finished my course, I have kept the faith" (2 Tim. 4:7). ("Our Testimony to the World," *Ensign,* May 1997, p. 84.)

SINGLE PARENTS

I mention next that very large group who are the single parents among us. Most of these are divorcees who carry exhausting burdens in fighting the daily battles that go with rearing children and seeing that their needs are met. For them this is a lonely duty. We must see that they are not left entirely alone. But at the same time, they are sensitive, and it is not right that others intrude and trample on those personal sensitivities. In dealing with them it is essential that the inspiration of the Lord be sought. But far better that we reach out to them with help in excess than that we neglect them.

Most of them are women who are struggling. They work for meager wages and face terrifying responsibilities in putting food on their tables and clothing on the backs of their children. They are a responsibility of the bishop and the Relief Society president. I hope that you will urge these officers to be kind and considerate, to be wise and careful, to be sensitive and prayerful and generous. We receive letters in the office of the First Presidency which indicate that this is not always the case. . . .

These single parents carry a burden the weight of which few of us really know. In the recent satellite broadcast conference a young mother, a divorcee with seven children, spoke to us. She told of an experience when one evening she walked across the street to carry something to a neighbor. As she left to return home and saw the lights in her own house and thought of those seven lively children with their difficult problems, all of them her responsibility, she felt a great weariness, a feeling of total inadequacy. In the dark of the night she lifted her eyes to heaven and pleaded with her Father in heaven that she might go to Him, if only for a night, to find comfort and strength for the trials of tomorrow. Tender was the response that came into her mind, almost as a revelation: "You cannot come to me, but I will come to you." . . .

God our Eternal Father . . . and His Beloved Son can come to the weary and the lonely by the power of the Spirit to comfort and sustain, to nurture and to bless. (Regional Representatives Seminar, March 31, 1989.)

Now to you single mothers, whatever the cause of your present situation, our hearts reach out to you. We know that many of you live in loneliness, insecurity, worry, and fear. For most of you there is never enough money. Your constant, brooding worry is anxiety for your children and their futures. Many of you find yourselves in circumstances where you have to work and leave your children largely to their own devices. But if when they are very small there is much of affection, there is shown much of love, there is prayer together, then there will more likely be peace in the hearts and strength in the character of your children. Teach them the ways of the Lord. Declared Isaiah, "All thy children shall be taught of the Lord; and great shall be the peace of thy children" (Isa. 54:13).

The more surely you rear your children in the ways of the gospel of Jesus Christ, with love and high expectation, the more likely that there will be peace in their lives.

Set an example for them. That will mean more than all the teaching you can give them. Do not overindulge them. Let them grow up with respect for and understanding of the meaning of labor, of working and contributing to the home and its surroundings, with some way of earning some of their own expense money. Let your sons save for missions, and encourage them to prepare themselves, not only financially, but spiritually and in an attitude to go out to serve the Lord without selfishness of any kind. I do not hesitate to promise that if you will do so, you will have reason to count your blessings. ("Stand Strong against the Wiles of the World," *Ensign*, November 1995, pp. 99–100.)

For you who are single parents, I say that many hands stand ready to help you. The Lord is not unmindful of you. Neither is His Church.

May He bless you, my beloved sisters who find yourselves in the situation of single parenthood. May you have health, strength, vitality to carry the heavy burden that is yours. May you have loving friends and associates to bear you up in your times of trial. You know the power of prayer as perhaps few others do. Many of you spend much time on your knees speaking with your Father in Heaven, with tears running down your cheeks. Please know that we also pray for you.

With all that you have to do, you are also asked to serve in the Church. Your bishop will not ask you to do anything that is beyond your capacity. And as you so serve, a new dimension will be added to your life. You will find new and stimulating associations. You will find friendship and sociality. You will grow in knowledge and understanding and wisdom, and in your capacity to do. You will become a better mother because of the service you give in the work of the Lord. ("Women of the Church," *Ensign*, November 1996, p. 69.)

SINGLES

It would be a beautiful world if every girl had the privilege of marriage to a good young man whom she could look upon with pride and gladness as her companion in time and eternity, hers alone to love and cherish, to respect and help. What a wonderful world it would be if every young man were married to a wife in the house of the Lord, one at whose side he would stand as protector, provider, husband, and companion.

But it doesn't work out that way in every case. There are some who, for reasons unexplainable, do not have the opportunity of marriage. To you I should like to say a word or two. Don't waste your time and wear out your lives wandering about in the wasteland of self-pity. God has given you talents of one kind or another. God has given you the capacity to serve the needs of others and bless their lives with your kindness and concern. Reach out to someone in need. There are so very many out there.

Add knowledge to knowledge. Refine your mind and skills in a chosen field of discipline. Never in the history of the world have women been afforded such opportunities in the professions, in business, in education, and in all of the honorable vocations of life. Do not feel that because you are single God has forsaken you. I repeat his promise quoted earlier, "Be thou humble; and the Lord thy God shall lead thee by the hand, and give thee answer to thy prayers." [D&C 112:10.]

The world needs you. The Church needs you. So very many people and causes need your strength and wisdom and talents. ("If I Were You, What Would I Do?" *BYU 1983–84 Fireside and Devotional Speeches*, September 20, 1983, p. 11.)

Many years ago I had a secretary who one morning was plainly in a bad mood. I said, "Something's wrong. Can I help?" She burst into tears and said, "It's my birthday. I am 35 today. What do I have to show for it?—a job yes, but no husband, no children, nothing of consequence."

I replied, "So you're 35? Happy birthday! According to actuarial tables you have more years ahead of you than you have behind you. Now with all you've learned over these 35 years you can build and grow and live a wonderful and productive and happy life. Lift your head. Smile and get happy and go forward."

Her dour face finally broke into a pleasant smile. I guess it was about five years later that she married, had a child and did many interesting and productive things. Thirty-five is not the end of life nor of the world. Neither is 40 or 50 or 60. As Madame Curie, the great scientist, is quoted as saying, "So little time and so much to do."

For you in this category it can be a wonderful season of your lives. You have maturity. You have judgment. Most of you have training and experience. You have the physical, mental, and spiritual strength to lift and help and encourage.

There are so many out there who need you. It is not enough to work at a word processor forty hours a week and feel that you have done all that you can do. You are needed. There are young people to be taught in the organizations of the Church. Refine your skills. Accept every challenge and assignment. Put time and effort into the preparation of your lessons. Keep your spiritual batteries at full charge and light the lamps of others. It is better to light one candle than to curse the dark. (Single Adult Fireside Satellite Broadcast, February 26, 1989.)

Included in the group we have designated as singles are several categories—those who have never married but who are relatively young and likely will; those who are older who have never married and whose chances for marriage are diminishing; those who have married and are divorced; and those who are widowed. Altogether they constitute about one-third of the adult membership of the Church. Their numbers are so large and their problems so serious that we cannot disregard them. . . .

I heard on a broadcast the other evening a song I have not heard in forty or fifty years. It was one of those tunes to which we danced when I was younger and less brittle. The opening lines of the lyrics say this: "You're nobody 'til somebody loves you, you're nobody 'til somebody cares."

Think about that for a minute. It applies to all of us. There is no substitute for appreciation and love. Without these two great blessings, life has little meaning. . . .

Somehow we have put a badge on this group. It reads "Singles." I do not know what else to call them, but I wish there were some other term. These are individuals, men and women, sons and daughters of God, not a mass of "look-alikes" or "do-alikes." The fact that they do not happen to be married does not make them essentially different from others. All of us are very much alike in appearance and emotional responses; in our capacity to think, to reason, to be miserable; in our need to be happy, to love, and to be loved.

I do not worry very much about the young men and women, including many returned missionaries, who are of such an age that in all likelihood they will be married within a relatively short time. I feel they should not be put under pressure by counsel from Church leaders to rush into it. But neither do I believe that they should dally along in a fruitless, frustrating, and frivolous dating game that only raises hopes and brings disappointment and in some cases heartache.

The young men should take the initiative in this matter. It goes without saying that they should be encouraged to live worthy of the companionship of a wonderful partner. They should be taught to put aside any thought of selfish superiority and recognize and follow the teaching of the Church that the husband and wife walk side by side with neither one ahead or behind. They should be interviewed occasionally to fortify them in their resolution to walk in paths of virtue while courting, and to maintain absolute fidelity one to another following marriage.

My greater concern is with those who are older and for whom the opportunities for marriage are discouragingly few.

We must be sensitive to the feelings of these people. Included in their number are many extremely able and faithful young women in their everyday vocational pursuits. But in the hearts of many of them there is a great loneliness unknown largely to the rest of us, but of which Church officers must be aware. These people do not want pity. They want to be regarded as the equal of others in handling opportunities and challenges. They do not want to be categorized as a unique and peculiar lot who do not fit in with the rest of us.

Great are their talents and tremendous is their capacity. They can make wonderful contributions. . . . We lived in a ward at one time where one of the Relief Society lessons each month was taught by such a woman. Following each such meeting my wife would glow with her enthusiasm for that teacher.

These people are not pariahs to be set aside. They are sons and daughters of God whose talents are to be cultivated and utilized. Of course there are some situations in which they cannot be used. But there are many situations where they can be used and ought to be used and both they and those who hear them will be profited in the process. . . .

We are neglecting many of these people. Among their numbers are so many who are talented and willing. They represent one of the great resources of the Church. (Regional Representatives Seminar, March 31, 1989.)

Keep marriage and motherhood in their true perspective. A happy marriage is the aim of every young woman. I know that some will be denied this opportunity. I urge you not to spend your time in self-pity. Rather, keep yourselves alive and vivacious in those activities which will bring satisfaction into your lives while associating with others who are vigorously pursuing lofty objectives. Remember always that you are not alone. There are thousands like you. And you are not helpless, a victim of fate. You can in large measure master your fate and strengthen your self-worth in reaching out to those who need and will appreciate your talents, your contributions, your help. ("Rise to the Stature of the Divine within You," *Ensign*, November 1989, p. 97.)

You classify yourself as the "singles." I feel some concern about the tendency in the Church to divide the members into various classes and groups. I do not look upon you as being essentially different from other members of the Church. You are men and women, holders of the priesthood, workers in the Relief Society. You are tremendously important to this work. The Church is much the stronger because of you. Your strong helping hands, and your willing hearts, have done so much to move forward the work of the Lord and bring to pass His eternal purposes. You are able, you are intelligent, you are faithful, you are devoted. Your present domestic situation may be different from that of others, but you certainly are not alone. I am told that you comprise about a third of the adult members of the Church. Just think of how much weaker this work would be without you. Think of how much stronger it is because of you. (Ellen Pucell Unthank Monument Dedication, Cedar City, Utah, August 3, 1991.)

Question: The emphasis on family, does that perhaps have a tendency to make a single Mormon or a divorced Mormon feel a little out of it?

President Hinckley: It may have that effect, I am sorry to say. Our hearts reach out to those people. We try to do everything we can to try to assist them. We have a great program for singles in the Church where they can mingle one with another and socialize together and meet companions. And that happens, not infrequently. It is a working program that accomplishes that result. But we know that some people will never marry and I am sure they feel the effects of that. Every normal man, every normal woman, I am confident, would like to be married to a good companion and be part of a good strong family. (Interview with Mike Wallace of *60 Minutes,* December 18, 1995.)

There are many women among us who are single. Generally, this is not of their own choice. Some have never had the opportunity to marry one with whom they would wish to spend eternity.

To you single women who wish to be married, I repeat what I recently said in a meeting for singles in this Tabernacle: "Do not give up hope. And do not give up trying. But do give up being obsessed with it. The chances are that if you forget about it and become anxiously engaged in other activities, the prospects will brighten immeasurably.

"I believe that for most of us the best medicine for loneliness is work, service in behalf of others. I do not minimize your problems, but I do not hesitate to say that there are many others whose problems are more serious than are yours. Reach out to serve them, to help them, to encourage them. There are so many boys and girls who fail in school for want of a little personal attention and encouragement. There are so many elderly people who live in misery and loneliness and fear for whom a simple conversation would bring a measure of hope and happiness." ("Women of the Church," *Ensign,* November 1996, p. 68.)

SPIRITUALITY

With the tremendous growth of the Church we become increasingly aware of the great magnitude of the affairs of this the Lord's kingdom. We have a comprehensive program for the instruction of the family. We have organizations for youth, for children, for mothers and fathers. We have a vast missionary system, a tremendous welfare operation, probably the most extensive genealogical program in the world. We must build houses of worship, hundreds and thousands of them. We must operate . . . schools, seminaries, institutes. The ramifications of our activities now reach around the world. All of this is the business of the Church. Sometimes the tendency is to handle it as we would ordinary business. But it is more than an organization of enterprises. It is more than a social body. These are but means to the accomplishment of its one true purpose.

That purpose is to assist our Father in heaven in bringing to pass his work and his glory, the immortality and eternal life of man. (See Moses 1:39.)

The forces against which we labor are tremendous. We need more than our own strength to cope with them.

To all who hold positions of leadership, to the vast corps of teachers and missionaries, to heads of families, I should like to make a plea: In all you do, feed the spirit—nourish the soul. " . . . the letter killeth, but the Spirit giveth life." (2 Cor. 3:6.) . . .

There is hunger in the land, and a genuine thirst—a great hunger for the word of the Lord and an unsatisfied thirst for things of the spirit. Ours is the obligation and the opportunity to nourish the soul. . . .

I make a plea that we constantly seek the inspiration of the Lord and the companionship of his Holy Spirit to bless us in keeping our efforts on a high spiritual plane. ("Feed the Spirit— Nourish the Soul," *Improvement Era*, December 1967, pp. 85–86.)

The older I grow the less concerned I become with quotas and statistics and percentages, and the more I become concerned with the kind of experience that the soul of man has in the Lord's church, and particularly in the Lord's holy house. (Temple Presidents Seminar, August 15, 1989.)

I think our people know a lot about the Word of Wisdom, they know a lot about paying their tithing, they know a lot about MIA, they know a lot about seminary, and they know a lot about the mechanics of our meetings. But I worry and am deeply concerned about whether they are being fed spiritually. That's my deepest concern. (Corpus Christi Texas Regional Conference, priesthood leadership session, January 6, 1996.)

Kipling once described our times as "these hot and godless days." . . . The spirit is as much a part of man as is his body. It too needs nourishment. This is the thing which gives refinement to man, which lifts him above the plane of the animal of the jungle, which motivates his finest deeds, which is divine in its essence. In the headlong materialistic rush in which the world is engaged it is being strangled and trampled. With it will go our liberty, the dignity of the individual, that altruism which makes life livable, the peace for which we long. We cannot survive without it.

Recently the newspaper magazine section which comes into many of your homes carried on its cover these words: "If America is to grow great, we must stop gagging over the word 'spiritual.' Our task is to rediscover and reassert our faith in the non-utilitarian values on which American life has rested from its beginning." (Laurence M. Gould, *This Week* magazine, August 7, 1966.)

I believe that. I believe it not only for America but for all nations. I commend it to you for your thoughtful consideration. I am convinced that no nation can for long base its progress solely on materialism. We need—oh, how we need—to re-enthrone God and "worship Him in spirit and in truth." ("Conquer or Be Conquered," BYU Commencement Address, August 19, 1966.)

If I were a bishop or stake president today, what would I do? I think that I would try to put my major efforts on building the spirituality of the people. I would work as hard as I knew how to work in building their faith in the Lord Jesus Christ, in God our Eternal Father, in the Prophet Joseph Smith and the restoration of this work and what it means and what it is all about. I would encourage my people to read the scriptures, to read the Book of Mormon, to read the New Testament. I would urge them with all the capacity I have to read quietly and thoughtfully and introspectively, if you please. I would urge them to read the teachings of the Prophet Joseph Smith. (Eugene Oregon Regional Conference, priesthood leadership session, September 14, 1996.)

We need to build ourselves spiritually. We live in a world of rush and go, of running here and there and in every direction. We are very busy people. We have so much to do. We need to get off by ourselves once in awhile and think of the spiritual things and build ourselves spiritually. If you have a study at home, lock yourselves in it. If you have a place in the basement where you can be by yourself, go there. Get by yourself and think of things of the Lord, of things of the Spirit. Let gratitude swell up in your hearts. Think of all the Lord has done for you. How blessed you are, how very blessed you are. Think of your duty and your responsibility. Think of your testimony. Think of the things of God. Just meditate and reflect for an hour about yourself and your relationship to your Heavenly Father and your Redeemer. It will do something for you. (Brigham City Utah Regional Conference, priesthood leadership session, February 22, 1997.)

STANDARDS

See also Values

We live in a day of shifting values, of changing standards, of will-o'-the-wisp programs that blossom in the morning and die in the evening. We see this in government, we see it in public and private morality, we see it in the homes of the people; we see it in the churches, and we even see it among some of our own members who are led away by the sophistry of men.

Men everywhere seem to be groping as men in darkness, casting aside the traditions that were the strength of our society, yet unable to find a new star to guide them. . . .

Some months ago I read a provocative article by Barbara Tuchman, a Pulitzer Prize-winning historian. Said she:

"When it comes to leaders we have, if anything, a super abundance—hundreds of Pied Pipers—ready and anxious to lead the population. They are scurrying around, collecting consensus, gathering as wide an acceptance as possible. But what they are not doing very notably is standing still and saying, '*This* is what I believe. This I will do and that I will not do. This is my code of behavior and that is outside it. This is excellent and that is trash.' There is an absence of moral leadership in the sense of a general unwillingness to state standards."

She continues, "Of all the ills that our poor . . . society is heir to, the focal one, it seems to me, from which so much of our uneasiness and confusion derive, is the absence of standards. We are too unsure of ourselves to assert them, to stick by them, if necessary in the cases of persons who occupy positions of authority, to impose them. We seem to be afflicted by a widespread and eroding reluctance to take any stand on any values, moral, behavioral or esthetic." ("The Missing Element—Moral Courage," *McCall's*, June 1967, p. 28.)

While standards generally may totter, we of the Church are without excuse if we drift in the same manner. We have standards—sure, tested, and effective. To the extent that we observe them, we shall go forward. To the extent that we neglect them, we shall hinder our own progress and bring embarrassment to the work of the Lord. . . .

The satisfying thing is that obedience brings happiness. It brings peace; it brings growth—all of these to the individual, and his good example brings respect for the institution of which he is a part.

Our adherence to these divinely given standards need never be an offensive thing to those about us. We need not contend with them. But if we will pursue a steady course, our very example will become the most effective argument we could ever advance for the virtues of the cause with which we are associated. ("Contend Not with Others, But Pursue a Steady Course," *Improvement Era*, June 1970, p. 40.)

[Our] standards have come from [the Lord]. Some of them may appear a little out of date in our society, but this does not detract from their validity nor diminish the virtue of their application. The subtle reasoning of men, no matter how clever, no matter how plausible it may sound, cannot abridge the declared wisdom of God. (*Be Thou an Example* [Salt Lake City: Deseret Book, 1981], p. 12.)

The Lord has given us counsel and commandment on so many things that no member of this church need ever equivocate. He has established our guidelines concerning personal virtue, neighborliness, obedience to law, loyalty to government, observance of the Sabbath day, sobriety and abstinence from liquor and tobacco, the payment of tithes and offerings, the care of the poor, the cultivation of home and family, the sharing of the gospel, to mention only a few. . . .

There may be those who will seek to tempt us away. There may be those who will try to bait us. We may be disparaged. We may be belittled. We may be inveighed against. We may be caricatured before the world. There are those, both in the Church and out, who would compel us to change our position on some matters, as if it were our prerogative to usurp authority which belongs to God alone.

We have no desire to quarrel with others. We teach the gospel of peace. But we cannot forsake the word of the Lord as it has come to us through men whom we have sustained as prophets. (*Be Thou an Example* [Salt Lake City: Deseret Book, 1981], p. 13.)

It is not always easy to live in the world and not be a part of it. We cannot live entirely with our own or unto ourselves, nor would we wish to. We must mingle with others. In so doing, we can be gracious. We can be inoffensive. We can avoid any spirit or attitude of self-righteousness. But we can maintain our standards. The natural tendency will be otherwise, and many have succumbed to it.

In 1856, when we were largely alone in these valleys, some thought we were safe from the ways of the world. To such talk, President Heber C. Kimball responded: "I want to say to you, my brethren, the time is coming when we will be mixed up in these now peaceful valleys to that extent that it will be difficult to tell the face of a Saint from the face of an enemy to the people of God. Then, brethren," he went on, "look out for the great sieve, for there will be a great sifting time, and many will fall; for I say unto you there is a test, a *Test*, a TEST coming, and who will be able to stand?" (Orson F. Whitney, *Life of Heber C. Kimball* [Bookcraft, 1945], p. 446.)

I do not know the precise nature of that test. But I am inclined to think the time is here and that the test lies in our capacity to live the gospel rather than adopt the ways of the world.

I do not advocate a retreat from society. On the contrary, we have a responsibility and a challenge to take our places in the world of business, science, government, medicine, education, and every other worthwhile and constructive vocation. We have an obligation to train our hands and minds to excel in the work of the world for the blessing of all mankind. In so doing we must work with others. But this does not require a surrender of standards. (*Be Thou an Example* [Salt Lake City: Deseret Book, 1981], p. 27.)

STEWARDSHIP

I invite you to look beyond the narrow boundaries of your own wards and rise to the larger vision of this, the work of God. We have a challenge to meet, a work to do beyond the comprehension of any of us—that is, to assist our Heavenly Father to save His sons and daughters of all generations, both the living and the dead, to work for the salvation not only of those in the Church, but for those presently outside, wherever they may be. No body of people on the face of the earth has received a stronger mandate from the God of heaven than have we of this Church. ("Rise to a Larger Vision of the Work," *Ensign*, May 1990, p. 97.)

We serve by His sufferance, knowing that at any time He chooses to do so, He can easily remove us. We are answerable to Him in this life, and will be held accountable when we are called before Him to make our report. I hope that we shall not be found wanting. I hope that when that time comes, I may have the opportunity of standing before my Beloved Savior to give an accounting of my stewardship, and that I may be able to do so without embarrassment, or apology, or excuse. I have so tried to conduct my life. I know that I am not a perfect man, that I have many weaknesses. But I can say that I have tried to do that which the Lord would have me do as His servant, and as the servant of every member of this Church throughout the world, and most particularly as the servant of my beloved President, our Prophet, Seer, and Revelator. ("'In . . . Counsellors There Is Safety,'" *Ensign*, November 1990, p. 51.)

We strive to keep the trust which has been placed in us. We know that someday we must stand before our Master and give an accounting of our stewardship. I hope and pray that we may do so without embarrassment or excuse. And I hope that we shall not be found to have been wanting in our sincerity, in our devotion, in our effort to handle well and faithfully the responsibility given us by the Lord. (Phoenix Arizona North/West Regional Conference, January 13, 1991.)

"And whoso is found a faithful, a just, and a wise steward shall enter into the joy of his Lord, and shall inherit eternal life" (D&C 51:19). Those words intrigue me. "A faithful, a just, and a wise steward." Every man here has a stewardship for others— faithful, just, and wise. Faithful in all he is asked to do. Just, even-handed, considerate of all for whom he has responsibility. Wise, with that wisdom which comes from the Lord. I would like to suggest that one verse to you as something you could write out and put on the mirror so that every morning you will see it and think of it and ponder it in terms of your responsibility. (Anchorage Alaska Regional Conference, priesthood leadership session, June 17, 1995.)

SUCCESS

Without preservation and cultivation of the spiritual, your material success will be as ashes in your mouths. ("Conquer or Be Conquered," BYU Commencement Address, August 19, 1966.)

The bane of my first-grade teacher's life was my friend Louie. He had what psychologists today might call some kind of an obsessive fixation. He would sit in class and chew his tie until it became wet and stringy. The teacher would scold him.

Louie eventually became a man of substance, and I have learned never to underestimate the potential of a boy to make something of his life, even if he chews his tie. ("Some Lessons I Learned as a Boy," *Ensign*, May 1993, p. 53.)

Men may become rich and famous, but if their home life is miserable because of selfishness and evil and abusive tactics and things of that kind, they are not successful, they are failures. I believe that with all my heart. The greatest job in this world is to build a home. I don't mean the physical structure, I mean the spiritual environment of a good home. (Eagle Gate 7th Ward Sacrament Meeting, September 17, 1995.)

You are moving into a competitive world. You are going to need all the wits that you have, all the brain capacity that you can possibly marshal, and all the skills you can develop if you are going to be successful in life. (Vista California Youth Fireside, March 23, 1996.)

The major work of the world is not done by geniuses. It is done by ordinary people, with balance in their lives, who have learned to work in an extraordinary manner. ("Our Fading Civility," BYU Commencement Address, April 25, 1996.)

The Lord would want you to be successful. He would. You are His sons and His daughters. He has the same kind of love and ambition for you that your earthly parents have. They want you to do well and you can do it. (Eugene Oregon Regional Conference, September 15, 1996.)

SUCCESSION TO THE PRESIDENCY

See also Church Government

We have maintained and followed the position that the keys and the authority of the priesthood, that authority without which there can be no true Church of Jesus Christ, were given to the Council of the Twelve Apostles in the very early days of the Church so that in the event of the death of the president the authority would remain and be passed on legally and properly for so long as the Church should continue.

For instance, in the great revelation on priesthood which we know as section 107 of the Doctrine and Covenants, which was received and recorded on March 28, 1835, the Lord spoke of the governance of his Church and said of the Twelve after speaking of the Presidency: "They form a quorum, equal in authority and power to" the presidency. (D&C 107:24.)

Two years later, on July 23, 1837, this principle was again affirmed through revelation: "For unto you, the Twelve, and those, the First Presidency, who are appointed with you to be your counselors and your leaders, is the power of this priesthood given, for the last days and for the last time." (D&C 112:30.)

Again on January 19, 1841, the Lord said through the Prophet Joseph: "I give unto you my servant Brigham Young to be a president over the Twelve traveling council;

"Which Twelve hold the keys to open up the authority of my kingdom upon the four corners of the earth, and after that to send my word to every creature." (D&C 124:127–28.) . . .

It is abundantly clear that the Lord placed the Council of the Twelve, with Brigham Young as its president, next to the Prophet Joseph Smith and gave unto them the keys and the authority to advance the Church under the direction of the Prophet while he was alive, and to govern after his death. ("The Joseph Smith III Document and the Keys of the Kingdom," *Ensign,* May 1981, pp. 20–21.)

The winter of 1843–1844 was a season of great tension in Nauvoo. Enemies were plotting the destruction of the Church. During that winter, on a number of occasions, Joseph assembled the Twelve in the upper room of his brick store on Water Street in Nauvoo. . . . I have time to quote from the record of only one who was present. There were many. Wrote he of Joseph Smith:

"This great and good man was led, before his death, to call the Twelve together, from time to time, and to instruct them in all things pertaining to the kingdom, ordinances, and government of God. He often observed that he was laying the foundation, but it would remain for the Twelve to complete the building. Said he, 'I know not why; but for some reason I am constrained to hasten my preparations, and to confer upon the Twelve all the ordinances, keys, covenants, endowments, and sealing ordinances of the priesthood' . . . for, said he, 'the Lord is about to lay the burden on your shoulders and let me rest awhile; and if they kill me . . . the kingdom of God will roll on, as I have now finished the work which was laid upon me, by committing to you all things for the building up of the kingdom according to the heavenly vision, and the pattern shown me from heaven.'" (Parley P. Pratt, "Proclamation," *Millennial Star,* 5 [March 1845]: 151.)

As you know, Joseph Smith was killed by the Carthage mob on June 27, 1844. On the following 8th of August a congregation of thousands assembled in Nauvoo. Sidney Rigdon, who had served as a counselor to Joseph Smith, spoke for an hour and a half, proposing that he be appointed guardian of the Church. There was no affirmative response. That afternoon Brigham Young spoke on behalf of the Apostles. Many present testified that he looked and sounded like the martyred Prophet. When, following his talk, a proposal was put that the Twelve lead the Church, having been given the keys by Joseph, the vote was overwhelmingly in favor.

Surely no one who is acquainted with the subsequent history can doubt the strength of that leadership. Work went forward on the temple and other projects. Then in February of 1846 the unparalleled movement began from Nauvoo on the Mississippi to Winter Quarters on the Missouri, and subsequently to this valley of the Great Salt Lake. So great was the faith of the tens of thousands involved, so strong their testimony, that many gave their lives rather than falter. Where could one find a more powerful witness for the validity of their leadership than in the actions of those who left their homes in Nauvoo to gather here in the valleys of the mountains in response to the call of the Twelve with Brigham Young at their head and subsequently as president of the Church? ("The Joseph Smith III Document and the Keys of the Kingdom," *Ensign,* May 1981, p. 21.)

From the tragedy of that 27th of June, 1844, when Joseph Smith sealed his testimony with his blood, from the confirmation that came into the hearts of the thousands assembled in Nauvoo on that subsequent August 8th, The Church of Jesus Christ of Latter-day Saints has gone steadily forward and has never taken a backward step. That same authority which Joseph held, those same keys and powers which were the very essence of his divinely given right to preside, were by him conferred upon the Twelve Apostles with Brigham Young at their head. Every president of the Church since then has come to that most high and sacred office out of the Council of the Twelve. Each of these men has been blessed with the spirit and power of revelation from on high. There has been an unbroken chain from Joseph Smith, Jr., to [the present]. ("The Joseph Smith III Document and the Keys of the Kingdom," *Ensign*, May 1981, p. 22.)

During this conference we shall be constituted as a Solemn Assembly to sustain as prophet, seer, and revelator and President of The Church of Jesus Christ of Latter-day Saints, the man who, under the plan of the Lord, has been chosen, ordained, and set apart to this most high and sacred office.

This transition of authority, in which I have participated a number of times, is beautiful in its simplicity. It is indicative of the way the Lord does things. Under His procedure a man is selected by the prophet to become a member of the Council of the Twelve Apostles. He does not choose this as a career. . . . The years pass. He is schooled and disciplined in the duties of his office. He travels over the earth in fulfilling his apostolic calling. It is a long course of preparation, in which he comes to know the Latter-day Saints wherever they may be, and they come to know him. The Lord tests his heart and his substance. In the natural course of events, vacancies occur in that council and new appointments are made. Under this process a particular man becomes the senior Apostle. Residing latent in him, and in his associate Brethren, given to each at the time of ordination, are all the keys of the priesthood. But authority to exercise those keys is restricted to the President of the Church. At his passing, that authority becomes operative in the senior Apostle, who is then named, set apart, and ordained the prophet and President by his associates of the Council of the Twelve.

There is no electioneering. There is no campaigning. There is only the quiet and simple operation of a divine plan which provides inspired and tested leadership.

I have been a witness, a personal witness, to this wondrous process. I give you my testimony that it is the Lord who selected Ezra Taft Benson to become a member of the Council of the Twelve almost forty-three years ago. It is the Lord who over these years has tested and disciplined him, schooled and prepared him. At the death of the prophet he was ready, not of his own choice nor of his own design. ("Come and Partake," *Ensign*, May 1986, pp. 46–47.)

Jesus Christ stands at the head of this church which bears His sacred name. He is watching over it. He is guiding it. Standing at the right hand of His Father, He directs this work. His is the prerogative, the power, the option to call men in His way to high and sacred offices and to release them according to His will by calling them home. He is the Master of life and death. I do not worry about the circumstances in which we find ourselves. I accept these circumstances as an expression of His will. ("God Is at the Helm," *Ensign*, May 1994, p. 59.)

TEACHING

Fundamental to the very program of the Church is the teaching of the gospel to the membership of the Church. In fulfillment of the obligation which was laid upon the Church in its inception, there has developed within the Church a system of great teaching organizations—the priesthood quorums, both Melchizedek and Aaronic, the far-flung church school system, and the auxiliaries: the Relief Society, the Sunday School, the Primary, and the MIA, all of which play so important a part in the education of our people. (Conference Report, October 1962, pp. 72–73.)

Your students deserve more than your knowledge. They deserve and hunger for your inspiration. They want the warm glow of personal relationships. This always has been the hallmark of a great teacher "who is the student's accomplice in learning rather than his adversary." This is the education worth striving for and the education worth providing. (Conference Report, October 1965, p. 52.)

There is an immortality in ideas and inspiration that a good teacher imparts to a receptive student, who in turn imparts to those who follow after him. ("The Second Hundred Years: A New Level of Achievement," BYU Address, August 28, 1975.)

I would like to remind you that every student failure is a teacher failure. Likewise, every student success is a teacher success. You are the bridge across which the frail feet of these youngsters must walk from the unknown to the known in their pursuit of truth. ("The Second Hundred Years: A New Level of Achievement," BYU Address, August 28, 1975.)

I hope no one will indulge in what I call "stodgy teaching"— that is, a dull recitation of facts, figures, hypotheses, and laws, with the expectation that the student will parrot back at examination time what the professor has mumbled through the term. Stretch your own minds, my dear brothers and sisters, and then stretch the minds of your students as you invite them to drink at the well of your knowledge. Open new and wonderful vistas before them. The nature of your particular discipline does not matter; it is concerned with life, and it ought to be made to live. ("The Second Hundred Years: A New Level of Achievement," BYU Address, August 28, 1975.)

We need to do a more thorough job in the teaching process to get the Spirit down into the hearts of the people. It is more than intellectual, it is more than a mental assessment. It must be a thing of the heart, a thing of the spirit. (Ireland Dublin Missionary Meeting, September 1, 1995.)

The Spirit of the Lord will overcome the effect of any differences . . . between him who is teaching and him who is being taught. ("Things Are Getting Better," *BYU Devotional Speeches of the Year*, April 8, 1976, p. 90.)

The young women of the Church need and deserve leaders and teachers of great capacity and faith, women to whom they can look with admiration and respect, women who are examples to girls who are growing and preparing for their missions in life, with their happiness in mind, with the future strength of the Church at stake, to give emphasis to this tremendous work. (Regional Representatives Seminar, April 1, 1988.)

We must strengthen ourselves and our people to get our teachers to speak out of their hearts rather than out of their books, to communicate their love for the Lord and this precious work, and somehow it will catch fire in the hearts of those they teach. (General Authority Training Meeting, April 2, 1996.)

We are coming to be recognized across the world for what we are, teachers of righteousness, teachers of truth, teachers of peace, teachers of goodness, teachers of salvation to the people of the world. How marvelous it is! (Japan Tokyo North, Japan Tokyo South, and Japan Sendai Missionary Meeting, May 18, 1996.)

I have spoken before about the importance of keeping the doctrine of the Church pure, and seeing that it is taught in all of our meetings. I worry about this. Small aberrations in doctrinal teaching can lead to large and evil falsehoods. (General Authority Training Meeting, October 1, 1996.)

TELEVISION

See also Media

Our critics point to the decay in our national life, and heaven knows that it is all too serious. But is it not a salutary thing that a recent poll taken by *TV Digest* indicated that 41 percent of the people of this nation think that the television networks have become too liberal in their portrayal of sex and other salacious material? ("The Miracle That Is America," Address to BYU Student Body, November 2, 1973.)

Is it the audience who selects the entertainment features that run on the networks? Of course not; it is the officers of those networks. It is true that they make those selections in terms of what they think will draw the largest audience and increase the rating points. But the choice in large measure is a subjective judgment. And in so doing they are pandering to that element of the society which enjoys the kind of titillating entertainment which leads to family and societal decay, and which disregards the tremendous residual of ethical and moral and spiritual strength in our people. ("Search for Excellence," Bonneville International Corporation Executives, February 6, 1989.)

If we could follow a slogan that says, "Turn off the TV and open a good book," we would do something of substance in strengthening another generation.

Don't misunderstand me. There are so very, very many things of value that come over television. But we can be selective and not be as dumb-driven slaves to the trash of the Hollywood writers and producers. ("Saving the Nation by Changing Our Homes," BYU Management Society, Washington, D.C., March 5, 1994.)

I regard television as perhaps the greatest tool ever discovered to teach and educate people in large numbers. But I decry the filth, the rot, the violence, and profanity that spews from television screens into our homes. It is a sad commentary on our society. The fact that the television set is on six or seven hours every day in the homes of America says something of tremendous importance. I feel sorry for those who are addicted to the tube. I believe it is an addiction. It becomes a habit as pernicious as many other habits. ("Saving the Nation by Changing Our Homes," BYU Management Society, Washington, D.C., March 5, 1994.)

I am suggesting that we spend a little less time in idleness, in the fruitless pursuit of watching inane and empty television programs. Time so utilized can be put to better advantage, and the consequences will be wonderful. ("We Have a Work to Do," *Ensign*, May 1995, p. 88.)

My dear young friends, do not rent trashy videotapes and watch them. Do not watch sleazy programs on television. It will not do you any good. It will just hurt you. Do not do it. Refrain from doing it. It will not do you any good. (Tulsa Oklahoma Youth Conference, July 14, 1996.)

I hope you don't just come home at night and seat yourselves in front of the television set and waste your time on that kind of thing. There's too much of better things to do. (Miami Florida Fireside, November 17, 1996.)

TEMPLE

See also Family History Work

I want to say that this temple is not only a thing of beauty and a joy to those who see it. It is a living expression of a testimony that God our Eternal Father lives, the ruler of the universe; that Jesus is the Christ, the Savior and Redeemer of the world, the only name given among men whereby we must be saved; that Joseph Smith was a prophet who was foreordained to this dispensation, spoken to by God the Father and the Resurrected Lord; that an angel has flown through the midst of heaven, having the everlasting gospel to preach to them that dwell upon the earth and to every nation and kindred and tongue and people; that a veritable "cloud of witnesses" has come to earth with keys and authority—John the Baptist, Peter, James, and John, Moses, Elias, and Elijah; that life is eternal, that love is eternal, that the family may be eternal; that we are our Father's children to whom he has offered that which he would have us have for our blessing, our happiness, our salvation, and our exaltation. ("'The Dawning of a Brighter Day,'" *Improvement Era*, February 1965, p. 114.)

Those who come to the temples to do work for the dead generally know very little of those in whose service they labor. They expect no thanks for that service. They come out of a sense of love and duty. There is an absence of selfishness, except as they desire to refine and enhance their own spirituality in the process. If there were more temple work done in the Church, there would be less of selfishness, less of contention, less of demeaning others. The whole Church would increasingly be lifted to greater heights of spirituality, love for one another, and obedience to the commandments of God. (Temple Presidents Seminar, August 15, 1989.)

The Lord has made it possible for us in these holy houses to receive our own [ordinances]. Then we have the opportunity and responsibility of extending these same blessings to those who have passed on without the privilege. But in the very process there comes into our own lives a refinement of character, together with increased spirituality. It is interesting to reflect on the fact that although many on the other side may not receive the ordinances done for them here, those who perform these ordinances will be blessed in the very process of doing so. (Temple Presidents Seminar, August 15, 1989.)

When I leave the office about 6 o'clock in the evening and drive from the parking ramp up on to Main Street and up to North Temple I see scores of people walking in the direction of this building, their little suitcases in hand. I say to myself, "These are the very pick and flower of the Church." These are they who understand the whole, broad mission of this work. They know that the Church is more than a social organization. They know that it involves more than meeting together to receive instruction. They know that it means more than recreation and sociability. They know that it is concerned with matters of eternity. They know that it deals with all of the children of God and their eternal well-being. (Temple Presidents Seminar, August 15, 1989.)

That which goes on in the House of the Lord, and which must be preceded by research, comes nearer the spirit of the sacrifice of the Lord than any other activity of which I know. Why? Because it is done by those who give freely of time and substance to do for others that which they cannot do for themselves, and for which they who perform this service expect no thanks or recompense. (Utah Genealogical Society Fireside, November 13, 1994.)

This house and others like it become the bridge between this life and the eternal life that lies beyond. (Salt Lake Temple Workers Devotional, June 11, 1995.)

I hope you are using the temple constantly, because you will gain blessings there that you cannot gain anywhere else on the face of the whole earth. The temple stands as a monument for all to see. It stands as a statement that we as a people believe in the immortality of the human soul. Everything that occurs in that temple is of an uplifting and ennobling kind. It speaks of life here and life beyond the grave. It speaks of the importance of the individual as a child of God. It speaks of the importance of the family as a creation of the Almighty. It speaks of the eternity of the marriage relationship. It speaks of going on to greater glory. It is a place of light, a place of peace, a place of love where we deal with the things of eternity. If there is any man here tonight who is not worthy to go into that holy house, I urge you to put your life in order so that you may go there and partake of the unique and wonderful blessings that we have there. (Taipei Taiwan Fireside, May 23, 1996.)

I hope that everyone gets to the temple on a regular basis. I hope your children over twelve years of age have the opportunity of going to the temple to be baptized for the dead. If we are a temple-going people, we will be a better people, we will be better fathers and husbands, we will be better wives and mothers. I know your lives are busy. I know that you have much to do. But I make you a promise that if you will go to the House of the Lord, you will be blessed; life will be better for you. Now, please, please, my beloved brethren and sisters, avail yourselves of the great opportunity to go to the Lord's house and thereby partake of all of the marvelous blessings that are yours to be received there. (Lima Peru Fireside, November 9, 1996.)

Temple Building

Temple building and the dedication of temples have gone on at such a pace in the last few years that some pay little attention and feel it is of small significance.

But the adversary has not been unmindful of it. The building and dedication of these sacred edifices have been accompanied by a surge of opposition from a few enemies of the Church as well as criticism from a few within. This has brought to mind a statement of Brigham Young in 1861 while the Salt Lake Temple was under construction. Evidently when someone with previous experience was asked to work on the Salt Lake Temple, he responded, "I do not like to do it, for we never began to build a Temple without the bells of hell beginning to ring."

To which Brigham Young replied, "I want to hear them ring again. All the tribes of hell will be on the move, if we uncover the walls of this Temple. But what do you think it will amount to? You have all the time seen what it has amounted to." (In *Journal of Discourses*, 8:355–56.) ("Rejoice in This Great Era of Temple Building," *Ensign*, November 1985, p. 54.)

When it was announced that we would build a temple in [Denver] and had selected a site on which it should stand, opposition rose against us. We gave up that site and tried another. Again we were thwarted. But we were determined to go forward, putting our trust in the Lord that He would guide us in accomplishing His purposes. Two other possible sites were selected. At the time, President Kimball and President Romney were both ill, and mine was a serious responsibility. I asked President Benson, then President of the Council of the Twelve, if we might go to Denver together, and there with Elder Russell Taylor, we looked over these sites. I give you my testimony that we were guided by the Spirit in choosing the ground on which that beautiful new structure now stands. . . .

We might expect that the adversary of righteousness would seek to thwart its construction and the work to be done therein. He had done so in the days of Kirtland when enemies threatened to push over the walls which were then being laid. He did so in the days of Far West when enemies drove our people from the state of Missouri. It was so in Nauvoo, where the temple had barely been completed when we were driven out. It was so here on this Temple Square when, during the forty years of the temple construction, there was one threat after another. ("The War We Are Winning," *Ensign*, November 1986, pp. 43–44.)

Today is the first Sunday of April 1993. Go back with me an even century to this same Temple Square. No, make it an even one hundred and one years. It is April conference of 1892. These grounds are crowded with people. The multitude is the largest ever assembled in this area of the West. There are thousands and thousands of them. All cannot get on the grounds, so large is the number. They are on surrounding streets. Some have climbed telephone poles; others, trees. The occasion is the placing of the capstone of the temple, the great round granite sphere which crowns the highest steeple on the east end. It is a day of celebration. Atop the ball is a bronze figure gilded with gold. The figure represents Moroni—prophet, writer, and compiler of the Book of Mormon. The figure represents the angel spoken of by John the Revelator when he declared with prophetic vision:

"And I saw another angel fly in the midst of heaven, having the everlasting gospel to preach unto them that dwell on the earth, and to every nation, and kindred, and tongue, and people,

"Saying with a loud voice, Fear God, and give glory to him; for the hour of his judgment is come: and worship him that made heaven, and earth, and the sea, and the fountains of waters." (Rev. 14:6–7.)

In the presence of that multitude, President Wilford Woodruff touched a switch. The capstone with the angel settled in place. President Woodruff led the multitude in a great and sacred shout: "Hosanna! Hosanna! Hosanna to God and the Lamb!"

There had been nothing before it and there has been nothing just like it since. ("This Peaceful House of God," *Ensign*, May 1993, p. 72.)

In July of 1847 Brigham Young had pointed out the location, only four days after the pioneers arrived in the valley. That spot had been marked by Wilford Woodruff. On April 6, 1853, the cornerstones were laid. All of you are familiar with the history of the years that followed—years of effort and heartbreaking disappointment; years of labor in sunshine and storm to bring great blocks of granite from these everlasting hills and to dress that stone, each piece according to a carefully designed pattern; years of unyielding faith in the pursuit of a goal.

These were years during which three other beautiful temples had been erected in this territory—in St. George, in Logan, and in Manti.

But the greatest dream of all centered here on Temple Square. And now by April of 1892 the exterior walls, steeples, and roof had been completed. Small wonder that the people shouted hosanna. A generation and more had passed since the work had commenced. Wilford Woodruff was now eighty-five and President of the Church. Before the vast crowd assembled on that day, Elder Francis M. Lyman made a motion that they now finish the interior and dedicate the temple one year from that day, April 6, 1893, forty years from the day of the laying of the cornerstones.

A mighty shout of approval filled the air.

But it was one thing to say yes in the excitement of the occasion, and another to actually accomplish the work. Some with practical minds and substantial experience said it could never be done.

The building was a shell. A mighty work of consecrated effort was commenced to finish the interior.

Floors were laid, partitions set in place, plumbing installed, and electrical lines run. And then came the tremendous finishing work.

Wooden lath by the mile was nailed to the framing. Lime by the ton was slaked to become plaster. Timber was cut, seasoned, sawed, and shaped into magnificently beautiful woodwork.

While preparing the ordinances for use in more modern temples, I have spent hours and days working in the magnificent fifth-floor Assembly Room of the Salt Lake Temple. I have marveled at the craftsmanship of those who built such strong and graceful structures as the four corner stairways of that room. I have appreciated architectural masterpieces across this world, but I have never seen more beautiful workmanship than is found in the House of the Lord. There are many fluted columns with delicately carved floral pieces at their crown. There are numerous intricate and artistic design works made in stone and wood and plaster. Nothing was spared to make this house of God a place of beauty.

It must have appeared impossible to get all of this done in a year's time. But craftsmen who had learned their exacting trades in Europe and the British Isles, and who had come as converts to these valleys of western America, exerted themselves unsparingly. Somehow it happened. Somehow it all came together, and this within a period of twelve months.

Wonder of wonders, and miracle of miracles, it was ready on the fifth of April. . . .

I stand in reverent appreciation and gratitude for this singular accomplishment. All of this was done in the days of the poverty of our people. . . .

A terrible storm arose that day. Rain fell in torrents, and the wind blew with savage fury. It was as if the forces of evil were lashing out in violent protest against this act of consecration.

But all was peace and quiet within the thick granite walls. The aged prophet, then eighty-six, led the way to the beautiful fifth-floor assembly room. The room was filled to capacity in this, the first of forty-one sessions. After appropriate preliminary expressions in music and speech, President Woodruff stepped to the pulpit at the east end of the room and offered the prayer of dedication.

It was a moving and powerful prayer. It was an expression of the hearts of those who love the Lord. ("This Peaceful House of God," *Ensign*, May 1993, pp. 72–73, 75.)

We have been criticized for the cost of [temples], a cost which results from the exceptional quality of the workmanship and the materials that go into them. Those who criticize do not understand that these houses are dedicated as the abode of Deity and, as Brigham Young stated, are to stand through the Millennium. ("This Peaceful House of God," *Ensign*, May 1993, p. 74.)

I have had a most unusual opportunity in my life. I think I have worked in almost every facet of the program of this Church. But I think the most satisfying experience of all has come from an assignment first received from President David O. McKay, to become involved in the temple program of the Church. In 1953 he called me to his office and told me of plans to build a temple in Zollikofen, Switzerland, and that he wished me to find a way to present the temple ceremony in various languages with a minimum of personnel.

Out of that assignment came the pioneer effort of the program now used in all but the Salt Lake and Manti temples. That is, the presentation of the endowment service using film or video.

Since that time I have never been without an interest in temples, and some responsibility concerning them. We now have 48 working temples. I have participated in the dedication or rededication of all but five of these 48 temples. I have visited all of these temples.

I have spoken literally hundreds of times in temple dedications. I have offered not a few dedicatory prayers in these sacred houses. I have listened to scores of choirs in a great variety of languages sing the Hosanna Anthem, and I have been emotionally touched as these choir members, standing immediately behind me, have broken down under the emotional stress of their sacred experience.

It has been my consuming desire to have a temple wherever needed so that our people, wherever they might be, could, without too great a sacrifice, come to the House of the Lord for their own ordinances and for the opportunity of doing vicarious work for the dead.

With the completion of the Mt. Timpanogos Temple, we will have 49 operating temples. We have seven others now in construction. We have announced eight others, concerning which preparatory work is being done. We have acquired nine more sites in various countries for the construction of temples, making a total of 73, and I wish it were a hundred. . . .

The Church is not complete without temples. The doctrine is not fulfilled without these sacred ordinances. People cannot have a fulness of that to which they are entitled as members of this Church without the House of the Lord.

The Lord has blessed us with the means, through the faithful consecrations of the Saints, to do that which we ought to do and must do. This is the greatest era of temple building in all the history of the world. But it is not enough. We must continue to pursue it until we have a dedicated temple within reach of our faithful people everywhere. (Temple Presidents Seminar, August 22, 1996.)

Tremendous sacrifice went into the construction of [the Logan Temple]. A young man went up to the sawmill to get a load of logs and on his way back the wagon tipped over into the river, he under the wagon. The water was very, very cold. He was there for thirty minutes before they could get the wagon turned over and get his body out. And miraculously enough he stood up and, before the day was over, climbed on his wagon and came down to this building site. It was thought that the extremely cold water stopped all of the bodily processes to a point that he did not die. . . . This place is a place associated with miracles. I hope we never lose sight of the fact that it is a place of miracles. (Logan Temple Workers Devotional, August 25, 1996.)

Temple Recommends

I fear that some people are granted temple recommends before they are really prepared for them. I feel that sometimes we unduly rush people to the temple. Converts and those who have recently come into activity need a substantial measure of maturity in the Church. They need understanding of the grand concepts of the eternal gospel. They need to have demonstrated over a period of time their capacity to discipline their lives in such a way as to be worthy to enter the House of the Lord, for the obligations there assumed are eternal. ("Keeping the Temple Holy," *Ensign,* May 1990, pp. 49–50.)

I submit that every man who holds the Melchizedek Priesthood has an obligation to see that the House of the Lord is kept sacred and free of any defilement. This obligation rests primarily and inescapably upon the shoulders of bishops and stake presidents. They become the judges of worthiness concerning those eligible to enter the temple. Additionally, each of us has an obligation—first, as to his own personal worthiness, and secondly, as to the worthiness of those whom he may encourage or assist in going to the House of the Lord. ("Keeping the Temple Holy," *Ensign,* May 1990, p. 50.)

Everything that occurs in the temple is eternal in its consequences. We there deal with matters of immortality, with things of eternity, with things of man and his relationship to his Divine Parent and his Redeemer. Hands must be clean and hearts must be pure and thoughts concerned with the solemnities of eternity when in these sacred premises.

Here is taught the great plan of man's eternal journey. Here are solemnized covenants sacred and everlasting. Entering the temple is a privilege to be earned and not a right that automatically goes with Church membership.

How does one earn that privilege? By obedience to the laws and ordinances of the gospel. ("Keeping the Temple Holy," *Ensign*, May 1990, p. 51.)

What a unique and remarkable thing is a temple recommend. It is only a piece of paper with a name and signatures, but in reality it is a certificate that says the bearer is "honest, true, chaste, benevolent, virtuous" and that he or she believes in doing good to all, that "if there is anything virtuous, lovely, or of good report or praiseworthy," he or she seeks after such. (A of F 13.) ("Keeping the Temple Holy," *Ensign*, May 1990, p. 52.)

One of my concerns is that not enough of our people are making the efforts to get a temple recommend, which becomes a symbol of their worthiness and the righteousness of their desires. (Heber City/Springville Utah Regional Conference, priesthood leadership session, May 13, 1995.)

Now is the time to get your lives in order that you may be worthy to go to the House of the Lord. Get a temple recommend. Get it now. If every man and woman in this hall tonight would make that resolution and go to work to be worthy of a temple recommend, your lives would be blessed, your homes would be blessed, you would feel the Spirit of the Lord in your homes. (Bogota Colombia Fireside, November 8, 1996.)

Let us work toward qualifying every member of this Church to hold a temple recommend. That is the passport to the House of the Lord. That is the passport to the place where we glimpse a little of heaven. That is the passport to the place where we lose ourselves in the service of others. That is the passport to the place where we always come away better men and women than we were when we entered. (Brigham City Utah Regional Conference, priesthood leadership session, February 22, 1997.)

I would hope that every Latter-day Saint who is old enough would have a temple recommend. It says something. It is a price-less, priceless thing to have a temple recommend. It says that we are faithful, that we are doing what we ought to be doing, that we are living the gospel, that we are sustaining our authorities, that we are observing the Word of Wisdom, that we are paying our tithing, that we are treating our families properly, that we are treating our neighbors properly, that we are the kind of people we ought to be. Perhaps you cannot get to the temple very often. But even if you cannot get to the temple, I would like to suggest that you go to your bishops and get a temple recommend and carry it with you and regard it as a precious and true thing. It is a credit card, if you please, with the Lord. (Jordan Utah South Regional Conference, March 2, 1997.)

Temple Work

Was there ever a man who truly loved a woman, or a woman who truly loved a man, who did not pray that their relationship might continue beyond the grave? Has a child ever been buried by parents who did not long for the assurance that their loved one would again be theirs in a world to come? Can anyone believing in eternal life doubt that the God of heaven would grant his sons and daughters that most precious attribute of life, the love that finds its most meaningful expression in family relationships? No, reason demands that the family relationship shall continue after death. The human heart longs for it. The God of heaven has revealed a way whereby it may be secured. The sacred ordinances of the house of the Lord provide for it. . . .

But there are uncounted millions who have walked the earth and who have never had the opportunity to hear the gospel. Shall they be denied such blessings as are offered in the temples of the Church?

Through living proxies who stand in behalf of the dead, the same ordinances are available to those who have passed from mortality. In the spirit world they then are free to accept or reject those earthly ordinances performed for them, including baptism, marriage, and the sealing of family relationships. There must be no compulsion in the work of the Lord, but there must be opportunity. ("Why These Temples?" *Ensign*, August 1974, pp. 39–40.)

Surely these temples are unique among all buildings. They are houses of instruction. They are places of covenants and promises. At their altars we kneel before God our Creator and are given promise of his everlasting blessings. In the sanctity of their appointments we commune with him and reflect on his Son, our Savior and Redeemer, the Lord Jesus Christ, who served as proxy for each of us in a vicarious sacrifice in our behalf. Here we set aside our own selfishness and serve for those who cannot serve themselves. Here we are bound together in the most sacred of all human relationships—as husbands and wives, as children and parents, as families under a sealing that time cannot destroy and death cannot disrupt. ("Why These Temples?" *Ensign*, August 1974, p. 41.)

We returned only a few days ago from Manila in the Philippines. There on an eminence where the ground falls away to the rear, affording a view of an entire valley, stands a beautiful and sacred temple. Here, as elsewhere, there is incised in the stone of one of the towers the words "Holiness to the Lord. The House of the Lord." . . .

In all of these new temples, the buildings have been opened to the general public prior to dedication. Tens and tens of thousands have gone through them. They have been free to ask any questions concerning them. These visitors have been respectful and reverent as they have partaken of the spirit of these sacred structures. As they have felt of that spirit and learned something of the purposes for which the temples have been built, these who have been our guests have recognized why, following dedication, we regard these buildings as sanctified and holy, reserved for sacred purposes and closed to the public.

Participating in these dedicatory services, one senses the true strength of the Church. That strength is in the hearts of the people, who are united by a bond of recognition of God as our Eternal Father and Jesus Christ as our Savior. Their individual testimonies are firmly established on a foundation of faith concerning things divine.

In each new temple we have had a cornerstone ceremony in harmony with a tradition that goes back to ancient times. Before the general use of concrete, the foundation walls of the building were laid with large stones. A trench would be dug, and stones would be placed as footings. Starting at a point of beginning, the foundation wall would be run in one direction to a cornerstone;

then the corner would be turned and the wall run to the next corner, where another stone was placed, from which the wall would be run to the next corner, and from there to the point of beginning. In many instances, including the construction of early temples in the Church, cornerstones were used at each junction point of the walls and put in place with ceremony. The final stone was spoken of as the chief cornerstone, and its placement became the reason for much celebration. With this cornerstone in position, the foundation was ready for the superstructure. Hence the analogy that Paul used in describing the true church:

"Now therefore ye are no more strangers and foreigners, but fellowcitizens with the saints, and of the household of God;

"And are built upon the foundation of the apostles and prophets, Jesus Christ himself being the chief corner stone;

"In whom all the building fitly framed together groweth unto an holy temple in the Lord." (Eph. 2:19–21.) ("Cornerstones of Our Faith," *Ensign*, November 1984, pp. 50–51.)

We are sometimes looked upon as provincial. Is there any group in all the world with a vision so broad and a work so comprehensive? I know of no other people so concerned with the eternal well-being of the sons and daughters of God of all generations. Surely the work that goes on in [temples] is the most unselfish of all work. Those who labor [there] do so, for the most part, in behalf of those beyond the veil of death. They do it because of a knowledge of the importance of eternal ordinances and covenants. They do it so that even the dead may exercise agency concerning the acceptance or rejection of sacred ordinances.

It is all part of the great pattern of the God of Heaven, who is our Eternal Father, and of His Son, who is our Savior and our Redeemer. ("An Ensign to the Nations," *Ensign*, November 1989, p. 54.)

I remind you of the absolute obligation to not discuss outside the temple that which occurs within the temple. Sacred matters deserve sacred consideration. We are under obligation, binding and serious, to not use temple language or speak of temple matters outside. I first went to the temple fifty-seven years ago. It was different from any other experience I had had in the Church. A young man of my association went about the same time. Thereafter, he was wont to use phrases from the language of the temple in a frivolous way. It was offensive. It was a betrayal of a sacred trust. I have watched him through the years. Once faithful, he has drifted from all Church activity and forsaken the faith of his fathers. I think that much of what has happened to him began with that small irreverential thing that he did in trivializing language which is not trivial. . . .

Said the Lord, "Remember that that which cometh from above is sacred, and must be spoken with care, and by constraint of the Spirit." (D&C 63:64.) And again, "Trifle not with sacred things." (D&C 6:12.) ("Keeping the Temple Holy," *Ensign*, May 1990, p. 52.)

Inside the temple a further sense of peace is experienced. The world is left behind with its clamor and rush. In the house of the Lord there is tranquillity. Those who serve here know that they are dealing with matters of eternity. All are dressed in white. Speech is subdued. Thoughts are elevated.

This is a sanctuary of service. Most of the work done in this sacred house is performed vicariously in behalf of those who have passed beyond the veil of death. I know of no other work to compare with it. It more nearly approaches the vicarious sacrifice of the Son of God in behalf of all mankind than any other work of which I am aware. Thanks is not expected from those who in the world beyond become the beneficiaries of this consecrated service. It is a service of the living in behalf of the dead. It is a service which is of the very essence of selflessness. ("The Salt Lake Temple," *Ensign*, March 1993, p. 5.)

This sacred edifice becomes a school of instruction in the sweet and sacred things of God. Here we have outlined the plan of a loving Father in behalf of His sons and daughters of all generations. Here we have sketched before us the odyssey of man's eternal journey from premortal existence through this life to the life beyond. Great fundamental and basic truths are taught with clarity and simplicity well within the understanding of all who hear. ("The Salt Lake Temple," *Ensign*, March 1993, pp. 5–6.)

[The temple] is a place of revelation. Here almost weekly the First Presidency of the Church and the Council of the Twelve Apostles have met since the time of dedication. Here there is earnest prayer with supplication for enlightenment and understanding. Here in these hallowed precincts there is discussion, quiet and restrained. And here is felt that inspiration which comes when men who are endowed with the highest authority of the eternal priesthood counsel together and seek the will of the Lord.

I was in that circle in that sacred room when President Spencer W. Kimball on a June day in 1978 pleaded with the Lord for direction on a matter fraught with tremendous consequences. It concerned the eligibility of all worthy men to receive the priesthood.

I can testify now, as I have testified before, that the spirit of revelation was felt on that occasion, and that the fruits which have flowed from that revelation have been sweet and wonderful for great numbers of people across the world.

The temple is also a place of personal inspiration and revelation. Legion are those who in times of stress, when difficult decisions must be made and perplexing problems must be handled, have come to the temple in a spirit of fasting and prayer to seek divine direction. Many have testified that while voices of revelation were not heard, impressions concerning a course to follow were experienced at that time or later which became answers to their prayers. ("The Salt Lake Temple," *Ensign*, March 1993, p. 6.)

Each temple built by The Church of Jesus Christ of Latter-day Saints stands as an expression of the testimony of this people that God our Eternal Father lives, that He has a plan for the blessing of His sons and daughters of all generations, that His Beloved Son, Jesus the Christ, who was born in Bethlehem of Judea and crucified on the cross of Golgotha, is the Savior and Redeemer of the world, whose atoning sacrifice makes possible the fulfillment of that plan in the eternal life of each who accepts and lives the gospel. Every temple, be it large or small, old or new, is an expression of our testimony that life beyond the grave is as real and certain as is mortality. There would be no need for temples if the human spirit and soul were not eternal. Every ordinance performed in these sacred houses is everlasting in its consequences. ("This Peaceful House of God," *Ensign*, May 1993, p. 74.)

In anticipation of the dedication of the [Vernal Utah] temple, let's get ready for it, you and I. Let's clean up our lives. Let's reach heavenward a little more. Let's be more faithful Latter-day Saints. Let us choose the right more frequently in all of our decisions. Let us walk more worthily before the Lord as His sons and daughters in anticipation of the day when we can gather together and worship in this completed house. (Vernal Temple Groundbreaking Ceremony, May 13, 1995.)

Joseph Smith . . . administered the first ordinances in the upstairs room of his brick store. Brigham Young pushed and pushed, although he knew that the Saints would have to leave Nauvoo, pushed and pushed for the completion of the temple so that all who could receive their ordinances would have opportunity to do so before they left. (Salt Lake Temple Workers Devotional, June 11, 1995.)

Missionary work is concerned with providing saving ordinances to our Father's living children throughout the world. Temple work is primarily concerned with service in behalf of the sons and daughters of God who have passed beyond the veil of death. God is no respecter of persons. If the living in all nations are deserving of the saving ordinances of the gospel, then those of all past generations must likewise be deserving. ("Of Missions, Temples, and Stewardship," *Ensign*, November 1995, p. 52.)

Our people cannot partake of all of the blessings of the gospel unless they can receive their own temple ordinances and then make these ordinances available to those of their kindred dead and others. ("Of Missions, Temples, and Stewardship," *Ensign*, November 1995, p. 52.)

I have a burning desire that a temple be located within reasonable access to Latter-day Saints throughout the world. We can proceed only so fast. We try to see that each temple will be in an excellent location, where there will be good neighbors over a long period of time. . . . The work is moving about as fast as we can go. It is my constant prayer that somehow it might be speeded up so that more of our people might have easier access to a sacred house of the Lord. . . .

These unique and wonderful buildings, and the ordinances administered therein, represent the ultimate in our worship. These ordinances become the most profound expressions of our theology. I urge our people everywhere, with all of the persuasiveness of which I am capable, to live worthy to hold a temple recommend, to secure one and regard it as a precious asset, and to make a greater effort to go to the house of the Lord and partake of the spirit and the blessings to be had therein. I am satisfied that every man or woman who goes to the temple in a spirit of sincerity and faith leaves the house of the Lord a better man or woman. ("Of Missions, Temples, and Stewardship," *Ensign*, November 1995, pp. 52–53.)

The temple ordinance is not just a ritual to go through, it is an act of solemn promising, . . . and we need to reflect on what we do and say in the House of the Lord concerning our attitudes and our behavior. (Charlotte North Carolina Regional Conference, priesthood leadership session, February 24, 1996.)

We performed somewhere in the neighborhood of six million ordinances last year in all the temples of the Church. We have nine and a half million members. Certainly we ought to have been able to perform an ordinance for every living member of this Church. (Temple Presidents Seminar, August 20, 1996.)

Yesterday I attended the funeral service of a beautiful woman whom I have known for a long time. She was a wonderful wife, a wonderful mother, a faithful Latter-day Saint, and an influence for great good in the community in which she lived. . . . As I said in that service, surely no one, no man or woman of reason, could ever think that the beauty of her character, her cultured and happy ways, the great knowledge which she worked so hard to attain, the companionship of her husband and children and grandchildren would all be lost as she stepped over the threshold from life to death.

As I have said before, every temple in this Church stands as a monument to our conviction, belief, and knowledge that the soul of man is immortal. . . . As the gospel is taught here to bless the lives of people, as ordinances are performed here, they become efficacious beyond the threshold of mortality.

I never confer the sealing authority upon a man that I do not think of the wonder of it all. Endowed with the keys of the holy priesthood and all of the powers of that priesthood, we confer the only authority on the face of the earth which reaches into the world beyond. No king, no president of a nation, no official of any entity in the world of which we are a part has any authority over matters beyond the grave. Everyone is helpless before the reach of death, but the humblest, good, righteous high priest who has received the sealing authority may bind in the heavens that which is bound on the earth. There is nothing else like it. (Temple Presidents Seminar, August 22, 1996.)

Without the spirit of dedication, without the spirit of sacrifice, without the spirit of consecration, temples could not function. That goes without saying. The work in the temple is essential, it is a work of personal sacrifice and individual consecration. There is nothing to compare in all the world with the proxy work that goes on, the vicarious work in behalf of the dead. . . . Adam offered sacrifice as he was commanded to do. Those sacrifices were of the herds and of the fields and the angel of the Lord asked him why and he said, "I know not except that the Lord has commanded me." (See Moses 5:6.) The angel went on to explain that it was in similitude of the Lamb of God, who would become the Redeemer of the world. Animal sacrifice was done away with the sacrifice of the Son of God. But the law of sacrifice and the law of consecration were not done away with and are still in effect, and in all of our history there has been no greater expression of sacrifice and consecration than in the building and maintaining of these sacred houses. (Logan Temple Workers Devotional, August 25, 1996.)

I hope we never lose sight of the fact that as we labor in [the temple] this is the House of God, that it is the House of the Lord Jesus Christ, that it is the house where the Holy Ghost ought to be comfortable to dwell and communicate. How sacred it must be kept. (Logan Temple Workers Devotional, August 25, 1996.)

We are responsible for the blessing, the eternal blessing, of all who have lived upon the earth, the uncounted, unnumbered generations of men and women who have lived upon the earth, all who today live upon the earth, and all who will yet live upon the earth. How great is our responsibility. We must stand a little taller and work a little harder to accomplish it. (Logan Temple Workers Devotional, August 25, 1996.)

I remember the time when I first came to Santiago. We had only a very few members of the Church here. We kept working and created the Nunoa Branch. And as the years passed we thought we were ready to have a stake of Zion. I came here to organize the stake, but when I interviewed all of the brethren I discovered they were not paying their tithing. I worried very much about what to do. The next morning we met in the Nunoa chapel and I said to the people, "You are not ready to have a stake. You are not paying your tithing. I will be back in six months and I would give you that time to start paying your tithing." I came back in six months. We organized the first stake in all of Chile. Since that time the work has rolled along in majesty and power until today we have some 400,000 Latter-day Saints in this land of Chile. We have 94 stakes of Zion. By early next year we will be ready to organize the 100th stake of Zion. What a glorious blessing that will be.

I make of that occasion a challenge for each of you this day to put your lives in order to be worthy to go to the House of the Lord and there to partake of the blessings that are peculiarly yours. Could there be a greater blessing in all the world than the sealing of husbands and wives, than the sealing of children to parents? My brethren and sisters, please do not pass up this great opportunity. It is worth everything. Please take advantage of it. Please get yourselves ready to go to the House of the Lord and there be sealed together as a family. There is that beautiful temple which is waiting for you. Please take advantage of it and God will bless you with happiness in your hearts and lives. (Santiago Chile Fireside, November 11, 1996.)

When the Washington D. C. Temple was dedicated in 1974, it was regarded as a place of great significance. I was in a press conference with President Kimball when a reporter asked President Kimball how much the building cost, and he told him. The reporter then asked, "Aren't you ashamed of yourself? The money that you have spent on this building would have gone so far in feeding the poor and those who are hungry and in distress in parts of the world." President Kimball nodded for me to answer. I responded, "We feed the poor. We take care of the needy. We reach out across the world to those in distress. We look after our own. We are doing the work of the Lord. This is a house of God, and nothing is too good for our Father in Heaven." (Washington Temple Workers Christmas Devotional, December 1, 1996.)

No person has all of the gospel until he is able to receive [the ordinances of the temple]. And the responsibility rests with us to see that the facilities are available. I do not know how much longer I am good for, but I hope to end out my days building temples of the Lord, taking the temples to the people so that they can have the marvelous blessings that are to be obtained here.

We are doing a very interesting thing in Santiago, Chile, and in São Paulo, Brazil. The temple opens early Friday morning. It is open the rest of the week, but on Friday morning it is open very early. It operates all day Friday, then all night Friday night. Then it is open all day Saturday, so that those who come can have all of the blessings that are available in that short time.

This is a great era of temple-building. We are reaching out everywhere that we can go to build the House of the Lord. He has blessed us with the means to do so. How grateful we are for the means to do so because of the faithfulness of our people in paying their tithes and offerings. I believe with all my heart that God has blessed us with something of an abundance in order to extend these sacred houses wherever our people are found. There will be a time, I am satisfied, when there will be temples in Africa, there will be temples all up and down South America, there will be more temples in Europe, there will be more temples in the Far East, there will be temples in Australia beyond the one which we now have in Sydney. We would like to see everyone have an opportunity to have relatively nearby, within a day's journey, a temple to which he or she might go and partake of the marvelous blessings there to be given. (Washington Temple Workers Christmas Devotional, December 1, 1996.)

TEMPTATION

In those early years, the milk we drank was not pasteurized. We, of course, did not have an automatic dishwasher, except that it was our automatic duty to wash the dishes. When we were diagnosed as having chicken pox or measles, the doctor would advise the city health department, and a man would be sent to put a sign in the front window. This was a warning to any who might wish to come to our house that they did so at their own peril.

If the disease were smallpox or diphtheria, the sign was bright orange with black letters. It said, in effect, "Stay away from this place."

I learned something I have always remembered—to watch for signs of danger and evil and stay away. ("Some Lessons I Learned as a Boy," *Ensign*, May 1993, p. 52.)

We cannot afford to be tainted by moral sin. We live in a world where temptation is constantly being thrown at us, particularly at you young people. It is on television. It is in magazines. It is in books. It is on videos which are readily available. Stay away from these things. They will only hurt you. When it comes to the moral law, you know what is expected of you. If you find yourself slipping under the pressure of circumstances, discipline yourself. Stop before it is too late. You will be forever grateful that you did. ("Stand True and Faithful," *Ensign*, May 1996, p. 92.)

You constantly are faced with difficult choices. Your problems are not new, but they are intensified. You are subjected to temptations that are attractive and appealing. You represent the future of this Church, and the adversary of truth would like to injure you, would like to destroy your faith, would like to lead you down paths that are beguiling and interesting, but deadly. ("Stand True and Faithful," *Ensign*, May 1996, p. 91.)

If you are tempted in any direction, remember that somewhere, someone's on his or her knees praying for the missionaries. That's true. That's absolutely true. Never forget it. You live where there is temptation. You live where there is a great letdown in morals. Rise above it. Stand tall. Be clean. Be pure. Be faithful. Be true. (Denmark Copenhagen Missionary Meeting, June 14, 1996.)

To you young people who face temptation, my plea to you is to be clean, to be pure, to be chaste. I make you a promise that if you will do so the time will come when you will thank the Lord with all your heart that you have chosen to behave yourselves. (Berlin Germany Regional Conference, June 16, 1996.)

TESTIMONY

See also Jesus Christ: A Testimony of Jesus Christ

A witness of the Lord is not obtained by observation of the accomplishments of men. Such observation makes reasonable a belief in his birth, life, death, and resurrection. But there is needed something more than a reasonable belief. There is needed an understanding of his unique and incomparable position as the divine Redeemer and an enthusiasm for him and his message as the Son of God.

That understanding and that enthusiasm are available to all who will pay the price. They are not incompatible with higher education, but they will not come only of reading philosophy. No, they come of a simpler process. The things of God are understood by the Spirit of God. (1 Cor. 2:11.) So declares the word of revelation. (Conference Report, April 1966, p. 86.)

Not long ago, while riding in a plane, I engaged in conversation with a young man who was seated beside me. We moved from one subject to another, and then came to the matter of religion. He said that he had read considerably about the Mormons, that he had found much to admire in their practices, but that he had a definite prejudice concerning the story of the origin of the Church and particularly Joseph Smith. He was an active member of another organization, and when I asked where he had acquired his information, he indicated that it had come from publications of his church. I asked what company he worked for. He proudly replied that he was a sales representative for IBM. I then asked whether he would think it fair for his customers to learn of the qualities of IBM products from a Xerox representative. He replied with a smile, "I think I get the point of what you're trying to say."

I took from my case a copy of the Doctrine and Covenants and read to him the words of the Lord expressed through Joseph Smith, words which are the source of those practices my friend had come to admire in us while disdaining the man through whom they had come. Before we parted, he agreed to read the literature I would send to him. I promised him that if he would do so prayerfully he would know the truth not only of these doctrines and practices which have interested him, but also of the man through whom they were introduced. I then gave him my testimony of my conviction concerning the prophetic calling of Joseph Smith. ("Joseph the Seer," *Ensign*, May 1977, pp. 64–65.)

The other day I was speaking with a friend concerning a mutual acquaintance, a man looked upon as highly successful in his vocation. "But what of his activity in the Church?" I asked. To which my friend responded, "He knows in his heart that it is true, but he is afraid of it. He is fearful that if he were to acknowledge his Church membership and live its standards, he would be cut off from the social circle in which he moves."

I reflected, "Like Peter who denied his own sure knowledge, the day will come, though possibly not until old age, when in hours of quiet reflection this man will know that he traded his birthright for a mess of pottage (see Gen. 25:34); and there will be remorse and sorrow and tears, for he will come to see that he not only denied the Lord in his own life, but also in effect denied him before his children who have grown up without a faith to cling to."

The Lord himself said, "Whosoever therefore shall be ashamed of me and of my words in this adulterous and sinful generation; of him also shall the Son of man be ashamed, when he cometh in the glory of his Father with the holy angels" (Mark 8:38). ("And Peter Went Out and Wept Bitterly," *Ensign*, May 1979, p. 66.)

Jesus, speaking to the Jews in the temple, said: "My doctrine is not mine, but his that sent me. If any man will do his will, he shall know of the doctrine, whether it be of God, or whether I speak of myself." (John 7:16–17.)

This is the wonder of this work, that every man may know for himself. He is not dependent on the teacher or the preacher or the missionary, except as they might instruct and bear witness. As Job declared long ago: "There is a spirit in man: and the inspiration of the Almighty giveth them understanding." (Job 32:8.)

Each man may know for himself, through the gift of the Holy Spirit, that it is true, and with as certain an assurance as that the sun will rise in the morning. (*Be Thou an Example* [Salt Lake City: Deseret Book, 1981], p. 7.)

The marvelous and wonderful thing is that any individual who desires to know the truth may receive that conviction. . . .

It will take study of the word of God. It will take prayer and anxious seeking of the source of all truth. It will take living the gospel, an experiment, if you please, in following the teachings. I do not hesitate to promise, because I know from personal experience, that out of all of this will come, by the power of the Holy Ghost, a conviction, a testimony, a certain knowledge.

People of the world seem unable to believe it, so many of them. What they do not realize is that the things of God are understood only by the Spirit of God. There must be effort. There must be humility. There must be prayer. But the results are certain and the testimony is sure. ("Faith: The Essence of True Religion," *Ensign*, November 1981, p. 8.)

There is a continuity and consistency in this work that is remarkable to witness and experience. Its strength and power lie in the ability of every member and every earnest investigator to know for himself or herself by the power of the Holy Spirit that it is true. Critics may wear out their lives in trying to deny or demean or cast doubt, but all who ask of God in faith have the assurance that by the voice of the Spirit will come the certainty that this work is divine. . . .

It is larger than any race or nation or generation. It encompasses all mankind. It is a cause without parallel. . . .

If we will pursue a steady course in carrying out [our] . . . responsibility, then we shall be participants with our Father in Heaven in the accomplishment of his eternal purposes. You and I may fail as individuals and miss the blessing. But his work cannot fail. There will always be those he will raise up to accomplish it. ("He Slumbers Not, nor Sleeps," *Ensign*, May 1983, pp. 7–8.)

I once listened to the experience of an engineer who recently had joined the Church. The missionaries had called at his home, and his wife had invited them in. She had eagerly responded to their message, while he felt himself being pulled in against his will. One evening she indicated that she wished to be baptized. He flew into a fit of anger. Didn't she know what this would mean? This would mean time. This would mean the payment of tithing. This would mean giving up their friends. This would mean no more smoking. He threw on his coat and walked out into the night, slamming the door behind him. He walked the streets, swearing at his wife, swearing at the missionaries, swearing at himself for ever permitting them to teach them. As he grew tired his anger cooled, and a spirit of prayer somehow came into his heart. He prayed as he walked. He pleaded with God for an answer to his questions. And then an impression, clear and unequivocal, came almost as if a voice had spoken with words that said, "It's true."

"It's true," he said to himself again and again. "It's true." A peace came into his heart. As he walked toward home, the restrictions, the demands, the requirements over which he had been so incensed began to appear as opportunities. When he opened the door, he found his wife on her knees praying.

Then before the congregation to whom he told this, he spoke of the gladness that had come into their lives. Tithing was not a problem. The sharing of their substance with God, who had given them everything, seemed little enough. Time for service was not a problem. This only required a little careful budgeting of the hours of the week. Responsibility was not a problem. Out of it came growth and a new outlook on life. And then this man of intellect and training, this engineer accustomed to dealing with the facts of the physical world in which we live, bore solemn testimony with moistened eyes of the miracle that had come into his life. ("It's True, Isn't It?" *Ensign*, July 1993, p. 5.)

The gaining of a strong and secure testimony is the privilege and opportunity of every individual member of the Church. . . . Service in behalf of others, study, and prayer lead to faith in this work and then to knowledge of its truth. This has always been a personal pursuit, as it must always be in the future. ("This Work Is Concerned with People," *Ensign*, May 1995, p. 53.)

The real strength of the Church lies not in the physical facilities which we own. . . . The strength of the Church lies in the conviction carried in the hearts of its members, by the individual members of the Church. It is the privilege, it is the opportunity, it is the obligation of every Latter-day Saint to gain for himself or herself a certain knowledge that this is the work of the Almighty, that God our Eternal Father lives and watches over His children when they look to Him in faith; that Jesus is the Christ, the Son of God, the Redeemer of all mankind, who rose from the dead to become the firstfruits of them that slept. That testimony . . . is the most precious possession that any of us can hold. . . .

If there are any lacking that testimony, you can get it; and you must get it. How? The Lord has said that he that doeth the will of the Father shall know of the doctrine, "whether it be of God, or whether I speak of myself." (John 7:17.) That's the way you gain a testimony. You do the will of the Father, and as certainly as you do the will of the Father you will know of the truth of the gospel, including the knowledge that Jesus is the Christ, the Son of God. (St. Louis Missouri Regional Conference, April 16, 1995.)

Speak out of the convictions in your hearts concerning the knowledge of the things of God. People can argue with you about the declarations you make on the doctrine based on scripture. But when you say, "I know . . ." there is no argument against that. . . . They can't refute you when you bear your testimony. And that is worthy of constant expression, so very, very important—testimony. (Mission Presidents Seminar, June 24, 1995.)

With all of our doing, with all of our leading, with all of our teaching, the most important thing we can do for those whom we lead is to cultivate in their hearts a living, vital, vibrant testimony and knowledge of the Son of God, Jesus Christ, the Redeemer of the world, the Author of our salvation, He who atoned for the sins of the world and opened the way of salvation and eternal life. I would hope that in all we do we would somehow constantly nourish the testimony of our people concerning the Savior. I am satisfied, I know it's so, that whenever a man has a true witness in his heart of the living reality of the Lord Jesus Christ all else will come together as it should. . . . That is the root from which all virtue springs among those who call themselves Latter-day Saints. (BYU Married Student Stakes Regional Conference, priesthood leadership session, February 10, 1996.)

It becomes each of us to acquire such a testimony. This is the very foundation of our faith. This is the thing upon which we build all else, the testimony which we carry in our hearts concerning our Eternal Father and His Beloved Son. We have many people coming into the Church . . . but [some] don't seem to have that testimony in their hearts and they stay for a little while and their faith grows cold and they are gone and all of the efforts of the missionaries are in vain. We must change that around. When the Lord was upon the earth . . . He fed the multitudes and they enjoyed being fed and they came back again, but instead of feeding them He talked with them about the gospel and many of them said, "This is an hard saying; who can hear it" (John 6:61), and they wandered off and left Him. And Jesus, I think with some sorrow in His heart, turned to his disciples and said, "Will ye also go away? Then Simon Peter answered him, Lord, to whom shall we go? thou hast the words of eternal life. And we believe and are sure that thou art that Christ, the Son of the living God" (John 6:67–69). "Lord, to whom shall we go? thou hast the words of eternal life. And we believe and are sure that thou art that Christ, the Son of the living God." That's what each one of us must be able to say, my brethren and sisters. Let us work on that. Let us do the will of the Lord and then we shall know that He lives. (Recife Brazil Fireside, November 15, 1996.)

I want to bear you my testimony. I know that God our Eternal Father lives. I know that. I know that He watches over us, His children. He is the great God of the universe. He is the Governor of the universe. And yet He listens to each of us, His children, and how thankful we ought to be. I know that Jesus is the Christ, the Redeemer of the world, He who wrought a great Atonement in behalf of each of us. I do not care what you remember from this meeting, but I hope that you will remember this, that you heard Gordon B. Hinckley say that he knows that God lives and that Jesus is the Christ, the Redeemer of the world, and that they appeared to the boy Joseph Smith, that the Book of Mormon is true, that the priesthood is upon the earth, and that we exercise it in behalf of the sons and daughters of God. That is my testimony and it is as real and as true as the sunrise in the morning. (Panama City Panama Fireside, January 20, 1997.)

I am thankful for so very many things. I am thankful for the knowledge which I have of God the Eternal Father. I am grateful to know that He is my Father. He is the great God of the universe. He is the Governor of the universe. He is over all and above all and yet, I may get on my knees and speak with Him and I am satisfied that He will listen and hear. What a wonderful blessing that is. I am grateful to know that I am a child of God, that I have a divine birthright, that whether I was born in the United States or Guatemala or Brazil or Japan, my Father in Heaven is my Father. I am grateful for the knowledge I have of the Lord Jesus Christ. "And this is life eternal, that they might know thee the only true God, and Jesus Christ, whom thou hast sent" (John 17:3). I can never thank my Savior enough. He has done for me what I never could do for myself. He has opened the way whereby I may have eternal life. I am so thankful for the knowledge of God and His Son which has come to us through the Prophet Joseph Smith. I am thankful for the Prophet Joseph. We sang a wonderful hymn, "Oh, how lovely was the morning! Radiant beamed the sun above" (*Hymns*, no. 26), which tells of when he went into the woods to pray and came out of those woods having spoken with the Father and the Son. I am grateful for all who ministered unto him; for the angel Moroni who delivered to him the plates from which the Book of Mormon was translated. I thank the Lord for this wonderful book which stands as another witness of the Lord Jesus Christ. I am thankful for the holy priesthood, the Aaronic Priesthood and the Melchizedek Priesthood which have been restored through John the Baptist and Peter, James, and John. This is not a reformation church, it is a restoration church, and how grateful we are for that. (Guatemala City Guatemala North and South Regional Conference, January 26, 1997.)

This is my opportunity to leave you my testimony of the gospel and the Lord Jesus Christ and God, my Eternal Father. Do I know that they live? Of course I do, and I think most of you do. I hope you do. I know with a certainty that God is my Eternal Father. . . . I do not know how He hears all of our prayers, I don't know that. I just know He does because I have my prayers answered. So do you. When you think about it, I think you would say that you have had yours answered. He is my Eternal Father and I know also that the day will come when I will have to make an accounting to Him of my life and what I have done with it, how I have used it, what I have accomplished, what good I have done in this world. The books will be opened and the record will be clear and we will be judged out of the record of our lives, of that I know. I know that He is merciful. I know that He is kind. I know that He loves His sons and daughters. I know that He wants us all to be happy. I know that He wants us to make something good of our lives. I am sure of that, I am confident of that, I know that.

I know that His Only Begotten in the flesh, His Beloved Son, is my Redeemer and my Savior and my Lord Jesus Christ, the Son of God, once the great Jehovah, who came to earth, born in a manger in a vassal state among a people where there was so much of hatred and meanness. He was the great Prince of Peace who taught love and kindness and forbearance, who went about doing good, healing the sick, raising the dead, causing the blind to see. He was my Savior who bled at every pore as He spoke to His Father in Gethsemane and died upon the cross for each of us and then came forth again the third day to become the first fruits of them that slept. He is my Savior and my Redeemer.

God the Father and the risen Lord appeared to the boy Joseph Smith in the grove of his father's farm and there told him to join none of the churches and to be patient and that the Lord would use him according to His way to accomplish His purposes. Then came the Book of Mormon under the hands of Moroni, a resurrected being. Then came the Aaronic Priesthood under the hands of John the Baptist. Then the Melchizedek Priesthood under the hands of Peter, James, and John. Other keys of the priesthood were restored under the hands of Moses, Elias, and Elijah. These things are true. They are true. God bless us to be faithful to the great knowledge that we have to cultivate within our hearts a spirit of testimony and to shape our lives accordingly and draw from our lives that great happiness which will be the blessing of each of us is my humble prayer, in the name of Jesus Christ, amen. (Weber State [Utah] Institute of Religion Devotional, April 15, 1997.)

THOUGHTS

I think I would like to speak to a text this morning. It comes from the Old Testament, from the book of Proverbs—"As [a man] thinketh in his heart, so is he." (Proverbs 23:7.)

You have heard it many times. I submit that it is profound in its implications. A man or woman largely becomes the product of his or her beliefs. Our behavior is governed by our thoughts, our beliefs. And these become our standards of conduct. (LDS Business College Devotional, February 5, 1991.)

You have a responsibility to keep your minds clean from bad and evil thoughts . . . from anything which would lower your thoughts into that which is filthy, instead of that which is beautiful and bright and wholesome. I invite each of you to inhale deeply, way down into the bottom of your lungs, the good, sweet, clean air that is about you. Up where you are there is no pollution. Isn't it wonderful? Isn't it good? Keep the pollution out of your lives. (Varsity Scouts, Arapahoe District, Denver Area Council, July 17, 1993.)

We are the creatures of our thinking. We can talk ourselves into defeat or we can talk ourselves into victory. (Utah Mayflower Society Dinner, November 16, 1994.)

Be clean in mind, and then you will have greater control over your bodies. . . . Unclean thoughts lead to unclean acts. ("'Be Ye Clean,'" *Ensign*, May 1996, p. 48.)

I remember going to President McKay years ago to plead the cause of a missionary who had become involved in serious sin. I said to President McKay, "He did it on an impulse." The President said to me: "His mind was dwelling on these things before he transgressed. The thought was father to the deed. There would not have been that impulse if he had previously controlled his thoughts." ("'Be Ye Clean,'" *Ensign*, May 1996, p. 48.)

If we think of the glory of God, if we have His work in mind, if we do not let our thoughts dwell on things of the world, then our whole bodies shall be filled with light and there shall be no darkness in us. Gone will be the darkness of evil. Gone will be the darkness of laziness. Gone will be all of those things that tear us down and retard us in our efforts. There shall be light and love and peace and goodness in our lives. (Taiwan Taipei Missionary Meeting, May 24, 1996.)

THRIFT

See also Debt; Self-Discipline; Work

We live in an age of persuasive advertising and of skillful salesmanship, all designed to entice us to spend. An extravagant husband or wife can jeopardize any marriage. I think it is a good principle that each have some freedom and independence with everyday, necessary expenditures, while at the same time always discussing and consulting and agreeing on large expenditures. There would be fewer rash decisions, fewer unwise investments, fewer consequent losses, fewer bankruptcies if husbands and wives would counsel together on such matters and seek counsel from others. ("Cornerstones of a Happy Home," Husbands and Wives Fireside Satellite Broadcast, January 29, 1984.)

I commend to you the virtues of thrift and industry. In doing so, I do not wish you to be a "tightwad," if you will pardon that expression, or to be a freeloader, or anything of the kind. But it is the labor and the thrift of people that make a nation strong. It is work and thrift that make the family independent. Debt can be a terrible thing. It is so easy to incur and so difficult to repay. Borrowed money is had only at a price, and that price can be burdensome. Bankruptcy generally is the bitter fruit of debt. It is a tragic fulfillment of a simple process. ("'Thou Shalt Not Covet,'" *Ensign*, March 1990, p. 4.)

I deplore waste. I deplore extravagance. I value thrift. I believe in prudence and conservatism. ("Rise to a Larger Vision of the Work," *Ensign*, May 1990, p. 96.)

I believe in the principle of thrift. We are witnessing in America tremendous business failures to a degree and of an extent we have not seen in a long while. Most of these are the fruits of imprudent borrowing, of debts so large they cannot be paid. We have seen billions upon billions lost in the failure of savings and loan institutions that have been forced to the wall because borrowers did not meet their obligations. We have seen strong banks shaken and brought to their knees because those to whom they loaned money could not pay their debts.

The assets of Eastern Airlines, once a great and proud American business institution, were recently auctioned to the highest bidder. It could not meet its obligations. Other airlines have gone under. Once Pan American was looked upon as the greatest commercial airline in the world. On more than one occasion I have flown Pan Am to Tokyo and other great cities of the

Orient, to Australia, to India and around the world, to Switzerland and Germany and to Britain, to the nations of South America and other places where this once mighty monarch was easily the best to be had. . . . It borrowed beyond its ability to pay and area by area it has sold its routes and is now in Chapter 11. ("Articles of Belief," Bonneville International Corporation Management Seminar, February 10, 1991.)

TITHING

Tithing is so simple and straightforward a thing. The principle, as it applies to us, is actually set forth in one verse of section 119 of the Doctrine and Covenants. That fourth verse consists of thirty-five words. Contrast that with the cumbersome and complex tax codes enacted and enforced by governments. In the one case it is a brief statement from the Lord, the payment left to the individual and motivated by faith. With the other it is a tangled web created by men and enforced by law. . . .

By way of personal testimony, while speaking of the financial resources of the Church, we reiterate the promise of the Lord given anciently through the prophet Malachi that he will open the windows of heaven upon those who are honest with him in the payment of their tithes and offerings, that there shall not be room enough to receive the promised blessings. Every honest tithe payer can testify that the Lord keeps his promise. ("The Miracle Made Possible by Faith," *Ensign*, May 1984, p. 47.)

Is the Church an institution of great wealth, as some claim?

The Church does have substantial assets, for which we are grateful. These assets are primarily in buildings in more than eighty nations. They are in ward and stake meeting facilities. They are in schools and seminaries, colleges and institutes. They are in welfare projects. They are in mission homes and missionary training centers. They are in temples, of which we have substantially more than we have ever had in the past, and they are in genealogical facilities. But it should be recognized that all of these are money-consuming assets and not money-producing assets. They are expensive to build and maintain. They do not produce financial wealth, but they do help to produce and strengthen Latter-day Saints. They are only a means to an end. They are physical facilities to accommodate the programs of the Church in our great responsibility to teach the gospel to the world, to build faith and activity among the living membership, and to carry forward the compelling mandate of the Lord concerning the redemption of the dead.

We have a few income-producing business properties, but the return from these would keep the Church going only for a very short time. Tithing is the Lord's law of finance. There is no other financial law like it. It is a principle given with a promise spoken by the Lord Himself for the blessing of His children.

When all is said and done, the only real wealth of the Church is the faith of its people. ("Questions and Answers," *Ensign*, November 1985, pp. 49–50.)

We *can* pay our tithing. This is not so much a matter of money as it is a matter of faith. I have yet to find a faithful tithe payer who cannot testify that in a very literal and wonderful way the windows of heaven have been opened and blessings have been poured out upon him or her.

I urge you . . . every one of you, to take the Lord at His word in this important matter. It is He who has given the commandment and made the promise. I go back to Nephi, who in that time of worry and concern said to his brothers: "Let us be faithful in keeping the commandments of the Lord; for behold he is mightier than all the earth." (1 Nephi 4:1.) ("'Let Us Move This Work Forward,'" *Ensign*, November 1985, p. 85.)

The fact is that tithing is the Lord's law of finance. It came of revelation from Him. It is a divine law with a great and beautiful promise. It is applicable to every member of the Church who has income. It is applicable to the widow in her poverty as well as to the wealthy man in his riches. . . . One need only compare it with the income tax to recognize the simplicity that comes of the wisdom of God in contrast with the complexity that comes of the wisdom of men. ("The Widow's Mite," *BYU 1985–86 Devotional and Fireside Speeches*, September 17, 1985, p. 9.)

On more than one occasion as a youth I heard President Heber J. Grant, his voice ringing with conviction, bear his witness concerning the sacred law of tithing and the marvelous promises which the Lord has made to those who are honest in paying their tithes and offerings. I was deeply impressed by what I heard.

Often quoted were these great words from the prophet Malachi: "Will a man rob God? Yet ye have robbed me. But ye say, Wherein have we robbed thee? In tithes and offerings.

"Ye are cursed with a curse: for ye have robbed me, even this whole nation.

"Bring ye all the tithes into the storehouse, that there may be meat in mine house, and prove me now herewith, saith the Lord of hosts, if I will not open you the windows of heaven, and pour you out a blessing, that there shall not be room enough to receive it.

"And I will rebuke the devourer for your sakes, and he shall not destroy the fruits of your ground; neither shall your vine cast her fruit before the time in the field, saith the Lord of hosts.

"And all nations shall call you blessed: for ye shall be a delightsome land, saith the Lord of hosts." (Mal. 3:8–12.)

Whenever I heard President Grant read these words from the Old Testament, I knew it was the Lord, the God of heaven, who made those remarkable promises. I knew that he was in a position to keep his promises. I have long since come to know that he does so. ("The Sacred Law of Tithing," *Ensign*, December 1989, pp. 2–4.)

I will always be grateful for a father and a mother who, as far back as I can remember, taught us to pay our tithing. In those days, in the ward in which we lived, the bishop did not have an office in the meetinghouse. We went to his home each December for tithing settlement. I can still sense my feelings of trepidation as I walked into that home as a very small boy to settle my tithing with Bishop John C. Duncan. The amount may have been only twenty-five cents, since we did not have very much in those lean times, but it was an honest 10 percent as we had figured it in our childish way, based on the little couplet that we would recite in Sunday School:

What is tithing? I will tell you every time.
Ten cents from a dollar, and a penny from a dime.

We never felt that it was a sacrifice to pay our tithing. We felt it was an obligation, that even as small children we were doing our duty as the Lord had outlined that duty, and that we were assisting his church in the great work it had to accomplish.

We did not do it with the expectation of material blessings, although we can testify that we have been so blessed. The Lord has opened the windows of heaven and poured out his blessings in marvelous measure. I know that he will bless all who walk in obedience to this commandment. ("The Sacred Law of Tithing," *Ensign*, December 1989, p. 4.)

I do not say that if you pay an honest tithing you will realize your dream of a fine house, a Rolls Royce, and a condominium in Hawaii. *The Lord will open the windows of heaven according to our need, and not according to our greed.* If we are paying tithing to get rich, we are doing it for the wrong reason. The basic purpose for tithing is to provide the Church with the means needed to carry on the Lord's work. The blessing to the giver is an ancillary return, and that blessing may not be always in the form of financial or material benefit. ("The Sacred Law of Tithing," *Ensign*, December 1989, p. 4.)

We hear some these days who say that because of economic pressures they cannot afford to pay their tithing. I recall an experience I had as a stake president some years ago. A man came to get his temple recommend signed. I questioned him in the usual way and asked, among other things, whether he was paying an honest tithing. He candidly replied that he was not, that he could not afford to because of his many debts. I felt impressed to tell him that he would not pay his debts until he paid his tithing.

He went along for a year or two in his normal way, and then made a decision. He talked about it some time later, telling me: "What you told me has proven to be true. I felt I could not pay my tithing because of my debts. I discovered that no matter how hard I tried, somehow I could not manage to reduce my debt. Finally my wife and I sat down together and talked about it and concluded we would try the promise of the Lord. We have done so. And somehow in a way we can't quite understand, the Lord has blessed us. We have not missed that which we have given to him, and for the first time in many years we are reducing our debt." ("The Sacred Law of Tithing," *Ensign*, December 1989, p. 4.)

In a revelation given on 8 July 1838, He indicated that His saints "shall pay one-tenth of all their interest annually; and this shall be a standing law unto them forever, for my holy priesthood, saith the Lord." (D&C 119:4.) The Brethren have interpreted the word *interest* to mean income. Beyond that they have not given interpretation. (Belle S. Spafford Conference on Women, February 23, 1990.)

I recall that when I was a boy I raised a question with my father, who was my stake president, concerning the expenditure of Church funds. He reminded me that mine is the God-given obligation to pay my tithes and offerings. When I do so, that which I give is no longer mine. It belongs to the Lord to whom I consecrate it. What the authorities of the Church do with it need not concern me. They are answerable to the Lord, who will require an accounting at their hands. ("Rise to a Larger Vision of the Work," *Ensign*, May 1990, p. 96.)

Those who pay tithing do not do so under the duress of legal compulsion. No one is disfellowshipped or excommunicated because he fails to pay. But hundreds of thousands, even millions of our people, do so faithfully, honestly, and willingly. They do so because of the conviction that each carries in his or her heart that the work is true and the law is divine. ("My Testimony," *Ensign*, November 1993, p. 53.)

Pay your tithes that you may be worthy of the Lord's blessings. I will not promise that you will become wealthy. But I bear testimony that the Lord does reward generously in one way or another those who keep His commandments. And I assure you that no investment counselor to whom you may go can promise you as the Lord has promised: "I, the Lord, am bound when ye do what I say; but when ye do not what I say, ye have no promise." (D&C 82:10.) The Lord honors His covenants. ("Pillars of Truth," *Ensign*, January 1994, p. 7.)

I am so thankful for the law of tithing. I believe in it with all my heart. My wife was going through some old papers the other day. What did she find? She found a tithing receipt for one of our boys. Twenty-three cents he paid in tithing that year as a little boy. I guess it cost the bishop more than that to write the receipt. I know it cost her more than that to mail it to our boy. She spent thirty-two cents to mail a twenty-three-cent tithing receipt to our son. But was it worth it, twenty-three cents? Was it worth the bishop's taking the time to sit down and write out that receipt? I do not know what [my son] has paid since. He has been a bishop, in a stake presidency, and other things. He is a banker. I guess he has paid in the aggregate many, many thousands of dollars. Why? Because the principle was implanted when he was a little boy. (Nottingham England Fireside, August 30, 1995.)

We were out at Canterbury Cathedral the other day and had a beautiful time. They are having a difficult time to get the funds to keep it up. When we were driving up to Nottingham from the south the other day, we stopped in the town of Hinckley just because the town and I happen to have the same name. We went to the old parish church there, built in the thirteenth century. I was appalled at what I saw in that beautiful old church. There was a coffee shop on one side and there was a shop on the other side that sold groceries and household items, all kinds of goods, within the church. Why? To get some money to maintain the church. What happened to the ancient law of the tithe? . . .

I hope you are paying your tithing, my fellow Latter-day Saints. The Church actually can get along without your money, but you can't get along without the blessings of the Lord. I mean that. And that has made it possible to carry forward this work. We are now constructing buildings all over the world. This work is established now in more than 150 nations. We are building more than 350 new buildings a year to accommodate the needs of the people. And what a marvelous thing to be able to say, wherever you go and find a Latter-day Saint meetinghouse, "I

was a part of that through the payment of my tithes and offerings." The Lord bless you to walk honestly with Him in that very
important matter. (Liverpool England Fireside, August 31, 1995.)

Some of you have money problems. . . . What is the cure? The
only thing I know of is payment of tithing. Now that doesn't
mean that you will have a Cadillac and a mansion. But it was
God who made the promise that He would open the windows of
heaven and pour down blessings upon those who walked honestly with Him in the payment of their tithes and offerings, and
He has the capacity to keep His promise. It is my testimony that
He does keep that promise. (Oahu Hawaii Regional Conference,
February 18, 1996.)

I have seen enough in my life to have a strong and firm testimony concerning the literalness of the promise that the God of
Heaven will open the windows of heaven and pour down blessings upon us if we will keep our side of the covenant [of tithing].
I do not think we will ever get a convert solid in this Church
until he or she pays tithing. . . . That will become the test of their
love for this work and their loyalty to it. I think somehow we
need to get that into their hearts, that tithing is an opportunity
and a blessing and not a discretionary thing that we can disregard with impunity. (Meeting with General Authorities and
Wives, April 10, 1996.)

I have wept as I have seen the poverty and the suffering of
the people in this part of the earth. My heart reaches out to them.
I do not know what the solution is, except the gospel of Jesus
Christ. I think it is the only thing that will help them and bless
their lives. If they, even living in poverty and misery, can look to
God with hope and faith, it will sustain them in their hours of
sorrow. Furthermore, I believe with all my heart that if they will
accept the gospel and live it, pay their tithes and offerings, even
though those be meager, the Lord will keep His ancient promise
in their behalf, and they will have rice in their bowls, and clothing on their backs, and shelter over their heads. I do not see any
other solution. They need a power greater than any earthly

power to lift them and help them. (Philippines Cebu Missionary Meeting, June 1, 1996.)

Many of you are under financial stress. You have big mortgage payments. I have seen some of the homes in which you live, and they are not shanties. Every month comes the time to pay. Those payments are very high in many cases. And the taxes are high. I hope that you are paying your tithing. You will have an easier time paying your bills if you live honestly with the Lord in the payment of your tithes and offerings. I have no doubt of that. (Jordan Utah South Regional Conference, March 2, 1997.)

TOLERANCE

Each of us is an individual. Each of us is different. There must be respect for those differences, and while it is important and necessary that both the husband and the wife work to ameliorate those differences, there must be some recognition that they exist and that they are not necessarily undesirable. There must be respect one for the other, notwithstanding such differences. In fact, the differences may make the companionship more interesting. ("Cornerstones of a Happy Home," Husbands and Wives Fireside Satellite Broadcast, January 29, 1984.)

Let us as Latter-day Saints cultivate a spirit of brotherhood in all of our associations. Let us be more charitable in our judgments, more sympathetic and understanding of those who err, more willing to forgive those who trespass against us. Let us not add to the measure of hatred that periodically sweeps across the world. Let us reach out in kindness to all men, even toward those who speak evil of us and who would, if they could, harm us.

In a word, let us more nearly live the gospel of the Master, whose name we have taken upon us. Let us move this work forward; let our lives be such as to be worthy of emulation. ("'Let Us Move This Work Forward,'" *Ensign*, November 1985, p. 85.)

In many communities where our people are in the majority, accusations are heard that we are intolerant, that we display an attitude of self-righteousness, and that we are uncooperative in advancing causes which are for the common good. . . . It has been reported that some parents, out of a desire to protect their children, have told them that they should not associate in school with those not of their faith.

It seems anomalous that some would keep their sons and daughters from so doing while they are in the elementary schools, and yet make great sacrifice when they grow older to send them into the mission field.

Let us not forget that we believe in being benevolent and in doing good to all men. I am convinced that we can teach our children effectively enough that we need not fear that they will lose their faith while being friendly and considerate with those who do not subscribe to the doctrine of this Church. Let us reach out to those in our community who are not of our faith. Let us be good neighbors, kind and generous and gracious. Let us be involved in good community causes. There may be situations, there will be situations, where, with serious moral issues involved, we cannot bend on matters of principle. But in such instances we can politely disagree without being disagreeable. We can acknowledge the sincerity of those whose positions we cannot accept. We can speak of principles rather than personalities. In those causes which enhance the environment of the community, and which are designed for the blessing of all of its citizens, let us step forward and be helpful. An attitude of self-righteousness is unbecoming a Latter-day Saint. (Regional Representatives Seminar, April 1, 1988.)

There is too much of intolerance in the world. There is too much of it in our own society.

I once listened to a beautiful prayer offered by a Greek-American in the manner in which he had been taught to pray. It was an expression of gratitude to the Almighty and a plea for His favor. It was concluded in the name of the Father and the Son and the Holy Ghost. His phrasing was not as my phrasing might have been, but I recognized his sincerity and told him of my appreciation.

I sat one evening at the table of a Jewish friend. The prayer which he uttered upon his guests and upon the table at which we sat was beautiful and moving. I was grateful for what I heard.

We can be appreciative in a very sincere way. Not only must we be tolerant, but we must cultivate a spirit of affirmative gratitude for those who do not see things quite as we see them. We do not in any way have to compromise our theology, our convictions, our knowledge of eternal truth as it has been revealed by the God of Heaven. We can offer our own witness of the truth, quietly, sincerely, honestly, but never in a manner that will give offense to others.

The strength of our position as we understand it will become the clearer and more precious as we allow others the same privilege of conscience that we so highly prize. We must learn to accord appreciation and respect for others who are as sincere in their beliefs and practices as are we. ("Out of Your Experience Here," *BYU 1990–1991 Devotional and Fireside Speeches,* October 16, 1990, p. 30.)

Teach [your children] tolerance. They need not surrender their own beliefs while extending tolerance to those with other beliefs.

Teach them civility toward others. Conflict between the races will fade when all of us recognize that we are all part of one great family.

Teach them respect—respect for others, respect for the property of others, respect for the opinions of others, respect on the part of men for women and women for men. ("Teach the Children," Southern Utah University Baccalaureate Address, June 3, 1994.)

We are of various doctrinal persuasions. While recognizing our theological differences, I think we are of one mind in our awareness of the evils and problems of the world and the society in which we live, and of our great responsibility and opportunity to stand united for those qualities in public and private life which speak of virtue and morality, of respect for all men and women as children of God, of the need for civility and courtesy in our relationships, and of preservation of the family as the divinely ordained basic unit of society.

While there are doctrinal differences, there is much of similarity among us. All of us carry in our hearts a desire to assist the poor, to lift the distressed, to give comfort, hope, and help to all who are in trouble and pain from whatever cause.

We recognize the need to heal the wounds of society and replace with optimism and faith the pessimism of our times. We must recognize that there is no need for recrimination or criticism against one another. We must use our influence to still the voices of angry and vindictive argument.

An article of the faith to which I subscribe states: "We claim the privilege of worshipping Almighty God according to the dictates of our own conscience, and allow all men the same privilege, let them worship how, where, or what they may" (Article of Faith 11). I hope to find myself always on the side of those defending this position. Our strength lies in our freedom to choose. There is strength even in our very diversity. But there is greater strength in the God-given mandate to each of us to work for the uplift and blessing of all His sons and daughters, regardless of their ethnic or national origin or other differences. . . .

May the Lord bless us to work unitedly to remove from our hearts and drive from our society all elements of hatred, bigotry, racism, and other divisive words and actions. The snide remark, the racial slur, hateful epithets, malicious gossip, and mean and vicious rumor-mongering should have no place among us.

May God bless us all with the peace that comes from Him. May He bless us with thankful hearts and with the will to mingle together with respect one for another, uniting our efforts to the blessing of the communities where we are fortunate to live. (National Conference of Christians and Jews Interfaith Services, November 20, 1994.)

[All people, regardless of their religious backgrounds, are] made of one blood, all nations of men for to dwell on all the face of the Earth. We all believe in the fatherhood of God; that we are all part of a great family . . . therefore, we are all brothers and sisters. We may disagree on our interpretation of God, but we can do so with respect and civility. (National Conference of Christians and Jews Banquet, February 21, 1995.)

How very heavy is the burden of human suffering, the suffering that comes of war, of so-called ethnic cleansing, of conflict in the name of religion, of foolish ideas of racial superiority, of intolerance, bigotry, and egotism.

When I was a small boy of perhaps seven or eight, I was sitting on the front porch of our home with some friends. A black family came walking down the street—a father, a mother, and two or three children. We boys made some disparaging remarks concerning them. I think they did not hear us. I hope they did not. But my mother did hear us. She marched us into the house, sat us down, and talked to us about respect and tolerance. I have never forgotten the lessons of that day.

I think often of Longfellow's couplet: "There is so much of bad in the best of us, and so much of good in the worst of us, that it ill becomes any of us to talk about the rest of us."

My heart has resonated with Paul's declaration to the men of Athens: "And [God] hath made of one blood all nations of men for to dwell on all the face of the earth" (Acts 17:26).

Each of us [from various religious denominations] believes in the fatherhood of God, although we may differ in our interpretations of Him. Each of us is part of a great family, the human family, sons and daughters of God, and therefore brothers and sisters. We must work harder to build mutual respect, an attitude of forbearance, with tolerance one for another regardless of the doctrines and philosophies which we may espouse. Concerning these you and I may disagree. But we can do so with respect and civility.

To those who are members of the church of which I am a member, I call attention to these words of Joseph Smith spoken in July of 1843: "If it has been demonstrated that I have been willing to die for a 'Mormon,' I am bold enough to declare before heaven that I am just as ready to die in defending the rights of a Presbyterian, a Baptist, or a good man of any other denomination; for the same principle which would trample upon the rights of the Latter-day Saints would trample upon the rights of the Roman Catholics, or of any other denomination . . ." (*History of the Church,* vol. 5, pp. 498.) This, I hope, can be my standard. . . .

Catholics, Protestants, Mormons, Greek Orthodox, Muslims, and people of various racial backgrounds and ethnic origins:

Thank you for the respect you exemplify and cultivate, for the tolerance you nourish, for the spirit of forbearance and civility which you demonstrate. We must continue, even more vigorously, to work unitedly for the common good, teaching our children to do likewise, so that the world, at least in some small measure, may be healed of its wounds and spared the scars of further conflict. (National Conference of Christians and Jews Banquet, February 21, 1995.)

I plead with our people everywhere to live with respect and appreciation for those not of our faith. There is so great a need for civility and mutual respect among those of differing beliefs and philosophies. We must not be partisans of any doctrine of ethnic superiority. We live in a world of diversity. We can and must be respectful toward those with whose teachings we may not agree. We must be willing to defend the rights of others who may become the victims of bigotry. ("This Is the Work of the Master," *Ensign,* May 1995, p. 71.)

We recognize the good that other churches do, and they do great good. I hope they recognize the good that we do. We have points of difference, very substantial differences concerning our theology, our doctrine, our ordinances. Such important matters as that we can disagree on without being disagreeable. We can be civil and gracious and kind and decent toward them. . . . There will be differences, as there have always been. But I think we have a good relationship. . . . We must recognize there are many wonderful people in other churches. That doesn't mitigate for one moment the impact of our message concerning the restoration of the gospel and the fact that the Lord has brought this Church forth in this dispensation for the blessing of His sons and daughters of all generations of time. (Anchorage Alaska Regional Conference, priesthood leadership session, June 17, 1995.)

Unfortunately, people can't seem to be tolerant and respectful of the views of others in so many cases. We must cultivate in this land an attitude of tolerance and respect for the beliefs and rights of others. We must cultivate an increased spirit of civility among people in their expressions one to another, and toward the beliefs and practices of others. We can disagree with people without being disagreeable. We can disagree without raising our voices and becoming angry and vindictive in our ways. We must learn to do so. We as a Christian community must practice a greater spirit of Christ in our lives, of love one for another, and extend that to all people regardless of whom they worship or how they worship, so long as they do not infringe upon the rights of others. (Interview with Gus Niebuhr of *New York Times*, July 17, 1995.)

As we move into another century, we must resolve to live together in a society of men and women of diverse backgrounds, interests, and cultures. We must live with respect and tolerance and understanding one for another. We can and should retain our individuality, and respect that of others, while nurturing together a great society dedicated to the blessing of all who reside here.

We must work cooperatively to maintain and enhance those elements of our common culture, those expressions of the arts which refine and elevate the human spirit. (Utah Centennial Statehood Day Celebration, January 4, 1996.)

We respect all other churches. We do not stand out in opposition to other churches. We respect all men for all the good that they do, and we say to those of all churches, we honor the good that you do and we invite you to come and see what further good we can do for you. We think that we have some significant things to offer which are not found in other churches, but, I repeat, we respect all men. We believe in worshiping God according to the dictates of our conscience and allow all men the same privilege, let them worship how, where, or what they may. (Seoul Korea Press Conference, May 22, 1996.)

The first Article of our Faith reads: "We believe in God, the Eternal Father, and in His Son, Jesus Christ, and in the Holy Ghost." That is our basic foundation belief. God is our Eternal Father—that is not in some philosophical sense, it is in a very real sense. God is the father of our spirits, and if He is the father of all people across the earth, then it follows naturally that we are all brothers and sisters and we ought to treat one another as brothers and sisters, with kindness and respect and love, with an implementation of the golden rule: "Therefore, all things whatsoever ye would that men should do to you, do ye even so to them" (Matthew 7:12). God is our father. We are His children. We sing, "I am a child of God." We do not think very much of what that means. It means so very much, that you and I, my dear brothers and sisters, have a divine birthright. There is something of divinity in each of us that is eternal and everlasting, and in the expression of that divinity we ought to stand tall and be clean and good and pure and a happy people. (Manila Philippines Fireside, May 30, 1996.)

Mr. Wallace: "How do you view non-Mormons?"

Response: "With love and respect. I have many non-Mormon friends. I respect them. I have the greatest of admiration for them."

Question: "Despite the fact that they haven't really seen the light yet?"

Reply: "Yes. To anybody who is not of this Church, I say we recognize all of the virtues and the good that you have. Bring it with you and see if we might add to it." ("'This Thing Was Not Done in a Corner,'" *Ensign,* November 1996, p. 51.)

TRUTH

It was said of old that "where there is no vision, the people perish: . . ." (Prov. 29:18.) Vision of what? Vision concerning the things of God, and a stern and unbending adherence to divinely pronounced standards. There is evidence aplenty that young people will respond to the clear call of divine truth, but they are quick to detect and abandon that which has only a form of godliness but denies the power thereof, "teaching for doctrines the commandments of men." (Matt. 15:9; see Joseph Smith 2:19.) ("A Charter for Youth," *Improvement Era,* December 1965, p. 1125.)

This is the kingdom of the Lord Jesus Christ restored in this the greatest dispensation of all time, to bless the people of the earth with the truth, the living truth of the living God. How we need men and women of strength and stature and faith and persuasiveness who will stand as advocates of the truth of God. ("Prepare to Lead," BYU *Speeches of the Year*, February 25, 1969, p. 7.)

History amply testifies that much of learning, including university learning, is not truth. What a tremendous challenge, what a marvelous opportunity is yours to lead young minds in an exploration of eternal truth. ("The Second Hundred Years: A New Level of Achievement," BYU Address, August 28, 1975.)

God has given us the *power of truth.*

President Joseph F. Smith once declared: "We believe in all truth, no matter to what subject it may refer. No sect or religious denomination [or, I may say, no searcher of truth] in the world possesses a single principle of truth that we do not accept or that we will reject. We are willing to receive all truth, from whatever source it may come; for truth will stand, truth will endure." (*Gospel Doctrine*, Salt Lake City: Deseret Book, 1939, p. 1.)

We have nothing to fear when we walk by the light of eternal truth. But we had better be discerning. Sophistry has a way of masking itself as truth. Half truths are used to mislead under the representation that they are whole truths. Innuendo is often used by enemies of this work as representing truth. Theories and hypotheses are often set forth as if they were confirmed truth. Statements taken out of context of time or circumstance or the written word are often given as truth, when as a matter of fact such procedure may be the very essence of falsehood. ("'God Hath Not Given Us the Spirit of Fear,'" *Ensign*, October 1984, p. 4.)

Ours ought to be a ceaseless quest for truth. That truth must include spiritual and religious truth as well as secular. ("The Continuing Pursuit of Truth," *Ensign*, April 1986, p. 2.)

There are people here who have in their hearts a love for truth, and when they hear it they will respond to it as you have responded in your hearts to a message of eternal truth. (Hyde Park Chapel Rededication, August 27, 1995.)

He has established His church, which carries the name of His divine Son, as the conservator and teacher of truth, that truth which will make and keep us free. ("To a Man Who Has Done What This Church Expects of Each of Us," *BYU 1995–96 Speeches,* October 17, 1995, p. 52.)

Cling to the Church. This is The Church of Jesus Christ of Latter-day Saints. This is the only true and living church upon the face of the whole earth, according to the word of revelation. Here lies the truth. (Ricks College Regional Conference, Rexburg, Idaho, October 29, 1995.)

Mine was the good fortune, the remarkable blessing to serve a mission for this Church in the British Isles more than sixty years ago. My first assignment was to Preston, Lancashire, where years earlier the first Latter-day Saint missionaries opened the work in that land. Poor and destitute, they arrived in Preston on Saturday, July 22, 1837. It was election day, Queen Victoria having recently ascended the throne. As they came down the road into the city, an election banner was unfurled. It read, "Truth Will Prevail." They adopted that as their motto. It has been our motto ever since. (Convocation for Honorary Degrees, BYU, March 5, 1996.)

I pray with all my heart that you will meditate and pray and experience the nurturing truth of the gospel, that your lives may shine with the radiance that comes from it. This work is true. This Church is true. The priesthood is true. Its power is among us. (Fukuoka Japan Fireside, May 19, 1996.)

If you have any question concerning the truth of this work, you do the will of God and you will know that it is true. (São Paulo Brazil Fireside, November 14, 1996.)

UNITY

The Lord said, Except ye are one, ye are not mine. (See D&C 38:27.) This great unity is the hallmark of the true church of Christ. It is felt among our people throughout the world. As we are one, we are his. ("Except Ye Are One," *Ensign*, November 1983, p. 5.)

It is now almost three years since I was called by President Kimball to serve as a counselor in the First Presidency of the Church. During a substantial part of that period I have humbly tried to carry a great and awesome responsibility. I have known something of loneliness and worry and deep concern. I have prayed earnestly for direction and strength and guidance. I have called on these my beloved brethren of the Twelve. They have freely and generously given of support, assistance, and inspired counsel.

There is unity in the First Presidency of the Church. There is unity between the Presidency and the Twelve, perfect unity. There is unity among the members of the First Quorum of the Seventy and the Presiding Bishopric. I am somewhat familiar with the history of this Church, and I do not hesitate to say that there has never been greater unity in its leading councils and the relationships of those councils one to another, than there is today. . . .

The work goes on in majesty and power. The kingdom grows, solidly and consistently. Testimony strengthens in the hearts and lives of the members of the Church across the world. Herein lies the great strength of this kingdom. ("Special Witnesses for Christ," *Ensign*, May 1984, p. 51.)

I want to assure you, as I have assured you in the past, that there is unity in the leadership of the Church. There is not the slightest divisiveness among the General Authorities. There is a great sense of loyalty among them—loyalty to you, loyalty to one another, loyalty to this cause, loyalty to God and his Eternal Son.

I love these my Brethren. Not one of them has ever hesitated to respond to any call that was made upon him. They have been willing to travel over land and sea, in sunshine or storm, to accomplish any task asked of them. They have lived up to the solemn charge given each at the time of his call—to put the interests of the kingdom of God ahead of all other interests. ("Live the Gospel," *Ensign*, November 1984, p. 86.)

I remember when President J. Reuben Clark, Jr., as a counselor in the First Presidency, would stand at this pulpit and plead for unity among the priesthood. I think he was not asking that we give up our individual personalities and become as robots cast from a single mold. I am confident he was not asking that we cease to think, to meditate, to ponder as individuals. I think he was telling us that if we are to assist in moving forward the work of God, we must carry in our hearts a united conviction concerning the great basic foundation stones of our faith, including the truth and validity of the First Vision as the record of this singular event is found in the history of Joseph Smith; of the truth and validity of the Book of Mormon as a voice speaking from the dust in testimony of Jesus the Christ . . . ; of the reality and power of the priesthood which was restored under the hands of those who held it anciently. . . . If we are to assist in moving forward the work of God, we must carry in our hearts a united conviction that the ordinances and covenants of this work are eternal and everlasting in their consequences; that this kingdom was established in the earth through the instrumentality of the Prophet Joseph Smith and that every man who has succeeded him in the office of President has been and is a prophet of the living God; and that there is incumbent upon each of us an obligation to live and teach the gospel as interpreted and taught by the prophet of our day. ("To the Bishops of the Church," *Ensign*, November 1988, p. 48.)

Loyalty to leadership is a cardinal requirement of all who serve in the army of the Lord. A house divided against itself cannot stand. (See Mark 3:25.) Unity is basic and essential. Declared the Lord, "If ye are not one ye are not mine." (D&C 38:27.) ("Keeping the Temple Holy," *Ensign*, May 1990, p. 51.)

UNWED PREGNANCY

See also Abortion; Chastity; Morality

When marriage is not possible, experience has shown that adoption, difficult though this may be for the young mother, may afford a greater opportunity for the child to live a life of happiness. Wise and experienced professional counselors and prayerful bishops can assist in these circumstances. ("Save the Children," *Ensign*, November 1994, p. 53.)

One major problem is the now-common phenomenon of children bearing children, of children without fathers. Somehow there seems to be in the minds of many young men, and some not so young, the idea that there is no relationship between the begetting of a child and responsibility for its life thereafter. Every young man should realize that whenever a child is begotten outside the bonds of marriage, it has resulted from violation of a God-given commandment reaching at least as far back as Moses. Further, let it be known clearly and understood without question that responsibility inevitably follows, and that this responsibility will continue throughout life. Though the mores of our contemporary society may have crumbled to a point where sexual transgression is glossed over or is regarded as acceptable, there will someday be accountability before the God of heaven for all that we do in violation of his commandments. I believe further that a sense of accountability must at some time bear upon every man who has fathered a child and then abandoned responsibility for its care. He must sometimes stop and wonder whatever became of the child he fathered, of the boy or girl who is flesh of his flesh and soul of his soul. ("Save the Children," *Ensign*, November 1994, p. 53.)

Every young man must be made to realize that in fathering a child he takes upon himself a responsibility that will endure as long as he lives. Let every young woman know that in giving birth to a child, she places upon herself a responsibility from which she will never be entirely free. How tragic is the desolate and ever increasing picture of illegitimate birth. With each such birth comes responsibility, to the mother, to the father if he stands up to it, and, inevitably, to society at large.

The lack of self-discipline and of a sense of responsibility, in my judgment, is one of the fruits of the increasing secularization of our society. I was appalled to read the other day that in one community a proposal was made that young women be paid a dollar a day for not becoming pregnant. How stupid. Where is our sense of values? (Provo City Community Centennial Service, August 4, 1996.)

VALUES

Be careful, in your headlong race for scientific progress, that you neglect not those values which will make that life worth living. Safeguard the family; preserve its integrity and sanctity. Labor for the peace that will come only as men recognize the Prince of Peace. Nourish the spirit. You can do it. You must do it. God will bless you in doing it. ("Conquer or Be Conquered," BYU Commencement Address, August 19, 1966.)

I was part of a graduating class of a sister institution in 1932. . . . That was a dark season, that year of 1932. It was at the bottom of the great worldwide depression. The unemployment rate was not the 5 or 6 or 7 percent over which we worry today, but more than 30 percent. Men saw their savings vanish, and some, with nothing to live for, took their own lives. Many with greater faith held on tenaciously as they sank into the pit of poverty.

It was into that world of economic distress that we of the class of '32 arrived, breathing something of an air of cynicism. Yet notwithstanding this, there was much joy in our lives. Cars were cheaper then, but few could afford one. But we dated, we danced, we had a lot of fun while worrying about life, and somehow we made it and pulled through. I can think of scores of my peers who had nothing in those days but who, somehow, with the blessings of heaven, went forward and became men and women of strength and substance as they walked a straight and steady course, guided by principles to which they held with steadfastness.

It was their beliefs and the motivation that came therefrom that pulled them through. Every one of us is largely the product of his or her beliefs. Our behavior is governed by these. They become our standards of conduct. ("This I Believe," *BYU 1991–92 Devotional and Fireside Speeches*, March 1, 1992, pp. 75–76.)

I am so bold as to say that the observance of four simple things on the part of parents would in a generation or two turn this nation around in terms of its moral values. They are simply these:

Let parents and children teach and learn together, work together, read together, and pray together. ("Saving the Nation by Changing Our Homes," BYU Management Society, Washington, D.C., March 5, 1994.)

Let the truth be taught, by example and precept, that to steal is evil, that to cheat is wrong, that to lie is a reproach to anyone who indulges in it. If we are to put civility back into our civilization, the process must begin in the home while children are very young. ("Teach the Children," American Mothers, Inc., Convention, May 1, 1994.)

I hope you will not feel that I am just one more in a long procession of preachers advocating today a return to old values. No! We are not returning—these values have always been taught here and are now being taught here. I anticipate they always will be. And you have become, by the goodness of your living, the shining example of the virtue of such values. ("Codes and Covenants," *BYU 1994–95 Devotional and Fireside Speeches*, October 18, 1994, p. 37.)

Question: Mormon values, your value system, apparently works. Compared with national averages, Mormons have fewer illegitimate children, less premarital sex, less adultery, more marriage, less divorce?

President Hinckley: We are trying to strengthen these values in our people. They are fundamental. We can't have a strong nation without a nation based on values. They are the very core of our civilization. (Interview with Mike Wallace of *60 Minutes*, December 18, 1995.)

This work stands as an anchor of stability, an anchor of values, in a world whose values are shifting. We stand for something. Our values find their roots in the teachings of the gospel of Jesus Christ. These are unchanging. They are today as they were when Jesus walked the roads of Palestine. They are as applicable now as they were then. They have been tested in the cauldron of human history, and they have not been found wanting. We expect great things of our people. This religion is demanding. It requires self-discipline. It requires study and courage and faith. People are responding to this as they feel the ground under them shake with uncertainties in a world of crumbling values. ("True to the Faith," Salt Lake Valley-Wide Institute Fireside, January 21, 1996.)

It's refreshing, always, to find people who stand up for standards and values that are tested and have been proved in the fires of history—such things as family solidarity, family loyalty, the importance of making something of one's life, and serving society to improve the world of which we are a part. (Interview with Peter Fritsch of *Wall Street Journal*, April 30, 1996.)

This Church and this gospel fill a need in the lives of the people. We live in a world of shifting values, moral values that are crumbling around the world, affecting every nation, including this nation. This Church stands as an anchor, a solid anchor of truth, in a world of shifting values. Every man and every woman who joins this Church and clings to its teachings will live a better life, will be a happier man or woman, will carry in his or her heart a great love for the Lord and His ways. (Manila Philippines Fireside, May 30, 1996.)

"A peculiar people." We're different. Of course, we're different from the world. If the world continues to go the way it is now going, we will become even more peculiar. We will stand for truth. We will stand for right. We will stand for honesty. We will stand for virtue. We will stand for personal cleanliness. We will be more and more a peculiar people. (Miami Florida Fireside, November 17, 1996.)

VIRTUE

See also Morality

This is the business of the Church—to open the vision of men to eternal verities, and to prompt them to take a stand for equity and decency, for virtue and sobriety and goodness. ("'Rise, and Stand Upon Thy Feet,'" *Improvement Era*, December 1968, p. 68.)

Strength to do battle begins with enlisting the strength of God. He is the source of all true power. Declared Paul to the Ephesians:

"Finally my brethren, be strong in the Lord, and in the power of his might.

"Put on the whole armour of God, that ye may be able to stand against the wiles of the devil.

"For we wrestle not against flesh and blood, but against principalities, against powers, against the rulers of the darkness of this world, against spiritual wickedness in high places.

"Wherefore take unto you the whole armour of God, that ye may be able to withstand in the evil day, and having done all, to stand." (Eph. 6:10–13.)

Brethren and sisters, the tide of evil flows. It has become a veritable flood. Most of us, living somewhat sheltered lives, have little idea of the vast dimensions of it. Billions of dollars are involved for those who pour out pornography, for those who peddle lasciviousness, for those who deal in bestiality, in perversion, in sex and violence. God give us the strength, the wisdom, the faith, the courage as citizens to stand in opposition to these and to let our voices be heard in defense of those virtues which, when practiced in the past, made men and nations strong, and which, when neglected, brought them to decay. ("Opposing Evil," *Ensign*, November 1975, p. 40.)

"We believe in being honest, true, chaste, benevolent, virtuous and in doing good to all men; indeed, we may say that we follow the admonition of Paul—We believe all things, we hope all things, we have endured many things, and hope to be able to endure all things. If there is anything virtuous, lovely, or of good report or praiseworthy, we seek after these things." (Article of Faith 13.)

That article of our faith is one of the basic declarations of our theology. During this great conference we have been reminded of many of the virtues set forth in that brief statement. We ought to reflect on it again and again. I wish that every family in the Church would write out that article of faith and put it on a mirror where every member of the family would see it every day. Then, whenever we might be tempted to do anything shoddy or dishonest or immoral, there would come into our minds with some force this great, all encompassing statement of the ethics of our behavior. There would be less rationalizing over some elements of our personal conduct which we try to justify with one excuse or another.

Some would have us believe that the area between good and evil is largely gray and that it is difficult to determine what is right and what is wrong. For any who so believe, I recommend this beautiful statement of Moroni found in the Book of Mormon: "For behold, the Spirit of Christ is given to every man, that he may know good from evil; wherefore, I show unto you the way to judge; for everything which inviteth to do good, and to persuade to believe in Christ, is sent forth by the power and gift of Christ; wherefore ye may know with a perfect knowledge it is of God." (Moro. 7:16.) ("'Fear Not to Do Good,'" *Ensign*, May 1983, p. 80.)

He who is disposed to shun virtue lacks appreciation of life, its purposes, and the happiness and well-being of others.

An observer of our plight has written the following: "We are witnessing the death of the old morality. The established moral guidelines have been yanked from our hands. . . . We are left floundering in a money-motivated, sex-obsessed, big-city dominated society. We must figure out for ourselves how to apply the traditional moral principles to the problems of our times. Many find this burden too heavy." (*Look*, Sept. 1963, p. 74.)

Challenging though it may be, there is a way to apply traditional moral principles in our day. For some unknown reason, there is constantly appearing the false rationalization that at one time in the long-ago, virtue was easy and that now it is difficult.

I would like to remind any who feel that way that there has never been a time since the Creation when the same forces were not at work that are at work today. The proposal made by Potiphar's wife to Joseph in Egypt is no different from that faced by many men and women and youth in our day.

The influences today may be more apparent and more seductive, but they are no more compelling. One cannot be shielded entirely from these influences. They are all about us. Our culture is saturated with them. But the same kind of self-discipline exercised by Joseph will yield the same beneficial result. Notwithstanding the so-called "new morality," notwithstanding the much-discussed changes in moral standards, there is no adequate substitute for virtue. God's standards may be challenged everywhere throughout the world, but God has not abrogated his commandments. ("'With All Thy Getting Get Understanding,'" *Ensign*, August 1988, p. 4.)

Is there a valid case for virtue in our world? It is the only way to freedom from regret. The peace of conscience which flows therefrom is the only personal peace that is not counterfeit.

And beyond all of this is the unfailing promise of God to those who walk in virtue. Declared Jesus of Nazareth, speaking on the mountain, "Blessed are the pure in heart: for they shall see God." (Matthew 5:8.) That is a promise, made by him who has the power to fulfill.

And again, the voice of modern revelation speaks an unmatched promise that follows a simple commandment:

"Let virtue garnish thy thoughts unceasingly." And here is the promise: "Then shall thy confidence wax strong in the presence of God. . . .

"The Holy Ghost shall be thy constant companion, . . . and thy dominion shall be an everlasting dominion, and without compulsory means it shall flow unto thee forever and ever." (D&C 121:45–46.)

May I comment on this marvelous promise. It has been my privilege on various occasions to converse with presidents of the United States and important leaders in other governments. At the close of each visit, I have reflected on the rewarding experience of standing with confidence in the presence of an acknowledged leader. And then I have thought, what a wonderful thing, what a marvelous thing it would be to stand with confidence—unafraid and unashamed and unembarrassed—in the presence of God. This is the promise held out to every virtuous man and woman. ("In Search of Peace and Freedom," *Ensign,* August 1989, p. 6.)

A week ago I had an interesting experience. Without any official assignment, I attended a stake conference in a rural area of southeastern Utah. The stake president and his wife had invited Sister Hinckley and me to stay at their home. While he conducted his Saturday afternoon meeting, we rode about the stake, visiting a half-dozen little towns, in each of which there is a Church meetinghouse. We noted that the lawns were green and the buildings nicely kept, although they are small and some of them are old. We drove about and looked at the homes, modest in their appearance, but in almost every case there was neatness and beauty with flowers in bloom. Having a free Saturday and Sunday, I had wanted to make this trip simply to thank the people for their faith and faithfulness and to express my love to them. Most of them are farm folk who work hard for a small return. But they know a great truth. They know the law of the harvest—"Whatsoever ye sow, that shall ye also reap." (D&C 6:33.)

They know that you do not reap wheat after sowing oats. They know that you do not get a racehorse from a scrub mare. They know that if you are to build another great generation, you must work with vision and faith. You must dream and plan, serve and sacrifice, pray and labor. After being with these wonderful people for two days, Sister Hinckley observed, "These are the kind who constitute the glue that holds the Church together." . . .

I repeat—I went among these people to express my gratitude and love. I felt a great overwhelming measure of love in return. Here in this stake of small rural wards, among people who made no pretense of sophistication, I found strength and faith and virtue. . . .

I do not wish to imply that I could not find such in cities and towns all over the world. Such people are to be found everywhere, but somehow there seemed so much larger a percentage of them among the folks whom we visited. Their feet were planted on the solid earth. They knew the meaning of work without respect to hours or season. ("Rise to the Stature of the Divine within You," *Ensign*, November 1989, pp. 94–95.)

There is no substitute for virtue. Keep your thoughts virtuous. Rise above the filth that's all around you in this world and stand tall in strength and virtue. You can do this and you will be happier for it for as long as you live. God bless you in cherishing, developing, and holding on to this great gift, the quality of personal virtue. (Utah Salt Lake City Missionary Meeting, December 18, 1995.)

Be clean. Be clean in your thoughts. It is not easy in the environment in which you live. But if you work at it, you can do it. You can shut out those influences which destroy your soul, your spirituality, and can destroy your very life. The sleaze, the filth, the terrible pornography that is sweeping over the earth like a flood—stay away from it. Do not rent videos of a sleazy, filthy nature and sit around and look at them. They will destroy you. Do not go to shows which will tear down your principles. Do not read literature which will destroy your high ideals. You are a son or daughter of God, and He expects marvelous things of you. Do not take the name of the Lord in vain. The Lord said, when He delivered the Ten Commandments to Moses: "Thou shalt not take the name of the Lord thy God in vain; for the Lord will not hold him guiltless that taketh his name in vain" (Ex. 20:7). . . . It is so common all around us. You do not have to do it. God has forbidden it. That is a commandment and it should have meaning for every one of us, my dear friends. Be clean from the stain of the world—the immorality which is so much around us, the filthy talk that comes of it—stay away from it. You may have to hear it once in a while, but you never have to repeat it. "Be ye clean, that bear the vessels of the Lord" (Isa. 52:11). You Aaronic Priesthood boys, you that bear the vessels of the Lord, be clean. Be clean in your dress. Look clean. I do not care whether it is green or white or purple, but let it be clean. Your faces, your hair—you are Latter-day Saints and you reflect this Church in all that you think and say and do, my dear young friends. Be clean. (Eugene Oregon Regional Conference, September 15, 1996.)

Be clean. You know what that means. Clean from the stains of the world. Clean from the world's evil things. Terrible language is used in high schools. You do not have to be a part of it. Don't you use terrible language. Don't do it. It will not do you a bit of good. Sleazy stuff will not help you. Be clean from the stain of the world and you will be blessed and magnified and helped in a wonderful way. (Tucson Arizona Youth Meeting, December 14, 1996.)

WAR

See also Peace

I make no defense of the [Vietnam] war from this pulpit. There is no simple answer. The problems are complex almost beyond comprehension. I seek only to call your attention to that silver thread, small but radiant with hope, shining through the dark tapestry of war—namely, the establishment of a bridgehead, small and frail now; but which somehow, under the mysterious ways of God, will be strengthened, and from which someday shall spring forth a great work affecting for good the lives of large numbers of our Father's children who live in that part of the world. Of that I have a certain faith.

I have seen a prototype of what will happen as I have witnessed the development of this work in others of the ancient nations of Asia—in Korea, in Taiwan, in Okinawa, in the Philippines, and in Japan. . . .

This marvelous membership is the sweet fruit of seed once planted in dark years of war and in the troubled days immediately following, when good men of the priesthood, both civilian and military, through the example of their lives and the inspiration of their precepts, laid a foundation on which a great work has been established.

May I read from a letter just received from one of our brethren in Vietnam:

"The other day in Phu Bai I saw a young member of the Church reading the paperback of *A Marvelous Work and a Wonder* (so that he would be qualified to teach any who might ask about the Church). The book was filthy, his hands were filthy, but he didn't see the dirt because he was reading so intently."

As I pictured that young infantryman in dirty battle dress, just returned from a dangerous jungle patrol, studying the gospel, two other pictures came to mind—the first, of the home in which he grew up, where there is constant prayer for his safety; the second, of the day when the clouds of war shall have lifted, when peace shall be in the land, and when there shall be congregations of the Church built upon foundations laid by such of our brethren there now. ("A Silver Thread in the Dark Tapestry of War," *Improvement Era*, June 1968, p. 50.)

War I hate with all its mocking panoply. It is a grim and living testimony that Satan, the father of lies, the enemy of God, lives. War is earth's greatest cause of human misery. It is the destroyer of life, the promoter of hate, the waster of treasure. It is man's costliest folly, his most tragic misadventure. . . .

But since the day that Cain slew Abel, there has been contention among men. There have always been, and until the Prince of Peace comes to reign, there always will be tyrants and bullies, empire builders, slave seekers, and despots who would destroy every shred of human liberty if they were not opposed by force of arms. . . .

Can anyone doubt that Hitler would have quenched the candle of freedom in every nation of Europe had he not been stopped? . . . Can anyone in this land be less than grateful for those who have given their lives that liberty might live?

I have stood at the Unknown Soldier's tomb in Arlington where are remembered the dead of this great nation. I have stood at the Cenotaph in Whitehall in London where are remembered the dead of Britain. I have seen the flame that always burns beneath the Arch of Triumph in Paris, in remembrance of the men of France who died in the cause of freedom. And I have felt a deep and moving sense of gratitude to those there remembered. I have stood beside my own brother's grave in the U.S. military cemetery in Suresnes, France, and thanked the Lord for the liberty preserved by the sacrifices of those who gave their lives in this great cause. I have walked reverently on that quiet ground known as the Punch Bowl in Hawaii where lie the remains of thousands who made the ultimate sacrifice.

When we opened the work in the Philippines and had no place to meet for that sacred service, we asked the American embassy for the privilege of meeting in the cemetery at Fort McKinley, on the outskirts of Manila. To me that quiet, green, beautiful ground is hallowed. There, row on row in perfect symmetry, stand fifteen thousand marble crosses, each marking the final resting place of a man who gave his life. Encircling that sacred ground are two great marble colonnades, extending from either side of a beautiful chapel. On these colonnades are inscribed in stone the names of some thirty-five thousand who died in the battles of the Pacific but whose remains were never found, "Comrades in arms whose resting place is known only to God."

I walked one of those silent corridors and there saw the name of a boy who grew up not far from where I lived, who laughed and danced and played ball and on the Sabbath administered the sacrament in the meeting house. Then he went away to war and his plane was last seen spiraling in flames into a distant sea. His mother received a telegram. Her dark hair turned gray and then white as she mourned the loss of her son. In such places, hallowed by the blood of patriots, I have thought of a scene in Maxwell Anderson's play, *Valley Forge*. Soldiers of the American Revolution, cold and hungry and despairing, bury a dead comrade in the frozen earth and General Washington says: "This liberty will look easy by and by, when nobody dies to get it." ("Lest We Forget," *BYU Speeches of the Year*, November 10, 1970, pp. 3–4.)

I am reading a book of history, a long and detailed account of the trickeries practiced by the nations involved in the Second World War. It is entitled *Bodyguard of Lies*, taken from the words of Winston Churchill who said: "In war-time, truth is so precious that she should always be attended by a bodyguard of lies." (*The Second World War*, vol. 5, *Closing the Ring*, Boston, Houghton Mifflin, 1951, p. 383.) The book deals with the many deceptions practiced on each side of the conflict. While reading it, one is again led to the conclusion that war is the Devil's own game, and that among its most serious victims is truth.

Unfortunately, the easy use of falsehood and deception goes on long after the treaties of peace are signed, and some of those schooled in the art in times of war continue to ply their skills in days of peace. Then, like a disease that is endemic, the evil spreads and grows in virulence. ("'An Honest Man—God's Noblest Work,'" *Ensign*, May 1976, pp. 61–62.)

What about the arms race, and particularly the nuclear arms buildup?

Again, it is a sad commentary on our civilization that the peace of the world hangs on a balance of terror. No one understanding the facts can doubt that a rash decision could lead to the extermination of the race. It is to be hoped that representatives of the great powers will continue to talk and will seek with sincere and earnest desire to find ways to ameliorate the terrible threat which hangs over the world.

I am of the opinion that if a catastrophe is to be avoided, there must be widely cultivated a strong and compelling will for peace on the part of men and women in all nations. Let us, who are followers of the Prince of Peace, pray with great faith, in His name, that the world may be spared a consuming catastrophe that could come from some misadventure. ("Questions and Answers," *Ensign*, November 1985, p. 52.)

WELFARE

I hope that during [the past year] no one in the entire Church went hungry, or without clothing, or shelter. If any of our people have so suffered, then to that degree we have failed in our stewardship. (Phoenix Arizona North/West Regional Conference, January 13, 1991.)

The principles under which [Church welfare] operates are as old as the gospel. It is an expression of the Golden Rule: "Whatsoever ye would that men should do unto you, do ye even

so unto them." (Matt. 7:12.) ("The State of the Church," *Ensign,*
May 1991, p. 52.)

*Question: What can only the bishop do as far as welfare needs in
the ward, and what should the quorum do for all the other needs concerning welfare?*

Essentially the bishop has the basic responsibility, if there is
an urgent need, of seeing that that need is taken care of in sup-
plying goods and medical care, whatever the case might be. The
elders quorum presidency has the responsibility of bringing to
the bishop's attention that this may be necessary, and backing up
the assignment of that individual to help him to earn his own
way, so to speak, to make some effort for that which he receives,
and to look after the welfare of the entire membership of the
quorum, including those who are not active. (Heber City/
Springville Utah Regional Conference, priesthood leadership
session, May 13, 1995.)

We are carrying on a great welfare/humanitarian service.
Our welfare program, as we know it today, was begun during
the Great Depression, and puts tremendous emphasis on self-
reliance. We try to teach our people to be self-reliant and, when
they can't take care of their own needs, to enlist the help of their
families. And when those needs cannot be met by the families,
then the Church moves in to help them. We have a great program that involves farm properties, ranching properties, field
properties where people can work and grow that which they eat.
We have flour mills, we have grain storage, we have meat processing plants, we have all of these things. We operate 99 storehouses, more than 100 employment centers, 46 thrift stores. In
1994, members donated the equivalent of over 150,000 days of
labor in such facilities to help those who are in distress and in
need. During the past ten years the Church has provided disaster
relief and self-reliance development in 109 countries. The value
has exceeded $30 million per year in humanitarian gifts to those
not of our faith in many parts of the world. There are, on an average, 400 humanitarian projects each year. (Edelman Public
Relations Luncheon, Harvard Club, New York, November 13,
1995.)

Question: You have your own welfare program?

President Hinckley: We have our own welfare program which is maintained as an effort to help people to help themselves. And through that welfare program we reach out to people in distress in many parts of the world. We have given millions, and millions, and millions of dollars worth of aid to people in distressed circumstances in Asia, in Africa, in Central and South America—

Question: With no objection from the membership?

President Hinckley: With no objection. With encouragement. (Interview with Mike Wallace of *60 Minutes*, December 18, 1995.)

We do have a great welfare program. We try to take care of the needs of our own people. So, where we are strongly established—in the United States, for instance—we have welfare farms that produce agricultural products. We have facilities to can and store those products. We have facilities for packaging, processing, and distribution. It's all part of an obligation we feel to take care of our own, while at the same time reaching out in a spirit of humanitarianism to people in distress, wherever they may be. (Interview with Dulcie Byby of *Manila Chronicle*, May 30, 1996.)

We believe in being benevolent, in reaching out to help others. We pay our fast offerings. That little practice which came of revelation if observed by all the people of the world would make government welfare programs unnecessary. . . . The German government, the English government, the United States government spend billions on taking care of those in need. It is a worthy undertaking. But how much easier, how much simpler, how much better if people followed the plan of the Lord. (Berlin Germany Regional Conference, June 16, 1996.)

The Congress and the President have recently enacted and signed new legislation concerning welfare. Hopefully, substantial good will come of it. But merely a new set of rules to deal with an old problem is unlikely to produce a cure. There must be a change of attitude, the taking on of a sense of accountability for one's actions. (Provo City Community Centennial Service, August 4, 1996.)

Catastrophes come to people sometimes when least expected—unemployment, sickness, things of that kind. The individual, as we teach, ought to do for himself all that he can. When he has exhausted his resources, he ought to turn to his family to assist him. When the family can't do it, the Church takes over. And when the Church takes over, our great desire is to first take care of his immediate needs and then to help him for so long as he needs to be helped, but in that process to assist him in training, in securing employment, in finding some way of getting on his feet again. That's the whole objective of this great welfare program. ("'This Thing Was Not Done in a Corner,'" *Ensign*, November 1996, p. 50.)

WIDOWS/WIDOWERS

See also Singles

For many of you, this is a great season for enjoying many of the finer elements of life. I have a friend who was left a widower. He was retired, left without the challenge of a daily job. He had never played the piano, but he began taking lessons. To master that instrument became an obsession that replaced his sorrow. He found happiness, usefulness, and companionship in his piano. It changed his outlook on life; it made him more cheerful and positive. (Single Adult Fireside Satellite Broadcast, February 26, 1989.)

Now to those of you who have lost a companion in death, our hearts go out to you with love and understanding. As a man once observed, "There exists no cure for a heart wounded with the sword of separation" (Hito Padesa, *Elbert Hubbard's Scrapbook*, p. 21).

With many of you there is the gnawing pain of bereavement and fear. To you the Lord has said, "Blessed are they that mourn: for they shall be comforted" (Matt. 5:4).

We know there are many days of loneliness and nights of longing. But there is also that which comes from Him who said, "I, even I, am he that comforteth you" (Isa. 51:12).

The Lord is your strength. He is available to you, and when invited, by His Spirit He will come to you.

You too have great talents to enrich the lives of others. You will find comfort and strength as you lose yourself in their service. Your own troubles will be forgotten as you help others with theirs. Your burdens will become lighter as you lift the burdens of the downtrodden and the oppressed. (Single Adult Fireside Satellite Broadcast, February 26, 1989.)

To you older women and men, who are widows and widowers, how precious you are. You have lived long and had much of experience. You have tasted the bitter and the sweet. You have known much of pain and sorrow and loneliness and fear. But you also carry in your hearts a sweet and sublime assurance that God our Father will not fail us in our hour of need. May the years that lie ahead be kind to you. May heaven smile upon you. May you draw comfort and strength from your memories, and may you, with your mature kindness and love, reach out to help those in distress wherever you find them. (Salt Lake Valley Single Adult Fireside, September 22, 1996.)

I wish to say a word to you older women, many of whom are widows. You are a great treasure. You have passed through the storms of life. You have weathered the challenges now facing your younger sisters. You are mature in wisdom, in understanding, in compassion, in love and service.

There is a certain beauty that shines through your countenance. It is the beauty that comes of peace. There may still be struggle, but there is mature wisdom to meet it. There are health problems, but there is a certain composure concerning them. The bad memories of the past have largely been forgotten, while the good memories return and bring sweet and satisfying enrichment to life.

You have learned to love the scriptures, and you read them. Your prayers for the most part are prayers of thanksgiving. Your greetings are words of kindness. Your friendship is a sturdy staff on which others may lean. ("Women of the Church," *Ensign*, November 1996, pp. 69–70.)

WOMEN

See also Motherhood

I am satisfied that [our Father in Heaven] loves his daughters as much as he loves his sons. President Harold B. Lee once remarked that priesthood is the power by which God works through us as men. I should like to add that motherhood is the means by which God carries forward his grand design of continuity of the race. Both priesthood and motherhood are essentials of the plan of the Lord.

Each complements the other. Each is needed by the other. God has created us male and female, each unique in his or her individual capacities and potential. The woman is the bearer and the nurturer of children. The man is the provider and protector. No legislation can alter the sexes. Legislation should provide equality of opportunity, equality of compensation, equality of political privilege. But any legislation which is designed to create neuter gender of that which God created male and female will bring more problems than benefits. Of that I am convinced.

I wish with all my heart we would spend less of our time talking about rights and more talking about responsibilities. God has given the women of this church a work to do in building his kingdom. That concerns all aspects of our great triad of responsibility—which is, first, to teach the gospel to the world; second, to strengthen the faith and build the happiness of the membership of the Church; and, third, to carry forward the great work of salvation for the dead.

This is a season for strength. I conclude with these stirring words of Moroni, written as he sealed his record to come forth in the dispensation of the fulness of times:

"Awake, and arise from the dust, O Jerusalem; yea, and put on thy beautiful garments, O daughter of Zion; and strengthen thy stakes and enlarge thy borders forever, that thou mayest no more be confounded, that the covenants of the Eternal Father which he hath made unto thee, O house of Israel, may be fulfilled.

"Yea, come unto Christ, and be perfected in him, and deny yourselves of all ungodliness." (Moro. 10:31–32.)

Put on thy beautiful garments, O daughters of Zion. Live up to the great and magnificent inheritance which the Lord God, your Father in Heaven, has provided for you. Rise above the dust of the world. Know that you are daughters of God, children with a divine birthright. Walk in the sun with your heads high, knowing that you are loved and honored, that you are a part of his kingdom, and that there is for you a great work to be done which cannot be left to others. ("Live Up to Your Inheritance," *Ensign,* November 1983, pp. 83–84.)

Of all the creations of the Almighty, there is none more beautiful, none more inspiring than a lovely daughter of God who walks in virtue, with an understanding of why she should do so, who honors and respects her body as a thing sacred and divine, who cultivates her mind and constantly enlarges the horizon of her understanding, who nurtures her spirit with everlasting truth. God will hold us accountable if we neglect His daughters. ("Our Responsibility to Our Young Women," *Ensign,* September 1988, p. 11.)

In that magnificent vision given Moses wherein the Lord spoke of His creations, of worlds made without number, and of the majesty and wonder of His work, He declared, "Behold, this is my work and my glory—to bring to pass the immortality and eternal life of man" (Moses 1:39).

The word *man* as used here is generic. It includes man and woman, for, as Paul said, "Neither is the man without the woman, neither the woman without the man, in the Lord" (1 Cor. 11:11).

I am confident that the daughters of God are as precious to Him as are His sons. They are as important a part of His eternal plan. It is obvious that there could be no continuity of the race without woman. ("Youth Is the Season," *New Era,* September 1988, p. 46.)

Only as I have grown older have I come to realize the great wealth of the home in which I was nurtured, a wealth measured not in dollars but in qualities more precious than dollars. My mother was an educator, the first Gregg shorthand teacher in Utah, a teacher of English. My father was not wealthy, but he was able to provide the substance of the modest living we enjoyed. When we children came along Mother left her profession and remained at home. There was a sense of security, an anchor of love that was felt and much appreciated, although seldom commented on.

My mother died while I was a student in this university. It was a dark and somber day for all of us of that family. But there was a residual that remained with us that gave us strength and guidance and discipline. From her I learned so many things, including respect for womanhood, together with an appreciation for the tremendous strength which she carried within her, including a bright and happy zest for life and a love for people, and incidentally, a tremendously beneficial love for literature, music, and art. From my family life I came to believe, as I still believe, that women have special attributes and qualities. I have come to believe that yours is a godly inheritance. (Belle S. Spafford Conference on Women, February 23, 1990.)

A letter came to the office addressed to President Benson. I wish to read a portion of it, and then perhaps comment on it. I will not use the writer's name. She may be listening somewhere, and I would not wish to embarrass her in any way. I will call her Virginia. With that change, I read a part of her letter:

"Dear President Benson,

"My name is Virginia. I am fourteen years old, and a matter has been on my mind a lot lately. In the scriptures I could not seem to find anywhere whether women may enter into the celestial kingdom if they are worthy. Also, when someone such as Joseph Smith had a vision of the celestial kingdom, he only seemed to see men there. I have prayed about it, but I felt that I needed your words. . . . In the scriptures, they talk about a woman being blessed if she is righteous, but not about celestial glory. This truly bothers me. If we are all Heavenly Father's children, then why do the scriptures say that men are to rule over women? And why in the scriptures was Eve created from Adam? I may be foolish, but I honestly do not understand. I love the gospel, and I am learning of its truth. I have a testimony, and I know that I have a divine purpose in life. But I suppose what I am asking, is—are men more important than women? And can women go to the celestial kingdom also? . . .

"I am still young and learning, and I need help in this matter. Thank you so much.

"Lovingly, Virginia."

Because President Benson is unable to speak to us, I will try to respond to your letter and in the process I speak to all. . . . Your letter was acknowledged by the secretary to the First Presidency. But I feel that it is so sincere in tone that it deserves a more complete answer. And perhaps the questions you ask are on the minds of many women—young women of your age, women of your mother's age, and women of your grandmother's age, be they single, married, or whatever their circumstances.

First, you ask whether women may enter into the celestial kingdom. Of course they may. They are as eligible to enter the celestial kingdom as are men, worthiness being the determining factor for both.

On February 16, 1832, Joseph Smith and Sidney Rigdon were given a remarkable vision. The Lord spoke with words both wonderful and challenging. Listen to Him:

"For thus saith the Lord—I, the Lord, am merciful and gracious unto those who fear me, and delight to honor those who serve me in righteousness and in truth unto the end.

"Great shall be their reward and eternal shall be their glory." (D&C 76:5–6.)

I am satisfied that He speaks here of His daughters as well as His sons. Infinite shall be the reward of each, and everlasting shall be his or her glory.

In this same revelation, Joseph Smith and Sidney Rigdon bear eloquent testimony concerning the Savior of the world, the Son of God. Listen to this:

"And now, after the many testimonies which have been given of him, this is the testimony, last of all, which we give of him: That he lives!

"For we saw him, even on the right hand of God; and we heard the voice bearing record that he is the Only Begotten of the Father—

"That by him, and through him, and of him, the worlds are and were created, and the inhabitants thereof are begotten *sons and daughters* unto God." (D&C 76:22–24; italics added.)

Note that in this tremendous declaration, both sons and daughters are mentioned.

While it is true that in the verses which follow, *man* is spoken of, I am confident that the word is used in a generic sense to include both men and women.

The revelation then speaks of those who receive the testimony of Jesus, who were baptized after the manner of His burial, and who keep the commandments, and promises that they "shall dwell in the presence of God and his Christ forever and ever." (D&C 76:62.)

"These are they whose bodies are celestial, whose glory is that of the sun, even the glory of God, the highest of all, whose glory the sun of the firmament is written of as being typical." (D&C 76:70.)

Are women included in those who shall partake of such glory? Most assuredly. As a matter of fact, in attaining the highest degree of glory in the celestial kingdom, the man cannot enter without the woman, neither can the woman enter without the man. The two are inseparable as husband and wife in eligibility for that highest degree of glory. If she lives worthy of it, hers will be a glory as celestial and eternal as his. Never doubt it, Virginia. Only live to be worthy of that glory which is available to you as well as to your brothers. . . .

Beyond the wonderful and descriptive words found in sections 76 and 137, we know relatively little concerning the celestial kingdom and those who will be there. At least some of the rules of eligibility for acceptance into that kingdom are clearly set forth, but other than that, we are given little understanding. However, I repeat that I am confident that the daughters of God will be as eligible as will be the sons of God. ("Daughters of God," *Ensign*, November 1991, pp. 97–98.)

In the sequence of events as set forth in the scripture, God first created the earth, "and the earth was without form, and void." (Genesis 1:2.) He then separated the light from the darkness, and the waters from the land. Then came the creation of vegetation of all kinds, giving the beauty of trees and grass, flowers and shrubs. Then followed the creation of animal life in the sea and upon the land.

Having looked over all of this, He declared it to be good. He then created man in His own likeness and image. Then as His final creation, the crowning of His glorious work, He created woman. I like to regard Eve as His masterpiece after all that had gone before, the final work before He rested from His labors.

I do not regard her as being in second place to Adam. She was placed at his side as an helpmeet. They were together in the Garden, they were expelled together, and they labored together in the world into which they were driven. ("Daughters of God," *Ensign*, November 1991, pp. 98–99.)

You ask whether men are more important than women. I am going to turn that question back to you. Would any of us be here, either men or women, without the other? The scripture states that God created man in His own image, male and female created He them. He commanded them together to multiply and replenish the earth. Each is a creation of the Almighty, mutually dependent and equally necessary for the continuation of the race. Every new generation in the history of mankind is a testimony of the necessity for both man and woman. ("Daughters of God," *Ensign*, November 1991, p. 99.)

May I express my gratitude to you faithful Latter-day Saint women, now numbered in the millions and found across the earth. Great is your power for good. Marvelous are your talents and devotion. Tremendous is your faith and your love for the Lord, for His work, and for His sons and daughters. Continue to live the gospel. Magnify it before all of your associates. Your good works will carry more weight than any words you might speak. Walk in virtue and truth, with faith and faithfulness. You are part of an eternal plan, a plan designed by God our Eternal

Father. Each day is a part of that eternity. ("Daughters of God," *Ensign*, November 1991, p. 100.)

I feel to invite women everywhere to rise to the great potential within you. I do not ask that you reach beyond your capacity. I hope you will not nag yourselves with thoughts of failure. I hope you will not try to set goals far beyond your capacity to achieve. I hope you will simply do what you can do in the best way you know. If you do so, you will witness miracles come to pass. (*Motherhood: A Heritage of Faith*, booklet [Salt Lake City: Deseret Book, 1995], p. 9.)

What a mighty congregation of women you are. . . . You live in many lands and you speak with a variety of tongues. But you understand with a single heart. Each of you is a daughter of God. Reflect on all the wondrous meaning of that one paramount fact.

He who is our Eternal Father has blessed you with miraculous powers of mind and body. He never intended that you should be less than the crowning glory of His creations.

I remind you of words spoken by the Prophet Joseph to the women of the Relief Society in April of 1842. Said he: "If you live up to your privilege, the angels cannot be restrain'd from being your associates" (Relief Society Minutebook, 28 April 1842, LDS Church Archives). What marvelous potential lies within you. ("Stand Strong against the Wiles of the World," *Ensign*, November 1995, p. 98.)

I believe this is the best season for women in all the history of the world. In opportunities for education, for the training of your hands and minds, there has never before been a time when doors were so widely opened to you as they are today.

But neither has there been a time, at least in recent history, when you have been confronted with more challenging problems. I need not remind you that the world we are in is a world of turmoil, of shifting values. Shrill voices call out for one thing or another in betrayal of time-tested standards of behavior. The moral moorings of our society have been badly shaken. . . . I cannot say enough of appreciation for your determination to live by the standards of the Church, to walk with the strength of virtue, to keep your minds above the slough of filth which seems to be moving like a flood across the world. Thank you for knowing there is a better way. Thank you for the will to say no. Thank you for the strength to deny temptation and look beyond and above to the shining light of your eternal potential. ("Stand Strong against the Wiles of the World," *Ensign*, November 1995, p. 99.)

Let me say to you sisters that you do not hold a second place in our Father's plan for the eternal happiness and well-being of His children. You are an absolutely essential part of that plan. . . .

Each of you is a daughter of God, endowed with a divine birthright. You need no defense of that position. ("Women of the Church," *Ensign*, November 1996, p. 67.)

You sisters are the real builders of the nation wherever you live, for you have created homes of strength and peace and security. These become the very sinew of any nation. ("Women of the Church," *Ensign*, November 1996, p. 68.)

What a resource are the women of The Church of Jesus Christ of Latter-day Saints. You love this Church, you accept its doctrine, you honor your place in its organization, you bring luster and strength and beauty to its congregations. How thankful we are to you. How much you are loved, respected, and honored. . . .

You bring a measure of wholeness to us. You have great strength. With dignity and tremendous ability, you carry forward the remarkable programs of the Relief Society, the Young Women, and the Primary. You teach Sunday School. We walk at your side as your companions and your brethren with respect and love, with honor and great admiration. It was the Lord who designated that men in His Church should hold the priesthood. It was He who has given you your capabilities to round out this great and marvelous organization, which is the Church and kingdom of God. I bear testimony before the entire world of your worth, of your grace and goodness, of your remarkable abilities and tremendous contributions. ("Women of the Church," *Ensign*, November 1996, p. 70.)

As I read the history of our people I am impressed that the men are named and remembered and honored. Too little honor is given the women.

Wallace Stegner was not a member of this Church. He was a student at the University of Utah when I was. He went on to become professor of creative writing at Stanford University and won a Pulitzer Award. He wrote considerably about our people. He wrote the story of the Mormon Trail. In his opening chapter he says this: "I shall try to present [the Mormons] in their terms and judge them in mine. That I do not accept the faith that possessed them does not mean I doubt their frequent devotion and heroism in its service, especially their women. Their women were incredible." (*The Gathering of Zion,* page 13.)

I believe that any honest and fair student of our history would come to the same conclusion. How absolutely magnificent were the women in the pioneer era of this Church. I begin, if you please, with Emma Smith, whom the Lord called "an elect lady" (D&C 25:3). Some few years ago I walked slowly about the Isaac Hale property in Pennsylvania. I thought of Emma's marriage, displeasing to her father. I looked at the burial place of her first child. I thought of her trying to get food on the table while Joseph and Oliver struggled with the translation of the Book of Mormon.

Wherever Joseph went, she went also. She did not have the same witness of this work that he had. But she had to carry much of the burden of his calling. She moved from one place to another, unable to establish a home until they settled in Nauvoo, and there her home was constantly filled with guests. When Joseph and Hyrum were killed in 1844, she was left alone with her children in a very uncertain situation. . . .

Hyrum's widow, Mary Fielding Smith . . . endured the long march from Nauvoo to the Missouri River. She was a part of the great migration which left Winter Quarters and traveled to the valley of the Great Salt Lake. Her little son Joseph was with her, and he drove the oxen during much of that long journey. She was a widow who walked in faith.

Oh, the faith of those pioneer women! They bore children, they cooked, they sewed, they laundered, they scrubbed by hand, they mended, they made what they wore and what their children wore. They nursed the sick, they dressed the dead. They fed the cattle, the chickens, the pigs. They worked from sunup to sundown. They even worked beside their husbands in building log houses wherever they stopped, in plowing the unbroken ground, in sowing seed and reaping a harvest. They brought culture and beauty into their homes. . . .

In Durban, South Africa, is a statue of a woman in heroic size. She represents the wives and mothers of the trekkers who made the long pilgrimage in the early days of that nation.

There is no man memorialized in that place, but only a noble and great woman. As I looked upon it I said to myself, "How wonderful that there should be memorialized this woman representative of her sisterhood, standing resolute and strong after having weathered every kind of hardship."

I wish we had a similar statue on Temple Square or some such place to memorialize the great, the noble, the quiet, unsung heroines who lived and died in that great odyssey of our people from New York to Ohio, from Ohio to Missouri, from Missouri to Illinois, from Illinois to Winter Quarters, and from Winter Quarters to this valley.

They of that generation are now gone. At least two other generations have come, and for the most part they have gone. But thumbing back through the pages of our history one cannot avoid exclaiming with Wallace Stegner, "Their women were incredible." (BYU Women's Conference Address, May 1, 1997.)

WORD OF WISDOM

One appreciates the incomparable wisdom of the Lord who in 1833 in a rural town on the frontier of America spoke these simple and encompassing words: " . . . tobacco . . . is not good for man, . . ." (D&C 89:8.)

He did not say that one would get lung cancer, develop heart or respiratory problems if he smoked. He did not produce mountainous statistics or recite case histories. He simply declared that " . . . tobacco . . . is not good for man, . . ."

That declaration was given as "a principle with promise," (V. 3.)

It was given as a warning and a forewarning, "in consequence of evils and designs which do and will exist in the hearts of conspiring men in the last days, . . ." (V. 4.) How aptly descriptive these words are in light of what we today observe. . . .

Can there be any doubt that it is a Word of Wisdom when great forces, with millions of dollars at their command and some of the cleverest minds in the art of advertising, promote that which sober men of science also now say "is not good for man"?

One cannot read the testimony without recognizing that true freedom lies in obedience to the counsels of God. . . .

The gospel is not a philosophy of repression, as so many regard it. It is a plan of freedom that gives discipline to appetite and direction to behavior. ("A Principle with Promise," *Improvement Era,* June 1965, p. 521.)

Be smart. Do not be so shortsighted as to indulge in the use of alcohol, tobacco, and drugs. It simply is not smart to do so. It is stupid, if you will pardon that harsh word, to use cocaine, marijuana, or any of the other drugs that rob you of control of your mind. After every drug-induced "high," there is a reactionary "low." Why spend money on that which can only harm you? Why become enslaved to a habit that can only hinder and short-circuit your future?

Beer and other forms of alcohol will do you no good. Their use will be expensive, will dull your conscience, and could lead to the disease called alcoholism, which is humiliating, dangerous, and even deadly. Tobacco will shorten your life. Studies show that it will enslave you, weaken your lungs, and statistically that it will shorten your life seven minutes for each cigarette smoked.

Be smart. Take the Lord at his word. His is the wonderful promise that those Saints who follow his counsel in these matters "shall find wisdom and great treasures of knowledge, even hidden treasures;

"And shall run and not be weary, and shall walk and not faint." (D&C 89:19–20.) ("Four B's for Boys," *Ensign,* November 1981, pp. 40–41.)

We receive numerous letters inquiring whether this item or that item is proscribed by the Word of Wisdom. If we will avoid those things which are definitely and specifically defined, and beyond this observe the spirit of that great revelation, it will not involve a burden. It will, rather, bring a blessing. Do not forget: it is the Lord who has made the promise. ("'Let Us Move This Work Forward,'" *Ensign*, November 1985, p. 85.)

The Word of Wisdom . . . is a divine code of health received through revelation in 1833. It proscribes alcohol and tobacco, tea and coffee, and emphasizes the use of fruit and grains. This Word of Wisdom came to us from the Father of us all, the God of heaven, for our blessing and the blessing of all who would observe it.

I regret that we as a people do not observe it more faithfully. But remarkable have been the blessings that have come of its observance to the degree that we have observed it. Newspapers across the nation have recently run reports on a significant California study. It was conducted by Dr. James Enstrom of the UCLA School of Public Medicine. It included a substantial number of active members of the Church—5,231 high priests and 4,613 of their wives. I quote now from a newspaper story:

"Compared to the other groups, the study found the Mormons had an average of 53 percent fewer fatal cancers . . . 48 percent fewer deaths from heart disease and 53 percent fewer fatal illnesses of all kinds." (*Salt Lake Tribune*, 12 Sep. 1990.)

Dr. Enstrom, speaking of the eight-year study, said that he "can predict that a very active, healthy-conscious 25-year-old *Mormon* male will live 11 years longer than the average American male of the same age." (Ibid., italics added.) ("*Mormon* Should Mean 'More Good,'" *Ensign*, November 1990, p. 53.)

I thank the Lord for a testimony of the Word of Wisdom. I wish we lived it more fully. But even though we do not, the Lord pours out His blessings upon those who try. . . . To me it is marvelous that beyond the promises of a physical nature is the promise of hidden treasures of knowledge concerning things divine and eternal. ("My Testimony," *Ensign*, November 1993, p. 53.)

I remember a report from the American Medical Association to the effect that heavy smokers die seven years before they would if they did not smoke. Seven years of life. That's as long as many persons spend in high school and college. Seven years—time enough to become a doctor, an architect, an engineer, a lawyer. Seven years in which to enjoy the sunrise and the sunset, the hills and the valleys, the lakes and the seas, the love of our children, the friendship of wonderful people we may know. What a statistical promise confirming the word of the Lord that the destroying angel shall pass by those who walk in obedience and will not slay them. (See v. 21.)

Then there is that other promise—that they shall have "great treasures of knowledge, even hidden treasures." (V. 19.) I think of an experience once told me by one of our Sunday School teachers. One Sunday while they were discussing the Word of Wisdom, someone asked what was meant by hidden treasures of knowledge.

The teacher stuttered and stammered and was saved by the bell. He told the class that they would consider the matter the following Sunday.

During the week he pondered the question but felt that he could not come up with an answer. Near the end of the week, he had lunch with a colleague. The man told him that at one time while traveling, he found himself passing a Mormon church building. He concluded to go in to see how the Mormons worshipped.

The man reported that it was a peculiar kind of service—that one after another stood up in the congregation, told of their experiences, expressed their gratitude, and then almost without exception testified that they knew that God lives, that Jesus Christ is His Son, our living Redeemer. The man drove up the highway that afternoon, saying to himself, *Surely these people have knowledge hidden from the world.*

Ponder that thought for a moment.

The Lord has given us a key to health and happiness—and has given it with a promise. It is a pillar of eternal wisdom. It is better to obey than to rationalize and sacrifice. ("Pillars of Truth," *Ensign,* January 1994, p. 6.)

Some people argue over whether it [the Word of Wisdom] is a commandment. I do not need to argue. As far as I am concerned, whether it is a commandment or counsel, that which the Lord counsels becomes a commandment to Gordon B. Hinckley. I hope it does to you. (Tacoma Washington Regional Conference, August 20, 1995.)

You cannot tamper with illegal drugs. We cannot afford to tamper with those things. Our bodies are the temples of our spirits. They are sacred. These are the creation of the Almighty. Man was formed in the image of God. As His son, as His daughter, we ought to take care of our bodies. Let us work with our children, teach our people, to not become shackled and enslaved by drugs which take possession until the individual no longer has power over himself and cannot control his own destiny. They are wrong, they are not good. (Charlotte North Carolina Regional Conference, priesthood leadership session, February 24, 1996.)

I feel so grateful for the Word of Wisdom. . . . What a remarkable thing it is. The Lord used those words "evil and conspiring men." Very interesting words, really. "Evil and conspiring men in the last days." Read the paper, listen to the radio, watch the television news, and you will see almost, not quite but almost, those words in the things that are taking place these very days in which we live. How thankful I am for the Word of Wisdom which is not only a law unto this Church but carries with it a great and marvelous promise that the destroying angel shall pass us by as the children of Israel and not slay us, and that we shall have great treasures of knowledge, even hidden treasures. That does not mean that we are going to be the smartest, wisest people on the earth in terms of the law or architecture or education or business or whatever. It means knowledge of the things of God which will come by the power of the Holy Spirit, the Holy Ghost. That is the promise of the Almighty. How thankful I am. (Potomac Virginia Regional Conference, April 27, 1997.)

WORK

See also Self-Discipline; Self-Reliance; Thrift

There is no substitute for [work]. Jehovah established the law when He declared, "In the sweat of thy face shalt thou eat bread." (Genesis 3:19.) . . .

Some years ago a Boeing 707 jet took off from Idlewild airport. It rose into the sky and then suddenly plunged into the Jamaica mud taking eighty-nine people to their deaths. The months of investigation that followed brought the conclusion that a workman in a New Jersey subcontractor's plant had carelessly handled a wire in putting together a servo mechanism that was assembled into the plane in the Boeing plant in Seattle. This all-important little wire, smaller than a pencil, connected with evident neglect, had caused a short circuit, wresting the plane from the control of the pilot and plunging it into the mud, with a fearsome loss of life and property.

Shoddy workmanship, lack of pride in labor, the repeated coffee breaks that rob employers of the time of those they hire are all characteristic of a flagrant dishonesty and a warped sense of obligation that afflicts so many of our people.

I should like to say to you tonight that one of the greatest values . . . is the virtue of honest work. Knowledge without labor is profitless. Knowledge with labor is genius. ("What Shall You Teach?" Address to BYU Faculty and Staff, September 17, 1963.)

Without labor there is neither wealth, nor comfort, nor progress. It was said of old, " . . . the drunkard and the glutton shall come to poverty: and drowsiness shall clothe a man with rags." (Prov. 23:21.)

We are commemorating this year the hundredth anniversary of the completion of this great Tabernacle in which we meet today. Not long before his death the late President John F. Kennedy spoke from this podium, as had many of his predecessors. At the conclusion of his address, the Tabernacle Choir sang with a majesty it has never excelled, "Mine eyes have seen the glory of the coming of the Lord. . . . His truth is marching on."

As the sound rolled through this historic house, touching the emotions of everyone here assembled, I felt a catch in my throat and a tingle in my spine, not alone for the presence in this building of the chief executive of the nation, not alone for the magnificent music of this choir, but more especially for the quiet men of faith and vision who a century ago laid the stone of the great buttresses which form the walls that encircle us and support the roof that shelters us. They were people possessed of a dream of destiny. This is their handiwork, prayerfully wrought. Notwithstanding the fact that they were largely isolated in this desert land, notwithstanding the fact that they erected this before ever the railroad came to this part of this country, they built with an excellence unsurpassed in our time. They possessed the skill, they nurtured the dream, and they labored with devotion to make this magnificent structure a reality. ("A Challenge from Vietnam," *Improvement Era*, June 1967, p. 53.)

I believe in the gospel of work. There is no substitute under the heavens for productive labor. It is the process by which dreams become reality. It is the process by which idle visions become dynamic achievements. We are all inherently lazy. We would rather play than work. We would rather loaf than work. A little play and a little loafing are good—that is one of the reasons you are here. But it is work that spells the difference in the life of a man or woman. It is stretching our minds and utilizing the skills of our hands that lifts us from the stagnation of mediocrity. ("Articles of Belief," Bonneville International Corporation Management Seminar, February 10, 1991.)

My mother was a gifted and wonderful woman. She was an educator; but when she married, she left her employment to become a housewife and mother. In our minds she was a great success.

We lived in what I thought was a large home in the First Ward. It had four rooms on the main floor—a kitchen, a dining room, a parlor, and a library. There were four bedrooms upstairs. The house stood on the corner on a large lot. There was a big lawn with many trees that shed millions of leaves, and there was an immense amount of work to be done constantly.

In my early childhood we had a stove in the kitchen and a stove in the dining room. A furnace was later installed, and what a wonderful thing that was. But it had a voracious appetite for coal, and there was no automatic stoker. The coal had to be shoveled into the furnace and carefully banked each night.

I learned a great lesson from that monster of a furnace: if you wanted to keep warm, you had to work the shovel.

My father had an idea that his boys ought to learn to work in the summer as well as in the winter, and so he bought a five-acre farm, which eventually grew to include more than thirty acres. We lived there in the summer and returned to the city when school started. ("Some Lessons I Learned as a Boy," *Ensign,* May 1993, p. 52.)

My father had a horse and buggy when I was a boy. Then one summer day in 1916, a wonderful thing happened. It was an unforgettable thing. When he came home that evening he arrived in a shining black brand-new Model T Ford. It was a wonderful machine, but by today's standards it was a crude and temperamental sort of thing. For instance, it did not have a self-starter. It had to be cranked. You learned something very quickly about cranking that car. You retarded the spark, or the crank would kick back and break your hand. When it rained, the coils would get wet, and then it would not start at all. From that car I learned a few simple things about making preparation to save trouble. A little canvas over the cowl would keep the coils dry. A little care in retarding the spark would make it possible to crank without breaking your hand.

But the most interesting thing was the lights. The car had no storage battery. The only electricity came from what was called a magneto. The output of the magneto was determined by the speed of the engine. If the engine was running fast, the lights were bright. If the engine slowed, the lights became a sickly yellow. I learned that if you wanted to see ahead as you were going down the road, you had to keep the engine running at a fast clip.

So, just as I'd discovered, it is with our lives. Industry, enthusiasm, and hard work lead to enlightened progress. You have to stay on your feet and keep moving if you are going to have light in your life. ("Some Lessons I Learned as a Boy," *Ensign*, May 1993, pp. 53–54.)

Work together. I don't know how many generations or centuries ago, someone first said, "An idle mind is the devil's workshop." Children need to work with their parents—to wash dishes with them, to mop floors with them, to mow lawns, to prune trees and shrubbery, to paint and fix up and clean up and do a hundred other things where they will learn that labor is the price of cleanliness and progress and prosperity. There are too many hundreds of thousands of youth in this land who are growing up with the idea that the way to get something is to steal it. Graffiti would soon disappear if those who spray it on had to clean it off.

I still remember an experience during my first year in high school. With some other boys I was eating lunch. I peeled a banana and threw the peeling on the ground. Just at that moment the principal walked by. He asked me to pick up the banana peeling. I say he "asked." There was a certain steely firmness in his tone. I got off the bench on which I was sitting and picked up the banana peeling and put it in the trash can. There was other litter around the can. He told me that while I was picking up my own trash, I could pick up the trash of others. I did it. I think I have never thrown another banana peeling on the ground. ("Saving the Nation by Changing Our Homes," BYU Management Society, Washington, D.C., March 5, 1994.)

Without hard work, nothing grows but weeds. There must be labor, incessant and constant, if there is to be a harvest. ("Farewell to a Prophet," *Ensign*, July 1994, p. 37.)

Work is the miracle by which talent is brought to the surface and dreams become reality. ("To a Man Who Has Done What This Church Expects of Each of Us," *BYU 1995–96 Speeches*, October 17, 1995, p. 55.)

WORLDLINESS

We see all around us a worldly creep that is destructive of faith. . . . I know that the temporal things of life are important. I know that the temporal affairs of the Church are important. I know that we as a people must live in the world. But I hope that we will not surrender ourselves to the world. Ours must be a warning voice. (General Authority Training Meeting, September 27, 1994.)

All of us live in the world. Of course we do. We cannot live a cloistered existence. But we can live in the world without partaking of the unseemly ways of the world.

The pull gets ever stronger. The adversary is clever and subtle. He speaks in a seductive voice of fascinating and attractive things. We cannot afford to let down our guard. . . . We need not run the wrong way. The right way is simple. It means following the program of the Church, bringing into our lives the principles of the gospel, and never losing sight of what is expected of us as sons of God with a great inheritance and a marvelous and eternal potential. ("Don't Drop the Ball," *Ensign,* November 1994, p. 48.)

I do not hesitate to say that if you pursue only your dream of recognition and monetary reward, and give no attention to these other items I will mention, you will not be successful in your living. ("A Three-Point Challenge," BYU Commencement Address, April 27, 1995.)

We have a different way of life. There is a difference. It is a way of life and it doesn't fit the mold that a lot of people have. So we are different and they use the word *weird*. . . . We live in the world, we are part of the world, but we don't need to take on all the ways of the world. That makes us appear different and I suppose weird. But we are not weird. (Interview with Bob Anderson of *60 Minutes,* December 6, 1995.)

"For the love of money is the root of all evil." [1 Timothy 6:10.] That's true. You get your mind on the things of the world and you lose the Spirit of the Lord in your work. It isn't money that He's talking about, it's the love of money, it's the covetousness, it's the greed, it's the desire to have more than you need which becomes the root of all evil. I hope you'll remember that all the days of your life. (Korea Seoul and Korea Seoul West Missionary Meeting, May 22, 1996.)

We live in a world of so much filth. It is everywhere. It is on the streets. It is on television. It is in books and magazines. It is everywhere. It is like a great flood, ugly and dirty and mean, engulfing the world. We have got to stand above it. (Berlin Germany Regional Conference, June 16, 1996.)

My message to the outside world would be that the world is slipping in its moral standards. That can only bring misery. The way to happiness lies in a return to strong family life and the observance of moral standards, the value of which has been proven through centuries of time. (Press Interview, *Berliner Zeitury*, June 16, 1996.)

There is so much of evil, enticing evil, in the world. Shun it, my brothers and sisters. Avoid it. It is as a dangerous disease. It is as a poison that will destroy you. Stay away from it. Stay completely away from it. (Manaus Brazil Fireside, November 16, 1996.)

YOUTH

To young people everywhere I should like to say that you need the Church, and the Church needs you. There is no better association than that with other young men and women of faith who recognize God as their Eternal Father and Jesus Christ as the living Savior of the world.

That association will give you strength. It will give you companionship. It will challenge your abilities. It will afford you opportunity for growth. In The Church of Jesus Christ of Latter-day Saints there is office and responsibility for all. (Conference Report, April 1967, p. 54.)

Since our last conference Elder Marion D. Hanks and I have been in Vietnam and other areas in Southeast Asia. In that troubled part of the world we have had many inspiring and sobering experiences, as we have met with our brethren in the armed forces. . . .

[There I met] a handsome boy, tall, clean-faced, wholesome in his look. I said lightly and half jokingly, "What are you going to do when you go home? Have you ever thought of it?"

A wistful sort of light came into his eyes. "Have I ever thought of it? I think of little else, sir. We're moving north again tomorrow, and if I can last another two months I know exactly what I'm going to do when I go home. I'm going to do three things. First, I'm going back to school and finish my education so that I can earn a living at something worthwhile.

"I'm also going to work in the Church and try to do some good. I've seen how desperately the world needs what the Church has to offer.

"And then I'm going to find me a beautiful girl and marry her forever."

I countered with a question, "Are you worthy of that kind of a girl?"

"I hope so, sir," he said. "It hasn't been easy to walk through this filth. It's been pretty lonely at times. But you know, I couldn't let my folks down. I know what my mother expects. I know what she's saying in her prayers. She'd rather have me come home dead than unclean."

I didn't sleep well that night. For one thing, it was terribly hot and the bed was not comfortable. For another, every few minutes a Phantom Jet would roar overhead. And beyond that was the statement of this young man who was about to go north again to face death.

I don't know whether he lived or died. . . . We met and talked with so many and our schedule was so heavy that I do not recall his name or where he was from, but I have not forgotten him. . . . I thought of him when I talked with a school dropout who had come to think it more important to buy an old jalopy than to go on with his education. I thought of him when I talked with two young people, the one a once-beautiful girl and the other a once-handsome young man, who had blighted their lives in walking a sordid trail of immorality.

I would that the Lord would give me the power to say something out of that young Marine's words to youth wherever they may be listening. . . . He mentioned three things he wanted to do, and then spoke indirectly of another he was already doing. Out of these I would like to formulate a challenge, a series of four challenges to youth. . . . Though these challenges may sound trite and old-fashioned, I hope you will not close your ears to them. . . . I therefore offer you these challenges:

1. That you prepare for usefulness.
2. That you serve with faith.
3. That you walk in virtue.
4. That you marry for eternity. ("A Challenge from Vietnam," *Improvement Era*, June 1967, pp. 52–53.)

I believe in our youth. I believe in their goodness and decency. I believe in their virtue. I have interviewed thousands of them on a personal and individual basis. Yes, there are some who have succumbed to evil, but they are a minority. . . .

I know of no experience more refreshing than to be with them and feel of their spirit. ("Be Not Afraid, Only Believe," *Improvement Era*, December 1969, p. 98.)

Your chances for a happy and lasting marriage will be far greater if you will date those who are active and faithful in the Church. Such dating is most likely to lead to marriage in the House of the Lord. ("Four B's for Boys," *Ensign*, November 1981, p. 41.)

You are youth of the noble birthright. You may not at this time know what that means. It means that behind you are great men and women who did wonderful and brave things. They made decisions that were not easy to make, and in many cases they paid a terrible price for those decisions, some of them even giving their lives rather than forsake the truth they had embraced. ("Four B's for Boys," *Ensign*, November 1981, p. 41.)

Never forget that you were chosen and brought to earth as a child of God for something of importance in His grand design. He expects marvelous things of you. He expects you to keep your lives clean from the sins of the world. You are the line through which will pass the qualities of your forebears to the posterity who will come after you. Did you ever see a chain with a weak link? Don't you become that weak link. (Youth Fireside Satellite Broadcast, December 5, 1982.)

These are bright and gifted and attractive youth. One cannot look into their faces and have any doubt concerning the future of this work. They are part of a marvelous generation whose numbers are constantly growing and whose faith is infectious. . . .

They are the certain promise of the future of the Church and of its growing strength and the fulfilling of its mission. Furthermore, they will bless the nations and the lands of which they are a part, for they are young men and women with ambition for education. They believe in the cultivation of the mind, of the development of their skills, of the need to master new technologies, to serve in the world of work into which they will move. . . .

They are the young men and women of faith who have been schooled in the scriptures. . . . They are familiar with the word of God as it has come through modern revelation. They are students who are acquiring both secular and religious education, learning by study and also by faith. They are examples of the power of that first great principle, faith in the Lord Jesus Christ. ("God Grant Us Faith," *Ensign*, November 1983, p. 52.)

Let us not worry and get all worked up about exotic excursions that now may not be possible. These might provide wonderful fun and young people, we all agree, need to have some fun under the direction of Church officers and teachers. But these officers and teachers, and these young men and women, are people of ingenuity who with faith and prayer can work out programs costing little in dollars that will yield tremendous dividends in wholesome recreation and faith-building activities. Perhaps we should be less concerned with fun and more with faith. (Belle S. Spafford Conference on Women, February 23, 1990.)

I have a great and compelling sense of gratitude and optimism about the youth of the Church. In saying this, I do not wish to imply that all is well with all of them. There are many who have troubles, and many who live far beneath the high expectations we have concerning them.

But even considering these, I have great confidence in our young people as a whole. I regard you as the finest generation in the history of the Church. I compliment you, and I have in my heart a great feeling of love and respect and appreciation for you. ("This Favored Season," *New Era*, September 1993, p. 4.)

Some time ago I read a letter to a newspaper editor which was highly critical of the Church. It included a question something like this: "When are the Mormons going to stop being different and become part of mainstream America?"

About this same time there came to my desk a copy of an address given by Senator Dan Coats of Indiana. He spoke of a report dealing with the problems of American youth. That report concluded:

"Suicide is now the second leading cause of death among adolescents. . . . More than a million teenage girls get pregnant each year. Eighty-five percent of teenage boys who impregnate teenage girls eventually abandon them.

" . . . Homicide is now the leading cause of death among fifteen- to nineteen-year-old minority youth. . . .

"Every year substance abuse claims younger victims with harder drugs. A third of high school seniors get drunk once a week."

The report reached a shocking conclusion. It said: "The most basic cause of suffering . . . is profoundly self-destructive *behavior.* Drinking. Drugs. Violence. Promiscuity. A crisis of behavior and belief. A crisis of character" (*Imprimis*, September 1991, p. 1).

When I read those statements, I said to myself, If that is the mainstream of American youth, then I want to do all in my power to persuade and encourage our young people to stay away from it. ("This Favored Season," *New Era*, September 1993, pp. 4–5.)

We are particularly proud of our youth. I think we have never had a stronger generation of young men and women than we have today. For the most part they are true to the faith of their forebears. Surrounded by forces that would pull them down and tremendous pressures to pull them away from time-tested virtues, they are going forward with constructive lives, nurturing themselves both intellectually and spiritually. We have no fears or doubts concerning the future of this work. (Press Conference, Salt Lake City, Utah, March 13, 1995.)

You are great young people. I have said again and again, we have the finest generation of young people ever in the history of this Church. I believe it. You know the gospel better. You come to seminary and you learn about the things of the Lord here. You know more about the gospel than those of my generation at your age did without any question. I am satisfied of that. Furthermore, you are intrinsically better. You are wonderful young people! (Skyline High School Seminary Fireside, Salt Lake City, Utah, April 30, 1995.)

Bring into the lives of our young people something more of spirituality. . . . There is more to the Aaronic Priesthood than sociality, essential as that is. Cultivate in the heart of every boy a sense of his relationship to the Lord as he becomes acquainted with the Savior of the world by knowing some elements of the atonement of the Redeemer through which eternal life is made possible for each of us. (Heber City / Springville Utah Regional Conference, priesthood leadership session, May 13, 1995.)

I look back to my own youth. Neither young men nor young women were doing much scripture reading at that time. What a marvelous change has been wrought. A new generation is arising who are familiar with the word of the Lord. Growing up in a worldly environment that is laden with immorality and filth of every kind, our youth, for the most part, are meeting the challenge of living in the world without partaking of the evils of the world. . . . It is wonderful to feel the pulse of this generation of young people. Of course, there are some who do not measure up. That has been the case since the time of the great war in heaven described by John the Revelator. The issue then was free agency as it is today. Then, as now, choices had to be made. . . .

That ancient struggle continues, the unrelenting battle that comes of free agency. Some, unfortunately, choose the wrong. But many, so many, choose the right, including so very many of our choice young men and young women. They deserve and need our gratitude. They need our encouragement. They need the kind of examples that we can become before them. ("We Have a Work to Do," *Ensign*, May 1995, pp. 87–88.)

I meet young people everywhere who are wonderful and faithful; youth who want to do the right thing and who indicate the reality of what I have been saying for a long time, that we've never had a better generation of young people in the Church than we have today. They are faithful. They are active. They're knowledgeable. They are a great generation, notwithstanding the environment in which many of them are growing up. (*Church News* Interview, June 7, 1995.)

Believe in yourselves, in your capacity to do things that are good and worthwhile and upstanding. You young men and women who are in school, believe in yourselves. Seek the Lord if you are stumbling. Believe in your capacity to learn and make something of your lives. Stand tall and go forward. I was interested in these words that I read the other evening and copied down. Moses, leading the children of Israel through the wilderness, heard them complain. They were always complaining, it seems to me. Forty years of complaining. Moses cried to the Lord because the people cried to him. "And the Lord said unto Moses, Wherefore criest thou unto me? speak unto the children of Israel, that they go forward" (Ex. 14:15). Don't stand around complaining. "Speak unto the children of Israel, that they go forward." That is a message for us in our day and time. This is the great day of opportunity for you young people, this marvelous time to be upon the earth. You stand at the summit of all of the past ages. You are exposed to all of the learning of all who have walked the earth, that learning being distilled down into courses where you can acquire knowledge in a relatively short time, that knowledge which men stumbled over in learning through all of the centuries past. Don't sell yourselves short. Don't miss your great opportunity. Get at it, work at it, study hard. The Lord has laid upon you a mandate, you young men and women of this Church, to acquire secular knowledge as well as spiritual knowledge, and that is defined very clearly and openly in the 88th Section of the Doctrine and Covenants. Take advantage of the opportunities that are yours; even if it entails sacrifice, take advantage. Be not faithless, but believing, in your capacity as a son or daughter of God to learn so that you may go forth to serve and make a contribution to the society of which you will become a part. Look up and go forward. (Smithfield/Logan Utah Regional Conference, April 21, 1996.)

I want to say to the young people, live your lives according to the principles of the gospel. You live in an age when there is so much of filth. You must not stoop down to that. You must rise above it. You must have the strength to say no and to stand tall. I promise you that if you will do so, those who would otherwise invite you to their kind of living will wish that they too had lived above those things. Be clean. Be pure in your lives. Watch the language that you use. Do not take the name of the Lord in vain and do not indulge in sleazy talk. And as you go forward with your lives, look for companionship among members of the Church. You will be much happier if you marry in the Church. You will be so much more secure in your marriage if you marry in the temple. (Copenhagen Denmark Fireside, June 14, 1996.)

Now because much has been given, much is expected of us. We asked your stake presidents yesterday about you young people in high school. They said it is a tough world in which you live, a very difficult environment. That is the case all over America with high schools. Profanity everywhere, vile profanity, sleazy, filthy language, drugs, alcohol, immorality, the whole story. Thank you for your strength. Thank you for your goodness. Thank you for your courage. Thank you for your efforts in hanging together, as it were, of going to institute, going to seminary, partaking of the blessings that are to be had there, not only in the teaching of the gospel but in the society in which you can mingle. (Eugene Oregon Regional Conference, September 15, 1996.)

Something that concerns me greatly is teen suicide. From 1950 to 1993 the homicide rates among young people tripled and suicide rates have quadrupled among children under fifteen years of age. That is an alarming figure, one that comes out of the *Wall Street Journal.* I fear that that statistic is correct. The murder rate in the United States is five times higher than in twenty-five other nations combined, while the suicide rate is twice as high. We are having too many suicides, particularly of young people. We must stay closer to our young people. The 55 percent of our young men who go on missions are probably not in this category, but the other 45 percent may be. If we could raise the number going on missions from 55 percent to 65 percent in the next few years, we would be doing a wonderful thing for the Church and a wonderful thing for our young people. (Jordan Utah South Regional Conference, priesthood leadership session, March 1, 1997.)

We cannot say it frequently enough. Turn away from youthful lusts. Stay away from drugs. They can absolutely destroy you. Avoid them as you would a terrible disease, for that is what they become. Avoid foul and filthy talk. It can lead to destruction. Be absolutely honest. Dishonesty can corrupt and destroy. Observe the Word of Wisdom. You cannot smoke; you must not smoke. You must not chew tobacco. You cannot drink liquor. You hold the priesthood of God. You must rise above these things which beckon with a seductive call. Be prayerful. Call on the Lord in faith, and He will hear your prayers. He loves you. He wishes to bless you. He will do so if you live worthy of His blessing.

You face great challenges that lie ahead. You are moving into a world of fierce competition. You must get all of the education you can. The Lord has instructed us concerning the importance of an education. It will qualify you for greater opportunities. It will equip you to do something worthwhile in the great world of opportunity that lies ahead. If you can go to college and that is your wish, then do it. ("Converts and Young Men," *Ensign,* May 1997, pp. 49–50.)

A Chosen Generation

And so I might continue with a picture familiar to all of you, but I return to Peter's great statement as I make a plea and offer a challenge: "Ye are a chosen generation." How very true that is. Notwithstanding all of the problems that we have, this, I believe, is the greatest age in the history of the world. And you young people of this generation are a part of it. You are the beneficiaries of it. Its fruits are here to bless your lives if you will grasp them and live worthy of them. . . .

Truly, my dear young friends, you are a chosen generation. I hope you will never forget it. I hope you will never take it for granted. I hope there will grow in your hearts an overpowering sense of gratitude to God, who has made it possible for you to come upon the earth in this marvelous season of the world's history. ("'A Chosen Generation,'" *Ensign,* May 1992, p. 70.)

I love the youth of the Church. I have said again and again that I think we have never had a better generation than this. How grateful I am for your integrity, for your ambition to train your minds and your hands to do good work, for your love for the word of the Lord, and for your desire to walk in paths of virtue and truth and goodness. ("This Is the Work of the Master," *Ensign,* May 1995, p. 70.)

You represent a great generation in the history of the world and in the history of this Church. In terms of the Church, I feel that you are part of the greatest generation we have ever had. You are better educated. You have gone through seminary, and are now participating in the Institute of Religion program. At a time when most young people do not pray, you do pray. You pray for understanding and enlightenment. You pray about your studies and the course of your lives. You pray about marriage, about finding a good companion and about going to the house of the Lord to have your marriage sealed under the authority of the holy priesthood. You pray for success in your studies and in other interests that you have.

Nearly every one of you desires to do the right thing. And in most instances you are doing it. You are trying to keep yourselves free from the corrosive stains of the world. It is not easy. It is a constant challenge. . . .

[But] the picture never looked brighter. The opportunities were never greater. This is a marvelous season in the history of the Lord's work. We are on stage, you and I, at this glorious season. We have so much to do, so very, very much to do to move forward the work of the Lord toward the marvelous destiny which He has outlined for it. . . . None has a more compelling responsibility than do you. You are young. You have energy. You have convictions in your hearts. You have associates with whom you can work and associates you can work upon. . . . I challenge you to stand for that which is right and true and good. The Church needs every one of you. It needs your strength. It needs your energy. It needs your enthusiasm. It needs your loyalty and devotion and faith. Regardless of your way of doing things in the past, I offer you a challenge to square your lives with the teachings of the gospel, to look upon this Church with love and respect and appreciation as the mother of your faith, to live your life as an example of what the gospel of Jesus Christ will do in bringing happiness to an individual. ("True to the Faith," Salt Lake Valley-Wide Institute Fireside, January 21, 1996.)

I was asked by an interviewer, "What do we have to offer the people of the Philippines?" We have happiness to offer to the people of the Philippines. Sin never was happiness. Transgression never was happiness. Evil never was happiness. Good means happiness. Brotherhood means happiness. Service to one another means happiness. What was it that Peter wrote concerning us of this generation? He said, "Ye are a chosen generation, a royal priesthood, an holy nation, a peculiar people; that ye should shew forth the praises of him who hath brought you out of darkness into his marvelous light." (1 Peter 2:9.) "A chosen generation." This is the greatest generation in the history of the world. How wonderful to be born at this time in the history of the earth. I hope you young people are grateful that this is the season of your lives. And for every one of you, this is the time when the God of heaven has moved in fulfillment of His ancient promise that He would usher in the fulness of the gospel in the Dispensation of the Fulness of Times. "A chosen generation." You're not just here by chance. You are here under the design of God. "An holy nation." I don't think that speaks of a particular nation—the Philippines, the United States, or anything of that kind—it speaks of a vast congregation of those who accept the gospel of Jesus Christ and try to live its teachings. (Cebu City Philippines Fireside, May 31, 1996.)

You are part of a marvelous generation, the best in the history of this Church. You read all about drugs and youth going down the road that leads to destruction. There are millions of them in this land. But I want to say that I believe with all my heart we have the finest generation of youth in this Church that we have ever had. I believe that. They know the gospel better. They know the scriptures a lot better than some of us. They are bright, energetic, faithful, clean, virtuous, and they have ambition. God bless you, my beloved young friends. I do love you. I want you to know that. I pray for you. I pray constantly that I can do something to help the young people of this Church move along to greater accomplishment while keeping the faith and being true to the traditions of their forebears. (Hailey 1st and 2nd Wards Sacrament Meeting, Sun Valley, Idaho, June 30, 1996.)

Young Men
See also Priesthood: Aaronic Priesthood; Scouting

We hear much these days of teenage sexual misbehavior. There is too much among our own youth.

Any boy who indulges in illegitimate sexual activity, as we define that in the doctrines and standards of this Church—and I think no one misunderstands what I mean when I say that—does himself irreparable damage and robs her with whom he is involved of that which can never be restored. There is nothing clever about this kind of so-called conquest. It carries with it no laurels, no victories, no enduring satisfaction. It brings only shame, sorrow, and regret. He who so indulges cheats himself and robs her. In robbing her, he affronts her Father in Heaven, for she is a daughter of God.

I know that this is strong language, plainly spoken. But I feel the trends of our times call for strong language and plain words. Jehovah did not speak ambiguously when he said, "Thou shalt not commit adultery." (Ex. 20:14.) ("Be Not Deceived," *Ensign,* November 1983, pp. 44–45.)

You young men who hold the priesthood, "be not faithless, but believing" in the tremendous thing that you have. This is no small or unimportant thing. This is not a gift that can simply be received and then put on a shelf. It is something to be lived for, to be nurtured, to be taken care of, to be expanded for good in its influence and power. You cannot do a mean or demeaning thing without discounting the strength and value and power of that priesthood. Keep yourselves, both young men and young women, on the highest plane of morality. You will be grateful if you do. (Ricks College Regional Conference, Rexburg, Idaho, October 29, 1995.)

Young Women

I next would like to say a few words to you young women, you who have crossed the threshold from childhood and early youth into the maturity of your later teens and early twenties. For you this must be a season for strength. It is a season that demands discipline of mind and of body. This is the season for preparation, and the Lord has said, "If ye are prepared ye shall not fear." (D&C 38:30.)

It is a time for education. The world that lies ahead of you will be fiercely competitive. Now is the time to train yourselves for possible future responsibilities.

Education is a tradition that has come down from our early history. We believe in the training of our youth, girls as well as boys. Brigham Young once said, "We have sisters here who, if they had the privilege of studying, would make just as good mathematicians or accountants as any man." (*Journal of Discourses,* 13:61.)

You have available to you tremendous opportunities for training your minds and your hands. You will wish for marriage and the companionship of a good husband. But none of us can foretell the future. Prepare yourselves for any eventuality. ("Live Up to Your Inheritance," *Ensign*, November 1983, pp. 81–82.)

The Church has been in the forefront in training the daughters of Zion and in giving them responsibility. We believe and have taught consistently from the earliest days of the Church that a woman's greatest mission in life is an honorable and happy marriage with the rearing of an honorable and happy family. That means mothering and nurturing in a very real and personal way, a way that is demanding both in time and energy. But this is not inconsistent with other activities. There are tremendous responsibilities for women in the Church as well as in the community consistent with and in total harmony with marriage, motherhood, and the rearing of good and able children.

It is important, therefore, that the girls in the Church have opportunity for and motivation to move forward in programs designed to improve their skills, to enhance their estimation of their own self-worth, and to broaden their knowledge of the gospel with consequent increase of faith. The generations are largely cast by the mothers who produce them. The story is told that Brigham Young was once asked what he would do if he had to choose between providing education for his sons or daughters. He replied that he would educate his daughters because they would become the mothers of his grandchildren. ("Youth Is the Season," *New Era*, September 1988, p. 47.)

It is so important that young women learn the ways of eternal truth, that virtue is attractive and all-important, that testimony is a pearl to be sought after and worn with dignity and pride, that they understand the incomparable blessings that come from temple marriage and a wholesome, rewarding family life.

Do we encourage education? By all means. Every young woman ought to refine her skills and increase her abilities, to broaden her knowledge and strengthen her capacity. ("Youth Is the Season," *New Era*, September 1988, p. 47.)

The young women of this generation not only have tremendous opportunities, but they also face terrible temptations. The pornography merchants cast their filthy lures in the direction of girls as well as boys. The exploitation of sex has become a marketable commodity employing every vile trick of the advertiser, every slick and seductive element that can be conjured up. Popularity is the siren's song. I recently read that the use of drugs in America is increasing more rapidly among young women than among young men.

It is so important that we increase our efforts to teach our young women the ways of eternal truth, to make virtue attractive and all-important, . . . to hold out the incomparable blessings that come from temple marriage and a wholesome, rewarding family life. ("Our Responsibility to Our Young Women," *Ensign*, September 1988, p. 10.)

Youth is the season to set the directions for life. And in the case of a young woman, her life will be immeasurably enhanced if she is exposed to and accepts those directions. Moreover, the posterity who follow after her will more likely be reared in "the nurture and admonition of the Lord" (Eph. 6:4; Enos 1:1) to their great benefit and blessing. When we save a girl, we save generations. No one can foretell the consequences of faithfulness in the life of a young woman.

It is important to emphasize the Aaronic Priesthood. It is important to encourage Scouting. But it is every bit as important to see that everything possible is done to afford every young woman in the Church an opportunity for growth and development, training and activity that will lead to faith, testimony, and virtuous and happy living. ("Our Responsibility to Our Young Women," *Ensign*, September 1988, p. 10.)

I want to say to young women here today, do not ever have any inferiority complex about your place in this world in which you live. You are a daughter of God, and I am satisfied that our Father in Heaven loves His daughters as much as He loves His sons. You hold up your heads and stand tall and walk in righteousness and faith and virtue and truth and do not let anybody put you down or sell you short. You are daughters of God. Live worthy of your divine inheritance, my beloved young women. You are not inferior in any sense. Under the gospel plan you are daughters of God. Each of us has our place in the great divine plan and we ought to magnify the calling and the field and the assignment and the qualities of good which we have within us. (Ricks College Regional Conference, Rexburg, Idaho, October 29, 1995.)

I urge each of you young women to get all of the schooling you can get. You will need it for the world into which you will move. Life is becoming so exceedingly competitive. Experts say that the average man or woman, during his or her working career, can expect to have five different jobs. The world is changing, and it is so very important that we equip ourselves to move with that change. But there is a bright side to all of this. No other generation in all of history has offered women so many opportunities. Your first objective should be a happy marriage, sealed in the temple of the Lord, and followed by the rearing of a good family. Education can better equip you for the realization of those ideals. ("Stand True and Faithful," *Ensign*, May 1996, p. 92.)

I have been asked about my feelings concerning young women serving missions, pursuing careers, and getting married. Get all three if you can. We believe in education. This Church encourages education. There is incumbent upon every member of this Church, as a mandate from the Lord, to get all the education you can get. That is important. Educate your minds and your hands to make a contribution to the society of which you will become a part. And if you do so you will bring respect and honor to the Church as well as bless your own lives. The Lord has told us to seek learning by the Spirit, by study, by faith. He has told us to learn of things beneath the earth, and on the earth, and above the earth—of kingdoms, of nations, of the things of the world. There is incumbent upon the Latter-day Saints a dictum from the Lord Himself to educate our minds and our hands.

Now, of course we also believe in marriage. I wish that every young woman in this Church could be married to a faithful, outstanding, wonderful young man who will treat her with kindness, who will love her and appreciate her and look after her. It does not happen to everyone, but that is the ideal. For those for whom this does not happen, I repeat, educate yourselves, make yourselves useful. Do not worry about marriage all the time. The less you worry about it, the more it is likely to happen. In the eternal plan of the Lord, you will be all right.

Concerning missions for young women, let me make it clear that you do not have the same obligation as do the young men of this Church. They have an incumbent obligation to go out and preach the gospel of Jesus Christ. If you want to go on a mission when you are twenty-one, speak to your bishop. The Church will go on loving you, respecting you, helping you, working with you whether you go on a mission or not. (Jordan Utah South Regional Conference, March 2, 1997.)

ZION

Many small efforts and little acts become the cumulative pattern of a great worldwide organization. . . .

I need not remind you that this cause in which we are engaged is not an ordinary cause. It is the cause of Christ. It is the kingdom of God our Eternal Father. It is the building of Zion on the earth, the fulfillment of prophecy given of old and of a vision revealed in this dispensation. ("An Ensign to the Nations," *Ensign*, November 1989, p. 53.)

"And the Lord called his people Zion, because they were of one heart and one mind, and dwelt in righteousness; and there was no poor among them." (Moses 7:18.)

If we are to build that Zion of which the prophets have spoken and of which the Lord has given mighty promise, we must set aside our consuming selfishness. We must rise above our love for comfort and ease, and in the very process of effort and struggle, even in our extremity, we shall become better acquainted with our God. ("Our Mission of Saving," *Ensign*, November 1991, p. 59.)

Our forebears dreamed of Zion. "Come to Zion," they said. "Even if you have to walk all the way. Come to Zion. Leave Babylon and gather to the mountains of Ephraim." No one can read the words of Brigham Young, John Taylor, or Wilford Woodruff without knowing that they thought of these mountain valleys as a great gathering place for people of one heart and one mind and one faith, a place where the mountain of the Lord's house should be established in the tops of the mountains and where all nations would flow unto it. (General Authority Training Meeting, September 27, 1994.)

There can never be in the foreseeable future a standing still or a failure to reach out, to move forward, to build, to enlarge Zion across the world. ("This Work Is Concerned with People," *Ensign*, May 1995, pp. 52–53.)

We can improve, and when all is said and done that's what this is all about: improvement, changing our lives so that we can help people change their lives and be better. And let's build Zion in the earth. That's what it is all about. (Tacoma Washington Regional Conference, priesthood leadership session, August 19, 1995.)

You are a fulfillment tonight of the great words of Jeremiah, who said, speaking in the name of the Lord, "I will take you one of a city, and two of a family, and I will bring you to Zion: and I will give you pastors according to mine heart" (Jeremiah 3:14–15). You are the fulfillment of that. This is Zion for you, where you live, and you are being fed by pastors with the message of the Lord, the very bread of life, as it were. How wonderful that you should be here and partake of these marvelous and great blessings. (Hyde Park Chapel Rededication, August 27, 1995.)

At one time the people of England, Ireland, Scotland, and Wales who joined the Church longed to gather to Zion. They paid a terrible price in dealing with it. Hundreds of them, thousands of them died on that long march from the Missouri River to the Valley of the Great Salt Lake. You do not have that anymore. You can live in comfort in your native land and build Zion here. This can become your Zion in a very real sense. (Nottingham England Fireside, August 30, 1995.)

Now, you are not perfect. It isn't likely that there will be a great hole left in the earth here as you are translated. You are not quite ready for that. But let us build Zion here. Let us cultivate the spirituality of the people. Let us teach faith. Let us teach the people to rely upon the Lord and to look to Him for strength and guidance and sustenance and love. He is our Father and our God. He is our Savior and our Redeemer. We are His disciples in whose footsteps we ought to walk. These, to me, are great and wonderful words from the 7th chapter of Moroni, the 26th verse: "And as sure as Christ liveth he spake these words unto our fathers, saying: Whatsoever thing ye shall ask the Father in my name, which is good, in faith believing that ye shall receive, behold, it shall be done unto you." That, to me, is a promise without parallel. (Brigham City Utah Regional Conference, priesthood leadership session, February 22, 1997.)

Aaronic Priesthood: includes keys of baptism, 34, 485; heritage of, exemplified by three rescuers, 481–82; bestowed by John the Baptist, 482; holds keys of ministering of angels, 483; counsel to holders of, 483–84; responsibilities accompanying, 484–85; as royal priesthood, 485; holds keys of repentance, 546; honoring, 721

Abortion, 1, 461–62

Abrahamic covenant, 147, 148

Abuse: of wives, 1–2, 322–23, 326, 331; of children, 2–4

Accountability: for choices, 55–58; for fulfilling Church callings, 65–66; for our stewardships, 146, 612–13; and welfare program, 687–88

Adoption: into everlasting covenant, 147–48; for children of unwed mothers, 673

Adultery, 5, 8

Adversity: inevitability of, 6; strength given for, 7; walking by faith through, 7

Agency, 54–55, 291, 715

Aging, 7–8

AIDS, 8

Airplane stories: landing gear reverts to redundancy system, 173–75; stewardess serves juice to Elder Hinckley, 184–85; motor fails, 195–96; in-flight conversation leads to family's conversion, 376–77; flying over pioneer route, 445–46; discussing gospel with prejudiced listener, 644; defective wiring causes crash, 704

Airport, President Kimball helps mother in, 240–41

Allen, James, Captain, 110

America, United States of: as choice land, 9–10, 18; fruitless criticism of, 10–11; having faith in, 11; strengths of, 11–13; has not sought territory in war, 12; Constitution of, 13–16; greatness of, lies in goodness, 16; moral decline in, 16–17, 19–20; is forgetting God, 18, 23; Judeo-Christian heritage of, 20–21, 23–24; secularizing of, 20–24; love of, 231

Anderson, Joseph, 286–87

Anderson, Maxwell, 231, 684

Anderson, William Robert, Commander, 188

Anger, 2, 24–26, 228–29, 330

Angels: ministering, of, 483; do not profane name of Deity, 496

Apathy, 31, 136, 138

Apostasy, 32, 125; drifting into, 136; spirit of, in Kirtland, 190

Apostles: ordained by Christ, 67, 79; receiving calling as, 79; restoration of office of, 79–80; responsibilities of, 80, 81, 83–84; character of, 81–82; keys held by, 82, 84–85; are not motivated by selfishness, 82–83; unanimity in decisions of, 84–85; authority of, in succession to Presidency, 614–15, 617; unity among, 671

Appreciation, expressing, 247–48

Argentina, 360

Ash tray, stolen, 268–69

Asia: growth of Church in, 98–99, 368; missionary work in, 372

Atonement of Christ: importance of remembering, 26–27; makes salvation possible, 27–28,

requires conviction of heart, 144;
described in letter, 243–44; of
Filipino man, 498–99

Cooke, Colonel, of Mormon
Battalion, 109–10

Cornerstone ceremony for temples,
633–34

Cornerstones of the Church, 111–12

Counselors: in First Presidency,
76–79; in presidencies
throughout Church, 93–95;
delegating responsibilities to,
309

Courage, 145–46; to set good
example, 180–81, 185; to be
obedient, 402–3

Courtesy, 131–33

Covenants: baptismal, 34–35, 146,
148; obligations inherent in, 138;
living up to, 146–49; renewed by
partaking of sacrament, 146–47,
149

Covetousness, 251–54, 708–9

Cowdery, Oliver, 80, 371, 546

Craftsmanship, 447, 627

Creator, Christ as, 273

Crime, 17, 20; rising rate of, 129;
cost of, 132

Criticism: spirit of, 149–51; facing,
without fear, 221

Critics of Church, 121–28, 290–91,
295–96, 409

Cross, symbol of, 182

Crucifixion of Christ, 27

Dart, John, 461–62

Dating, 711

De Tocqueville, Alexis, 16

Deacons quorum, 485

Death: temple answers mystery of,
151–52; mother's, lessons in,
152; role of, in eternal life, 152,
153; victory over, through
Atonement, 152, 153–54; as
"great reliever," 153; is not the
end, 173; relevance of Christ
pointed out by, 272

Debt: Church avoids, 120–21;
Saints counseled to avoid,
154–55, 522, 653; reasonable,
155; dangers of, 653–64; family
reduces, after paying tithing,
657–58

Delegation of responsibilities, 309,
311, 598

Denver Temple, 625

Depression, the Great, 17, 30, 155

Disagreement, civility in, 131

Discernment, 678

Disciplinary councils, 95–96

Discipline versus punishment, 417,
418, 422, 577

Discouragement, 156

Discrimination, 222

Dishonesty: inherent in adultery, 5;
engendered by covetousness,
251–54; costs of, 266, 268;
temptation of, 269; of shoddy
workmanship, 704

Dispensation of the fulness of
times, 156–58, 549

Diversity, strength in, 661, 664

Divine nature, 158–61

Divorce, 161–63, 209, 329

Doctrine: teaching, 310–11, 565;
scriptures as source of, 572;
standard for, lies in scriptures,
574; safeguarding purity of, 620

Doctrine and Covenants, 102,
163–65; preface to, 503–4

Documents, forged, 194–95

Dominion, unrighteous, 219–20,
327–28

"Dropping the ball," 579–80